Praise for *The Handbook of Language and Globalization*

Winner of the 2011 British Association of Applied Linguistics Book Prize.

"An enlightening and engaging collection by eminent international scholars. A major resource for the study of theoretical and pragmatic approaches to Global English, including concerns about 'marginalization' and 'murder' of languages."
Braj B. Kachru, Professor Emeritus, University of Illinois

"This *Handbook* provides a fascinating exposition of the complex, multidimensional nature of globalization as it pertains to the world's languages. Coupland has marshalled authors at the forefront of their fields who offer a diversity of approaches and do not flinch from disputes and challenging questions. I suspect that this *Handbook* will transform the discourse on globalization within linguistics and will impel a reconsideration of whether linguistic diversity is inevitably impacted by global processes."
Margaret Florey, Resource Network for Linguistic Diversity

Blackwell Handbooks in Linguistics

This outstanding multi-volume series covers all the major subdisciplines within linguistics today and, when complete, will offer a comprehensive survey of linguistics as a whole.

Already published:

The Handbook of Child Language
Edited by Paul Fletcher and
Brian MacWhinney

The Handbook of Phonological Theory, Second Edition
Edited by John A. Goldsmith,
Jason Riggle, and Alan C. L.
Yu

The Handbook of Contemporary Semantic Theory
Edited by Shalom Lappin

The Handbook of Sociolinguistics
Edited by Florian Coulmas

The Handbook of Phonetic Sciences, Second Edition
Edited by William J.
Hardcastle and John Laver

The Handbook of Morphology
Edited by Andrew Spencer
and Arnold Zwicky

The Handbook of Japanese Linguistics
Edited by Natsuko Tsujimura

The Handbook of Linguistics
Edited by Mark Aronoff and
Janie Rees-Miller

The Handbook of Contemporary Syntactic Theory
Edited by Mark Baltin and
Chris Collins

The Handbook of Discourse Analysis
Edited by Deborah Schiffrin,
Deborah Tannen, and Heidi E.
Hamilton

The Handbook of Language Variation and Change
Edited by J. K. Chambers,
Peter Trudgill, and Natalie
Schilling-Estes

The Handbook of Historical Linguistics
Edited by Brian D. Joseph and
Richard D. Janda

The Handbook of Language and Gender
Edited by Janet Holmes and
Miriam Meyerhoff

The Handbook of Second Language Acquisition
Edited by Catherine J.
Doughty and Michael H. Long

The Handbook of Bilingualism and Multilingualism, Second Edition
Edited by Tej K. Bhatia and
William C. Ritchie

The Handbook of Pragmatics
Edited by Laurence R. Horn
and Gregory Ward

The Handbook of Applied Linguistics
Edited by Alan Davies and
Catherine Elder

The Handbook of Speech Perception
Edited by David B. Pisoni and
Robert E. Remez

The Handbook of the History of English
Edited by Ans van Kemenade
and Bettelou Los

The Handbook of English Linguistics
Edited by Bas Aarts and April
McMahon

The Handbook of World Englishes
Edited by Braj B. Kachru;
Yamuna Kachru, and Cecil L.
Nelson

The Handbook of Educational Linguistics
Edited by Bernard Spolsky and
Francis M. Hult

The Handbook of Clinical Linguistics
Edited by Martin J. Ball,
Michael R. Perkins, Nicole
Mller, and Sara Howard

The Handbook of Pidgin and Creole Studies
Edited by Silvia Kouwenberg
and John Victor Singler

The Handbook of Language Teaching
Edited by Michael H. Long
and Catherine J. Doughty

The Handbook of Language Contact
Edited by Raymond Hickey

The Handbook of Language and Speech Disorders
Edited by Jack S. Damico,
Nicole Mller, Martin J. Ball

The Handbook of Computational Linguistics and Natural Language Processing
Edited by Alexander Clark,
Chris Fox, and Shalom Lappin

The Handbook of Language and Globalization
Edited by Nikolas Coupland

The Handbook of Hispanic Linguistics
Edited by Manuel
Díaz-Campos

The Handbook of Language Socialization
Edited by Alessandro Duranti,
Elinor Ochs, and Bambi B.
Schieffelin

The Handbook of Intercultural Discourse and Communication
Edited by Christina Bratt
Paulston, Scott F. Kiesling, and
Elizabeth S. Rangel

The Handbook of Historical Sociolinguistics
Edited by Juan Manuel
Hernández-Campoy and Juan
Camilo Conde-Silvestre

The Handbook of Hispanic Linguistics
Edited by José Ignacio Hualde,
Antxon Olarrea, and Erin
O'Rourke

The Handbook of Conversation Analysis
Edited by Jack Sidnell and
Tanya Stivers

The Handbook of English for Specific Purposes
Edited by Brian Paltridge and
Sue Starfield

The Handbook of Language and Globalization

Edited by

Nikolas Coupland

WILEY-BLACKWELL

A John Wiley & Sons, Ltd., Publication

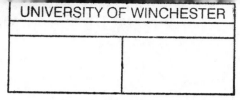
This paperback edition first published 2013
© 2013 Blackwell Publishing Ltd except for editorial material and organization © 2013 Nikolas Coupland

Edition History: Blackwell Publishing Ltd (hardback, 2010)

Blackwell Publishing was acquired by John Wiley & Sons in February 2007. Blackwell's publishing program has been merged with Wiley's global Scientific, Technical, and Medical business to form Wiley-Blackwell.

Registered Office
John Wiley & Sons Ltd, The Atrium, Southern Gate, Chichester, West Sussex, PO19 8SQ, UK

Editorial Offices
350 Main Street, Malden, MA 02148-5020, USA
9600 Garsington Road, Oxford, OX4 2DQ, UK
The Atrium, Southern Gate, Chichester, West Sussex, PO19 8SQ, UK

For details of our global editorial offices, for customer services, and for information about how to apply for permission to reuse the copyright material in this book please see our website at www.wiley.com/wiley-blackwell.

Library of Congress Cataloging-in-Publication Data

The handbook of language and globalization / edited by Nikolas Coupland.
    p. cm. – (Blackwell handbooks in linguistics)
Includes bibliographical references and index.
ISBN 978-1-4051-7581-4 (hardcover : alk. Paper) ISBN 978-1-118-34717-1 (paperback : alk. Paper)
1. Language and languages—Globalization—Handbooks, manuals, etc.   2. Languages in contact—Handbooks, manuals, etc.   3. Linguistic change—Handbooks, manuals, etc.   4. Sociolinguistics—Handbooks, manuals, etc.   I. Coupland, Nikolas, 1950–
    P130.5.H358 2010
    306.44–dc22

                                                                        2010003118

A catalogue record for this book is available from the British Library.

Cover image: August Macke, Playing Forms, 1914. Städtisches Kunstmuseum, Bonn. Photo © Erich Lessing/akg-images.
Cover design by Workhaus

Set in 10/12 pt Palatino by Toppan Best-set Premedia Limited
Printed in Malaysia by Ho Printing (M) Sdn Bhd

1   2013

Contents

Illustrations

Acknowledgments

This volume found its origins in a research programme titled 'Language and Global Communication' funded by the Leverhulme Trust (Grant F/00 407 / D) to the Centre for Language and Communication Research at Cardiff University, 2001–2007 (see http://www.cf.ac.uk/encap/globalcomm). Colleagues and I are very grateful to the Trust for their support.

My former colleague Theo van Leeuwen, coordinated, directed and inspired the programme for four years until a career move took him away form Cardiff, at which point I took on the coordinating role, but with Theo's continuing guidance and involvement. About 14 Cardiff colleagues played some significant part in the programme's development and in the dissemination of its findings, although not all of them appear in the pages of the Handbook.

Under the aegis of the 'Language and Global Communication' programme, one international conference and a regular series of workshops were held, and several of the contributors to the present volume participated in those events. The Leverhulme Trust has therefore supported this volume in more ways than might be initially apparent, which, once again, I very gratefully acknowledge.

I am particularly grateful to my colleague Adam Jaworski for the leading role he has played in many aspects of our work on globalisation, and not only in his pioneering research in the sociolinguistics of global tourism.

As seems to be inevitable with Handbook-length projects, this volume has been a long time coming. I thank the earliest on-time contributors for their patience, and colleagues at Wiley-Blackwell for theirs too, also for their professional guidance.

Every effort has been made to trace copyright holders and to obtain their permission for the use of copyright material. The publisher apologizes for any errors or omissions in the above list and would be grateful if notified of any corrections that should be incorporated in future reprints or editions of this book.

NC
July 2009

Introduction: Sociolinguistics in the Global Era

NIKOLAS COUPLAND

The End of Globalization?

The gestation period of this Handbook has been an interesting time for observers of globalization. The international 'credit crunch,' apparently triggered by irresponsible over-lending in the United States but in reality the result of financial laxness on a wider scale, has led to severe economic retrenchment in many parts of the world. Several nation-states have moved to restrict some of the more obvious excesses of global capitalism, initially in the banking and finance sectors. But there are indications of a more general global wariness about flows of money and people, which suggests that national authority and national political initiative are not, after all, in terminal decline. There has also been repeated visible political resistance to fast capitalist globalization: for example the estimated 35,000 people who marched in London in March 2009 in opposition to the agenda of the G20 summit – a meeting of the leaders of the twenty most economically powerful nations – under the slogans "Put people first" and "Jobs, justice, climate." Should we conclude that, after all, this is not such a "runaway world" (Giddens 2002) of rampant globalization?

Academic commentators, including several contributors to this Handbook, observe that, whatever globalization is, it isn't an altogether new phenomenon. Indeed, 'it's nothing new' proves to be one of the least new things to say about globalization, but it is an important observation. As, for example, Mufwene (this volume) points out, colonization in its various modes has been characteristic of more aggressive and more benign encounters between peoples throughout history. Colonization in different eras and contexts meant transnational expansion of economic, military, and cultural sorts. It certainly reshaped global arrangements, including linguistic ones. We are also historically familiar with 'empire,' old and new (Hardt and Negri 2000), in the British case from the mid-seventeenth century, and many have interpreted globalization as latter-day imperialist hegemony, often in the form of westernization or Americanization or McDonaldization (or

The Handbook of Language and Globalization, First Edition. Edited by Nikolas Coupland.
© 2013 Blackwell Publishing Ltd except for editorial material and organization © 2013 Nikolas Coupland.
Published 2013 by Blackwell Publishing Ltd.

other, even more inventive, neologisms of this kind – see Mooney, this volume). So why all this fuss about globalization now?

As Kellner (1989) points out, large-scale shifts to more globally based economic arrangements were predicted and theorized well before our own time. Key voices on *both* sides of early ideological debates about capitalism predicted an increasing globalization of capitalist markets. Adam Smith, for example, anticipated the emergence of a (beneficial and liberalizing, in his view) world market system, while Karl Marx saw global emancipation for the proletariat in the demise of national interests and frameworks and in the onset of internationally grounded revolution. Transnational interdependencies and influences are, once again then, 'nothing new.'

So, as we embark on an exploration of language and globalization, do we in fact believe that globalization currently exists as a new social condition, or that it deserves extensive treatment across the disciplines? Is globalization an economic experiment in retreat, or perhaps a faddish academic concept of the 1990s that refers to historical social processes we were already pretty familiar with? In the rest of this section I would like to make a pitch for the social reality of globalization and for its contemporary importance – both as a social mode that we need to keep probing and as a focus for some new ways of understanding language in society. We have to concede that globalization is complex and multi-faceted, and difficult to delimit chronologically. The concept is often over-consolidated, over-hyped, and under-interpreted. But I want to argue (drawing on the views of many others) that it is an indispensable concept, particularly if we take it as shorthand reference to a cluster of changed and still fast changing social arrangements and priorities which are indeed distinctive and (despite opinions to the contrary) *indeed new*. Having done this, I will try to map out, in four sections that outline the four parts of this volume, how the forthcoming chapters inform our understanding of the many productive and necessary links between 'language' and 'globalization.'

What, then, might persuade us to take globalization seriously and to accept that social analysis needs to be framed in relation to an already globalized and increasingly globalizing world? We might start with a quasi-ethnographic appeal to lived experience and perceptions of social change, say, over the last forty or fifty years. What macro-level social changes have impacted on us (or, at least for the purposes of this initial sketch, on the 'us' defined by the privileged lives lived in the west or the north, and through British eyes)? Answers will be tropes of lifespan discourse: "Back then, things were different..."; "I remember the days when ..." But such autobiographical fragments would point to the sorts of social change that constitute globalization. I venture some of my own fragments below.[1] I would say that we have experienced:

- an increasing mediation of culture and greater cultural reflexivity
- the proliferation and speeding up of communication technologies
- a large shift to service-sector work, globally dispersed
- the decline of the (British) Establishment

- failing trust in professional (medical, legal, political) authority
- the growth of the middle class but the accentuation of the rich/poor divide
- greater subservience to global market economics, in the face of its demerits
- an upsurge in consumer culture and many new forms of commodification
- more emphasis on individualism and on projects of the self
- an upsurge in ecological politics and sensibilities on a world-wide scale
- a reduction of the grosser inequalities through gender and sexual orientation
- developing ethnic pluralism, especially in urban settings
- increasingly familiar cultural landscapes, widely dispersed
- national boundaries becoming (perhaps until recently) more permeable
- massively increasing demographic mobility, often for economic reasons
- a shift towards more globally based risks, threats and conflicts.

If a list of this sort were supported by research evidence (and a substantial body of work does support many of these claims), then we could easily recognize three familiar dimensions or application domains of globalization within them: *economic, political* and *cultural* globalization (see the discussion of these dimensions in Garrett's chapter, this volume). There are financial motivations, motivations linked to production and consumption, behind many of the changes we might otherwise assume to be 'cultural,' for example in the commodification of history as heritage or in the shaping of globally familiar metropolises. The circulation of global capital is what has homogenized the cities we take to be "world cities" (Friedmann 1986). A sense of local culture often has to be worked up in opposition to, or even within, the mechanisms of, globalized systems – for example when 'the local' is performed for mass audiences on TV or in tourism (Coupland 2009a).

When we observe that people are far more mobile today than in earlier decades (although of course there are severe social class and national restrictions on who actually *is* more mobile), we are reacting not only to technological developments but to how mass media have allowed us to visualize the world's 'distant places' as being within our reach. When we observe that ecological awareness is a development of recent decades, we are seeing how the risks and threats of global economic upscaling, and of course of mobility as part of that, have come to be resisted in newer oppositional discourses. If we see the British Establishment in decline, this is because of wholesale shifts in global political, economic, and cultural *systems*, which need to be seen as interwoven dimensions of how the world has come to be. If there has been some emancipation around gender and sexuality, this has been achieved through activity across transnational networks of various sorts, and so on. My point is simply that there are some general principles at work behind our individual perceptions of relatively recent social change, and that the concept of globalization invites us to reflect critically on changes which are significant, not least in their recency, reach, depth and systematicity.

As Lechner and Boli (2004) point out, there is the difficulty that the word 'globalization' has already become something of a global cliché (and, again, see Garrett's investigation, in this volume, into the variable inferred meanings and associations of the word 'globalization'). To that extent it is difficult to avoid the objection that subjective generalizations about change may represent a sort of leakage from journalistic or political usage back into personal perceptions and accounts. In fact it is interesting to speculate that, under globalization, mass-mediation reaches deeper into individual psyches and everyday social practice than we might assume. All the same, it would take an impressive level of cynicism to conclude that there was 'nothing new' behind contemporary observations of recent social change and 'nothing new' in the contemporary wave of globalization. It is not part of my brief to review objective sociological evidence in support of the fact that the world has changed, although we live in an era when astounding statistics routinely surface, pointing at least to new *scales* of global interdependencies in contemporary life.[2] At some point too, we need to trust the preponderance of informed opinion in academic literatures. After two decades of claim and counter-claim, globalization theory has achieved a relatively stable consensus, agreeing to set aside several more radical and totalizing arguments but holding to a middle ground. The consensus (though probably not in the chapters of this volume) is that, while globalization is certainly not without precedent, its scale and scope *are* new and detectable in changes over recent decades – and most clearly so since the 1980s. Globalization has certainly has not run its course.

In relation to history and the periodization of globalization, Robertson (1992) noted that McLuhan's idea of 'the global village' (a phrase coined in 1960) and some general notion of global 'shrinkage' entered public as well as academic consciousness fairly soon after World War II. The war itself was an event which clearly encouraged new ways of conceptualizing world orders and systems. Robertson summarizes his own conception of globalization in exactly these terms: the compression of the world and the intensification of consciousness of the world as a whole. Some key historical events are most commonly associated with the consolidation of the global (or globalized) era. In the anglophone world, these include the beginning of sustained right-wing/conservative periods of political office (Margaret Thatcher in Britain from 1979 and Ronald Reagan in the USA from 1981) and aggressive shifts towards free market, neo-liberal ideologies and policies.[3] In many regions formerly dependent on manufacturing and heavy industry, this period was also associated with rapid and damaging deindustrialization and the outsourcing of manufacturing to cheaper markets in other countries. This shift is in turn linked to a rise in service-sector work and to more emphasis being placed on 'the knowledge economy' (see Heller, this volume, on the new economy), which are inherently more globally structured activities.

The ending of the Cold War (in the late 1980s) and the dissolution of the USSR (in 1991) provided even more self-evident shifts in 'world systems' (in the sense of Wallerstein 1974) and opened up global markets for western cultural and commercial initiatives. Global participation in the internet (from the mid 1990s: see n. 2) and the exponential development of new, globally networked, communication technologies in the same period added to the mix. Therefore, while there are of course historical precursors, over earlier centuries, to most of the general *sorts* of social process we take to define globalization – demographic mobility, transnational interchange, colonial activity, and even the technologizing of communication, most obviously with the advent of printing – there are also compelling arguments that what we have seen, since 1980, has been of quantitatively and qualitatively different orders. It is in the phenomenal expansion of transnational, global mobility and in the massively increased intensity of commercial and cultural exchange and exploitation that we find a warrant for conceiving of globalization as 'something new,' and indeed (in the words of Appadurai 1996: 27) as something "strikingly new."

Globalization theory is, however, more convincing when it is more nuanced, more cautious, and more contextually refined. Appadurai and many others nowadays have resisted simple linear accounts of globalization, as encountered for example in the McLuhan type of claim to the effect that the world is becoming culturally smaller or more uniform. As Appadurai says:

> Most often the homogenization argument subspeciates into either an argument about Americanization or an argument about commoditization, and very often the two arguments are closely linked. What these arguments fail to consider is that at least as rapidly as forces from various metropolises are brought into new societies they tend to become indigenized in one way or another: this is true of music and housing styles as much as it is true of science and terrorism, spectacles and constitutions. (Appadurai 1996: 29)

This is a persuasive argument that, under the rubric of globalization, we need to explore the *tensions* between sameness and difference, between centripetal and centrifugal tendencies, and between consensus and fragmentation. (This perspective is shared by many contributors to the Handbook, and these tensions are as important in relation to linguistic processes as in other domains.) Globalization is non-linear, just as it is *not* uniformly and (ironically enough) *not* universally and *not* globally experienced. It is better theorized as a complex of processes through which difference as well as uniformity is generated, but in relation to each other. Globalization often produces hybridity and multiplicity (Hall 1996, 1997; Kellner 1989), and the multi-directionality of change has been summarized in the awkward but widely used concept of glocalization (Bauman 1998a, 1998b; Robertson 1995; see Shi-xu, this volume), which expresses the interaction of globalizing and localizing shifts. Importantly, however, it is in the appeal to hybridity and social complexity that we see how it is also necessary to approach globalization from the perspective of late modernity or post-modernity (Bauman 1982), and vice versa.

Different views are held about whether late modernity and globalization (or, more accurately, the social condition of globality) can be, or need to be, distinguished theoretically. But many of the key conditions associated with late modernity – heightened cultural reflexivity and social complexity, indeterminacy and hybridity in personal and social identities, changed thresholds of risk and trust, increased emphasis on individual life-projects and responsibilities, detraditionalization and the decline of institutions (see for instance Beck 1992,

1999; Giddens 1991, 1994; Harvey 1989) – are much easier to appreciate if we situate them in the dynamics of a more globally connected world. As I noted above, mass-mediation, for example, is a powerful factor in the dense representation of cultural difference, and people are more likely to construe alternatives to their inherited selves against this complex backdrop of images and social types. Individualization, in Beck's thesis, is a demonstrable consequence of heightened levels of global consumption, and so on. So globalization matters in the analysis of the transition from modern to late modern social arrangements, and (as many contributors to this book show) there are many specifically sociolinguistic elements to late modernity; late modernity in fact places new emphases on language, meaning, and social semiotics.

Still following an historical track, it is often observed that the earliest tangible evidence of globalization was in economics, where the impact of transnational flows of money and influence became obvious from the 1980s onwards, to some extent challenging the autonomy and authority of states and national governments. Globalization theory has often posited 'the decline of the nation–state' (Evans 1997; Hardt and Negri 2000; Ohmae 1995) – again, with the risk of over-generalization. National governments of course can – and do – continue to dictate swathes of policy within their own confines, and national boundaries and identities remain significant in many social dimensions. But there are increasingly troublesome domains where states have only limited opportunities to act conclusively on their own, for example in relation (as Beck has recently pointed out)[4] to transnational terrorism, global warming, or economic globalization itself. These are, once again, issues within our own individual realms of experience, and the concept of globalization provides a route into the critical assessment of several of the defining characteristics of our lives.

Appadurai's (1996) concept of "financescapes" (or financial landscapes) was an attempt to point to the new global architecture of financial systems – commodity speculation and rapidly shifting global currency markets – in the same way in which he encouraged us to be aware of new global "ethnoscapes," "mediascapes," "technoscapes," and "ideoscapes" (ideational and ideological landscapes: see Block's discussion of some of these concepts in the present volume). We find a compelling instance of how these 'scapes' work together under globalization in Hardt and Negri's account (2000: 253–4) of the demographic consequences of globalized macroeconomic arrangements: ghettos, favelas, and shantytowns appearing in 'First World' cities, and stock exchanges, banks, and large corporations emerging in 'Third World' localities for example.

Probably the key insight from the now voluminous literature on globalization is the need to understand socio-cultural arrangements in terms of different forms of *mobility* and *flow*. Hannerz (1992, 1996), for example, develops the view that we can no longer conceive of cultures as neatly bounded entities. Cultures diffuse and flow into each other, constructing, and responding to, complex hierarchical relationships that he calls "centres" and "peripheries" (Hannerz 1992: 218; see Blommaert and Dong, this volume). Cultural centers are sources of authority and taste that peripheries often revere and seek to emulate. In Hannerz's view, globally powerful economic and political centers need not always be cultural centers, and vice versa, so that we need a multi-dimensional "world systems" model. France, for example, Hannerz claims, is an authoritative cultural center in many respects, more so than it is a political center. He argues that Japan has tended to keep a lower cultural profile despite its economic successes. Hannerz theorizes a constantly evolving pattern of cultural influence and change which is very *un*likely to lead simply to cultural homogenization, although it could include what he calls stable forms of "creolization" or cultural hybridity. Some peripheries develop to become centers, and cultural values and markets themselves evolve and change in the flow of "cultural traffic."

As we shall see, flow has been picked up as an orienting concept by sociolinguists too, and it will be useful to refine the term's application. Bartelson (2000) tries to distinguish three ways in which global flows have been conceptualized: namely in terms of *transference*, *transformation* and *transcendence*. Transference is the most material and most readily interpretable form of flow – the movement or exchange of things across pre-existing boundaries and between pre-constituted units. Demographic migration and the dissemination of cultural formats and products are straightforward examples of transference. Although transference is very much a characteristic of global social arrangements, it is not different in kind from processes that have been labelled 'internationalization' or 'political/economic/cultural interdependence.' The 'nothing new' comment on globalization seems mostly applicable to globalization seen as transference, notwithstanding the important objection that the scale and intensity of contemporary transference is unprecedented. Globalization as transformation implies a more radical change, whereby flows modify the character of the whole global systems in which they function. Boundaries and units are themselves refashioned, as well as things flowing across and between them. In the third scenario, transcendence, "globalisation is driven forward by a dynamic of its own and is *irreducible* to singular causes within particular sectors or dimensions" (Bartelson 2000: 189, original emphasis). This abstract, third condition is strongly echoed in Hardt and Negri's (2000) notion of "empire," but also (as Bartelson points out) in Lash and Urry's (1994) argument that contemporary information and communication structures are reconstituting the world as networks of flow rather than (as we might say) as "flows of things" and through signs rather than objects, which of course provides an entrée into linguistics and semiotics.

These, then, are some of the concepts and interpretive stances that have emerged from theoretical work on globalization. Many others are picked up and debated in the following chapters, several of which incorporate their own reviews of globalization theory. My intention in this section has been simply to illustrate the resourcefulness of globalization theory and to suggest that, *prima facie* at least, social changes associated with globalization are perceptually salient for most of us and pose significant contemporary personal and intellectual challenges. Academic disciplines across the social sciences and humanities do need to (continue to) engage with globalization, and of course to (continue to) contribute to its analysis in circumstances of rapid social change.

Globalization theory has reached a point where it is quite widely recognized that we need to distinguish different disciplinary and interdisciplinary perspectives, indeed different *discourses*, on globalization (Robertson and Khondker 2009). It is in response to this challenge that the contributors have offered their work to the Handbook. In introducing an earlier and much smaller collection of work on sociolinguistics and globalization (Coupland 2003b), I commented that linguists were, at that time, "late getting to the party," in the sense that commentaries and treatises on globalization were already in full spate across other disciplines,[5] but non-existent in sociolinguistics. The present volume is able to demonstrate the considerable distance that sociolinguistics has travelled in just a few years, to the extent that linguistic perspectives on globalization do now constitute an independent discourse of globalization, albeit one that helps to synthesize and refine many others.

In the remainder of this Introduction I shall try to map out the different ways in which 'language' and 'globalization' are brought together in the four parts of the present volume and to anticipate some of the key insights that emerge from the wealth of new material that follows.

Global Multilingualism, World Languages and Language Systems

In Part I of the Handbook we find perspectives that have an impressive history within sociolinguistics. Proponents of 'nothing new' can legitimately point to rich traditions in the sociology of language that have dealt extensively with multilingual systems and with language contact processes and cases. These include classic studies by Michael Clyne, Ralph Fasold, Charles Ferguson, Joshua Fishman, Heinz Kloss, William Mackey, William Samarin, William Stewart and others (for a related review, see Ammon 1989; also Ammon, this volume). To pick out just one landmark study, Stewart (1970) reported a succinct but limited notational system designed to capture systemic relationships between languages and a taxonomy of language 'types': *vernacular, standard, classical, pidgin and Creole*. Original conceptualizations like Stewart's laid the ground for systematic descriptive accounts of languages in communities and languages in contact, and these early initiatives have been massively extended in recent scholarship; see for example Apel and Muysken (1987), Kachru (1992), Myers-Scotton (2002), Pavlenko and Blackledge (2004). The sociology of language has always been interested in the relative vitality of languages and communities, and in language death and attrition internationally. It might be tempting to argue that, even if globalization itself refers to a new and newly important social condition, we can account for 'language and globalization' simply by extending the remit of a traditional sociology of language. As we shall see, however, this is to understate significantly what is required.

In response to globalization, the most obvious requirement is for a sociology of language that can model relationships among languages on a global scale. In his opening paper, Mufwene[6] does extremely valuable ground-clearing work, reviewing the concept of globalization and its relationship with earlier processes of colonization and bringing a critical eye to the widely debated concept of 'global English.' Mufwene is a strong proponent of the 'nothing new' stance, certainly in relation to 'world languages,' and perhaps also in relation to 'language and globalization.' He is skeptical about the need to defend the concept of 'world language' at all, and he argues that, throughout history, we have seen languages expand and fragment. His account of 'global English,' as others call it, finds close parallels with Latin, which came to be favored mainly for its association with international trade but then diversified into different Romance varieties. The world, he argues, is not heading towards monolingualism, and English is not a "killer language" (see also Mufwene 1994, 2008).

It is therefore useful to assess the orientations that subsequent chapters in Part I take, implicitly or explicitly, to Mufwene's stance, which will strike some as laissez-faire and as rather apolitical. In fact, however, De Swaan is, rather similarly, matter of fact and certainly not romanticizing in his overview of global language systems (compare De Swaan 2001; also Crystal 2000 and Winford 2003). De Swaan assesses the relative "communication values" of different languages in the "world system," their "prevalence" and their "centrality," and proceeds to explain and predict the changing fortunes of languages – what, in the terminology of classical sociology of language, is referred to as ethnolinguistic vitality, language maintenance, and language shift (see Fishman 1991). De Swaan's top-down model captures the apparently rational and pragmatic decisions people make when they decide to invest in particular languages or to leave them behind. The world's linguistic system is described as an evolving set of relationships among languages as their utility values change.

Skutnabb-Kangas and Phillipson trust less in rational choice and take a more overtly political approach in their assessment of the prospects of the world's languages (see also Phillipson 1992, 1993; Skutnabb-Kangas 2000). They align against "linguistic neo-imperialism," "linguistic genocide," and "crimes against humanity in education." Ammon, again, reviews the concept of 'world languages' (and compare Ammon, Mattheier, and Nelde 1994); and, like De Swaan, he attempts a synthesis of the ranking of languages within a global linguistic system by referring to previous accounts. Ammon debates lingua franca uses of English (compare House 2003, Jenkins 2007, Seidlhofer 2004) in which the authentic 'Englishness' of English arguably ceases to be an issue. Ricento then asks whether countries can and should protect their national linguistic resources, opposing globalist neo-liberal discourse and assumptions. He reflects on the early linguistic history of North America and on language policies in South Africa, India and elsewhere, concluding that neo-liberal claims – that an 'open market' will liberate people to make informed linguistic choices and will lead to more democratic arrangements – are not supported by historical evidence.

It is clear, then, that some authors are much more vociferous than others on the topic of how global languages, and English in particular, come to be imposed on an expanding range of territories and on other languages. Ammon and De

Swaan model global systems in which languages have different capital values and vie for recognition and for speakers, while both Ricento and Skutnabb-Kangas and Phillipson bring more human and ethical considerations to the fore. Mufwene stresses that linguistic globalization, however we define it, is an historically continuous and rather unexceptional process. Ricento frames his arguments in relation to recent globalization theory more than the others do. Even so, there is consensus across the Part I chapters I have mentioned so far – at the level of theory. All these contributors develop analyses couched in terms of relativities of ethnolinguistic vitality – what we could reductively describe as balance sheets of global linguistic entitlement and opportunity, where world languages (if they can be named so) are shown to be winning out at the expense of others. Similar approaches are found in other important existing accounts, including Brutt-Griffler's *World English* (2002), Gordon's *Languages of the World* (2005), Graddol's two volumes analyzing future global trends within English and other languages – *The Future of English* (1997) and *English Next* (2006) – Maurais and Morris's *Languages in a Globalizing World* (2003), Nettle and Romaine's *Vanishing Voices* (2000), and Wright's *Language Policy and Language Planning: From Nationalism to Globalization* (2004).

As we will see in later chapters, however, there are authors who want to take issue with the broad orientation found in all these works. For example Blommaert (2006, 2009, and also later in this volume) argues that sociolinguistics has settled into a dominant but reductive mode of describing the spread of linguistic variables over restricted horizontal spaces, in the general manner of Labovian variationism (see Labov 1972 and Coupland 2007 for a review); but he thinks that this is also apparent in the sociolinguistic field of language contact. His objection is that this perspective gives us only a restricted account of space and time, when globalization theory stresses how time and space have themselves been radically reconfigured. Blommaert is concerned that systems approaches pay very little attention to the particular functions of communicative repertoires under conditions of mobility. In her chapter, later in the volume, Heller similarly challenges some of the assumptions underlying rights-based appeals to linguistic ownership and autonomy. Going back to some conceptual distinctions that we considered a little earlier, we might say that contact models in sociolinguistics have tended to deal with flows as *transference* – as movement of codes and people across pre-defined and unchanging boundaries – rather than in terms of *transformation* and *transcendence*. The underlying issue is whether in fact we need more theory, and different theory, in the sociolinguistic framing of globalization, or whether it is sufficient to widen the scope of existing treatments. These debates come back in the subsequent parts of the book.

Still on the theme of global languages, Pool takes us in a different direction. He offers a pro-active vision of "panlingual globalization" in which, through marketing and other strategies, the world's 7,000 or so existing languages might be protected, offsetting the drift (*pace* Mufwene) towards global monolingualism through English. He then discusses and illustrates a set of semantic principles according to which panlingual translation might be facilitated. In some ways, a brave new world of linguistic engineering sits rather well with the commodification of language that others see as a hallmark of linguistic globalization. But in any account of 'world languages' it is crucial to recognize that languages other than English have their own claims to this status (compare the concluding discussion in Block's chapter). As Mufwene argues, even without the focused global intervention of the sort Pool envisages, it is a mistake to predict a world unilingual in English without close investigation of shifts being experienced by other languages and their users. Part I of the Handbook would ideally contain chapters reflecting on many other languages and national settings, 'majority' and 'minority' alike, and on their shifting patterns of vitality. Chapters in the other parts of the book do, however, bring in detailed commentaries on many of them – for instance Bhatt's observations on South Asia and West Africa, Heller's observations on La Francophonie, Kramsch and Boner's references to Tanzania, Mooney's analysis of the linguistic bases of global religions, Pennycook's remarks on popular culture in various global settings, Shi-xu's commentary on China, van Leeuwen and Suleiman's reference to Egypt and Arabic.

As detailed case studies in Part I, we have Mar-Molinero's assessment of the spread of global Spanish and Busch's account of the development of new national languages in eastern Europe, the former Yugoslavia in particular. Each of these two case studies raises issues of general importance. Mar-Molinero points to a mix of centralized language policy initiatives, particularly by Spain, and to grassroots initiatives, particularly centered on popular music, which is helping to promote varieties of Spanish globally. The power of vernacularity has been underestimated in language systems approaches, which mainly seek to map out the status of 'whole languages.' Yet one of the themes that emerge strongly in the later parts of the Handbook is the need to attend to the globalization of *genres* and *styles* of particular languages, as well as – or in preference to – commentaries on 'whole languages' themselves. It can be argued that, under globalization, languages are evolving and spreading less and less as coherent uniform linguistic systems. Mar-Molinero explains that 'Spanglish' and *Livin' la vida loca* play a key role in the transnational appeal of Spanish, but also in shifting evaluations of what matters as 'language' in global communication.

Busch describes shifts in the other direction in eastern Europe – shifts whereby codes formerly institutionalized as 'majority languages' have been repositioned and decentered as 'minority languages' (such as Russian in the Baltic states) and whereby varieties rise to prominence as new 'national languages.' Like Mar-Molinero, she points to the limitations of top-down measures in implementing language planning, even under authoritarian conditions, but again to the importance of understanding the language-ideological basis of demarcating one language from another (see also Gal 2006). Busch quotes Bakhtin's view that a 'national language' is an ideologically saturated object and an expression of a world view, rather than a strictly linguistic category.

In Part I, therefore, we are already seeing some significant disputes, both within key contributors' positions on global multilingualism and between the ways in which that broad area of scholarship and others make sense of 'the sociolinguistics of globalization'. There are different levels of political engagement: Is the global expansion of particular languages something we should regret and oppose, or something inevitable and familiar? There is disagreement over units of analysis: Is linguistic globalization about the fates of languages, regarded as bounded linguistic systems within changing social and sociolinguistic systems, or is it about ways of using language, new repertoires, diffusing genres and styles, and changing ideologies around language use? There is disagreement about the necessary theoretical infrastructure: To what extent should sociolinguistics refashion its own theory in response to the new challenges posed by globalization? Or can we get by with what we have? These are some of the debates around which a sociolinguistics of globalization is being carried forward, and there are many more to come in the volume. The terrain is too challenging and too interesting for us to expect bland consensus.

Global Discourse in Key Domains and Genres

Part II of the Handbook shifts focus from language regarded as a system (and from language systems functioning in global systems) to language regarded as social action – or from languages to discourses. In his 2006 book, Fairclough sets out a Critical Discourse Analysis (CDA) agenda relating to globalization (see also Fairclough 2009). He espouses a realist position, accepting that there are objective facts of globalization to be observed and measured, but he says that these objectivities are generally "much too complex to be fully controlled by any human intervention" (2006: 28). Hence critical attention needs to be given to how the discourses that drive forward the objective changes we associate with globalization are constructed – or selected – and consumed. For Fairclough and for all critical analysts of discourse, discourses do have social consequences. Discursive change, in Fairclough's view, often presages and facilitates real social change. The key elements for Fairclough are the (pro-globalization) discourse of "globalism" and the way it is impacting on patterns of work, government, politics, and personal identity in different social settings. In fact globalism is, he says, a new *order* of discourse – a new structured configuration of discourses, genres and styles, based on neo-liberal political assumptions (ibid., p. 29).

Related issues concerning markets and values inescapably feature in many chapters; they are dealt with most directly in Part III. In Part II, contributors explore instead some of the key communicative genres and practices that globalization has not only facilitated but brought into being. We might also say that these are some of the key discourses through which globalization has *itself* been brought into being: discourse practices associated with mass media (Androutsopoulos; van Leeuwen and Suleiman), tourism (Jaworski and Thurlow), language teaching (Block), global terror (Hodges), and global religion (Mooney).

Androutsopoulos describes the main characteristics of 'Web 2.0,' where the internet becomes more radically interactive via content-sharing and social networking sites and platforms. He shows how engagement with the interactive web involves new forms of textual and symbolic manipulation and appreciation. In Androutsopoulos's chapter we immediately see that a sociolinguistics of new media needs to be elaborated, both descriptively and theoretically. Textual resources, including the ones Androutsopoulos refers to as "spectacles," are inherently multi-modal rather than strictly linguistic, for example video clips that become a focus for interactive reassessment and critical comment among networks of users. Associated web pages show complexities of visual syntax and trans-modal relations. Androutsopoulos argues that users and analysts alike need to be sensitive to intertextual relationships, because meanings are often made by appropriating pre-existing resources and embed them in new environments (see Johnson and Ensslin's (2007) concept of "intermediality"). We also have to be alert to heteroglossic relationships, because users often take particular stances, sometimes oppositional or "vari-directional," to materials that they comment on. Older sociolinguistic themes emerge too, but they require new interpretations. Androutsopoulos traces new ways in which the interactive web positions vernacular varieties such as the Bavarian dialects of German.

Van Leeuwen and Suleiman share the view that sociolinguistic analyses of globalized mass media need to be multimodal and focused on local-global tensions. They start from the view that analysis of glocalization processes is often over-generalized, for example in the idea, contrary to the McDonaldization hypothesis, that global mass media are always localized and indigenized. They prefer a case-by-case approach, which can be sensitive to just what is globally uniform and what is locally specific in particular media products, for instance the many national versions of *Cosmopolitan* magazine (see Machin and van Leeuwen 2007; also Machin and van Leeuwen, this volume). In the case examined in detail here, that of an Egyptian superhero comic, *Zein*, van Leeuwen and Suleiman find that "becoming global" is not considered legitimate, so that the comic ultimately fails, commercially and in its reception by critics. That is, the clearly USA-sourced genre of superhero comics proves to be "unlocalizable," even though the *Zein* data that van Leeuwen and Suleiman analyze are in themselves designed as highly globalized texts.

Van Leeuwen and Suleiman's approach to analysis and their concerns about premature generalization are significant for a sociolinguistics of globalization, as well as for sociolinguistics generally. A specifically linguistic/discursive approach to globalization offers the resource of detailed critical commentary on particular instances, of a sort that is not available to most other social science treatments. As Labov said about the sociolinguistic approach that he pioneered, in the detail of empirical investigation "we encounter the possibility of being right" (Labov 1972: 259), and this is a particularly precious resource in an area of theory that tends towards the grandiose. (Later on in the run of chapters, Mooney makes a similar appeal for sociolinguistics not to set aside its traditional concerns with linguistic detail and specific cases.)

Jaworski and Thurlow share the commitment to analytic particularity, and also to analyzing discursive *practice* – or what we might call the 'coming to be' of globally situated communicative interaction. They also show how careful analysis of discursive events can illuminate, refine, or challenge some of the more abstract and general claims about global social processes. So this is not empirical particularism as an alternative to social theory, or linguistic analysis in the service of social theory. It is the attempt to understand the general in the context of the particular and to expose the theoretical significance of local discursive practices – the perspective that motivates CDA as a discipline. Jaworski and Thurlow analyze tourism encounters (and see Jaworski and Thurlow 2010; Jaworski et al. 2010; Thurlow and Jaworski 2010), which they see as a focal genre of "banal globalization," the everyday textual realization of global capitalism. But they also draw attention to the fact that "language," in many different ways, becomes a central practice in the performance of tourism and comes to be associated with particular exchange values, especially in interactions between tourists and "hosts" or "locals." They identify particular act-types that are structurally linked to the economic frameworks of global tourism, for instance "tourist teases" and "tourist greetings." This is language (discourse) constituting globalization.

Reflecting, partly autobiographically, on the institutions and priorities of English language teaching around the world, Block argues that a globalized ideoscape dominates contemporary practice (and see Block and Cameron 2002; Canagarajah 1999). This provides an opportunity to assess the implementation of glocalization in language education contexts – how westernized and homogenized teaching materials and approaches are and to what extent they accommodate presumed or actual local cultural context. Block points out that, in the past, English language teaching materials have tended to realize British and American cultural ideologies, while more cosmopolitan and global consumerist values have now started to be represented. Global cultural flows are coming to be incorporated in teaching materials (for instance engagement with global celebrities and lifestyles), and those texts constitute a flow mechanism in its own right. In fact there are interesting resemblances between Block's description of the social representations found in more cosmopolitan teaching texts and the intuited list of social changes with which I began this introduction.

There is no clearer or more chilling instance of a discourse that drives social change and new global relations – Fairclough's CDA agenda – than the discourse of the George W. Bush administration referring to 'the war on terror.' Bush's rhetoric, as analyzed by Hodges (and compare Hodges and Nilep 2007), forces new global disjunctions between 'them' and 'us,' between terrorists and victims, and between Islamic fundamentalists and (at least by implication) rational westerners. That discourse, Hodges shows, was a device for constructing different interpretations of global relations – for example when Bush identified the 9/11 attacks on the World Trade Center as a triggering event for a legitimate 'war on terror,' which Bush and others then took as a warrant for military exploits in Iraq and elsewhere. The discourse becomes available for recontextualization or application in other contexts, for example by Serbian intellectuals who rationalize their own conflict with Bosnian and Kosovar Muslims.

Discourse is of course not only a means of obscuring and manipulating political processes; it needs to provide means of disambiguating veiled or double-voiced meanings. We might associate this function with CDA itself; but, as Hodges shows, there are many voices, not least voices in the mass media, interested in renegotiating the 'war on terror' discourse and its presuppositions. If we stand back from the detail of Hodges's commentaries on these processes, it becomes possible to see global international relations and conflict as a series of complex flows of contested meanings. This is arguably where we find the most pressing case for a linguistic perspective on globalization, particularly in the form of critical analyses of discourse.

Religion itself is a casualty of the 'war on terror' discourse, in the sense that it looms in the background of contemporary global antagonisms and is non-specifically implicated in conflict discourses (see the attribution 'fundamentalist,' mentioned above, and the discussion of fundamentalism in Mooney's chapter). It is important, then, to review the wider links between language, discourse, place, and religion and to reflect on their changing inter-relationships under globalization. This is what Mooney offers in her chapter: a critical and comparative sociolinguistic reassessment of world religions and of their globalizing forms and functions. Religious systems are discourses, variably amenable to change and to hybridization and with different historical connections to global zones and languages. These discourses are, as Mooney shows, increasingly carried to people via satellite, cable TV, and the internet (which includes virtual reality domains), creating global "religious marketplaces." Televangelism, for example, is a genre broadcast mainly through English, which shows that religion is not at all immune to the general pressures we saw discussed in Part I. But it is the corporatization and technologization of religion that stand out perhaps as being most significant; the internet, as Mooney suggests at one point, may be in the process of becoming a metaphor for the divine.

Language, Values, and Markets under Globalization

Many chapters in Part I and Part II of the Handbook have made reference to the economic basis of contemporary globalization, as I did in my introductory remarks on globalization theory in this chapter. The forces that reconfigure patterns of multilingualism are to a large extent economic, as for example when the 'value' of English consists in the access it is often perceived to give to wider markets, and hence to financial advancement of different sorts. International tourism is above all, as Jaworski and Thurlow emphasize, a global economic system, and so is global English language teaching. As we have just seen, even religion may be tending that way. Sociolinguists have for some time used Bourdieu's "symbolic capital" framework (Bourdieu 1991) and his analysis of neo-liberalism as economic fatalism (Bourdieu and Wacquant 1999; Fairclough 2006, 2009). But a sociolinguistic conception of *le marché linguistique* was established as early as the 1970s (see Sankoff and Laberge 1978).

In Part III, although sociolinguistic engagement with markets is 'nothing new,' we do see many of the new ways in which markets and values have taken on significance in relation to globalization. This involves taking a broader view of 'values,' one which spans monetary and material value as well as cultural values of various sorts. Two general issues are addressed in this part of the book. First, how does globalization create new value systems in which language is implicated (including new values for language use and for the language varieties themselves)? Secondly, how are the discourses of globalization valued in different places and under different conditions?

Heller critiques the role of language in the globalized new economy. The new economy has come about through the relocation of heavy industry and manufacturing out of former industrialized areas; it is evident in the rise of service-sector and niche markets in their place. Heller's research has been extremely influential in pointing out new demands made on language use and new value frameworks around varieties and multilingualism, especially in new economy work practices (Duchêne and Heller 2007; Heller 2007; see also Cameron 2000). In her chapter here, Heller explains how language comes to be commodified, treated as a marketplace skill or as resource that bears little relation to older understandings of the fact that ways of speaking are historically structured into communities through socialization. Sociolinguistics has repeatedly shown the local value of minority linguistic varieties within their own community settings, indexing ingroup allegiance and ethnolinguistic distinctiveness. But in new economy settings, minority varieties can be treated as shortcuts to cultural authenticity, for example in international tourism contexts (see Jaworski and Thurlow). Heller then widens the debate, cycling back to the issues discussed in Part I. She argues that rights-based and ecologically framed arguments against "killer languages" make assumptions which are strongly locked into nationalist assumptions and out of step with changed, globalized social circumstances. In fact she argues that we need a new sociolinguistics, one that deals with language as a resource and not with language as a system.

A similar case is made by Blommaert and Dong, who urge us to see language as a set of mobile, trans-locally operative resources rather than as localized and "sedentary" sociolinguistic patterns. Blommaert and Dong lobby for a difficult concept of sociolinguistic scales (compare Blommaert, Collins, and Slembrouck 2005), which superimposes a vertical hierachization of value onto language varieties and uses in their particular 'horizontal' (social and geographical) locations. In ways reminiscent of Gumperz's theory of conversational inferencing (Gumperz 1982), they point to the indexical importance of sociolinguistic fragments or truncated repertoires (alongside the importance of whole varieties, traditionally conceived) as the focus of assessments of linguistic adequacy or acceptability. These theoretical resources are needed, Blommaert and Dong argue, to account for changing and uneven patterns of attributed value when people and ways of speaking and texts "travel." If we return to Bartelson's three-way reinterpretation of flow, Blommaert and Dong's dissatisfaction with distributional sociolinguistic accounts is similar to Bartelson's comment that contemporary globalization entails something more significant than 'transference.' Blommaert and Dong insist that global flow disrupts the landscapes over which movement happens, and this is what is implied in Bartelson's concepts of "transformation" and "transcendence."

Those indexical fragments or 'bits' of language, as in the accent-shifts that Blommaert and Dong comment on in their Beijing example, are also the stuff of variationist sociolinguistics, and particularly of approaches to the social meaning of variation referred to under the heading of 'style' (Coupland 2007). Johnstone considers the apparent paradox that regional variation at the level of accents or dialect (for example of English) continues to be socially and stylistically meaningful and noteworthy in the contemporary context of globalization, where what others have called 'superdiversity' reigns. How can small-scale local meanings be significant in the vast sociolinguistic marketplaces of the globalized world? Johnstone argues that dialect indexicality is actually a *consequence* of globalization rather than representing a series of fitful attempts to maintain a sense of the local in the face of global homogenization (although one could argue that this is likely too). Johnstone's point is that, under globalization, very local linguistic forms and styles are resemioticized, given new ideological values and loadings, particularly in stylized usages and in performance frames of different sorts. They become the focus of discourses of differentiation and they are culturally noticed or enregistered (Agha 2006). Johnstone then goes on to discuss dialect "enregisterment" processes and outcomes in Pittsburg, USA, as elements of the process of producing 'the local,' much of it mass-mediated.

Valuing the local is, from one point of view, an ecological sensitivity, and we saw in relation to arguments about global multilingualism that a general valuing of 'diversity where it exists' motivates many language maintenance efforts. There is, however, an important distinction to be drawn between valuing 'one's own difference' (which surfaces in nationalist discourses and in some sorts of language-rights arguments, and which endorses sometimes questionable, essentialist claims about linguistic ownership) and valuing diversity for its own sake. The latter position is a far 'deeper' ecological stance, especially when it is applied to the biosphere as a whole rather than to 'languages' or 'language varieties,' which are social constructs rather than organic entities. Stibbe presents the arguments for bringing a deep ecology framework to sociolinguistics: an ecolinguistics that will expose how particular ways of using language conspire in the destruction of the planet. Language is seen as a barrier to ecological understanding and action. Stibbe reviews the history of ecolinguistics in its different waves before commenting on the spread of discourses he considers hegemonic – including the globalist discourse of progress and consumerism, which Fairclough analyses (see above). But he also comments on how environmental discourses themselves often embed consumerist and anthropocentric attitudes that militate against their authors' own ambitions.

A particular paradox of glocalization is how to reconcile the need to establish universal principles – say, of linguistic self-determination, or of health care entitlement, or of environmental protection – with the need to respect and attune to particular global environments with unique histories and cultural values. As Stibbe says, there is a risk of positively intended discourses becoming hegemonic. This is precisely what Shi-xu documents in his analysis of western versus Chinese discourses of human rights. He shows that the historically limited but fast evolving Chinese human rights discourse is based in particular philosophical traditions and colonial experiences. Shi-xu documents the many recent institutional resources established to support such a discourse, but explains that China has not been well placed to engage constructively with strident and culturally hegemonic (and would-be universalist) western demands.

In a similar vein, we might expect the precise meanings of the very concept of 'globalization' to have different resonances in relation to different domains of global activity (of the sorts we have been discussing), but also in different parts of the world, in different languages, and in culturally specific discourses. In fact Mufwene (in the second endnote to his chapter) discusses semantic non-equivalences between French "mondialization" and English "globalization." Taking a quantitative empirical (questionnaire-based but open-ended) line on this question, Garrett is able to show some systematic differences in the way university students in Australia, China, Japan, New Zealand, the UK, and the USA construe, and react evaluatively to, the term 'globalization.' Chinese and New Zealand respondents, for example, give the most positive and most negative reactions, respectively. While Garrett finds globalization to be taken to refer overall to cultural dimensions more than to economic and other ones, cultural issues in globalization are more salient to Japanese and USA respondents than to others – "global unity and cooperation" being uppermost in the way they specify that cultural significance. Americans show a relatively strong awareness of their country being the main force behind globalization, but rather little preoccupation with economic issues and issues of power and exploitation. As well as exposing some very revealing national trends, Garrett's study is valuable in cautioning against an over-confident use of one of the two core concepts we are debating in this volume.

Finally in Part III, Kelly-Holmes explores the processes of global marketing, and she focuses on the brand that has often been taken to represent the apogée (or nadir) of globalized commercialism: *McDonald's*. Marketing is the strategic use of image and language text to promote and differentiate a brand; McDonald's used the slogan "I'm lovin' it" as their first global advertising theme. The slogan ostensibly conjures up values of harmony and straightforwardness and, as Kelly-Holmes says, it cleverly manages the tension between McDonald's being a global corporate giant and the implied intense localness of enjoying a fast hamburger. The vernacularity and informality of the sloganized utterance and the visual style of its textual representation are, as Kelly-Holmes shows, further parts of the brand's "unique selling proposition." The slogan has appeared in seven languages other than English, showing a degree of strategic localization (compare Kelly-Holmes 2005). Most of these languages are, however, easily predicted from De Swaan's and other models of global language systems. As Kelly-Holmes says, global marketing relies on and exploits global language hierarchies in predictable ways. But a coherent and 'clean' brand image is maintained through the multilingual versions, through McDonald's consistency of visual design and stylistic manipulations.

Language, Distance, and Identities

In the final part of the Handbook we have a series of chapters devoted to the analysis of language and meaning "across distance" and to the effects of distance on the experience of personal and social identities. This work responds to the observation that globalization involves a compression of time and space (Giddens 1994, 2002). Social relations, and even forms of intimacy, become possible across distance, but they still have to be negotiated through complex and sometimes restrictive forms of mediation. This theme is a particular challenge to sociolinguistics, in that the discipline's founding insights into identity have mainly been linked to 'community,' which has in turn been theorized as local, face-to-face mutual engagement (in speech communities, in social networks, or in communities of practice). There have been efforts to retheorize the traditional but unrewarding concept of 'speech community' and to move on from the 'sociolinguistics of community' that has been built around it (Coupland 2010; Patrick 2002; Pratt 1987; Rampton 2006, 2009). These theoretical developments have been necessary, partly to take account of more mobile trajectories and flows of populations, and partly to build less essentializing models of social identities, premised on 'authentic' cultural membership (Bucholtz 2003, Coupland 2003a, Eckert 2003). But the detailed analysis of sociolinguistic identities 'at distance,' in specific domains, is a new undertaking.

In a contribution that draws together many of the key insights of other chapters of the Handbook, Kramsch and Boner explore a critical, post-modern approach to communication across distance and culture. They alert us to the fact that concepts of flow and transcultural exchange, like the old notion of "intercultural communication" (Kramsch 1998), may conceal global inequalities (compare Blommaert and Dong) and cultural fragmentation. In their empirical study of interactions that were set up between members of an American economic development NGO and local people in order to help establish entrepreneurial projects in Tanzania, they are able to demonstrate the consequences of some fundamental mismatches in the way participants orient to planning processes. It turns out that NGO members and local people have, for example, different understandings of the core linguistic concepts of 'help' and 'need.' Behind negotiations to establish new forms of partnership there are different, culturally based understandings of other concepts too – such as 'friend,' which might imply on the one hand participation in fast moving commercial partnerships and networks, and on the other hand 'slow-time' relations of trust with other people in local face-to-face networks. Globalization, Kramsch and Boner explain, tends to instrumentalize relationships in the drive towards new entrepreneurial activity, and to set up "imaginary solidarities." Discursive exchange, they say, comes to involve "shadows" – only fleetingly or marginally detectable assumptions and implications.

In his chapter, Bhatt takes a more historical perspective, but similarly critiques the partly veiled assumptions attached to the use of English in India and Nigeria in the colonial era, before going on to discuss the complex implications of language choice for identity negotiation in post-colonial contexts. Bhatt takes us into the classic sociolinguistic controversy – paralleled in discussions of English as a lingua franca (on which see above) – of whether and how it is possible to construct genuinely *post*-colonial identities and subjectivities through use of 'the colonial language,' English. Bhatt takes an interdisciplinary perspective, citing arguments from literary studies and from critical and cultural theory. But he bolsters them with sociolinguistic commentaries on English syntactic and pragmatic features that index "acts of resistance." This helps to pin down the concept of cultural hybridity, so often appealed to in post-colonial cultural studies, defining it as the transfer of specific features from indigenous local languages into English usage.

Gender and sexuality have generally been treated as culturally bound, 'within-community' issues, both in sociolinguistics and elsewhere. In successive chapters, Piller and Takahashi, then Leap, set out to assess the impact of a globalization perspective on these very well established sociolinguistic fields. Piller and Takahashi consider the way patterns of transnational migration – which, as we have already seen, are prone to leaving important and often troublesome legacies, bound up with language competence and language evaluation – impact on particular groups of migrant women. Relevant groups include care-workers, women employed in catering and tourism sectors, and sex workers. Piller and Takahashi show that variable levels of competence in English have different social consequences for individuals, as for example when Filipina domestic workers in Taiwan are able to use their relatively high linguistic competence to renegotiate power differentials with their employers. But the authors also track covert category distinctions, which define some sorts of employment – for example "white (migrant) women's work." Leap reviews the history of "gay language," noting the urban North Atlantic associations of legitimated gay stances and lifestyles in many parts of the world (compare Leap and Boellstorff 2004). As in the case of 'migrant women,' this can lead to a situation where English competence has a particular status within what Leap calls the "global circuit" of same-sex cultures. But local sexual cultures vary in their endorsement of western 'gay liberation politics,' as well as in their normative speaking conventions for gay encounters – as is demonstrated for example in the case of 'Bahasa gay' in Indonesia, or in a convention, prevalent in French gay practice, of using English lexis for iconic commodities. This variation can lead to unanticipated social hierarchies and patterns of social exclusion as people move through the global circuit.

Although globalization theory in its more extreme forms has prematurely declared the demise of the nation-state (a theme I have already touched upon), many people would have reservations about the claim that traditional ethnic identities are in terminal decline. We saw some contributors arguing for a position where the grander potential social realignments associated with globalization theory become the focus of empirical sociolinguistic research, and of research that is accountable to its data (as sociolinguistics has always been). In the case of ethnicity, it would seem sensible *not* to presume that all local ethnic sensibility is 'impossible' or 'naively essentialist' in a globalizing world, but also *not* to presume that our cultural provenances 'naturally' or even 'normally' lock us into particular social identities. At the levels of sociolinguistic theory and analysis, we should expect 'identity' to be a more demanding and multi-layered concept – needing to be subdivided at least into the dimensions of 'feeling,' 'knowing,' and 'doing' rather than being treated as some composite form of 'being.' (I argue this case in detail in Coupland 2007; but see also the discussion of different identity sub-processes in Machin and van Leeuwen's chapter, below.) We should expect specifically ethnic identities to interact with, and possibly to compete with, other social dimensions of identification, and we should also expect these relativities to be particularly important under circumstances of global flow.

In the spirit of these reservations, Maher explores what he calls "metroethnicities" and the linguistic usage associated with them, "metrolanguage." Drawing theoretical support from Butler (1997), Hall (1997), Pennycook (in this volume) and others, Maher explores some of the complexities of performative identity among young global urbanites. He argues that metroethnicity is characteristic of fast moving and fluid urban spaces in "world cities" like Tokyo. It involves playful and ephemeral signification, sometimes centered on global celebrities like the UK-born footballer David Beckham, but with eclectic indexical appropriations of ethnic and national styles such as 'a Thai accent' or 'an Irish genealogy.' Metroethnicity and metrolanguage, says Maher, are performed in the pursuit of what is cool, and to that extent they construct "lite" identities – playful and commodified identities rather than socially fixed or embedded identities.

Maher's written account is performed within the genre norms of metroethnicity itself, and something of the same feeling of metacultural *jouissance* (a term which I do not use in its Lacanian – or in any other specific – sense) comes through in Pennycook's account of global popular culture shifts and appropriations. Pennycook focuses on the cyclical flows associated with hip hop and rap music – a truly globalized set of genres, carried through a different sort of global circuit. He comments, for example, on developments in French language hip hop over the last twenty years, which has spawned distinctive scenes outside of France itself, including in West Africa and Canada. Hip hop culture proves to be an ideal locus for exploring trajectories of globalization and localization and ways in which linguistic resources are selectively redeployed and freshly coined in the construction of new hybridities (see also Pennycook 2007). Pennycook celebrates the new transcultural relationships and identities that surface and the potential for transgressive and oppositional stances – not least for an opposition to national language norms and policies.

Global distance of a very different sort is entailed when people become onlookers, observing mediated spectacles of human tragedy in far-off places. Chouliaraki is interested in how these events are mass-mediated and in how they impact on media consumers. Global media bring to us versions of human disasters across geographical distance and across cultural differences, but often there is also a gulf between the context of suffering and the context of observation, between the powerlessness of those who suffer and the privileged circumstances of the observers. The power of mediating institutions such as TV news, and the motivational power of the texts themselves, also impinge directly. Chouliaraki analyzes, in relation to six particular instances, these contexts and processes of production and consumption and the public readiness to take action in support of the suffering. There are different types or modes of representation. One is "adventure news," which is told in classical narrative form, keeping viewers "distant" from the catastrophic event. Chouliaraki then identifies a quite different mode, which she calls "ecstatic" news coverage: this is familiar to most of us from the manner of constructing the television coverage of the 9/11 attacks on the World Trade Center in New York. In this mode normal temporal arrangements are suspended, creating a feeling of timelessness. Chouliaraki argues that, in this frame, disaster television creates its own sense of the historical and triggers empathetic engagement from viewers. She is therefore able to show how global publics can be differently positioned by the global media reporting of disasters (compare Chouliaraki 2006); spectators can sometimes be constructed as moral agents who need to judge globally significant events, and to act.

In the Handbook's final chapter we stay in the domain of global media, with Machin and van Leeuwen's analysis of "lifestyle identities." They consider the case of *Cosmopolitan* magazine and comment on the identities that *Cosmo* constructs for its female readers, across its wide global range of publication contexts. Machin and van Leeuwen then find that young women interviewees in different global settings tend to recycle these values and identities in their responses to researchers who interview them. Lifestyle identities are based on ideologies of choice and consumerism, on the assumption that one can 'be' whatever one chooses – namely on the basis of commodities purchased and consumed and by building lifestyles organized around these choices. There are resonances here with the analyses of identity discussed in other chapters of Part IV – not so much in the specific 'contents' of those 'identities' as in the underlying processes appealed to. Machin and van Leeuwen observe that the way we theorize identity is influenced by the social conditions we experience around us, and therefore by specific judgments of what matters *qua* 'identity.' They draw a fascinating contrast between, for example, the *Cosmo*-reading women's repertoire of 'lifestyle' categories and distinctions for their own identities and bureaucratic, statist categories and distinctions used in employment and immigration contexts. 'Functionalist,' consumption-focused routes into identity, centered on lifestyle and choice, are fully consistent with mass-mediated and globalized discourses, which continually offer us commodified versions of ourselves, if only we make the right choices. As Machin and van Leeuwen conclude, just how much agentive freedom we have in exercising these choices remains a moot point.

NOTES

1 I comment in greater detail on a similar list, and discuss some supporting sociological evidence pertaining to Britain, in Coupland 2009b.
2 We cannot fail to react to statistics like the following: there has been a 342 percent increase in global usage of the internet between 2000 and 2008 (quoted at http://www.internetworldstats.com/stats.htm), and 1.6 billion international tourist arrivals worldwide are forecast by the World Tourism Organization by 2020, compared with 924 million in 2008 (reported at http://www.unwto.org – both sites accessed 8 July 2009).
3 There is the considerable irony that, in Thatcher's case, the drive to free-market economics coincided with aggressive nationalistic stances, not least in relation to 'protecting British sovereignty' in Falklands War. Hall interprets Thatcher's orientation to the Falklands as "living the past entirely through myth" and "reliving the age of the dictators, not just as farce but as myth" (1997: 177), and this once again points to the non-linearity of globalization processes.
4 http://www.guardian.co.uk/commentisfree/2008/jan/15/politics.eu (consulted 8 July 2009).
5 Important sources that have not come up so far in the present discussion include Beck, Giddens and Lash 1994; Castells 1996; Cohen 1997; Featherstone 1990; Featherstone and Lash 1995; Held et al. 1999; Hobsbawm and Ranger 1983; McGrew and Lewis 1992; Papastergiadis 2000; and Scott 1997 (although this is still far from being a comprehensive list).
6 In the remainder of this Introduction, authors' names not accompanied by dates refer to chapter contributions to the present volume.

REFERENCES

Agha, A. (2006) *Language and Social Relations*. Cambridge: Cambridge University Press.

Ammon, U. (ed.) (1989) *Status and Function of Languages and Language Varieties*. Berlin: Mouton de Gruyter.

Ammon, U., Mattheier, K. J., and Nelde, P. H. (eds) (1994) *English Only? In Europa In Europe En Europe*. Tübingen: Niemeyer.

Apel, R., and Muysken, P. (1987) *Language Contact and Bilingualism*. London: Edward Arnold.

Appadurai, A. (1996) *Modernity at Large: Cultural Dimensions of Globalization*. Minneapolis: University of Minnesota Press.

Bartelson, J. (2000) Three concepts of globalization. *International Sociology* 15(2): 180–96.

Bauman, Z. (1982) *Intimations of Postmodernity*. London: Routledge.

Bauman, Z. (1998a) On glocalization: Or globalization for some, localization for some others. *Thesis Eleven* 54(1): 37–49.

Bauman, Z. (1998b) *Globalization: The Human Consequences*. Cambridge: Polity.

Beck, U. (1992) *Risk Society: Towards a New Modernity*. London: Sage.

Beck, U. (1999) *What is Globalization?* Cambridge: Polity.

Beck, U., Giddens, A., and Lash, S. (1994) *Reflexive Modernization: Politics, Tradition and Aesthetics in the Modern Social Order.* Oxford: Polity Press.

Block, D., and Cameron, D. (eds) (2002) *Globalisation and Language Teaching.* London: Routledge.

Blommaert, J. (2006) *Discourse.* Cambridge: Cambridge University Press.

Blommaert, J. (2009) *A Sociolinguistics of Globalization.* Cambridge: Cambridge University Press.

Blommaert, J., Collins, J., and Slembrouck, S. (2005) Spaces of multilingualism. *Language and Communication* 25(3): 197–216.

Bourdieu, P. (1991) *Language and Symbolic Power.* Cambridge: Polity.

Bourdieu, P., and Wacquant, L. (1999) On the cunning of imperialist reason. *Theory, Culture and Society* 16(1): 41–58.

Brutt-Griffler, J. (2002) *World English: A Study of Its Development.* Clevedon: Multilingual Matters.

Bucholtz, M. (2003) Sociolinguistic nostalgia and the authentication of identity. *Journal of Sociolinguistics* 7(3): 398–416.

Butler, J. (1997) *Excitable Speech: A Politics of the Performative.* New York and London: Routledge.

Cameron, D. (2000) Styling the worker: Gender and the commodification of language in the globalized service economy. *Journal of Sociolinguistics* 4(3): 323–47.

Canagarajah, S. (1999) *Resisting Linguistic Imperialism in English Teaching.* Oxford: Oxford University Press.

Castells, M. (1996) *The Rise of the Networked Society.* Oxford: Blackwell.

Chouliaraki, L. (2006) *The Spectatorship of Suffering.* London: Sage.

Cohen, R. (1997) *Global Diasporas.* Seattle, WA: University of Washington Press.

Coupland, N. (2003a) Sociolinguistic authenticities. *Journal of Sociolinguistics* 7, 3: 417–31.

Coupland, N. (ed.) (2003b) *Sociolinguistics and Globalisation* (thematic issue of *Journal of Sociolinguistics* 7(4)).

Coupland, N. (2007) *Style: Language Variation and Identity.* Cambridge: Cambridge University Press.

Coupland, N. (2009a) The mediated performance of vernaculars. *Journal of English Linguistics* 37(3): 284–300.

Coupland, N. (2009b) Dialects, standards and social change. In M. Maegaard, F. Gregersen, P. Quist, and J. N. Jørgensen (eds), *Language Attitudes, Standardization and Language Change*, 25–50. Oslo: Novus.

Coupland, N. (2010) The authentic speaker and the speech community. In C. Llamas and D. Watts (eds), *Language and Identities*, 99–112. Edinburgh: Edinburgh University Press.

Crystal, D. (2000) *Language Death.* Cambridge: Cambridge University Press.

De Swaan, A. (2001) *Words of the World: The Global Language System.* Cambridge: Polity.

Duchêne, A., and Heller, M. (eds) (2007) *Discourses of Endangerment: Ideology and Interest in the Defense of Languages.* London: Continuum.

Eckert, P. (2003) Elephants in the room. *Journal of Sociolinguistics* 7(3): 392–7.

Evans, P. (1997) The eclipse of the state? Reflections on stateness in an era of globalisation. *World Politics* 50(1): 62–87.

Fairclough, N. (2006) *Language and Globalisation.* London: Routledge.

Fairclough, N. (2009) Language and globalisation. *Semiotica* 173: 317–42.

Featherstone, M. (ed.) (1990) *Global Culture: Nationalism, Globalisation and Modernity.* London: Sage.

Featherstone, M., and Lash, S. (1995) Globalisation, modernity and the spatialization of social theory: An introduction. In M. Featherstone, S. Lash and R. Robertson (eds), *Global Modernities*, 1–24. London: Sage.

Fishman, J. A. (1991) *Reversing Language Shift: Theoretical and Empirical Foundations of Assistance to Threatened Languages.* Clevedon: Multilingual Matters.

Friedmann, J. (1986) The world city hypothesis. *Development and Change* 17(1): 69–84.

Gal, S. (2006) Migration, minorities and multilingualism: Language ideologies in Europe. In C. Mar-Molinero and P. Stevenson (eds), *Language Ideologies, Policies and Practices: Language and Future of Europe*, 13–27. Basingstoke: Palgrave Macmillan.

Giddens, A. (1991) *Modernity and Self-Identity: Self and Society in the Late Modern Age*. Cambridge: Polity.

Giddens, A. (1994) Living in a post-traditional society. In U. Beck, A. Giddens, and S. Lash (eds) *Reflexive Modernization: Politics, Tradition and Aesthetics in the Modern Social Order*, 56–109. Oxford: Polity Press.

Giddens, A. (2002) *Runaway World: How Globalisation Is Shaping Our Lives*. London: Profile Books.

Gordon, R. G. (2005) *Ethnologue: Languages of the World*. Dallas: SIL International. (Available online at http://www.ethnologue.com.)

Graddol, D. (1997) *The Future of English?* London: British Council.

Graddol, D. (2006). *English Next: Why Global English May Mean the End of 'English as a Foreign Language.'* London: The British Council. (See also http://www.britishcouncil.org/files/documents/learningresearch-english-next.pdf).

Gumperz, J. J. (1982) *Discourse Strategies*. Cambridge: Cambridge University Press.

Hall, S. (1996) Introduction: Who needs 'identity'? In S. Hall and P. du Gay (eds), *Questions of Cultural Identity*, 1–17. London: Sage.

Hall, S. (1997) The local and the global: Globalization and ethnicity. In A. D. King (ed.), *Culture, Globalization and the World System*, 19–40. Minneapolis: University of Minnesota Press.

Hannerz, U. (1992) *Cultural Complexity: Studies in the Social Organization of Meaning*. New York: Columbia University Press.

Hannerz, U. (1996) *Transnational Connections*. London: Routledge.

Hardt, M., and Negri, A. (2000) *Empire*. Cambridge, MA: Harvard University Press.

Harvey, D. (1989) *The Condition of Postmodernity*. Oxford: Blackwell.

Held, D., McGrew, A. G., Goldblatt, D., and Perraton, J. (1999) *Global Transformations: Politics, Economics and Culture*. Cambridge: Polity.

Heller, M. (ed.) (2007) *Bilingualism: A Social Approach*. London, Palgrave Macmillan.

Hobsbawm, E. J., and Ranger, T. O. (eds) (1983) *The Invention of Tradition*. Cambridge: Cambridge University Press.

Hodges, D., and Nilep, C. (eds) (2007) *Discourse, War and Terrorism*. Amsterdam: John Benjamins.

House, J. (2003) English as a lingua franca: A threat to multilingualism? *Journal of Sociolinguistics* 7(4): 556–78.

Jaworski, A., and Thurlow, C. (eds) (2010) *Semiotic Landscapes: Language, Image, Space*. London: Continuum.

Jaworski, A., Thurlow, C., Ylänne, V., and Lawson, S. (2010) *Language, Tourism and Globalization: The Sociolinguistics of Fleeting Relationships*. London: Routledge.

Jenkins, J. (2007) *English as a Lingua Franca: Attitudes and Identity*. Oxford: Oxford University Press.

Johnson, S., and Ensslin, A. (2007) Language in the media: Theory and practice. In S. Johnson and A. Ensslin (eds), *Language in the Media*, 3–22. London: Continuum.

Kachru, B. B. (ed.) (1992) *The Other Tongue: English Across Cultures*. Urbana: University of Illinois Press.

Kelly-Holmes, H. (2005) *Advertising as Multilingual Communication*. Basingstoke and New York: Palgrave Macmillan.

Kellner, Douglas (1989) *Critical Theory, Marxism and Modernity*. Cambridge, UK

and Baltimore, MD: Polity Press and
Johns Hopkins University Press. (See
also http://www.gseis.ucla.edu/
faculty/kellner/papers/theoryglob.htm
– consulted 8 July 2009).

Kramsch, C. (1998) *Language and Culture*.
Oxford: Oxford University Press.

Labov, William (1972) *Sociolinguistic
Patterns*. Philadephia: Pennsylvania
University Press.

Lash, S., and Urry, J. (1994) *Economies of
Signs and Space*. London: Sage.

Leap, W., and Boellstorff, T. (eds) (2004)
*Speaking in Queer Tongues: Globalization
and Gay Language*. Urbana: University of
Illinois Press.

Lechner, F., and Boli, J. (2004) General
introduction. In F. Lechner and J. Boli
(eds), *The Globalization Reader*, 1–4.
Malden, MA: Blackwell.

Machin, D., and van Leeuwen, T. (2007)
Global Media Discourse. London:
Routledge.

Maurais, J., and Morris, M. A. (eds) (2003)
Languages in a Globalizing World.
Cambridge: Cambridge University
Press.

McGrew, A. G., and Lewis, P. (eds) (1992)
*Global Politics: Globalization and the Nation
State*. Cambridge: Polity.

Mufwene, S. (1994) New Englishes and
criteria for naming them. *World Englishes*
13: 21–31.

Mufwene, S. (2008) *Language Evolution:
Contact, Competition and Change*. London:
Continuum.

Myers-Scotton, C. (2002) *Contact
Linguistics: Bilingual Encounters and
Grammatical Outcomes*. Oxford: Oxford
University Press.

Nettle, D., and Romaine, S. (2000)
*Vanishing Voices: The Extinction of the
World's Languages*. Oxford: Oxford
University Press.

Ohmae, K. (1995) *The End of the Nation
State: The Rise of Regional Economies*. New
York: The Free Press.

Papastergiadis, N. (2000) *The Turbulence of
Migration*. Cambridge: Polity.

Patrick, P. (2002) The speech community.
In J. K. Chambers, P. Trudgill and N.
Schilling-Estes (eds), *The Handbook of
Language Variation and Change*, 573–97.
Malden, MA: Blackwell.

Pavlenko, A., and Blackledge, A. (2004)
*Negotiation of Identities in Multilingual
Contexts*. Clevedon: Multilingual
Matters.

Pennycook, A. (2007) *Global Englishes and
Transcultural Flows*. London: Routledge.

Phillipson, R. (1992) *Linguistic Imperialism*.
Oxford: Oxford University Press.

Phillipson, R. (2003) *English Only?
Challenging Language Policy*. London:
Routledge.

Pratt, M. L. (1987) Linguistic utopias. In N.
Fabb, D. Attridge, A. Durant, and C.
MacCabe (eds), *The Linguistics of Writing*,
48–66. Manchester: Manchester
University Press.

Rampton, B. (2006) *Language in Late-
Modernity: Interaction in an Urban School*.
Cambridge: Cambridge University
Press.

Rampton, B. (2009) Speech community and
beyond. In N. Coupland and A.
Jaworski (eds), *The New Sociolinguistics
Reader*, 694–713. Basingstoke: Macmillan.

Robertson, R. (1992) *Globalisation: Social
Theory and Global Culture*. London: Sage.

Robertson, R. (1995) Glocalization:
Time–space homogeneity–heterogeneity.
In M. Featherstone, S. Lash, and R.
Robertson (eds), *Global Modernities*.
27–44. London: Sage.

Robertson, R., and Khondker, H. H. (2009)
Discourses of globalization: Preliminary
considerations. *International Sociology*
13(1): 25–40.

Sankoff, D., and Laberge, S. (1978) The
linguistic market and the statistical
explanation of variability. In D. Sankoff
(ed.), *Linguistic Variation: Models and
Methods*, 239–50. New York: Academic
Press.

Scott, A. (ed.) (1997) *The Limits of
Globalisation: Cases and Arguments*.
London: Routledge.

Seidlhofer, B. (2004) Research perspectives on teaching English as a lingua franca. *Annual Review of Applied Linguistics* 24: 209–39.

Skutnabb-Kangas, T. (2000) *Linguistic Genocide in Education or Worldwide Diversity and Human Rights?* Mahwah, NJ: Lawrence Erlbaum Associates.

Stewart, W. (1970) A sociolinguistic typology for describing national multilingualism. In J. Fishman (ed.), *Readings in the Sociology of Language*, 531–45. The Hague: Mouton.

Thurlow, C., and Jaworski, A. (2010) *Tourism Discourse: Language and Global Mobility*. London: Palgrave Macmillan.

Wallerstein, I. (1974) *The Modern World System I: Capitalist Agriculture and the Origins of the European World-Economy in the Sixteenth Century*. New York: Academic Press.

Winford, D. (2003) *Introduction to Contact Linguistics*. Malden, MA: Blackwell.

Wright, S. (2004). *Language Policy and Language Planning: From Nationalism to Globalisation*. London: Palgrave.

Part I Global Multilingualism, World Languages, and Language Systems

1 Globalization, Global English, and World English(es): Myths and Facts

SALIKOKO S. MUFWENE

Introduction

Today's world is claimed to be economically and culturally more globalized than ever before, thanks to faster and more reliable means of transportation and communication, which have facilitated greater human traffic and the exchange of larger volumes of information and goods. This concurrent evolution has also led to increased mutual cultural influences across national and regional boundaries, which prompted some experts to claim that the world has been homogenizing by convergence, at the expense of cultural diversity. To be sure, the directions and volumes of traffic are not necessarily symmetrical. The players or partners involved in the relevant world-wide networks of interconnectedness and interdependence do not hold equal economic powers; it is the more powerful who control which populations and commodities (including languages) are transported more freely, and in which directions. Thus, to the eyes of many, globalization is no more than McDonaldization and Americanization (largely through the world-wide diffusion of Hollywood movies); and the spread of English is no less than a part of this trend (for such views, propounded in one form or another, see for instance Crystal 2000, 2004; Nettle and Romaine 2000; Skutnabb-Kangas 2000; Phillipson 2003; Hagège 2006). Some linguists have thus claimed that a 'global English' is bound to emerge which should facilitate communication world-wide, alongside – or perhaps superseding – 'indigenized' or 'world Englishes.' According to the same futurologists, the more widely this 'global English' spreads, the more likely it is to drive other languages to extinction, just as has been witnessed in North America and Australia.

However, neither economic globalization nor language spread is new in the history of mankind. What is especially striking today is both the scale and the speed at which these processes are evolving. I submit that examining them comparatively, with more historical depth than is exhibited in the current linguistics

The Handbook of Language and Globalization, First Edition. Edited by Nikolas Coupland.
© 2013 Blackwell Publishing Ltd except for editorial material and organization © 2013 Nikolas Coupland.
Published 2013 by Blackwell Publishing Ltd.

literature, should help us sort out myths and facts about how English is actually spreading and whether it is justified to expect the consequences of the process to be uniform all over the world. I therefore invite the reader to be patient and to review with me a selective, informative history of mankind from the point of view of colonization, which will help us assess more critically the spread of English. This history will explain why we need not fear the emergence of a 'global English,' let alone of a time when it might function as the world's exclusive or dominant vernacular. I will start by articulating from the outset the interpretation of globalization that really bears on language endangerment.

What Is Globalization and What Is New about It?

Answers to the above questions vary and depend largely on what particular aspects of the manifold phenomenon called 'globalization' a scholar chooses to focus on. If we start with the characterization of globalization both as "the process of becoming global" (Keohane and Nye 2000) and as "the state that results from this process," then we must also articulate what the word *global* means. Although most dictionaries privilege its meaning as 'world-wide' (as in *global warming*), we cannot ignore its other interpretation as 'all-inclusive' or 'comprehensive' (as in *global war* – which is different from *world war* – and as in *global problem/ solution*).[1] Thus there can be globalization at the local level, consisting of interdependences which obtain among the different components of the industry or economic structure of a city, or at the regional level, for instance when neighboring countries form economic alliances, such as in the now very successful case of the European Union.[2]

Globalization need not be thought of exclusively or primarily at the world-wide level. This level differs from the local especially in scale. Although the two may be claimed to differ also in complexity, this is not necessarily the case, unless one conceives of world-wide globalization as an economic system in which all the components of national industries are fully integrated, in complementary ways. The reality is that most of Africa and a great deal of the Pacific Islands remain on the margins of the present world-wide economic system. Moreover, only some industries (such as car and computer manufacture) are distributed complementarily over different parts of the world. However, the relevant trade networks, which should connect the missing links, do not include all parts of the world – especially not those still lagging in transportation infrastructure.

Telecommunications, transportation, shipping, and banking are indeed among the handful of industries that can be claimed to instantiate world-wide globalization *qua* networks of interconnectedness and interdependence. These particular industries also make it obvious that the world is not equally interconnected; countries with the highest globalization index are more centrally connected than others, and the so-called 'global cities' are more interconnected than other places. One can likewise argue that world-wide globalization is simply a geographically expanded version of glocalization, although students of multiculturalism discuss the latter as if it were a consequence of world-wide globalization. As cultures, and therefore languages, travel primarily and the most naturally with people, these observations prompt us to assess critically claims that English is becoming a global language (see the sections "The Fallacy of 'Global English'" and "Will there be an English-only Europe?" below).

One may also argue that the most primitive forms of globalization in human economic history can be traced back all the way to the beginnings of agriculture, when farmers colonized the hunter–gatherers and some complementarity and interdependence arose in modes and kinds of food production. The evidently monumental differences between, on the one hand, the forms of cooperation and trade that emerged then and, on the other, today's international industrial conglomerations and networks of trade amount to differences in scale and complexity rather than to differences in kind or spirit. The goal remains for different partners to specialize in what they produce best, or more extensively, and to buy the remaining commodities from other parties, thereby improving and maximizing production through cooperation. That the spirit of this practice has remained fundamentally the same is evident in the asymmetrical power relations which obtain between partners – namely in the tendency for the economically and/or militarily more powerful to dominate the weaker ones. This tendency may entail the adoption of cultural practices, including the language, of the more powerful by the weaker party. However, things have not always proceeded this way in human history (see below). For our purposes, this perspective should help us not only to determine the places where English has spread, but also to assess discriminately the communicative functions it serves and to establish whether its impact on the indigenous languages has been uniform around the world. On the other hand, it is evident that non-local globalization can be related to colonization, as explained below – except where partnership is negotiated between equals.

Complexity in local globalization may have started also with the emergence of towns and cities. Life in such larger agglomerations has required a certain amount of interdependence through complementary organization – such as with housing, food and water supplies – and adequate communication and transportation networks in order for the residents to function adequately. The cities' specialization in industries, as opposed to farming and hunter–gathering, also led to an interdependence between rural and urban environments, although the division of labor and some amount of cooperation in food production varied from one part of the world to another, according to particular times in history. All this anticipated the emergence of nation–states, in which national economies would be coordinated (and even planned, to the extent that this was possible) in ways that can be described as involving globalization. As a matter of fact, we can say that the more globalized a city's or nation's economic system is, the higher its globalization or glocalization index is, and the more centrally or significantly it can participate in the world-wide global economic network. The so-called 'global cities' (such as New York, London, Paris, Tokyo, Frankfurt, Los Angeles, Chicago, and São Paulo) are those with a high glocalization index, and they function not only as major world financial centers but also as primary ports of entry and as principal diffusion centers in the spread of world-wide trends. They are also places that can best highlight differences in the ways English and other major languages have spread around the world, especially through the extent of the contrast between them and the surrounding rural areas. Otherwise the characteristics of interconnectedness and interdependence associated with world-wide globalization are generally extensions of those that apply in glocalization.

'Global cities' also remind us that world-wide globalization started with long-distance trading practiced at an early date by, for example, the Babylonians, the Egyptians, the Phoenicians, the Chinese (on the Silk Road), and, later, the Greeks and the Romans (Cowen 2001): essentially they remind us that enterprises started from economically and politically powerful cities. Then as now, the size of the world was largely determined by how far technology enabled the traders to go and their respective languages to travel with them. In the Middle Ages the Arabs and the Chinese definitely expanded the size of that world-trade, as the former sailed across the Mediterranean as well as eastwards and southwards along the Indian Ocean, while the latter sailed southwards in the Pacific and westwards in the Indian Ocean. Further improvements in transportation technology would lead to the European Great Explorations of the fifteenth century and to the consequent colonization of most of the rest of the world by Europeans (see for instance Osterhammel and Peterson 2005). Since then, world-wide globalization has changed in respect of how far away the colonizers and traders traveled from their homelands, how fast they journeyed, how much commodity and human traffic actually took place, how much more complex the exchange system has become, and how asymmetrical the share of profits has been between partners.[3]

Long-distance trade involved not only exchanges of commodities, but also traffic of people and ideas, and hence of cultures. This produced language spread, which sometimes transformed the vernacular a into lingua franca, as has been the case in history with Akkadian, Aramaic, Greek, Latin, Arabic, Malay, Swahili, Nheengatu (Lingua Geral), Quechua, and Mobilian, to name but a few (see Ostler 2005 for many more examples), before the age of modern European languages. Out of the latter, English has emerged as a pre-eminent world language and, being 'indicted' by linguists for the loss of several indigenous languages, especially in North America and Australia, it has been mischaracterized as the 'killer language' par excellence. I will return to most of the issues related to this topic from the next section onward. I would just like to conclude this section with some comments on the role of urbanization in language coexistence and competition, which will explain why the impact that the usage of English as a vernacular has exerted, in particular on indigenous languages in North America, may not be replicated in former British exploitation colonies, especially those of Africa.

Cities have usually been contact settings, where individuals of different ethno-linguistic backgrounds have migrated either from rural areas or from other cities, typically in search of better economic opportunities. It is probably around them that one can most easily defend the hypothesis that, due to complex webs of interconnectedness and interdependence among residents and among the industries in which they (hope to) function, globalization *cum* glocalization is homogenizing places culturally, hence linguistically. Cities also happen to be the nodes that connect different nations in the world-wide network of interconnectedness and interdependence more commonly associated with globalization. If it is true that globalization as a process is homogenizing the world, cities should be the focus of any serious empirical study. I argue below that, despite similarities in the way the (international) airports and highways of cities are structured, in the way night life is experienced, in the names of major hotels (Hilton, Hyatt, Sheraton, Holiday Inn), or in the fact that cities display McDonald's eateries – a phenomenon which some scholars have characterized as Americanization – there are still many cultural differences between them, which make it inaccurate to claim or predict the end of cultural diversity (see for instance Tomlinson 1999; Marling 2006; Florida 2005). Cities filter cultural influence from outside and adapt it to local traditions. Even if their cultures change significantly under outside influence, they retain a certain amount of substrate or element that keeps them from becoming replicas of each other. In other words, even 'global cities' maintain individualities in the peculiar ways they adapt to changes and outside influences, which keeps world-wide globalization from making our planet culturally uniform. Thus although some 'global cities' may be claimed to become anglophone or Americanized, they are not undergoing the process in a uniform way, or to the same extent. One cannot rely to the same extent on the usefulness of English as a lingua franca in Tokyo as in Paris or Amsterdam – at least not yet today.[4]

Colonization and Globalization

As observed by some economic historians (Mignolo 2000; Cowen 2001; Osterhammel and Peterson 2005), modern-day regional and world-wide economic globalization can be associated with, or traced back to, colonization in the sense of political and economic domination of a territory and its population(s) by citizens of another territory. Interestingly, today's most central players in world-wide globalization include nations that evolved out of settlement colonization – whereby Europeans resettled or founded new homelands in territories outside Europe, eliminated or marginalized indigenous populations, developed highly glocalized economic systems that they intended to be better than in the Europe they emigrated from (Crosby 1986), and imposed socioeconomic world orders that reflect 'occidentalism' or westernization. Other players are nations such as the United Kingdom and France, which built powerful economic systems thanks to huge colonial empires, especially through the exploitation of colonies whose production of vital raw materials they controlled exclusively up to the mid-twentieth century. Germany and Japan of course stand out as miraculous developments after World War II.

Discussing world-wide globalization in relation to colonization of any kind (trade, settlement, or exploitation) provides an enlightening historical perspective. It makes obvious various layers of human traffic that account for geographic and demographic patterns of language distribution today. To be sure, higher living standards and regional wars have increasingly contributed to population movements and contacts, especially through the free relocation of individuals or families, through tourism, deportations, and refugeeism. However, the world is still more heavily marked by the high volumes of human traffic associated with various layers and styles of documented colonization, which may well be claimed to have connected various regions and to have introduced various degrees of interdependence. As I will show below, these migrations have borne on the vitality of languages – both those of the indigenous populations and those the migrants – in various ways, constantly changing the 'linguascape' (or the spatial distribution of languages) of the world. Our era cannot be the only time when populations have worried about the impact of the languages of the dominant populations on those of the dominated or marginalized ones.

Among the older cases of population dispersal, the Indo-European and Bantu expansions may be the best known ones to date. Both groups dispersed gradually, over millennia, to resettle in new territories, where their languages eventually prevailed over most of the indigenous ones. In both cases, regardless of whether proto-Indo-European or proto-Bantu consisted each of one single language (a dubious assumption) or of a cluster of related language varieties, the cost of the Pyrrhic victory was further diversification, largely triggered, as it seems, by substrate influence from the indigenous languages. This became evident at a later date, in the spread and diversification of one Indo-European language, Latin.

As indicated above, trade contributed to the spread of many languages as lingua francas. In other cultural respects, it also facilitated the diffusion of the Phoenician alphabet and of the Arabic graphic representation of numbers. In most cases, the languages of trade hardly replaced those they came in contact with, unless there was a concurrent wave of colonization and settlement that spread a given language as a vernacular, as in the case of Arabic in North Africa – but not in south and southeast Asia. Vernacular shifts have typically resulted from settlement colonization, as I intend to show below regarding the geographic expansion of English. For now, suffice it to mention also the successful spread of varieties of Chinese in China, which was a consequence of the Han settlement colonization of East Asia, although several minority languages have survived the invasion. However, note that the Chinese trade-colonial expansion in Southeast Asia during the period between the thirteenth and the fifteenth centuries was not matched by a similar language spread. On the contrary, the Peranakan Chinese – an economically powerful group, comparable to that of Creoles of European descent or of mixed ancestry in Latin America – speak now as their vernaculars some indigenous languages of their trade colonies, and chiefly Malay.[5] (See Ostler 2005 for similar considerations.)

The spread of Latin, which has often been invoked as an earlier example of a 'global language' (for example by Crystal 1997), is worth explaining here, as it will help us address the question of whether we can actually speak of a 'global English.' While it is true that Latin spread in the world around the Mediterranean and North Sea (including England, Belgium, and Germany) thanks to the Roman Empire (a notorious colonial enterprise), it is also noteworthy that it became a vernacular only in southwestern Europe and in Romania. Actually this vernacular shift, which, I maintain, is more typical of settlement colonies, appears to have occurred most significantly after the Romans had left the Western Roman Empire (Polomé 1983; Janson 2004) – which obviously had been neither a settlement nor a typical exploitation colony. As explained in Mufwene (2008), this was an interesting colonization, in a style of its own, fitting typologically just between the two.

Unlike settler colonists, the Romans abandoned their western empire when they thought it better to protect Rome against the invading Germanics. However, they had ruled in a manner that rewarded some retired officers by granting them land in the provinces. These former officers continued to speak Latin as an emblem of their status. The Romans had also Romanized the indigenous ruling class, through which they administered their colonies (though they had a few Roman administrators too), and they rewarded quite handsomely some of these natives, who served Rome's interests, with important offices in the empire – all the way to senatorial and even imperial positions (Garnsey and Saller 1987). It was in fact these indigenous rulers, the emergent Roman-style cities, and to some extent the Christian missions (on which see below) that perpetuated the usage of Latin as a vernacular after the collapse of the Western Roman Empire. From the emergent cities, Vulgar Latin gradually spread to the rural areas, along with the Roman-style economy and culture it was associated with (Landa 2000). This process appears to have occurred over several centuries, during which Latin was influenced by the Celtic and other languages it was displacing. Meanwhile, Classical Latin, used by intellectual elites, remained a lingua franca, a status it has maintained to date at the Vatican. Its life was thus not so different from that of Classical Greek in the Byzantine Empire or in modern Greece, where it is no longer used as a lingua franca today (modern dialects evolved from Dimotiki and Katharevousa varieties are now spoken as vernaculars).

The vernacularization of Vulgar Latin in the Romance countries in today's continental Europe is indeed a geographical and demographic expansion, very similar to that of English, centuries later, in Ireland – where one had to wait until the rule of Oliver Cromwell and the introduction of potato farms in the seventeenth century for English to start spreading as a vernacular. Although it had been introduced to Ireland earlier, in the ninth century, before the change to settlement colonization in the seventeenth, English had remained a lingua franca within a small elite class of traders in and around Dublin and some other towns. (See also Leith 2007 for a discussion of the spread of English in the British Isles from the point of view of colonization.)

In the wake of the collapse of the Western Roman Empire in the fifth century, Latin was only the language of former Roman administrators and legionaries (most of whom were indigenous) and, later, of scholarship and of Catholic liturgy. It is also debatable whether, by using Classical Latin, the clergy played a more important role – albeit a negligible one – in the vernacularization of the Romans' language than scholars did. After all, the missionaries proselytized in some of the indigenous vernaculars spoken by the masses of the population. Until the beginning of the second millennium, the Christian/Catholic schools had succeeded only in producing an elite class of speakers of Classical Latin (Landa 2000), which makes the history of the vulgarization of Latin, then mostly an urban peculiarity, similar to that of English in Ireland before the seventeenth century.

Note also that the school system played a less important role in the spread of English in Ireland as a vernacular than migrant workers on the potato plantations owned by English entrepreneurs did. Although they learned it naturalistically, without the benefit of (much) school education, the migrant workers – and the plantations – gave a lucrative value to English, at least for the common people, just as the Roman-style emergent cities in southwestern Europe did to Latin, the language of their modern economy. I will show below how the spread of English outside Europe is very much correlated to the English colonial expansion, varying in ethnographic functions according to the colonization style applied in different territories.

The European Colonial Expansion since the Fifteenth Century

As explained in Mufwene (2005, 2008), the European colonial expansion since the fifteenth century is, in a number of ways, an extension of the Indo-European dispersal since about 6,000 years ago, at least in the way the latter has been explained by Renfrew (1987). The more recent wave of colonization differs from the older one in the following respects:

1   the role of trade and industrial expansion in triggering massive and often planned population movements;
2   the role played by proprietor companies in the initial peopling of the colonies (including the importation of European indentured servants, of black African slaves, and of Asian and black African contract laborers after the abolition of slavery);
3   the larger size of the colonized territories and the longer distance that separated them from the homelands;
4   the diversity of colonization styles (notably between settlement and exploitation colonies);
5   the speed of the demographic and economic transformation of the colonies; and
6   the complexity and incredible volumes of the new economies.

The linguistic consequences have also been rapid and more extensive, although varying according to colonization styles too (see below).

Although nowadays there is more European traffic in search of warm beaches for relaxation, European explorers (similar to our astronauts), traders, and colonists from the fifteenth to the nineteenth century were seeking socioeconomic solutions to European problems (Crosby 1986; Diamond 1997). Some of these entailed settling new territories such as the Americas, the southern tip of Africa,

Australia, New Zealand, the Falkland Islands, and Algeria, among a host of other, smaller places south of the Mediterranean. Even these solutions had earlier precedents in the colonization, for sugar cane cultivation, of islands closer to continental Europe, such as the Azores, Madeira, and the Canary Islands (Schwartz 1985) – at a time when the only European world powers were the Spaniards and the Portuguese, who competed with the Arabs, the Turks during the early Ottoman Empire, and the Chinese in the Far East. Then Portuguese dominated, as a language of trade and diplomacy, from the western coast of Africa all the way to Japan, and from the fifteenth to the eighteenth century (Ostler 2005). This is a reminder, to those worried about today's expansion of English as the foremost world-wide language, that we must really figure out what is the same and what is different in this latest wave of demographic expansion of an (Indo-)European language. Even after other European nations, especially England, France, and Holland emerged in the seventeenth century as major maritime powers and engaged themselves in the colonial enterprise, Portuguese remained the primary trade language on the west African coast (Huber 1999); in fact it was replaced (the fastest) only here, where it was not spoken as a vernacular (not counting Cape Verde and the Bight of Biafra Islands, where it would evolve into Creole varieties). Thus Portuguese has been maintained in places such as Diu, Daman, Goa, and Korlai (in India), Batticalhoa (in Sri Lanka), and Macao (in China), where it has served as a vernacular even among the Christianized natives whom the Portuguese lived with, albeit as a 'creolized variety' (Clements 1996; Ansaldo 2009).

Noteworthy is also the fact that the effects of Portuguese on the vitality of indigenous languages have not been the same from Brazil to Mozambique. The variation is correlated with the fact that Portuguese has functioned as a dominant vernacular only in Brazil, in the Netherlands Antilles, and in the eastern Atlantic islands, as well as in the few settlement concessions on the coast of the Indian Ocean mentioned above and in Macao. Outside Brazil, it evolved into vernaculars identified as Creole varieties, thus displacing the non-European vernaculars among its speakers. In Brazil, its negative impact on the indigenous languages is less extensive than that of English in North America, although it is probably just a matter of time before all native American languages will disappear, as most pre-Indo-European and Celtic languages in Europe have.

This evolution is unlike that observed in Asia and in the black African mainland, including Mozambique, where the indigenous languages have generally survived their contacts with the European colonial languages. European exploitation colonies have generally fostered both individual and societal multilingualism, the colonial languages being typically used as lingua francas, but rarely as vernaculars, by the small minorities of natives who speak them fluently. Colonial languages used as vernacular thus function as emblems of socioeconomic achievement and status – privileges enjoyed only by a small minority in the Third World, where the economy has been on the decline for the past half century. Otherwise multilingualism, in forms that clearly associate different languages with different ethnographic functions, is not only the norm in many parts of the world, but also a strong protector of the indigenous languages against the spread of colonial languages. (See also Ostler 2005 for a similar observation.)[6]

European colonization started everywhere with some coastal trade posts and/or settlement concessions. Gradually, but much faster than with the Indo-European expansion, these initial colonies evolved and expanded into major settlement colonies.[7] Where European settlers became majority populations, especially in North America and Australia, their cultures prevailed, albeit in new, indigenized forms. Some of their languages also prevailed as the dominant vernacular, since competition among European settlers often worked to the definitive advantage of one colonial group, for instance the Anglos in North America and the Portuguese in Brazil. The indigenous languages were displaced, be it through the extinction of their speakers – through wars and genocides (such as in the Caribbean), and/or through ills (as in North America; see Crosby 1992, Boyle 2007) – through population mixings (as in Brazil and in European settlements in Asia), through further expansions into lands reserved for the natives (Banner 2005, for the United States), or through the assimilation of the natives. The last process occurred much later than in the case of other European immigrants (Mufwene 2008; Mufwene and Vigouroux 2008).

A similar linguistic evolution took place in plantation or slave depot colonies of the Caribbean, to some extent the east Atlantic, and the Indian Ocean, where the European economic system prevailed but the new majority populations were non-European and non-indigenous, and where the new economic regime originally thrived with the help of African slave labor and was sustained later with contract laborers. European languages not only prevailed – at the expense of both indigenous and most other non-indigenous languages – but also evolved into several divergent vernacular varieties, now disfranchised as Creole ones.[8]

On the other hand, Europeans did not develop an interest in full control of the economic resources of Africa and Asia until the nineteenth century. Due to climatic conditions (at least in the case of Africa, see Diamond 1997), the colonization style then changed to an exploitation regime in which only a handful of European colonial administrators and representatives of relevant companies would live in the colonies, for short terms, to exploit raw materials and have them processed in the metropole (see also Leith 2007). These colonial agents communicated with the indigenous populations through other non-European colonial auxiliaries, many of them recruited locally, to whom scholastic varieties of European languages were taught.

The 'Macaulay doctrine' (1835) in India, which is fairly representative of European colonial linguistic practices and policies, promoted the education of masses of Indian children in the indigenous languages, reserving education in English only for a privileged few (Brutt-Griffler 2002). We must bear in mind that the spread of a language as a vernacular depends more on its practice in the home and on its genuine 'transmission' through interactions with children and immigrants than on teaching a scholastic or standard variety of it as a lingua franca in schools. As explained in Mufwene (2005, 2008), this difference between exploitation and settlement colonies in the 'transmission' of European colonial languages is correlated with a significant difference between the linguistic consequences of European geographical expansion. In settlement colonies, where some colonial languages have prevailed as vernaculars, these have also driven to extinction not only most of their European competitors, but also the languages brought over by slaves and contract laborers.[9]

In exploitation colonies, where European languages function as official languages and as lingua francas commanded only by minority socioeconomic elites, most of the indigenous languages continue to be spoken. Unlike in settlement colonies, the norm has been societal and individual multilingualism, with relatively clear geographical and ethnographic divisions of labor in the usage of indigenous vernaculars, indigenous varieties of lingua franca, and European languages. I focus below on the differential evolution of English and on its varying impact on indigenous language outside the British Isles.

The British Empire, the British Commonwealth, and the Emergence of English as a Pre-Eminent 'World Language'

The colonization of the world entailed fierce competition among Europeans, often engaging them in wars with each other, such as the one between France and England in the Caribbean and in Canada and between both these nations and Spain in the Caribbean. Eventually the Spaniards maintained most of Latin America and the Portuguese settled in Brazil and in their African colonies, aside from minor settlements in Asia. Apart from Lebanon, Cambodia, and the exploitation colonies of Africa, the French kept some of their Caribbean and Indian Ocean Islands, having lost for instance Mauritius, Trinidad, St Kitts, and Grenada to England in the eighteenth century, and Haiti to its Independence in 1804. They faired no better in North America, where they also lost Nova Scotia to the English, and Louisiana to the United States (at that date Louisiana included the whole area bounded by the Rocky Mountains to the west, the Mississippi and Missouri Rivers to the east, the Gulf of Mexico to the south, and Quebec to the north), managing to keep just a little more than Quebec from today's Canada. The Dutch traded New Netherland (mostly today's State of New York) for Surinam in the seventeenth century, and they settled in the Netherlands Antilles and Indonesia, losing today's South Africa and Sri Lanka to the United Kingdom in the eighteenth century. Having lost the United States in the late eighteenth century, the United Kingdom capitalized on building the British Empire (with the colonization of Australia and New Zealand and the confiscation of territories seized from France at the outcome of the Napoleonic wars in the early nineteenth century). The empire was replaced by the British Commonwealth soon after World War II and the subsequent independence of many former colonies.

In the colonies, the change of colonial rule generally entailed a shift of official languages. In settlement colonies, this change also corresponded to a vernacular shift up to the Creole varieties, for instance in Trinidad, where the English Creole has driven the French one out. An important exception is Mauritius, where both French and Mauritian Creole have acquired the status of 'national languages' and English functions as a statutory official language. Many educated Mauritians are often more fluent in French than they are in English and enjoy socializing in it – which should remind us that language spread and evolution hardly proceed uniformly everywhere, as the ecologies of appropriation and practice vary from one territory to another. Nonetheless, the status of English as the main vernacular and business language in the United States, which emerged as a dominant military and economic power with World War I, just consecrated the hegemony of English as the world-wide language of trade, business, and eventually scholarship and diplomacy (see below). Meanwhile Russian was spreading in eastern Europe and in Siberia as the official language of the emergent Soviet Union.

By the middle of the twentieth century, a few European colonial languages had emerged as 'world languages,' in the sense of languages spoken as vernaculars or as lingua francas outside their homelands and by populations other than those ethnically or nationally associated with them. These included English, French, Russian, and Spanish. When the demographics include non-native speakers, the majority of whom inhabit former exploitation colonies and who use these languages only as official language or lingua franca, the total number of English speakers, estimated by some to around 1 billion, dwarfs the number of speakers of other European languages. It is noteworthy that French, which had emerged in the eighteenth and nineteenth centuries as an elite language of 'high culture' spoken at royal and imperial courts, even as far as Russia, and as the diplomatic language of Europe in particular, has been losing ground to English since the United States became the dominant economic and military power of the twentieth century – an evolution which has increased its momentum with the new wave of world-wide globalized economy after the collapse of the Soviet Union (in the late 1980s).

I submit that, as in the case of that earlier 'world language,' Latin, it was the association with trade and (more) lucrative business that favored English over its competitors, both in the United States and around the world. French had the misfortune of being associated with the elite class and with a metropolis that had lost to its anglophone rivals, Britain and the United States, on the colonial scene. Recall that, centuries earlier, Classical Latin, which was used by the European intelligentsia all the way up to the eighteenth century, also lost to its competitor, Vulgar Latin, which was associated with urbanity, trade, and the then 'modern' working class. Eventually the indigenized varieties that evolved from this 'Latin of the people' were not only hailed as national languages, but also promoted as languages of scholarship. France and Spain in particular went as far as to set up academies that dictated (not always successfully) the best ways in which educated people should express themselves in their respective languages.

It is important to emphasize that the status of a language as a 'world language' is not determined by demographics alone. Mandarin Chinese, which is the world's foremost 'major language' because it has more native speakers than English or

Spanish, does not necessarily count as a 'world language.' It is just a major language, and maybe the foremost major language. This largely has to do with the fact that its function as a lingua franca is limited to China and the Chinese Diaspora. Similar considerations apply to Hindi, whose total number of native speakers is close to 200 million and which functions as lingua franca in parts of India and, to some extent, in parts of the Indian Diaspora – but not outside the Indian population.

On the other hand, overlooking variation across nations, Arabic counts as a 'world language' to the extent that it is used as a religious/ritual language wherever Islam is practiced; but it does not have that status of lingua franca associated with English and French as languages of business/trade and scholarship which are also used by non-native speakers. Arabic is thus reduced to the same status as Spanish, which outside Spain is spoken mostly in Latin America, as the dominant vernacular. Arabic has prevailed primarily as a vernacular language in parts of the Middle East and in North Africa, since the settlement colonization of the region by the Arabs from the seventh century onwards.

It thus appears that what has made English the foremost 'world language' is its function as lingua franca, a status which La Francophonie, as the Organization of Francophone States, wishes French had reached to the same extent, against the odds articulated above (Mufwene 2008). It is this evolution that has led some scholars (see below) to characterize English as a 'global language,' that is, as a pre-eminent 'world language.' However, it will still be informative to learn more about its expansion as a post-colonial language and about the emergence of the varieties disfranchised as 'indigenized Englishes.'

World Englishes

The heading of this section has to do with (an advocacy for) the recognition of diverse modern English varieties as legitimate, wherever they are spoken, as long as their speakers abide by some local communal norms. The spread of English has proceeded generally at the cost of its structural integrity. English has become assimilated or indigenous – it has 'indigenized' – everywhere (Mufwene 2009), changing its features in response to the previous communicative habits of its new speakers, and meeting new communicative needs. The relevant literature has generally made a three-way distinction among the outcomes of the evolution of English since the seventeenth century:

1 'native Englishes,' spoken in the United Kingdom, North America, Australia, and New Zealand (that is, in its original homeland and in the settlement colonies where populations of European descent have become demographic majorities);
2 'Creole/pidgin Englishes,' which developed especially in the Caribbean and on the islands of the Pacific; and

3   'indigenized/nativized Englishes,' which evolved in India and in other former exploitation colonies.[10]

The structural differences between various 'world Englishes' are due not to the nature of the restructuring processes that led to their emergence but to a number of ecological factors, including:

1   the kinds of input varieties that the new speakers were exposed to: in the case of the varieties disfranchised as 'indigenized/nativized Englishes,' scholastic varieties as opposed to vernacular ones;
2   the modes of language 'transmission' involved: through teaching in school in the case of indigenized Englishes, through intuitive learning in the other cases; and
3   patterns of interaction with native speakers of the metropolitan kind (of which there was very little in the case of Creole varieties) versus interaction mostly among non-native speakers (as in the incipient stages of Creole varieties and in the post-colonial autonomization of 'indigenized Englishes').

In sum, the differences are due to the way in which variation in the contact ecologies influenced the appropriation of English by its new speakers. In the case of 'native Englishes,' English mostly became a kind of *koine* – or *koine*-ized – among its traditional speakers, who found themselves interacting regularly with speakers of other dialects (Mufwene 2001; Schneider 2007). The new, colonial variety was appropriated by other speakers after the critical period in the speciation process, changing little afterwards (Mufwene 2008; Trudgill 2008).

Whatever the most accurate account of the speciation process is, the end result is that there are several English varieties spoken around the world today, although some are treated as less legitimate than others. Several varieties are not mutually intelligible, owing to differences both in the particular earlier colonial forms of the koines they have evolved from and to the varying extents to which they have diverged from the relevant initial koines. For instance, as noted above, 'indigenized Englishes' generally started from artificial scholastic varieties and diverged under the influence of the indigenous languages spoken by the elite populations who used them (primarily as lingua francas). Creole varieties started from non-standard forms of *koine* spoken by the indentured servants and early Creole slaves with whom the Bozal slaves – who appropriated colonial vernacular languages as their own – interacted.

An important difference between 'Creole' and 'native' Englishes lies in the fact that the latter evolved in settings where populations of European descent became demographic majorities, whereas the Creole varieties evolved in ecologies where African slaves or non-European contract laborers became overwhelming majorities quite early in the evolution of the colonies and influenced the new vernacular languages by giving them features of the ones they had previously spoken.[11] To be sure, even where 'native Englishes' evolved, populations of English descent have become minorities, being overwhelmed demographically by populations from continental Europe. However, the latter did not shift to English as early as the African slaves on the plantations. By the 'founder principle' (Mufwene 1996, 2001), those who shifted later, after the critical period during the divergence process, exerted less influence on the emergent colonial varieties than those who had done it earlier.

Since the end of World War II, and even more so after the disintegration of the Soviet Union, English has spread all over the world, so to speak, having become a convenient lingua franca of trade and scholarship in continental Europe and in many places elsewhere that have not been colonized by England or the United Kingdom. Kachru (1983) refers to these new territories as the "Expanding Circle," where English, identified among teachers as a 'foreign language,' is used strictly as lingua franca for communication with outsiders, but is not an official language (see also Swaan 2007). This is set in contrast both with what Kachru calls the "Inner Circle" – a territory corresponding to the United Kingdom and its former settlement colonies, where English is spoken as the (dominant) vernacular – and with what he calls the "Outer Circle" – a territory corresponding to the former exploitation colonies, where English, identified among teachers as 'second language,' functions as an official language and serves as lingua franca for communication both among members of the elite class and with the outside world.

This world-wide geographical expansion beyond the United States and the British Commonwealth has led some scholars (for instance Crystal 1997; McArthur 1998; McCrum et al. 2002; Pennycook 2007) to characterize English as a 'global language,' comparable to Latin after the collapse of the Western Roman Empire. As noted above, colonial varieties of the Romans' language continued to be used as the vernacular of the emergent Roman-style towns and as the lingua franca of international trade (for instance in the Hanseatic League), whereas the standard variety – Classical Latin – functioned as the language of scholarship, but had a less successful 'story' from the point of view of language evolution. In any case, an important question is whether it is justified to speak of a 'global English' any more than of a 'global Latin.'

The Fallacy of 'Global English'

As global as English has been claimed to be, it is not evenly distributed around the world. The average population speaking it fluently in the 'Outer Circle' countries hardly exceeds 20 percent. India, the most populous country of the lot, stands out with only 30 percent of English speakers, and the Philippines is rather exceptional with its proportion of 46 percent speakers (Kingsley 2008). The number of those who speak English as a foreign language is even smaller in countries of the 'Expanding Circle.' As travelers to places such as Japan and Taiwan must have noticed, one cannot visit just any country around the world and hope to get by with English only, especially in rural areas. Even more striking is the fact that the proportion of confident speakers is way below the expected yield, considering all the energy, time, and money invested in teaching and learning English as a foreign language in countries such as Japan and South Korea. Overall, the extent of the spread of English in the 'Expanding Circle' correlates more or less with the extent to which particular countries participate in the world-wide globalized economy, which is in turn correlated with each country's glocalization index. In places that are still on the margins of economic globalization, the presence of English remains scant, especially where the rural population still exceeds the urban one. Although one will always come across peddlers who manage to speak some English at craft markets and in other touristic areas, for commercial purposes, the proportion of educated people who still do not speak English (confidently) is too high to be overlooked.

On the other hand, as is well explained by McArthur (1998), the expression 'English as a global language' has misled some into speaking of 'global English,' analogously to speaking of 'world English' (translated from the French *anglais mondial*). The suggested reference is to what the proponents expect to be a universal standard, used as lingua franca by all speakers of various English varieties ('native' and 'non-native'), some of which are not mutually intelligible. Crystal (1997), who appears to have started the trend, also identifies this variety as "world standard spoken English" (WSSE). He expects it to arise from the will to overcome the diversity that has ensued from the world-wide spread of English, as described above.

If WSSE were to arise spontaneously, or could do so at all, it would be the first such evolution toward linguistic uniformity in the history of language spread and contact. The universal trend has been for the prevailing language to diversify, especially in the spoken form, as is made evident by the history of English itself and, before it, by that of Latin. Worse for the wishful thinking, even Standard English itself, which is controlled by several institutions, has diversified. It seems utopian to me to conjecture that speakers of 'native Englishes' will be accommodating, midway, all those other populations speaking their language with a foreign element, and will thus contribute to the development of some WSSE, in order to guarantee mutual intelligibility.

The conjecture is disconnected from the way English has been spoken (and written/read) in international interactions. Typically, speakers of 'native Englishes' have spoken their varieties with some arrogance; the burden has been on speakers of 'non-native Englishes,' which are generally treated as 'deviations' from the metropolitan norms (see Swaan 2007, citing Quirk 1990), to 'improve' their intelligibility – not the other way around. The only time when the accommodation has proceeded in the other direction has been when people from the 'Inner Circle' have found themselves residing in the 'Outer Circle': especially their children have made most of the adjustments, the way children of (im)migrants normally adjust, in any host setting, even to a stigmatized variety.

Crystal completely overlooks the fact that the vast majority of speakers of English world-wide do not speak a standard variety (local or regional). Therefore they have no motivation for, nor would they be particularly invested in, speaking some sort of Standard English in cross-cultural interactions that are normally informal.[12] However 'global' the English language has become – in the sense of being a language that is spoken almost anywhere on our planet and permeates so many diverse domains of modern life (McArthur 1998) – it will continue to 'indigenize' everywhere, acquiring local characteristics in the same way it has done to date.

To be sure, it is legitimate to speak of 'English as a global language,' as this phrase underscores the fact that English has spread geographically so as to serve especially as an international lingua franca in various domains, in a way in which no other world language ever has. On the other hand, the notion of a global English with uniform structural features all over the world is a utopia we may as soon forget about. It is not even consistent with the process of world-wide economic globalization itself, which has speeded the spread of English on a planetary scale. Note that English is not even the only language of the global economy, since manufacturers trade in different languages, making sure that they secure profitable markets everywhere they can. Thus American companies use German to trade with the Germans in Germany and Japanese to trade with the Japanese in Japan. The others do just the opposite in trading with anglophone countries. It just so happens that, thanks to colonial history, there are so many such countries. In a way, one can argue that English has spread as a business language not only because of American military and economic hegemony, but also because almost any country in the world would like to trade with the United States, the United Kingdom, and many other important members of the former British Commonwealth. As much as the British Council has been accused of spreading English, it is responding to demands for the language. The need for this asset is created elsewhere, especially in the way world-wide global economy has evolved.

On the other hand, economic globalization has not produced, nor is it producing, socioeconomic uniformity. On the contrary, it has replaced old forms of diversity with new ones, producing several local adaptations in modes of production and consumption (Tomlinson 1999, 2007), along with various forms of economic inequity (Stiglitz 2002; Blommaert 2003; Florida 2005, 2007). The so-called 'McDonaldization' of the world has proceeded with adaptations to local tastes and customs, using local major languages rather than English everywhere. (Don't count on English to order your meal at a McDonald's in France or Brazil!) The world-wide distribution of Hollywood movies has been more in the interest of profits than in the service of American English and culture. Movies have generally been translated into several major languages, and the plots have often been modified to the tastes of local markets (Marling 2006). The evidence suggests that the practice of English in all the 'circles' – 'inner,' 'outer,' and 'expanding' – is always embedded in local cultures and is always influenced by the previous linguistic habits of the new speakers. We may as well brace ourselves for more diversity. Crystal (1997) and McArthur (1998) are not at all mistaken in comparing the spread of this imperial language to that of Latin, which has speciated into the Romance languages – and, I may add (along with Posner 1996 and Trask 1996), further into the Romance Creoles.

Will there Be an English-Only Europe?

A concomitant of the myth of the emergence of a 'global English' has been the growing fear that, because it is increasingly being used as the lingua franca of western Europe and of the European Union, English is endangering the vitality of other continental European languages and driving western Europe toward monolingualism (Phillipson 2003,[13] Hagège 2006). Noteworthy is also the literature on language endangerment that has painted English as the 'killer language' par excellence, likely to displace indigenous languages everywhere. On the example of North America and in Australia, the geographical expansion of English has been feared to eliminate linguistic diversity and to push in the direction of world-wide monolingualism (see for instance Crystal 2000, 2004; Nettle and Romaine 2000; Skutnabb-Kangas 2000).

What has been totally ignored in this respect is the political and apparently also ethnographic distinction, which Kachru (1983) so aptly captures, between the 'Inner Circle,' the 'Outer Circle,' and the 'Expanding Circle.' From the point of view of language vitality, the usage of English as a vernacular in the 'Inner Circle' must be distinguished from usage as an official language and as an important lingua franca of the intra-national elite in the 'Outer Circle,' as well as from its status as a foreign lingua franca, used for communication with outsiders by nationals of the 'Expanding Circle.'[14] It is the vernacular function of English in places where it has also prevailed as the dominant or only language of the economy that has fostered nation-wide monolingualism. Both in the 'Outer Circle' and in the 'Expanding Circle' multilingualism has been the norm; English is still far from evolving into a lingua franca of the majority; and the fear that it will drive indigenous languages to extinction remains an unsubstantiated myth.

Members of the 'Expanding Circle' such as Japan and Taiwan, whose highly glocalized economies function in the local vernaculars, appear to have realized that they need English only at the interface with the world-wide globalized economy, in which it is wise to trade in the buyer's language (as was also observed by Ostler 2005). This also explains why only those who are likely to interact with the outside world are seriously interested in speaking English (fluently). From an ethnographic perspective, the goal for learners/speakers seems to be the acquisition/command of the foreign language for communication with the foreign market or places one visits as a tourist, rather than the acquisition of a new vernacular in lieu of the current one. Those who emigrate to Anglophone territories make the necessary adjustments after resettling. Depending on whether or not they settle in host communities where they can continue to speak their heritage languages, they may maintain them or they may gradually become less competent in them. Even if the immigrants shift to English as their (dominant) vernacular, they constitute, typically, (small) minorities compared to the populations left behind in their homelands. Thus they, collectively, constitute no threat to the vitality of their heritage languages – and certainly not more so than the massive migrations, free and forced alike, which were associated with the

European colonization and settlement of parts of the world between the sixteenth and the nineteenth centuries and with the large ethnic Diasporas that this process has created.

It is also noteworthy that the gap between countries of the economic North (including Australia) and countries of the economic South keeps increasing, although polities such as Singapore, Brazil, and China are crossing the divide. Many parts of the world, including large pockets of China, still remain on the margins of world-wide economic and cultural globalization. Even after such countries participate in this complex network, local aspects of their economies will continue to function in their national languages, as is obvious from places such as the Netherlands and the Scandinavian countries. More significant is actually the fact that most of the populations in countries that are on the margins of world-wide globalization are still rural, generally outside of tourist traffic routes, and not directly involved in international trade. Even if school children learn a little bit of English, for them the language is just a subject similar to geography and history; it is not necessarily associated with potential benefits of travel abroad and jobs that require competence in this 'second' or 'foreign' language. The little knowledge acquired is lost as quickly as that of various other subjects learned in school, which lack practical applications to the subjects' lives. It is ludicrous to suggest that teaching English as a foreign language in Third World schools is endangering the relevant indigenous languages.

Even in places such as Japan, which have a high glocalization index, the people who take advantage of English classes are mostly those who wish to visit anglophone countries or to get senior white-collar jobs for which competence in the foreign language is an asset. Because English is not needed as an alternative vernacular or as lingua franca for communication among Japanese in Japan, just as it is not in many other countries of the 'Expanding Circle,' the majority of learners are not particularly invested in the language, especially since they can earn a decent living in their heritage language.

In countries of the 'Outer Circle,' the fact that English is needed only in the small white-collar sector of the industry and the rest of the economy functions in the indigenous languages, compounded by the fact that lucrative white-collar jobs are not likely to increase, has kept in check the spread of English within the overall population. Every person who has gone to high school has undoubtedly learned the (ex-)colonial language, but not everybody feels invested in practicing it, which spells atrophy on the (little) competence acquired in school. Not even call centers in India and the Philippines have contributed to spreading English any further. As large as the number of jobs they provide may sound, one must remember that India and the Philippines are densely populated nations. The market is still very limited, already saturated, and accessible to people who have already invested in English anyway and are apt to learn a stage variety, used only at work but not for socialization with one's fellow countrymen.

As a matter of fact, the call centers of India and of the Philippines are showing that people do not just decide to stop speaking their heritage language, especially while they continue to live with relatives who still function in them (Mufwene

2005, 2008). Practical multilingualism for professional purposes does not of necessity spell the death of one's heritage language(s). Such death occurs insidiously, when the socioeconomic structure of the relevant populations forces them to communicate more often in a dominant language other than their ancestral one, without them realizing what the long-term effect of their communicative practices is, namely loss of the capacity to use their respective heritage languages. In many parts of the Anglophone world, English is no more dangerous to the indigenous languages than McDonald's eateries are to their traditional cuisines. There are certainly endangered languages in the 'Outer' and 'Expanding Circles', but (the spread of) English has nothing to do with their condition.

Conclusions

The claim that economic globalization has helped spread English as a lingua franca around the world is certainly not groundless. However, it makes more sense when the process is related to colonization, to which globalization is originally connected. Much of the impetus that today's globalization has given to the spread of English is also largely attributable to the earlier role that colonization played in expanding the language geographically and demographically.

It is true that English has become the kind of global language that Latin came to be after the collapse of the Western Roman Empire. Equally true is the fact that English has evolved in a way similar to Latin, indigenizing into new vernaculars in the settlement colonies (both as 'Creole' and as 'native Englishes') and speciating into national and international varieties of lingua franca in the 'Outer' and 'Expanding Circles' (both as 'pidgin' and as 'indigenized Englishes'). However, just like with Latin, its evolution is not in the direction of a uniform 'global English'. This is significantly due to variation in the ecologies of its appropriation, which include:

1   the extent of the interactions the new speakers have had with speakers from the 'Inner Circle';
2   the specific languages English has come in contact with; and
3   the particular uses to which it has been put.

Rather than driving the world toward monolingualism, the differential evolution of English appears to be substituting a new form of diversity for an older one.

ACKNOWLEDGMENTS

I am grateful to Cécile B. Vigouroux for our numerous discussions on globalization and migrations, as well as for her critical and constructive feedback on a draft of this essay. I am solely responsible for the remaining shortcomings.

NOTES

1   As aptly pointed out by Chaudenson (2008), this evolution of the meaning of 'global' as 'world-wide' or 'universal' is related to that of the word *globe* in its etymological meaning of 'round body, ball, sphere,' is used also to represent 'planet Earth.' The persistence of 'comprehensive' and 'globular' among the meanings of 'global' should remind us that economists may have been mistaken in equating 'globalization' almost exclusively with what French linguists call *mondialisation* (Mufwene 2005) and with what Skutnabb-Kangas (2000) explains as 'universalization.' I argue below that what today is more specifically designated, especially by multiculturalists, as 'glocalization' – 'local globalization' – is perhaps where we all should start in order to make sense of how globalization as a world-wide phenomenon works, albeit in a patchy way. I even go so far as to propose a glocalization index: a measure (however inexplicit at this stage) of the degree of integration and strength of the domestic economic system of a territory. The index largely determines whether or not the territory functions as one of the centers, is on the margins, or is somewhere else on the continuum of interconnectedness and interdependences that characterize the world-wide networks of economic globalization.

2   Other examples include ASEAN (Association of SouthEast Asian Nations, involving Brunei, Cambodia, Indonesia, Laos, Malaysia, Myanmar, the Philippines, Singapore, and Vietnam), NAFTA (North American Free Trade Agreement, involving the United States, Canada, and Mexico), and MERCOSUR/MERCOSUL (Mercado Commún/Commun del Sur/do Sul 'Southern Common Market' involving Argentina, Brazil, Paraguay, and Uruguay).

3   In a yet unpublished paper, Chaudenson (n.d.) highlights the role that rivers played as the earliest highways of long-distance trade, with canoes serving as the earliest, primitive vehicles for long-distance transportation. As a matter of fact, a closer examination of trade networks in the Hellenistic Empire created by Alexander the Great and in the Roman Empire shows how roads connected with rivers and rivers with seas, to ensure the smooth transportation of humans and commodities between on the one hand Athens and Rome and, on the other, the colonies. Then the saying "all roads lead to Rome" acquires fuller historical meaning.

4   Florida (2007) observes that, even within themselves, cities do not evolve uniformly either, displaying disparities between neighborhoods in their responses to pressures or demands of globalization.

5   This is somewhat reminiscent of the invasions of England by the Scandinavians during the ninth to the thirteenth century – which did not lead to the replacement of English by either Norse or Danish.

6   As explained in Mufwene (2005, 2008) and in Mufwene and Vigouroux (2008), this does not mean that indigenous languages, especially minority ones, are not endangered at all. They are typically threatened by other, major indigenous languages, notably by urban vernaculars and/or by regional lingua francas, which are associated with cash economy and modernity.

7   To be sure, the colonization associated with archaic Greece and then with the Roman Empire was already faster than in the earlier phases of the Indo-European dispersal, a few millennia earlier. As noted in the section on "Colonization and Globalization," changes in speed are correlated with improvements in technology, especially in modes

of transportation, and with military differences between the colonists/colonizers and the natives (Cowen 2001; Osterhammel and Peterson 2005). In the case of the Americas, the Europeans were also assisted by the deadly germs they brought with them, to which the natives were not (sufficiently) immune (Crosby 1992).

8   As explained in Mufwene (2001), this disfranchising has had more to do with colonial political ideologies, in which linguists have been trapped, than with any peculiar ways in which language restructuring proceeded in the case of Creole vernaculars, which are clearly new, non-standard varieties of Indo-European languages spoken by non-European majorities who in general have also been marginalized socio-economically.

9   Hawaii is exceptional because of the particular time when and way in which it was colonized, although the new English varieties now spoken by descendants of the contract laborers are also disenfranchised as Creole or pidgin. Unlike the slaves in the Caribbean and in the Indian Ocean, the Hawaiian contract laborers were not ethnically mixed and their descendants are still identified by their traditional ethnicities, namely as Chinese, Japanese, Korean, or Filipino. They have also maintained cultural ties with their 'nations' of origin.

10   The same literature is also ambivalent about the acrolectal English varieties of the Caribbean, which are the vernaculars adopted by non-negligible proportions of the populations, although these populations constitute minorities. In any case, overlooking them in the present discussion bears little on the accuracy of the position I defend below against the notion of a global English. After all, the typology is essentially sociological, if not political. It contributes little to understanding why and how English has evolved differentially during its spread around the world (Mufwene 2001).

11   Linguists have generally been ill at ease with this explanation, as they had rather not address this racial bias in accounts of the emergence of Creoles. The very fact of arbitrarily isolating 'Creoles' or 'basilectal varieties' from their 'acrolects' in a universe where most of the populations are to be situated somewhere on a continuum between these extreme analytical constructs confirms the bias that these linguists deny. Speakers of 'native Englishes' too can be plotted on continua between the 'standard' and 'non-standard' varieties. Assuming that colonial 'native Englishes' are also contact-based English, 'Creoles' are really the counterparts of non-standard 'Englishes' in North America, Australia, and the like, except that they are spoken predominantly by populations of non-European descent (Mufwene 2008).

12   This is a phenomenon particularly well grasped by House (2003). Many speakers of English, especially from the 'Expanding Circle,' do not see the language as a marker of cultural or social identity, although it is evidently an asset. The reality is that, although speakers normally make adjustments to each other, usage of English as an international lingua franca is not associated with a particular community of practice, which would foster the emergence of a common norm. Television and the radio are not interactive enough to produce it; communication on the Internet is not of the kind that can go beyond simply familiarizing its users with diversity; and professional conferences are not regular enough to fulfill Crystal's dream. As well pointed out by Florida (2007), world-wide globalization is not eradicating locality. This is precisely where the action of evolution lies.

13   The heading of this section was obviously borrowed from the title of Phillipson's book, which expresses a fear that I believe to be exaggerated. However, my discussion covers many other parts of the world, to which the same considerations apply.

14   See Mufwene (2005, 2008), and a good deal of the literature on 'world Englishes' – particularly Kachru, Kachru, and Neslon (2006), and Schneider (2007).

REFERENCES

Ansaldo, U. (2009) *Contact Languages, Ecology and Evolution in Asia*. Cambridge: Cambridge University Press.

Banner, S. (2005) *How the Indians Lost Their Land: Law and Power on the Frontier*. Cambridge, MA: Belknab Press.

Blommaert, J. (2003) A sociolinguistics of globalization. Commentary. *Journal of Sociolinguistics* 7: 607–23.

Boyle, J. (2007) Language eradication among the Native North Americans. Paper presented at the 11th African, African American, Native American, Caribbean and the Americas Heritage Conference. Northern Illinois University, Chicago.

Brutt-Griffler, J. (2002) *World English: A Study of its Development*. Clevedon: Multilingual Matters Ltd.

Chaudenson, R. (2008) On the futurology of linguistic development. In C. B. Vigouroux and S. S. Mufwene (eds), *Globalization and Language Vitality: Perspectives from Africa*, 171–90. London: Continuum Press.

Chaudenson, R. (n.d.) *L'Eau et les langues*. Unpublished manuscript.

Clements, J. C. (1996) *The Genesis of a Language: The Formation and Development of Korlai Portuguese*. Amsterdam: Benjamins.

Cowen, N. (2001) *Global History: A Short Overview*. Cambridge: Polity.

Crosby, A. W. (1986) *Ecological Imperialism: The Biological Expansion of Europe, 900–1900*. Cambridge: Cambridge University Press.

Crosby, A. W. (1992) Ills. In A. L. Karras and J. R. McNeill (eds), *Atlantic American Societies: From Columbus through Abolition 1492–1888*, 19–39. London: Routledge.

Crystal, D. (1997) *English as a Global Language*. Cambridge: Cambridge University Press.

Crystal, D. (2000) *Language Death*. Cambridge: Cambridge University Press.

Crystal, D. (2004) *The Language Revolution*. Cambridge: Polity.

Diamond, J. (1997) *Guns, Germs, and Steel: The Fates of Human Societies*. New York: W. W. Norton.

Florida, R. (2005) The world is spiky: Globalization has changed the economic playing field, but hasn't leveled it. *Atlantic Monthly*, October, 48–51.

Florida, R. (2007) Pity the tri-city Toronto. *Globeandmail.com*, Opinions. December 22.

Garnsey, P., and Saller, R. (1987) *The Roman Empire: Economy, Society, and Culture*. Berkeley: University of California Press.

Hagège, C. (2006) *Combat pour le français: au nom de la diversité des langues et des cultures*. Paris: Odile Jacob.

House, J. (2003) English as a lingua franca: A threat to multilingualism? *Journal of Sociolinguistics* 7: 556–78.

Huber, M. (1999) Atlantic Ceoles and the lower Guinea Coast: A case against Afrogenesis. In M. Huber and M. Parkvall (eds), *Spreading the Word: The Issue of Diffusion among the Atlantic Creoles*, 81–110. London: University of Westminster Press.

Janson, T. (2004) *A Natural History of Latin: The Story of the World's Most Successful Language*. Oxford: Oxford University Press.

Kachru, B. (1983) *The Indianization of English: The English Language in India*. New Delhi: Oxford University Press.

Kachru, B., Kachru, Y., and Neslon, C. (eds) (2006) *The Handbook of World Englishes*. Malden, MA: Blackwell.

Keohane, R. O., and Nye, J. S. (2000) Globalization: What's new? What's not?

(And so what?) *Foreign Policy* 118: 104–19.

Kingsley, B. (2008) World Englishes in global contexts. The Braj and Yamuna Kachru Distinguished Lecture in the Linguistics Sciences. University of Illinois at Urbana-Champaign, October 9.

Landa, M. de (2000) *A Thousand Years of Nonlinear History*. New York: Swerve Editions.

Leith, D. (2007) English – Colonial to postcolonial. In D. Graddol, D. Leith, J. Swaan, M. Rhys, and J. Gillen (eds), *Changing English*, 117–52. London: Routledge.

Marling, W. H. (2006) *How 'American' is Globalization?* Baltimore: Johns Hopkins Press.

McArthur, T. (1998) *The English Languages*. Cambridge: Cambridge University Press.

McCrum, R., Cran, W., and McNeil, R. (2002) *The story of English*, 3rd edn. London: Faber and Faber/BBC Books.

Mignolo, W. D. (2000) *Local Histories/Global Designs: Coloniality, Subaltern Knowledges, and Border Thinking*. Princeton, NJ: Princeton University Press.

Mufwene, S. S. (1996) The Founder Principle in creole genesis. *Diachronica* 13: 83–134.

Mufwene, S. S. (2001) *The Ecology of Language Evolution*. Cambridge: Cambridge University Press.

Mufwene, S. S. (2005) *Créoles, écologie sociale, évolution linguistique*. Paris: L'Harmattan.

Mufwene, S. S. (2008) *Language Evolution: Contact, Competition, and Change*. London: Continuum Press.

Mufwene, S. S. (2009) The indigenization of English in North America. T. Hoffmann and L. Siebers (eds), *World Englishes: Problems, Properties, Prospects*, 335–68. Amsterdam: Benjamins.

Mufwene, S. S., and Vigouroux, C. B. (2008) Colonization, globalization, and language vitality in Africa: An introduction. In C. B. Vigouroux and S. S. Mufwene (eds), *Globalization and Language Vitality: Perspectives from Africa*, 1–31. London: Continuum Press.

Nettle, D., and Romaine, S. (2000) *Vanishing Voices: The Extinction of the World's Languages*. Oxford: Oxford University Press.

Osterhammel, J., and Peterson, N. P. (2005) *Globalization: A Short History*. Princeton: Princeton University Press.

Ostler, N. (2005) *Empires of the World: A Language History of the World*. New York: Harper Collins.

Pennycook, A. (2007) *Global Englishes and Transcultural Flows*. London: Routledge.

Phillipson, R. (2003) *English-Only Europe? Challenging Language Policy*. London: Routledge.

Polomé, E. (1983) The linguistic situation in western provinces of the Roman Empire. *Principat* 29: 509–53.

Posner, R. (1996) *The Romance Languages*. Cambridge: Cambridge University Press.

Quirk, R. (1990) Language varieties and standard language. *English Today* 6(1): 3–10.

Renfrew, C. (1987) *Archaeology and Language: The Puzzle of Indo-European Origins*. Cambridge: Cambridge University Press.

Schneider, E. (2007) *Post-Colonial Englishes: The Dynamics of Language Diffusion*. Cambridge: Cambridge University Press.

Schwartz, S. B. (1985) *Sugar Plantations in the Formation of Brazilian Society: Bahia, 1550–1835*. Cambridge: Cambridge University Press.

Skutnabb-Kangas, T. (2000) *Linguistic Genocide in Education – Or World-Wide Diversity and Human Rights?* Mahwah, NJ: Lawrence Erlbaum.

Stiglitz, J. E. (2002) *Globalization and its Discontents*. New York: W.W. Norton and Co.

Swaan, J. (2007) English voices. In D. Graddol, D. Leith, J. Swaan, M. Rhys, and J. Gillen (eds), *Changing English*, 5–38. London: Routledge.

Tomlinson, J. (1999) *Globalization and Culture*. Chicago: University of Chicago Press.

Tomlinson, J. (2007) Cultural globalization. In G. Ritzer (ed.), *The Blackwell Companion to Globalization*, 352–66. Malden, MA: Blackwell.

Trask, R. L. (1996) *Historical Linguistics*. London: Arnold.

Trudgill, P. (2008) Colonial dialect contact in the history of European languages: On the irrelevance of identity to new-dialect formation. *Language in Society* 37: 241–54.

2   Language Systems

ABRAM DE SWAAN

The human species is divided into some 6,000 groups, each one of which speaks a different language and does not understand any of the others. Yet this fragmentation is overcome by people who speak more than one language and thus ensure communication between different groups. Multilingual speakers have kept together humanity, separated as it is by so many language barriers.

Accordingly, a language (sub-)system consists of a set of 'language groups,' each one being defined by a common language and all being connected to one another through the mediation of multilingual speakers. Such multilingual connections between language groups do not occur haphazardly but constitute a surprisingly efficient, strongly ordered, hierarchical network, which ties together – directly or indirectly – the 6.5 billion inhabitants of the earth at the global level. This ingenious pattern of connections between all language groups on earth constitutes the world language system.[1] In addition to the political, economic, ecological, and cultural dimensions of the 'world system,' this world-wide constellation of languages constitutes its linguistic dimension, with a periphery, a 'semi-periphery,' and a 'core.'[2]

The vast majority of the languages in today's world – some 98 percent of them – survive in quite marginal positions within the global language system: these are the 'peripheral languages' and, although there are thousands of them, altogether they are spoken by less than 10 percent of mankind. They are languages of memory; they function almost entirely without script, media, or records.

The small, peripheral language groups tended to be connected mostly to adjacent communities, as intermarriage and local trade taught local people to speak the language of the nearby villages. But, since they were increasingly confronted by teachers, policemen, officials, and traders from the nearest city, such people are now more likely to acquire one and the same second language: the medium of government and of the market. This is, in each case, the language which is 'central' to a cluster of these peripheral language groups, like a planet surrounded by so many moons. The speakers of Frisian, Papiamento, Limburgish, and Sranan Tongo, for example, only rarely speak each other's language and, if they know a

The Handbook of Language and Globalization, First Edition. Edited by Nikolas Coupland.
© 2013 Blackwell Publishing Ltd except for editorial material and organization © 2013 Nikolas Coupland.
Published 2013 by Blackwell Publishing Ltd.

second language, that tends to be Dutch, which is both the central language in their group and the language of the state.

There may be some 150 languages (about 3 percent of the total) that occupy this central or 'planetary' position in the global language system. Taken together, they are spoken by 95 percent of mankind. These central languages are used in schools; they appear in print, in newspapers, in textbooks, and in fiction; they are current on the internet; and they are spoken on the radio and on television. Most often they are used in parliament, in the bureaucracy, and in courts. They usually are 'national' languages, and quite often such a language constitutes the official language of the state that rules the area. For each central language there exists a standard version, regulated by a standardized grammar, syntax, vocabulary, orthography, and pronunciation. Much of what has been said and written in these languages is recorded and preserved for posterity. Usually there is also a recognized corpus of classical texts, which embody the sediment of the use of the language by preceding generations.

Quite a few speakers of a central language are multilingual: first of all, there are those whose native speech is one of the peripheral languages and who in due course have acquired the central language. In fact everywhere in the world the number of this type of bilinguals is on the increase, as a result of the spread of elementary education and of the printed word, as well as of the impact of radio broadcasting. The complementary type – that of native speakers of the central language who have learned one of the peripheral languages – is much less common. Apparently, *language learning occurs mostly upward.*

By the same token, native speakers of a central language tend to acquire a second language, which is usually more widely spread and higher up in the hierarchy. At this level, each cluster of central language groups is connected, through multilingual speakers, to a very widespread language group, which occupies a 'supercentral' position within the system – much like planets (each with its own moons) circling around a sun. The supercentral language serves purposes of long-distance and international communication. There are about a dozen of these: Arabic, Chinese, English, French, German, Hindi, Japanese, Malay, Portuguese, Russian, Spanish, Swahili, and Turkish. All these languages, except Swahili, number more than 100 million speakers; Mandarin Chinese (in its written version) and English (including foreign speakers) each number around a billion users. Each supercentral language connects the speakers of a cluster of central languages. Thus La Francophonie consists in the language groups that communicate through French as their supercentral language.

If an Arab and a Chinese, or a Spaniard and a Japanese, meet, they will almost certainly make themselves understood in one and the same language – one that connects the supercentral languages with one another and therefore constitutes the pivot of the world language system. This 'hypercentral' language, which holds together the entire constellation, is, of course, English, in the hub of the linguistic galaxy – like a black hole devouring all languages that come within its reach. English has not always held that position. It has only done so for little more than the half of a century, and one day it may lose its hypercentral function again.

However, in the next decades English is only likely to gain many more speakers, on account of the dynamics of language spread.

The Communication Potential of a Language: The Q-Value

The relatively autonomous dynamic of a language constellation also results from the interplay of individual expectations. If people anticipate that a language will become current in their section of the world language system, they will not hesitate to adopt it themselves; but if, on the other hand, they suspect that in their environment one language will be abandoned for another, they themselves will use it less, will neglect to teach it to their children, and will favor the new language. Nowadays these expectations may affect not only regional or national languages but also those spoken on a continental or even on a global scale, as is demonstrated by the current fate of French and Russian as second languages – in francophone lands (the lands of La Francophonie) and in the 'near abroad' of the former Soviet Union, respectively.

Suppose that one person were to choose the language which seemed most useful, the one which offered the greatest possibilities of communication, either directly or through the mediation of an interpreter or translator. The language selected will be the one that is most prevalent in the relevant language constellation, offering an opportunity for direct communication with the largest number of people in it – and all the more if that language has also been acquired as a foreign one by a large number of bilingual individuals; for these can provide an indirect connection with a third language, through interpretation or translation. The constellation will be global, continental, or regional, as the case may be.

The utility of a language, i, for a given speaker in a constellation or sub-constellation, S, can be expressed in terms of its 'communication value,' Q_i, which indicates its potential to link this speaker with other speakers in S. The 'prevalence,' p_i, of language i refers to the number of speakers, P_i, who are competent in i, divided by all the speakers, N^S, in constellation S. 'Centrality,' c_i, refers to the number of *multilingual* speakers, C_i, who speak language i, divided by all the *multilingual* speakers in constellation S, M^S. The communication or Q-value equals the product of the prevalence (p_i) and the centrality (c_i) of language i in constellation S.

The formula can be written as follows:

$$Q_i = p_i \times c_i = (P_i/N^S) \times (C_i/M^S)$$

A numerical example may illustrate the calculation of Q_i.

Imagine a system S with four languages: i, j, k, and l. Suppose there are 150 speakers who only know language i, 100 who only speak j, 250 who only speak k, and 200 who only know l. Moreover, 10 speakers are competent in the combination i *and* j, 30 in i *and* l, 20 in j *and* l, 30 in k *and* l, and 10 in i, j, and l.

It follows that the total number of speakers (N^S) in the constellation S is 800, and the total number of multilingual speakers (M^S) in S is 100. The prevalence of language i (p_i) is calculated by adding the number of monolingual speakers of i (150) to the number of multilingual speakers of i in i *and* j, i *and* l, and i, j *and* l (50 in all): $P_i = 200$. The number of multilingual speakers who also speak i (C_i) is 50. Equally, $P_j = 140$, and C_j is 40; $P_k = 280$, and C_k is 30; $P_l = 290$ and C_l is 90.

$$Q_i = (P_i/N^S) \times (C_i/M^S) = (200/800) \times (50/100) = 0.125$$

Accordingly, $Q_j = 0{,}07$; $Q_k = 0{,}105$; $Q_l = 0{,}32625$.

Language l, with bilinguals from all other three languages, clearly scores highest, due to its high centrality; it is indeed positioned as the central language of the constellation. The Q-value of a repertoire with several languages may be calculated in a similar manner.[3]

The current scarcity and unreliability of statistics on language competencies do not permit a more elaborate measure. A simpler measure would lack validity. Elsewhere, I have published the Q-values of the official languages of the member states in the European Union/Community since 1975.[4] As might be expected, English obtained the highest score. Although German was much more current as a mother-tongue, the large number of multilingual speakers competent in English gave the latter the greatest prevalence and, necessarily, the strongest centrality. The case of French is of special interest, since it had a weaker prevalence than German (and certainly than English), and yet, because so many more Europeans had learned French, not German, as a foreign language, French still obtained a higher Q-value than German until around 1995, when German overtook it.

Apparently this measurement reflects the rough assessments based on the rather vague estimates that people make when considering which foreign language to learn. In fact, these estimates also reflect the anticipated decisions of others – in other words, the future state of the constellation. When such expectations reinforce one another, they result in a stampede towards the language expected to win; and the language in question will in fact win because of those very expectations. The world-wide preference for English as a foreign language is the most spectacular example.

This touches upon the very core of the political economy of language, a speciality so far hardly developed. Since a language has utility, it constitutes a good in the economic sense. But what sort of good? First, language is not consumed by being used. On the contrary, the more people use it, the better it serves each one of them. Language is freely accessible to all – no price can be exacted for using it. Moreover, it cannot be created by one person alone, and not everyone needs to collaborate in order to create or maintain it (so no one has a veto). These characteristics define a language as a collective good.

But there is more: not only does a language not lose its utility when more speakers use it; all users actually *gain* from an increase in its use. A similar effect also occurs with standards for new products, as in the case of operating systems like Apple or Windows for computers or Blu-ray and HDD for DVD-players: their value for each user increases with the number of users – a phenomenon known as 'external network effect' and also displayed by languages. However, while technical standards are incorporated in a consumer product that must be purchased and this fact allows for the exclusion of those who will not pay, no one can be excluded from a collective good such as a language. Languages, displaying as they do the properties of collective goods and also producing external network effects, thus constitute a special category: they are 'hypercollective' goods.

This hypercollective quality can trigger a stampede from one language to another, although the movement can be retarded by the time and the effort required in order to learn the new language and by the impossibility to forget the old tongue quickly. The abandonment of a language can be prevented only when a critical mass of speakers is committed to preserving it, so that a minimal Q-value will be guaranteed. Individual users will of course be tempted to abandon the old language and to adopt the new one as they assign a superior Q-value to the latter. Acting in this way, they procure an advantage for themselves, but simultaneously they reduce the value of the old language for those who continue to use it. A 'guaranteed' Q-value therefore requires measures to be taken in order to prevent people from switching languages, and this necessitates either collective action from language speakers of the language or compulsory state intervention (as France briefly imposed in recent times). This argument provides the foundation for an economic theory of language politics – and even for an economic theory of ethnic politics.

The hypercollective nature of a language applies also to its past. One might imagine that all communication leaves a sediment in the form of texts, either in human memory or in physical record of one form or another – written or printed on paper, or recorded in digital form. The totality of these memorized, written, or otherwise recorded texts constitutes the cumulative cultural capital of that language – a capital accessible only through the language itself. This capital is hypercollective in nature, for the simple reason that the more people contribute to it and draw from it, the more useful the capital becomes for each one of them. Clearly, with the disappearance of a language, the corresponding cultural capital would lose its value.

At this point one might envisage the elaboration of an economic theory of culture – of linguistic culture at the very least. Once again, two issues must be confronted: on the one hand, the individual temptation to switch and, on the other, the need for collective action or public constraint so as to prevent such 'defections.'

Languages define areas of communication. Beyond these limits, cultural practices and products travel with greater ease the less they depend on language: the visual arts cross much more easily than, say, poetry. For language-bound culture to transcend linguistic barriers, either the services of specialized bilinguals such as translators are required, or a foreign audience that has learned the language of the original version.

Language both insulates and protects the language-bound cultural elites in its domain: on the one hand, what they produce does not, on its own, transpire to the outside world; on the other hand, cultural production in other languages cannot penetrate that domain and compete there directly – it requires local competence in these foreign languages or translation into the domestic language.

This insulation operates more intensely for the less widely spread languages. As a result, the cultural elites concerned are faced with a dilemma: to adopt a more widely spread second language and compete with many more producers, on a much larger market – the 'cosmopolitan strategy'; or to stick to their less widely spread language and compete with only a few others for a much more restricted public – the 'local strategy.' Thus, say, Surinamese, Frisian, or Antillean authors face the dilemma of choosing between, respectively, Sranan, Frisian or Papiamento on the one hand, and Netherlandish[5] on the other. At the next system level, Dutch authors, in turn, have had to confront the choice between publishing in Netherlandish or English.

The case for remaining with the smaller language is usually better argued for and more explicitly advocated than its opposite – the choice of the larger language. The arguments most commonly presented for the first case are three-fold. First, the small idiom is threatened, it would even disappear as people abandon it in increasing numbers, and it would eventually meet 'language death.'[6] Next, the same argument may be generalized from language to all indigenous verbal practices and products: these are bound to disappear unless the language in which they are embedded continues to be spoken and understood. The phenomenon would erode the sense of personal identity and of identification with the community. Finally, linguistic imperialism and the pursuit of cultural hegemony are only abetted by 'defectors' from the smaller language group who adopt the more widely spread language.[7] Choosing the larger language, on the other hand, will not just improve career prospects for its new practitioners, it will also open up a larger world with broader knowledge, a more varied culture, and a greater diversity of lifestyles and moral options.

Recorded Language as Collective Cultural Capital

The dilemmas of a choice between the local and the cosmopolitan position within the global language system have been clarified through the notions of the hyper-collective character of languages and of the Q-value of language repertoires. The next concept to be introduced, that of 'collective cultural capital' – that is, the totality of available texts in a given language – allows us to demonstrate the dilemmas of collective action that are involved in the effort to preserve the cultural heritage, embedded as it is in language.

First, under what conditions do authors and speakers prefer the free exchange of language-bound products, or texts, and when will they choose to protect their community from the linguistic encroachments that may well result from the free exchange of texts with a larger language community? And, second, under what conditions will they resort to collective measures in order to protect their common language?

In the international exchange of language-bound culture goods – that is, texts – transport costs play a minor role, decreasing to almost zero for electronic transmission. In this respect, texts are the international commodity par excellence. What can make foreign texts costly is the expense of translation. Interpreters or translators produce a version of a foreign text in the domestic idiom. Many members of the domestic public do not need translation services, being themselves competent in the foreign language. Learning an additional language is comparable to purchasing a second home in another country or opening a branch office there – and saving on transport expenses as a result.[8] Acquiring a foreign language allows one to operate on two national markets and to save on translation costs.[9] Like transportation costs and import duties, the costs of translation or of foreign language acquisition also function as a barrier protecting indigenous authors – that is, domestic producers of texts in the local language. As a consequence, a community where competence in a foreign language (especially one with a higher *Q*-value) is relatively scarce provides authors with a natural 'protective' barrier. Their captive audience finds itself restricted to domestic or translated texts, very much like consumers who must either buy goods produced domestically or pay transport costs and import duties. A somewhat chauvinistic public may not mind this situation too much, preferring products with a strong *couleur locale*.

Authors who grew up with a peripheral language – one with a low *Q*-value – may find it to their advantage to write in it, if their (captive) audience is mostly monolingual. Their foreign competitors find themselves hampered by the costs of translation, which are quite forbidding in small language communities.

The consumers of language-dependent culture, on their part, are best served by the most varied supply of texts, accessible at the lowest cost. In the smaller language communities, the supply of domestic texts is necessarily limited. Even much larger societies are often unable to produce textual genres that require an extensive infrastructure, a very high investment, or a mass audience – for instance scientific publications, TV series or spectacular films.[10] They are dependent on translated imports.

An author in a small language community has three options:

1 to accept the limitations of the domestic audience: a low–risk and low-gain proposition;
2 to learn a foreign tongue with a high *Q*-value well enough to be able to compose texts in it: a major and high-risk investment;
3 to find a foreign publisher who will commission a translation into the high-Q language (this, too, requires a considerable and risky investment – on the part of the publisher).

But, in options (2) and (3), the potential gains are proportional: a chance of large circulation on a much larger market.[11] However, the two cosmopolitan strategies require good connections with foreign publishers and literati, in other words they demand transnational social capital.[12]

The users of texts in the more peripheral languages who want to transcend the limitations of domestic supply equally face two options: either they pay for translation or they learn the language with the higher *Q*-value.

In western Europe and in the US, almost all foreign language learning occurs in secondary school and the vast majority of the relevant age cohort does indeed attend full daytime education at that level.[13] As a result, the investment is compulsory, and the effort is made at the very start of one's career as a consumer of language-bound cultural goods. In other parts of the world, secondary school attendance is much lower. Sending a child to a school where foreign languages are offered is left to the parents who can afford it, or taking private language courses depends on the adult individual's decision.

Whether a foreign language is compulsory in school or not, the motivation to learn it increases when attractive cultural products are unavailable in translation into one's own peripheral language. On the other hand, the incentive for publishers to translate texts in the more peripheral language decreases if increasing numbers of potential readers and spectators from that language area are also fluent in the more central language.[14]

In conclusion, restrictions on the translation and dissemination of foreign language-bound products will, paradoxically, increase the public's motivation to learn a foreign language – an effect that may be much reinforced by the increased prestige of such foreign products.

Protectionism and Free Trade in Cultural Exchange

There is, however, one *caveat*: authors in small languages have some reason to be worried by foreign competition; but so do their readers, who may come to fear that eventually their indigenous authors will be forced out of the field through the impact of translated and imported texts. Concern may grow that in the end this will lead to a general erosion of the mother tongue and of domestic culture in general – or, in the terms of this analysis, to an overall depreciation of the original investment in mastery of the mother tongue. In other words, the short-term preferences of individual consumers may damage their collectively accumulated cultural capital in the long run. Moreover, given the low marginal costs of translated texts, the arguments from international trade theory about 'dumping' may well apply in the case of cultural exchange too.[15] Television and movie conglomerates in the very large language communities, such as the USA, can afford to export comedy series and films at negligible rates, preventing the small countries at the receiving end from developing a domestic entertainment industry that can compete – even if only internally – with foreign imports. In fact, producers in Europe have petitioned the European Commission, at times successfully, to impose tariffs or quotas on imported films. Many EU states subsidize the translation of domestic literature for export. Governments may also decide to subsidize domestic production, because they consider certain texts as especially valuable: they are 'merit goods,' quite independently of actual demand. Merit goods can be defined as commodities that one agrees *others* should be using. The prestige of high art and high tradition may radiate towards people who themselves have no part in them. Equally, citizens from small countries who find themselves abroad may have a collective interest in the prestige of their national culture, even if they do not particularly care for it themselves, as individuals.

The situation is entirely different for the former French and British colonies, especially in Africa, where the erstwhile colonial language remains the most central (but usually not the most prevalent) and the predominance of texts in the ex-colonial language actually hinders the emergence of cultural and scientific production in the indigenous languages. On the other hand, in many countries the former colonial language remains the only medium of exchange at the national level and therefore greatly facilitates communication at the global level.

The unequal relations of power and prestige that prevail between different languages in a given constellation – for example between the higher, supercentral language and the central or even peripheral languages that must compete with it – also exist between the different versions of a single language – for instance between the standard version and the dialects of the domestic periphery (the 'countryside,' the 'backwoods,' the *'banlieu'*). And sometimes 'local' authors who write in the 'dialect,' or singers and comedians who speak it, occupy a separate niche, being sheltered by the limited intelligibility of their language variety to outsiders, and by its low prestige elsewhere.

The users of a language with high Q-value, on the contrary, profit from the position their language occupies in the encompassing constellation of languages. Their advantage is a clear case of what economists would call 'location rent.'[16] Whenever an outsider acquires their mother tongue, they profit, as the 'communication value' of their language increases without any effort on their part. The tremendous advantages of this position may be seen when one looks at the exports of language-bound cultural goods from the US and Britain. This privilege is not won by birthright alone, it can also be acquired: quite a few writers, many singers and actors, legions of scientists and scholars have made the effort to acquire fluency in English and reaped the rewards that go with it. Nor does it come solely from a location in the English-speaking heartland, the US and the UK. An astonishing number of writers from peripheral societies where English prevails in some form have gained world-wide stature through their mastery of English prose. Success with the native English public often brings with it recognition from a world-wide audience, which has learned English as a foreign language. Next comes translation into the many languages that are linked to English through interpreters and translators. Not only the rent from linguistic capital enter the equation, but also the rent from the social capital based on a strategic position in the network of international cultural exchange.

The authors in the large languages have little to fear from foreign competition: translation costs operate as a protective barrier. The effort demanded from foreign authors who want to write directly in English serves as a formidable barrier, protecting native authors. Moreover, the numbers of people who have learned to understand English grow at a spectacular pace, adding to the audience of

English-language authors.[17] It goes without saying that, under these conditions, the US and the UK are well advised to support free cultural exchange across the globe, even if they must do so unilaterally.[18]

The position of cultural consumers who learned English as their mother tongue is as privileged as that of the producers, if not more so: competition from abroad brings consumers only more variety in supply, while they need not fear at all for the survival of their own language and culture. On the contrary, all over the world tens of millions of students are busy learning English every day; in the process they improve their own position in the language constellation of the world and, unbeknownst to them, they also improve the value position of all other English speakers. All the while, native English speakers hardly realize what enviable blessing is bestowed upon them through the sheer accident of their having the mother tongue they have and through the learning efforts of a myriad of unknown foreigners.

These benefits are almost entirely undeserved and unjustified; but so are most of the advantages and detriments that befall nations as accidents of geography and history: location, climate, natural resources, trade routes … Recently, a movement aiming to right the wrongs of language hegemony has spread across the western world: it advocates the right of all people to speak the language of their choice, to fight 'language imperialism' abroad and 'linguicism' at home, to strengthen 'language rights' in international law. Alas, what decides is not the right of human beings to speak whatever language they wish, but the freedom of everyone else to ignore what one says in the language of one's own choice.[19] If, on the other hand, people wish to communicate beyond the narrow circle of their linguistic peers, they have little choice but to learn the (super)central language that links them to wider circles of communication.

Monoglossia, Polyglossia, and Heteroglossia

The users of a language share it as a hypercollective good. Having constituted a language community over the centuries, they have gradually accumulated a collection of texts recorded or memorized in their language.[20] Just as every speaker added benefits to all others, every new text increases the collective cultural capital.

In principle, a language community should be willing to subsidize new speakers to join its ranks, since these would increase the Q-value of the language for all members. Language courses for recent immigrants are indeed routinely subsidized in Israel and in EU countries such as the Netherlands. For the same reasons, it would be rational for the British or the American government – or for the French or German, for that matter – to sponsor courses abroad in their respective languages. But actually many students who find themselves out there are willing to pay for textbooks and tuition anyway, since they want to improve the Q-value of their repertoire by adding a widely spread language.

Most governments subsidize foreign language learning in secondary schools at home. This, too, is rational, both for the individual who acquires a repertoire with higher *Q*-value and for the collectivity, since the domestic language grows in value: its centrality increases through the gain of multilinguals in the ranks of its speakers – namely students who have mastered a foreign language. In other words, all speakers of a language profit from the language learning efforts made only by some among them; they gain opportunities to find interpreters between the foreign language learned and their own, and this is reflected in an increase in centrality, a factor in the *Q*-value of their language. The same applies to speakers of the foreign language – again, without any activity on their part, since the *Q*-value of that language also grows with the increase of its multilingual speakers. Where hypercollectivity prevails, language learning is a win–win game, with benefits for every one. The gain comes at a cost, however: the expense and effort of language learning itself. And there may be a hidden cost in the long run, namely desertion from the language with the smaller *Q*-value.

Polyglossia,[21] the coexistence of several languages in one society, often in distinct social domains, may constitute a lasting sociolinguistic equilibrium. But, under certain conditions, people may begin to abandon the language with the lesser *Q*-value – usually an indigenous language, often their mother tongue. In one domain after another, growing numbers of speakers choose the more central language for their use, commonly a more recent arrival in the area. A slow stampede out of the domestic tongue and toward the dominant language is underway. This is what sociolinguists call 'language death' or 'language extinction.' It is difficult not to depict the process as a tragic loss. The metaphor of death or extinction conjures up the image of a lost species. A biological species, however, may be saved by conserving the habitat where it finds its niche. For a language to survive, a considerable number of people must maintain their speech, and maybe their ways of life, against the inroads of a changing social and linguistic environment: a rather more precarious task.

As speakers in the community of the original language become bilingual in increasing proportion, the added *Q*-value of being fluent (not only in the exogenous but also) in the indigenous language begins to diminish, since more and more people who speak it can also be reached through the other medium – until no one is left who speaks the domestic language only, and competence in it no longer adds to one's *Q*-value.[22] Children may now learn the new language at an ever earlier age, with increasing facility, and they may even adopt it as their mother tongue instead of the original language. This is by no means unusual. On the contrary, it is the 'normal' course of affairs in processes of nation formation and colonization. A powerful center extends its political, economic and cultural control over the periphery, be it adjacent or overseas, and its language spreads across the new territories. This process has occurred in the French *province* with Breton, Flemish, and Occitan and throughout the 'Celtic fringe' of the British Isles with Welsh, Scots, and Irish; it has also happened all over Latin America, under the impact of Spanish; while the small languages of memory in India and Indonesia, in South Africa and Senegal, in Nigeria and Congo (Zaire) are under the triple impact of the supercentral former colonial languages, of the (super)central domestic languages, and of the popular, vehicular 'pidgins.'

From an individual perspective, it is entirely rational for people to opt for the language with the larger Q-value. Only the costs of second-language learning and the emotional costs of abandoning one's mother tongue will impede the transition to the dominant language. Once the great majority of the original language community has become bilingual and diglossia is well-nigh complete, another stage sets in, one that may well be called 'heteroglossia': the original language no longer adds much to the Q-value of individual repertoires (in fact, it adds less than its 'maintenance' costs) and it is increasingly being abandoned, as the dominant language takes over.

However, at this point other considerations may become predominant: with the surrender of the indigenous language, the corresponding collective cultural capital becomes increasingly inaccessible. Either the texts must be translated into the dominant language, or the collective cultural stock is lost. In this case the individual cultural capital, predicated as it is on the collective capital, must be written off. (Of course, the new speakers of the hegemonic language acquire access to the collective cultural stock of their new language community in the process, and they may well consider this to be an adequate compensation for their loss). Since it usually does not pay for someone to translate endogenous texts into the hegemonic language on one's own, a collective effort for cultural conservation must be made by the members of the language community in dissolution. But those who speak and act for this disbanding language community will most likely prefer to salvage the language not by translating its heritage, but by preventing the members of the community from deserting it in the first place: they will insist that a collective effort should be made to maintain the idiom, even if only as a second language. There will be pressure upon adults to continue to use it and upon children to go on learning it as their parents did.[23] Clearly a community with an effective coordinating agency, for instance a political authority of its own, is in a much better position to impose its policies than a collectivity that must rely on voluntary compliance.[24]

Authors, as producers of texts, have a larger stake in the original language and in the conservation of its cultural stock than others, because of their costly investment in language skills and in knowledge of the accumulated texts. Moreover, the switch to the dominant language as a full means of expression requires from them a much larger effort than from those who only speak it, hear it, and read it. And, finally, if and when the domestic language is maintained by a sufficiently large audience, this provides the indigenous authors with a protected market for their texts and gives them an added interest in maintaining the original language.

Thus, unless they make up their mind to become cosmopolitans, venturing into the high-Q language community, authors will feel compelled to defend the domestic language. Translators and interpreters, too, have a vested interest in slowing down the spread of the dominant language and in preventing desertion from the original language, so as to maintain a clientele for their services. It should therefore come as no surprise that specialized producers and translators of texts are among the first to defend the domestic language, together with politicians, who wish to preserve their local support base, and community leaders or clergymen, who do not want to see their congregation disband as its unifying language evaporates.

The 'tipping point' in the transition from diglossia to heteroglossia comes when those who speak both the indigenous and the exogenous language find that the costs of maintaining the local language begin to outweigh the latter's dwindling additional Q-value.[25] This occurs when a considerable majority of the community has already become bilingual. Once desertion sets in, parents no longer teach the mother tongue to their children and no longer make an effort to speak it 'correctly' themselves. If the language is to survive at all, individual language maintenance is no longer enough. Young adults must be pressured into the much larger effort of learning what has by then become the language of their elders.

In general, the gains that speakers may reap from the addition of new users of their language find their counterpart, under obverse conditions, in the increasing losses that the remaining speakers suffer once others begin to desert their language. Since language is a hypercollective good and cultural stock constitutes a collective good for the language community, language maintenance raises problems of collective action and confronts individual language users with its concomitant dilemmas: it would indeed make sense for everyone separately to maintain the original language if many others could be counted on to act likewise. However, since one cannot be sure that the others will do so, in each individual case maintenance of the original language appears not to be worth the effort. In such situations people often profess publicly their allegiance to the collective heritage, while in private they neglect their inherited language and culture and they try to improve their children's career prospects by securing proficiency in the dominant language.[26]

On the whole, when the language community also constitutes a state, its government can avert a stampede out of the national language, even when a high degree of diglossia prevails. A government can do so by safeguarding the domains of domestic politics, national culture, education, law, and so forth as the preserve of the indigenous language, and by preventing the exogenous language from usurping all the prestigious functions. In short, it is the state that can keep its official language 'robust.' Thus some European countries – like the Netherlands, Luxembourg, and Denmark – are rapidly approaching a state of universal multilingualism and pervasive diglossia, where up to 80 percent of the population is more or less competent in English. But at present there are no signs of abandonment or neglect of the national languages in these countries. The domestic language continues to function in a series of distinct social domains, while English dominates in others. Even if switching between the two languages is frequent, the one hardly encroaches upon the other.[27] Still, even if there is no reason for alarm, there is sufficient cause to remain alert: English could make inroads into new domains of speech, and the national languages could continue to lose prestigious functions. But, most probably, European languages will prove vital enough to maintain their specific domains under the pressure of English.

The Case of the European Union

In a sociolinguistic perspective, the European Union represents a subsystem of the global language system, but one with a multitude of strongly anchored national traditions. From the outset, the official language of every member state was recognized as an official language of the European Community and, later, of the European Union. In 1956, the six founding members contributed four languages: Dutch, French, German, and Italian – an almost manageable number. Without much discussion, French was accepted as the working language of the Community's budding bureaucracy, as it had been the language of diplomacy until the end of World War II and the sole language of the European Coal and Steel Community, which preceded the EC. In those post-war years the Germans and the Italians kept a low profile, and the Dutch (even counting in the Dutch-speaking Flemish of Belgium) were not numerous enough to insist upon the use of their language in the administration.

The first great expansion of the European Community in 1973 brought in the British, the Irish (almost all of them native English speakers), and the Danes, who for the vast majority had learned English in school. In fact, English quickly became another working language of the Commission's bureaucracy and an informal lingua franca in the European Parliament. The Germans still did not push their language too much and, being generally more fluent in English than in French, they may have helped to promote English against French.[28] Since then, French has been surpassed by English as the language of the European bureaucracy. German comes a far third, and other languages hardly play any role in day-to-day administration.[29]

With the addition of Greece in 1981, of Portugal and Spain in 1986, and of Austria, Finland, and Sweden in 1995, the set of official languages in the European Union grew to nine, then to eleven – a number that became increasingly difficult to cope with for the translation and interpretation services. On May 1, 2004, ten new states joined the Union: Cyprus, the Czech Republic, Estonia, Hungary, Latvia, Lithuania, Malta, Poland, Slovenia and Slovakia; by January 1, 2007, Bulgaria and Romania had also joined. The twelve new members increased the number of EU citizens from 390 million (EU15) to 486 million (EU27) and brought the number of official languages to twenty-three (Irish was belatedly accepted as a language of the Union, and the (Greek) Cypriots did not add a language of their own).

From the 1960s on, secondary education had been rapidly expanding throughout Europe. Quite independently of each other, the member states made sweeping reforms of their secondary school systems, and in the process most of them reduced the number of compulsory foreign languages taught, henceforward prescribing only English or leaving the choice entirely to the students, who almost everywhere opted for English anyway.[30] As a result of the expansion of secondary education, there are now more citizens in the Union than ever before who have studied one or more foreign languages. This situation encompasses French, German, Spanish, and Italian. But of course the numbers of English students have grown most spectacularly. Of all high-school students in the EU25, about 25 percent learn German or French, some 10 percent learn Spanish, and less than 5 percent learn Russian. But almost 90 percent of all pupils in secondary education learn English (*Key Data* 2005: C8). The accession of so many central and eastern European countries has strengthened the position of German vis-à-vis French, but English also leads in the new member countries, albeit with a slight margin.

For the present purposes of our analysis, four levels of communication are to be distinguished within the European Union. In the first place, the official, public level consists mainly of the sessions of the European Parliament and of the external dealings of the European Commission. Here the founding treaty applies, which recognizes all the official languages of the member states as languages of the Union; moreover, the principle holds that decisions by the EU should be published in all these languages, since they affect the laws of the constituent states. In the second place, there is the level of the Commission bureaucracy, where the officials have more or less informally adopted a few 'working languages' in their everyday contacts and internal correspondence. Then there is a third level, of transnational communication, which is neither official nor institutional: this is the 'civic' level of the citizens of Europe, where several languages compete for predominance in various areas of the Union and in many different domains of communication. English no doubt is paramount at this level too, but French still rivals it in southern Europe, and in central Europe English competes with German.

The fourth level is that of domestic communication within each present (and future) member country. There the official language is the mother tongue of a large, if not vast, majority – the language taught in school at all levels and protected by the national state in every way. Nevertheless, these 'central' or official national languages increasingly coexist with a supercentral language used for transnational communication; at present this is, in every country, English, which is spoken by a fast growing proportion the population.

In fact, while all twenty three official languages of the Union are used at the first level – for public and ceremonial occasions, for important official documents, and in correspondence with the citizens – only two languages, English and French, are used at the second level, of informal communication in the corridors of Parliament and in the meeting rooms of bureaucracy. When it comes to the third level, that of civil Europe, statistics and survey data all concur that English is the first language of transnational communication, while German, French, and maybe Spanish play secondary roles in the corresponding regions and have a limited scope in cultural or commercial exchanges.

At the fourth level, within each member country, the national language continues to function at most levels of domestic social interaction, while transnational functions are carried out by the supercentral language(s) ensuring all-European communication. As long as each state continues to act as the protector of its national language, there is no immediate threat from the supercentral language, not even when a large majority of citizens has learned it as a foreign language. A state of diglossia, a precarious equilibrium between two languages in one society, will prevail. Either pidginization, for instance with English, or a complete takeover by English seem quite unlikely. This is because the national languages of Europe tend to be quite 'robust,' strengthened as they are by the support of the state and its bureaucracy, by the media, by the schools, and by a thorough codification in dictionaries, in grammars and in a literary corpus. Such state languages appear to be as permanent and constant, as completely rule-governed, and as clearly demarcated from adjacent languages as the state itself claims to be.

The rise of English as the lingua franca of Europe cannot be understood solely in the context of that subcontinent. This first second language of the European Union is spoken nowhere on the mainland as a first language. It was the position of English as the linking language of the British Empire and as the national language of the United States, the hegemonic power since 1945, that gave it the decisive head start in Europe in1973. French, which had a similar position as a global ex-colonial language in the francophone world (La Francophonie), still could not muster equal prevalence and centrality and was easily surpassed by English in terms of global *Q*-value. Had the Germans supported the French, their two languages might have become the major media of the EU; but the Germans chose tacitly to support English against the old-time rival, French, and now they protest the neglect of German in the EU.

The actual predominance of English as the second language of the member societies, as the lingua franca of international traffic, and as the informal language of choice within the Union's institutions (with the exception of the French-speaking European Court) is difficult to reconcile with the formal construction of the European Union as a combination of relatively autonomous states. Any recognition of the actual inequality among the languages of the Union clashes with the official precept of equal status for every member state, and thus risks to offend all nations except the UK. This fact has provoked some striking rhetoric about 'unity in diversity' and about the need for students to learn as many different languages as possible. But, in the meantime, almost every Union initiative unwittingly tends to promote English, as it increases cultural or commercial exchange between the nations of Europe unavoidably in English. Even the campaign for the promotion of linguistic diversity, by further increasing the confusion of tongues, only serves to profile English as the sole solution: the more languages, the more English. This is the outcome of the mutually reinforcing expectations that people form about the language choices other people will make. The slow stampede towards English as a foreign language has now reached the tipping point not only in Africa, in the Middle East, in India and in China, but, in the same global context, also in Europe.

English as the Hub of the World Language System

English, and French too, have survived in former colonies to a surprising degree. Apart from a host of local and contingent factors, this is due to the variety of indigenous languages in almost all of these newly independent countries. As a result, the colonizers and the indigenous administrators spoke the colonial language as their common medium. And the liberation movement saw itself forced to adopt the same language, often much against its actors' will, for the sake of keeping their ranks united. When independence came in countries as diverse as Senegal and India, the victorious nationalist movement insisted on a single, indigenous, national language, and met with vast support among the population. In the ensuing national debate, the question was which indigenous language to select. And the answer invariably was: 'not yours.' Even if a language was understood by three quarters of the population, such as Wolof in Senegal, the Wolof speakers who were ethnic Serrer or Malinké would happily continue to use Wolof but refused to recognize it as the language of the land. The speakers of the Dravidian languages of southern India would rather hold on to English than adopt Hindi officially. This 'language envy' prevented the adoption and the spread of a common indigenous language and favored the former colonial medium. Moreover, as the ex-colonial language still seemed to offer the best opportunities on the labor market at home and abroad, citizens who could afford it would continue to profess their support for a native language in public, but privately would opt for an English school for their children: a remarkable instance of 'private subversion of the public good,' as David Laitin has called it.[31]

In many of these countries there existed a popular lingua franca, rarely written, but widely spoken all across the land: Wolof in Senegal, Pidgin in Nigeria, Hindustani in India, Malay in Indonesia, Swahili in Tanzania and Kenya [...] However, these 'bazaar languages' were often considered too lowly to serve as the idiom of the newly independent nation. Only in Tanzania was Swahili adopted as the national language; and, in Indonesia, Malay was transformed into *bahasa Indonesia* and very successfully introduced throughout the archipelago. In other countries, however, both the indigenous administrators and the liberation fighters had a vested interest in the former colonial language and may have tacitly favored it to secure an advantage for themselves. In South Africa, a dozen languages were officially recognized, but the ensuing fragmentation effectively excluded all of them, leaving just English – the language of the ANC and of the former elite (with the exception of the speakers of Afrikaans, who were white and rural for the most part). The same principle was at work again: the more languages, the more English.

In the course of the twentieth century, English has become the hypercentral language of the world language system. Even if there are languages with more speakers, such as (probably) Mandarin and Hindi, English remains the most central one, on account of the many multilinguals who have it in their repertoire. This has nothing to do with the intrinsic characteristics of the English language; on the contrary, its orthography and pronunciation make it quite unsuitable as a world language. It is a consequence of the particular history of the English-speaking nations and of reciprocal expectations and predictions about the language choices that prospective learners across the world will make. Even if the hegemonic position of the US were to decline, English would continue to be the hub of the world language system for quite some time, if only because so many millions of people have invested so much effort in learning it and for that very reason expect so many millions of other speakers to continue to use it.

NOTES

1   Karl W. Deutsch (1966) pioneered a global and systemic vision of international communication networks. The theoretical perspectives that are presented here are elaborated in De Swaan 2001.
2   Wallerstein 1974.
3   For a detailed discussion, see De Swaan 2001, pp. 33–40.
4   Cf. De Swaan 2001; for the most recent data, see De Swaan 2007.
5   'Netherlandish' and 'Dutch' are here used as synonyms, denoting the language spoken in the Netherlands and in Flanders (i.e. the Flemish part of Belgium). In the literature one sometimes also encounters the term 'Netherlandic.' The spelling and vocabulary of Dutch are standardized under the auspices of the joint *'Nederlandse Taalunie.'*
6   See Dorian 1989; Hindley 1990; Uhlenbeck 1994; Hale et al. 1992, Ladefoged 1992.
7   Cf. Phillipson 1992. See also Clayton 1999, who points out that not only the imperialist strategy of imposing the conqueror's language, but also the "pragmatic" strategy of mobilizing domestic languages in support of imperial rule may bolster the conqueror's position.
8   A similar effect operates in the multinationalization of firms; see Carnoy 1993, p. 71: "The greatest pressure on automobile firms to become global, however, is still protectionism – the power of national political aims imposing themselves on comparative prices." Since duties and other trade restrictions make it more costly to import or export, "the general effect will be to increase the costs of using external markets relative to multinational control" (p. 60). In other words, it will probably pay to open a branch office or a subsidiary plant in the protectionist country.
9   To readers, the advantage of learning a highly central language may not only reside in the opportunity to read its literature, but also in the opportunity to read the translations that have been made into it from a multitude of other languages.
10   Already in 1980, almost two thirds of all chemical and almost three quarters of all medical articles were published in English, and adding five other languages would account for well over 90 percent of publications in these fields; see Laponce 1987, pp. 66–8. Except in the USA, television entertainment is for a very large part imported, and imports come overwhelmingly from the United States; see Varis 1984; Biltereyst 1992, p. 523.
11   For statistics on translations from Netherlandish, see Heilbron 1995.
12   Heilbron (1995) and Casanova (1999) have applied the notion of a world language system to the network of translations. Casanova has shown how Paris functions as the hub of a network that elevates literary works from peripheral and central languages to the supercentral level of French *belles lettres*, while Heilbron has demonstrated that literary works from the smaller languages enter world literature by being translated into English and other world languages, and from there they are introduced in smaller languages. Similar movements have been observed in popular music, films, etc.

13   In 1990, 93 percent of young people in Europe speaking some foreign language had learned it at secondary school; see *Eurobarometer* 1991.

14   There is a countertendency: as the cultural elites, fluent in the foreign language, are familiar with these foreign texts and performances, their prestige may convince others that these products are indeed desirable, and the demand for translated versions may increase accordingly among those sections of the public that have not learned the foreign language. The relative impact of the two tendencies is a matter of empirical investigation.

15   'Dumping' refers to the practice of selling goods at marginal or lower cost on separate – that is, usually foreign – markets (so that on the home market the full price may still be fetched).

16   See Muth 1968.

17   For brevity's sake I have limited this discussion to the case of English; however, Arabic and Spanish – both growing international language communities – and French, a stagnant one at best – would provide interesting cases on their own.

18   This, again, is a tenet of classical international trade theory since David Ricardo and John Stuart Mill; see Bhagwati 1988, pp. 24–33.

19   Cf. Skutnabb-Kangas and Phillipson 1994.

20   '*En Afrique, chaque vieillard qui meurt est une bibliothèque qui brûle*' ('In Africa, when an old person dies, it is as if a library went up in flames', author's translation): Hompate Bâ, quoted in Diongue 1980, p. 53.

21   The term is a variation on an expression coined by Ferguson (1959): 'diglossia,' a concept he restricted to the coexistence of two registers of the same language in different domains of one society. Later the term was used in a broader sense, for the coexistence of two languages rather than registers of a single language.

22   The prevalence $p_{\{i,j\}}$ for a two-language repertoire $\rho_{i,j}$ is defined as the proportion of all speakers in the language constellation S who have either language i or language j or both in their repertoire. When all j-speakers have learned the language i, $p_{\{i,j\}} = p_i$. Equally, $c_{\{i,j\}}$ is defined as the proportion of *multilingual* speakers who have either i or j or both in their repertoire. Unless there are speakers of a third language in the constellation who also speak j, but not i, or speakers of j who also speak some third language, but who do not speak i – which is rare in the actual constellations under study – it is the case that $c_{\{i,j\}} = c_i$. As a result:

$$Q_{\{i,j\}} = p_{\{i,j\}} \cdot c_{\{i,j\}} = p_i \cdot c_i = Q_i$$

Competence in language j no longer adds to the Q-value of a speaker of i.

23   It is customary to argue that no one is individually motivated to contribute any effort towards this collective objective. However, in this case too, many of the activities required are not just a 'sacrifice' but may well be rewarding in themselves: admonition, rebuke, scandalization, ostracization, joining in demonstrations, participating in riots, or even participating in terrorist attacks may generate individual satisfaction. In general, informal negative social sanctions quite often are a pleasure to apply. Cf. De Swaan 1988, p. 5.

24   See Laitin 1987, 1989.

25   See Schelling 1978; Laitin 1993.

26   No one has depicted these dilemmas more starkly than David Laitin (1993).

27   The public is much concerned with the appearance of foreign, mostly English, loan words in the vocabulary. But such additions to the lexicon leave the morphological

'hard core' of the language, its grammar, syntax, and prononciation, mostly unaffected; see Hagège 1987, pp. 27–89. The resilience of many European languages is demonstrated by the adoption of English verbs, such as 'delete' or 'save' in computer speech, which are then conjugated according to the rules of the borrowing language, e.g. in Dutch: '*Ik heb de file geseefd*' ('I saved the file'). Surprisingly, the tense and the word order are also spontaneously transformed into perfectly correct Dutch, a feat that students often fail at in formal translation exercises.

28   See Bellier 1995, esp. p. 245; Ammon 1996, p. 262. Nevertheless, at least since 1991, the German government has regularly insisted on the adoption of German as the third language of the European Commission's bureaucracy, and in the fall of 1999 it actually collided with the (then) Finnish presidency of the Union on this issue.

29   See Schlossmacher 1994; also Mamadouh 1995.

30   See Van Deth 1979.

31   Laitin 1992, pp. 152–3.

REFERENCES

Ammon, U. (1996) The European Union (EU – formerly European Community): Status Change of English during the last fifty years. In J. A. Fishman, A. W. Conrad, and A. Rubal-Lopez (eds), *Post-Imperial English: Status change in Former British and American Colonies, 1940–1990*, 241–67. Berlin and New York: Mouton de Gruyter.

Bellier, I. (1995) Moralité, langue et pouvoirs dans les institutions européennes. *Social Anthropology* 3(3): 235–50.

Bhagwati, J. (1988) *Protectionism*. Cambrigde, MA: MIT Press.

Biltereyst, D. (1992) Language and culture as ultimate barriers? An analysis of the circulation, consumption and popularity of fiction in small European countries. *European Journal of Communication* 7: 517–40.

Carnoy, M. (1993) Whither the nation–state? In M. Carnoy, M. Castells, and S. S. Cohen, *The New Global Economy in the Information Age: Reflections on Our Changing World*, 1–17. University Park: Pennsylvania State University Press.

Casanova, P. (1999) *La République mondiale des lettres*. Paris: Éditions Du Seuil.

Clayton, T. (1999) Decentering language in world-system inquiry. *Language Problems and Language Planning* 23(2): 133–56.

De Swaan, A. (1988) *In Care of the State; Health Care, Education and Welfare in Europe and the United States in the Modern Era*. Cambridge: Polity.

De Swaan, A. (2001) *Words of the World: The Global Language System*. Cambridge, UK and Malden, MA: Polity/Blackwell.

De Swaan, A. (2007) The language predicament of the EU since the enlargements. In U. Ammon, K. J. Mattheier, and P. H. Nelde (eds), *Sociolinguistica: International Yearbook of European Sociolinguistics, Vol. 21: Linguistic Consequences of the EU-Enlargement*, 1–21. Tübingen: Max Niemeyer Verlag.

Deutsch, K. W. (1966) *Nationalism and Social Communication: An Inquiry into the Foundations of Nationality* [1953]. Cambridge, MA: MIT Press.

Diongue, M. (1980) *Francophonie et langues africaines en Sénégal*. Dakar: Ecole Normale Supérieure des Bibliothèques.

Dorian, N. (ed.) (1989) *Investigating Obsolescence: Studies in Language Contraction and Death*. Cambridge: Cambridge University Press.

Eurobarometer (1991) Young Europeans in 1990. Brussels: European Coordination Office 34(2).

Ferguson, C. A. (1959) 'Diglossia.' *Word* 15(2), 325–40.

Hagège, C. (1987) *Le Français et les siècles*. Paris: Odile Jacob.

Hale, K., Krauss, M. Watahomigie, L. J., Yamamoto, A. Y., Craig, C., LaVerne Masayesva, J. and England, N. C. (1992) Endangered languages. *Language* 68(1): 1–42.

Heilbron, J. (1995) Nederlandse vertalingen wereldwijd; Kleine landen en culturele mondialisering. In J. Heilbron, W. de Nooy, and W. Tichelaar (eds), *Waarin een klein land ... Nederlandse cultuur in internationaal verband*. Amsterdam: Prometheus.

Hindley, R. (1990) *The Death of the Irish Language: A Qualified Obituary*. London: Routledge.

Key Data on Teaching Languages at School in Europe. [2005] Brussels: Euridice European Unit.

Ladefoged, P. (1992) Another view of endangered languages. *Language* 68(4): 809–11.

Laitin, D. D. (1987) Linguistic conflict in Catalonia. *Language Problems and Language Planning* 11(2): 129–46.

Laitin, D. D. (1989) Linguistic revival: Politics and culture in Catalonia. *Comparative Studies in Society and History* 31(3): 297–317.

Laitin, D. D. (1992) *Language Repertoires and State Construction in Africa*. Cambridge: Cambridge University Press.

Laitin, D. D. (1993) The game theory of language regimes. *International Political Science Review* 14(3): 227–40.

Laponce, J. A. (1987) *Languages and their Territories*. Toronto: University of Toronto Press.

Mamadouh, V. (1995) *De talen in het Europese parlement*. Amsterdam: Instituut voor sociale geografie, Unversiteit van Amsterdam [Amsterdamse sociaal-geografische studies, 52].

Muth, R. F. (1968) Rent. In D. L. Sills (ed.), *International Encylopedia of the Social Sciences*, Vol. 13, 458–9. New York and London: MacMillan/Free Press.

Phillipson, Robert (1992) *Linguistic imperialism*. Oxford/New York: Oxford University Press.

Schelling, T. C. (1978) *Micromotives and Macrobehavior*. New York: Norton.

Schlossmacher, M. (1994) Die Arbeitssprachen in den Organen der Europäischen Gemeinschaft. Methoden und Ergebnisse einer empirischen Untersuchung. In U. Ammon, K. J. Mattheier, and P. H. Nelde (eds), *Sociolingistica: International Yearbook of European Sociolinguistics, Vol. 8: English only? In Europe*, 101–22. Tübingen: Max Niemeyer Verlag.

Skutnabb-Kangas, T., and Phillipson, R. (eds) (1994) *Linguistic Human Rights: Overcoming Linguistic Discrimination*. Berlin and New York: Mouton de Gruyter.

Uhlenbeck, E. M. (1994) The threat of rapid language death: A recently acknowledged global problem. In *The Low Countries: Arts and Society in Flanders and the Netherlands, 1993–1994*, Vol. 1: 25–31. Rekkem, Belgium: Stichting Ons Erfdeel.

Van Deth, J.-P. (1979) *L'Enseignement scolaire des langues vivantes dans les pays membres de la communauté européenne: Bilan, réflexions et propositions*. Bruxelles: Didier.

Varis, T. (1984) The international flow of television programs. *Journal of Communication* 34(1): 143–52.

Wallerstein, I. (1974) *The Modern World-System: Capitalist Agriculture and the Origins of the European World-Economy in the Sixteenth Century*. San Francisco: Academic Press.

3 The Global Politics of Language: Markets, Maintenance, Marginalization, or Murder?

TOVE SKUTNABB-KANGAS AND ROBERT PHILLIPSON

Prospects for the World's Languages

Today's prospects for the maintenance and further development of all existing spoken and written languages and sign languages in the world have been estimated as bleak. The latest (16th) edition of *Ethnologue*, the world's most complete catalogue of languages, lists 6,909 "known living languages" on its website (http://www.ethnologue.org/).[1] Most of the world's languages are very small in terms of numbers of speakers. UNESCO experts (see below) estimate that 96 percent of the world's languages are spoken by 4 percent of the world's population (see Skutnabb-Kangas 2000, chapter 1 on numbers). The languages with the largest numbers of 'native' speakers are today (Mandarin) Chinese, Spanish, Hindi, and English, in this order (see *Ethnologue*, and also resources at http://www.terralingua.org). At least some 4,500 of the world's spoken languages are indigenous (Oviedo and Maffi 2000).

UNESCO's Safeguarding Endangered Languages website (www.unesco.org/culture/en/endangeredlanguages) estimates that "over 50 percent of some 6,700 languages spoken today are in danger of disappearing," and that "[o]ne language disappears on average every two weeks." Some of the facts that, UNESCO suggests, may be reasons for this disappearance are that 90 percent of the world's languages are not represented on the internet, and that 80 percent of African languages have no orthography. According to more pessimistic, but still realistic, estimates, there might be only 300 to 600 oral languages left in 2100 as unthreatened languages, transmitted by the parent generation to children (see Krauss 1992). These would probably include most of the languages that have more than

The Handbook of Language and Globalization, First Edition. Edited by Nikolas Coupland.
© 2013 Blackwell Publishing Ltd except for editorial material and organization © 2013 Nikolas Coupland.
Published 2013 by Blackwell Publishing Ltd.

one million speakers today (Gunnemark 1991: 169–71 gave their number as 208 languages), and a few others. Almost all languages about to disappear would be indigenous, and most of today's indigenous languages would disappear, with the exception of very few, which are strong numerically (for example Quechua, Aymara, Bodo, Mapuche) and/or have official status (like Māori, some Saami languages). UNESCO's reaction so far has been mainly to support the listing and documentation of these languages; much more important is to try to influence the conditions that lead to their endangerment in the first place. The poor and power-less economic and political situation of indigenous peoples and minorities (IMs), who often live in the world's most diverse ecoregions, is one of the important background factors; habitat destruction through logging, the spread of agricul-ture, the use of pesticides and fertilizers, deforestation, desertification, overfish-ing, and so on often compel IMs into forced assimilation and/or migration or destitution. Formal education and media in dominant languages are the most important direct factors behind the macroeconomic, techno-military, social and political causes of linguistic genocide.

Most of the figures above are about spoken languages. What about sign lan-guages? How many are there? The World Federation of the Deaf's Fact Sheet on sign language(s) gives no figures (http://www.wfdeaf.org/documents.html). *Ethnologue* lists 114 sign languages, but there are many more. Every country in the world has deaf people,[2] and they have developed sign languages everywhere. Since the deaf have been much more isolated from each other than oral people, they may have developed even thousands of sign languages. Each country that has so far recognized 'sign languages' has recognized one and one only. Since there are somewhat over 200 states in the world, the number of the world's official sign languages would be over 200 when all states have recognized at least one (see Branson and Miller 1998 for hierarchizing processes among sign languages). Just as official, spoken 'languages' are the ones connected to the most powerful dialects, imperilling others, most of the world's sign languages may also be made to disappear. Using this verbal construction implies agency by something or someone – languages do not 'just' disappear by themselves, of old age, or because they are not seen to be fit for a postmodern digitalized age, or because people opt out of them 'voluntarily.' Many states actively seek to eliminate or to 'murder' minority languages. Misinformation to the parents of deaf children about cochlear implants may also create the belief that these children would come to 'hear' through implants; therefore many parents mistakenly think that there is no need for sign languages.

Most of the figures for speakers/signers and for 'native speakers,' second lan-guage users, and so on are seriously unreliable for two main reasons: one is conceptual, the other is economic–political. First, the whole concept of 'a lan-guage' is unclear. What has been seen as one language can 'become' several languages, either fast, because of political machinations ('Serbocroat' reverted to 'Serbian' and 'Croatian,' and 'Bosnian' was 'invented' – all within a decade), or over time (vulgar Latin branched out into Italian, Portuguese, Spanish, French, Romanian, and so on: Janson 2007). The borders between 'languages' and 'dialects,' and between one language and another, are sociopolitical constructions. This fact has made some linguists claim that 'languages' do not exist (Makoni and Pennycook 2007a; Mühlhäusler 1996; Reagan 2004). Still, even these linguists habitually refer to languages – we cannot in practice manage without the concept. Secondly, census and other data about languages, mother tongues, first languages, competence in various languages, and so on have never been reliably collected except for small sub-samples of various populations. It might be possible to do it, but that would require economic investment, conceptual clarification, and training. Besides, with reliable figures, demands for language-based services from governments might grow considerably, and not all governments are interested in offering them. Chaudenson (2003) states that the official figures for French as a second language world-wide are fraudulent. Of the various figures available for the numbers of native/first/home-language English speakers (compared in Skutnabb-Kangas 2000: 39) and second-language English users, scholars who regard the expansion of English as unproblematic tend to produce the highest ones. For any language planning purposes, and also in education, figures have to be used, and we have tried to find the most reliable ones while admitting their relative unreliability. To analyze the reasons for languages being maintained, marginalized, or murdered requires a situated framework which places languages in the historical, economic, and political context of 'globalization,' which we see as entailing linguistic neo-imperialism.

From Colonization to Corporate Globalization

The present-day strength of English, French, Spanish, and Portuguese in the Americas, in Africa, in Asia, in Australasia and in the Pacific is a direct consequence of European expansion throughout the world since 1492 and of successive waves of colonization. The languages have accompanied political and economic influence, being invariably backed up by military might. The promotion and hierarchization of languages often dovetailed with missionary activity: Christianity thus accompanied several European languages world-wide, just as Arabic has been an integral part of the spread of Islam, and Russian of Soviet communism. While Europeans were experiencing industrialization and the consolidation of 'national' (that is, dominant) languages, they were deeply involved in overseas expansion, which contributed to economic boom in Europe. Many of the features of what is now known as globalization were presciently described by Marx and Engels in their *Communist Manifesto* of 1848 (1961). This text stressed global economic markets, class interests, and ideological legitimation of an oppressive world order.

The project of global dominance has been articulated since before the USA achieved its independence; for instance George Washington saw the United States as a "rising empire" (Roberts 2008: 68). US national identity was forged through massive violence, the dispossession and extermination of indigenous peoples, the

myth of unoccupied territory, the surplus value extorted from slave labor, and an active process of national imagination used to form a common identity, one deeply permeated by religion (Hixson 2008).

The project of establishing English as the language of power, globally and locally, is central to this empire. The 'manifest destiny' that colonial Americans arrogated to themselves has been explicitly linked, since the early nineteenth century, to English being established globally: "English is destined to be in the next and succeeding centuries more generally the language of the world than Latin was in the last or French in the present age" (John Adams to Congress, 1780, cited in Bailey 1992: 103). "The whole world should adopt the American system. The American system can survive in America only if it becomes a world system." (President Harry Truman, 1947, cited in Pieterse 2004: 131).

The role of scholars in facilitating US empire is explored in Neil Smith's *American Empire. Roosevelt's Geographer and the Prelude to Globalization* (2003), which traces the shift through territorial, colonial dominance (the invasion of the Philippines in 1898) to the attempt to dominate globally through "a strategic recalibration of geography with economics, a new orchestration of world geography in the pursuit of economic accumulation" (2003: xvii–xviii). Academia services the "global needs of the political project, perpetuating a system in which [...] global power is disproportionately wielded by a ruling class that remains tied to the national interests of the United States" (ibid., p. xix). In US colonies and in the British Empire, English was privileged and other languages marginalized. Today's global ruling classes tend to be proficient in English.

In the twenty-first century, 'empire' has increasingly figured in the political discourse of advocates and critics. Engler's *How to Rule the World. The Coming Battle over the Global Economy* (2008) distinguishes clearly between the "corporate globalization" of the final decades of the twentieth century and its successor, "imperial globalization" based on military dominance.

Alternatives to Economic Globalization (2002: 19) lists the following eight key features of *economic/corporate globalization* (neo-liberalism):

1   promotion of hypergrowth and unrestricted exploitation of environmental resources to fuel that growth;
2   privatization and commodification of public services and of remaining aspects of the global and community commons;
3   global cultural (and, we would add, linguistic) and economic homogenization and the intense promotion of consumerism;
4   integration and conversion of national economies, including some that were largely self-reliant, to environmentally and socially harmful export-oriented production;
5   corporate deregulation and unrestricted movement of capital across borders;
6   dramatically increased corporate concentration;
7   dismantling of public health, social and environmental programs already in place;
8   replacement of the traditional powers of democratic nation–states and local communities by global corporate bureaucracies.

Alternatives to Economic Globalization fails to mention language among the features listed under "cultural homogenization," despite referring to a global monoculture and to the unrestricted flow of production and marketing, "needed" by large multinational corporations. It seems that not even the best globalization experts are aware of the tendencies toward linguistic homogenization and of the threats to linguistic diversity mentioned above. Much of the literature on English as a "global" or "international" language has tended to be celebratory and failed to situate English within the wider language ecology or to explore the causal factors behind its expansion (on these subjects, see Phillipson 1992 and 2008a and Pennycook 1998). Influential work by Crystal, Fishman, and Graddol is critically analyzed in Phillipson 2000, and books on the world language system by De Swaan and Brutt-Griffler are critically analyzed in Phillipson 2004. One of the controversial questions today is to what extent corporate globalization is leading toward greater homogenization or greater diversification (for instance through localization), as some researchers claim. For instance Mufwene (2008: 227) claims that McDonaldization does not lead to uniformity because the "McDonald menu is partly adapted to the local diet." Even if McDonald's in India may serve vegetarian burgers in Hindi, this reduction to superficial adaptation disregards completely the structural and process-related aspects of homogenization (see n. 3 for examples; also, for a discussion of McDonaldization, see Hamelink 1994; Ritzer 1996; and Definition Box 6.3 in Skutnabb-Kangas 2000).[3] Linguistic glocalization needs to be discussed in a politico-economic framework which relates the hierarchization of languages to global and local power relations.

A typical example of special pleading for English can be found in a book by a political scientist who argues for the formation of an EU "super-state" and cites the familiar trope of English as lingua franca, along with young people's consumerism and global business integration (Morgan 2005: 57). He seems unaware that there are *many* 'lingua francas' in Europe; or that the "common transnational youth culture" is essentially American and that the convergence of "business practices" derives from the US corporate world and from the conceptual universe it embodies. It is false to project English as though it is 'neutral,' English as a mere tool that serves all equally well, in whatever society they live. The phrase 'English as a lingua franca' generally decontextualizes users and seems to imply symmetrical, equitable communication, which is often not the case. It conceals the actual functions that the language performs, English as a *lingua academica*, *lingua bellica*, *lingua culturalis*, *lingua economica*, and so on (Phillipson 2008b). It also ignores the Anglo-American semantics and grammar embedded in the language (Wierzbicka 2006; Mühlhäusler 2003). It fails to explore the hegemonic practices of the currently dominant capitalist language or to theorize English linguistic neo-imperialism.

Linguistic Neo-Imperialism

Imperialism needs careful definition if it is to be used analytically. This principle guided the definition of linguistic imperialism as a variant of linguicism

(Skutnabb-Kangas 1988: 13) operating through structures and ideologies and entailing unequal treatment for groups identified by language (Phillipson 1992). For Harvey (2005: 26), capitalist imperialism

> is a contradictory fusion of *'the politics of state and empire'* (imperialism as a distinc-
> tively political project on the part of the actors whose power is based in command
> of a territory and a capacity to mobilize its human and natural resources towards
> political, economic, and military ends) and *'the molecular processes of capital accumula-*
> *tion in space and time'* (imperialism as a diffuse political–economic process in space
> and time in which command over and use of capital takes primacy). (Emphasis
> added)

The first of these components of the "contradictory fusion" is the top-down process of what a state, a combination of states, or an institution such as a corpo-ration or a university does to achieve its goals – which includes the way it manages linguistic capital. The second is the way "economic power flows across and through continuous space, toward or away from territorial entities (such as states or regional power blocs) through the daily practices of production, trade, com-merce, capital flows, money transfers, labour migration, technology transfer, cur-rency speculation, flows of information, cultural impulses, and the like" (ibid.). Most of these processes are crucially dependent on language, and constituted by language.

English can be seen as the *capitalist neo-imperial language* that serves the interests of the corporate world and of the governments it influences (Phillipson 2008a, 2009). This dovetails with the language being activated through *molecular processes of linguistic capital accumulation in space and time*, in a dialectic process at the inter-section of economics, politics, and discourses. So far as linguistic neo-imperialism is concerned, the 'political mode of argumentation' refers to decision-making, language policy, and planning, whereas the 'economic mode of argumentation' refers to the working through of such decisions at all levels, to the implementation of language planning decisions, to the actual use of English in myriad contexts.

When English increasingly occupies territory that hitherto was the preserve of national languages in Europe or Asia, what is occurring is *linguistic capital accu-mulation*, over a period of time and in particular territories, in favor of English. When Singaporean parents gradually shift from an Asian language to the use of English in the home, this represents linguistic capital accumulation. If users of German or Swedish as languages of scholarship shift to using English, similar forces and processes are at work. When considering agency in each of these exam-ples, the individuals concerned opt for the neo-imperial language because they perceive that this linguistic capital will serve their personal interests best, in the false belief that this requires the sacrifice of their own language. When language shift is subtractive, and if this affects a group and not merely individuals, there are serious implications for other languages. If domains such as business, the home, or scholarship are 'lost,' what has occurred is in fact *linguistic capital dispossession*.

Analysis of the interlocking of language policies with the two constituents of Harvey's "contradictory fusion" can highlight both the corporate agendas, which serve political, economic, and military purposes, and the multiple flows that make use of English for a range of purposes. New discourses and technologies are adopted and creatively adapted, but in a rigged, so-called 'free' global and local market. The active promotion of other major international languages such as Chinese, French, Japanese, and Spanish also aims to strengthen the market forces and the cultures associated with each language; but at present the linguistic capital invested in these languages does not seriously threaten the current pre-eminence of English. A Chinese global empire may be on the way.

International language promotion itself needs to be seen in economic terms, dovetailing as it does with media products and many commercial activities. TESOL (the Teaching of English to Speakers of Other Languages) – teaching materials, examinations, know-how, teachers, and so on – is a major commercial enterprise for the British and for the Americans and a vital dimension of English linguistic neo-imperialism. "The English language teaching sector directly earns nearly £1.3 billion for the UK in invisible exports and our other education related exports earn up to £10 billion more" (Lord Neil Kinnock, Chair of the British Council, in the Foreword to Graddol 2006 – a work that charts many variables in the global linguistic mosaic, challenges British monolingual complacency, and aims, as Kinnock stresses, to strengthen "the UK's providers of English language teaching" and "broader education business sectors"). The major publishing houses are now global. For instance "Pearson Education's international business has been growing rapidly in recent years, and we now have a presence in over 110 countries" (http://www.pearson.com/index.cfm?pageid=18). The website of Educational Testing Services of Princeton, NJ, which is responsible for the TOEFL (Test of English as a Foreign Language) for language proficiency, declares as their mission: "Our products and services measure knowledge and skills, promote learning and educational performance, and support education and professional development for all people worldwide" (www.ets.org, About ETS).

The entrenchment of English in many countries world-wide and for many cross-national purposes leads Halliday (2006) to make a distinction between indigenized and standardized Englishes, which he categorizes as "international" and "global":

> English has become a world language in both senses of the term, international and global: international, as a medium of literary and other forms of cultural life in (mainly) countries of the former British Empire; global, as the co-genitor of the new technological age, the age of information. [...] they obviously overlap. [...] International English has expanded by becoming world Englishes, evolving so as to adapt to the meanings of other cultures. Global English has expanded – has become 'global' – by taking over, or being taken over by, the new information technology, which means everything from email and the internet to mass media advertising, news reporting, and all the other forms of political and commercial propaganda.

Halliday's "international" is an unfortunate label, since he is in effect referring to *local* forms and uses of English, comprehensible within a country, for instance. His terms also elide the anchoring of *global* English in the English-dominant countries, where this is the primary *national* language and one that also opens international doors. This terminology is a minefield which obscures power relations and hegemonic practices, nationally and internationally.

Why Are Languages 'Disappearing'? The Role of Formal Education

Having situated language hierarchization and the linguistic capital accumulation enjoyed by speakers of some languages but not of others, we now ask why languages are 'disappearing' and what role formal education plays in this linguistic dispossession. An important distinction is between languages and speakers. Some languages live on, especially in a written form, even when there are no native speakers (that is, speakers who have learned the language in early childhood, from parents or other caretakers) or second/foreign-language speakers. Sanskrit and Hebrew in the 1800s and many indigenous languages today in Australia, Canada, and the United States are examples.

Secondly, what happens to languages can be analyzed in terms of several interacting continua. In theorizing language policy, many disciplines need to be considered. One continuum describing the status of languages has linguistic genocide at one end and maintenance and further development (including many types of hybridization), with full Linguistic Human Rights (LHRs), at the other end. Often used concepts such as language marginalization, attrition, and extinction would be closer to the genocide end of the continuum. Each of these positions can be the result of open and planned language policy or a side-effect of other policies, intentional or unintentional. In economic terms, for instance, the relative conditions for languages are influenced by factors such as:

- the relative isolation of the speakers from speakers of other languages (Fishman 1966);
- the self-sufficiency of the group (the extent to which they need to trade with others for basic needs; whether they can grow and collect what they need all year round, and so on: Nettle 1999);
- the availability of jobs without the need to migrate;
- the existence of material resources of interest to outsiders in the area, and their exploitation (logging, oil, mining, and the like).

Negative, stigmatizing attitudes (for instance referring to the languages of 'Others' as dialects), the invisibilization of certain languages, even demographically large ones, and a lack both of knowledge and of awareness about languages among those who make decisions – all contribute to marginalization. 'They' only have dialects, whereas 'we' have languages – just as 'they' have tribes, 'we' have nations, 'they' chiefs, 'we' presidents, 'they' witch doctors, 'we' real doctors; 'they' still need to be 'developed,' 'civilized,' and taught democracy, good governance, and human rights – by 'us' (Sachs 1992).

The availability of (at least primary) formal education without needing to leave the area is decisive for the future of the children. But education through the medium of a dominant foreign language can encourage language shift, triggering language attrition at group level as well as at individual level, especially when secondary education is outside the area and delivered in the dominant language (see Jhingran 2009). The example below, from the education of the Nenets in the Russian Federation, illustrates not only the phenomenon of language shift and some of the connections to the reasons listed above; it also illustrates that education of indigenous/tribal and minority (IM) children in a dominant language can cause linguistic and educational harm (in the UN Genocide Convention's sense, for which see below). There are thousands of similar examples from all over the world.

> In the Russian Federation, in Siberia, the Far East and the North of the European part of Russia there are at least 35 endangered languages still in use (Kazakevitch 2004: 9). Tundra Nenets (about 25,000 speakers) is "the strongest" among them, "partly due to the relatively large size of the ethnic group (over 32,000) and partly to the fact that the majority of the Nenets still keep to their traditional occupation – reindeer herding – and hence lead a nomadic or half-nomadic life […]. Up to now in some districts children come to school speaking only Nenets. As soon as the children are able to speak Russian it becomes the only means of school instruction. Nenets is taught as a subject both in primary and in secondary school. Unfortunately, Nenets classes don't have any significant influence on the language preferences of the pupils who stay at a boarding school for 9–11 years and visit their families only during holidays. After finishing secondary school many of these choose to speak mostly Russian. Luckily for the language, not all Nenets children finish secondary school: some leave school after grade 4, 5 or 6 and return to their families with their traditional occupations. Of course there are exceptions, but on the whole it should be stated *that the level of education is in inverse proportion to the degree of mother tongue use* (our emphasis). The level of education of a speaker determines if not his/her competence in his/her ethnic language, then the ethnic language competence of his/her children. As a rule, children of well-educated Nenets parents (even those who are concerned with protection and preservation of the ethnic language – such as school teachers of Nenets, language planners, language and folklore researchers) have poor or no command of Nenets." (Dunbar and Skutnabb-Kangas 2008)

Linguistic Genocide and Crimes against Humanity in Education

It is a fact that mainly dominant-language medium education for IM children

* prevents access to education, because of the linguistic, pedagogical and psychological barriers it creates;

- may lead to the extinction of indigenous languages;
- contributes thereby to the disappearance of the world's linguistic diversity;
- often curtails the development of the children's capabilities, perpetuates poverty, and causes serious mental harm;
- is organized against solid research evidence about how best to reach high levels of bilingualism or multilingualism and how to enable IM children to achieve academically in school (Magga et al. 2005).

This subtractive education through the medium of a dominant language can have harmful consequences socially, psychologically, economically, and politically. It can (and it does, especially for indigenous/tribal children) cause both serious physical harm: impoverished living conditions – with unemployment and with housing and health problems – and, partially through these conditions, alcoholism, suicide, criminality, including incest, and so on – and very serious mental harm: social dislocation; psychological, cognitive, linguistic, and educational harm; and, partially through it, also economic, social and political marginalization (see Dunbar and Skutnabb-Kangas 2008). This kind of education may thus participate in linguistic and cultural genocide, according to two of the five definitions of genocide – II(b) and II(e) – in the United Nations' 1948 *International Convention on the Punishment and Prevention of the Crime of Genocide* (E793, 1948):

> ARTICLE 2
>
> In the present Convention, genocide means any of the following acts committed with *intent to destroy*, in whole or in part, a national, ethnical, racial or religious group, as such [...]
>
> ARTICLE II(b): causing serious bodily *or mental* harm to members of the group [...]
>
> ARTICLE II(e): forcibly transferring children of the group to another group. (Emphasis added)

Most indigenous/tribal students (with some exceptions, for instance Saami, Māori), many national minority and most immigrant minority students in the world are being taught through the medium of dominant languages, in *submersion* programmes. Dominant-language-only submersion programmes "are widely attested as the least effective educationally for minority language students" (May and Hill 2003: 14).[4] Sociologically and educationally, submersion models for IM children fit the two UN definitions of genocide quoted above (see Magga et al., 2005) – in particular subtractive submersion models for IM children, where a dominant language is learned at the cost of the mother tongues – but also, to a certain extent, many early-exit transitional weak models (for definitions, see Skutnabb-Kangas and McCarty 2008).[5]

It is also clear that, even if mother tongues are to some extent used as teaching languages, basic educational and linguistic goals may not be achieved. Kathleen Heugh (2009) shows that, when children have been taught in their own languages for only a few years, an *early* transition to the international language of wider communication (ILWC) across Africa is accompanied by:

- "poor literacy both in the first and in the second language (L1 and L2; Mothibeli 2005; Alidou et al. 2006; HSRC [Human Sciences Research Council] studies in South Africa 2007);
- poor numeracy/mathematics and science (HSRC 2005, 2007);
- high failure and drop-out rates (Obanya 1999, Bamgbose 2000);
- high costs/wastage of expenditure (Alidou et al. 2006)."

> If learners switch from an African MT [mother tongue] to FL/L2 [foreign-language/ second-language] medium, they may seem to do well until half way through grade/ year 4. After this, progress slows down and the gap between L1 [first-language] and L2 [second-language] learner achievement steadily widens. We now know from comprehensive studies in Second Language Acquisition [...] in Scandinavia, Australia, Russian Federation, India, North America, and especially in Africa that it takes 6–8 years to learn enough L2 to be able to learn through the L2. (From a Power Point presentation leading to Heugh 2009)

Funding for education in the post-colonial period has seen World Bank policies perpetuating the dominance of European languages at the expense of local ones, and generating educational failure. The integration of the linguistic/educational dimension with cultural and economic globalization is insightfully explored in Rassool (2007). The case study of Pakistan (Rassool and Mansoor 2007) shows that the use of English as the sole medium of higher education (for only 2.63 percent of the population) ensures the cultural alienation of the elite from the rest.

> The global cultural economy is interdependent and, despite the dominant position occupied by English, in practice, it has an organically interactive multilingual base. A narrow monolingual nationalism [a reference to Urdu, TSK and RP], an under-resourced educational system as well as unequal access to English as international lingua franca, therefore, [are] counter-productive to national growth. (Ibid., p. 240).

All strong multilingual education models (both for IMs and for linguistic majority children) use mainly an IM language as the main teaching language during the (many) first years. The longer this period is, the better the results are in terms of high levels of bilingualism or multilingualism and general school achievement.[6]

Part of the conclusion in Dunbar and Skutnabb-Kangas 2008 – an expert paper for the UN Permanent Forum on Indigenous Issues (PFII)[7] – runs as follows:

> That States persist in such [subtractive] policies, given such knowledge, has been described as a form of linguistic and/or cultural genocide. [...] In Dunbar and Skutnabb-Kangas 2008 we consider the possibility that such policies, implemented in the full knowledge of their devastating effects on those who suffer them, constitute

international crimes, including genocide, within the meaning of the United Nations' 1948 Convention on the Prevention and Punishment of the Crime of Genocide (the 'Genocide Convention'), or a crime against humanity. [...] [S]ubtractive education [...] is now at odds with and in clear violation of a range of human rights standards, and in our view amount[s] to ongoing violations of fundamental rights. It is at odds with contemporary standards of minority protection. In our view, the concept of 'crime against humanity' is less restrictive [than genocide], and can also be applied to these forms of education. In our view, the destructive consequences of subtractive education, not only for indigenous languages and cultures but also in terms of the lives of indigenous people/s, are now clear. The concept of 'crimes against humanity' provides a good basis for an evolution that will ultimately lead to the stigmatization through law of subtractive educational practices and policies.

Linguistic and Cultural Diversity and Biodiversity: Correlational and Causal Relationships

A central argument for the maintenance of all languages is as follows. If we continue as at present, most of the world's indigenous languages will be gone by 2100. One serious implication for diversity is that most of the world's linguistic diversity resides in the small languages of indigenous peoples. Most of the world's mega-biodiversity is in areas under the management or guardianship of indigenous peoples (for example the 'biodiversity hotspots'). The international organization Terralingua

> supports the integrated protection, maintenance and restoration of the biocultural diversity of life – the world's biological, cultural, and linguistic diversity – through an innovative program of research, education, policy-relevant work, and on-the-ground action. (www.terralingua.org)

Terralingua's home page of November 27, 2007 states:

> People who lose their linguistic and cultural identity may lose an essential element in a social process that commonly teaches respect for nature and understanding of the natural environment and its processes. Forcing this cultural and linguistic conversion on indigenous and other traditional peoples not only violates their human rights, but also undermines the health of the world's ecosystems and the goals of nature conservation.

The World Resources Institute, the World Conservation Union, and the United Nations Environment Programme (1992: 21) also articulate the interconnectedness of diversities:

> Cultural diversity is closely linked to biodiversity. Humanity's collective knowledge of biodiversity and its use and management rests in cultural diversity; conversely conserving biodiversity often helps strengthen cultural integrity and values.

One reason for maintaining all the world's languages is that linguistic (and cultural) diversity and biodiversity are correlated, and very likely also causally related. Much of the knowledge about how to maintain biodiversity is encoded in the small languages of indigenous and local peoples. By killing them we kill the prerequisites for maintaining biodiversity. (For details, see Harmon 2002, Maffi 2001, Skutnabb-Kangas 2000, 2003, Skutnabb-Kangas et al. 2003, Skutnabb-Kangas and Phillipson 2008a, 2008b).

Linguistic Human Rights in Market-Oriented Globalization

Market and non-market values of languages and diversity

How do human rights fare in corporate globalization? In an article entitled "Justice for sale. International law favours market values," Mireille Delmas-Marty (2003) discusses the dangerous conflict between legal concepts based on the one hand on 'universal' *market values*, on the other hand on genuinely universal *non-market values*. The latter include individual and collective human rights as a part of the universal common heritage of humanity.

The epistemology of human rights law and philosophically oriented political science are now starting to accept that normative rights should be stipulated at least in relation to some parts of this heritage (in their terminology, 'common public assets'). Still, the legal protection of market values is "incommensurably stronger" than the protection of non-market values. Delmas-Marty exemplifies this with the fact that there is no universal international court individuals could turn to when their (non-market-value-based) human rights have been violated. "Individual rights are entirely a matter for states, and reports are the only form of monitoring" (ibid.). This monitoring does not support educational linguistic human rights strongly.[8]

On the other hand, laws based on market values, spread by organizations like the WTO (World Trade Organization) and WIPO (World Intellectual Property Organization), are being developed extremely rapidly,[9] with harsh sanctions for violations. Through his discussion of "market failure," economist François Grin (2003: 35) offers excellent arguments for resisting market dominance for public or common assets/goods like cultural products:

> Even mainstream economics acknowledges that there are some cases where the market is not enough. These cases are called 'market failure.' When there is 'market failure,' the unregulated interplay of supply and demand results in an inappropriate level of production of some commodity.

In Grin's view, many public goods, including minority language protection, 'are typically under-supplied by market forces' (ibid.). The level becomes inappropriately low. Therefore it is the duty of the state(s) to take extra measures to increase it.

Some researchers disagree that there is such a duty. Edwards, for instance, argues that, for minorities, the communicative and symbolic values of language "are separable, and it is possible for the symbolic to remain in the absence of the communicative" (1984: 289). According to this view, even if minority members no longer know their language and cannot communicate in it, they can still remain, and feel that they are, members of the minority. Since "the symbolic value of language is essentially a private ethnic marker" (ibid.), governments should take no action to enable minorities to maintain their languages, "on the grounds that matters of ethnicity are best left to those directly concerned" (ibid., p. 299); "public institutions" like schools should not "promote private ethnicity" (ibid., p. 300). Grin's careful opinion is that "this view is probably mistaken, and there are strong analytical reasons for state intervention – unless one were to argue that linguistic diversity is a bad thing in itself" (Grin 2003: 34). Edwards omits to say that schools strongly promote the "private ethnicity" of the linguistic majority by using this majority's language as teaching language.

Can states leave the responsibility for languages and linguistic diversity unconsidered in this way? States *can* be neutral in relation to religions, but *not* in relation to languages (see for instance Kymlicka and Grin 2003: 10), because all states must function through the medium of *some* language or languages. A state or federation that does not actively support minority languages is in fact supporting (the dominance of) the official language(s) unjustly.

A European Parliament Resolution of 2003[10] exemplifies the attempt to build bridges between the market and cultural products, through suggestions for exempting cultural goods and services and education from market laws. According to Point 16 of this resolution, cultures (here including languages) and education have a dual nature, as both economic and cultural goods, and "must therefore be made subject to special conditions." The market "cannot be the measure of all things, and must guarantee in particular diversity of opinion and pluralism" (ibid.). Point 18 "[c]alls on the European Union to place an unmistakable stress, in the context of the WTO and GATS, on the nature of cultural services and products as cultural goods, and to exempt them from trade liberalization."

Another of Delmas-Marty's (2003) vital claims is this: "The market is replacing the nation, superseding the state and becoming the law: under the law of the market, law itself becomes a marketable commodity." With many others (such as Zygmunt Bauman), Delmas-Marty sees this development as a danger, since "the market is replacing the nation, superseding the state and becoming the law"; "the law is ill-equipped to deal with non-market values"; and "the only concepts that apply universally are market-related."

François Grin (2004)[11] differentiates between *market and non-market values for private and social purposes*. Most of the discourse on the worth of linguistic diversity and of knowledge of several languages has been about societal and, to some extent, private market values. The common but misguided claims about the negative correlation between linguistic diversity and economic growth as a causal relationship are effectively counteracted by Paulin Djité (2008) among others; multilingualism has *social market value*, as many studies show. Even English-dominant countries appreciate this:

> English is not enough. We are fortunate to speak a global language but, in a smart and competitive world, exclusive reliance on English leaves the UK *vulnerable* and dependent on the linguistic competence and the goodwill of others […] Young people from the UK are at a *growing disadvantage* in the recruitment market. (The Nuffield Foundation 2000; emphasis added)

Another social market benefit flows from the relationship between creativity, innovation, and investment, which can be a result of good mother-tongue-based multilingual education (MLE). Creativity precedes innovation, also in commodity production; investment follows creativity. High levels of multilingualism can enhance creativity: high-level multilinguals as a group do better than corresponding monolinguals on tests measuring several aspects of 'intelligence' (a contested concept, of course), creativity, divergent thinking, cognitive flexibility, and so on; and good MLE mostly leads to high-level multilingualism. In knowledge societies, diverse knowledges and ideas (meaning results of creativity) give access to markets and produce market value, whereas homogenization of various kinds is a market handicap. Positive globalization means context-sensitive localization, as opposed to corporate McDonaldized one-size-fits-all homogenization. A somewhat similar analysis, which grades European and some other countries in terms of their innovation and creativity potential, is Florida and Tinagli 2004. The chain they present is as follows: tolerance entices diversity/difference, which entices creativity, which develops competitiveness, which brings money. In Singapore, English means money. In today's Africa, Chinese means money.

Using one's (well-known) mother tongue instead of other languages and thus being more fluent, accurate, efficient, fast in finding the right expressions, is a great advantage for those who are able to do so when negotiating, regardless of whether it is about business or about details of formulation in political meetings at different levels (*private market value*). Here mother-tongue speakers, especially of English but also of French, are today free-riders at the expense of all of us others (van Parijs 2003: 167–8). In a large-scale Swiss study, Grin concludes that, whereas each additional year of formal education adds on an average 4.5 percent to the net earnings, knowledge of an additional language generally adds more; the additional earnings in the study were between 4 and over 20 percent, depending on "a person's L1, the L2 considered, L2 skills level, gender, type of job, etc." (Grin 1999: 194; see also Grin and Sfreddo 1997).

Many of the beautiful pronouncements about the historical, aesthetic, philosophical, and other values of linguistic and cultural diversity for the whole of humankind, about languages as the libraries of humankind, and other 'Unescoese' statements exemplify *social non-market values*. Social non-market-value arguments have often been labeled and rejected as romantic, non-realistic, elitist, moralistic, essentializing, and the like (see Skutnabb-Kangas 2009). The enjoyment of feeling at ease when using one's mother tongue reflects *private non-market values*. Issues around ethnic and linguistic identity are a central aspect of these values.

An example of a combination of the values could be a European Union meeting, with interpretation. People might feel more confident (*private non-market value*) and might be objectively more competent when speaking their own language, without recourse to a 'dumbed-down,' less exact Euro-English (*private market value*). A meeting with really good interpreters avoids costly misunderstandings and is more efficient (*social market value*) and more just and equal (*social non-market value*).

With the help of these distinctions, it is easier to classify many positivistic and post-modernist arguments against the maintenance of linguistic diversity. It is relatively easy to discuss the private *market* value of various languages, including the topic of maintaining or not maintaining certain specified mother tongues. But it is difficult to use rational choice theories on issues which are mainly seen as representing private *non-market* values if these are seen as non-values. Most of those who argue against diversity do not accept that using the mother tongue, or even having competence in several languages, can or should have any private non-market value. As long as a numerically small mother tongue does not give you a better job with a higher salary than shifting to a numerically and politically more powerful language, there are, according to this line of thought, few arguments for maintaining these mother tongues. And bilingualism is often not considered as a real option; the thinking here is often an 'either/or' one: either the IM language or the dominant language (Kond-medium or English-medium schooling in India, not MLE with Kond, Oriya and English: Mohanty et al., Skutnabb-Kangas et al. 2009).

It seems to be shortsighted to reject any of the (market or non-market, private or social) arguments for reasons why IM languages should be supported: all of them are useful in various ways.

Moral and Welfare Considerations: Costs of Diversity

Many researchers whose mother tongue is a dominant language have never experienced any threat to their language. As a result, they are much less aware than dominated-language speakers of the *non-market* values of their *own* languages, and, consequently, of those of other people. At the same time, they are often not aware (or do not want to be aware) of the *market* benefits that they themselves have access to because of being speakers of dominant languages. Often they take both these benefits and the fact that others are learning their language in a non-reciprocal way, for granted, and they are not willing in any way to compensate for these non-earned benefits; they are linguistic free-riders. To compensate would be fair, even in terms of the types of justice that the legal system accepts. Several researchers have started discussing issues in these terms of economic compensation (for instance Grin 2003, 2004; van Parijs 2003).

The costs of non-multilingualism and of non-maintenance of languages and linguistic diversity, as well as the enormous human and economic wastage caused by present non-education (for example concerning EFA – Education for All – and Millennium Goals),[12] have received too little attention. These costs of non-action and of a 'business-as-usual' attitude have not been properly weighed against the costs of maintaining linguistic diversity, partially through MLE and LHRs. The costs issues can be discussed within several paradigms.[13]

Grin (2003: 24–7) differentiates between *moral considerations arguments* and *welfare considerations arguments* in answering the question why anybody, including society as a whole, should bother about maintaining IM languages. Most of the legal discourse, including the considerations about LHRs, refers to moral norms about the right to live in one's own language, even if the extent of the ensuing rights is debated (ibid., pp. 24–5). In contrast,

> the emphasis of the welfare-based argument is not on whether something is morally 'good' or 'bad,' but on whether resources are appropriately allocated. The test of an 'appropriate' allocation of resources is whether society is better off as a result of a policy (ibid., p. 25).

In a moral discourse, in most cases the question of compensation has not even arisen, and the question of what kind of rights, if any, should be granted to speakers of IM languages, seems to depend on how 'nice' the states are. This is a shaky foundation for human rights, as Fernand de Varennes rightly observes (1999: 117):

> Moral or political principles, even if they are sometimes described as 'human rights,' are not necessarily part of international law. They are things that governments 'should' do, if they are 'nice,' not something they 'must' do. Being nice is not a very convincing argument and is less persuasive than rights and freedoms that have the weight of the law behind them.

In a welfare-oriented discourse, one can calculate in much more hard-core terms (often, but not necessarily always, involving cash) who the winners and losers are. Here "the question is whether the winners, who stand to gain from a policy, can compensate the losers and still be better off [than without the policy]" (Grin 2003: 25). This is an empirical question, not a moral one.

Many of the issues discussed can be, and have been, labeled in an either/or way, which often seems non-productive – we should rather have continua, or both/and. Both market and non-market values, private and social, have to be considered, among other things because languages are both economic and cultural goods. If markets are to decide, market failure is certain to promote mainly dominant languages; therefore the implementation of strong linguistic human rights in relation to IM languages is a necessary duty of states. It is not a question of protecting individuals, collectivities, or languages – but all of these; it is not a question of having a territoriality or personality principle, but a context-sensitive combination of both (Henrard 2000; see also Skutnabb-Kangas 2006, 2007).

One can argue for this even within a liberal political philosophy; but it is only within a more critical political and philosophical paradigm that one can use a more proactive argument. If the fate of research-based suggestions for the education of IM children is decided by market-value-based laws, both formalized and non-formalized, then the human rights, including LHRs, of IM people(s) do not stand a chance – unless the rights are formulated in terms of cost–benefit analyses that show the economic market value both of granting these rights and of mother-tongue medium education. If even human rights law is a 'marketable commodity,' we, as researchers, have to discuss whether and how it is possible to market 'our commodity' more effectively and efficiently while keeping our integrity.

When assessing the empirical question of why one should maintain minority languages, Grin asks both what the costs and benefits are if minority languages *are* maintained and promoted, and what the costs (and benefits) are if they are neither maintained nor promoted. Some of his conclusions, which we endorse, are as follows (Grin 2003: 26):

- "diversity seems to be positively, rather than negatively, correlated with welfare";
- "available evidence indicates that the monetary costs of maintaining diversity are remarkably modest";
- "devoting resources to the protection and promotion of minority cultures" (and this includes languages) "may help to stave off political crises whose costs would be considerably higher than that of the policies considered" (namely the peace-and-security argument);
- "therefore, there are strong grounds to suppose that protecting and promoting regional and minority languages is a sound idea from a welfare standpoint, not even taking into consideration any moral argument."

Strong research evidence shows that educating IM children mainly through the medium of their mother tongue should last minimally eight years to deliver positive results. Everything else is irrational, costly, and a short-sighted compromise. Experience obviously needs to be contextualized (see Skutnabb-Kangas and Heugh 2010).

UNESCO's project on the Atlas of the World's Languages in Danger of Disappearing (www.unesco.org/culture/en/endangeredlanguages/atlas) has as its goal "to raise awareness on language endangerment and the need to safeguard the world's linguistic diversity." The latest UNESCO plans seem to take this seriously, also in education.[14]

NOTES

1   All websites are active as of January 2010.
2   The term 'deaf' refers to biological deafness, whereas 'Deaf' (with capital D) is used about conscious cultural deafness.

3 For Hamelink, McDonaldization involves "aggressive round-the-clock marketing, the controlled information flows that do not confront people with the long-term effects of an ecologically detrimental lifestyle, the competitive advantage against local cultural providers, the obstruction of local initiative" – all of which "converge into a reduction of local cultural space" (1994: 112). In Ritzer's definition, the "basic dimensions of McDonaldization" are "efficiency, calculabity (or quantification), predictability, increased control through substitution of nonhuman for human technology, and the seemingly inevitable by-product of rational systems" (rational in the Weberian sense) "– the irrationality of rationality" (1996: 33).

4 This is a study commissioned by the Māori Section of the Aotearoa/New Zealand Ministry of Education, http://www.minedu.govt.nz/.

5 See Dunbar and Skutnabb-Kangas 2008 for a legal and sociological discussion of the "intention" required in Article 2.

6 See e.g. Ramirez, Yuen, and Ramey 1991; and Thomas and Collier 2002, the largest ever study of various educational alternatives, with over 210,000 children – in this case, Spanish-speaking children in the USA; for summaries of the research, see e.g. Collier 1989 and Cummins 2009 (and the references in it).

7 For the Permanent Forum for Indigenous Issues (PFII), see www.un.org/esa/socdev/unpfii/. For recent arguments, see Skutnabb-Kangas and Dunbar 2010.

8 For a detailed discussion and exemplification of this part of the article, see Skutnabb-Kangas 2004.

9 This happens mainly through the 1994 agreement on TRAPS (trade-related aspects of intellectual property rights). Even primary education is now being treated as a commodity and can come in under TRAPS; the fact that education is for a fee in over 100 countries is an important issue here (Tomaševski 2001; see also http://www.tomasevski.net/). The internationalization of European higher education has gone under the label 'the Bologna Process' since 1999. Forty-six European states are committed to it, Australia and the USA acting as observers, out of self-interest, since foreign students in higher education are big business for them and Europe is, potentially, a serious competitor (the increasing use of English in European higher education symbolizes this fact). This European process is a direct result of education being increasingly considered a service that can be traded, under the aegis of the WTO and, more specifically, of GATS – the General Agreement on Trade in Services. Member states have been legally committed to this 'liberalization' process since 1995, but there is a fundamental unresolved tension between education as a human right and trading in educational services (Devidal 2004, De Sequira 2005). In the many Bologna policy documents, which are written exclusively in English, language policy is never mentioned – even if the EU has twenty-three official languages (Phillipson 2003). There is nothing on bilingual degrees, or on multilingualism: 'internationalization' means 'English-medium higher education' (Phillipson 2006).

10 The European Parliament Session document from 15 December 2003 (A5-0477/2003) from the Committee on Culture, Youth, Education, the Media and Sport contains a "Draft European Parliament Resolution on preserving and promoting cultural diversity: The role of the European regions and international organizations such as UNESCO and the Council of Europe" (2002/2269(INI)), and an Explanatory Statement. The text was adopted by the Parliament.

11 Grin's home page, http://www.unige.ch/eti/recherches/ecole/organisation/departements/dfr/dfr-corps-enseignant/pages-personnelles/francois-grin.html, is a goldmine for articles on language economics.

12   See http://www.unesco.org/education/efa/ed_for_all/ and http://www.un.org/millenniumgoals/goals.html.

13   One further development of the reasoning of economics Nobel laureate Amartya Sen has been applied to education, poverty, and the medium of education in Mohanty 2000 and in Magga et al. 2005.

14   See e.g. points 14–18 of the document at: http://unesdoc.unesco.org/images/0016/001614/161495e.pdf.

REFERENCES

Alidou, H., Aliou, B., Brock-Utne, B., Diallo, Y. S., Heugh, K., and Wolff, H. E. (2006) *Optimizing Learning and Education in Africa: The Language Factor. A Stock-Taking Research on Mother Tongue and Bilingual Education in Sub-Saharan Africa.* Paris: Association for the Development of Education in Africa (ADEA). Available at: http://www.adeanet.org/adeaPortal/adea/biennial2006/doc/document/B3_1_MTBLE_en.pdf.

Alternatives to Economic Globalization. A Better World Is Possible (2002) A Report of the International Forum on Globalization. San Francisco: Berrett-Koehler Publishers.

Dunbar, R., and Skutnabb-Kangas, T. (2008) Forms of education of indigenous children as crimes against humanity? Expert paper written for the United Nations Permanent Forum on Indigenous Issues (PFII). New York: PFII. [In the PFII system: "Presented by Lars-Anders Baer, in collaboration with Robert Dunbar, Tove Skutnabb-Kangas and Ole Henrik Magga"]. Available at: http://www.un.org/esa/socdev/unpfii/documents/E_C19_2008_7.pdf.

Bailey, R. W. (1992) *Images of English.* Cambridge: Cambridge University Press.

Bamgbose, A. (2000) *Language and Exclusion: The Consequences of Language Policies in Africa.* Münster, Hamburg and London: Lit Verlag.

Branson, J., and Miller, D. (1998) Nationalism and the linguistic rights of Deaf communities: Linguistic imperialism and the recognition and development of sign languages. *Journal of Sociolinguistics* 2(1): 3–34.

Chaudenson, R. (2003) Geolinguistics, geopolitics, geostrategy: The case of French. In J. Maurais and M. A. Morris (eds), *Languages in a Globalising World*, 291–7. Cambridge: Cambridge University Press.

Collier, V. P. (1989) How long? A synthesis of research on academic achievement in a second language. *TESOL Quarterly* 23: 509–31.

Cummins, J. (2009) Fundamental psychological and sociological principles underlying educational success for linguistic minority students. In Skutnabb-Kangas, Phillipson, Mohanty, and Panda (eds), 19–35.

de Sequira, A. C. (2005) The regulation of education through the WTO/GATS. *Journal for Critical Education Policy Studies* 3(1). Available at: www.jceps.com.

de Varennes, F. (1999) The existing rights of minorities in international law. In M. Kontra, R. Phillipson, T. Skutnabb-Kangas, and T. Várady (eds), *Language: A Right and a Resource. Approaching Linguistic Human Rights*, 117–46. Budapest: Central European University Press.

Delmas-Marty, M. (2003) Justice for sale. International law favours market values. *Le Monde Diplomatique* (English version), August.

Devidal, P. (2004) Trading away human rights? The GATS and the right to education: A legal perspective. *Journal for Critical Education Policy Studies* 2(2). Available at: www.jceps.com.

Djité, P. G. (2008) From liturgy to technology. Modernizing the languages of Africa. *Language Problems and Language Planning* 32(2): 133–52.

Edwards, J. (1984) Language, diversity and identity. In J. Edwards (ed.), *Linguistic Minorities. Policies and Pluralism*, 277–310. London: Academic Press.

Engler, M. (2008) *How to Rule the World. The Coming Battle over the Global Economy*. New York: Nation Books.

Fishman, J. A. (1966) *Language Loyalty in the United States. The Maintenance and Perpetuation of Non-English Mother Tongues by American Ethnic and Religious Groups*. London, The Hague and Paris: Mouton and Co.

Florida, R., and Tinagli, I. (2004) *Europe in the Creative Age*. London: Demos.

Graddol, D. (2006) *English Next. Why Global English May Mean the End of 'English as a Foreign Language.'* London: British Council.

Grin, F. (1999) *Compétences et récompenses: La Valeur des langues en Suisse*. Fribourg: Editions Universitaires.

Grin, F. (2003) Language Planning and Economics. *Current Issues in Language Planning* 4(11): 1–66.

Grin, F. (2004) On the costs of cultural diversity. In P. van Parijs (ed.), *Linguistic Diversity and Economic Solidarity*, 189–202. Bruxelles: De Boeck-Université. [Also available at: http://www.unige.ch/eti/elf/.]

Grin, F., and Sfreddo, C. (1997) *Dépenses publiques pour l'enseignement des langues secondes en Suisse*. Geneva: CSRE-SKBF.

Gunnemark, E. V. (1991) *Countries, Peoples and Their Languages. The Geolinguistic Handbook*. Gothenburg: Geolingua.

Halliday, M. A. K. (2006) Written language, standard language, global language. In B. B. Kachru, Y. Kachru, and C. B. Nelson (eds), *The Handbook of World Englishes*, 349–65. Malden, MA and Oxford, UK: Blackwell.

Hamelink, C. J. (1994) *Trends in World Communication: On Disempowerment and Self-Empowerment*. Penang: Southbound and Third World Network.

Harmon, D. (2002) *In Light of Our Differences: How Diversity in Nature and Culture Makes Us Human*. Washington, DC: The Smithsonian Institute Press.

Harvey, D. (2005) *The New Imperialism*. Oxford: Oxford University Press.

Henrard, K. (2000) *Devising an Adequate System of Minority Protection: Individual Human Rights, Minority Rights and the Right to Self-Determination*. The Hague, Boston, London: Martinus Nijhoff Publishers.

Heugh, K. (2009) Literacy and bi/multilingual education in Africa: Recovering collective memory and knowledge. In Skutnabb-Kangas, Phillipson, Mohanty, and Panda (eds), 103–24.

Hixson, W. L. (2008) *The Myth of American Diplomacy. National Identity and US Foreign Policy*. New Haven: Yale University Press.

Janson, T. (2007) *A Natural History of Latin. The Story of the World's Most Successful Language*. Oxford: Oxford University Press.

Jhingran, D. (2009) Language contexts in India: Implications for primary education. In Skutnabb-Kangas, Phillipson, Mohanty, and Panda (eds), 263–82.

Kazakevitch, O. (2004) Language endangerment in the CIS: Seeking for positive tendencies. In O. Sakiyama and F. Endo (eds), *Lectures on Endangered Languages 5*, 3–20. Suita, Osaka: The Project "Endangered Languages of the Pacific Rim."

Krauss, M. (1992) The world's languages in crisis. *Language* 68(1): 4–10.

Kymlicka, W., and F. Grin (2003) Assessing the politics of diversity in transition countries. In F. Daftary and F. Grin (eds), *Nation-Building, Ethnicity and Language Politics in Transition Countries*, 5–27. Budapest and Flensburg: Local Government and Public Service Reform Initiative, Open Society Institute and ECMI (European Centre for Minority Issues).

Maffi, L. (ed.) (2001) *On Biocultural Diversity. Linking Language, Knowledge and the Environment*. Washington, DC: The Smithsonian Institute Press.

Magga, O. H., Nicolaisen, I., Trask, M., Dunbar, R., and Skutnabb-Kangas, T. (2005) Indigenous children's education and indigenous languages. Expert paper written for the United Nations Permanent Forum on Indigenous Issues. [Also available at: http://www.tove-skutnabb-kangas.org/en/index-en.html, as: PFII_Expert_paper_1_Education_final.pdf].

Makoni, S., and Pennycook, A. (2007a) Disinventing and reconstituting languages. In Makoni and Pennycook (2007b), 1–47.

Makoni, S., and Pennycook, A. (eds) (2007b) *Disinventing and Reconstituting Languages*. Clevedon, UK: Multilingual Matters.

Marx, K., and Engels, F. (1961) The Communist Manifesto *[1848]*. In A. P. Mendel (ed.), *Essential Works of Marxism*, 13–44. New York: Bantam.

May, S., and Hill, R. (2003) *Bilingual/Immersion Education: Indicators of Good Practice*. Milestone Report 2. Hamilton: Wilf Malcolm Institute of Educational Research, School of Education, University of Waikato.

Mohanty, A. K. (2000) Perpetuating inequality: The disadvantage of language, Minority mother tongues and related issues. In A. K. Mohanty and G. Misra (eds), *Psychology of Poverty and Disadvantage*, 104–17. New Delhi: Concept Publishing Company.

Mohanty, A. K., Panda, M., Phillipson, R., and Skutnabb-Kangas, T. (eds) (2009)
Multilingual Education for Social Justice: Globalising the Local. New Delhi: Orient Blackswan.

Morgan, G. (2005) *The Idea of a European Super-State. Public Justification and European Integration*. Princeton, NJ: Princeton University Press.

Mothibeli, A. (2005) *Cross-Country Achievement Results from the SACMEQ 11 Project – 2000 To 2002. A Quantitative Analysis of Education Systems in Southern and Eastern Africa*. Edusource Data News No. 49 (October). Johannesburg: The Education Foundation Trust.

Mufwene, S. S. (2008) *Language Evolution. Contact, Competition and Change*. London and New York: Continuum.

Mühlhäusler, P. (1996) *Linguistic Ecology. Language Change and Linguistic Imperialism in the Pacific Region*. London: Routledge.

Mühlhäusler, P. (2003) *Language of Environment – Environment of Language. A Course in Ecolinguistics*. London: Battlebridge.

Nettle, D. (1999) *Linguistic Diversity*. Oxford: Oxford University Press.

The Nuffield Foundation (2000). *Languages: The Next Generation. The Final Report and Recommendations of the Nuffield Languages Inquiry*. London: The Nuffield Foundation.

Obanya, P. (1999) *The Dilemma of Education in Africa*. Dakar: UNESCO Regional Office.

Oviedo, G., and Maffi, L. (2000) *Indigenous and Traditional Peoples of the World and Ecoregion Conservation. An Integrated Approach to Conserving the World's Biological and Cultural Diversity*. Gland, Switzerland: WWF International and Terralingua.

Pennycook, A. (1998) *English and the Discourses of Colonialism*. London and New York: Routledge.

Pennycook, A. (2007) The myth of English as an international language. In Makoni and Pennycook (2007b), 90–115.

Phillipson, R. (1992) *Linguistic Imperialism.* Oxford: Oxford University Press.

Phillipson, R. (2000) English in the new world order: Variations on a theme of linguistic imperialism and 'world' English. In T. Ricento (ed.), *Ideology, Politics and Language Policies: Focus on English*, 87–106. Amsterdam: John Benjamins.

Phillipson, R. (2003) *English-Only Europe? Challenging Language Policy.* London: Routledge.

Phillipson, R. (2004) Review article "English in globalization: Three approaches" (books by De Swaan, Block and Cameron, and Brutt-Griffler). *Journal of Language, Identity, and Education* 3(1): 73–84.

Phillipson, R. (2006) English, a cuckoo in the European higher education nest of languages? *European Journal of English Studies* 10(1): 13–32.

Phillipson, R. (2008a) The linguistic imperialism of neoliberal empire. *Critical Inquiry in Language Studies* 5(1): 1–43.

Phillipson, R. (2008b) Lingua franca or lingua frankensteinia? English in European integration and globalisation. *World Englishes* 27(2): 250–84. [This is a 'forum' consisting of the article, responses by seven scholars, and a closing word by Robert Phillipson.]

Phillipson, R. (2009) *Linguistic Imperialism Continued.* New Delhi: Orient Blackswan and New York/London: Routledge.

Pieterse, J. N. (2004) *Globalization or Empire.* New York and London: Routledge.

Ramirez, J. D., Yuen, S. D., and Ramey, D. R. (1991) *Executive Summary: Final Report: Longitudinal Study of Structured English Immersion Strategy, Early-Exit and Late-Exit Transitional Bilingual Education Programs for Language-Minority Children, Submitted to the U. S. Department of Education.* San Mateo, CA: Aguirre International.

Rassool, N. (2007) *Global Issues in Language, Education and Development: Perspectives from Postcolonial Countries.* Clevedon: Multilingual Matters (Series Linguistic Diversity and Language Rights).

Rassool, N., and Mansoor, S. (2007) Contemporary issues in language, Education and development in Pakistan. In Rassool, 218–41.

Reagan, T. (2004) Objectification, positivism and language studies: A reconsideration. *Critical Inquiry in Language Studies: An International Journal,* 1(1): 41–60.

Ritzer, G. (1996) *The McDonaldization of Society. An Investigation into the Changing Character of Contemporary Social Life*, rev. edn. Thousand Oaks, CA, London, and New Delhi: Pine Forge Press.

Roberts, A. (2008) *A History of the English-Speaking Peoples since 1900 [2006].* New York: Harper Perennial.

Sachs, W. (ed.) (1992) *The Development Dictionary. A Guide to Knowledge as Power.* London: Zed Books.

Skutnabb-Kangas, T. (1988) Multilingualism and the education of minority children. In T. Skutnabb-Kangas and J. Cummins (eds), *Minority Education: From Shame to Struggle*, 9–44. Clevedon, Avon: Multilingual Matters.

Skutnabb-Kangas, T. (2000) *Linguistic Genocide in Education – Or Worldwide Diversity and Human Righs?* Mahwah, NJ and London, UK: Lawrence Erlbaum Associates. [South Asian updated edition: Delhi, Orient BlackSwan, 2008.]

Skutnabb-Kangas, T. (2003) Linguistic diversity and biodiversity: The threat from killer languages. In C. Mair (ed.), *The Politics of English as a World Language. New Horizons in Postcolonial Cultural Studies*, 31–52. Amsterdam and New York: Rodopi.

Skutnabb-Kangas, T. (2004) The right to mother tongue medium education: The hot potato in human rights instruments. Opening Plenary, Second Mercator International Symposium "Europa 2004: A new framework for ALL languages?" Tarragona, Spain, 27–28 February 2004.

Available at: http://www.ciemen.org/
mercator/pdf/simp-skuttnab.pdf [*sic*].

Skutnabb-Kangas, T. (2006) Language
policy and linguistic human rights. In T.
Ricento (ed.), *An Introduction to Language
Policy. Theory and Method*, 273–91.
Oxford: Blackwells.

Skutnabb-Kangas, T. (2007) Language
planning and language rights. In M.
Hellinger and A. Pauwels (eds),
*Handbook of Language and Communication:
Diversity and Change*, 365–97. Berlin and
New York: Mouton de Gruyter
(Handbooks of Applied Linguistics 9).

Skutnabb-Kangas, T. (2009) MLE for global
justice: Issues, approaches,
opportunities. In Skutnabb-Kangas,
Phillipson, Mohanty, and Panda (eds),
36–62.

Skutnabb-Kangas, T. and Dunbar, R. (2010)
*Indigenous Children's Education as
Linguistic Genocide and a Crime Against
Humanity? A Global View. Gáldu Čála.
Journal of Indigenous Peoples' Rights* No 1,
2010. Guovdageaidnu/Kautokeino:
Galdu, Resource Centre for the Rights of
Indigenous Peoples (http://www.galdu.
org). As an e-book, free of charge:
http://www.e-pages.dk/grusweb/55/.

Skutnabb-Kangas, T. and Heugh, K. (2010)
Multilingual education works when
'peripheries' take the centre
stage. In K. Heugh and T. Skutnabb-
Kangas (eds), *Multilingual Education
Works. From the Periphery to the
Centre*. New Delhi: Orient
BlackSwan.

Skutnabb-Kangas, T., and McCarty, T.
(2008) Clarification, ideological/
epistemological underpinnings and
implications of some concepts in
bilingual education. In J. Cummins and
N. H. Hornberger (eds), *Encyclopedia of
Language and Education, Vol. 5: Bilingual
Education*, 2nd edn, 3–17. New York:
Springer.

Skutnabb-Kangas, T., and Phillipson, R.
(2008a) A human rights perspective on
language ecology. In A. Creese, P.
Martin and N. H. Hornberger (eds),
Encyclopedia of Language and Education,

Vol. 9: Ecology of Language, 2nd edn,
3–14. New York: Springer.

Skutnabb-Kangas, T., and Phillipson, R.
(2008b) Language ecology. (Revision). In
J.-O. Östman and J. Verschueren (eds),
Handbook of Pragmatics. Amsterdam:
Benjamins.

Skutnabb-Kangas, T., Maffi, L., and
Harmon, D. (2003) *Sharing a World of
Difference. The Earth's Linguistic, Cultural,
and Biological Diversity*. Paris: UNESCO
Publishing (UNESCO, Terralingua and
World Wide Fund for Nature). [Also
available at: www.terralingua.org/
RecPublications.htm.]

Skutnabb-Kangas, T., Phillipson, R.,
Mohanty, A. K., and Panda, M. (eds)
(2009) *Social Justice through Multilingual
Education*. Bristol: Multilingual Matters.

Smith, N. (2003) *American Empire.
Roosevelt's Geographer and the Prelude to
Globalization*. Berkeley and Los Angeles,
CA: University of California Press.

Thomas, W. P. and Collier, V. P. (2002) *A
National Study of School Effectiveness for
Language Minority Students' Long Term
Academic Achievement*. George Mason
University, CREDE (Center for Research
on Education, Diversity and Excellence).
Available at: http://www.crede.ucsc.
edu/research/llaa/1.1_final.html.

Van Parijs, P. (2003) Linguistic justice. In
W. Kymlicka and A. Patten (eds),
Language Rights and Political Theory,
153–68. Oxford: Oxford University Press.

Tomaševski, K. (2001) *Free and Compulsory
Education for All Children: The Gap
between Promise and Performance*. Lund:
Raoul Wallenberg Institute of Human
Rights and Humanitarian Law and
Stockholm, Swedish International
Development Cooperation Agency
(Right to Education Primers 2).

Wierzbicka, A. (2006) *English: Meaning and
Culture*. Oxford: Oxford University
Press.

World Resources Institute, World
Conservation Union and United Nations
Environment Programme (1992) *Global
Biodiversity Strategy: Policy-Makers' Guide*.
Baltimore: WRI Publications.

4 World Languages: Trends and Futures

ULRICH AMMON

The Concept of 'World Language': Ranks and Degrees

There are reasons to underline that the plural in the title is meant seriously. Titles referring to, or dealing with, English only as a world language (for instance Crystal 1997a/2003; but see also Graddol 2006) suggest that no other language deserves this attribute, or at least will no longer in the near future. Some even hint at the possibility that English may suffice, in future, as the only foreign language people have to know. Thus Crystal (1997a: 19), with a touch of enthusiasm, envisions a world

> in which intelligibility and identity happily coexist. This situation is the familiar one of bilingualism – but a bilingualism where one of the languages within a speaker is the global language [English], providing access to the world community, and the other is the regional language, providing access to the local community [any of the other languages].

In this world every non-anglophone would be bilingual, with English as the additional language, and anglophones could satisfy their communicative as well as their identity needs through their native tongue alone. However, while English is doubtlessly the predominent world language, a few other languages also have a global reach, which their speakers experience when they travel around the world and lecture to audiences in their own language, or communicate with individuals other than emigrants or expatriates. This has been possible with languages like French or German for over a hundred years, and has become true of languages like Spanish, Japanese or Chinese in more recent times.

This chapter aims to draw attention to the plurality of 'world languages' (or 'global languages'). This requires an adequate conceptual specification, which allows for ranks or degrees of global reach (or 'globality') of languages. For this purpose it seems useful to distinguish 'global function' from 'global status,' and

The Handbook of Language and Globalization, First Edition. Edited by Nikolas Coupland.
© 2013 Blackwell Publishing Ltd except for editorial material and organization © 2013 Nikolas Coupland.
Published 2013 by Blackwell Publishing Ltd.

again from 'factors that influence global function.' Thus Spanish, for example, is not very different from English in global status, being spread over three or four continents (depending on the delimitation of continents) and over twenty-one countries, in which it is both the official language and the native language of the majority of the population; but is clearly less predominant in global function. It also trails English considerably in factors that influence global function, for example in the economic strength of its speakers – a respect in which Spanish amounts to only about a fourth of what English amounts to, if one measures the two in terms of the Gross Domestic Product (GDP) of all their respective native speakers (3,204 versus 12,717 billion $ in 2005; see table 4.4 below). We would nevertheless include Spanish into the plurality of world languages with which we deal here, on the grounds that one finds those who speak it as a foreign language in countries around the world.

A concept of 'world language' which is useful for our purposes would be based on its *global function*, which means 'use for global communication' and can be specified further with respect to the two concepts of 'international' and 'interlingual' communication. International communication by definition transcends different nations, in other words it occurs between individuals or institutions (or individuals representing institutions) of different nations. If both sides share the same language as native speakers – say, French in the case of a Frenchman and a Quebecois – the choice of this language is natural. The more interesting case for our purposes is the choice of a language for international communication in cases where at least one side consists of native speakers of a different language – for example that of French between a Frenchman and an Italian, or between an Italian and a Greek. Language choice is then 'interlingual' – to use an uncommon but self-explanatory term. It seems adequate for our purposes to focus on international and at the same time interlingual communication; and this is what the phrase 'international communication' will mean in what follows. It can be specified, if necessary, as international communication *in the narrower sense*, to be distinguished from international communication *in the wider sense*, where both sides are native speakers of the same language.

The concept of 'international communication' requires a decision as to whether to include only the citizens or all the inhabitants of countries; a limitation to the former might be more to the point. The specification of international communication as being 'in the narrower sense' requires, in addition, a distinction between native and non-native speakers of languages; in other words it requires us to decide about the in-between category of 'second-language speakers,' who – roughly speaking – make everyday use of the language but have acquired it at a later stage in life (usually after puberty). These should probably be counted as native speakers if they claim the language as their (second) mother tongue, especially if they have native-like skills (but discrepancies between claims and skills may need extra consideration). Otherwise they should be classified as foreign-language speakers. Again, this category should be distinguished from that of mere language learners (present or previous learners), who have (virtually) no skills in the language. Most of the data available for our purposes do not allow for such distinctions; nevertheless, being sensitized to them can at least sharpen our critical judgment.

There are, in addition, important further distinctions within interlingual communication. It can either be *asymmetrical*, if the language is used between native and non-native speakers, or *symmetrical*. Of the latter, the case most relevant for our purposes is that of using the language as lingua franca, which means that it is non-native to all participants. A symmetric form which is more limited in applicability is that of *polyglot dialogue* (or *passive bilingualism*), where participants use actively their different native languages and understand those of the other(s) too. Mixed forms are of course possible among groups of more than two participants.

On the basis of these distinctions we can now define a language as being more international the more extensively it is used for international communication (in the narrower sense). In addition, a lingua franca which extends over several languages can be given more weight than a language of bilateral asymmetric use. It is such usage, as lingua franca, that distinguishes English most noticeably from other languages. Quantification can comprise the number of individuals or the number and size of institutions involved, as well as the frequency and length of communicative events. But quantity alone does not fully capture ranks or degrees in a language's functioning as an 'international language' – or, a fortiori, as a 'world language.' Geographical distance and the distribution of speakers, institutions, and communicative events are relevant too – or perhaps even linguistic diversity, that is, the linguistic distance between the languages involved. In the face of this complexity of dimensions, it is easy to see that precise operationalization and the measurement of world languages in rank or degree can vary widely. In addition, the available data, including those presented hereafter, often rely on gross simplification and on indicators of dubious validity and reliability, instead of being based on direct observations.

World Languages and Their Ranking Order

Heinz Kloss (1974) and William Mackey (1976) have been among the pioneers who suggested indicators and factors of language status in a community, including the global community. David Dalby – who sees the *linguasphere*, that is, the "languages extended around the planet by humankind," as "the single most influential layer of the biosphere" – highlights what he calls the "arterial languages" (2002: 1f.). The metaphor suggests their international function, but Dalby defines them only by number of speakers, as spoken by at least 1 percent of mankind, and thus arrives at twenty-nine languages in 2002. Abram De Swaan's typology (2001: 2–4; compare also Chapter 1 of this volume) comes closer to international function. Within what he calls the "global language system," he sees all "languages […] connected by multilingual speakers," in "a strongly ordered, hierarchical pattern." The higher up languages are in this hierarchy, the greater the number of other languages (and speakers per language) to which they are connected through multilingual speakers. English is the "'hypercentral language' at the hub that holds the entire constellation together." Following in rank are the "super-central," the "central" and, finally, the "peripheral languages." The eleven super-central languages are Arabic, Chinese, French, German, Hindi, Japanese, Malay (specified as *bahasa indonesia*), Portuguese, Russian, Spanish, and Swahili (in alphabetical order). "All […], except Swahili, have more than one hundred million speakers and each serves to connect the speakers of a series of central languages." It is important to stress the *directness* (or immediacy) of connection, since all languages are, in today's "globalized" world, connected indirectly, via chains of multilingual speakers. English may be the only language connected to (virtually) all other languages *directly*, since every language community contains some multilinguals with English in their repertoires.

It is important to add that, in De Swaan's model, the non-native (not the native) languages in multilinguals' repertoires are crucial for connections. His criterion for the "centrality" of a language refers to the extent to which that language is known (or used) non-natively (though he adds the number of native speakers, which he calls languages' "prevalence," as another component of languages' "communicative value"). The focus on non-nativeness corresponds to our above definition of international communication (in the narrower sense), on which we suggest to base the ranking order, or the degree, of languages' internationality or globality. Thus a language with no native speakers at all can well be an international or a world language – if it is directly connected to many or to all other languages via multilinguals, as was true for Latin as a European international language during and beyond the Middle Ages, or as was planned for Esperanto. The number of native speakers is, by itself, no valid criterion for the internationality or globality of a language, though it is (as will be shown shortly) a rough indicator of such a status, as well as a factor which influences it. The focus on non-native speakers corresponds to our intuition that French or English are international or world languages rather than Hindi; or rather than Hindi and Urdu, combined as a single language – or even rather than Chinese, in spite of the latter languages' higher numbers of native speakers (see table 4.3 below).

The functional criterion allows for the distinction between written, oral, oral and written, and perhaps other modes of language use (for instance the gestural mode for hearing-impaired persons), and thus for important distinctions between historical and recent international languages – such as between classical Chinese or medieval Latin, which mainly served for written international communication, and modern English, which is written and spoken globally.

Also, if function is seen as essential for international or world languages, mere knowledge of a language is, strictly speaking, not sufficient; nor is mere study – which, again, is not identical with knowledge. The extent of knowledge or study of a language as a foreign one can, however, serve as an indicator of internationality or globality, on the basis of assumptions of strong positive correlations with use (which, however, ask for corroboration). Such indicators can be specified as to geographic reach and density, in order to show that languages can be international but regionally restricted, or global but with regional differences in density.

Non-Native Speakers

One of the seemingly best indicators of the internationality or globality of languages is the extent of their study as a foreign language. Assessing it is, however, far from easy, since available data are often flimsy and of dubious quality. Methods of data collection remain unclear in most cases, and there is always the danger of exaggerated figures when they are issued by a country in which the language has official status, because higher figures are assumed to attract more learners. Therefore specifying the languages which are presently studied around the globe in school, at the tertiary level, or in adult education (that is, in *formal studies*, as opposed to informal studies unaccounted for) remains to a considerable extent speculative, notwithstanding the arbitrariness of delimiting an open-ended ranking order. Table 4.1 contains the likely – though incomplete – ranking order of our choice, with rough estimates of learner numbers added (in million). Languages which could perhaps be added to a more comprehensive list would

Table 4.1   Number of non-native learners of major languages world-wide

1	English	750 < 1,000, perhaps >1,000[a]
2	French	82.5
3	Chinese	30 (with other estimates hardly above 3)[b]
4	German	16.7
5	Spanish	14
6	Italian	3 < 14
7	Japanese	3
8	Russian	?[c]

SOURCES:
- English: Crystal 1997a: 61/2003: 68f.; 1997b: 360
- French: http://www.diplomatie.guv.fr... (accessed June 18, 2009)
- Chinese: Graddol 2006: 63
- German: StADaF 2005: 15
- Spanish: *Enciclopedia del Español en el mundo* 2006: 25, 27
- Italian: estimate made by Andrea E. Samà, head of the cultural department of the Italian Embassy in Berlin
- Japanese: Japan Foundation 2008: 1

NOTES

[a] Crystal estimates non-native speakers at 530–830 million (1,200–1,500 million total, minus 670 "native or native-like" speakers) and, respectively, perhaps >1,000 (yet with cautions in 2003: 68). But numbers have most likely increased meanwhile (see Graddol 2006).

[b] Markus Taube in the Chinese Department at the University of Duisburg-Essen, and *Fachverband Chinesisch*, estimate numbers as hardly above 3 million.

[c] No useful figures could be gathered for Russian.

Table 4.2 Five countries with the highest number of foreign language students (in thousands)

German	Spanish	Japanese
Russia 3,322	USA 6,000	Korea 911
Poland 2,208	France 2,220	China 684
France 2,261	Brazil 1,000	Australia 366
Ukraine 760	Germany 453	Indonesia 273
Hungary 604	Italy 302	Taiwan 191

SOURCES: StADaF 2005: 8–15; *Enciclopedia del español en el mundo* 2006: 25–7; Japan Foundation 2008: 5.

be Portuguese, Dutch, Korean, Arabic, and Esperanto. The data, which are imprecise for various reasons, refer to the year 2005 and thereabout.

Main areas of study can be roughly determined by countries with the highest numbers of students, which are given in table 4.2 for the three languages for which data were available country by country.

Numbers of foreign-language learners need to be seen in relation to numbers of native speakers. More native speakers of a language imply that the pool of potential foreign-language learners is smaller. In consequence, same absolute numbers of foreign-language learners do not necessarily mean same density. Same numbers, globally, for Chinese (with a vast number of native speakers) mean a higher density than for other languages.

For each language, density varies around the globe. The map below (which is based on data from StADaF 2005: 8–15) illustrates this statement for German, for which formal foreign-language studies have been confirmed for 114 countries in 2005. This map shows the density of studies of German as a foreign language – that is, the number of students in relation to the countries' total population. Quartiles range from 0–0.008 percent (Guinea; first quartile) to 0.4–6.7 percent (Slovakia; fourth quartile): density of studies is, for example, 838 times higher in Slovakia than in Guinea. In the map, countries are pictured as homogeneous units, which can be misleading in the case of large territories – for instance Russia, where population density varies widely.

Density of study as a foreign language and, to a lesser extent, even absolute numbers of students are rough indicators of languages' degree of international function, as has been confirmed by fragmentary data: for German, in the western part of eastern Europe; for Russian, in the eastern and central parts of Asia; for French, in western Europe and in western and northern Africa; for Spanish, in non-hispanophonic America and in parts of western Europe; or, for Japanese and Chinese, in East Asia and in the Pacific region.

While overall numbers for French, German, Italian, and Russian seem to be stagnating or even declining – though with regional differences, and not for

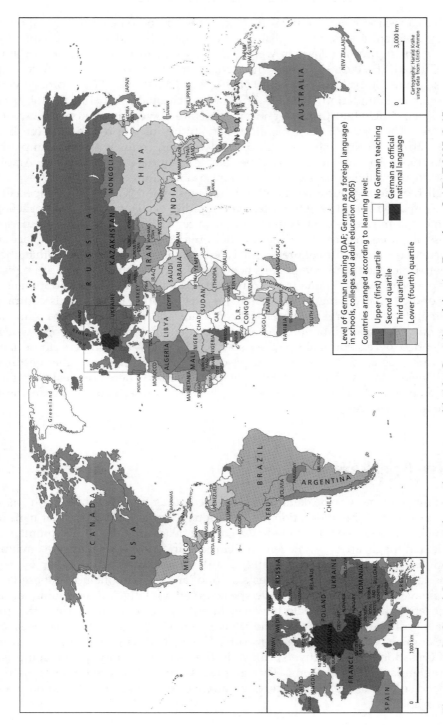

Figure 4.1 Studies of German as a foreign language worldwide: Quartiles of density. Data from StADaF 2005: 8–15

French as a second language in West Africa – they seem to be on the rise, though on very different scales, for English, Chinese, Spanish, and Japanese. Thus, for example, the figures for German were 20.2 million in 2000, but only 16.7 million in 2005 (StADaF 2005: 15), while the figures for Japanese show the following increase (in million): 1.62 (1993), 2.10 (1998), 2.36 (2003), 2.98 (2006), probably >3 (2008) (Japan Foundation 2008: 1) – if data are reasonably reliable. A look back into history shows that Chinese and Japanese are newcomers among the world languages. They are not even mentioned in studies of world-wide foreign language learning during the first half of the twentieth century, as for example in Fränzel (1939). For similar reasons, especially Portuguese but perhaps also Arabic may show up in the same league in the foreseeable future.

English obviously outranks all other languages by far. Numbers are especially hard to pin down, because of the extent and rapidity of change (see Graddol 2006). Even more important is the fact that skills acquired in English are mostly superior to those acquired in other languages, either on account of its privileged place in the curricula or on account of preferential choice for it among learners. Both higher numbers of learners and better skills acquired determine the position of English as the preferred world lingua franca, and even its nativization – its adoption as a native or quasi-native language in certain regions. All other languages, in contrast, serve mainly for bilateral asymmetrical communication and function as a lingua franca only in special situations, for example at conferences of philology, which are attended by exceptionally skilled speakers. In many encounters, these languages are used only for symbolic purposes, such as greetings and other gestures of politeness, while serious work takes place in English. There is a wealth of fractional data, but (to our knowledge) no globally representative ones on these functional differences.

Native Speakers

The number of native speakers (often referred to as 'numerical strength') is a useful indicator of the internationality of languages only for living or for natural languages, as cases like that of medieval Latin (a dead language) or Esperanto (an artificial language) attest. And even for living natural languages there are obvious exceptions, like Hindi (or Hindi and Urdu), Bengali, and (to a lesser extent) Indonesian – if those who speak it as a second language are included: these languages have great numbers of native speakers but a relatively low rank in terms of internationality. On the whole, however, internationality and numerical strength correlate positively. Table 4.3 lists the twelve numerically strongest languages, or rather language communities, of the world. The 'second-language' speakers, who have been added to the native speakers in the second column, do not comprise real foreign-language speakers. The languages are ranked according to native (first) and second-language speakers, with native speakers alone as a subordinate criterion, in 2005.

Table 4.3 Number of native and native plus second-language speakers of major languages world-wide (in millions; ranking order according to native plus second-language speakers)

2005				1984		1964	
Rank	Language	Number of speakers		Rank	Number of speakers	Rank	Number of speakers
1	Chinese	873	1,051	1	700	1	515
2	Hindi+Urdu	425	588	4	194	3	185
3	English	309	508	2	391	2	265
4	Spanish	322	382	3	211	4	145
5	Russian	145	255	5	154	5	135
6	Arabic	206	246	8	117	8	90
7	Bengali	171	211	11	102	9/10	85
8	Portuguese	177	192	6	120	9/10	85
9	Indonesian	23	163	10	110	?	
10	Japanese	122	123	9	117	7	95
11	German	95	123	7	119	6	100
12	French	65	115	12	63	11	65
13	Italian	62	62	13	?	12	55

SOURCES: *Ethnologue* 1984/2005; Muller 1964.

Comparison of different points in time show that the following languages have overall risen in rank: Hindi and Urdu, Arabic, Bengali, and Portuguese (sometimes declining in-between); the following languages have declined in rank: English, Japanese, French, Italian, and especially German; while the rest have maintained their rank – namely Chinese, Spanish, and Russian. Indonesian remains an unclear case for lack of data.

Economic Strength

A large number of native speakers is an indicator and, like other indicators, it is at the same time a factor enhancing a language's internationality. The reason is that acquisition of such a language promises communicative access to numerous individuals and to their culture. Smaller languages can, however, also appear attractive to learners, especially if their speakers have economic strength, which often correlates positively with scientific or cultural wealth. Therefore the total economic strength of languages is perhaps an even more reliable indicator of their international or global rank than numerical strength. One way of measuring it is by total Gross Domestic Product (GDP) of the speakers, usually native or native

Table 4.4 Economic strength of major languages world-wide, in terms of native speakers'GDP (in billion $)

	2005		1987	
	Rank	*GDP (billion $)*	*Rank*	*GDP (billion $)*
English	1	12,717	1	4,271
Japanese	2	4,598	2	1,277
German	3	3,450	3	1,090
Spanish	4	3,204	5	739
Chinese	5	2,400	7	448
French	6	2,215	6	669
Italian	7	1,207	9	302
Arabic	8	984	8	359
Portuguese	9	872	10	234
Russian	10	584	4	801
Hindi + Urdu	11	215	11	102
Bengali	12	113	13	28
Indonesian[a]	13	38	12	65

SOURCES: *Ethnologue* 1984/2005; *Fischer Weltalmanach* 1990/2007.
NOTES
[a] Without second-language speakers.

and second-language speakers – though foreign-language speakers could be considered, too, but have not been so far, probably because calculation is difficult. Table 4.4 contains native speakers' GDP world-wide, which was calculated for each country in proportion to shares of the language's native speakers in the country's population, and then summed up. The table includes, for comparative purposes, the same languages as table 4.3: the numerically strongest languages, not all of which would rank among the economically strongest thirteen. Only the first ten languages in table 4.4 are also the ten economically strongest ones world-wide.

The comparison between table 4.4 and table 4.3 reveals that some languages rank considerably higher in economic strength than in number of native speakers, notably Japanese, German, French, and Italian (whose main countries are also members of the G7 group of the world's economically strongest countries). It seems likely that economic strength is one of the reasons, or rather abstract causes, why these languages keep being studied as foreign languages around the world.

Table 4.4 also illustrates the conspicuous distance of English from the following languages. Even Chinese, it seems, hardly has a chance to catch up with English in the foreseeable future, since English can summon the US, Britain, and numerous other countries, including a growing segment of India. This is certainly one of the main reasons why China, which is sometimes pictured as the future linguistic competitor of the anglophone countries, has made English a generally obligatory school subject and thus virtually adopted it as its main international language, which no other large country has done with Chinese.

Comparison of the numbers for 2005 with those for 1989 shows that the following languages have risen in economic strength: Chinese and Italian (2 ranks), Portuguese and Spanish (1 rank). Russian has declined (4 ranks), while English, Japanese, German, French, Arabic, and Hindi and Urdu have maintained the same rank. Bengali and Indonesian cannot be judged, the latter being a special case, for which the method of counting speakers seems to have changed in the source. For Chinese, Portuguese, and Spanish, the function of international languages has probably increased, and for Russian it has decreased, in line with the economic rank. The international function of English, and perhaps also of Japanese, have increased, while that of German, French, and Italian has probably decreased, in spite of unchanged – or, in the last case, even improved – economic rank. Corroboration for these assumptions is, however, fractional. It can be based, among other possibilities, on numbers of non-native speakers and on the role in science communication (on which see below) as indicators.

Official Status

Number and geographic distribution of countries with official status of language are other potential indicators. Their reliability is, however, limited, because of the enormous variety in the size of countries; because languages can play an important role in a country without having official status (see for instance Crystal 1997a: 56, for English in Kenya and Tanzania); and because communication between countries with the same official language is often mainly international *in the wider sense* (see the section on the concept of 'world language' above). The number of countries can especially be misleading if it is presented on a global map without indication of differences in population density.

Official status in international organizations (rather than countries) takes us closer to international function. The following languages are official and working languages of the United Nations (UN): Chinese, English, French, Russian, Spanish (all since 1945), and Arabic (since 1973). Most documents appear in all of them. We do not know, however, to what extent they are read by non-native speakers; we can only guess that texts in English are much preferred to others. The status of official and working language of the UN enhances to some extent a language's desirability in the linguistic training of diplomats. Translation and interpretation in the UN and its various organs are, however, done in a wider array of languages, including all of those we have identified as international in table 4.1 above (for a somewhat dated but still largely valid documentation, see Tabory 1980: 239). Important international communication in the narrower sense, notably oral, takes place in informal meetings and encounters, for which interpretation is unavailable. There English is definitely the preferred language. We can but guess at

Table 4.5   Number of countries and continents with official language status world-wide

	Language	Countries	Continents[a]
1	English	50	6
2	French	29	5
3	Arabic	22	2
4	Spanish	21	3
5	Portuguese	8	3
6	German	7	1
7	Chinese/Italian	3	1
8	Bengali	2	1
9	Hindi + Urdu	2	1
10	Russian	2	2
11	Indonesian/Japanese	1	1

SOURCE: Banks 2007.
NOTES
[a] Counts on continents are based on a division into six: Africa, Asia, Australia and Pacific, North America, South America, and Europe.

frequency of choice in the case of other languages and assume that French comes second – at a distance. Basically the same ranking order can be observed in other international constellations or organizations, the differences between them depending on the respective regional international languages. The European Union, for example, has twenty-three official languages for communication between institutions and member states (they are called 'official and working languages'), but internal institutional work takes place in the actual working languages (what are called the 'procedural languages'), which are mainly English, to a considerable but diminishing extent French, at a greater distance German, and very rarely Spanish and Italian.

Economy

In the section above we moved to what could be called the 'terrain' of diplomacy – to be distinguished from its 'domain,' which in sociolinguistics has the meaning of 'type of situation (with basically same attributes).' A terrain can comprise a variety of very different domains. We will deal here only with two such terrains, namely economy and science. Unlike in the case of domains, serious attempts at a taxonomy of terrains seem to be missing in sociolinguistics. Other examples of terrains – obviously with considerable overlap among them, and some of them being also treated as domains – would be (perhaps) education, culture, religion, sports, holidays, tourism, or the media.

In recent years, the most globally distributed companies of any original home country – the so-called 'global players' – have adopted English as their official, or at least co-official, company language. This does not mean, however, that other languages are not used internationally for economic purposes. Especially smaller companies continue to use their own national language where it seems possible, either because they try to avoid the additional costs of handling a foreign language or because their economic exchanges are regionally limited. The latter circumstance usually allows them to preserve a structure with a continued clear dominance of their home base – in contrast to the global players, whose branches in various countries enjoy considerable autonomy (this is monocentric versus multicentric company structure). As one would expect, international languages other than English are used in trade and other economic exchanges mainly in the regions where they are a preferred subject of study (see table 4.2 and the map in Figure 4.1). In some countries, companies can get explicit advice about the reach of their own language. Thus the Chamber of Commerce in Hamburg regularly issues such advice for Germany on the basis of a survey of German companies and of their linguistic experience. Table 4.6 offers an overview of the languages which can be used by German companies abroad.

It should, however, be noted that the data in table 4.6 refer only to business correspondence – as other data do, which come up with great numbers of languages. Still other data, largely fragmentary and anecdotal, reveal that, for business negotiations and treaty texts, English is the generally preferred language. It is also the language which has expanded more than any of the others during the sixteen years period covered by table 4.6. The expansion of the other languages is largely due to the break-up of countries (Soviet Union and Yugoslavia), or, for Portuguese, the exaggerated impression of an expansion is created by the fact that data for a number of countries were missing in 1989.

Science

Science is the terrain where English has become, and has been noticed to be, especially prominent – or even dominant, to hint at the possibility of unfavorable implications (see Ammon 2002). Here French and German once ranked on the same level, and the older generation of French and German academics still remember being able to use their respective language regularly, for publishing in international journals or for presentations at international conferences. Now they cannot do it any longer; they have to use English – especially in the natural sciences, but also in the social sciences and in the humanities, even if to a lesser extent.

The shares of a language in scientific publications world-wide are a convenient, but of course rough, indicator of that language's course of development. Figure 4.1 gives a long-term overview of the five major scientific languages' shares

Table 4.6   Number of countries for which languages can be used for correspondence by German companies (figures for 1989 in brackets)[a]

	Sole language or co–language	Sole language	Co–language
1 English	137 (122)	52 (64)	85 (58)
2 French	58 (57)	18 (25)	40 (32)
3 German	37 (26)	1 (1)	36 (25)
4 Spanish	28 (26)	16 (17)	12 (9)
5 Russian	23 (1)	– (–)	23 (1)
6 Arabic	17 (12)	– (–)	17 (12)
7 Portuguese	13 (8)	– (–)	13 (?)
8 Italian	9 (4)	– (–)	9 (4)
9 Dutch	7 (8)	– (–)	7 (8)
10 Chinese	3 (–)	– (–)	3 (–)
11 Croatian	2 (–)	– (–)	2 (–)

SOURCE: Handelskammer Hamburg 2005.

NOTES

[a] Table 4.6 includes only languages which can be used for two or more foreign countries (excluding Germany). Twenty-four more languages are given for single countries. It seems worth stressing in our context that the latter are also used internationally (in the narrower sense defined above, see p. 102), though not globally. The above data have been collected from a source which reflects a German vantage point, and they may suggest an exaggerated reach of German. They show, nevertheless, the international reach of a considerable number of languages – that is, their usefulness beyond their 'own' countries (where they have official status). Just compare numbers of countries in tables 4.5 and 4.6. There are various studies of foreign-language needs of companies in different countries which regularly come up with a considerable number of languages, for example twenty-eight for German companies in a comprehensive study (Schöpper-Grabe and Weiß 1998: 245).

in natural science publications during a time span of over a hundred years. Chinese is a newcomer, which rose to 1 percent only in 1999 and continued as follows: 1.5 percent in 2000 and 2001; 1.8 percent in 2002; 2 percent in 2003; 2.1 percent in 2004.

It should be added that we do not have the real proportions, since data have not been collected directly, but through the most comprehensive periodical bibliographies or bibliographical databanks. Formerly such bibliographies existed in a number of countries with different languages, but now the English-speaking countries pretty much monopolize them. Thus for example German bibliographical databanks like *Chemisches Zentralblatt* or *Physikalische Berichte* were absorbed respectively by *Chemical Abstracts* in 1969 and by *Physics Abstracts* in 1978.

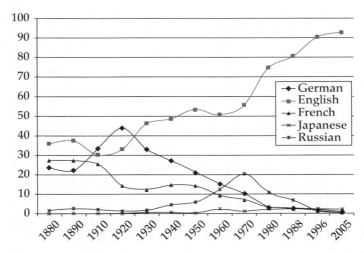

Figure 4.2 Shares of languages in science publications, 1880–2005: overall average percentage for biology, chemistry, medicine, physics, and mathematics. Sources: Tsunoda 1983; Ammon 1998; the author's own analysis, with the help of Abdulkadir Topal and Vanessa Gawrisch, of *Biological Abstracts*, *Chemical Abstracts*, *Physics Abstracts* and *Mathematical Reviews*

It has been convincingly shown, in the case of citation indexes, that they are skewed in favor of English in the sense that titles in this language are over-represented (Sandelin and Sarafoglou 2004). The same appears to be likely for most of the bibliographical databanks. Nevertheless, there can be no doubt that English carries home by far the lion's share in total scientific publications. The titles included in the Anglo-Saxon databanks might even be better indicators of international and global scientific communication than those excluded, since they focus on publications with the highest 'impact factor.'

The situation is slightly different in the social sciences, where shares of other languages are more noticeable (see Figure 4.3), and more so for the humanities. For the latter, other languages than English still play a noticeable international role, especially in various branches of archaeology, music, theology, history, philosophy, and in the own subject, i.e. the respective languages' linguistics, literature and philology (Ammon 1998: 170–9).

English also serves as a medium of teaching in non-anglophone countries, mainly in the sciences – especially at tertiary level (Ammon and McConnell 2002), but also, and to a growing extent, at secondary level (for Malaysia, see Gill 2007) – while study programs in other foreign languages, for instance French or German, are scarce. Even countries which are known for their vigorous defence of the own language's international rank have introduced study programs in English – for example France and Germany had introduced 555 and respectively 674

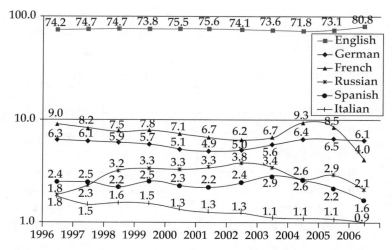

Figure 4.3   Shares of languages in publications of the social sciences, years 1880–2006: overall average percentage for anthropology, political science, economics, and sociology. Shares of other languages are smaller than 1 percent during entire time span. Sources: *International Bibliography of the Social Sciences*, IBSS; the author's own analysis, with help of Vanessa Gawrisch

such programs by 2008. (See http://www.campusfrance.org/en/b-agence/espacedoc_infos.htm#forma_en, and http://www.daad.de/deutschland/studienangebote/internationalprogrammes/07535.de.html, both in October 2008.) In particular, these countries hope that the English-language programs may even have the side-effect of propping up their own language's international rank by attracting foreigners. Students begin their studies in English and partially continue that way, but they also have to learn the country's own language – French or German. Skills in that language often are a prerequisite for the degree and are tested at the end of studies. Anyway, rudimentary language skills are nearly unavoidable for the purpose of everyday life in the country. In this way the number of learners and the global reach of other languages may increase through English-language study programs.

The Rise and Stabilization of a Single, World Lingua Franca

Although it seems obvious that a number of languages function internationally and globally, especially those whose native communities are numerically and – what is even more important – economically strong or whose languages have had a tradition of being studied abroad, it is necessary not to overlook differences and proportions. There is virtually no descriptive parameter or indicator for the international or global rank of a language which, if applied to today's languages world-wide, does not place English at the top (see Crystal 1997b; De Swaan 2001; Maurais and Morris 2003; Graddol 2006). The overall explanation for this unique position is complex and can here only be hinted at. It is also speculative to a considerable extent, because the weight of factors is largely unknown. It makes sense to distinguish various strands of explanation, especially the socio-economic, the political, the technical (or technological), the communicative (or interactional), and the psychological (or attitudinal and cognitive).

Socio-economically, the long-lasting economic superiority of the anglophone countries, with Britain leading in the eighteenth and nineteenth century and the US in the twentieth, has formed the crucial pillar. Politically and ideologically, Britain's colonialism, driven as it was by economic motives and by ideas of its own cultural superiority and religious zeal, was accompanied and supported by the export and imposition of Britain's own language (Phillipson 1992). To be fair, it needs to be pointed out that all European countries were prone to act in the same way but they were unable to do so, or less successful at it. In recent times, access to virtually all countries world-wide, the political prerequisite of 'globalization,' gave an additional push to the predominance of English, since regions of special protection for other languages were eliminated (for instance eastern Europe for German and Russian). In addition, practically all countries or private institutions world-wide have upgraded English in their curricula for school or tertiary education. English has been made an obligatory subject of study – often the only obligatory foreign language, or the only one offered, or the one to which most study time has been allotted; or it has become the preferred choice for the majority of students, and in quite a few cases the language of instruction.

Technologically, growingly efficient means of transport and communication (media, the internet, and the like) have allowed for ever more intensive international and global contacts. Technology has not developed, however, practical machines for automatic translation or interpretation between languages; nor are these in the pipeline for the foreseeable future, in spite of considerable technical progress in this direction.

Rules of communication and interaction between individuals of different linguistic background favor the choice of one and the same language (see Crystal 1997a/2003). They discourage exclusion of participants for reasons of communicative efficiency or politeness, and hence they call for the choice of the best and most generally known language (van Parijs 2001). As a consequence of frequent use by non-native speakers, the national connotation of that language – that is, its association with native countries – has worn off, and the language has acquired a touch of neutrality, similar to what was once planned for Esperanto. This tendency has been supported by claims to national neutrality from the side of prominent linguists, especially of anglophone background, or from other sides (see the section on the concept of 'world language' above).

The question of national neutrality has been raised in the context of studies on 'world Englishes' (Jenkins 2003) or on 'international English' (Seidlhofer 2003), which focus on the use of English by non-native speakers. These studies, or an important subset of them, aim not only at systematically analyzing and describing non-native speakers' linguistic peculiarities of English but, over and above, at making them generally acceptable, at least for international communication. This perspective may seem forbiddingly utopian in the face of the huge variability among, and difficulty of delimiting, communicatively functional peculiarities from the communicatively dysfunctional 'anything goes.' It would, in my view, require codifying these peculiarities, or at least a core set of them, and acknowledging them as variants of a multi-central global language – expanding the idea of pluricentric languages with a variety of norms which diverge regionally or nationally, but only to an extent that does not preclude communication. It seems possible, and also reasonable, to conceive of attempts to acknowledge and upgrade international English as the first steps towards developing a real global lingua franca. This would have to be not just a variety of English but a language in its own right, though certainly one mainly based on English (whose impact on other languages world-wide is noticeable even today: see for instance House, Baumann, and Probst 2004). Only then, and not as a mere variety of English, could such a language be a real lingua franca – that is, a non-native language for all its users (notwithstanding the possibility of re-nativization). Its conceptualization as a "hybrid language" (House 2003: 573) can be understood as leading in the same direction. Then this language should be named, accordingly, not by a compound name with the element 'English' in it, but by an independent new name, say, 'Globalish,' designed to express its major function (for details, see Ammon 2003). To non-anglophones, such a solution would appear to be fairer not only than 'global English' (Crystal 1997a/2003), but also than 'international English' or 'world English,' and thus it would mitigate resentment by diminishing national inequalities with respect to norm control of the language and to access to it.

The costs and hardships of language learning will keep working in favor of a single predominant language. Linguists do not want to hear about these hardships; they insist instead on valuable investment and on satisfaction, or even pleasure – but the growing abstinence of native speakers of English, including linguists, from foreign-language learning tells another story. Because of these costs and hardships, which put limits to human multilingualism, sets of competing languages function, to some extent, like zero-sum games: the rise of one can entail the fall of the others. Thus the rise of English as a world language can cause the fall of competitor languages. But there are also more indirect connections. The upgrading of minority languages can cause the shrinkage of international languages other than English; English is not affected but its predominance can, as a consequence, even increase. If a minority language becomes the language used at school, as has happened in many places, especially within the EU, students still have to learn and use the country's national official language. Their first real foreign language is then their third language at school, a role for which they choose almost always English – otherwise they would fear that they overstretch their language learning capacity; besides, they feel that skills in English are indispensable. The same regularity applies in the case of second official languages, if they are obligatory school subjects. They, too, can have the effect of giving English an indirect extra boost and of causing shrinkage in the study of other international or global languages.

The Rise of New and the Continuation of Traditional Subordinate and Bilateral World Languages

Are we heading towards a world with only one single international and world language, all the other languages being confined to their own language communities – that is, a world in which practically none of them is being used for international, let alone global, communication or studied as a foreign language? There are reasons to assume that this is not a realistic scenario for the foreseeable future. Not even David Graddol (2006) goes so far, although his predictions, which extend up to the middle of the twenty-first century, amount to an overall growing predominance of English as a world language. His warning, made to the anglophone world, against abstinence from foreign-language learning implies that he foresees the continuance of other international – or even world – languages. Following demographic and economic prediction, and especially the rise of the *BRIC* states (Brazil, Russia, India, and China; though *CIRB* might be the more realistic ranking order), Graddol foresees the growing importance of Chinese, Russian, Portuguese, "Indic" (obviously, and highly questionably, Hindi), and also Spanish, and the "slow relative decline of Japanese and most European languages" (Graddol 2006: 62f.).

While especially Chinese and Spanish seem to be indeed on the rise, his predictions about the future of the other languages appear more uncertain. Graddol's methods are, basically, scenario planning and extrapolation from previous development, about whose reliability he may, in spite of some scepticism, be too confident. The poor predictability of economic developments, for which the recent financial crisis provides an example, and the considerable stability of the economic ranks of language communities (see table 4.4) are reasons to be cautious about predictions concerning language status and function.

This said, it seems, first, unlikely that any other language can 'dethrone' English as the clearly predominant world language, and as especially the world lingua franca, in the foreseeable future. Secondly, it seems likely that other languages than English will continue to be used internationally or globally, mainly for bilateral contact, for the following reasons (perhaps among others, such as persistent anti-American sentiments):

• Because skills of English will spread more slowly and will remain poorer than would be necessary for the substitution of other international languages: numbers of learners should not be equaled with numbers of individuals with skills.

- Because communication in English only will not be fully accepted in relevant situations by native speakers of other international or world languages, especially from economically powerful communities, even if they have sufficient skills in English.

Language use has more functions than communication and cognition, and the choice of a language can be refused or resented even if its use were efficient for the present purpose. The attitudes which mainly come into play here are not only related to the identity function of language. They can, in addition, derive from assumptions of lack of fairness – and not only in communication (van Parijs 2001), but also in establishing international relations. The former kind of assumptions is easy to comprehend. As to the latter, the idea seems to spread in various countries that knowledge of one's own language abroad enhances the diffusion of one's own values and of favorable attitudes towards one's own country, and consequently helps to improve economic and other international relationships. Therefore knowledge of one's own language abroad should be promoted rather than sacrificed to, or substituted by, use of English as a global language.

Vice versa, countries find it easier to establish contacts with another country from the outside if they know that country's own language than if they try to do it through English as a foreign language. They consider it especially advantageous to follow the rule that, if you want to sell, you had better be as polite as to choose the buyer's own language. Thus even British companies are eager to hire personnel with foreign language skills, and students who have acquired them in addition to their professional expertise enjoy excellent job opportunities (Durrell 2004: 29). Recently, since 2005, the number of students of foreign languages, especially French and German, has increased in Britain after years of decline (www.cilt.org/research/statistics/education, accessed in September 2008). The English-language study programs in France and Germany have yielded to criticism concerning the neglect of one's own language and have in most cases led to the introduction of demands for its acquisition as an obligatory component. A good many students are eager to expand their knowledge of foreign languages beyond English, because they consider this to be a valuable qualification.

For all these reasons, it appears likely that other languages besides English will gain, or maintain, international or global function. The gist of their use will probably be bilateral, but the possibility of multilateral usage, including as a lingua franca in special situations, remains, irrespective of the role of English as the predominant world lingua franca.

REFERENCES

Ammon, U. (1998) *Ist Deutsch noch internationale Wissenschaftssprache? Englisch auch für die Lehre an den deutschsprachigen Hochschulen.* Berlin and New York: Mouton de Gruyter.

Ammon, U. (2003) Global English and the non-native speaker. Overcoming disadvantage. In H. Tonkins and T. Reagan (eds), *Language in the Twenty-First Century*, 23–34. Amsterdam: John Benjamins.

Ammon, U. (ed.) (2002) *The Dominance of English as a Language of Science. Effects on the Non-English Languages and Language Communities*. Berlin and New York: Mouton de Gruyter.

Ammon, U., and McConnell, G. (2002) *English as an Academic Language in Europe. A Survey of Its Use in Teaching*. Frankfurt am Main, Berlin, Bern, Bruxelles, New York, Oxford, and Vienna: Lang.

Banks, A. S. (2007) *Political Handbook of the World: 2007*. Washington, DC: CQ Press.

Biological Abstracts (1927–2005) Philadelphia. Available at: www.campusfrance.org/en/b-agence/espacedoc_infos.htm#forma_en.

Chemical Abstracts (1907–2005). Columbus, OH: Chemical Abstracts.

Crystal, D. (1997a) *English as a Global Language*. Cambridge: Cambridge University Press. [2nd edn: 2003.]

Crystal, D. (1997b) World languages. In Crystal, D. (ed.), *The Cambridge Encyclopedia of Language*, 2nd edn, 359–61. Cambridge: Cambridge University Press.

Dalby, D. (2002) The Linguasphere Register of the World's Languages and Speech Communities. Available at: www.linguasphere.org/book.html.

De Swaan, A. (2001) *Words of the World. The Global Language System*. Cambridge: Polity.

www.diplomatie.gouv.fr/en/france-priorities_1/francophony-french-language_1113/french-language_1934/promoting-french_4450/global-initiatives_4451/promoting-and-teaching-french-abroad_6881.html?var_recherche=french+learners.

Der Fischer Weltalmanach 1990/2007. Frankfurt am Main: Fischer Taschenbuch Verlag.

Durrell, M. (2004) Perspektiven für den Deutschunterricht und die Germanistik im Vereinigten Königreich Großbritannien und Nordirland. *Jahrbuch für Internationale Germanistik* 35(1): 19–25.

Ethnologue. Languages of the World (1984), 10th edn. Dallas, TX: SIL International. [15th edn: 2005.]

Enciclopedia del Español en el Mundo (2006). Madrid: Instituto Cervantes (Annuario del Instituto Cervantes 2006–7).

Fränzel, W. (1939) Die lebenden Sprachen im Sprachunterricht der Welt. *Internationale Zeitschrift für Erziehung* 8(2): 104–28.

Gill, S. K. (2007) Shift in language policy in Malaysia: Unravelling reasons for change, conflict and compromise in mother-tongue education. *AILA Review* 20: 106–22.

Graddol, D. (2006) *English Next. Why Global English May Mean the End of 'English as a Foreign Language.'* London: British Council.

Handelskammer Hamburg (ed.) (2005) *Exportnachschlagewerk K und M: Konsular- und Mustervorschriften*, 36th edn. Hamburg: Dieckmann.

House, J. (2003) English as a lingua franca: A threat to multilingualism? *Journal of Sociolinguistics* 7: 556–78.

House, J., Baumann, N., and Probst, J. (2004) English as a lingua franca and its influence on other languages. *Translator* 10(1): 83–108.

International Bibliography of the Social Sciences: Sociology (1951–2005); *Economics* (1952–2005); *Political Science* (1953–2005); *Social and Cultural Anthropology* (1955–2005). London and Chicago: Tavistock and Aldine.

Japan Foundation (2008) *Survey Report on Japanese-Language Education abroad 2006: Present Condition of Overseas*

Japanese-Language Education. Summary. Tokyo: The Japan Foundation.

Jenkins, J. (ed.) (2003) *World Englishes. A Resource Book for Students.* London and New York: Routledge.

Kloss, H. (1974) Die den internationalen Rang einer Sprache bestimmenden Faktoren. Ein Versuch. In H. Kloss (ed.), *Deutsch in der Begegnung mit anderen Sprachen,* 7–77. Tübingen: Narr.

Mackey, W. F. (1976) *Bilinguisme et contact des langues.* Paris: Klincksieck.

Mathematical Reviews (1940–2005). Providence, RI: American Mathematical Society.

Maurais, J., and Morris, M. A. (eds) (2003) *Languages in a Globalising World.* Cambridge: Cambridge University Press.

Muller, S. H. (1964) *The World's Living Languages. Basic Facts of Their Structure, Kinship, Location and Number of Speakers.* New York: F. Unger.

van Parijs, P. (2001) Linguistic justice. *Politics, Philosophy and Economics* 1: 59–74.

Phillipson, R. (1992) *Linguistic Imperialism.* Oxford: Oxford University Press.

Physics Abstracts (Science Abstracts Series A) (1898–2005) Piscataway, NJ: Institute of Electrical Engineers.

Physikalische Berichte (1920–1978). Braunschweig: Vieweg.

Sandelin, B., and Sarafoglou, N. (2004) Language and scientific publication statistics. *Language Problems and Language Planning* 28(1): 1–10.

Schöpper-Grabe, S., and Weiß, R. (1998) *Vorsprung durch Fremdsprachentraining. Ergebnisse einer Unternehmensbefragung.* Cologne: Deutscher Instituts-Verlag.

Seidlhofer, B. (2003) *A Concept of International English and Related Issues: From 'Real English' to 'Realistic English'?* Strasbourg: Council of Europe.

StADaF [Ständige Arbeitsgruppe Deutsch als Fremdsprache] (2005) *Deutsch als Fremdsprache weltweit. Datenerhebung 2005.* Berlin, Bonn, München, Köln: Auswärtiges Amt, Deutscher Akademischer Austauschdienst, Goethe-Institut, Zentralstelle für das Auslandsschulwesen.

Tabory, M. (1980) *Multilingualism in International Law and Institutions.* Alphen aan den Rijn and Rockville, ML: Sijthoff and Noordhoff.

Tsunoda, M. (1983) Les Langues internationales dans les publications scientifiques et techniques. *Sophia Linguistica* 13: 144–5.

5 Language Policy and Globalization

THOMAS RICENTO

Introduction

The following definition of globalization comes from Scheuerman (2008):

> Covering a wide range of distinct political, economic, and cultural trends, the term 'globalization' has quickly become one of the most fashionable buzzwords of contemporary political and academic debate. In popular discourse, globalization often functions as little more than a synonym for one or more of the following phenomena: the pursuit of classical liberal (or 'free market') policies in the world economy ('economic liberalization'), the growing dominance of western (or even American) forms of political, economic, and cultural life ('westernization' or 'Americanization'), the proliferation of new information technologies (the 'Internet Revolution'), as well as the notion that humanity stands at the threshold of realizing one single unified community in which major sources of social conflict have vanished ('global integration').

While this definition suffices as a general description of a complex bundle of phenomena in political, economic, social, cultural, and technological spheres, how the term is used and understood in public and academic discourse is quite variable. Norman Fairclough (2006), for example, cites the work of Held et al. (1999), who distinguish three approaches to globalization found in the academic literature: 'hyperglobalist,' 'sceptical,' and 'transformationalist.' According to Fairclough, "hyperglobalists see globalization as the emergence of a single global market which is supplanting the nation-state as the primary economic and political unit" (2006: 15). Neo-liberals regard this phenomenon positively, as human progress, while others (such as radicals and neo-Marxists) regard it negatively, as the triumph of global capitalism. In contrast to this perspective stand the skeptics, who believe that the level of global economic integration was higher in the late nineteenth century and "that the contemporary evidence indicates regionalization (with Europe, East Asia, and North America as the main [...] economic blocs) rather than globalization, and the continuing economic power of

The Handbook of Language and Globalization, First Edition. Edited by Nikolas Coupland.
© 2013 Blackwell Publishing Ltd except for editorial material and organization © 2013 Nikolas Coupland.
Published 2013 by Blackwell Publishing Ltd.

nation–states" (ibid., p. 15). Finally, the transformationalists agree with the hyper-globalists that contemporary globalization is unprecedented, but they argue that it is much more complex and multidimensional; that the nation–states have been radically transformed in character, but not supplanted; and that the effects of globalization are contingent and unpredictable (ibid.).

Among scholars in language policy studies, all three approaches can be found, although the (critical) hyperglobalist and transformationalist positions tend to dominate current research. Good examples of these approaches in research on English as a global language can be found in Canagarajah (1999) and Pennycook (2007). The mainstream neo-liberal approach is characterized by Fairclough as the "globalist" discourse of globalization, "which represents it in reductive neo-liberal economic terms within a strategy to inflect and re-direct actual processes of globalization in that direction" (2006: 40). Steger (2005; cited in Fairclough 2006: 40) describes six core claims of 'globalism':

- Globalization is about the liberalization and global integration of markets.
- Globalization is inevitable and irreversible.
- Nobody is in charge of globalization.
- Globalization benefits everyone.
- Globalization furthers the spread of democracy in the world.
- Globalization requires a war on terror.

Steger describes globalism as a 'story' (or narrative), a discourse and an ideology. This view of globalization has been promoted by influential journalists such as Thomas L. Friedman, who writes for the *New York Times*. In his best-selling book *The Lexus and the Olive Tree* (2000), Friedman provides a fairly clear explanation of how he understands globalization:

> The driving idea behind globalization is free-market capitalism – the more you let market forces rule and the more you open your economy to free trade and competition, the more efficient your economy will be. Globalization means the spread of free-market capitalism to virtually every country in the world. Therefore globalization also has its own set of economic rules – rules that revolve around opening, deregulating and privatizing your economy, in order to make it more competitive and attractive to foreign investment.

Fairclough (2006: 9–10) claims that "globalist" discourse "represents the highly complex phenomenon of globalization reductively as purely economic, as a particular form of capitalism and a particular view of what capitalism should – must – be like." He goes on to point out that the Friedman extract given above is vague about agency: "Who or what 'spreads' free-market capitalism? Who produces or enforces the 'rules'?" (ibid., p. 10). The notion that capitalism is a rule-governed (and, by implication, logical) system that operates independently of "rule-makers" or other powerful agents is just the sort of "hidden" presupposition that characterizes much of the globalist discourse in the mainstream media. To this core argument that globalization (as described by Friedman and others) is 'the only game in town,' other discourses attach notions such as that it benefits more people than it harms, or that it is somehow a key ingredient in democracy and the best way to improve living standards in poor countries, and so on.

The present chapter explores answers to the following questions: To what degree are languages imbricated in the processes of globalization? Can (and should) countries protect their national linguistic resources, or should they 'open their markets' and promote languages such as English in order to enhance access to technology, trade, and the like? As Crystal (2003: 9) points out, "a language has traditionally become an international language for one chief reason: the power of its people – especially their political and military power." The conquests of the British, Greeks, Romans, Moors, Spanish, Portuguese, and French caused English, Greek, Latin, Arabic, Spanish, Portuguese, and French to spread across Europe, Africa, Asia, and the Americas; and that history, with its legacy, persists in many guises to the present day. As to whether states can or should 'protect' their national language(s) or have an 'open market' policy with regard to global languages such as English, history suggests that the attempts by states to control language markets have both succeeded and failed, and to varying degrees. Viewed over the long arc of recorded history, language change may be seen, from one perspective, as a virtually agentless process, restricted and shaped by rules of 'universal grammar.' However, if we investigate the political and social dimensions of language spread, we can learn how human agency has accelerated change with regard to the structures, use, relative status and longevity of languages (see Brutt-Griffler 2002).

The globalist discourse on the inevitability and progressive nature of globalization is not new. Yet, from Columbus' plunder and enslavement of the native inhabitants of Hispaniola to the passing of NAFTA (the North America Free Trade Agreement) by the US Congress in 1994, the goal of imperial powers has always been to *increase control* over markets and to *protect the wealth* of the monarch or corporation. To demonstrate some of the ways in which globalist discourse has become non-ideological (that is, 'common sense' truth), we can look at recent history in the US: NAFTA, of which the Uruguay Round was passed by the US Congress in 1994, has little to do with free trade (since it deals mostly with intra-company transfers); it was opposed by organized labor and by the general population (at least in the US, as measured by contemporary public opinion polls); it led to the loss of millions of unskilled jobs in the US, Canada, and Mexico; and it has resulted in significant environmental degradation. Yet, despite these facts, analyses of mainstream media commentary on NAFTA reflect the globalist values described above by Steger (2005). Here is an extract from an editorial, A35, titled "If Nafta Loses," written by the liberal *New York Times* columnist Anthony Lewis on November 5, 1993:

> The arguments made against Nafta by such significant opponents as the United Auto Workers seem to me to come down to fear of change and fear of foreigners. [...] Unions in this country, sad to say, are looking more and more like the British unions

that have become such a millstone around the neck of the Labor Party: backward, unenlightened [...] The crude threatening tactics used by unions to make Democratic members of the House vote against Nafta underline the point.

A corollary to the globalist discourse on globalization (reflected in Lewis' column) is that, in democracies, the views of the people expressed through collective organizations such as labor unions can be easily dismissed by the liberal main-stream media as ignorant, xenophobic, or uninformed, without the slightest concern for hypocrisy on the part of those who do the dismissing (such as Anthony Lewis). Yet the evidence that NAFTA has been injurious to workers in the US, Canada, and Mexico is by now well documented (for documentation on the nega-tive effects of NAFTA on wages, employment, and the environment in Mexico, the US, and Canada, as well as for a discussion on the contents of NAFTA and on the public and media reaction to it, see Mitchell and Schoeffel (2002), Chapter 8, notes 18–24, at www.understandingpower.com). From a factual (as opposed to globalist rhetorical) perspective, it is impossible to sustain the case that NAFTA has been a net gain in economic, social, and environmental terms for the majority of the population in Canada, the US, or Mexico, *unless* one subscribes to the (usually implicit) ideology of 'free market capitalism,' reflected in globalist dis-course, that success – that is, 'progress' – is measured by the degree to which the owners of capital – corporations, banks, chief executive officers, share-holders – increase their wealth relative to the general population. For example, according to Barlow and Clarke (1998: 50),

> Despite robust economic growth, the [Council on International and Public Affairs]'s study reveals that the real wages of US workers have declined by 19.5 percent from their level of twenty-five years ago. Indeed, virtually all of the income gains during the past decade have reportedly gone to the top 5 percent of American families, thereby dramatically increasing inequality and poverty in the country.

As far as wealth is concerned, according to a report by the World Institute for Development Economics Research of the United Nations University (2006), data from the Federal Reserve's Survey of Consumer Finances

> found that the richest 1 percent of Americans held 32 percent of the nation's wealth in 2001. (This excludes the billionaires in the Forbes list, who control roughly another 2 percent of the nation's wealth.) This tops the inequity in every country but Switzerland, among the 20 nations that measure these wealth disparities and are cited in the report. (*New York Times*, December 6, 2006)

For additional data on the growing gap in wages and wealth in the US, see Mitchell and Schoeffel (2002), Chapter 10, notes 5, 8, 15, 65–9, and 101 (at www. understandingpower.com).

If, then, we understand the economic dimension of globalization (which domi-nates public discourse in the US) as something quite different from an idealized open, equal-access, uncontrolled, 'market driven' system – that is, as a system in which decisions about capital flows are *not* based on principles of participatory democracy, in which the interests or desires of the people *do not* determine (or even influence) policy, and in which 'efficiency' comes to mean that *some* people (not everyone) benefit to an extraordinary degree – then we should be skeptical about laissez-faire claims applied to the trajectories and fates of minority or marginalized languages as if they were simply buffeted about (and marginalized, or made obsolete) by the 'invisible hand' of social change, human creativity and desire, and unfettered personal decision-making. I am not arguing for cause and effect between economic systems and the status of languages, or that languages have the same characteristics as commodities. What I am arguing, however, is (1) that globalization has real effects on societies and on their languages, effects which can be measured; and (2) that the globalist discourse identified by Fairclough also affects the way people (including academics, journalists, and politicians) think and talk about language(s) in everyday life, which also has real effects on language policies and practices over time.

The Role of English in Globalization

Since English has become (or at least it is argued by many scholars and pundits to be) the pre-eminent 'global' language, it is appropriate that we focus on English in considering how it came to be regarded as such, and what it might mean to say that English is a global language. The case of English has perhaps been studied and argued about more than that of any other language over the past several decades (for a discussion of some of the major themes and controversies, see *Journal of Language, Identity and Education* 2004, Vol. 3, No. 2). When it is often claimed that no other language in history has been so widely used, it is inevitable that the H-word (hegemony) will be invoked, rightly or wrongly. Consider the facts, culled from various sources, which might offer support for the claim of hegemony. Crystal (2003), relying on the latest editions of the *Encyclopedia Britannica Yearbook* and *Ethnologue: Languages of the World*, as well as on census data (where available), makes the following claims:

- There are 75 territories in which English has held or continues to hold a special place as an official or co-official language, and where it is used as a first or second language (these territories are listed in Crystal 2003: 62–5).
- On the basis of the 2001 census, the total population of these territories is 2.24 billion people (one third of the world's population).
- The number of users of English as a first language totals 329,140,800; the number of users of English as a second language totals 430,614,500.
- If the various English-derived pidgins and Creoles are counted in the category of English as a first language (80 million people), then the total number of first-language users of English is about 400 million.
- Since far more people use English as a second or foreign language (L2) than as a native or first language (L1), the ratio of native to non-native English speakers is 1:3.

- The annual population growth rate in countries with large numbers of L2 English users (Cameroon, India, Malaysia, Nigeria, Philippines) is considerably higher than the population growth rate in the principal L1 English users (Australia, Canada, New Zealand, UK, USA); in the period 1996–2001, the average difference was 2.4 percent versus 0.88 percent, respectively.

What is particularly interesting about these data is the fact that the world of the future will see a decline in the number of first-language users of English. In a widely cited article, Graddol (1999: 60–1), relying on data from the *Sex and Age Quinquennial* (United Nations Population Division) dataset for 1950–2050 (1998 revision) and using the (then) current estimates of L1 English speakers in 56 countries with a total population of about 337 million speakers, calculates that, whereas in 1950 over 8 percent of the world's population spoke English as their first language, by 2050 the proportion will be less than 5 percent.

What do these data suggest about the English 'market' in global terms? First, languages *qua* languages have no power, since, if English in and of itself conferred power on its users, there would be far less poverty among the large numbers of L2 English speakers. Rather, the richest and most militarily powerful nation in the world – the US – happens to be home to about 75 percent of the world's *native* English speakers. Three out of the seven G7 countries – namely the US, the United Kingdom, and Canada – are predominantly L1 English-speaking countries. (The G7 stands for the 'Group of Seven' finance ministers formed in 1976, and the other countries of the group are France, Germany, Italy, and Japan.) This high correlation between economic and military power and the dominance of English plays itself out in virtually all the important sectors of international banking, finance, diplomacy, media, cinema, technology, and in publications in many fields (especially science, economics, and technology). It is an official or working language in virtually all of the major international organizations, including the United Nations, the Association of Southeast Asian Nations, the Commonwealth, the Council of Europe, the European Union, the North Atlantic Treaty Organization, the World Bank, and the International Monetary Fund. English is the only official language of the Organization of Petroleum Exporting Countries and the only working language of the European Free Trade Association (Crystal 2003: 87). But this is just the tip of the iceberg. According to Crystal (ibid., pp. 87–8), about one third of the 12,500 international organizations in the world (the number 12,500 comes from the Union of International Associations 1996) list the languages they use in an official or working capacity. Crystal took a sample of 500 from these organizations (from the beginning of the alphabet) and found that 85 per cent of them (424) made official use of English. The next most common language identified was French, which 245 countries (49 percent) used officially. Amazingly, according to Crystal, one third of the sample (169 countries) use *only* English to carry on their business. The only other languages to be used in more than 10 percent of the organizations were Arabic, Spanish, and German.

In addition to its influence in the economic and political arena, English has also had an enormous impact through media in this language (broadcast and print).

Although, according to the World Association of Newspapers in 2005, the US ranked fourth (behind China, India, and Japan) in daily newspaper circulation (48.3 million, compared to 93.5 million in China), according to a study done by Wallechinsky and colleagues (1977: 114), the top five newspapers in terms of influence on a world scale were all in English: *New York Times, Washington Post,* and *Wall Street Journal,* followed by two British newspapers, *The Times* and *The Sunday Times* (Crystal 2003: 92–3). In the area of popular culture, English has traveled to virtually every corner of the globe through music, film, sports, and entertainment. Pennycook (2007) rightly notes that English is not a monolithic language, but rather has been (and continues to be) adapted, modified, destabilized, and transformed in the many contexts of its use around the world, including in popular musical idioms such as rap and hip-hop (see for instance Pennycook 2007; the 2007 special issue of the *Journal of Language, Identity, and Education* 6(2): *Glocal Linguistic Flows: Hip-Hop Culture(s), Identities, and the Politics of Language Education*). Further, even the construct of 'world Englishes,' popularized by Kachru (1986), fails to take into account "all those other Englishes which do not fit the paradigm of an emergent national standard, and in doing so," it "falls into the trap of mapping centre linguists' images of language and the world on to the periphery" (Pennycook 2007: 22–3). Canagarajah (1999: 180) argues that Kachru's attempt to systematize the varieties of English around the world has left out "many eccentric, hybrid forms of local Englishes as too unsystematic." Yet, despite the admirable postmodern move toward deconstructing the idea that English is 'one thing' and toward repositioning its multifarious speakers as adapters, resisters, and transformers of the English imaginary (thereby mitigating the effects of English hegemony), connections of English with technology, economy, education, and culture continue to operate in their numerous diasporic and hybridic manifestations world-wide.

Even if we wish to argue that the existence of a global lingua franca (English) in fields such as science has certain advantages, it cannot be denied that the dominant status of English in scientific discourse and publication has coincided with the rise of the US as a (now solitary) superpower and with all that this entails in the economic, political, and military domains. In a detailed analysis of language use in scientific publications over the course of one century in American, German, French, and Russian bibliographies, Hamel (2007) found that, up until about 1925, German was the preferred language of scientific publications. English surpassed German around 1930 (46 percent in English versus 33 percent in German), and it gradually increased its share, so that, by 1996, 90.7 percent of scientific publications were in English, 2.1 percent were in Russian, 1.7 percent were in Japanese, 1.3 percent were in French, and 1.2 percent were in German. In an analysis of publications in several natural sciences – undertaken in 1996, adapted from Ammon (1998), and cited in Hamel (2007: 58) – the disparity between publications in English and eight other languages is even more striking. For example, 94.8 percent of all publications in physics between 1992 and 1997 were in English (the next highest language represented was Japanese, which had 1.7 percent). A similar pattern emerges with regard to publications in social sciences and humanities worldwide: between 1974 and 1995, publications in English increased from 66.6 percent to 82.5 percent, and the second most common language was French, which decreased from 6.8 percent to 5.9 percent during this period. The only 'free-market' choice available to scientists has been, essentially, to publish in English (and be read), or not to publish (or to publish in a language few people would read). To paraphrase a famous sentence by Adam Smith, markets are efficient and effective mechanisms in a context of *perfect liberty*, that is, when people have equal knowledge about their options, access to them, and the unfettered ability to fulfill their needs and human potential. If you are a scientist with limited English proficiency, your choices with regard to fulfilling your needs and desires are clearly constrained (see Flowerdew 2007; Englander 2009). If you desire to become a scientist and have no English proficiency or opportunity to acquire it, your dream will remain a dream. It is more than obvious that, with regard to many domains of human activity, some languages are far more 'equal' than others, and that the 'English market' (to take one example) is simply not available for the vast majority of the world's population as a means of social mobility beyond very restricted, (usually) local domains, if at all – even though it is estimated that one third of the world uses English in some fashion.

Spanish and English in the New World

Those who see the domination of English in academic publishing as unproblematic argue that language change, including language shift and loss, is always and everywhere natural, inevitable, and necessary, just as globalization (reflected in globalist discourse) is beneficial and necessary. However, acceptance of such a view requires us to examine what is meant by the terms 'natural,' 'inevitable,' and 'necessary.' The process of displacement of people, along with their cultures and languages, has no doubt been a feature of human society for a very long time. Yet, whereas on the subject of how various humanoid sub-groups of the genus *Homo sapiens* (Neanderthal, Cro-Magnon, and so on) succeeded each other we can only speculate – and such speculation is based mainly on the analysis of anatomical differences in fossils, for instance variation in cranium size and form, or features of the vocal tract (see Lieberman et al. 1969) – thanks to the development of vernacular literacy 700 years ago, we have written records of how, in much more recent times, certain groups of descendants from our ancestor *Homo sapiens* (and of course, their languages), *were* actually eradicated by other groups of descendants from *Homo sapiens*, as technologies of transportation and weaponry provided European explorers with the means to impose their will – and their germs – on the 'less advanced' peoples in the Americas, Africa, Oceania, and Asia. Consider the words of Christopher Columbus upon first encountering the Arawak people on October 12, 1492 (Zinn 1980: 1):

> They [...] brought us parrots and balls of cotton and spears and many other things [...] They willingly traded everything they owned [...] They do not bear arms, and

do not know them for I showed them a sword, they took it by the edge and cut themselves out of ignorance. They have no iron. Their spears are made of cane [...] They would make fine servants [...] With fifty men we could subjugate them all and make them do whatever we want.

On the grounds of his exaggerated claims and lies (including the presence of great amounts of gold in Hispaniola), Columbus was given seventeen ships and twelve hundred men for his second expedition. He and his men found no gold, so (having guns and swords, and the will to use them in the name of God and Queen), they settled for filling up their ships with Arawak men, women, and children, all to be sold as slaves in Spain (one third of the first shipment died before reaching Spain). When too many slaves died in captivity, Columbus and his men ordered all persons aged 14 or over to collect a certain amount of gold every three months. Indians who were found without a copper token around their neck which signaled that they had delivered some gold had their hands cut off, and they bled to death (Zinn 1980: 4). In two years, through murder, mutilation, or suicide, half of the 250,000 Indians on Haiti were dead. When it was clear that no gold had remained, the Indians were taken as slave labor; they were made to work at a ferocious pace on estates known as *encomiendas* and died by the thousands. By the year 1515 there were perhaps 50,000 left; by 1550 there were 5,000, and a report of the year 1650 shows that none of the original Arawaks or their descendants remained on the island (Zinn 1980: 4–5).

The story of the barbarism of Columbus was reported by the Dominican priest Bartolomé de las Casas (1971), who chronicled in lavish (and often grue-some) detail the devastation brought by the Spanish onto the Taino and Arawak peoples and their lands. He wrote that, when he arrived on Hispaniola in 1508, "there were 60,000 people living on this island, including the Indians; so that from 1494 to 1508, over three million people had perished from war, slavery, and the mines. Who in future generations will believe this? I myself writing it as a knowl-edgeable eyewitness can hardly believe it..." (cited in Zinn 1980: 7). Indeed, 450 years later, Samuel Eliot Morison, eminent Harvard historian and expert on Columbus, mentions the enslavement and killing in his 1954 book *Christopher Columbus, Mariner* – but, as Zinn points out (ibid.), he refers to this important fact only in passing, in one single sentence: "The cruel policy initiated by Columbus and pursued by his successors resulted in complete genocide" (Morison 1954: 129). Then Morison sums up his view of Columbus in the book's final paragraph (pp. 198–9):

He had his faults and his defects, but they were largely the defects of the qualities that made him great – his indomitable will, his superb faith in God and in his own mission as the Christ-bearer to lands beyond the seas, his stubborn persistence despite neglect, poverty and discouragement. But there was no flaw, no dark side to the most outstanding and essential of all his qualities – his seamanship.

The relevance of this commentary made by Morison on Columbus is to show how the ideology of globalist discourse on globalization tends to omit or trivialize the devastating facts of cultural contact initiated by those who come to be known (and to describe themselves) as history's 'winners.' The passage also requires us to ask ourselves whether this history (reproduced many times, on other continents and territories, in 'modern days') was 'inevitable,' 'natural,' and 'necessary' (see Mühlhäusler 2003), and, if so, what that might reveal about the implicit (mainstream) beliefs about human nature that attach to the ideology of globalist discourse (for instance social Darwinism).

The policies of Columbus were duplicated by other 'brave explorers' of the New World: Cortes in Mexico, Pizarro in Peru, and the English settlers in Virginia and Massachusetts (Zinn 1980: 11). What was the impact of the European conquest on the languages of North America? At the time when the Spanish arrived on the North American continent, 500 different native American languages may have been spoken by a native population of 30–40 million people (Leap 1981: 129) – a number that was reduced to 400,000 by 1920 (Molesky 1988: 37). This lowering was the result of diseases contracted from the white settlers, wars, massacres, and the ongoing encroachment of European settlers into native lands. In the 1990 census, 26 languages/language families with 1,000 or more speakers were counted (Waggoner 1993). At first, native Americans were given the 'choice' between resettling in alien territories, so as to make room for the white settlers, and facing certain slaughter. Later on they were given the 'choice' of attending government-sponsored boarding schools in order that "their barbarous dialects should be blotted out and the English language substituted" (J. D. Atkins, annual report for 1887, cited in J. Crawford 1992: 48). Punishments for native language use continued in the US into the 1940s and 1950s, and effective bilingual programs were dismantled by the Bureau of Indian Affairs, replaced by the imposition of monolingual English instruction at reservation schools, with disastrous results (Crawford 1989: 26). In the absence of this historical perspective, it may seem obvious to some that Native Americans should *want* to learn English (adapt!) and forgo the learning of their ancestral languages – because this is the 'smart thing to do,' because it is more practical, because English is the language of the workplace, and so on. By this reasoning, 'smart' laid-off auto-workers in Ohio and Michigan (partly as a result of NAFTA) would do well to learn Spanish, so as to be able to steal across the Mexican border and to find work in *maquiladoras*, earning $10 a day with no benefits – since their English (apparently) isn't helping them to find work in the US. (According to the Wikipedia, "A maquiladora or maquila is a factory that imports materials and equipment on a duty-free and tariff-free basis for assembly or manufacturing and then re-exports the assembled product, usually back to the originating country": http://en.wikipedia.org/wiki/Maquilladora.)

The fact that Columbus continues to be honored in North America with a holiday bearing his name provides powerful evidence that history is written by the victors of 'globalization.' "History," writes Henry Kissinger in his first book, *A World Restored* (1957), "is the memory of states" (cited in Zinn 1980: 9) – and, I would add, of their collective perspective on what 'counts' in terms of the relative worth of human lives, cultures, and their languages. We should never forget how both Spanish and English became the dominant languages of the Americas when we engage in academic discussions about whether or not English – or Spanish – is still an imperial or (now) a post-imperial language (see for instance Fishman et al. 1996). The most important point is that the historical record described above has largely disappeared from the dominant narratives about the origins and development of the Americas; what has come down to the present day, in mainstream accounts, is an exclusionary narrative about the 'American people,' 'American values,' the 'American ethos,' 'American ways of thinking,' and so on, which reflects a *particular* and self-serving construction of US 'Americanism' (for a fuller analysis, see Ricento 2003).

The fact that alternative, more inclusive, accounts (such as Zinn 1980) are labeled 'critical' means that these accounts are marginalized as minority, non-mainstream, or 'ideological' views. The relatively few aboriginal languages in the Americas that have survived through centuries of oppression and suppression continue to teeter on the brink of extinction, with but a few exceptions (see Ricento 1996 for data on native American languages in the US, and Ricento and Cervatiuc (2010) for data on First Nation languages in Canada). In language policy documents and in academic discourse, native American languages are often referred to as 'heritage' languages, along with other languages with long histories in North America, including Spanish, that should more accurately be called *American* languages, of equal status to that of English – if status is equated with years of presence on the North American continent (see Ricento 2005 for a discussion of 'heritage' languages in the US). This is why it has been said that 'he who controls the past controls the future, and he who controls the present controls the past.'

While there have been notable attempts to reframe the discourse of the American past and present with regard to aboriginal languages (for instance McCarty 2002), in much of the academic discourse concerned with language policy there is a tendency to operate in the present tense, without an understanding of the fact that the past continues to have an effect on the present (see Wiley 2006; Ricento 2005); the ideologies that attach to globalist discourse (described earlier) influence 'commonsense' attitudes about the nature of language(s) – that is, attitudes which regard them as commodities with relative (market) value, used by groups with relative (human) value. If languages are reduced to 'things' that can be counted and assigned a market value, then their loss can be accounted for by their (apparent) relative worth or worthlessness in defined (and highly controlled) markets. There have been a few notable attempts in the language policy literature to show how and why languages should *not* be treated as commodities; for example Grin (2006: 84) argues that "linguistic environments exhibit many forms of market failure [...] in fact it could be argued that almost every form of market failure occurs when it comes to the provision of linguistic diversity." It is for this reason, Grin argues, that states and international organizations need to work cooperatively to develop language policies which can level the playing field for speakers of minority or less powerful languages.

Comparative Case Studies

The value of any language depends on who is using it, for what purpose, and in what context. Thus English (or Spanish, Mandarin, Arabic, and so on) has high value for many people who use it (including those for whom it is a first or native language, or those for whom it is a second or third language), and less value for many others, who have limited proficiency in it or little opportunity to use it. State institutions may pay attention to languages to the extent that the latter serve to maintain or enhance the interests of powerful (usually dominant) groups in the state. It is well understood that institutions evolve, and are managed, so as to enhance and maintain the power of particular interests through various instruments of governmentality (Foucault 1991). Rose (1996) describes governmentality as an "array of *technologies of government*," which can be analyzed in terms of the various strategies, techniques, and procedures by which programs of government are enacted. States and their governments are not always successful, however, at imposing their will through overt, top-down, centralized approaches to language planning. Let us consider several examples in which the stated goals of states have *not* fully succeeded in the area of language planning; and let us consider how history and the effects of globalization continue to cast a large shadow on the attempts of newly independent states to regain their pre-imperial linguistic identities.

Blommaert (2006: 248) describes the attempt made by the Tanzanian government to establish socialist hegemony in the 1960s through the spread of Swahili – which, it was hoped, would contribute to the marginalization of English. While

> thirty years of concentrated efforts toward the goal set forth in the 1960s resulted in the generalized spread of Swahili [...] neither English nor local languages and 'impure' varieties of Swahili disappeared, and in the eyes of language planners, this meant that Tanzanians had still not fully become *Ujamaa*-socialists but still displayed adherences to bourgeois values (through English) and to pre-socialist modes of life (through local languages).

While Swahili was dominant in the political domain and in primary school education, in other domains, for instance local ones, or post-primary education, "people continued to use local languages or other newly emerged forms of communication" (Msanjila 1999, cited in Blommaert 2006: 248–9). There is no doubt that global pressures in favor of English played a role in its continued use in education. The point here is that, while states can be effective in controlling language use in some domains through governmentality, other pressures and factors may limit their control in other domains. Blommaert (2006: 249–50) uses the example of Tanzania to argue that "language policy [...] should be seen as a [...] niched *ideological* activity, necessarily encapsulated in and interacting with many others, regardless of how dominant it may seem at first sight." What is particularly interesting about the situation in Tanzania is that the hegemony of English in education persisted *even* after national independence was achieved – which indicates the enormous penetrating power associated with English in the domains of economy, politics, technology, and education beyond the borders of Tanzania.

In South Africa, as in Tanzania and other African states that achieved political independence from colonial domination, English continues to play an important role in political, cultural, and educational life because of its international power. In South Africa the use of African languages in education has a long history, "but its association with apartheid Bantu Education (BE) from the 1950s has triggered its rejection by the very ones for whom it would appear to be pedagogically beneficial" (Lafon 2008: 37). The western-style formal education introduced by Christian missionaries in the nineteenth century achieved a high level of excellence over time and, according to chief Albert Luthuli (2006: 20, cited in Lafon 2008: 37), "except in the matter of language, there was not much difference between black and white education." However, after the election of the Nationalist Party in 1948 and the imposition of BE as part of its apartheid policy, education for Africans was separated from 'mainstream' education in terms of syllabus and language (Lafon 2008: 39). The curriculum was based on the idea of "an ordained hierarchy of races," which aimed to "isolate [Africans] and convince [them] of their permanent inferiority" (Luthuli 2006: 35). As Lafon (2008: 39) puts it:

> Language was becoming a slave of politics: in 1961, the previously united language committees were split into separate boards, and the development of each language was henceforth conducted in an isolated way. The development of African languages as LoL/T [language of learning and teaching] was constrained within a pedagogy that has been characterised as 'uncreative literacy.'

For nearly fifty years, the system of racially segregated schooling widened the gap between the education of Africans and that of whites; for many Africans, BE meant inferior education and became emblematic of the apartheid regime. As a result of this history, a deeply ingrained negative attitude toward the use of African languages as a medium of instruction has developed – an attitude that persists to the present day. While the unification of the education system in 1991 extended schooling to all children and upgraded the facilities, nonetheless it developed into a bifurcated system, in which dysfunctional and impoverished schools are used by the majority of South African children and "a small number of well resourced schools [are] used by the privileged minority" (Botsis and Cronje 2006–7: 50). This bifurcated system is reflected in the school language policies (Lafon 2008: 45):

> the use of African languages as LoL/T is restricted to underprivileged schools whilst the privileged schools invariably and regardless of their population will have English (more and more rarely Afrikaans) as LoL/T. The continuing systematic association between these two parameters is crucial. The use of African languages as LoL/T is clearly construed by African parents and the public at large as embodying poor quality education.

Hence the 'rush to English' in the 1990s was not so much an aversion for instruction through the medium of African languages as it was a movement toward higher-quality education, better equipped schools, better trained teachers, and so on. More and more primary schools have moved to English as a medium of instruction, so that, by 2004, out of 25,736 South African schools in the Department of Education, only 6,542 had an African language as their primary medium of instruction, compared to 16,796 having English (cited in Lafon 2008: 46).

English represents far more than a 'language' among others in South Africa. Rather, English (through European eyes) was the vehicle through which "not only the geographical and political space of Africa […] was constructed […] but also African history, languages and traditions" (Makoni and Pennycook 2007: 4). The two authors argue that, in order truly to begin the process of decolonization, it is necessary to "disinvent" and "reconstitute" languages that were, after all, *written* and largely constructed, and even named, by Europeans. The elevation of nine African languages as official languages, alongside Afrikaans and English, in the South African Constitution (1996) must be understood within a broader historical context, in which Africa was "a continent without languages" (Samarin 1996: 390):

> Africans used language in a linguistic sense to communicate with each other, and we have learned that these are beautifully complex and awesomely elegant means of verbal expression, not the primitive jabberings that they were first taken to be. But they were not languages in the socio-cultural sense. There is little in our knowledge of Africa to suggest ethnolinguistic self consciousness. Thus we can say before literacy there were no languages.

While Europeans invented discrete 'languages' and projected them as indigenous to putative 'native speakers,' such 'languages' where often experienced as mixtures of local and foreign discourses (Makoni and Pennycook 2007: 14). "When the constructed languages were introduced into local communities they had the effects of creating, and at times, accentuating, social differences." As these languages could only be acquired through formal education, "those who acquired them tended to have higher social status" (ibid.). Makoni and Pennycook show similar patterns of construction, followed by social hierarchization, with other languages, for example Fijian, Yoruba, or Tagalog. The attempt to give equal status to African languages, to English, and to Afrikaans (RSA Constitution 1996) perpetuates an idea of 'language' which is based on the western construct of discrete scripts, sound systems, and lexical systems. As Makoni and Pennycook point out: "By rendering diversity a quantitative question of language enumeration, such approaches continue to employ the census strategies of colonialism while missing the qualitative question of where diversity lies" (ibid., p. 16).

A final example concerns the contemporary roles of English on the Indian subcontinent. The English language assumed a pivotal position during the Raj in India (1858–1947). It separated British rulers from their subjects, but also Indians who spoke English from those who did not. This legacy – of a division between Indians who speak, and are educated in and through, English, and Indians who are educated in vernacular languages – persists to the present day in Indian society. According to Crystal (2003), on the basis of data from the 2001 census, only one third of 1 percent of the Indian population are L1 English speakers (that is, 350,000 people out of a total population of 1,029,991,000), while 200,000,000 Indians, a number which represents about 20 percent of the total population, use English as a second language. Yet, even though English is clearly a minority language throughout India, those who are educated in it from primary school have a decisive advantage over those who are educated through the medium of the local vernacular language. This is because the prestigious science-based disciplines at the tertiary level, such as computer science, engineering, the hard sciences, pharmacy, and medicine tend to be available only in English. The English proficiency of students educated through schooling in the vernacular is generally deficient at the level of high-school completion, which prevents these students from entering such professions (Ramanathan 2005: 6). Ramanathan concludes that,

> by validating the role of English as much as it does at the tertiary realm and beyond, the general socio-educational apparatus is also simultaneously sending out implicit messages about the generally low regard it has for the Vernaculars both within the apparatus as a medium of instruction and in the larger social world to which the apparatus is inextricably tied. (Ibid., p. 35)

There is a clear association between social class and medium of instruction: students schooled in the vernacular in the K-12 years are typically lower-income children, while English-medium instructed children tend to be middle class and have access to better higher education and careers. Thus, as we saw was the case in South Africa, English is associated with higher socio-economic status and a better life, while vernacular languages are devalued – even though all K-12 students in India have the option of being educated either in one of India's fifteen nationally recognized languages or in English (Gupta et al. 1995; Pattanayak 1981). Thus the English–vernacular divide helps to maintain the class structure in India more than sixty years after India gained independence from British rule.

Globalization and Language Policies: Paradoxes and Possibilities

In considering the complex relations between language policies and globalization, I have shown the various roles that English has played as an imperial, national, and indigenized language in North America, Africa, and the Indian subcontinent, especially during the post-World War II period. In all of these settings, English has enjoyed a privileged status vis-à-vis other languages, whether in the US, UK, Canada, Australia, and New Zealand, where it is a majority language, a national language, or a first/native language, or in South Africa, Tanzania, and India, where it is a minority language with special status. While English is not the only imperial language that continues to exert influence in Africa and elsewhere, it is, world-wide, the imperial language that has gained by far the largest number of users as a second or foreign language. From a global perspective, the number of people who use English as their first or native language is decreasing, while the number of people who use it as a second or third language for various purposes – in local, translocal, or transnational contexts – is increasing. Scholars who study English through the lens of cultural studies demonstrate the ways in which English has been taken up, transformed, and incorporated, together with local languages, into the lyrics of popular musical forms such as rap and hip-hop (Pennycook 2007). While to 'use English' may mean many things, "to have a command of English sufficient to rap in the language may, in some contexts, imply a very particular class background" (Pennycook 2007: 113).

We have seen how in schooling, at the K-12 and tertiary level, proficiency in English serves as a gatekeeper and marker of socio-economic class, not only in developing countries but also in industrialized countries of Asia and Europe. This is particularly the case in the 'hard' sciences, economics, business, and technology. When physicians trained in English interact with non-English speaking patients, the resulting miscommunication can have lethal consequences. In a study of communication between patients, nurses, and physicians in Cape Town, South Africa, A. Crawford (1999: 29) found that "it is not possible to isolate the patient disempowered in terms of the language barrier from the whole biomedical discourse in which patients occupy a disempowered position." The problem in South Africa stems from wide divisions based on social class, race, and gender as much as it stems from language. As was discussed earlier, in South Africa, English as a medium of education is associated with relative economic privilege, while an education delivered through the medium of an African language is usually reserved for the underprivileged. The relatively lower status of African languages harkens back to conditions during apartheid, when Bantu education was institutionalized to maintain racial (and linguistic) segregation. However, despite the ongoing attempts to elevate the status of African languages, most notably by enshrining nine African languages as co-equal official languages, with English and Afrikaans, in the South African Constitution, the legacy of English in South Africa (which pre-dates official apartheid), combined with the perceived benefits of learning English as a language of wider communication, tends to sustain the appeal – and power – of English in contemporary society.

The perception that English is *the* global language will probably continue as long as American economic and military power remain strong in relation to the other powerful economic blocs in Europe and Asia; the benefits of communicating in English will continue to accrue disproportionately for those who have access to education in English at the secondary and tertiary level. For the most part, the notion that a world connected through a common language might foster common understanding and facilitate broad-based cooperation among states, that it would help to reduce the gap between its 'haves' and 'have-nots,' that it would reduce the conflict between states – or between ethnolinguistic groups within states – has not been demonstrated. That this is so should not be surprising, if we consider the disconnect between the rhetorical promise of the globalist discourse, dominant in the US and in other wealthy states, and the actual policies and practices of these states, which are designed to benefit the few at the expense of the many, including in those wealthy states themselves. A common global language does not entail common values or beliefs, not to mention lending itself to the promotion of progressive values of social justice and equal economic opportunity; to understand the nature and effects of power, we need to investigate the ways in which neo-liberal values and beliefs are instantiated, taken up, and rendered influential *through* language as reflected in societal discourses, and especially in the dominant institutional discourses within a society. As Norman Fairclough has ably demonstrated in *Language and Globalization* (2006), the critical analysis of texts can be integrated within a political and economic analysis of globalization to show how the (self)-promotion of the economic and political interests of liberal democracies is falsely portrayed as universally beneficial in everyday mainstream media and official political discourse. In order to begin to diminish the pernicious effects of state capitalism on the lives of billions of people in less developed countries, we need first to understand how the interests of large globalized corporations and banks, already protected and promoted by international organizations such as the World Bank and the International Monetary Fund, are also supported and promoted by the neo-liberal mainstream media in wealthy nations. The findings of critical discourse analysis, combined with a critical examination of the real economic effects of globalization, can help us to understand better why the gap between the richest and the poorest countries continues to grow despite claims from proponents of 'globalist discourse' that globalization is the best means available to alleviate poverty around the world.

REFERENCES

Ammon, U. (1998) *Ist Deutsch noch internationale Wissenschaftssprache? Englisch auch für die lehre an den deutschsprachigen Hochschulen.* Berlin: Mouton de Gruyter.

Barlow, M., and Clarke, T. (1998) *MAI (the Multilateral Agreement on Investment) and the Threat to American Freedom.* New York: Stoddart.

Botsis, H., and Cronje, F. (2006–7) *Education.* 2006/2007 South African survey. South African Institute of Race Relations, Human Sciences Research Council.

Blommaert, J. (2006) Language policy and national identity. In T. Ricento (ed.), 238–54.

Brutt-Griffler, J. (2002) *World English: A Study of Its Development.* Clevedon: Multilingual Matters.

Canagarajah, A. S. (1999) *Resisting Linguistic Imperialism in English Teaching.* New York: Oxford University Press.

Crawford, A. (1992) "We can't all understand the whites' language": An analysis of monolingual health services in a multilingual society. *International Journal of the Sociology of Language* 136: 27–45.

Crawford, J. (1989) *Bilingual Education: History, Politics, Theory and Practice.* Trenton, NJ: Crane Publishing Co.

Crawford, J. (ed.) (1992) *Language Loyalties: A Source Book on the Official English*

Controversy. Chicago: University of Chicago Press.

Crystal, D. (2003) *English as a Global Language*. Cambridge: Cambridge University Press.

de las Casas, B. (1971) *History of the Indies*. New York: Harper and Row.

Englander, K. (2009) Transformation of the identities of non-native English-speaking scientists as a consequence of the social construction of revision. *Journal of Language, Identity, and Education* 8: 35–53.

Fairclough, N. (2006) *Language and Globalization*. Abingdon and New York: Routledge.

Fishman, J. A., Conrad, A., and Rubal-Lopez, A. (eds) (1996) *Post-Imperial English: Status Change in Former British and American Colonies, 1940–1990*. Berlin: Mouton de Gruyter.

Flowerdew, J. (2007) The non-anglophone scholar on the periphery of scholarly publication. *AILA Review* 20: 14–27.

Foucault, M. (1991) Governmentality. In G. Burchell, C. Gordon, and P. Miller (eds), *The Foucault Effect: Studies in Governmentality*, 87–104. Chicago: University of Chicago Press.

Graddol, D. (1999) The decline of the native speaker. *AILA Review*, 13: 57–68.

Grin, F. (2006) Economic considerations in language policy. In T. Ricento (ed.), 77–94.

Gupta, R., Abbi, A., and Agarwal, K. (eds) (1995) *Language and the State: Perspectives on the Eighth Schedule*. New Delhi: Creative Books.

Hamel, R. E. (2007) The dominance of English in the international scientific periodical literature and the future of language use in science. *AILA Review* 20: 53–71.

Held, D., McGrew, A., Goldblatt, D., and Perraton, J. (1999) *Global Transformations: Politics, Economics and Culture*. Cambridge: Polity.

Kachru, B. (1986) *The Alchemy of English*. Oxford: Pergamon.

Lafon, M. (2008) Asikhulume! African languages for all, a powerful strategy for spearheading transformation and improvement of the South African education system. In *Les Nouveaux Cahiers de L'IFAS. IFAS Working Paper* 11, Chapter 3. Available at: http://www.africavenir.com/publications/occasional-papers/LAFON_asikhulume.pdf.

Leap, W. L. (1981) American Indian languages. In C. A. Ferguson and S. B. Heath (eds), *Language in the USA*, 116–44. Cambridge: Cambridge University Press.

Lieberman, P. H., Klatt, D. H., and Wilson, W. H. (1969) Vocal tract limitations on the vowel repertoires of the rhesus monkey and other non human primates. *Science* 164: 1185–7.

Luthuli, A. (2006) *Let My People Go: The Autobiography of Albert Luthuli*. Cape Town: Tafelberg.

Makoni, S., and Pennycook, A. (2007) Disinventing and reconstituting languages. In S. Makoni and A. Pennycook (eds), *Disinventing and Reconstituting Languages*, 1–41. Clevedon: Multilingual Matters.

McCarty, T. (2002) *A Place to Be Navajo: Rough Rock and the Struggle for Self-Determination in Indigenous Schooling*. Mahwah, NJ: Lawrence Erlbaum.

Mitchell, P. R., and Schoeffel, J. (eds) (2002) *Understanding Power: The Indispensable Chomsky*. New York: New Press.

Molesky, J. (1988) Understanding the American linguistic mosaic: A historical overview of language maintenance and language shift. In S. L. McKay and S. C. Wong (eds), *Language Diversity: Problem or Resource*, 29–68. Boston, MA: Heinle and Heinle.

Morison, S. E. (1955) *Christopher Columbus, Mariner*. Boston: Little, Brown and Company.

Msanjila, Y. (1999) The use of Kiswahili in rural areas and its implications for the future of ethnic languages in Tanzania. Doctoral dissertation, University of Dar es Salaam, Tanzania.

Mühlhäusler, P. (2003) English as an exotic language. In C. Mair (ed.), *The Politics of English as a World Language*, 67–86. Amsterdam: Rodopi.

Pattanayak, D. P. (1981) *Multilingualism and Mother-Tongue Education*. Bombay: Oxford University Press.

Pennycook, A. (2007) *Global Englishes and Transcultural Flows*. Oxford: Routledge.

Ramanathan, V. (2005) *The English– Vernacular Divide: Postcolonial Language Politics and Practice*. Clevedon: Multilingual Matters.

Ricento, T. (1996) Language policy in the United States. In M. Herriman and B. Burnaby (eds), *Language Policies in English-Dominant Countries*, 122–58. Clevedon: Multilingual Matters.

Ricento, T. (2003) The discursive construction of Americanism. *Discourse and Society* 14: 611–37.

Ricento, T. (2005) Problems with the 'language-as-resource' discourse in the promotion of heritage languages in the USA. *Journal of Sociolinguistics* 9: 348–68.

Ricento, T. (ed.) (2006) *An Introduction to Language Policy: Theory and Method*. Malden, MA: Blackwell.

Ricento, T., and Cervatiuc, A. (2010) Language minority rights and educational policy in Canada. In J. Petrovic (ed.), *International Perspectives on Bilingual Education: Policy, Practice,*

Controversy, 21–42. Charlotte, NC: Information Age Publishing.

Rose, N. (1996) Governing 'advanced' liberal democracies. In A. Barry, T. Osborne, and N. Rose (eds), *Foucault and Political Reason: Liberalism, Neo-Liberalism and Rationalities of Government*, 37–64. London: UCL Press.

Samarin, W. (1996) Review of Adegbija Efurosibina: Language attitudes in Sub-Saharan Africa: A sociolinguistic overview. *Anthropological Linguistics* 38: 389–95.

Scheuerman, W. (2008) Globalization. In E. N. Zalta (ed.), *The Stanford Encyclopedia of Philosophy*. Available at: <http://plato. stanford.edu/archives/fall2008/entries/ globalization/>.

Steger, M. (2005) *Globalism: Market Ideology Meets Terrorism*. Lanham: Rowman and Littlefield.

Waggoner, D. (1993) Navajo dominant among Native American languages spoken by 331,600. In D. Waggoner (ed.), *Numbers and Needs: Ethnic and Linguistic Minorities in the United States*, Vol. 3, no. 5, p. 2. Washington, DC.

Wallechinsky, D., Wallace, I., and Wallace, A. (eds) (1977) *The Book of Lists*. London: Cassell.

Wiley, T. G. (2006) The lessons of historical investigation: Implications for the study of language policy and planning. In T. Ricento (ed.), 135–52.

Zinn, H. (1980) *A People's History of the United States*. New York: Harper and Row.

6 Panlingual Globalization

JONATHAN POOL

Predicting Unilingual Globalization

The complex relationship between globalization and linguistic diversity (Mufwene 2004) makes it difficult to predict the changes in the distribution of languages that will accompany future advances in world social integration. Figure 6.1 shows one highly simplified idea of their relationship. Here progress in information and communication technology (ICT) is modeled as promoting global interactivity among communities, and this in turn encourages shifts from low-density (smaller and less resource-endowed) second and native languages to high-density ones. This causal relationship would make one expect a decline in linguistic diversity as globalization proceeds. However, the same technological progress facilitates the development of tools and resources usable for the maintenance and cultivation of low-density languages and the creation of viable communities out of linguistic diasporas. Such progress could allow linguistic diversity and globalization to thrive together.

If globalization can both promote and diminish linguistic diversity as shown in Figure 6.1, the net impact of globalization may depend on human motivations. The more the world's population wants to participate in linguistic diversity and the more the native speakers of low-density languages want to maintain and transmit them, the more they will exploit ICT for these purposes, and thus the more directly globalization and linguistic diversity will co-vary.

Most of the evidence seems to predict an inverse relationship, because linguistic diversity, maintenance, and revitalization are not generally popular ideals. Low-density languages throughout the world have been dying, only rarely showing resistance (UNESCO 2003: 2–4). Typically, parents do not demand that these languages be transmitted to their children; children do not insist on learning them; and schools do not require pupils to learn them. Often speakers of low-density languages even try to prevent their children from learning and using them, in part because they are under the influence of denigrating opinions held by outsiders

The Handbook of Language and Globalization, First Edition. Edited by Nikolas Coupland.
© 2013 Blackwell Publishing Ltd except for editorial material and organization © 2013 Nikolas Coupland. Published 2013 by Blackwell Publishing Ltd.

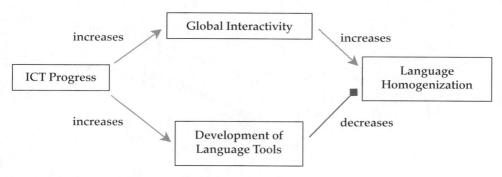

Figure 6.1   Globalization and unilingualization. Created by author

(Eidheim 1969; Harrison 2007). The world's population, as a whole, treats low-density languages as inferior, or at best superfluous (Crystal 2000: 27). People decide, given this opinion, that assimilation within and across generations to high-density languages confers net benefits on those who assimilate, if the cost of assimilation is not excessive. Globalization decreases that cost by creating opportunities for immersive learning of high-density languages. These combined forces have led to predictions that something between half and 90 percent of the world's living languages will die within the next century (Woodbury 2006; UNESCO 2003: 2). Weaker forms of these forces appear to be reducing the use of medium-density languages in science, diplomacy, business, and other domains (Phillipson 2008).

Even if linguistic diversity became much more popular, this change might not suffice to produce a positive globalization–diversity relationship. Suppose that, in general, any benefits conferred by linguistic diversity were dispersed, but all its costs were imposed on those who maintain low-density languages. In other words, suppose that the choice whether to learn, use, document, and enrich low-density languages took the form of a collective action dilemma, each native speaker of such a language finding himself/herself in a situation modeled by Figure 6.2 (see De Swaan 2004: 579). In this dilemma, if everybody cultivates the language everybody is at A, and if nobody does so everybody is at C. Everybody prefers A to C. But any individual at A can reach B, thus enjoying increased benefits, by defecting (not cultivating). If all individuals yielded to that incentive, the outcome would change and everybody would be at C. The language would probably atrophy and die.

Strategies for Panlingual Globalization

Those who reluctantly predict linguistic homogenization accompanying globalization need not simply despair; they can try to render their prediction false. Consider the following examples of action strategies.

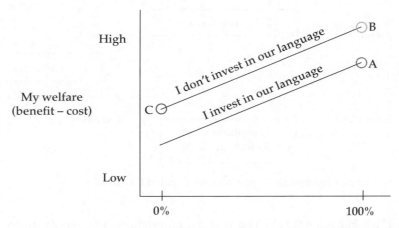

High

My welfare
(benefit – cost)

Low

0%   100%

Fraction of other speakers of our language investing in it

Figure 6.2   Low-density language dilemma. Created by author

Strategy 1: Marketing multilingualism

Persuade the world's population that the existence of about 7,000 languages (Gordon 2005) is a boon rather than a curse. This is the strategy attempted by Nettle and Romaine (2000), Crystal (2000), Abley (2003), and Harrison (2007). When languages die, they argue, the world loses:

1 irreplaceable knowledge of history, medicine, nature, and productive methods encoded in languages' lexicons;
2 evidence for the scientific understanding of language and the human mind;
3 diverse ideas arising from languages' differing systems of knowledge representation; and
4 the respect, tolerance, sophistication, and enjoyment that develop (or could develop) from people learning to live in a multilingual world.

They further argue that cultural and biological diversity and diverse identities, all of which are already widely appreciated, depend on linguistic diversity, which should therefore be valued for its effects even by those who do not value it intrinsically.

This strategy, if effective, would make the world want linguistic diversity; but that want would not by itself stop the erosion of linguistic diversity. An increased popular appreciation of linguistic diversity might merely make the slopes in Figure 6.2 steeper, as in Figure 6.3. In this case the predicted (equilibrium) outcome would be the same, and overcoming the dilemma would require additional strategies.

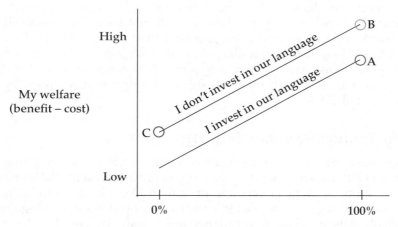

Figure 6.3 Low-density language dilemma with diversity popular. Created by author

Strategy 2: Ecolinguistic compensation

Design mechanisms to internalize the benefits of low-density language cultivation. This strategy would give financial support to those who keep their native languages alive and vibrant. The world could absorb the costs of the analysis, documentation, instruction, and other activities that the cultivators require (UNESCO 2003). Beyond that, the world could treat active native speakers of low-density languages as service providers and pay them compensation.

Consider a numerical example. Suppose that keeping the 5,000 lowest-density languages alive and vigorous costs $5,000,000,000 per year ($1,000,000 per language per year) and yields benefits (knowledge, identity, tolerance, and so on) worth $30,000,000,000 per year (1/20 of 1 percent of the gross world product). If the native speakers of those languages total 1,000 persons each, or 5,000,000 altogether (a plausible estimate, given that only about 400 languages have 10,000 speakers or more), then each native speaker incurs a cost, on average, of $1,000 per year. Let us assume that they have no special affection for their native language, so they share the benefits of their cultivation equally with all the others in the world. If so, the annual benefit enjoyed by each native speaker is $5 ($30,000,000,000, split among the 6,000,000,000 persons in the world).

In this example, without a subsidy, native speakers who cultivated a low-density language would incur a cost of $1,000 for a benefit of $5 annually. An ecolinguistic compensation policy could pay the maintainers of a low-density language $2,000 per year each. This would give them 200 percent returns on their investments, while still leaving the rest of the world with a $20,000,000,000 annual net benefit ($30,000,000,000 in gross benefit, minus $10,000,000,000 in compensation costs).

Compensation mechanisms have been analyzed as a means of making dominant languages more equitable for those who do not speak them natively (Van Parijs 2007) and of making official-language policies fair and efficient (Pool 1991; Ammon 2006: 333–6). A close parallel is that of ecological compensation mechanisms (also known as payments for environmental services, or markets in biodiversity services); these have been in use for about thirty years (Ferraro and Kiss 2002; Jenkins et al. 2004).

Strategy 3: Linguistic subsidiarity

Reorganize social life to make linguistic communities more self-governing and socioeconomically autonomous. This strategy would aim to make the world more like a community of language communities than like a community of nation–states, territories, religions, ideologies, or other subpopulations. A self-governing and internally cohesive low-density language community could make its language official and treat it as the main medium of education, commerce, publication, and other social interaction, more easily than is possible where the language is merely that of a minority. With the progress of telecommunications, non-contiguous communities such as those formed by linguistic diasporas become more feasible. The strategy would not only make jurisdictional and transactional boundaries more coincident with language boundaries, but also, as proposed by Bastardas (2002), transfer authority from world bodies to single-language local units of government as much as is practical (the subsidiarity principle), thereby making the languages of those units useful and used. According to Mufwene (2002), utilization, particularly in a person's work, is the critically necessary condition for the survival of a low-density language.

Strategy 4: Panlingual transparency

Create language processing systems that automatically translate utterances among all the languages of the world. This strategy would attempt to produce a real-world counterpart to the fictional "Babel fish" of Adams (1979: 51–2). Such systems would allow anybody who knows any language to understand thoughts and emotions expressed in any other language. In this situation, the incentives for assimilation to high-density languages would be diminished, with the amount of diminution depending on the quality of the translation.

Research and development in machine translation have been active for about half a century (Hutchins 2006; Trujillo 1999), the goal almost always being to translate between particular pairs or small sets of (generally high-density) languages. A few systems under current development apply to larger sets of languages, but never to more than about 50 (see for example http://translate.google.com; http://www.langtolang.com).

Attempts to realize panlingual – or even massively multilingual – translation have mostly involved human effort rather than automatic processing; these projects have mainly focused on particular bodies of text, such as the Universal

Declaration of Human Rights (UDHR 2008), and the user interfaces of particular computer application programs, such as search engines (for instance http://www.google.com/support/bin/static.py?page=searchguides.html&ctx=preferences&hl=en#searchlang). However, some approaches to language modeling, including machine-translation interlinguas (Schubert 1992; Dorr et al. 2006) and typological grammar engineering (Bender and Flickinger 2005), might make automatic translation efficiently extensible to any number of languages.

As these four strategies illustrate, panlingual globalization might be pursued in radically diverse ways (see Fettes 2003; Tonkin 2003). At their simplest, Strategy 1 is cultural, Strategy 2 is economic, Strategy 3 is political, and Strategy 4 is technological. It is plausible that the most effective approach to panlingual globalization would combine these and other strategies, rather than relying on only one.

Engineering Panlingual Globalization

Any strategy for panlingual globalization is likely to arouse doubts because it aims at an outcome which was never experienced and is far from current reality. For example:

1   How could the world be persuaded to value linguistic diversity highly?

2   If ecolinguistic compensation were paid, how could one know who is eligible for the payments and how much to pay each of them?

3   Aren't there far too many entrenched interests aligned with existing jurisdictional boundaries to make linguistic subsidiarity achievable?

4   Don't the still laughable automatic translations between high-density languages, after half a century of effort, show that panlingual translation is simply too difficult?

5   More fundamentally, might efforts to preserve low-density languages inadvertently devalue medium-density ones and thereby hasten global unilingualism (De Swaan 2004)?

To best evaluate these doubts, one can attempt to implement each strategy. This brings us from the stage of envisioning panlingual globalization to the stage of engineering it. The following discussion will focus on an actual attempt to begin engineering panlingual transparency (Strategy 4).

In late 2006, the University of Washington's Turing Center (http://turing.cs.washington.edu), with the support and collaboration of Utilika Foundation (http://utilika.org), began investigating the possibility of translation among thousands of languages. Even though, as mentioned above, existing automatic translation systems are limited to about 1 percent of the world's languages, they have produced results far inferior to expert human translations. As one example, consider the translations of an English sentence into French produced by nine systems currently offered to the public, shown in table 6.1. Ambiguities like those involved

Table 6.1 Automatic translations from English into French. Created by author

Role	Text
Source	Both speakers stopped talking after the warning light went on
Target, PITS (http://translation2. paralink.com)	Les deux speakers ont arrêté de parler après que la lumière d'avertissement a continué
Target, SYSTRANet (http://www. systranet.com)	Les deux haut-parleurs ont cessé de parler après que le voyant d'alarme se soit allumé
Target, Babylon Online Translator (http://translation.babylon.com)	Les deux orateurs ont cessé de parler après le voyant s'est passé
Target, Live Search Translator (http://microsofttranslator.com)	Les deux orateurs cessé de parler après que le voyant d'avertissement a
Target, Google Translate (http:// translate.google.com)	Les deux intervenants ont cessé de parler après le voyant d'alerte s'est passé
Target, PROMT Translator (http:// www.online-translator.com)	Les deux orateurs ont arrêté de parler après que la lumière d'avertissement a continué
Target, SDL FreeTranslation.com (http://ets.freetranslation.com)	Les deux orateurs ont arrêté de parler après que la lumière d'avertissement a continué
Target, Reverso Translation (http://www.reverso.net)	Les deux orateurs(locuteurs) ont arrêté de parler après que le témoin lumineux a continué
Target, InterTran (http://www. tranexp.com:2000/Translate/ result.shtml)	Tous les deux interlocuteurs arrêtions parler à la suite les voyant lumineux êtes allé one

in 'speaker' and 'go on,' which human translators easily resolve, often defeat machines. (French *haut-parleurs* refers to amplifying devices. French *a continué* and *s'est passé* can be translated 'went on,' but this sense is not applicable here.) If automatic translation is difficult for the most richly endowed languages, there is reason to be pessimistic about automatic translation from every language into every other language.

After investigating some alternatives, the Turing Center researchers concluded that they could design a system to perform one type of translation more or less panlingually: lexical translation. The system would translate lexemes, the elements of the lexicons (vocabularies) of languages. For example, the system would not translate "Both speakers stopped talking after the warning light went on."

Instead it would translate the lexemes "both," "speaker," "stop," "talk," "after," "the," "warn," "light," "go," and "on." It might also translate "warning," "warning light," and "go on," since they, too, may be considered lexemes (they may appear as entries in dictionaries).

This project of panlingual lexical translation (PanLex) was massively multilingual from the beginning and is rapidly extensible to cover all languages (being limited only by the available data). In compensation, PanLex translates lexemes and makes no attempt to translate sentences, paragraphs, or longer discourses. We might describe it as initially wide but shallow; most translation systems, by contrast, begin deep but narrow. Other systems may be asked, "You don't cover my language, so what good can you do for me?"; PanLex may be asked, "You cover my language, but you translate only lexemes, so what good does that do for me?"

The hypothesis underlying PanLex was that lexical translation is more useful than one might imagine. Some utterance types often consist merely of sequences of lexemes. Web search queries, library-style subject headings, entries in book indices, user-interface labels ('copy,' 'undo,' and the like), social tags on the Web, list entries (places, events, hobbies, interests, etc.), weather-forecast summaries, telegrams, SMS text messages, baby talk, and foreigner talk are among them. Moreover, utterances that generally contain morphology and syntax may be converted to sequences of lexemes, and the sequence and context may make them fully or partly intelligible. Grammatically conveyed information, such as time, number, illocutionary force, or evidentiality, may be expressed with lexemes (such as 'yesterday,' 'many,' 'question,' or 'allegedly'), and, if not so expressed, may still be successfully inferred. Even in situations where purely lexical translation is insufficient, it may be easily and inexpensively supplemented; this would result in a family of equivalent controlled languages (Pool 2006) with minimalistic syntax, which would avoid the structural ambiguities of natural languages. For example, communicators might supplement 'man, bite, dog' with annotations to specify which of the verb's arguments is the agent and whether the statement is an assertion, a question, or a recommendation. The idea that simple annotation techniques may have great expressive power is akin to one of the assumptions of the Semantic Web Initiative (Berners-Lee et al. 2001): that human communication references massive numbers of things, but only a few relationships among those things.

PanLex draws on various lexical resources, including dictionaries, wiktionaries, glossaries, lexicons, word lists, terminologies, thesauri, wordnets, ontologies, vocabulary databases, named-entity resources, and standards. Despite their different names and formats, they all assert facts of the type "Lexemes A, B, C, … , and N share at least one meaning common to them all." The fact that they share a meaning makes them synonyms if they belong to the same language, or translations if they belong to different languages.

There are thousands of these resources in existence, and they report the equivalences of millions of lexemes in thousands of languages. One of the first resources usually bestowed on any low-density language is a dictionary or word list. Such

Figure 6.4   Simple lexical resource. Source: http://www.erlang.com.ru/euskara/ ?basque. Author: Kirill Panfilov. © Erlang. Data retrieved 26 January 2010. Used with permission

a resource usually translates between that language and some higher-density language, such as English, French, Spanish, Russian, German, Hindi, or Tok Pisin. However, any arbitrary pair or larger set of languages might be covered. For example there are resources linking Greek with Catalan, Nepali with Esperanto, and Turkish with Azerbaijani. About 300 multilingual resources are being developed in the Wiktionary project (Wikimedia Foundation 2008); each wiktionary has a single source language and translates lexemes into an unlimited set of other languages. There are also specialized resources, sometimes organized as thesauri with taxonomies of meanings expressed in multiple languages; one example is the Food and Agriculture Organization's thesaurus (FAO 2008), which expresses about 28,000 meanings related to agriculture and nutrition in Arabic, Czech, Mandarin, German, English, French, Hindi, Hungarian, Italian, Japanese, Lao, Western Farsi, Polish, Portuguese, Slovak, Spanish, and Thai. Finally, there are monolingual resources (thesauri and wordnets) that identify synonyms.

PanLex defines concepts pragmatically. When a resource asserts that some lexemes share a meaning, PanLex assigns a new identifier to that meaning, leaving for later the question whether it is the same meaning as any meaning from any other resource. The simplest bilingual word lists, such as the one shown in Figure 6.4, give no information about a lexeme except its lemma (its dictionary or citation form). PanLex accordingly treats a lemma in a language as a lexeme. While some other systems might analyze English 'tear' (eye water) as one lexeme and 'tear' (rip) as another, PanLex treats 'tear' as a single lexeme. More complex resources, like the one shown in Figure 6.5, provide additional facts about lexemes and meanings. PanLex recognizes four fact types that often appear in complex lexical

پاتا pātā

پاتا pātā, s.f. (6th) The funeral service (from A فاتحه) (E.) Sing. and Pl.; (W.) Pl. پاتاوی pātāwī. پاتا کول pātā kawul, or پاتا ویل pātā wa-yal, verb trans. To offer up prayers for the dead, to perform the funeral service, to make an exordium.

Figure 6.5 Complex lexical resource. Source: Digital South Asia Library. Author: Henry George Raverty, in *A Dictionary of the Puk'hto, Pus'hto, or Language of the Afghans: With Remarks on the Originality of the Language, and Its Affinity to Other Oriental Tongues* (Williams and Norgate, 1867, p. 146). Used with permission

resources: definition, domain, meaning identifier, and word class. It also recognizes a generic fact type, which consists of an arbitrary attribute–value pair. This can be used for otherwise unrecognized facts such as etymology, argument frame, register, and usage.

PanLex recognizes a range of language varieties. Most are ordinary natural languages, such as Burmese and Zulu, but the system can accommodate ethnic dialects, controlled natural languages (Pool 2006), artificial languages (Blanke 1989; Libert 2000 and 2003), and the controlled vocabularies embodied in standards. For example, the ISO 639 standard (SIL 2008) is treated as a language variety in PanLex. This standard identifies nearly 8,000 three-letter codes to represent the human languages of the world; each code is a lexeme in the ISO 639 language variety.

Logically, the main facts recorded by PanLex are assignments of meanings to lexemes. These facts, called 'denotations' in the PanLex terminology, take the form "authority A asserts that lexeme L has meaning M." From two or more denotations, one can derive assertions about translations and synonyms. If some authority says that lexeme A has meaning X and also says that lexeme B has meaning X, then that authority considers A and B to be translations or synonyms. The entire collection of the denotations can be interpreted geometrically or tabularly. Geometrically, it has the logical form of an undirected graph, as in Figure 6.6. The graph contains nodes (points) of two types: lexemes and meanings. Edges (lines) represent denotations; each edge connects one lexeme node with one meaning node. If a resource asserts a fact about translations or synonyms, the fact is

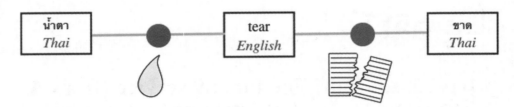

Figure 6.6   Graphical interpretation of denotations. Created by author

Table 6.2   Tabular interpretation of denotations. Created by author

Meaning	Language	Lexeme
1	English	tear
1	Thai	น้ำตา
2	English	tear
2	Thai	ขาด

represented as a single meaning node connected to two or more lexeme nodes. Tabularly, the collection of denotations can be viewed as a three-column table, as in table 6.2, with each row representing a denotation. An asserted translation or synonymy is represented as two or more rows with the same meaning and distinct lexemes. The denotations are actually stored in a relational database, so that users can efficiently use the system as a translation engine.

Prototypes, Experiments, and Results

In the effort to make PanLex a useful system, its developers have faced three principal challenges.

The *first challenge* has been to collect enough lexical facts from enough language varieties to make PanLex realistically large. About 600 lexical resources have been consulted to date. Although these resources are in machine-readable form, most were created for human readers and rely on the readers' knowledge and intuitions. For example, dictionaries commonly use symbols such as '~' to indicate that a part or all of a headword is to be repeated, but the repeated item may vary irregularly. Translations into phrases containing commas, such as 'there, there,' are often intermixed in the same resource with translations into multiple synonymous expressions, such as 'often, frequently,' and with translations into disjunctions with shared constituents, such as 'soccer, football field.' Resources are often constructed over many years, and formats change while the work is in progress.

Multilingual resources are often collaborations among teams or persons who follow different conventions of punctuation, capitalization, and orthography. Moreover, a world-wide conversion of character encoding from multiple conflicting systems to a single coherent standard, Unicode (Unicode 2007), has been in progress since 1991, but many digitized resources remain encoded under pre-Unicode standards, some of them poorly defined. Finally, even resources that are consistently organized and well encoded exhibit incompatibilities, for instance in diacritical marks and in other aspects of spelling. Automatically combining facts attested by multiple resources requires that, if two facts refer to the same lexeme, the lexeme be identifiable as the same. All of these problems require that extensive normalization be performed on data contributed by resources.

Notwithstanding these obstacles, as of April 2009 (about 2.5 years after the project was launched), the database contains about 27,400,000 denotations. They assign, in total, about 10,100,000 meanings to about 12,300,000 lexemes in about 1,300 language varieties. On the basis of these facts it is possible to perform about 204,500,000 different translations (102,200,000 pairs of lexemes, each translatable in both directions). Here 'translations' include intralingual translations ("Lexeme B is a synonym of lexeme A"), which constitute about 5 percent of the total.

The *second challenge* has been to fill gaps in the data with artificial intelligence. The data provide only a small fraction of the translations that users might want, even among the lexemes already in the database. To get translations from any lexeme into any language variety, users require not only attested facts, but also automated inference from those facts. Consider the case in which somebody wants to translate the Icelandic word '*hnappur*' into Arabic (Figure 6.7). The database currently assigns three meanings to '*hnappur*'; there are other denotations assigning one or more of these meanings to nine other lexemes, but none of those lexemes is in Arabic. So, without automated inference, the system cannot translate '*hnappur*' into Arabic. Simple two-hop translation, namely translation with only one intermediate lexeme, is one kind of inference, though it is susceptible to errors. We reach five Arabic lexemes by translating in two hops from '*hnappur*.' The gray disks in Figure 6.7 represent meanings, and the letters labeling them represent lexical resources. Thus, in this example there are five resources participating in two-hop translations from '*hnappur*' into Arabic. We are translating through some ambiguous lexemes such as 'stud,' 'key,' and '*touche*,' and nothing guarantees that the meanings they share with '*hnappur*' are equivalent to the meanings they share with Arabic lexemes. But some of the Arabic lexemes have more connections to '*hnappur*' than others do, and inference routines invented at the Turing Center use such path redundancy as evidence of validity. Three-hop connections provide even more evidence. For example, Esperanto '*klavo*' = Hungarian '*billentyü*' = Arabic 'مفتاح.'

Experiments were conducted with inference algorithms applied to an early version of the database, containing about 1,300,000 lexemes (Etzioni 2007). One of the simpler algorithms assumed that any hop on any path exhibits a uniform probability of semantic shift. Another assumption was that cliques (sets of three or more lexemes that are all pairwise translations of each other) have a high

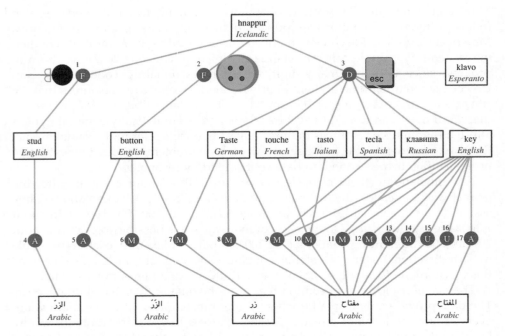

Figure 6.7   Illustration of the need for translation inference. Created by author

probability (about 80 percent, based on tests) of sharing a real meaning. An example of such a clique in Figure 6.7 is '*hnappur*,' 'button,' and 'Taste,' where resource F asserts a shared meaning between '*hnappur*' and 'button,' resource D, between '*hnappur*' and 'Taste,' and resource M, between 'button' and 'Taste.' Two algorithms derived inferred translations beyond the attested ones for three language pairs: English–Russian, English–Hebrew, and Turkish–Russian. Persons who were bilingual in these pairs judged the correctness of all the translations without knowing which ones were attested and which were inferred. On average, the judges considered about 92 percent of the *attested* translations correct and about 80 percent of the combined attested and inferred translations correct. With this reduction in precision, the system was able to increase the number of translations by 33 percent for English–Russian, 80 percent for English–Hebrew, and 215 percent for Turkish–Russian.

Inference can also draw on external data. In one set of experiments (Sammer 2007), the attested translations were supplemented with monolingual corpora of news articles. Given an ambiguous lexeme (such as 'plant' in English) and translations from it into two other languages, the system determined what fraction of the words found near the target words in the two languages' corpora represented translations of each other. This fraction was positively associated with the lexemes in question sharing a meaning.

Work continues on improved inference algorithms. Initial results on an early version of the data indicate that inference based on redundant paths can expand the sets of translations in a multilingual dictionary by about 50 percent without any increase in error. Given that users reported about 8 percent of attested translations to be erroneous, algorithms that combine translations from multiple sources may be able to discover new translations (increasing 'recall') while also eliminating some errors (increasing 'precision').

One of the main goals for translation inference is making it efficient. As Figure 6.7 suggests, a person might easily want an inference algorithm to consider more-than-two-hop paths when extracting translations. However, experiments conducted at the Turing Center have found multi-hop inference too complex for real time implementation. Solutions being investigated include precomputation of translations, implementation of the system on clusters of several computers operating in parallel, random sampling instead of exhaustive search for some inference operations, and redefining the problem of translation as a problem of discovering universal meanings and their panlingual expressions. The idea behind this last approach is to discover from the data the real meanings that appear to be most universally expressed in the world's languages and to identify for each meaning an expression in each language. Then users who specify (for instance with an unambiguous lexeme) one of the universal meanings could obtain its expression in any language instantly, because a time-consuming inference process would not be required.

The *third challenge* has been to show that translations derived from PanLex can produce benefits. The project has pursued this goal by means of two main tactics. One is to show that the translations can make searching the Web more effective, and the other is to show that people can exchange intelligible messages with each other using only translated lexemes.

The search project involved constructing a special Web search engine for images. Launched in September 2007 (Hickey 2007) and made available for public use (http://www.panimages.org), PanImages helps the user formulate and submit multilingual search queries for images. PanImages guides users to type lemmata, helps them choose meanings for the chosen lexemes, and gives them choices among the attested and inferred translations of those lexemes. Users can thereby discover images whose labels are in languages the users don't know, but which are nonetheless relevant to them. The service can also help users (1) to improve the precision of their image-search results by avoiding highly ambiguous query words; and (2) to find culturally specific images (Colowick 2008; Etzioni 2007). PanImages is still an experimental prototype, but it has had about 200,000 visitors in its first year of existence.

A second project investigated lemmatic communication. This is communication in which one person (the 'encoder') constructs sequences of lexemes that represent the meaning of a message. An automated system translates the lexemes into another language, and another person (the 'decoder') attempts to understand the intended message. The success of this method of communication depends largely on the encoder's avoidance of ambiguous lexemes. For example, in table 6.3 the

Table 6.3   Example of successful lemmatic communication. Created by author

Source sentence	Encoding	Translation	Decoding
Washing hands regularly is effective in the reduction of the spread of infectious diseases	regularly, wash, hand, effectively, reduce, infectious disease, spread	regelmäßig, waschen, Hand, wirkungsvoll, reduzieren, Infektions-krankheit, ausbreiten	Regelmäßiges Händewaschen reduziert wirkungsvoll die Ausbreitung von Infektions-krankheiten

Table 6.4   Example of failed lemmatic communication. Created by author

Source Sentence	Encoding	Translation	Decoding
The trial ended with a lengthy sentence	trial, end, with, lengthy, sentence	essai, fin, avec, long, phrase	L'essai s'est terminé par une longue phrase

encoding and the translation from English into German introduce no major distortion in meaning, so the decoded sentence easily conveys the intended meaning. In table 6.4, however, ambiguous lexemes in the encoding lead to a translation that describes the last sentence of an essay, instead of the outcome of a criminal case.

In an experiment on lemmatic communication (Everitt 2010), Spanish and Hungarian-speaking subjects read passages and converted their sentences to sequences of lexemes. Other subjects read the lexeme sequences and converted them back into passages consisting of sentences. There were three conditions:

1   The lexemes were automatically translated from Spanish into Hungarian or vice versa between the encoding and decoding stages; the translation was crude, a given lexeme being always rendered identically, regardless of its context.

2   The lexemes were not translated; encoding and decoding subjects spoke the same language.

3   As with condition 2, the lexemes were not translated, but they were randomly reordered – a simulation of word-order differences among languages. The quality of the decoding was rated by another set of subjects.

As expected, both the reordering and the translation interfered with the task. Still, in all conditions, subjects succeeded in producing final sentences that bore close or moderate resemblance to the original sentences almost half the time or more.

On the basis of the subjects' errors and comments, the investigators hypothesized that improvements to the system and user interface could further increase the success of lemmatic communication. The contemplated improvements include more intelligent automatic translation, warnings when encoders choose ambiguous lexemes, options for decoders to see alternate translations, and opportunities for decoders to ask encoders to clarify or try again. The experiment and its pretests revealed that a major issue facing encoders is efficiency. It is difficult to design an encoding interface that allows people to select lexemes from a database as rapidly as they can type free text. However, intelligent interfaces might learn to anticipate the next lexeme and accelerate the selection process, perhaps even exceeding the pace of free-text writing.

Work continues in an effort to make lemmatic communication practical. The Turing Center is developing an application, PanMail, which will allow people to send messages to each other through the internet across all language boundaries, using lemmatic communication. Additional research is under way for designing graphical and other language-independent expressive methods, which can supplement lemmatic communication.

Applications that deliver useful results also create opportunities to collect system-improving knowledge from users. Persons who use systems based on PanLex in order to get translations will sometimes know (or believe) that the translations they get are incorrect, or will be able to perform translations that the system cannot. Experimenting with user-contribution features in the PanImages application, the Turing Center has obtained a few thousand corrections and additions from users. However, these include many jocular, sarcastic, semi-literate, and other low-quality contributions. Obtaining data from many dispersed users requires quality management.

As the PanLex project addresses these three major challenges, its system development can be understood as taking place on three corresponding layers. Layer 1 is the database of attested denotations and auxiliary facts. Layer 2 consists of versions of the database that employ various inference routines developed at the Turing Center for the discovery of unattested translations, universal meanings, and expressions of universal meanings. Layer 3 consists of the applications and experiments that build on the other layers to provide practical services, conduct research, collect additional data, and improve the quality of the existing data.

Future and Related Work

PanLex began as an in-house database for prototypes and experiments designed by one team. Efforts are now under way to move the database and related tools into an institutional and technical environment suitable for easy access to researchers and end-users world-wide. In the envisioned future, the problem of lexical translation inference and the goal of building applications that rely on it will be treated as objects of collaborative and competitive research at multiple institutions. Users anywhere will be able to access the database, add resources to it, and use, evaluate, and improve inference algorithms operating on it. Someone who has constructed a dictionary that translates the words of low-density language A into higher-density language B will, by contributing the dictionary's data to PanLex, enable the speakers of A to translate words from their language not only into B, but into thousands of other languages. If this capability, in combination with projects implementing other strategies of panlingual globalization, motivates actions that breathe new life into dying languages, the intuitions underlying PanLex will be shown to have been well founded.

There appear to be opportunities for mutually beneficial collaboration between PanLex and other projects with similar aims. Collections of digital lexical resources include: Wiktionary (http://www.wiktionary.org/); wordgumbo (http://www.wordgumbo.com/index.htm); FreeLang (http://www.freelang.net/), FreeDict (http://sourceforge.net/project/showfiles.php?group_id=1419); Dicts.info (http://www.dicts.info/); Digital Dictionaries of South Asia (http://dsal.uchicago.edu/dictionaries/); Majstro Aplikaĵoj (http://www.majstro.com/Web/Majstro/sdict.php); Ergane (http://download.travlang.com/Ergane/); Logos (http://www.logos.it); OneLook (http://www.onelook.com/); Langtolang (http://www.langtolang.com/); Lingoes (http://www.lingoes.net/en/translator/index.html); Rosetta Project (http://rosettaproject.org); EUdict (http://www.eudict.com/); SensAgent (http://dictionary.sensagent.com/); OmegaWiki (http://www.omegawiki.org/); WinDictionary (http://www.windictionary.com/); LingvoSoft (http://www.lingvozone.com/); and Webster's Online Dictionary (http://www.websters-online-dictionary.org/). A much larger collection is that of the printed dictionaries in the world's libraries. Projects that digitize books (including dictionaries), such as Project Gutenberg (http://www.gutenberg.org/wiki/Main_Page) and the Google Books Library Project (http://books.google.com/googlebooks/library.html), are other potential content contributors. Relevant standards with which PanLex wholly or partly complies include Unicode (Unicode 2007) and OLIF (http://www.olif.net/documentation.htm). The Global WordNet Association (http://www.globalwordnet.org/) and Language Grid (http://langrid.nict.go.jp/en/index.html) are other related initiatives.

Mutually beneficial terms of collaboration may be tricky to negotiate with compilers of lexical resources. Many such resources are deployed as advertising-supported services that seek to maximize human visitors in order to generate revenue. PanLex, by contrast, seeks to achieve panlingual *transparency*, in which users get efficient translation without spending time personally choosing and using tools on translation Web sites. The two models might be difficult to reconcile (see Kilgarriff 2000). Moreover, the legal rules under which providers of lexical resources operate are obscure (Zhu et al. 2002; Kienle et al. 2008) and globally unharmonized (Fernández Molina 2004). There is little relevant case law, and apparently none on lexical resources. Creators of translingual dictionaries sometimes assert claims that their contents are protected by copyright, even while they borrow liberally from other dictionaries on the theory that lemmatic translations, part-of-speech identifications, and other borrowed facts are inherently ineligible for copyright protection. The designers of PanLex hope to avoid disputes while developing forms of mutually rewarding collaboration, which may facilitate pan-lingual communication.

Conclusion

Massive linguistic extinction may not be a necessary consequence of globalization. Several strategies are available for making panlingual rather than unilingual glo-balization a reality. The PanLex project is an attempt to implement one of those strategies. When several such projects have produced results, work can begin to combine them and to study their interactions. Until then, pronouncements on the inevitable demise of the world's languages will be premature.

ACKNOWLEDGMENTS

Research, suggestions and comments from Susan M. Colowick are gratefully acknowledged.

REFERENCES

NOTE Accessibility of all internet resources mentioned below has been confirmed on January 26, 2010.

Abley, M. (2003) *Spoken Here: Travels among Threatened Languages*. Boston: Houghton Mifflin.

Adams, D. (1979) *The Hitchhiker's Guide to the Galaxy*. London: Pan Books.

Ammon, U. (2006) Language conflicts in the European Union. *International Journal of Applied Linguistics* 16: 319–38.

Bastardas i Boada, A. (2002) World language policy in the era of globalization: Diversity and intercommunication from the perspective of 'complexity.' *Noves SL. Revista de Sociolingüística* (Summer issue): 1–9. Available at: http://www6.gencat.cat/llengcat/noves/hm02estiu/metodologia/a_bastardas1_9.htm.

Bender, E. M., and Flickinger, D. (2005) Rapid prototyping of scalable grammars: Towards modularity in extensions to a language-independent core. In R. Dale, K. F. Wong, J. Su, and O. Y. Kwong (eds), *Proceedings of the 2nd International Joint Conference on Natural Language Processing IJCNLP-05 (Posters/Demos)*, 203–8.

Berners-Lee, T., Hendler, J., and Lassila, O. (2001) The semantic Web. *Scientific American* 284(5): 34–43.

Blanke, D. (1989) Planned languages: A survey of some of the main problems. In K. Schubert (ed.), *Interlinguistics: Aspects of the Science of Planned Languages*, 63–87. Berlin: Mouton de Gruyter.

Colowick, S. M. (2008) Multilingual search with PanImages. *Multilingual* 19(2): 61–3. Available at: http://turing.cs.washington.edu/PanImMultilingual.pdf.

Crystal, D. (2000) *Language Death.* Cambridge: Cambridge University Press.

De Swaan, A. (2004) Endangered languages, sociolinguistics, and linguistic sentimentalism. *European Review* 12: 567–80.

Dorr, B. J., Hovy, E. H., and Levin, L. S. (2006) Machine translation: Interlingual methods. In K. Brown (ed.), *Encyclopedia of Language and Linguistics*, Vol. 7, 2nd edn, 383–94. Oxford: Elsevier. Available at: ftp://ftp.umiacs.umd.edu/pub/bonnie/Interlingual-MT-Dorr-Hovy-Levin.pdf.

Eidheim, H. (1969) When ethnic identity is a social stigma. In F. Barth (ed.), *Ethnic Groups and Boundaries*, 39–57. Boston: Little, Brown.

Etzioni, O., Reiter, K., Soderland, S., and Sammer, M. (2007) Lexical translation with application to image search on the Web. In B. Maegaard (ed.), *Proceedings of Machine Translation Summit XI.* Available at: http://turing.cs.washington.edu/papers/EtzioniMTSummit07.pdf.

Everitt, K., Lim, C., Etzioni, O., Pool, J., Colowick, S., and Soderland, S. (2010) Evaluating lemmatic communication. trans-kom 3. Available at: http://www.trans-kom.eu/ihv_03_01_2010.html.

FAO [Food and Agriculture Organization of the United Nations] (2008) *AGROVOC Thesaurus.* Available at: http://www.fao.org/agrovoc.

Ferraro, P. J., and Kiss, A. (2002) Direct payments to conserve biodiversity. *Science* 298: 1718–19.

Fernández-Molina, J. C. (2004) The legal protection of databases: Current situation of the international harmonization process. *Aslib Proceedings: New Information Perspectives* 56: 325–34.

Fettes, M. (2003) The geostrategies of interlingualism (=ch. 3). In J. Maurais and M. A. Morris (eds), *Languages in a Globalising World*, 37–46. Cambridge: Cambridge University Press.

Gordon, R. G., Jr (ed.) (2005) *Ethnologue: Languages of the World*, 15th edn. Dallas: SIL International. Available at: http://www.ethnologue.com/.

Harrison, K. D. (2007) *When Languages Die: The Extinction of the World's Languages and the Erosion of Human Knowledge.* New York: Oxford University Press.

Hickey, H. (2007) A rose is a rozsa is a 薔薇: Image-search tool speaks hundreds of languages. Available at: http://uwnews.washington.edu/ni/article.asp?articleID=36524.

Hutchins, J. (2006) Machine translation: History. In K. Brown (ed.), *Encyclopedia of Language and Linguistics*, 2nd edn, Vol. 7, 375–83. Oxford: Elsevier. Available at: http://www.hutchinsweb.me.uk/EncLangLing-2006.pdf.

Jenkins, M., Scherr, S. J., and Inbar, M. (2004) Markets for biodiversity services: Potential roles and challenges. *Environment* 46: 32–42.

Kienle, H., German, D., Tilley, S., and Müller, H. (2008) Managing legal risks associated with intellectual property on the Web. *International Journal of Business Information Systems* 3: 86–106.

Kilgarriff, A. (2000) Business models for dictionaries and NLP. *International Journal of Lexicography* 13: 107–18.

Libert, A. (2000) *A Priori Artificial Languages.* München: Lincom Europa.

Libert, A. (2003) *Mixed Artificial Languages.* München: Lincom Europa.

Mufwene, S. S. (2002) Colonization, globalization and the plight of 'weak' languages. *Journal of Linguistics* 38: 375–95.

Mufwene, S. S. (2004) Language birth and death. *Annual Review of Anthropology* 33: 201–22.

Nettle, D., and Romaine, S. (2000) *Vanishing Voices: The Extinction of the World's Languages.* Oxford: Oxford University Press.

Panfilov 2008. Кирилл Панфилов, "Баскско-русский словарь." Available at: http://www.erlang.com.ru/euskara/?basque-eurus.

Phillipson, R. (2008) Lingua franca or lingua Frankensteinia? English in European integration and globalization. *World Englishes* 27: 250–84.

Pool, J. (1991) The official language problem. *American Political Science Review* 85: 495–514.

Pool, J. (2006) Can controlled languages scale to the Web? In *Proceedings of the 5th International Workshop on Controlled Language Applications (CLAW 2006)*. Available at: http://turing.cs.washington.edu/papers/pool-clweb.pdf.

Raverty, H. G. (1867) *A Dictionary of the Puk'hto, Pus'hto, or Language of the Afghans*, 2nd edn. London: Williams and Norgate. Available at: http://dsal.uchicago.edu/dictionaries/raverty/index.html.

Sammer, M., and Soderland, S. (2007) Building a sense-distinguished multilingual lexicon from monolingual corpora and bilingual lexicons. In B. Maegaard (ed.), *Proceedings of Machine Translation Summit XI*. Available at: http://turing.cs.washington.edu/papers/SammerMTSummit07.pdf.

Schubert, K. (1992) Esperanto as an intermediate language for machine translation. In J. Newton (ed.), *Computers in Translation*, 78–95. London: Routledge.

SIL International (2008) *ISO 639–3*. Available at: http://www.sil.org/iso639-3/default.asp.

Tonkin, H. (2003) The search for a global linguistic strategy. In J. Maurais and M. A. Morris (eds), *Languages in a Globalising World*, 319–33. Cambridge: Cambridge University Press.

Trujillo, A. (1999) *Translation Engines: Techniques for Machine Translation*. London: Springer.

UDHR in Unicode (2008) Unicode Consortium. Available at: http://www.unicode.org/udhr/.

UNESCO (2003) Ad hoc expert group on endangered languages. Language Vitality and Endangerment, International Expert Meeting on UNESCO Programme Safeguarding of Endangered Languages. Available at: http://www.unesco.org/culture/ich/doc/src/00120-EN.pdf.

Unicode Consortium (2007) *The Unicode 5.0 Standard*. Upper Saddle River, NJ: Addison-Wesley.

Van Parijs, P. (2007) Tackling the anglophones' free ride: Fair linguistic cooperation with a global lingua franca. *AILA Review* 20: 72–86.

Wikimedia Foundation (2008) Wiktionary. Available at: http://www.wiktionary.org.

Woodbury, A. C. (2006) What is an endangered language? Linguistic Society of America. Available at: http://www.lsadc.org/info/pdf_files/Endangered_Languages.pdf.

Zhu, H., Madnick, S. E., and Siegel, M. D. (2002) The interplay of Web aggregation and regulations. In *Proceedings of Law and Technology, LAWTECH 2002*. Track 375–853.

7 The Spread of Global Spanish: From Cervantes to *reggaetón*

CLARE MAR-MOLINERO

Introduction

In this chapter I explore the impact of globalization on the Spanish language today and argue that Spanish is indeed a global language in its range of world-wide uses and status. I will begin with a brief explanation of the spread of Spanish, which has led to its wide geographical and demographic extension today. I will show in what ways Spanish merits the description of 'global' language within the contemporary global linguistic hierarchy. I will then look at how sociolinguistic processes typical of globalization are impacting on, or being harnessed by, Spanish. I will identify the agents influencing these globalization processes, showing how international 'pan-Hispanic' language policies and planning, particularly by Spain, have a major role in these processes, but arguing, also, that there are contrasting – and sometimes counter – grassroots influences which exert authority over the Spanish language in its global spread; these are notably led by US Latinos and transmitted through popular culture such as popular music.

The Spread of Spanish

With over 400 million speakers across the world (Gordon 2005), Spanish is obviously a major world language. Spanish is the official or national language of twenty-one states, and it is widely used in international organizations and events. Estimates as to how many people speak Spanish inevitably vary, pointing to the unreliability of many language censuses. Too often censuses simply reflect the population size of a country where Spanish is the official language. When questionnaires or interviews seek to discover more nuanced information, self-reporting can hide very different attitudes and behavior toward a language, from the desire to hide ethnic origins to a wish to exaggerate linguistic competence. Questions about 'mother tongue,' 'language,' and even 'speaking a language' can be misleading and can result in significant differences in the totals produced.

The Handbook of Language and Globalization, First Edition. Edited by Nikolas Coupland.
© 2013 Blackwell Publishing Ltd except for editorial material and organization © 2013 Nikolas Coupland.
Published 2013 by Blackwell Publishing Ltd.

Bearing in mind these limitations, the SIL International's publication, *Ethnologue*, currently in its fifteenth edition (Gordon 2005), is a generally respected source for linguistic data. The latest edition reports a total of 420 million speakers of Spanish, which includes 350 million 'native' speakers (see below for further discussion of the marked difference between first-language (L1) and second-language (L2) speakers), placing Spanish among the most widely spoken languages, after Chinese, English, and Hindi for total numbers (and, significantly, before English for native speakers). Importantly, too, with the exception of Spain (as well as of Equatorial Guinea and of the Philippines, where speakers of Spanish are now very reduced), all the principal Spanish-speaking states border on other Spanish-speaking states. This has been important in terms of language spread and of maintaining the presence of the language.

In two important studies on the economic significance of the Spanish language, Moreno-Fernández and Otero (2007; 2008) have analyzed national censuses and looked at Spanish-speaking migration and diasporas across the world. They have combined their findings in these areas with statistics about learners of Spanish, to arrive at an even higher number of Spanish-speakers. They suggest that, by including anyone who can communicate in Spanish, from native speakers to mere language learners, they arrived at a number of 438,979,000 speakers world-wide (Moreno-Fernández and Otero 2008: 75).

How did the local vernacular of the Castile region become such a widely spoken world language? The history of the development of and domination, in Spain, of a distinct variety called 'Castilian,' and then its emergence as 'Spanish,' the national language, mirrors very closely the development and consolidation of the Spanish nation–state. Throughout the nation-building process, national identity was closely linked to linguistic identity.[1] The spread of the Spanish language was further reinforced by the process of rapid Spanish colonization in Latin America. Language played a significant role in the consolidation of Spain's American empire. Not only did Castilian/Spanish quickly dominate over the thousands of existing indigenous languages as the language of power, of administration, of public life, and especially of the church, but it was a particularly suitable medium for communication across such enormous geographical distances because of its highly developed literacy. This spread of a print community, albeit from the ruling elites, created an "imagined" community (Anderson 1992) of a Spanish-speaking world in the Americas. The idea of 'pan-Hispanism,' *Hispanidad*, or of a 'Spanish-speaking world' can be said to date back to these beginnings.

In the same way in which the Spanish language had been the great unifier of a vast Spanish Empire during the colonial days, its total integration and permanence in Latin American society was also assured from the period of independence onward. The presence in Latin America of a ruling elite made up exclusively of people of European descent, unlike in many other ex-colonial situations, ensured the maintenance of Spanish as the language of power. However, the link between Spanish and national identity was very different from the one found in Spain.

Spanish, of course, was not the unique national language in any of the new independent Latin American republics; and it was not their 'own,' as they *all* used Spanish. Nor was Spanish in any way an original indigenous language of the region. It was, on the contrary, the imposed, imperialist language, of the very enemy whom the wars of independence had just defeated. And yet, despite this, Spanish did indeed serve a nation-forming role in Latin America, as it had done previously in Spain, thereby reinforcing its dramatic spread across the world (Mar-Molinero 2000). Within the new and highly constructed independent republics there was an urgent need to create a sense of national identity – a desired uniqueness that could distinguish Ecuadorians from Peruvians, Argentineans from Uruguayans, Mexicans from Guatemalans, and so on. Most of these new states, such as Mexico, Peru or Venezuela, were in fact highly artificial national entities, containing as they did many different ethnic groups, cultures, and histories. Most also contained many different linguistic groups. For this reason, the role of the Spanish language was seen to be one of unifying the disparate groups under the banner of their new (imposed) national identity. In some of the republics, even a particular form of Spanish was emphasized: Mexican Spanish, Argentinean Spanish, and the like (Sánchez and Dueñas 2002). Spanish was taught in schools and used in all forms of written communication, notably in constitutions, in laws, and in the church. Furthermore, Spanish was the official, and often also the 'national' language recognized in the republics' new constitutions. On the whole, it was not until well into the twentieth century that some of these states began to recognize the existence of other, non-Spanish languages as national, or even as co-official (see Alvar 1986; Hamel 2006).

In the twentieth century, urbanization, industrialization, and technological advances led to the rapid decrease, or even death, of indigenous languages in Latin America and to the total consolidation of Spanish in all the independent republics. Education systems and greater access to literacy in general also helped to promote the learning and use of Spanish to the detriment of the indigenous languages, which until recently have scarcely been taught and do not have a tradition of literacy[2] (Morales-González and Torres 1992).

From the twentieth century on, internal migration from rural areas, where traditionally local indigenous languages are spoken, to many large Latin American cities, where the use of Spanish prevails, had a significant impact on language use and on the spread of Spanish. So, too, had the immigration out of Spanish-speaking Latin America into the United States, which produced an ever growing Spanish-speaking population there. This US Spanish-speaking community has very different features from those of the earlier Spanish colonization. The spreading process of the Spanish language outlined so far was characterized by dominance and elite imposition. In contrast, US Latino communities are frequently characterized by marginalization and discrimination; they are the under-privileged in a dominantly anglophone society. In spite of this, Spanish has nonetheless maintained and reinforced a firm footing in the US since the mid-twentieth century, when large groups of Spanish speakers started to migrate there legally and illegally.[3]

The phenomenon highlights the changing nature of language spread in the late twentieth century, since this was the result of greater proximity and accessibility to their homelands offered to immigrant groups by advances in transportation and by sophisticated technological communications. The existence of trains, motorways, aeroplanes, telephones, televisions, and email, some or all of which are now available even to the poorest immigrants, has changed the relationship of the immigrants with their host country and their sense of identity. In particular, a change has been witnessed in the nature of language spread, from its being an imposed, 'top-down' colonizing process to its becoming (in many cases) a more 'bottom-up,' infiltrating phenomenon.

The American 'melting-pot,' with its demand for instant integration into American culture, language, and identity, has been greatly challenged by this phenomenon. It is a phenomenon found across the world, to a greater or lesser extent, in places experiencing large influxes of immigration. In particular, many of the member states of the European Union have seen waves of immigrants whose links with their homelands have prevented a total assimilation and who often eventually return to their countries of origin – a pattern with inevitable consequences for language use and behavior.

Thus language spread has been affected by many of the forces of globalization, both in terms of how immigrants do or do not integrate themselves into the host societies and in terms of how permanent they perceive their settlement to be. Moreover, globalization has brought with it a role for global languages, which are crossing borders and taking over in domains where local languages were previously used. This process, in turn, has seen an expansion in the role of world languages and a decrease, even death, of a multitude of smaller, more local languages (Crystal 2000; Mühlhäusler 1996).

'Global' Spanish

I have previously discussed the Spanish language's status as a global language in detail (Mar-Molinero 2004) and concluded that, in many respects, as a result of its spread, Spanish today meets the essential criteria commonly used to describe a language as 'global,' albeit it is in a considerably less dominant position than global English. I will briefly summarize these conclusions below.

The size of the population alone is not enough to determine the influence and global role of a language. It is also necessary to ask who the speakers are, and to make distinctions between certain categories which are indeed very different. While the category 'mother tongue' proposes a very debated concept, we can acknowledge that the majority of those who live in Spain and in nearly all the Latin American countries where Spanish is the official language, as well as a part of the Spanish-speaking community in the US, acquire Spanish as their first language. The proportion of these people will be lower in some Latin American countries such as in Paraguay, Guatemala, and Bolivia, where there is a strong presence of indigenous languages. In such countries, as in many other parts of

Latin America and in some parts of Spain, for instance in Catalunya, there are linguistic minority groups, which nonetheless learn Spanish very early on in their lives (usually when they go to school) and speak it to a high level of competence. Together, these two groups make up a very high percentage of the linguistic community referred to as 'Spanish speakers.' As we have seen, the vast majority of Spanish speakers speak Spanish as their first language, and relatively few speak it as a second language; however, a significant increase among learners of Spanish as a foreign language has been occurring in recent years (Bugel 2006; Del Valle and Villa 2006; Instituto Cervantes 2000; Marcos Marín 2006).[4] Included in this group are those who learn Spanish as part of their education curriculum, or in adult life, for purposes such as business or international communication. It is to this group that we should look when assessing the level of the global role of Spanish, as this is the group that represents those with a perceived need, motivation, and desire to learn Spanish voluntarily and enthusiastically. Such people are led by the need to understand Spanish because this language is used in an increasing range of domains and areas on the international stage. We will examine these in turn below.

In terms of the legal, political, and economic significance of Spanish, as we have noted, twenty-one countries recognize it as their official or national language, and Spanish is also an official language in many international bodies such as the United Nations and its offshoots (like UNESCO), or the European Union. Of course, official recognition does not always guarantee actual use in these organizations. Likewise, in judging global political and economic impact, it is important to ask how politically significant the various Spanish-speaking states are in the global pecking order. Many of the Latin American republics are still relatively poor and underdeveloped, with notably high levels of illiteracy. Therefore the economic clout of the users of Spanish varies – from the relatively significant economy of Spain to the expanding markets of, say, Chile, Mexico, and some of the Mercosur countries, and to the very poor and weak economies of countries like the Dominican Republic or Guatemala. In terms of economic power, we should also – increasingly – consider the role and importance of Spanish speakers in the US, which will be discussed below.

A particularly clear indicator of the global role of a language is its selection for use in scientific, academic, and technological communications, which by definition aim to reach international audiences. Despite a noticeable increase in the material reported from Spaniards and Latin Americans in academic and scientific publications, and despite strong participation on the internet (see Marcos Marín 2000 and 2006), the pattern for Spanish speakers continues to be to publish and communicate above all in English (and sometimes in French or German) rather than in their mother tongue (Martin Mayorga 2000).

In one area which is particularly significant in terms of global communication, the internet, there are signs of increase in the use of Spanish (and, more generally, in the use of languages other than English). Marcos Marín (2006) notes that, according to his statistical sources, between 2000 and 2004 Spanish has risen from a percentage of around 10 among the languages used on the internet to a proportion of 15 to 20 percent. He warns that numbers vary widely between sources, hence these data are only approximate; but he is confident that they represent, overall, a situation where Spanish is the third most used language, after English and Chinese. This is an important change from the 1990s, when Spanish lagged behind Japanese and German, in fifth place.[5]

Another key element in the promotion and spread of the Spanish language and culture is the international media. While these remain predominantly in English, there is a growing number of respected newspapers and radio and television stations in Spanish across the world and, in particular, an increasing number of them is available in the US (Carreira 2002; Morales 2001). Cable and satellite television has increased enormously for Spanish speakers, especially in the US, but also world-wide. Once again, the role of the internet is important in the provision of many on-line media broadcasts, including on-line newspapers, radio, and television.

Spanish is the language of the education system in all the countries where it is also an official language; and, as noted, Spanish is widely taught elsewhere as a foreign language, particularly in the US, where it is the first foreign language (see Instituto Cervantes 2000). Increasingly Spanish is offered in other secondary curricula across the world, most notably in the Far East (Japan), Australia, and Europe; and particularly in Brazil (Bugel 2006), although in almost all of these places it is the second foreign language, after English. The active and vigorous work of the Instituto Cervantes across the world has helped to underpin this take-up of Spanish as a foreign language, and it reinforces a Spanish-speaking cultural presence. Indeed, cultural production in Spanish is another area where the profile of the language can be, and is being, raised, both through the activities of such organizations as the Instituto Cervantes and through the current popularity of Latin music and bands, which will be discussed below. Tourism on the one hand and, once again, the US Latino community on the other are partly responsible for this upsurge in awareness of a Hispanic culture.

In the Instituto Cervantes' Centro Virtual *El español en el mundo: Annuario 2000*, the on-line *anuario* of the state of the Spanish language across the world, we are given some interesting and revealing data about the increased level of learning and use of Spanish in various countries. The reasons given for this increase in the demand for learning Spanish as a foreign language, it is suggested, are political (for instance the emergence of the southern Latin American 'Common Market,' Mercosur), economic (as well as Mercosur, the expanding investment by Spanish companies in Brazil and other parts of Latin America) and cultural (the boom in Hispanic culture world-wide in recent years). This so-called boom in Hispanic culture includes both book and record publishing. It is notable also for the sudden popularity, both in America and in Europe, of Latin-style bands and pop groups and of salsa dance classes and club evenings. While the pop-stars themselves do not, all of them or always, sing in Spanish, the positive attitudes that their connection with a Spanish-speaking world brings certainly increase an interest in Spanish and a desire to learn it among tourists and leisure seekers from the developed world.

Publishing in Spanish is also an upward-moving trend, reflecting the provision of Spanish teaching on the one hand and better literacy across the Spanish-speaking world on the other – along with a genuine increase in the popularity of reading in Spanish (Carreira 2002). Concerning, more specifically, the Spanish-reading market in the US, Carreira reports:

> [P]ublishing houses like HarperCollins, Random House, Lectorum and others are rushing to translate popular English titles [...] Book distributors are also gobbling up titles from Argentina, Spain and Mexico to sell to libraries, universities and retail chains like Wal-Mart and Target. (2002: 42)

The cumulative effect of this spread of published and broadcast Spanish across various media is likely to be a wider sense of identity among Spanish speakers, which the print and the electronic/recorded word would link together to form an 'imagined,' shared community.

Spanish and Globalization

The rapid growth and presence of Spanish world-wide, beyond the national borders of Spanish-speaking countries, bring the language into contact with processes that typically characterize globalization. Spanish as a product or as a commodity is promoted and enhanced by global media and communications, and the language itself, in all its varieties, is affected by global phenomena. Today the processes involved in globalization bring languages together more frequently, and sometimes unexpectedly. In sociolinguistic terms, the effects on language contact and language spread are also different. Whereas in the past we might have spoken, typically, of the relatively discrete phenomena of language shift, revival, or death, today we should consider such key processes of globalization as those identified by Coupland (2003: 467): "interdependence, compression across time and space, disembedding and commodification."

The spread of Spanish means that the global "interdependence" of Spanish-speaking communities – among themselves and between them and other parts of the world system – has a significant impact on the language itself. These communities share media and cultural production, in particular those available through fast technological forms of communication such as satellite television, film, recorded music, and the internet. Increasingly there are signs that the Spanish-speaking language community responds collectively to new linguistic needs, such as when it operates on the internet by creating and/or borrowing, particularly from English, new words and terms. Associated with the same phenomenon is Coupland's second concept: the "compression across time and space" experienced by the Spanish-speaking world in spite of its expansive size and territory, as electronic communications (telephones, text messages, emails) make geographical and temporal distances insignificant. Furthermore, the "disembedding" referred to by Coupland arises with the transfer of culturally specific items of speech, which originated in one Spanish speech community, to another, and with the consequent adaptation or re-embedding of such items. Coupland (ibid., p. 468) cites Giddens (1991: 18), who explains this concept as "the 'lifting out' of social relations from their local contexts and their re-articulation across indefinite tracts of time-space." For example, the language, practices, and social behavior portrayed in *telenovelas* (TV soaps) produced by Mexicans and performed by Venezuelan actors to scripts written by Colombians can be seen and interpreted, simultaneously, by audiences in Spain, in Puerto Rico, and even in the US.

Such processes are the result of phenomena typically associated with globalization: 'new' migration (that is, migration patterns which increasingly display a circular movement, frequent contacts with the 'home' country, and transnational networks); high tech media and communications (mobile phones, satellite television, emails, and the internet); and modern rapid transportation systems. The concepts of time and space have been altered forever, with inevitable consequences for the basic unit of communication – the language.

However, language processes do not happen in a vacuum and are not without agency, as Hamel (2006), Phillipson (1992), and Mar-Molinero (2006a and b) noted (among others). In the rest of this chapter I will examine the contrasting and sometimes conflicting agents that I identify as instrumental in influencing the nature and character of contemporary global Spanish. In so doing I will explore the "language authority" (Gal and Woolard 2001; Woolard, 2007) of Spanish, and I will argue that Spanish operates globally both as an 'anonymous,' top-down, public language driven by dominating institutional and government policies, and also as an 'authentic,' grassroots, bottom-up language.[6]

Language Policies and Planning from 'above': The Influence of Spain on Global Spanish

The clearest illustration of the authority of Spanish as a language imposed from above is that of the various initiatives taken by the current (and previous) Spanish government and by the associated Spanish business ventures. Two overarching aims, in my opinion, guide Madrid's international policy in matters of language: on the one hand, the desire to maintain a position of leadership in the Spanish-speaking world, as custodian of *castellano* ('Castilian'); on the other, a recognition of the growing economic value of 'selling' the Spanish language. To underpin these goals, Spain has evolved a 'pan-Hispanic' language policy, intended to touch Spanish speakers across the world.[7]

The principal guardians of the Spanish language (the *castellano* from Spain) are two powerful institutions funded and fostered by the Spanish government: the Real Academia de la Lengua Española (RAE)[8] and the Instituto Cervantes (hereafter referred to as 'the Cervantes').[9] The former is part of a network of language academies: the Asociación de Academias de la Lengua Española (ASALE). ASALE functions throughout the Spanish-speaking Latin America, yet its main policy guidance derives from the RAE in Spain. Together, these two institutions – the

RAE and the ASALE – hold regular *Congresos de la lengua española*, sponsored by the Spanish and, from time to time, by various Latin American governments, at different venues across the Spanish-speaking world, with the purpose of promoting and controlling discussion and debate about the Spanish language.

Both the RAE and the Cervantes claim to support a wider concept of 'Spanish' than the one corresponding merely to the variety spoken in Spain. The RAE has recently launched various updated publications which explicitly intend to cater for a wider pan-Hispanic community (Paffey and Mar-Molinero 2009). In particular, the RAE has produced in 2005, in conjunction with the ASALE and the Cervantes, the *Diccionario panhispánico de dudas* (*DPD*). The Cervantes for its part has pledged its commitment to serving the wider Spanish-speaking world and has published yearly *Anuarios* entitled *El español en el mundo*. More recently, it has produced the *Enciclopedia del español en el mundo*.

Nonetheless, these institutions remain, I would argue, fundamentally representative of their national government and they resist any real weakening of their own powerful leadership in the Spanish-speaking world – in part by ensuring that they are seen as *the* authority on Spanish language, and in part by promoting a 'neutral' or anonymous variety of Spanish as the norm and standard, yet one which is overwhelmingly based on the variety spoken in central Spain. As Marcos Marín has written:

> Speaking in Spanish identifies the members of this [Spanish-speaking] community both to themselves and to those outside. It is typical that the sense of linguistic unity, which is very much in the minds of those who come from Spanish America, is constantly reinforced, and that Spanish today has an internal coherence which is indeed superior to that of other world languages. This is not something that has happened by chance; it is the result of a desire for linguistic unity which contemporary media must reinforce.[10]

The RAE reminds us that:

> The principal mission of the Academy […] is to ensure that the speakers of the Spanish language, as they subject it to constant adaptation according to their needs, do not break the language's essential unity, which is maintained throughout the Spanish-speaking world.[11]

The RAE remains the leader and the hub of initiatives on Spanish language policy and of their direction. This includes the recent move to promote a 'pan'-Hispanic language policy. Such a policy is shaped on the terms of the RAE – and hence of the Spanish government – and has the ultimate mission of maintaining 'unity' and guarding against the perceived threat of fragmentation that many diverse Spanishes represent. Notably, at the most recent *Congreso de la lengua española*, in Cartagena, Colombia, in 2007, no contributions were invited from the Spanish-speaking community in the US, although there were papers and participants from everywhere else in the Spanish-speaking world – including participants from non-Castilian language communities in Spain, or papers on "Spanish in Brazil."

As I will discuss later, for many of these guardians of 'Standard' Spanish and Spanish 'unity,' the US situation is seen as posing a particularly worrying threat, one that suggests a loss of authority and a loss of neutrality.

The Cervantes, too, while in its cultural activities and publications emphasizes its commitment to Spanish across the world and to promoting a corresponding pluralism, in fact seeks to reinforce a single, standard variety of Spanish in its all-important language teaching courses, which are hosted in the Aula Virtual del Español (the AVE). This variety comes from Spain and is proposed as the only model for Spanish language learners. Its choice is described and justified as follows:

> The principal variety of the AVE, the one which is normative for the corpus presented to the students as a model of the language they should reproduce, is central peninsular Spanish. [...] [C]entral peninsular Spanish was chosen because it is not in contact with other languages and has the fewest differentiating characteristics as regards the shared language. [...] Its selection as the principal variety is based on the fact that central peninsular Spanish has sufficient demographic importance and status among the Spanish-speaking community through media and cultural expressions.[12]

Evident from the stated objectives of the RAE and of the Cervantes are the beliefs that a standard single variety of Spanish is a neutral medium of social participation and that language variation would be an impediment to this goal.

Moreover, government departments, overseas embassies, language institutions, cultural bodies, and universities also contribute to the intricate, multilateral networks of agents for the effective management of language spread which make up the implicit and explicit language policies in Spain – albeit to a lesser degree than the RAE and the Cervantes. Private business interests in Spain have also woken up to the huge commercial opportunities offered by the Spanish-speaking markets and by the selling of the Spanish language. Business companies also work frequently with governmental agencies, often in order to make their presence visible on major websites, as happened in three recent and particularly high-profile examples, EducaRed, Campusred and Universia, which have the support of Telefónica and the Banco Santander Central Hispano (Marcos Marín 2006: 46).

In general, commercial interests, which are often led from Spain, are seizing the opportunities to sell and commodify *Latinidad*, as an increasing world-wide demand for things perceived as 'Latino' make this a very lucrative market. Many top popular tourist locations are Spanish-speaking and 'Latino'-packaged – for instance Spain itself, Cuba, the Dominican Republic, and the Mexican 'Mayan Riviera.' Once again, it is often companies from Spain that are promoting and investing heavily in these locations. With this popularity goes the need and desire to have contact with the language and to learn it, at least for basic communicative and popular cultural purposes. As Marcos Marín comments:

> [Take together] Spanish television channels, video courses, radio, movies in Spanish, and the whole market of dubbing, publishing, newspapers, and magazines, all of the

production of educational materials, and it will be apparent that the economic volume of Spanish in the United States is greater than that of any other Spanish-speaking country or any other country in the world.[13]

But he also continues with a very important cautionary comment stressing the interconnectivity of the spread and significance of Spanish across all of the Spanish-speaking world.

> The claim that nowadays Spanish would continue to exist in the world even if it were only for the United States is, although true, nevertheless dangerous, because, without the rest of the Hispanic world, Spanish in the United States would make little sense. *It is the whole that matters.* [My emphasis][14]

Glocalization and Counter-Spread of Global Spanish

As Norman Fairclough (2006) has argued, the processes of globalization not only produce top-down imposition of language spread policies, but also globalization from below. He suggests that this may be the case of "individuals or groups in specific places in many cases defending themselves against negative effects of processes of globalization or taking advantage of new possibilities offered by these processes" (ibid., p. 121). He continues: "Globalization makes available new resources for local action which include new discourses and practices and identities (including genres and styles) in which these discourses are internalized and operationalized" (ibid.). In the present section of the chapter I will explore how the US Latino situation makes a good example of this kind of globalization from below, originating from very local bases and creating new genres and styles, both of Spanish and of its related cultural products. Fairclough further argues:

> The impetus for globalization from below comes from situated action in particular places, but through the dialectic of place and space these places are 'glocalized,' so that resources for situated actors are less and less purely local and increasingly global. (ibid., p. 139)

We find clear examples of such 'glocalization' of Spanish with the impact of the US Latinos both within the Spanish-speaking world and beyond. The way in which the Latino communities in the US are marginalized and left on the periphery (geographically, socially, and politically), and yet they increasingly project their voices, especially culturally and linguistically, places them in "contact zones," as these are defined and developed by Mary Louise Pratt (1987; 1992). Contact zones are, namely, "social spaces where cultures meet, clash and grapple with each other, often in contexts of highly asymmetrical relations of power" (Pratt 1999: 6). To understand and analyse them, Pratt argues for a "linguistics of contact," which "will be deeply interested in processes of appropriation, penetration or co-optation of one group's language by another – and in how or whether to distinguish among those three kinds of contact" (Pratt 1987: 61). The emergence of a powerful external marketing of Spanish in response to world-wide demand for *Latinidad* and, in particular, to the perceived increasing importance of the US Latino market suggests that, with global Spanish, all three kinds of contact can be identified. Furthermore, I would argue that the three processes are not only on many occasions initiated by dominant Anglo groups from outside the Latino communities, but also that US Latinos have made the reverse contact from within their communities through forms of glocalization, taking their varieties of Spanish into English-speaking domains in the US and beyond.

Spanish in the US: Global versus Local Standards

Spanish in the US clearly experiences the struggles and conflicts of existing in contested spaces – 'contact zones' – with the result that different language authorities converge. On the one hand, and indisputably, the authority of English is ever-present; but we have also seen how the spread of global Spanish is increasingly brought to the doors of the US Latino communities through media, advertising, commerce, and education by non-Latino agents such as big business or the Spanish government's language policies. However, the Spanish of these communities is also heard and stimulated in part by the very weight of belonging to a global Spanish-speaking community, in part by the numbers of (constantly renewed) native speakers and their geographical concentrations. Far from making a wholesale shift to English, as happened typically with the languages of US immigrant communities in the past, US Latino communities have preserved Spanish as a significant feature, allowing it to develop particular characteristics in its newly established environments.[15] Therefore US 'Spanishes' do not necessarily resemble the national varieties used in the places of origin of their speakers, nor are they much influenced by the elitist and distant corpus of Standard Spanish from Spain. On the contrary, they are authentic identity markers of their speakers. US 'Spanishes' conflict with the hegemony of English around them, but they also oppose the imposition of an anonymous, neutral Spanish from above and from outside, and they resist attempts from both sides to appropriate them.

Apart from the inevitable pressure on the US Latino community to learn English and to shift to an increasing use of it, maintaining any particular, local form of US Spanish is also challenged by the onslaught of other Spanishes, which seek dominance and question the legitimacy and authenticity of any new local variety. This does not occur in discrete, 'black and white,' ringfenced ways. The contest takes place in contact zones, where the level of penetration between the languages (different Spanishes and English) or the level of appropriation will vary according to a range of typical sociolinguistic features: gender, generation, networks, social context, and so on.

In consequence, a common feature in these US Spanish-speaking communities is, unsurprisingly, a range of types of code-switching and code-mixing. Some label this phenomenon as 'Spanglish,' intending to signal a totally new code or language. For others, this is a label which deliberately intends to suggest a negative and unacceptable phenomenon, namely a degenerative fragmentation of the cherished norm – as can be seen in the reaction of the 'guardians' of Standard Spanish mentioned earlier (see Del Valle 2006). For others still, 'Spanglish' is a crusading term, designed to claim autonomy and authority in separation from the imposition of a global anonymous Spanish; this attitude can be seen in the work and campaigning of Ilan Stavans (2003). However, a less ideologically oriented examination of the characteristics that have led to the coining of 'Spanglish' is more likely to arrive at the conclusion which Marta Fairclough draws when she argues that 'Spanglish' cannot be considered to have experienced "grammaticalization" – which she describes as taking place when languages are in contact and undergo a process whereby they become a new mixed code or language (rather than being merely two languages that alternate; Fairclough 2003: 186). She also suggests that 'Spanglish' is a "natural linguistic process *that cannot be either imposed or halted*" (my emphasis).[16]

Nonetheless, as Fairclough and many others have noted, varieties of US 'Spanishes,' or 'Spanglish' in this looser sense, are evident daily, in many walks of life. Fairclough has noted that, in the media in particular, there are examples both of neutral Standard Spanish and of many non-standard or regional varieties and, significantly, of code-switching and 'Spanglish.' It comes as no surprise to discover for example that, in the media's use of Spanish, it is in news items that the language is at its most neutral and standard, while *telenovelas*, comic strips, women's magazines and children's programmes deploy code-switching or Spanglish to the highest degree. The linguistic hierarchy implied here is clear; nonetheless, the diffusion of non-standard US Spanish has a significant impact on an increasingly wide, even global audience. Crucially, it is to the younger generation that much of this kind of language is directed and designed to respond. As Fairclough says,

> the programmes that choose to incorporate code-switching are those designed for children and young people [...] who speak the hybrid language *Spanglish* [...] [and] follow pop culture and their idols, like Ricky Martin and his musical hit *Livin' la vida loca*.[17]

While not everyone would agree that this is in fact a 'language,' the significant facts here are that its ownership goes to the younger generation and that the outlets for it are created through mass media. In the examples given above, however, we can still see that what promotes this use of Spanish is large international commercial interests (the Warner brothers, or the pop music industry). In the following section I will explore the very important role that music is currently playing in the spread of Spanish and I will argue that it, too, contests the ownership and authority of global Spanish.

With music we have a particularly good example of the wider issues of cultural identity which the US Latino voices struggle to bring out from their local communities, and which grapple with the mainstream Anglo norms. This process is resulting in a growing international awareness of a different Spanish, authentic but increasingly authoritative. Latino music operates in the 'contact zone' of conflicting communities and cultures, in a postmodern world of globalization where cultural and linguistic authority are being contested.

Popular Music and Counter-Global Spanish

Latin music[18] of all sorts has of course been popular in the US and in other parts of the western world for a long time, but from at least the early '90s it has seen a growing popularity, which has led to what may best be called now a 'boom.' As Morales writes,

> Afro-Cuban music thrived in New York, and, to a lesser extent, in Los Angeles, through the '50s and '60s, then retreated into the status of an extremely popular ethnic music in the '70s and '80s only to reemerge in the '90s as a bona fide 'American' music. (2002: 156)

In all this music there are signs of an intricate linking, crossovers, and even hybridization of forms between the Latino roots (often from the specific countries of origin of various groups) and the Anglo mainstream – a process leading to what Morales describes as musical 'Spanglish.' The parallels with linguistic 'Spanglish' are strong. Many of the artists themselves show this hyphenated identity and ambivalent relationship with their audiences and sponsors, with the result that their music and its market are characterized by the typical processes of globalization – for instance disembedding from local roots and development of hybrid genres and forms.

Much of the best known, mainstream Latin music of recent years which has hit the charts and sold by millions, not only in the US but world-wide – such as music by Ricky Martin, Jennifer López, Enrique Iglesias, Cristina Aguilera, Shakira, or Buena Vista Social Club – is financed and promoted by large international (non-Latino) companies and 'sanitized' to suit a non-Spanish/Latino audience. A large part of this music was originally recorded and performed in English, with just the occasional Spanish word thrown in. Interestingly, this tendency has changed; many of the artists named above have also, or mostly – or, in the case of Buena Vista Social Club, even exclusively – sung in Spanish. Many earlier successful recordings in English by Latino artists have been re-released using Spanish or a mixture of Spanish and English. J-Lo is now promoting herself as a 'Latina'/Spanish-speaking singer and actress. Shakira is strongly committed to singing and recording in Spanish. Cristina Aguilera has re-positioned herself as a 'Latina' (given her Ecuadorian connections) and is learning Spanish. Even Madonna has recently chosen to release some of her music in Spanish (there is for example her Spanish version of "Don't cry for me Argentina"), clearly wishing to identify with this popular (and lucrative) market.

Such popularity of the Latino music contributes to the spread of Spanish-based global culture and presents a further problem for language purists, as it rarely contains standard elite Spanish. Typically the lyrics will be colloquial, often specific to the variety spoken in the area, region, or country of the singer; they will bear marks of social class and age; and, increasingly, they will be identifiable with US 'Spanishes,' and therefore full of code-switching. And yet this, more than many other forms, is the form of Spanish most often heard and most likely to reach a vast global audience. It reflects the kind of language spoken among many of the music's followers and fans. It is also the language that many non-Spanish-speaking fans will learn as they listen to the music and will certainly believe to be Spanish. Ironically, it could be agued that this language is instrumental in motivating many, particularly younger people across the world, to want to learn Spanish and to share in this cultural boom (which also includes dance, film, and fashion).

Latin music is not limited to the US Latino communities; in fact its success has attracted artists from many 'Latin'/Spanish-speaking countries, from Mexico in Central America, from the Caribbean Islands, from South America, and from Spain itself, prompting them to engage with it and to make records in the different styles. Nonetheless, the most likely prime audience available to such artists, at least in the first instance, is the US Latino market. As a result, *rock en español*, hip hop, tropical pop, and *reggaetón*[19] receive further transnational influences, which bring the music and the lyrics to the Spanglish melting-pot.[20]

Conclusion

As we have seen, Spanish is spread widely across the world and is spoken by many millions. The indications are that this pattern is designed to increase, through native speakers (among whom the birth rate is high) and through others' enthusiasm to learn Spanish. Some of this attraction is the direct product of the kind of Spanish which is heard and marketed through contemporary popular Latino music, with its special varieties of the language. Thus the voice of localized Spanish is globalized, rubbing shoulders with the dominant, elitist standard promoted and protected by the Spanish government and its language agents through pan-Hispanic policies. It would nevertheless be hard to disagree with the claim, made by Moreno-Fernández and Otero (2008): 68), that Spanish

> is a linguistically homogeneous language. [...] The basis of the relative homogeneity is found in the simplicity of its vocalic system (five elements); the range of its consonantal system, which is shared by the entire Hispanic world; the dimension of its shared lexical heritage (basic lexicon); and the elemental syntax community.

Whether the glocalized forms of Spanish being exported from the Latino communities of the US are beginning to challenge this homogeneity and pose a genuine possibility of fragmentation remains to be seen.

ACKNOWLEDGMENTS

Parts of the discussions elaborated here have appeared in different forms and for different purposes previously, particularly in Mar-Molinero 2004, 2006b, and 2008. I am grateful to Nikolas Coupland for the opportunity to bring these different arguments and contentions together as a whole by contributing to this current volume.

NOTES

1   For a fuller discussion of the relationship between the Castilian language and Spanish nation-state building, see Del Valle and Gabriel-Stheeman 2002; Lodares 2001; Mar-Molinero 2000; Siguan 1992.

2   Quechua and Nahuatl (the languages of the Inca and the Aztec empires respectively), served imperial purposes of their own and developed forms of writing. Indeed, because Quechua evolved as a *lingua general*, it began to be written in Roman script and taught in the universities.

3   We should also note that this immigration was not in fact the first one to bring Spanish speakers to the US; a small community of Spanish-speakers has lived in parts of the southwest from the times before this territory was US-governed – from the days of the Spanish Empire and of independent Mexico.

4   Moreno-Fernández and Otero (2008: 81) suggest there are around 23 million non-native Spanish speakers "made up of speakers of Spanish as a second or foreign language and users of various bilingual mixes (7.8 milllion) and foreign residents in Spanish-speaking countries in the process of acquiring Spanish (1.8 million)."

5   See Marcos Marín 2006, ch. 2, for a full discussion of the level of use of Spanish on the internet, both in terms of content and in terms of metalanguage; of data on the volume of ownership over vehicles of electronic communication and on their use in the Spanish-speaking world; and of the impact such use may have on the Spanish language itself.

6   For a fuller discussion of these processes, see Mar-Molinero 2008.

7   For further discussions of this concept, see Del Valle 2007 and 2008, and Paffey and Mar-Molinero 2009.

8   For a fuller discussion of the role of the RAE in Spanish language policy, see Paffey 2007.

9   For a fuller discussion of this institite, see Mar-Molinero 2006a.

10   *Hablar en español identifica a los miembros de esa comunidad, entre sí y ante el resto. Es característico que la conciencia de la unidad lingüística, muy viva en el pensamiento de los próceres de la América Hispánica, se haya visto continuamente reforzada y que el español tenga hoy una coherencia interna verdaderamente superior a la de otras lenguas de difusión mundial. No se trata de algo casual, sino del resultado de una voluntad de unidad lingüística, que los medios actuales deben reforzar* (Marcos Marín 2006: 46–7). All translations in this chapter are mine.

11   *La Academia [...] tiene como misión principal velar porque los cambios que experimente la Lengua Española en su constante adaptación a las necesidades de sus hablantes no quiebren la esencial unidad que mantiene en todo el ámbito hispánico* (Real Academia Española 1995, Articulo 1°).

12   *La variedad principal del AVE y norma del corpus que se propone al alumno como modelo de lengua para su reproducción es el español peninsular central.* [...] *[S]e optó por el español peninsular central por no estar en interacción con otras lenguas y tener menos elementos diferenciadores con respecto a la lengua común.* [...] *La selección de esta variedad como principal está fundamentada en que el español peninsular central tiene suficiente importancia demográfica y proyección hacia el conjunto de la comunidad hispanohablante a través de manifestaciones culturales y medios de comunicación.* [...] *[E]l español general o estándar recoge los rasgos comunes y compartidos por sus variedades.* Available at: http://ave.cervantes.es/trat.htm.

13   *... canales de televisión en español, cursos de video, de radio, películas en español, todo el mercado de doblaje, editoriales, periódicos y revistas, toda la producción educativa integral en español, y se verá que el volumen económico del español en los Estados Unidos es superior al de cualquier país hispanohablante o cualquier país del mundo* (Marcos Marín 2006: 41).

14   *La afirmación de que el español subsistiría hoy en el mundo aunque sólo fuera por los Estados Unidos, aunque sea cierta, con todo, es peligrosa, porque sin el resto del mundo hispánico, el español no tendría sentido en los Estados Unidos tampoco.* Es el conjunto el que importa (ibid.).

15   I will not repeat here the well documented and well known debates about the intergenerational transmission of Spanish within the US, nor do I have space to explore the detailed studies of the different and sometimes convergent varieties of US Spanishes here. See e.g. Billis 2005; García et al. 2001; Niño-Murcia et al. 2008; Roca 2000; Zentella 2002.

16   *Si bien hay lenguas en contacto que sufren un proceso de gramaticalización y se convierten en un nuevo código mixto, es decir una nueva lengua (no dos idiomas que alternan) el* Spanglish *en Estados Unidos se encuentra lejos de consumar ese proceso de gramaticalización. El polémico* Spanglish *parece ser un fenómeno esporádico, cuyo uso resulta muy personal y sumamente difícil de cuantificar; es un proceso lingüístico natural* que no se puede ni imponer ni detener (ibid.).

17   *Por lo general, son los programas dirigidos principalmente a los niños y a la juventud los que optan por incorporar el CC [cambio de código]. A (...) Son también ellos quienes hablan una lengua híbrida que es el* Spanglish. *Los jóvenes son los seguidores de la cultura pop y sus ídolos, como Ricky Martin y su éxito musical* Livin' la vida loca (Fairclough 2003: 199).

18   For fuller discussions of the phenomenon of Latino music, and especially of its impact today, see for example Cepeda 2000; Morales 2002; Flores 2000; Glasser 1995; and Rivera 2003.

19   It is claimed that *reggaetón* is a hybrid product of Jamaican reggae and dance halls which was taken to Panama by Jamaican workers helping to build the Panama Canal. However, it only began to gain popularity in the '80s and, more significantly, in the '90s, when it was introduced into Puerto Rico. There it was further mixed with *bomba* and *plena* and, finally, with US hip-hop. Importantly, *reggaetón* normally has raps in Spanish, often exclusively in Spanish. Initially the music was popular in Puerto Rico, and it was soon transported, too – to Colombia and the Dominican Republic, and, of course, to the US. Today it is a global commercial success, with tracks such as Daddy Yankee's 'gasolina,' which are number one hits all over the world. Anglo and mainstream rap and rock artists have also joined the bandwagon.

20   For a discussion of the impact of popular music – specifically hip hop – on global Englishes which offers both similarities and contrasts with the example of Spanish discussed here, see Pennycook 2007.

REFERENCES

Alvar, M. (1986) *Hombre, etnia, estado: Actitudes lingüísticas en Hispanoamérica.* Madrid: Gredos.

Anderson, B. (1992) *Imagined Communities: Reflections on the Origins and Spread of Nationalism*, 2nd edn [1983]. London and New York: Verso.

Billis, G. D. (2005) Las comunidades lingüísticas y el mantenimiento del español en Estados Unidos. In L. Ortiz López and M. Lacorte (eds), *Contactos y contextos lingüísticos: El español en Estados Unidos y en contacto con otras lenguas*, 29–55. Madrid: Vervuert.

Bugel, T. (2006) *A Macro- and Micro-Sociolinguistic Study of Language Attitudes and Language Contact: MERCOSUR and the Teaching of Spanish in Brazil.* Unpublished doctoral dissertation, University of Illinois at Urbana-Champaign.

Carreira, M. (2002) The media, marketing, critical mass, and other mechanisms of linguistic maintenance. *Southwest Journal of Linguistics* 21(2): 37–54.

Cepeda, M. E. (2000) "Mucho loco for Ricky Martin": On the politics of chronology, crossover, and language within the Latin music 'boom.' *Popular Music and Society* 24(3): 55–71.

Coupland, N. (2003) Introduction: Sociolinguistics and globalisation. *Journal of Sociolinguistics* 7(4): 465–73.

Crystal, D. (2000) *Language Death.* Cambridge: Cambridge University Press.

Del Valle, J. (2006) US Latinos, *la hispanofonía* and the language ideologies of high modernity. In C. Mar-Molinero and M. Stewart (eds), *Globalization and Language in the Spanish-Speaking World: Macro and Micro Perspectives*, 27–47. Basingstoke and New York: Palgrave Macmillan.

Del Valle, J. (2008) The pan-Hispanic community and the conceptual structure of linguistic nationalism. *International Multilingual Research Journal* 2(1–2): 5–27.

Del Valle, J. (ed) (2007) *La Lengua? Patria Común? Ideas e ideologías del español.* Madrid: Vervuert–Iberoamericano.

Del Valle, J., and Gabriel-Stheeman, L. (eds) (2002) *The Battle over Spanish between 1800 and 2000: Language Ideologies and Hispanic Intellectuals.* London and New York: Routledge.

Del Valle, J., and Villa, L. (2006) Spanish in Brazil: Language policy, business and cultural propaganda. *Language Policy* 5: 369–92.

Fairclough, N. (2003) El (denominado) Spanglish en Estados Unidos: Polémicas y realidades. *Revista Internacional de Lingüística Iberoamericana* 1(2): 185–284.

Fairclough, N. (2006) *Language and Globalization.* Abingdon and New York: Routledge.

Flores, J. (2000) *From Bomba to Hip-Hop: Puerto Rican Culture and Latino Identity.* New York: Columbia University Press.

Gal, S., and Woolard, K. A. (2001) Constructing languages and publics: Authority and representation. In S. Gal and K. A. Woolard (eds), *Languages and Publics*, 1–13. Manchester and Northampton, MA: St Jerome.

García, O., Morín, J. L., and Rivera, K. (2001) How threatened is the Spanish of New York Puerto Ricans? In J. Fishman

(ed), *Can Threatened Languages Be Saved?*
44–73. Clevedon and New York:
Multilingual Matters.

Giddens, A. (1991) *Modernity and Self-Identity. Self and Society in the Late Modern Age*. Cambridge: Polity.

Glasser, R. (1995) *My Music is My Flag: Puerto Rican Musicians and Their New York Communities, 1917–1940*. Berkeley, Los Angeles, and London: University of California Press.

Gordon, R. G., Jr (ed.) (2005) *Ethnologue: Languages of the World*, 15th edn. Dallas, TX: SIL International. [Online version available at: http://www.ethnologue. com/; accessed on August 28, 2008.]

Hamel, R. E. (2006) The development of language empires. In U. Ammon, N. Dittmar, K. J. Mattheier, and P. Trudgill (eds) (2006), *Sociolinguistics: An International Handbook of the Science of Language and Society*, Vol. 3 [*Handbucher zur Sprach- und Kommunikationswissenschaft 3*], 2240–58. Berlin and New York: Walter de Gruyter.

Instituto Cervantes (2000) *El español en el mundo: Anuario 2000*. Madrid: Instituto Cervantes, Plaza Janés.

Lodares, J. R. (2001) *Gente de Cervantes: La historia humana del idioma español*. Madrid: Taurus.

Marcos Marín, F. (2006) *Los retos del español*. Madrid and Frankfurt: Iberoamericana and Vervuert.

Marcos Marín, F. (2000) La lengua espanola en internet. In Instituto Cervantes, 299–359.

Mar-Molinero, C. (2000) *The Politics of Language in the Spanish-Speaking World: From Colonisation to Globalisation*. London and New York: Routledge.

Mar-Molinero, C. (2004) Spanish as a world language: Language and identity in a global era. *Spanish in Context* 1(1): 3–20.

Mar-Molinero, C. (2006a) The European linguistic legacy in a global era: Linguistic imperialism, Spanish and the

Instituto Cervantes. In C. Mar-Molinero and P. Stevenson (eds) (2006), *Language and the Future of Europe: Ideology, Policies and Practice*, 76–91. Basingstoke and New York: Palgrave Macmillan.

Mar-Molinero, C. (2006b) Forces of globalization in the Spanish-speaking world: Linguistic imperialism or grassroots adaptation? In C. Mar-Molinero and M. Stewart (eds), *Globalization and Language in the Spanish-Speaking World: Macro and Micro Perspectives*, 8–27. Basingstoke and New York: Palgrave Macmillan.

Mar-Molinero, C. (2008) Subverting Cervantes: Language authority in global Spanish. *International Multilingual Research Journal* 2(1–2): 27–48.

Martin Mayorga, D. (2000) El español en la sociedad de la información. In Instituto Cervantes, 359–75.

Morales, A. (2001) El español en Estados Unidos: Medios de comunicación y publicaciones. In Instituto Cervantes, Centro Virtual Cervantes, *Anuario 2001*. Available at: http://cvc.cervantes.es/ lengua/anuario/anuario_01/morales/ p03.htm (accessed on January 18, 2010).

Morales, E. (2002) *Living in Spanglish: The Search for Latino Identity in America*. New York: St Martin's Griffin.

Morales-Gónzalez, D. and Torres, C. (eds) (1992) *Educational Policy and Social Change: Experience from Latin America*. Westport and London: Praeger.

Moreno-Fernández, F., and Otero, J. (2007) *Demografía de la lengua española*. Madrid: Instituto Complutense de Estudios Internacionales.

Moreno-Fernández, F., and Otero, J. (2008) The status and future of Spanish among the main international languages: Quantitative dimensions. *International Multilingual Research Journal* 2(1–2): 67–84.

Mühlhäusler, P. (1996) *Linguistic Ecology: Language Change and Linguistic Imperialism in the Pacific Region*. London and New York: Routledge.

Niño-Murcia, M., Godenzzi, J. C., and Rothman, J. (2008) Spanish as a world language: The interplay of globalized localization and localized globalization. *International Multilingual Research Journal* 2(1–2): 48–67.

Paffey, D. (2007) Policing the Spanish language debate: Verbal hygiene and the Spanish Language Academy. *Language Policy* 6(3–4): 313–32.

Paffey, D., and Mar-Molinero, C. (2009) Globalisation, linguistic norms and language authorities: Spain and the panhispanic language policy. In M. Lacorte and J. Leeman (eds), *Español en Estados Unidos y otros contextos de contacto. Sociolingüística, ideología y pedagogía [Spanish in the United States and Other Contact Environments. Sociolinguistics, Ideology and Pedagogy]*, 159–73. Madrid: Iberoamericana/ Vervuert (Lengua y Sociedad en el Mundo Hispánico 21).

Pennycook, A. (2007) *Global Englishes and Transcultural Flows*. Abingdon and New York: Routledge.

Phillipson, R. (1992) *Linguistic Imperialism*. Oxford: Oxford University Press.

Pratt, M. L. (1987) Linguistic utopias. In N. Fabb, D., Attridge, A., Durant, and C. McCabe (eds), *The Linguistics of Writing: Arguments between Language and Literature*, 48–66. Manchester: Manchester University Press.

Pratt, M. L. (1992) *Imperial Eyes. Travel Writing and Transculturation*. London and New York: Routledge.

Pratt, M. L. (1999) Arts of the contact zone. Paper delivered to the Modern Languages Association (MLA). Available at: http://web.nwe.ufl. edu/-stripp/2504/pratt.html/.

Real Academia Española (1995) *Estatutos y reglamento de la Real Academia Española*. Madrid: Real Academia Española.

Rivera, R. Z. (2003) *New York Ricans: From the Hip Hop Zone*. New York: Palgrave Macmillan.

Roca, A. (ed) (2000) *Research into Spanish in the United States*. Somerville: Cascadilla Press.

Stavans, I. (2003) *Spanglish: The Making of a New American Language*. New York: Harper Collins.

Sánchez, A., and Dueñas, M. (2002) Language planning in the Spanish-speaking world. *Current Issues in Language Planning* 3(3): 280–305.

Siguan, M. (1992) *España plurilingüe*. Barcelona: Ariel.

Villa, D. (2000) Languages have armies and economies too: The presence of US Spanish in the Spanish-speaking world. *Southwest Journal of Linguistics* 19: 144–54.

Woolard, K. A. (2007) La autoridad lingüística del español y las ideologías de la autenticidad y el anonimato. In Del Valle (ed.), 129–43.

Zentella, A. C. (2002) Spanish in New York. In O. Garcia and J. A. Fishman (eds), *Multilingual Apple: Languages in New York City*, 2nd edn, 167–203. Berlin and New York: Mouton de Gruyter.

8 New National Languages in Eastern Europe

BRIGITTA BUSCH

Introduction

In the transformation process that took place in central and eastern Europe in the 1990s, the taboo of the inviolability of state borders, which had dominated the political post-Wold War II order in Europe, was abandoned and large multilingual entities disintegrated into new states which considered themselves to be nation–states. This disintegration caused new majority–minority relationships and a new definition of status for languages spoken and written in the successor states of entities like the Yugoslav Federation, the Soviet Union, or the Czechoslovak Republic. Languages that had formerly been dominant state languages became minority languages with a low status in certain contexts (for instance Russian in the Baltic states), and former regional or minority languages were raised to the status of official languages (for instance Estonian in the Estonian Republic). Alongside the flag, the code of arms, the national anthem, and other insignia, the state language was considered a central element in the affirmation of 'new' national identities. The efforts of imposing a single, uniform language, both at the discursive and at the formal linguistic level, were closely connected with processes of delineation and assertion.

The present chapter focusses on the example of former Yugoslavia in order to analyze processes related to the affirmation of new state and national languages in the context of globalization. The example is particularly interesting because there a common multi-variety standard, Serbocroatian, was split into different 'new' national languages. This process is characterized by conflicting forces at work. Whereas the political elites in the new nation–states referred to strategies and tools of language policy and language planning traditionally linked to nation-building, the process in fact took place in a situation where the role of the nation-state was already being challenged by a group of simultaneous factors – for instance the end of the bipolar world division; the acceleration of European integration, which was accompanied by an accentuation of the center–periphery divide; the dynamics of globalization, with its new configuration of spaces and

The Handbook of Language and Globalization, First Edition. Edited by Nikolas Coupland.
© 2013 Blackwell Publishing Ltd except for editorial material and organization © 2013 Nikolas Coupland.
Published 2013 by Blackwell Publishing Ltd.

scales; the deregulation of the economic sphere; the multi-directionality of migration and communication flows. While forces centripetal with reference to the nation-state aimed at constructing and imposing a unitary language, centrifugal tendencies were simultaneously working toward the decentering of these national languages.

Unification versus Division: Language Policies in the Space of Former Yugoslavia

Linguistically, the southern Slav space is usually described as a language continuum which begins in the Alps in the north and stretches down right to the shores of the Black Sea. Segmentation into different languages was determined by extralinguistic factors and depended on the political centers of these languages (Neweklowsky 2000). Phases of divergence and convergence alternated according to various political parameters (Bugarski 2004). The number of officially recognized languages in the area varied. Until World War II there were three south Slavic languages: Slovenian, Serbocroatian, and Bulgarian. In 1944, when the Federal Yugoslav Republic of Macedonia was founded, the number rose to four. To regroup the varieties spoken in the area of this member republic into an official standard language and to name it 'Macedonian' was a compromise between the Serbian side, which claimed that the Macedonian dialects were Serbian, and the Bulgarian side, which insisted on them being Bulgarian (ibid.).

The common norms for the standard Serbocroatian (or Croatoserbian) language had already been accepted by Serbs and Croats in the middle of the nineteenth century, when Vuk Karadžić (1787–1864), who was active during the rule of the Austro-Hungarian monarchy, codified it. From the very beginning of its codification and unification by Vuk Karadžić, this language was differentiated into two national varieties: an eastern one – Serbian; and a western one – Croatian. In the so-called 'second Yugoslavia' (1943–92) – the history of the which can be characterized as a sensitive, sometimes fragile equilibrium between centralistic and federalistic forces – an agreement was signed in 1954 concerning language use in the Bosnian, Croatian, Montenegrin, and Serbian member republics of the Socialist Federal Republic of Yugoslavia (SFRJ). The agreement confirmed that Serbocroatian/Croatoserbian was the official language of these four republics and allowed for variation at the lexical, syntactic, and phonetical level; such variation can be exemplified by the parallel and equal use of ekavian and jekavian variants.[1] Within the logic of imagining the space of south Slavic languages as a continuum, ekavian is usually attributed to the eastern parts (mainly Serbia), and jekavian to the western areas (Croatia, Bosnia, Montenegro).

The notion of a 'language continuum' stems from dialectology and opposes the idea of clear-cut language boundaries. It was arrived at through information gathered from carefully chosen informants (mostly elderly people in rural areas who have not left their original settlement). The results would map a network of 'isoglosses' (an isogloss being a line marking the limit of use of a specific linguistic feature), and these in turn indicate the territorial distribution of particular systemic features (phonological, morphological, lexical); hence isoglosses depict idioms as continua rather than as entities clearly demarcated by borders. Although linguistic theory asserts that borders can be drawn by means of denser bundles of isoglosses, it does not define the density or the degree of difference which may justify the concept of 'language border.' The linguistic border is not a clearly demarcated line, but rather a zone of transition (Melis 1996: 177). Chambers and Trudgill (1980) suggested defining the notion of 'language border' within a continuum as the point where total communication breakdown occurs. This is, however, equally problematic, since inter-comprehension is a variable which also depends on language ideologies and on extralinguistic factors such as communication interests.

That the 'language continuum' was a type of construct ideally designed to promote the socialist notion of unity in diversity became clear in the course of more recent Yugoslav history, when the 'Croatian Spring' movement of the 1970s stipulated the recognition of a separate Croatian language and, in support of this claim, emphasized the tradition of a distinct Croatian literary language which went back for centuries. In his historical account of the linguistic situation in the south Slavic space, Škiljan (2001: 96) draws attention to the fact that the notion of a dialect continuum gives only a partial representation of a more complex whole, because, in addition to dialects and synchronically with them, different other idioms were also present throughout history. Migration and social transformations like urbanization produced a local co-presence of different idioms across the south Slavic space. Different successive state administrations – such as those of the Ottoman Empire, of the Austro-Hungarian monarchy, or of the kingdom of the Serbs, Croats, and Slovenes – imposed different official and administrative languages. A range of liturgical languages – Latin, Old Church Slavonic, Arabic, Hebrew, each one with its distinct writing system – entered the everyday life of the south Slavic space, which was already linguistically diverse; and so did various languages of literary production, with their systemic features – supradialectal or supra-vernacular. Each of these idioms was linked to a network of speakers, had a certain communicative efficiency, and was attached to different forms of symbolic power. As individuals participated in different networks, considerable mixing and overlapping occurred.

The first indications of the disintegration of the Yugoslav state became apparent in the middle of the 1980s, when the centers of the member republics gained political importance over the central state. The communist party split into six ethno-national parties, which were eager to control the public sphere in their relative territories (Puhovski 2000: 42). Borders and their representation on maps became a central topic in political and media discourses (Dragičević-Šešić 2001: 72). The division of the Yugoslav federation was argued for by emphasizing the existence of different kinds of boundaries: the political, the ethnical, the religious, and the linguistic. Considerable effort was made to construct these different kinds of boundaries as congruent and to reify them as 'natural' dividing lines, endowed both with an external dimension – that of separating between states – and with an internal dimension – that of excluding 'others' from the national consensus (Hodžić 2000: 24). At the same time the existence of a standard Serbocroatian language, common yet pluricentric (or multi-various), was questioned; it was postulated instead, in Croatia as well as in Serbia, that separate national languages had 'always' existed, and complaints were made that the right to use one's own language had been denied by the Yugoslav state. The existence of language boundaries and of distinct national speech communities was argued for by pinning down possible linguistic differences between these national languages.

In the socialist as well as in the western world the (nation–)state as a bounded unit has been taken for granted as a point of departure in research, and social sciences have largely operated on the assumption of an unproblematic division of space and of 'naturally' discontinuous territories (Newman and Paasi 1998: 195). Referring to ethnic conflicts, Bourdieu makes the point (1982: 138) that borders are not to be considered as a "natural" category, but as social and political constructs. He emphasizes that the drawing of borders is linked to constructing, deconstructing, and reconstructing social groups. This process, he states, is in turn connected with a particular vision of the world, which is affirmed through demarcation from other world visions; and there is a dialectical relationship between these world visions and social practices. Pushing Bourdieu's argument a little further, the drawing of borders also has a dimension of discursive constructedness, as discursive acts are socially constitutive in a variety of ways, being largely responsible for the production, the maintenance, and the transformation of social conditions. Discursive acts are socially constitutive in a variety of ways, being largely responsible for the production, the maintenance, and the transformation of social conditions. Or, as Wodak and colleagues put it, "through linguistic representation in various dialogic contexts, discursive practices may influence the formation of groups" (1999: 8). Thus it can be argued that language boundaries are not only social and political constructs, but also discursive ones (Busch and Kelly-Holmes 2004).

Similarly, in linguistic theory the assumption of a speech community was for a long time taken for granted as a frame of departure for research. Such an assumption implies that the social, cultural, territorial entities in which people live can be differentiated according to linguistic criteria; it implies therefore some notion of boundedness. There have been different approaches toward a definition of speech community. One approach takes the characterizing feature to be "interaction by means of speech" (Bloomfield 1965: 42) or, more narrowly, direct and indirect communication via the common language. Fishman points out that the notion of speech community is not necessarily tied to the use of a single speech variety, but rather to "density of communication and/or symbolic integration [...] regardless of the number of varieties employed" (Fishman 1971: 234). Other approaches are centerd around "shared social attitudes towards language" (Labov 1972: 120) or are based on the self-evaluation of speakers "who regard themselves as using the same language" (Halliday et al. 1964: 140). Authors point out that extralinguistic criteria enter such definitions. For instance Bloomfield concedes that his definition is only of relative value, since cleavages between adjoining speech forms can be primarily of political, not linguistic, nature. Furthermore, as the possibility of communication can range from zero to a delicate adjustment (Bloomfield 1965), Fishman mentions social and cultural criteria which enter into the notion of speech community and make the definition problematic (Fishman 1971). In sociolinguistics there is thus a large consensus that the notion of speech community is also – or even primarily – a social and political construct, no less than the notion of language border is. Bringing into play the concept of language ideologies, Woolard (1998: 18) states: "simply using language in particular ways is not what forms social groups, identities or distinctions (nor does the group relation automatically give rise to linguistic distinction); rather ideological interpretations of such uses of language always mediate these effects."

Following this line of thought, the 'new' national languages postulated in the process of disintegration of former Yugoslavia cannot be considered to be natural formations, but rather unitary languages in the Bakhtinian sense:

> A unitary language is not something given [*dan*] but is always in essence posited [*zadan*] – and at every moment of its life it is opposed to the realities of heteroglossia. […] We are taking language not as a system of abstract grammatical categories, but rather language conceived as ideologically saturated, language as a world view, even as a concrete opinion, insuring a maximum of mutual understanding in all spheres of ideological life. Thus a unitary language gives expression to forces working toward concrete verbal and ideological unification and centralization, which develop in vital connection with the process of sociopolitical and cultural centralization. (Bakhtin 1981: 270f.)

Whereas the periods when Serbocroatian was the dominant official language were characterized by pluri-centrism occurring under conditions of changing power relationships, in the post-Yugoslav phase former sub-centers become new poles of centralization working toward linguistic unification vis-à-vis the inside and toward a maximization of difference vis-à-vis the outside.

Sociolinguistic approaches differentiate between ethnic languages, national languages, and official languages. In the *International Handbook of Sociolinguistics*, Barbour (2004: 288) reserves the phrase 'national language' for languages which, "whether they are official languages or not, have a clear role in national identity." This link with constructions of national identity applies to the concept of 'civic nation' (*Staatsnation*), which follows the model of the French Revolution, as well as to the one of 'ethnic nation' (*Kulturnation*), which is to be taken in the Herderian sense. Whereas the notion of official language is necessarily bound up with that of sovereign power within a determined territory and with questions of legal status, the notion of national language is tied to discursive constructions of nationhood and people – *demos* or *ethnos* – and to symbolic functions attributed to language. The phrase 'national language' is also anchored in the Marxist historical approach to linguistic theory, since it refers to the literary language or to the standard variety which originated in the so-called 'nationality language' (*jazýk naródnosti*), and the latter encompassed all the varieties of a language in the pre-standardization phase. In this approach, national language is considered to be not only a means of communication but also a strong means of cohesion.

Constructing/Inventing the National Languages

The dissolution, step by step, of the Socialist Federal Republic of Yugoslavia began in 1990 with the outbreak of armed conflicts and led to the formation of new states which declared their independence: Slovenia, Croatia, Macedonia, Bosnia–Herzegovina (BiH), the Federal Republic of Yugoslavia (later, Serbia and Montenegro), Montenegro, and Kosovo. For Bosnia and Herzegovina alone, it is estimated that up to 250,000 persons were killed during the war or are reported missing. Approximately half of the population was forced to leave their homes, either seeking refuge in another country or being displaced internally. While most of the newly founded states followed a more or less traditional nation-state model, the Dayton Peace Accords of 1995 left Bosnia–Herzegovina with a rather complex structure. The agreement divided the state into two areas, known as 'Entities' – the Federation of Bosnia–Herzegovina (FBiH) and the Serb Republic (Republika Srpska, RS) – both still placed under international administration. Whereas Serbocroatian/Croatoserbian had been the official language in the member republics of Croatia, of Bosnia–Herzegovina, of Serbia and of Montenegro during the period of the Socialist Federal Republic of Yugoslavia, the newly founded nation-states declared Croatian (1990) and Serbian (1992) as the official languages of the respective states and Bosnian, Croatian, and Serbian (1993) as the official languages of Bosnia–Herzegovina.

The ground for the language division was prepared by nationally oriented elites. In Croatia, leading cultural institutions published in 1967 the so called "Declaration on the name and position of the Croatian literary language," which called for the recognition of Croatian as a separate language. In Serbia, in a Memorandum of 1986, the Serbian Academy of Sciences and Arts expressed concern about Serbian minorities in Croatia being denied the right to "use their own language and script" (Greenberg 2004: 11). In Croatia, a number of handbooks of linguistic advice for the general public had already appeared in the 1980s and were circulated among journalists and school teachers. Differential dictionaries were not an entirely new phenomenon in the area; what was new was their number, and the fact that they did not address a specialized circle (translators, linguists) but targeted a large general public through cheap pocket editions (Okuka 1998: 88). It is interesting to note that there are considerable differences between these dictionaries, not only in the number of lexical items they list, but also in general orientation: some represent an extreme attempt at purism, drawing as they do on lexical items which stem from the language reform introduced by the totalitarian NDH[2] state during World War II, others are more "moderate" (ibid.; Langston 1999: 186f.). The aims of such dictionaries and handbooks, as authors formulated them, were "to bear witness to the existence of a separate Croat language" (Brodnjak 1991; compare Langston 1999: 187) and to assist people who were "striving to speak good Croatian in daily life to demonstrate their national consciousness also by means of language" (Pavuna 1993; compare Langston 1999: 180).

Later on dictionaries and language advice handbooks started to appear in Bosnia in a similar way, emphasizing turcisms as inherently Bosnian and stressing differences in orthography between what is considered the Bosnian language and what is considered the Croatian and the Serbian language. In a Bosnian language handbook which also lists "correct" and "incorrect" words, language is coupled with national duty and loyalty, as expressed in the foreword: "we expect from you that you know your language and care for it" (Halilović 1996: 7). Analyzing the new school dictionary of the Bosnian standard language, Durić (2003) estimates that 70 percent of the lexical items listed can be considered as turcisms.

Script choice and spelling systems can mark proximity and distance between two speech communities, as they are constitutive parts of language regimes (Coulmas 2005: 7). In Serbia, 'difference' was mainly defined through promoting the Cyrillic script. The constitutional amendments adopted in 1989 still allowed the Latin script for ethnically mixed regions, but they prescribed that the official script in Serbia should be Cyrillic. Consequently Latin inscriptions disappeared from public spaces, form state controlled media, and from school manuals. The Latin was reduced, roughly, to the private domain. The defence of the Cyrillic was a topic not only in the media, but also in intellectual circles; for example, at the University of Belgrade a society for the protection of the Cyrillic was founded with the aim to "prevent the annihilation of the Cyrillic script as the first step in the annihilation of the Serbian national identity" (Jakšić 2001: 14). The Cyrillic script served as a symbol of proximity to the eastern and orthodox sphere, while the exclusive use of the Latin script and the rejection of turcisms were evoked in an attempt to legitimate Croatian efforts to locate the newly founded state as an integral part of western Europe, on the imaginary geographical map and as part of the centuries old European *Schicksalsgemeinschaft* – a community determined by historical destiny – based on Christian values (Skopljanac Brunner et al. 2000).

Parts of the scientific community in linguistics and slavistics were not immune against the nationalistic virus, and they fueled the debate by supplying arguments that could be used to forge language ideologies. There was a tendency to reify languages or to use metaphors and personifications, by speaking for example of a "cultural and emotional individuality" of languages (Katičić 2001: 26). In this context, the ongoing debate whether a common language still exists or had ever existed is highly significant. Already in the 1970s, the Croatian linguist Brozović coined the phrase "middle-south-Slavic diasystem," which was defined as a common linguistic substance. Monnesland (2003) shows that, although the term 'diasystem' is not in use in international linguistic terminology, it became popular in the south Slavic space, in an attempt to avoid the term 'language.' There seemed to be a larger consensus that 'something' was common, but there was a problem of naming it. Some pleaded for 'Serbo-Croat(ian)' or 'Croato-Serb(ian)' (according to continuity), others for 'middle-south-Slavonic (according to the geo-geographical position) or for Newshtokavian (according to the dialectal basis; Brborić 2003:

36). A similar debate is taking place around the name of the standard language in use in Bosnia–Herzegovina. The question is whether it should be 'Bosnian' – a regional rather than ethnic name – or 'Bosniac' – which comes from the self-chosen ethnic name of Muslims, in accordance with the idea of deriving a lingonym from an ethnonym (Brborić 2003; Jurić-Kappel 2003).

Designing and Implementing Language Policies

With the proclamation of independent states on the territory of former Yugoslavia, the postulated national languages gained official status as dominant state languages within the new territories. The implementation of corpus and acquisition planning could thus rely on the power of legislative and administrative structures. The war situation reinforced the position of the state authorities due to the possibility of imposing emergency regulations and of evoking a firm national consensus. The outbreak of the war interrupted the information and communication flows between the now separated states, and not only in the public domain but also in private sphere, as postal and telecommunication services were cut. This almost total isolation favored the constitution of separate national public spheres with their specific national discourses, in which newly coined terms and changing linguistic and signifying practices gradually become an obstacle to mutual understanding.

In implementing language policies and corpus planning, authorities traditionally rely on three main pillars: administration, education, and the media. Administration and education are sectors in which prescriptive language use can be implemented immediately – at least in written communication, which can be easily monitored and controlled. In the case of national languages in the space of former Yugoslavia, numerous examples for such prescriptive implementation efforts can be cited. The following example shows that, even in authoritarian conditions, top-down measures in language planning can hardly be enforced when they do not gain acceptance. In 1993, when the war in Bosnia–Herzegovina was raging, the potentates in Republika Srpska – the Serbian part of Bosnia-Herzegovina – aligned their efforts at 'language cleansing' to the 'motherland,' not only by adopting the Cyrillic script but also by prescribing the ekavian variant for public use in 1993. In fact the authorities were well aware that the ekavian variant, which is widely spread in Serbia, was not used in the Serbian part of Bosnia in daily practice. The idea was that the "ekavica should be given back to the people to which it belongs [...] in order to liberate it form foreign influences."[3] All media were compelled by law to employ exclusively the *ekavica* (that is, ekvian) and the Cyrillic script. This enforced ekavization ended in a fiasco, and in 1998 the Republica Srpska authorities had to revise their decision and to reallow the use of the jekavian variant in the public domain.

In the state of Bosnia–Herzegovina there are now three emotionally loaded standards in use in the public domain. Although differences are being accentuated – especially at the lexical level and in the script – these differences do not exclude mutual comprehension. In the Serbian and Croatian part of Bosnia–Herzegovina, language policies endeavored to fortify the links with the respective 'mother-lands.' In Republika Srpska, Serbian is prescribed as the medium of instruction. In the Federation, either Bosnian or Croatian is the official language of instruction, depending on the majority population in the respective area. While 'minority' children may in principle attend classes in the curriculum and language of the local majority, with all its nationalistic elements, in practice the politics of separation have led to two widespread phenomena in BiH education: the bussing of children to 'mono-ethnic' schools outside of their area of residence; and the 'two-schools-under-one- roof' system.

The role of the media in the discursive construction of national identities has been widely acknowledged, mainly with reference to the post-World War II media system in western Europe, which is based on a strong public-service broadcasting sector. National radio and television have been understood as playing a "dual role, serving as the political public sphere of the nation–state, and as the focus for national cultural identification. [...] Broadcasting has been one of the key institutions through which listeners and viewers have come to imagine themselves as members of the national community" (Morley and Robins 1996: 10). Media have an impact on language policy at different levels: first of all, by using language as one of the semiotic modes in communicating, the media contribute to language change, since they provide linguistic resources; or, as Bourdieu suggests in speaking more generally about the literary field, they "produce means of production," "word and thought associations," and, moreover, all the forms of discourse that are seen as "authoritative" and can be cited as examples of "correct language use" (Bourdieu 1982: 35). Secondly, even if media independence has been one of the basic principles of the modern state, state authorities have had a certain possibility of control and intervention through media laws, licensing procedures, frequency and paper allocations, subsidies. National laws and regulations can also intervene at the level of language use. An example of this kind of intervention is the French legislation concerning the limitation of anglicisms in the public domain, which was copied by a number of eastern European countries in the 1990s (Busch 2004: 151). Furthermore, media production depends on available resources; it can be seen as a moment in a chain of communicative events which often revert to national news agency material and to press releases issued by official sources. Finally, the media have always been engaged in metalinguistic discourses. And metalinguistic discourses gain in importance especially at times when language change is being promoted by top-down methods and when the affirmation of language boundaries is at stake. They can contribute to creating an environment for policing language use and for the spread of language purism, linking 'correct' language use to national loyalty and stigmatizing 'wrong' language use as deviant.

Several large international research projects dealt with the role of national broadcasting institutions and of state controlled print media during the war in the propagation of hate speech and in the development of ethnic stereotypes on the territory of former Yugoslavia (Skopljanac Brunner et al. 2000). Okuka (1998),

Langston (1999), and Langston and Peti-Stantić (2003) cite numerous examples of metalinguistic discourses in the political sphere (speeches, declarations, party programs) and in the media – discourses in which strategies of differentiation, of emphasizing language boundaries between Serbian and Croatian and Bosnian, of evoking the idealized past of a 'pure' language are apparent. Nevertheless, oppositional voices were also present, especially through the independent media, in which sarcastic comments on language purism were frequent (Busch 2001: 158). In Serbia the mainstream media immediately abandoned the practice of using two alphabets and began to use exclusively the Cyrillic script, for print as well as for subtitling. In the publishing sector subsidies were directly tied to employing the Cyrillic script. An extreme example of an overtly prescriptive language policy aiming at cementing differences via the media was the Croatian Radio and Television (HRTV) in the early1990s. The HRTV produced a handbook that listed desired Croatian and undesired 'foreign' words; journalists who opposed it were sacked under the pretext of being unable to speak 'correct' Croatian. Language use in war reporting was strictly prescribed; for instance the *Jugoslovenska narodna armija* ('the Yugoslav national army,' JNA) had to be called the "Serbian communist occupator" (Thompson 1999: 159). Temporarily the state TV followed a policy that attempted to make the symbolic boundaries – which had been discursively constructed between the Croatian and the Serbian language – coincide with communication boundaries. Speakers of Serbian were subtitled into Croatian in TV and in films (Škiljan 2002: 278).

Language ideology approaches draw attention to the fact that the process of demarcating one language from another – the external demarcation – has a counterpart in the drawing of internal boundaries, in the definition of who the legitimate speakers are (Gal and Woolard 2001). In other words the process of external differentiation is linked to a process of internal homogenization, which results in exclusions. From the perspective of the individual speaker, this means that his/her linguistic practices function as markers of belonging to a defined group. At all the different levels of linguistic practice – the vocabulary, the phonological system, the syntax, the script, or the orthography – certain characteristics can become shibboleths.

Before the disintegration of the Yugoslav Federation it was possible to use the allegedly eastern ekavian and the allegedly western jekavian variants, as well as the Cyrillic or the Latin script, throughout the whole Serbocroatian space. Especially in urban environments, one person could even use, say, jekavian in speaking and ekavian in writing. In population censuses, citizens could choose to declare their affiliation to a specific ethnicity (the Serbian, the Croatian, the Roma, the Muslim …) or opt for a Yugoslav identity. In the national hubris of the first years after the proclamation of the new states, it was impossible to avoid the ascription of an unambiguous and exclusive identity on the basis of national belonging. One of the well known markers for ascriptions of ethnic affiliation was the usage of the two variants of the word 'thousand,' which had so far functioned as synonyms: whereas *tisuća* became a marker of belonging to Croatian, that is, the western side, *hiljada* became a marker of Serbian, on the eastern side. But neither is inherently characteristic for one side or the other. Such linguistic practices, which function as a kind of shibboleth, are in fact pragmatic phenomena, patterns of language use that are interpreted by speakers and listeners through ideologies about pragmatics (Gal 2006: 17). In political and media discourses, an environment was created that propagated linguistic purism and linguistic loyalty toward the nation. Against the ongoing processes of differentiation due to the heteroglossic nature of linguistic practice, the unitary language – in this case, the national language – needs to be policed in order to be kept distinct and 'pure.' Although 'wrong' language usage could entail severe consequences such as loss of employment, there were also strategies for undermining purism and policing – for instance reverting to vernaculars or local dialects, or naming one's own language '*naš jezik*' ('our language').

To summarize: in their concepts, the new states followed the 'old' models of (nation–)state building – models based on a (discursively) constructed unity between territory, people, and language. An important factor in this process was the construction of language boundaries and of the language community by means of ideologies, myths, and metalinguistic discourses which emphasize differences. In this national paradigm the standard language and its 'purity' were considered to be means of creating a sense of belonging and of proving loyalty. Also, in their choice of instruments for the implementation of national language policies, the new nation–states drew on traditional repertoires such as the status definition in the legal system, or on the language used in administration, in education, and in the media. These factors contributed to a centripetal movement, which anchored the new national languages or re-emphasized established state languages. The national language is, in the Bakhtinian sense, "ideologically saturated," "a world view," "a unitary language" giving "expression to forces working towards concrete verbal and ideological unification and centralisation" (Bakhtin 1981: 74).

Challenging the National Languages

Whereas centralizing forces, firmly rooted in the paradigm of the monolingual nation–state, viewed language as homogenous, counter-moves acting toward the affirmation of heteroglossia were present right from the beginning in the process of affirmation of national sovereignty. Three types of discourse linked to particular imaginations of society, as Heller and Labrie (2003: 16) described them in Canada's case, can be discerned in different phases of history, but are also simultaneously present today: the traditionalist (*traditionaliste*), the modernizing (*modernisant*) and the globalizing (*mondialisant*). The traditionalist discourse propagated by elites is based on the construction of belonging to a socially homogeneous group, which is the legitimate bearer of religious and moral values expressed through a linguistic conservatism and purism. The modernizing discourse is oriented toward the modern nation–state, in which language severs as a factor of national unity and cohesion. The emergent globalizing discourse considers the economy as a key factor in the valorization of linguistic practices and promotes multilingualism, cultural and linguistic diversity, and the commercialization of cultural and linguistic resources. In the south Slavic space these three strands of discourse can be identified as co-present; thereby the globalizing is strongly oriented toward Europe and expressed as affiliation to the European economic and cultural space (Busch 2001).

Homogenization in language use is much more difficult to implement today, under the conditions of globalization, where communication and media flows have become more diverse and multi-directional than in previous times, when communication was organized around a national public sphere, as described by Habermas (1990). In social science globalization is interpreted as changes in the scales on which social activities take place (Jessop 2002). The nation-state looses its central position as a reference point in the economic and political order. Not only global, but also regional economic blocks, cross-border regions, regions within states, cities, and so on gain in importance in the actual process of the re-scaling of particular spatial entities. The notion of interlocked scales and of re-scaling has been introduced into linguistics, for instance by Fairclough (2006) in reference to orders of discourse, or by Blommaert, Collins, and Slembrouck (2005). These different, socially constructed spaces develop their own language regimes, characterized by sets of norms and expectations about communicative interactions, by orders of indexicality.

The central position of states in the formulation and implementation of language policy and language planning is being challenged by the different levels of scale, and the number of potential actors in the field is thus being multiplied. At a supranational level, European and international institutions have increasingly integrated language policy in their agenda – the OSCE (Organization for Security and Cooperation in Europe) mainly with regard to minority languages; the Council of Europe (CoE) principally in connection with education policies and human rights; and most recently the European Union in relation to the comprehensive language plan that also encompasses the languages of migration and of the Union's trade partners. The two main legal instruments guaranteeing linguistic rights, the Council of Europe's Charter for Regional and Minority Languages and the Framework Convention for the Protection of National Minorities, were finalized precisely with a view to counteracting nationalism in the transition process across eastern Europe. Signing both documents was seen as a precondition for entry into the Council of Europe and obliged the candidate countries to recognize in their legislation that they were not constituted in a purely monolingual and mono-national way.

The introduction of market economy accelerated a power shift from state institutions to the private sector. In the media and communication sector, this reconfiguration became obvious particularly fast. Corporate mergers, strategic alliances, and the convergence of the media and of communication and entertainment industries changed ownership structures and contributed to altering information and communication flows and to intensifying the spread of globalized cultural products in the countries of eastern Europe. In parallel, a globalized terminology is integrated into institutional and individual linguistic practices, as Fairclough (2006) demonstrates in the case of Romania, and becomes a marker of belonging to a global elite. Other factors in the decentering of unitary language are the products provided by globalized language learning industries, software enterprises, communication and media industries. What software is available in what languages and scripts, and to what linguistic norms the most widely spread text processing programs comply, is mainly driven by market interests.

In parallel with the efforts toward linguistic demarcation made by the national media in the successor states of former Yugoslavia, there emerge developments that re-group the Serbocroatian speaking realm into one. Such developments are not motivated by nostalgia as much as by market considerations which aim at maximizing audiences, at creating a public for advertising, and at avoiding language marked as a particular national standard. Commercial interests guide for instance the policy of the Novi Sad-based (Serbian) yellow press magazine *Svet plus*, a magazine featuring mainly celebrity gossip, which claims to be the diaspora magazine with the highest circulation rate between Athens and Stockholm. A similar strategy of maximizing audiences by addressing the whole south Slavic space can be observed in the case of the Belgrad-based company Pink TV. Pink TV, sometimes referred to as 'Balkan MTV,' could profit from the large Serbian home market and build a media empire that reaches now even beyond former Yugoslavia. Pink TV advertises specific cultural practices and values; it promotes new trends in fashion and music; it reaches audiences from Slovenia to Bulgaria, also covering Bosnia–Herzegovina, Montenegro, and Serbia; and it is highly popular in the diaspora.

Emphasis on the local can also contribute to undermining aspirations of imposing a unitary language. Using regional vernaculars or local dialects is no longer necessarily indexical of a traditionalist orientation, but it can represent a rejection of national categorizations, especially when communication flows develop a trans-local dimension that transgresses state borders. This change in connotation is linked to the fact that language has become a tradeable commodity – at the local level, in the form of a commercialization of authenticity (Heller 2003). Similarly, regional multilingualism can become an asset in opening spaces beyond the national. Media in the successor states of the former Yugoslavia have become both more local – a process which includes the use of local varieties on the Slavic continuum – and more trans-local. In the sector of civic media, this strategy of addressing and linking audiences within the entire (virtual) linguistic space as a heterogeneous trans-local public is understood as a possibility of 'dis-enclaving' the space culturally. Linguistically this is achieved through the direct representation of different voices and discourses by means of their own modes of expression. The rise of multilingual formats in the media was a response to processes of ethnicization. Such formats make visible the co-presence of different languages, which also has a transformative effect on the discourse itself.

In the multilingual area of Vojvodina as well as in the regions around Skopje or Istria, several multilingual media initiatives have been active at least for some time (Karlsreiter 2003). In the multilingual radio programs different languages alternate, often within one time slot; speakers use the language they prefer to speak in; and the moderators take care that the program can be followed by listeners with different language backgrounds. In multilingual areas like the Vojvodina or Skopje it can be assumed that part of the population has at least some understanding of more than one language. Bilingual and multilingual media products address simultaneously audiences which are usually separated; journalists have to keep in mind the interests and needs of both – the positions which are being negotiated have to be acceptable to both.

In the past years there has been a growing number of media which address the otherwise fragmented audiences across the Balkan area, in a trans-local move. One of these is Cross Radio, a project which promotes program exchange both between different radio stations in the space of the former Yugoslavia and between stations that produce programs in urban centers with a significant diaspora. Cross Radio focuses on culture, with the idea of promoting a transnational – and thus 'de-provincialized' – cultural space. Consequently different codes and registers can be heard in the programs, which are re-broadcast by stations from Pristina, via Belgrade, Zagreb, and Ljubljana, to Zurich, and are also directly accessible to a wider public through the internet. In the print sector there is a range of cultural magazines and periodical publications which run along similar lines.

Finally, communication flows have become more multi-directional, in the public as well as in the private domain. Satellite technologies and the internet render media products more easily and more rapidly accessible to de-territorialized audiences on a global scale. Mobile phones, computer-mediated communication and increased travel facilities enhance interpersonal communication even across long distances. This reconfiguration of communication flows contributes to the emergence of new spaces of identity beyond the national one (Morley and Robins 1996) and allows people to engage in transidiomatic practices (Jacquemet 2005). In migration research, a diaspora is no longer primarily seen as a homogenous group depending on a motherland, but as a socially differentiated nexus of persons living in a variety of complex lifeworlds (*Lebenswelten*). In linguistics, research was mainly framed in terms of language loss and language change, whereas since the 1990s there has been a distinct focus on questions of lingo-cultural hybridity, language crossing, and linguistic liminality (Rampton 1995).

National Languages and Language Change

The centripetal forces working toward the unitary national language and the centrifugal forces tending toward heteroglossia, reinforced by the processes of glocalization, represent the framework in which change in linguistic practices takes place. There are only a very few empirical studies dedicated to the change of language use in the space of former Yugoslavia, and it is difficult to say how much the effort to promote unitary languages has actually brought about changes in daily language practices. Langston (1999) presents a study based on a corpus which he obtained from text samples taken in 1996/97 from different Croatian media, which he compares to samples taken in 1985. He concludes: "Noticeable changes in lexical usage in the Croatian media have indeed taken place since the break-up of the Yugoslav state, but on whole they are relatively minor. [...] Differences may also be observed in the usage of the state-controlled or more nationalistic media versus that of the independent press" (Langston 1999: 188f.). Jahn (1999: 353), investigating language attitudes in the Istrian peninsula, observed considerable differences according to political attitudes, and generally concluded that "people feel linguistically insecure" and tend to avoid the standard variety whenever possible. From their questionnaire-based survey, Langston and Peti-Stantić (2003) draw the preliminary conclusion that the survey indicates "a significant level of resistance towards change" and that "Croatian language reform is still a work in progress, and it will be some time before we see what will become part of the standard language and what will be rejected" (p. 56).

Most of the work on language change focuses, however, on the lexicon, which reacts in a seismographic and intense way because of changing practices and needs of naming. Kunzmann-Müller (2003) compares language change at the lexical level in different south Slavic languages, on the basis of corpuses derived from media texts. She concludes that changes in the language of the media are more noticeable in Bulgaria than in the space of former Yugoslavia; and she attributes this state of things to the fact that, in the latter, the media enjoyed a higher degree of freedom in the times of socialism. In terms of linguistic practices, this means that an ideologically less loaded media language was closer to the spoken language. Concerning changes in grammar, Kunzmann-Müller concludes that elements from non-standard varieties brought into the 'new' national language are more likely to find acceptance than historical forms reactivated in top-down corpus planning. Gustavsson (2003) compares three grammars actually in use in Bosnia–Herzegovina, in Croatia, and in Serbia. According to his summary, the most noticeable differences can be found in grammatical terminology, in the choice of script, and in the use of the old Slavonic phoneme *jat* (which separates between ekavian and jekavian); as far as the description of the linguistic system is concerned, differences are minor. Generally speaking, the topic of language change is one of the research foci in Slavistics today. Zybatow (1995) criticizes research on this topic on the grounds that is mainly based on the analysis of lexical changes and does not pay heed to changes in connotations, in communication practices, in text genres and their discursive location, or in meta-linguistic attitudes. He pleads for a pragmatics-based concept of analyzing linguistic change.

What Sue Wright (2004: 53), referring to Bakhtin, claims for standard languages in general applies well to the new national languages of eastern Europe: "Standardisation is in part a fiction. We have imagined languages in the same way that we have imagined communities. [...] There is a perpetual tension as centripetal forces of convergence compete with centrifugal forces of differentiation." The work on language change, still scarce as it is, suggests that imposing national languages was successful to some extent, at a symbolic level, which is visible for instance in practices of naming and in the use of highly marked lexical items. Linguistic practice shows that the heteroglossia of daily life works effectively toward decentering any kind of unitary language, even in ideologically saturated contexts of policing. Under the condition of globalization, the process of decentering possibly gains in momentum, as daily life is influenced by processes of rescaling that foreground the supranational, subnational, and transnational levels with their corresponding linguistic practices. One could summarize the recent developments in eastern Europe by subsuming them to a struggle between different concepts: at the level of national policies, the traditional concept of the connection between language and territory – in which space is conceived as bounded, as a static 'container' for social relations, for communication, and for language practices – has been prevailing, while economic players and the lifeworlds reflect the globalized practices. From this perspective, language is linked to another notion of space and place: space defined by common social and linguistic practices, and place defined as an intersection of different practices and different networks in which small-scale language regimes develop.

NOTES

1   The distinction between 'ekavian' and 'jekavian' relates to the notation of the old Slavonic sound 'jat,' which can be reproduced either as 'e' or as 'je' – as e.g. in the variants of the word for 'river': *rijeka* (jekavian) and *reka* (ekavian).
2   The fascist NDH state (Nezavisna Država Hrvatska/Independent Croatian State) introduced a language reform which aimed at marking the difference between a Serbian and a Croatian language. In the course of this reform an etymological orthography was propagated and internationalisms were labelled 'serbisms.'
3   Alternativna informativna mreža (AIM), September 13, 1993. For the AIM archive see: http://www.aimpress.ch/. This example is also discussed in Bugarski 1995.

REFERENCES

Bakhtin, M. (1981) *The Dialogic Imagination,* edited by Michael Holquist. Austin, TX: University of Texas Press.

Bakhtin, M. (1984) *The Dialogical Principle,* edited by Tzvetan Todorov. Manchester: Manchester University Press.

Barbour, S. (2004) Nationalsprache und Amtssprache. In U. Ammon, N. Dittmar, K. J. Mattheier, and P. Trudgill (eds), *Soziolinguistik. Ein internationales Handbuch zur Wissenschaft von Sprache und Gesellschaft*, 2nd edn, Vol. 1, 288–96. Berlin: Mouton de Gruyter.

Blommaert, J., Collins, J., and Slembrouck, S. (2005) Spaces of multilingualism. *Language and Communication* 25: 197–216.

Bloomfield, L. (1965) *Langauge History [1933]*. New York: Rinehart and Winston.

Bourdieu, P. (1982) *Ce que parler veut dire. L'Economie des échanges linguistiques.* Paris: Fayard.

Brborić, B. (2003) Standardni jezik i jezički standard: aktualne retrospektive. *Wiener Slawistischer Almanach* (special issue) 57: 9–37.

Brodnjak, V. (1991) *Razlikovni rječnik srpskog I hrvatskog jezika*. Zagreb: Hrvatska sveučilišna naklada.

Bugarski, R. (1995) *Jezik od mira do rata*. Beograd: Slovograph.

Bugarski, R. (2004) Language and boundaries in the Yugoslav context. In B. Busch and H. Kelly-Holmes (eds), *Language, Discourse and Borders*, 21–38. Clevedon, Buffalo, Toronto, and Sydney: Multilingual Matters.

Busch, B. (2001) Grenzvermessungen: Sprachen und Medien in Zentral-, Südost- und Osteuropa. In B. Busch, B. Hipfl, and K. Robins (eds), *Bewegte Identitäten – Medien in transkulturellen Kontexten*, 145–73. Klagenfurt: Drava.

Busch, B. (2004) *Sprachen im Disput. Medien und Öffentlichkeit in multilingualen Gesellschaften*, Klagenfurt: Drava.

Busch, B., and Kelly-Holmes, H. (eds) (2004) *Language, Discourse and Borders in the Yugoslav Successor States*. Clevedon: Multilingual Matters (Current Issues in Language and Society series).

Chambers, J. K., and Trudgill, P. (1980) *Dialectology*, Cambridge: Cambridge University Press.

Coulmas, F. (2005) Changing language regimes in globalizing environments. *International Journal of the Sociology of Language* 175(6): 3–15.

Dragičević-Šešić, M. (2001) Borders and maps in contemporary Yugoslav art. In N. Švob-Đokić (ed.), *Redefining Cultural Identities*, 71–87. Zagreb: Institute for International Relations.

Durić, R. (2003) Školski Rječnik bosanskog jezika Dž. Jahića i standardizacija leksike u bosanskom jeziku na općekomunikacijskoj razini. *Wiener Slawistischer Almanach* (special issue) 57: 65–85.

Fairclough, N. (2006) *Language and Globalization*. Abingdon and New York: Routledge.

Fishman, J. (1971) *Sociolinguistics. A Brief Introduction*. Rowley, MA: Newbury.

Gal, S. (2006) Migration, minorities and multilingualism: Language ideologies in Europe. In C. Mar-Molinero and P. Stevenson (eds), *Language Ideologies, Policies and Practices: Language and the Future of Europe*, 13–28. Basingstoke: Palgrave Macmillan.

Gal, S. (2001) Linguistic theories and national images in nineteenth-century Hungary. In Gal and Woolard (eds), 30–46.

Gal, S., and Woolard, K. (2001) Constructing languages and publics. Authority and representation. In Gal and Woolard (eds), 1–13.

Gal, S., and Woolard, K. (eds) (2001) *Languages and Publics: The Making of Authority*. Manchester: St Jerome Publishing.

Greenberg, R. D. (2004) *Language and Identity in the Balkans. Serbo-Croatian and its Disintegration*. Oxford: Oxford University Press.

Gustavsson, S. (2003) O trima "srednjejužnoslavenskim" gramatikama. *Wiener Slawistischer Almanach* (special issue) 57: 87–95.

Habermas, J. (1990) *Strukturwandel der Öffentlichkeit [1962]*. Frankfurt am Main: Suhrkamp.

Halilović, S. (1996) *Gnijezdo lijepih riječi: pravilno – Nepravilno u bosanskome jeziku*. Sarajevo: Baština.

Halliday, M. A. K., McIntosh, A., and Strevens, P. (1964) *The Linguistic Sciences and Language Teaching*. London: Longman.

Heller, M. (2003) Globalization, the new economy, and the commodification of language and identity. *Journal of Sociolinguistics* 7: 473–92.

Heller, M., and Labrie, N. (2003) Langage, pouvoir et identité: Une étude de cas, une approche théorique, une méthodologie. In M. Heller and N. Labrie (eds), *Discours et identité. La Francité canadienne entre modernité et mondialisation*, 9–41. Cortil-Wodon: Editions Modulaires Euopénnes (EME).

Hodžić, A. (2000) Preoccupation with the 'other.' In N. S. Brunner, S. Gredelj, A. Hodžić, and B. Krištofić (eds), *Media and War*, 19–41. Belgrad: Argument.

Jacquemet, M. (2005) Transidiomatic practices: Language and power in the age of globalization. *Language and Communication* 25: 257–77.

Jahn, J.-E. (1999) New Croatian language planning and its consequences for language attitude and linguistic behavior – The Istrian case. *Language and Communication* 19: 329–54.

Jakšić, B. (2001) The disintegration of Yugoslavia and the division of language. Unpublished paper presented at the International Conference "Language–Society–History: The Balkans," Thessaloniki, 11–12 November 2001.

Jessop, B. (2002) *The Furtue of the Capitalist State*. Cambridge: Polity.

Jurić-Kappel, J. (2003) Bosanki ili bošnjački? *Wiener Slawistischer Almanach* (special issue) 57: 95–101.

Karlsreiter, A. (2003) *Media in Multilingual Societies: Freedom and Responsibility*, Wien: Office of the Representative on Freedom of the Media (OSCE).

Katičić, R. (2001) Croatian linguistic loyalty. *International Journal of the Sociology of Language* 147: 17–29.

Kunzmann-Müller, B. (2003) Syntaktischer Wandel in den südslawischen Sprachen. *Wiener Slawistischer Almanach* 52: 129–44.

Labov, W. (1972) *Sociolinguistic Patterns*. Oxford: Blackwell.

Langston, K. (1999) Linguistic cleansing: Language purism in Croatia after the Yugoslav break-up. *International Politics* 36: 179–201.

Langston, K., and Peti-Stantić, A. (2003) Attitudes towards linguistic purism in Croatia: Evaluating efforts at language reform. In M. Dedaic and D. N. Nelson (eds), *At War with Words*, 247–83. Berlin: Mouton de Gruyter.

Melis, L. (1996) Frontière linguistique. In H. Goebl, P. H. Nelde, Z. Stary, and W. Wölk (eds), *Kontaktlinguistik. Ein internationales Handbuch zeitgenössischer Forschung*, Vol. 1/2, 175–180. Berlin: Walter de Gruyter.

Monnesland, S. (2003) O pojmu "dijasistem." *Wiener slawistischer Almanach* (special issue) 57: 153–61.

Morley, D., and Robins, K. (1996) *Spaces of Identity. Global Media, Electronic Landscapes and Cultural Boundaries*. London and New York: Routledge.

Neweklowsky, G. (2000) Soziolinguistische Forschung zum Serbokroatischen und seinen Nachfolgesprachen. In *Sociolinguistica* 14: 192–6.

Neweklowsky, G. (2006) Die südlsavische Region. In U. Ammon, N. Dittmar, and K. J. Mattheier (eds), *Soziolinguistik. Ein internationales Handbuch zur Wissenschaft von Sprache und Gesellschaft*, Vol. 3, 1824–36. Berlin: Mouton de Gruyter.

Newman, D., and Paasi, A. (1998) Fences and neighbours in the postmodern world: Boundary narratives in political geography. *Progress in Human Geography* 22: 186–207.

Okuka, M. (1998) *Eine Sprache, viele Erben. Sprachenpolitik als Nationalisierungsinstrument in Ex-Jugoslawien*. Klagenfurt: Wieser.

Pavuna, S. (1993) *Govorimo li ispravno hrvatski? Mali razlikovni rječnik*. Zagreb: Integra.

Puhovski, Ž. (2000) Hate silence. In Brunner, Gredelj, Hodžić, and Krištofić (eds), 41–53.

Rampton, B. (1995) *Crossing: Language and Ethnicity among Adolescents*. London: Longman.

Škiljan, D. (2001) Languages with(out) frontiers. In N. Švob-Đokić (ed.), *Redefining Cultural Identities*, 87–101. Zagreb: Institute for International Relations.

Škiljan, D. (2002) *Govor nacije. Jezik, nacija, Hrvati*. Zagreb: Golden Marketing.

Skopljanac Brunner, N., Gredelj, S., Hodižić, A., and Krištofić, B. (2000)

Media and War. Zagreb and Belgrade: Centre for Transition and Civil Society Research, Agency Argument.

Thompson, M. (1999) *Forging the War. The Media in Serbia, Croatia, Bosnia and Herzegovina*. London: University of Luton Press.

Wodak, R., de Cillia, R., Reisigl, M., Liebhart, K., Hofstätter, K., and Kargl, M. (1998) *Zur diskursiven Konstruktion nationaler Identität*. Frankfurt am Main: Suhrkamp.

Woolard, K. (1998) Introduction. Language ideology as a field of inquiry. In B. Schieffelin, K. Woolard, and P. Kroskrity (eds), *Language Ideologies. Practice and Theory*, 3–51. New York: Oxford University Press.

Wright, S. (2004) *Language Policy and Language Planning: From Nationalism to Globalization*. Basingstoke: Palgrave Macmillan.

Zybatow, L. (1995) *Russisch im Wandel. Die russische Sprache seit der Perestrojka*. Berlin: Harrasowitz Verlag.

Part II Global Discourse in Key Domains and Genres

9 Localizing the Global on the Participatory Web

JANNIS ANDROUTSOPOULOS

Introduction

Given the importance of digital communications technologies as backbone of the network society (Castells 2000), the WorldWideWeb no doubt constitutes one of the "key social domains for language use in a globalizing world" (Coupland 2003: 466). Yet research on language and globalization has not systematically addressed the web, just as the emerging scholarship on computer-mediated discourse has paid little attention to the relationship of globalization and language online. Situating itself at the interface of these two fields, the present chapter draws attention to some linguistic practices that can be observed on the contemporary spaces of computer-mediated discourse that are commonly labelled 'web 2.0.'[1] The main objects of analysis are 'vernacular spectacles' – that is, multimedia content that is produced outside media institutions and uploaded, displayed, and discussed on media-sharing websites such as *YouTube*. Focusing on spectacles that rely on, and modify, textual material from popular culture, I argue that spectacles provide new opportunities to engage with global media flows from a local perspective. This engagement is both receptive and productive, in other words it is not limited to viewing and commenting online but extends to producing spectacles and displaying them to web audiences. I shall argue that spectacles create novel opportunities for the public staging of vernacular speech in the digital age. Yet vernacular spectacles are not made of language alone. Their meaning emerges through language and other semiotic modes, in a tension between appropriated material and its local recontextualization.

The framework and findings presented in this chapter are part of a broader engagement with the study of computer-mediated discourse (CMD). My approach advocates a combination of sociolinguistic and discourse analysis with ethnographic procedures, and it encompasses both screen and user-based data – that is, systematic observation of online discourse activities as well as direct contact with internet users (Androutsopoulos 2008). Empirically, the first part of this chapter draws on extended observation of web 2.0 environments, and the second

The Handbook of Language and Globalization, First Edition. Edited by Nikolas Coupland.

part focuses on two videos and their online comments. Such limitation to online data is the norm in CMD research (Herring 2004), but it is not uncontested from a broader methodological perspective. Jones (2004) argues that understanding the context of computer-mediated communication requires shifting attention from the screen to the social activities in which CMD is embedded. At the crossroads of sociolinguistics and popular culture, Pennycook (2007) advocates complementing textual analysis by the study of discourse production and reception practices. While I in principle endorse such a combination, I also make a case for the legitimacy of 'plain' textual analysis combined with ethnographic observation of online activities. While providing little insight into social life in front of the screen, a screen-based approach focuses on the contexts that emerge through ongoing online activities and layers of digital text.

I begin this chapter by situating my approach in language and globalization research and by introducing concepts that are central to my analysis. The following two sections outline some concepts and distinctions I find useful for the language-focused study of web 2.0 environments.[2] I proceed in three steps: First I outline characteristics of contemporary web communication that I consider consequential for language and discourse online, namely participation and convergence. I then identify four dimensions of language in contemporary web environments: organization, self-presentation, interaction, and spectacle. Subsequently I focus on three concepts for the analysis of discourse in these environments: multimodality, intertextuality, and heteroglossia. These form a background against which to examine the dialogue and the tension between globally available texts and their local recontextualizations. Two Bavarian versions of US American popular culture texts are then analyzed in order to illustrate how global content is locally treated in media productions 'from below,' and what role dialect has to play in this process.

Localization, Recontextualization, and Vernacularity

Scholars across disciplines have argued that globalization is not a unidirectional process by which linguistic or cultural elements are diffused and uncritically adopted (Crane 2002; Fairclough 2006: 32–6; Machin and van Leeuwen 2007, ch. 2; Pathania-Jain 2008: 132–42). An equally important aspect is how the global is localized, that is, appropriated and productively used as a medium of local expression, providing a resource for local negotiations of identities and relationships. From a sociolinguistic angle, instead of just thinking of a 'global' language and its impact on 'local' ones, attention is directed to the circulation of linguistic resources and their re-embedding in new sociocultural environments (Blommaert 2003, 2005; Pennycook 2007). According to one account, globalization creates a reorganization of norms in which 'mobile' codes "become local resources, embedded in local patterns of value-attributions" (Blommaert 2005: 139).

The aspect of global/local interdependence I focus on is 'semiotic mobility': the circulation of signs across time and space, their disembedding from and re-embedding into social and semiotic contexts (Blommaert 2003: 611, 2004: 128; Chouliaraki and Fairclough 1999: 83; Coupland 2003). From this angle, cultural globalization is an increased circulation of cultural artefacts across national and ethnolinguistic borders (Crane 2002), sometimes leading to "transnational globalized art forms" (Blommaert 2004: 131) such as reggae or hip hop (Alim et al. 2009). Semiotic mobility and local adaptation involve, by definition, a (usually complex and extensive) process of mediation, and they are situated within some form of popular culture such as radio talk, popular music, or lifestyle magazines. This goes to reinforce the suggestion that "it is hard to see how we can proceed with any study of language, culture, globalization and engagement without dealing comprehensively with popular culture" (Pennycook 2007: 81). In formal terms, globally circulating signs are theorized at two levels of granularity. New genres or discourse patterns are situated at a broader level, for instance in news discourse, in the communications and service industry, or in popular music. At a microlinguistic level we have linguistic features, usually (but not exclusively) lexical items that spread across dialects or languages. In one typical case of late modern linguistic globalization, lexis and discourse markers of English origin are 'borrowed' and structurally integrated into the grammar and the pragmatics of recipient languages up to the point of becoming indecipherable to the original speakers. There is an implicational relationship between the two levels, such that locally adapted lexis is often found in adapted genres or discourse styles, as for instance with English borrowings and code-mixing in African hip hop (see Higgins 2009 for a recent discussion).

In my analysis, semiotic mobility is situated within the web, regarded as 'mediascape' – that is, a large and complex repository of images and narratives (Appadurai 1996). This repository enables those with adequate technological access and competence to actively appropriate signs and texts, thereby acting as mediators between global resources and local audiences. Indeed, a novelty of the web 2.0 era (which is discussed in greater detail in the next section) is the capacity it creates for a large number of people to become 'intertextual operators' who digitally modify multi-modal text, for instance by adding subtitles, by replacing the original audio track, and so on. These media practices are closely related to localization and recontextualization in my data.

The term 'localization' has different meanings in the academic and professional literature, in translation studies among other domains (Cronin 2003). I use it here as a generic counterpart to globalization. By localization I mean a discourse process by which globally available media content is modified in a (more or less salient) local manner, involving some linguistic transformation to a local code and an orientation to a specific audience, defined by means of language choice. Localization in this sense is a specific type of construction of 'linguistic locality' as a response to globalized popular culture. Semiotic material from 'elsewhere' is made to speak 'from here' and 'to here,' drawing on a range of semiotic resources for its new indexical grounding. Localness is a scalar construct, its scope depending on situated contrast; it usually indexes a space below the nation-state level, but this can range from a large region to a small locality (Johnstone et al. 2006; Androutsopoulos 2010).

On content-sharing sites such as *YouTube*, localization often takes the shape of the recontextualization of popular texts. At home in a range of disciplines, the concept of recontextualization signifies the fit, into a new setting, of social practices that have been lifted from a previous, perhaps 'original' context. With regard to globalization, the terms 'decontextualization' and 'recontextualization' (alongside 'disembedding' and 're-embedding') are widely used to signify relations of "colonization and appropriation" (Fairclough 2006: 33–5) or the adaptation of mediated cultural patterns to new reception communities (Androutsopoulos and Scholz 2002, with regard to hip hop). I also draw on the theorizing of recontextualization undertaken by Bauman and Briggs (1990) in performance studies, which offers useful analytical options. They understand recontextualization as the re-embedding of text in a (new) situational context, and they identify six dimensions of that transformation which I will draw on in the analysis of recontextualized spectacles: framing; form; function; indexical grounding; translation; emergent structure of a new context.

In the web environments I focus on, recontextualization means that globally available media material is given new form, function, and meaning while still bearing traces "from its earlier context" (Bauman and Briggs 1990: 75). Vernacularity is a key aspect of this process. I discuss vernacularity here in two senses. The first is offered by the notion of vernacular literacies, classically defined as literacy practices that are not part of educational or professional institutions but are relatively free from institutional control, rooted in everyday practice, serving everyday purposes, and drawing on vernacular knowledge (Barton and Hamilton 1998). A lot of literacy practices in the new media among young people in the western world are vernacular in that sense (see for instance Snyder 2002). I argue that vernacular digital literacies are 'landing points' of globally circulating signs and texts; they are the sites where these signs and texts are locally reworked, drawing on the affordances of contemporary digital media to manipulate and publish content – music, speech, and video. Secondly, in a sense familiar to sociolinguists, 'vernacular' refers to local varieties of language, those that are the first to be acquired: the most local and informal, uncodified, and often classified as non-standard (Coupland 2009). The relevant relation between the two is that vernacular practices of digital literacy can be a site of vernacular linguistic expression. The well documented role of the new media as a site of written and public usage of vernaculars (for overviews, see Androutsopoulos 2006a, 2010) is explored in this chapter on the terrain of spectacles and their comments.

This sketches out an exploratory framework for the forthcoming discussion. As this discussion suggests, my concern is less with global semiotic flows as such than with the local recontextualization of globally available signs. From this angle, the relevance of content-sharing platforms to the relationship between language and globalization is not (just) that they facilitate the global circulation and availability of semiotic material, but that they constitute playgrounds for the display and negotiation of local responses to such material.

Web 2.0: Participation, Convergence, and the Rise of Vernacular Spectacles

A phrase often used for convenience rather than for its explanatory potential, 'web 2.0' lacks a widely accepted definition (Scholz 2008). It is often exemplified by lists of characteristics such as "rich user experience," "user participation," "dynamic content," "scalability" (Wikipedia 2009). Hinchcliffe (2006) posits as "key aspects" of web 2.0 its "rich and interactive user interfaces," "data consumption and remixing from all sources, particularly user generated data," and an "architecture of participation that encourages user contribution." Another way of exemplifying web 2.0 is by a juxtaposition to 'web 1.0,' a post-hoc label for the condition of the WorldWideWeb until the turn of the century (O'Reilly 2005). In that early era, the web was predominantly a medium of information retrieval. Content was professionally produced for consumption by users who could not do much more than surf, read, and print out. Interpersonal communication was carried out on applications that predated the web and operated separately from it, such as e-mail, newsgroups and Internet Relay Chat (IRC), to which much early scholarship on language on the internet was devoted. Thus a broad distinction between internet applications for interpersonal communication and the web as a unidirectional, information-oriented medium persisted throughout the 1990s. This dichotomy collapses during the 2000s, as a new generation of websites integrate applications for interpersonal communication and tools for the management of user-generated content. Typical web 2.0 environments such as social networking and media-sharing sites[3] offer an infrastructure to be appropriated and 'filled in' by users who generate almost all the content (excluding online advertisement and commercial banners): users edit and upload new texts, comment on or modify texts by other users, and create links between different kinds of texts (on condition of having adequate hardware and software and access to the internet). In that sense, the web developed from "publishing" to "participation" (O'Reilly 2005), and web 2.0 environments are indeed shaped by an "architecture of participation that encourages user contribution" (Hinchcliffe 2006).

Such accounts might be useful points of departure for a language and discourse-centered approach; indeed the emphasis on user participation ties in well with the sociolinguistic interest in the public visibility of vernaculars, with the increased informality of public discourse, and with sociolinguistic change generally. The boost of vernacular multi-literacies in web 2.0 environments exemplifies what the participatory web is all about. However, the tendency to mingle technology and society makes these accounts less useful. Moreover, a sociolinguistic angle may uncover characteristics that are less pronounced in broader discussion, yet potentially more consequential for language use.

Research on computer-mediated discourse has not yet engaged systematically with web 2.0 environments, referencing them, if at all, as sites of future scholarship (Baron 2008, Thimm 2008, Rowe and Wyss 2009; but see Boyd 2008). Besides participation, contemporary web environments are characterized by processes of convergence between formerly separate applications, modes, and activities. Drawing on media studies (Jenkins 2006), I use 'convergence' as a broad cover term that encompasses more specific processes of *integration, embedding*, and *modularity*. By 'integration' I mean the co-existence of various communication modes on a single platform (as in personal messages, instant messaging (IM), wall posts, and groups on *facebook*). By 'embedding' I mean the ability to place digital content, especially videos, on a web page. Multimedia texts are combined with other texts (such as blog entries) and commented upon by users, and thus constantly recycled. 'Modularity' refers to the way in which web pages are composed of a number of different elements – different in terms of origin, authorship, affordances, conditions of production and so on – which are puzzled together within a design template.[4]

These processes complicate the media and semiotic composition of web environments. As a result of integration, what used to be isolated modes of computer-mediated communication (CMC) is now replicated on multi-mode platforms. Embedding and modularity make web pages multi-layered and multi-authored. These processes have in common a blurring of boundaries between genres and participation roles: professional and user-generated discourse may now appear side by side, and the blend sometimes leads to informal writing styles being positioned as voices of expertise. For instance, commercial web services position user contributions such as reviews and ratings as a complement to, or even substitute for, professionally authored content. Processes of convergence thus lead to increasingly heterogeneous discourse spaces, in which different language styles, genres, and voices co-exist.

However, rather than thinking of web 2.0 as something entirely new (as the label might misleadingly suggest), it is more productive to assess its novel aspects against previous stages of CMD. I organize this assessment around four dimensions of language in contemporary web environments: *organization, interaction, self-presentation*, and *spectacle*.

A considerable part of user activity on the 'participatory web' sets forth linguistic (and semiotic) practices of self-presentation and interaction that are fundamental to all CMD. Profile pages on social networking sites may be viewed as a continuation of personal homepages, which initiated the practice of self-presentation on the early Web (Döring 2002), and interactive written discourse in newsgroups and Internet Relay Chat sets a yardstick for current modes of web-based interpersonal communication. However, there are differences within this continuity. Self-presentation on today's profile pages is more serialized and standardized in terms of design than on earlier homepages. Standardization is understood here as the imposition of uniformity on design. The design options available to blog authors and profile makers are limited to a few alternative layouts, a fixed number of background colors and typefaces, and so on. Templates enable the creation of blogs and profile pages in a few simple steps. Likewise, contemporary forms of online talk largely share with their predecessors in web forums and newsgroups a relative lack of institutional regulation and a proliferation of the features that have come to characterize informal written language online: spoken-like and vernacular features, traces of spontaneous production, innovative spelling choices, emoticons (signs that represent a facial expression by means of punctuation marks), and the like. But new patterns of discourse organization emerge as well, for instance comments on published content, which were popularized on blogs and are now ubiquitous on content-sharing sites. Online interaction today also seems more densely interspersed with multimedia than at earlier stages of CMD. Embedded videos that prompt short exchanges among 'friends' on social networking sites are an example.

A further dimension of language that has always been fundamental to the web is the organization of web interfaces through hypertext links. Its neglect in CMD scholarship reflects researchers' focus on interpersonal communication rather than on edited websites, but it is also symptomatic of a broader lack of attention to visual communication (van Leeuwen 2004). Website interfaces consist in large part of multiple navigation bars, which are composed of bare nouns or verbs, or of nominal or verbal phrases. On *YouTube* for instance, the navigation bar above the video screen reads *Home, Videos, Channels, Community*. These are set in blue lettering against a light grey background. At the top right, we find *Sign Up, Quick List, Help, Sign In*; below the video are placed the items *Rate, Share, Favorite, Playlists, Flag*. Each of these clickable items links the video page to another video, a specific user activity, or another area of the website. The organizational dimension of language on web interfaces consists of isolated lexical items, and coherence is constituted within "visual syntax" (van Leeuwen 2004: 17), together with choices in typography and color. However, the design of web interfaces also raises some important sociolinguistic issues, such as the choice of languages for localized versions of global corporate websites (Kelly-Holmes 2006) and the language style of emblematic items in web design (Androutsopoulos 2006b).

The main innovation in web 2.0 environments are the 'spectacles': multi-modal content that is uploaded by users on media-sharing sites and often embedded in other web pages. My interest is primarily in video, but the concept is meant to encompass other types of digital content such as music or photography, which may not involve language at all. The spectacle metaphor suggests that these items are displayed to an audience; are viewed rather than read; are mainly perceived and consumed as entertainment; and prompt responses, which are usually expressed in comments. With their video-sharing platforms in operation since 2005, spectacles are relatively new to the web, because their production, circulation, and consumption require technological standards that were not available on a large scale until very recently. On today's content-sharing sites, each spectacle is hosted on a dedicated web page, which features usage statistics (views, geographical spread of web hits), lists of similar content, a commenting option, and other elements such as video responses. This page is the immediate textual environment of a spectacle and therefore an integral part of the analysis that follows.[5]

The significance of web 2.0 spectacles to a sociolinguistics of globalization is grounded in a number of facts. First, spectacles extend the dimensions of language online. While spoken language was marginal so far in CMD, being limited to video conferencing and online phone calls, it now gains a much wider presence. Spectacles don't simply feature spoken language, but language that is digitally edited, generically diverse, and often a hybrid drawing on different sources. More importantly, vernacular spectacles are at the core of a flourishing culture of media production from below. They are a site of grassroots media creativity that takes different shapes in terms of originality, reworking, and appropriation: people's own, amateur footage, pirated material (for example stretches of broadcast, snatches of concerts filmed on mobile phones), and, not least, vernacular productions which capitalize on the digital appropriation and manipulation of mass media resources.[6]

Spectacles are embeddable and can be combined with other textual elements on virtually any web page. They therefore have a high potential for constant circulation and recycling. Even though vernacular spectacles are mostly of low-budget quality, some become very popular, occasionally leading to mainstream broadcasting. In my observations of *YouTube* I have come across several cases of (German, Greek, or English) spectacles with millions of views and thousands of comments, which provide hints to the offline dissemination or broadcast of these videos. Drawing on the concept of 'primary texts,' introduced by John Fiske (1987) in the analysis of television discourse, we may say that the participatory web is a site for the extra-institutional emergence of new primary texts of vernacular origin. Becoming a primary text on a media-sharing website depends on popularity, not on a specific semiotic make-up. Spectacles of any type – original footage, pirated material, or intertextual modification – may in principle develop into a focal point of attention for millions of users in one particular country, or even world-wide. Such popularity is sociolinguistically significant, considering that spectacles may provide a site for the unregulated mediation of vernacular speech, thereby extending the prevalence of vernacular language in computer-mediated discourse (Androutsopoulos 2006b, 2007, 2010).

However, primary vernacular spectacles lack the contextualization devices usually available to the broadcast program. In Fiske's framework, primary texts are accompanied by an array of 'secondary' texts such as announcements, advertisements, and reviews, which market a primary text and suggest preferred readings (in other words, interpretations). With vernacular spectacles, the absence of such secondary texts is partially compensated for by the adjacent comments. In quantitative terms, comments can be understood as indicators of attention to, and engagement with, a spectacle on the part of the users. In qualitative terms, comment authors may provide background information, engage in identity debates triggered by the spectacle, or 'echo' scenes and voices of the spectacle in a manner reminiscent of audience practices during or after reception. Comments can be thought of as "encasing events" (Goffman 1986: 262) which contextualize

Table 9.1 Four dimensions of language in social networking sites (SNS) and content sharing sites (CSS). Compiled by author

Dimension	Main characteristic	Agency	Typical site
Organization	Constitutes web interfaces as part of web design	Site designer	SNS and CSS
Self-presentation	Resource for profile pages and other sites of user presentation	Individual user	SNS
Spectacle	Part of multimedia material people upload and make available	User	CSS (and embedded in SNS)
Interaction	Means for interpersonal communication and comments on 'prompts'	Multi-authored	SNS and CSS

the 'encased' video clip. I argue below that comments do a diverse discursive work, which contributes to the recontextualization of a spectacle.

Key characteristics of these four dimensions of language in web 2.0 environments are summarized in table 9.1.[7] While I suggest that spectacles are central to the current stage of digital discourse, what characterizes contemporary web environments is the co-existence of and interplay between all four dimensions of language. Organization, self-presentation, spectacle, and interaction are constantly interrelated in practice, and it is therefore useful to think of processes of globalization and localization as involving in principle all four dimensions.

Exploring Spectacles: Analytical Concepts for Web 2.0 Research

I approach the web as a 'sociolinguistic ecology,' in which participants use available linguistic resources, across different modes of computer-mediated communication, to accomplish social activities (Androutsopoulos 2006b). While rejecting technological determinism, namely the assumption that communications technologies determine language production (Hutchby 2001), this approach does take into account the constraints of different technologies of mediation. Linguistic practices in CMD are therefore theorized as the outcome of the relation between media constraints and user agency within specific socio-cultural settings. This approach challenges two principles explicitly or implicitly shared by many studies of language and new media. The first is the analytical restriction to a single communication mode such as email or instant messaging. This practice entails a risk of technological determinism, as it implicitly foregrounds the impact of that mode on language usage. It also hinders an understanding of how multiple modes are coordinated by individual users within a web environment. The second is the decontextualization of written language from its digital surroundings. This is common practice in studies of language variation, linguistic economy, and language change in CMC, in which the multi-modal embedding of linguistic data is usually not considered; indeed, the relative 'modal poverty' of frequently used data from IRC or IM favors this analytical disembedding. However, in view of the semiotically rich environments and of the co-existence of language styles in web 2.0, an analysis is required that contextualizes the microlinguistic level in its multi-modal context and does not reduce that context to the communications technology used, but rather treats it as assembled and emergent. This, in turn, calls for analytical concepts which "can be applied cross-modally" (van Leeuwen 2004: 15) to both language and image (and sound), and which address relations between modes, texts, and codes.

Three such concepts, I argue, are multi-modality, intertextuality, and heteroglossia. Even though not systematically used in CMD research, these concepts are familiar ground in sociolinguistics and discourse studies. My understanding of multi-modality is shaped by the framework created by Kress and van Leeuwen (2001); my understanding of heteroglossia, by the framework created by Bakhtin (1981) and by his reception in sociolinguistics – for instance Rampton (1995) and Bailey (2007); and my understanding of intertextuality, by Bakhtin again, and by text linguistics. I briefly introduce them below, focusing on their application to spectacles. Figure 9.1, featuring the video screen of one of the two German recontextualized spectacles to be analysed below (see section 6), shall accompany the discussion.

Multimodality – broadly defined as the combination of semiotic modes in the production of meaning (Kress and van Leeuwen 2001) – operates across different components of a spectacle page. Spectacles consist of rich combinations of image, spoken and written language, music and sound. The video depicted in the screenshot consists of the following layers: the music of a global pop song, new German lyrics, a sequence of still images, and superimposed subtitles of the lyrics. The rest of this web page is made up of different modules (for instance the list of "related videos" to the right), featuring distinct combinations of language, image, color, and typography. Spectacles are complex multi-modal texts within a complex multi-modal environment, and the way they work the tension between the global and the local will often rely on multi-modal combinations rather than on language alone.

On a second level of analysis, spectacles and spectacle pages can be viewed as webs of intertextual relations. *YouTube* videos are frequently intertextual in that they rely on, and modify, existing texts (antecedent, or referenced texts). The

Figure 9.1   Screenshot of "Schwappe Productions – An Preller." Source: http://www.youtube.com/watch?v=icmraBAN4ZE

spectacle in Figure 9.1 brings together elements of different antecedent texts of recognizable origin: a pop tune, a collage of pictures and graphics found on the web. The intertextuality of spectacles implies decomposability into separate parts or layers, each of a different provenance, each bringing its own connotations. At the same time, videos are part of a network of intertextual relations on the spectacle page. Its most obvious aspect is the relation of the video to its video responses (if available) and to its comments. Other elements on the page, such as the channel information box on the top left and the sets of "related" and "promoted videos" on the right, are also intertextually linked to the video. Video-sharing sites therefore require a detailed intertextual analysis of relations constituted within a spectacle, between it and its antecedent texts, as well as among various components of the spectacle page.

An analysis of spectacle pages as composites of intertextually fabricated videos, multi-authored comments, and a professionally designed user interface implies that these pages will be quite heterogeneous in sociolinguistic terms. The norms that govern the language of the website interface have nothing to do with the linguistic and stylistic choices of spectacles, and these in turn are independent from the linguistic choices of the comments. Analytical concepts commonly used in CMD studies, such as language variation or code-switching, are in my view insufficient to address such heterogeneity. While language variation analysis has been used to study relations between standard and dialect or written and spoken usage in CMD, web 2.0 environments also confront us with unexpected co-occurrences and juxtapositions of language styles that result from media convergence and are interwoven with their multi-modal environment.[8] I therefore find it more useful to think of web 2.0 environments as heteroglossic. In a recent paper, Bailey (2007: 257) defines heteroglossia as "(a) the simultaneous use of different kinds of forms or signs, and (b) the tension and conflicts among those signs, based on the sociohistorical associations they carry with them." Unlike variation and code-switching, heteroglossia encompasses all kinds of linguistic difference across all levels of linguistic and discourse structure. Moreover, as the concept is socially not formally defined, it "directs the analyst to historical social relations, rather than just details of surface form" (Bailey 2007: 269).

Using heteroglossia, we may look at web 2.0 platforms as sites of tension and contrast between linguistic resources that represent different social identities and ideologies. In particular, a number of potential sites of heteroglossic articulations can be identified in and around spectacles. The intertextuality that characterizes some vernacular spectacles involves a tension between voices or perspectives. In the example (Figure 9.1), this tension comes about between the female African-American voice of the original pop song and the male, dialect-speaking voice of the Bavarian recontextualization (see below). A contrast between spectacle and comments in terms of linguistic choices may reflect the tension between globally circulating content and its local consumption, or between a local performance and equally local responses to it. While the style choices of spectacles are fixed and displayed to an audience, those of comments are emergent and interactively shaped. Comment authors may style-shift to align themselves with – or to distance themselves from – the language styles of the local spectacle; and, within a stretch of comments, participants will sometimes mobilize heteroglossic contrasts to con-textualize conflicting views and stances (Androutsopoulos 2007). On a different level, spectacle and comments may contrast with the linguistic design of the web interface, reflecting the tension between user-generated discourse and professional choices of website localization. Heteroglossia offers considerable analytical versatility, which suits the multi-layered co-existence of language styles and voices in web environments.

Recontextualized Spectacles: Local Responses to Global Media Content

Spectacles, then, are shaped by multimodal, intertextual, and heteroglossic relations, and these can be seen as forming a nexus within which recontextualization is situated. Recontextualization involves the appropriation and reworking of globally circulating media material into a local code for a local audience. In the case of spectacles, this involves the manipulation of different media and modes, intertextual tensions within popular culture, and heteroglossic contrasts of revoicing and re-imaging. Even though some of these processes have long preceded digital culture, their workings with spectacles crucially draw on the affordance of contemporary digital media to manipulate and publish music, speech, and video.

One example I documented in a recent case study (Androutsopoulos 2009) is a Greek *YouTube* spectacle entitled "To krasaki tou Tsou" ("Choo's little wine"). Originally an entry to an amateur video clip competition, it consists of three layers of digital text: first, a Japanese song from the soundtrack of a Hollywood movie (*Kill Bill II*); second, new video footage, namely an amateur parody of Chinese martial arts movies (of the *Crouching Tiger, Hidden Dragon* type); finally, Greek subtitles with a phonetically approximate, 'surface translation' of the Japanese lyrics. To the Greek-speaking viewers for whom this is intended, the subtitles make the (undecipherable) Japanese lyrics to be heard as a sort of 'Japanese Greek.' For example the song's refrain, in transliterated Japanese: *Janomeno kasa hitotsu*, is subtitled in Greek as: *Γενομένο, το κρασάκι του Τσου – jenoméno to krasáki tu Tsu* ("ripe, Choo's little wine"). In the corresponding movie frame, a group of comically 'oriental' characters fondle a bottle of wine. Unlike in usual subtitling, the Japanese lyrics and the Greek subtitles lack a semantic or pragmatic relationship. The coherence of the multi-modal text is constituted in the relation between the moving image and the Greek subtitles, on a frame-to-frame, verse-to-verse basis. The heteroglossic contrast between the language heard and the language read is at the core of the trash humor of this spectacle.

This is one example of how a globally known pop-culture text is recontextualized in a vernacular spectacle. The Greek makers of that video are not alone in this practice. My *YouTube* observation uncovered thousands of videos that go by the label 'misheard lyrics,' and a culture of 'fake' subtitles seems to have been one of *YouTube*'s trends in the last two years.[9] Not all of these are so elaborate as to feature their own video footage. A popular technique is the phonetic subtitling of video excerpts (music video clips, Bollywood movies) or of songs (often with a cartoon figure voicing the subtitles in a speech bubble). This procedure always involves phonetic subtitling and maintains the original sound and voice, but is not dependent on a particular language pair: some 'misheard lyrics' appropriate Bollywood films or German rock music and localize them for an English-speaking audience, others even take English-language pop songs and allocate them fake (that is, phonetically similar but semantically divergent) English subtitles.

Phonetic subtitling (with or without new video footage) is one among several semiotic techniques that can be used to recontextualize media material, for a new audience and to a new purpose. Another technique is dubbing or re-dubbing, that is, superimposing a new voice over the original footage. This is popular with German *YouTube* users, who are fond of re-dubbing snatches of Hollywood films in Bavarian or Swabian dialect.[10] A third option is a cover version or a restaging involving a translation of the antecedent together with new footage. Yet another option is to maintain the original tune, replacing the lyrics and adding new footage. All these different options offer glimpses into what one could term 'techniques of guerrilla double-voicing in the digital age.' Vernacular spectacle makers appropriate conventional techniques of localizing media content, such as dubbing, translating, and subtitling, in order to stage a dialogue between the voices of the original material and their own reworkings.[11] Interpreting these productions is often quite complex, as their heteroglossic ambiguities and multimedia layers may raise questions of humor, parody, ethnic representation, and stereotyping (see Jenkins 2006: 292–3).

Discussing the importance of *YouTube* "as a key site for the production and distribution of grassroots media" (Jenkins 2006: 274), Henry Jenkins draws attention to parody as a key mode "for reworking mass media materials for alternative purposes" (2006: 282). Localization is one such purpose, and the workings of parody in recontextualized spectacles may involve techniques of intertextuality and language play which look back to local pre-digital traditions. For example, the Japanese–Greek video echoes traditional vernacular practices of jocular appropriation of 'foreign' linguistic material by the Greek-speaking community, and elaborates this tradition, by means of digital technology, into a multimedia text, which, despite (or perhaps thanks to) its 'trash' aesthetic, gained mass popularity in Greece during 2008. This popularity is indicated by the statistics available on the spectacle page (in terms of numbers of views and comments), but also by the comments unfolding underneath the spectacle. In that case study I found that comments contextualize the spectacle by offering a range of insights into its production, reception, and subsequent offline dissemination: the local video was apparently screened on nation-wide television programs, and the Japanese song, heard afresh through the lenses of the *YouTube* parody, was played in cafés. As a consequence, in the analysis of the transformations involved in recontextualization, I consider (with Bauman and Briggs 1990) how comments contribute to the emergence of local framing, indexical grounding, and a new function of recontextualized spectacles.

Two 'Bavarian' Recontextualizations on *YouTube*[12]

Against this backdrop, the present section offers a detailed analysis of two local transformations of globally available semiotic material. Both examples are German-language videos that appropriate US American antecedents. They were initially selected from a larger set of *YouTube* videos, tagged (or self-categorized) as 'Bavarian.' The first example is a local adaptation of a so-called "fast food freestyle" (see Appendix for sources). The original version is apparently a *YouTube* classic, online since November 2006 and available in different copies, the most popular approximating 6 million views at the time of writing.[13] In this amateur video we see a young man rapping a fast-food order through a drive-thru intercom, accompanied by human beatbox. The local version is entitled "Mc Donalds rap (bayerisch)." The second example is a cover version of "Umbrella" by Rihanna, a pop song released in late March 2007. The local version, online since August 2007, is entitled "An Preller" (a Bavarian dialect expression). It combines a karaoke version of the original tune with new lyrics and a video that consists of a sequence of still images.

All video material tagged as 'Bavarian' can be understood as claiming some relation to that region, culture, or language.[14] By focusing on these recontextualized videos, we examine how this relation is established in a dialogue between the original and the local version, as well as between spectacle and comments. Both examples could be lumped together as local appropriations of US American popular music, but they are in fact quite different in terms of the provenience and status of the antecedent texts. "Umbrella," with numerous top positions in singles charts around the world during 2007, epitomizes the global circulation of US American pop music.[15] Its presence on *YouTube*, in various amateur videos rather than in the official video clip, is secondary to its dissemination via broadcast channels. The fast-food freestyle exemplifies a different pattern of global circulation. The original vernacular spectacle gained international popularity on *YouTube* (including in Germany, as is evidenced by the video's audience map), and the Bavarian response is also posted and consumed on that platform. This raises questions concerning the global status of different spectacles, which will be taken up in my concluding discussion. The two cases also differ in terms of popularity, as expressed in views, comments, and video responses. On all counts, "An Preller" is much more popular than the Bavarian freestyle.[16]

The following discussion moves from the textual correspondences of the lyrics to the multi-modal composition of the spectacles, then to the linguistic resources used in the local versions, and finally to the contextualization work of the comments. To begin with, the Bavarian fast-food freestyle is a translation that remains quite faithful to the propositional content of the referenced text, with some stylistic allowance for context and rhyme (see Excerpt 1).[17]

Excerpt 1   Versions of "Fast food freestyle" lyrics: original text followed by an English gloss, for ease of comparison

Original text (as posted on the spectacle page):

1   I need a double cheeseburger and hold the lettuce
2   don't be frontin' son no seeds on the bun
3   we be up in this drive thru order for two
4   i got the cravin' for a number nine like my shoe

Gloss of 'Bavarian' version (author's translation):

1   I want a double cheeseburger but without salad
2   don't feel fooled no sesame on the bread
3   we're sitting in the drive through order for two
4   the craving for a size nine chicken is there

'Bavarian' version (as posted on the spectacle page):

1   I mog an dobblkäsburger aber ohne zalood
2   fühl di ned veroarschd kan sesam aufm brot
3   mir höggn in der durchfahrt bestelln für zwaa
4   die begierde nach am neuner chickn is da

Line 2 of the translation omits the original address term and selects a different verb. Line 4 omits the simile ("like my shoe") but maintains the numerical size of the order. Consider also line 7, "dr pepper for my brother, another for your mother," translated as "*coca cola für mei Buu, noch eins für ma kuh.*" Here a soft drink not available in Germany is substituted by a different brand; the recipient of the soft drink is rendered as *Buu* /'bu:/, a dialect word for 'boy' or 'mate' that also happens to facilitate rhyme; in the same line, "mother" is rendered by *Kuh* ('cow'), a substitution apparently dictated by rhyme. However, the original wording – "your mother" – echoes (in my reading) the African-American tradition of the sounds and dozens, an allusion lost in the translation. Nonetheless, the translation basically maintains the same semantic line; it tells the same story in the same genre, injecting some local flavor by means of referential choices and use of dialect.

However, the two versions do not *show* the same story as far as their multimodal composition is concerned. Table 9.2 displays the sequential organization of the two videos, following the segmentation of the lyrics. In the original version we only see the driver rapping his order at the intercom. We hear the human beatbox and the voices of two (invisible) service personnel, their responses apparently prompting the rapper to repeat his order slower and then again faster. These short dialogic sequences separate the four takes of the freestyle stanza.

In the Bavarian version we see the two youngsters, identified in the opening credits as "Peter and Eggi," in front of the camera, in a living-room. The cover version maintains the rhythmic structure of the beatbox and the repetition of the stanza at different speeds, but the last two segments of the original are omitted and the interludes are designed differently, with the rapper giving instructions (lifted from the original) to the beatboxer. The brackets[18] of the Bavarian version are more elaborated than those of the original. The opening bracket features a sequence of title images (the Bavarian flag and the fast food company logo, with a German slogan) which contextualize the version's local anchoring and its relation to a pretext. The closing bracket features a farewell to the camera and a list of end credits. Thus the local version lacks a naturalistic setting, but elaborates its framing by introducing its own contextualization elements.

In the case of "Schwappe Productions – An Preller", the music is the only common semiotic mode between the original song and the local video. The lyrics are now delivered by a male voice, and the visual part consists of a sequence of still images cut together to the music. The recontextualized song maintains the original's pop-song structure (intro–stanza–chorus–stanza–chorus–bridge–chorus–outro), but its content and delivery are of poor quality by professional standards. In terms of verbal content, "An Preller," which roughly translates into

Table 9.2   Versions of "Fast food freestyle" video clips. Compiled by author

Segment	Original version		Bavarian version	
	Time		*Time*	
opening bracket	–	–	0.00	Image: Bavarian flag + title: *Mc Donald's – bayerisch Peter and Eggi*
			0.05	Image: McDonalds logo with German slogan, *ich liebe es*
			0.09	Both boys: *Bolero!*
freestyle	0:01	*Big mac!* + beatbox	0.11	Beatbox + *hunger!* ('hunger')
	0.10	**1st take**	0.20	**1st take**
interlude	0.31	Rapper: *That's about it!*	0.39	Both: *Knusper!* ('crispy')
	0.34	Reply by personnel	0.41	Rapper: *Slow down Peter*
	0.38	Rapper: *We'll slow it down for you* Reply by personnel		
freestyle	0.44	*Big mac!* + beatbox	0.43	Beatbox
	0.55	**2nd take**	0.52	**2nd take**
interlude	1.22	Request by personnel	1.15	Both: *Knusper!* ('crispy')
	1.25	Rapper: *Speed this one up*	1.16	Rapper: *Speed up Peter*
freestyle	1.28	*Big mac!* + beatbox	1.18	Beatbox
	1.35	**3rd take**	1.26	**3rd take**
interlude	1.44	Interruption and dialogue with personnel	–	–
freestyle	2.01	*Big mac!* + beatbox	–	–
	2.08	**4th take**		
closing bracket	2.26	End titles	1.42	Both: *knusper!* ('crispy')
	2.25	Beatboxer to rapper: *say crispy!*	1.45	Beatboxer: *yippie*
	2.27	Rapper: *Crispy*	1.46	Rapper: *Bolero!*
	–		1.47	End titles

'being pissed,' is probably best described as a narrative of binge-drinking culture (see Excerpt 2). Delivered from a first-person perspective, it explicitly claims collective regional validity by narrating what people do "at the weekend in Bavaria" (line 1). The story and the accompanying images abound in emblems of localness, such as the *Mass*, the Bavarian beer mug.

Excerpt 2   "An Preller," first stanza and chorus (as seen in subtitles):

1   Am Wochenend in Bayern / gengan die Leid gern feiern
2   I mach des a recht gern / Noch ist der Absturz fern
3   Aber dann kaffst da a Mass / Und scho steigt der Spaß
4   Nach Nummer 8 jedoch / Hat der Spaß boid a Loch
5   I hob / scho wieder an Rausch in der Fotzn / Hearst des is doch echt zum Kotzen
6   Koaner versteht mi wei i so lall / Zefix bin I scho wieder prall
7   Draußt werds scho langsam wieder heller / Aber mi drahts nur oibe schneller
8   Wei i hob scho wieder an so an Preller! / i hob scho wieder an so an Preller!

Gloss:

1   At the weekend in Bavaria / People like to have a party
2   I like that too / the crash is still far away
3   But then you buy a *Mass* / And the good times are rising high
4   But after number 8 / Soon there's a hole in good times
5   I've got / Once again a buzz in my face / Can you hear, this really sucks
6   Nobody understands me because I'm babbling / Darn, I'm so full once again
7   Outside it gets lighter / But my head's spinning around ever quicker
8   Because I'm pissed again / I'm pissed again

In its visual dimension, "An Preller" (henceforth AP) is a *bricolage* (Chandler 1998) that incorporates visual bits and pieces of very different origin, which gain new meaning in their dialogic relationship to the lyrics. A number of bracketing elements offer explicit local cues. The opening bracket and the first stanza are visualized by Bavaria's chequered blue–white flag and the *Mass*. The split screen at 0:06,[19] also seen in Figure 9.1, uses the spatial opposition between 'given' and 'new' (Kress and van Leeuwen 1996) to visualize the contrast between the original song and the recontextualized version: an umbrella to the left, its lining in the colors of the Bavarian flag, is juxtaposed to the Bavarian *Mass*. Visual references to binge drinking and its consequences draw on different sources, such as animated emoticons, a staple feature of web discussion forums (for instance at 0:17, 0:20, 0:27, 0:33), but also images from German mainstream and popular culture[20] and, not least, an image of Mickey Mouse (0:51). Rather than a purist local representation, the video's visual part is an intertextual amalgam of materials from regional, national and transnational digital culture, sequentially arranged and cut to the lyrics.

Both local versions claim to be 'Bavarian,' most obviously so through their titles and tags; however, from a social dialectological perspective, they do not feature the same dialect. AP is cast in a levelled, urban Bavarian, and the local freestyle is in Franconian dialect, as many commentators point out. In both cases, the singing voice is markedly different from Standard German, and its dialect features in phonology, lexicon, and – partially – syntax are regular enough to constitute it as dialect voice. Bavarian dialect is made even more prominent in AP through the title, which is a dialectal pun on *Umbrella*, and through the subtitles.[21] Both videos feature additional little moments of heteroglossia. In the local free-style, the rapper's instructions to the human beatbox ("slow down Peter, speed up Peter") come in English, taking up the responses of the original rapper to the service personnel, but also echoing a broader convention of English code-switching at skeletal points of German rap songs. AP features bits of written Standard German on displayed signs and image captions (for instance at 3:31, 3:36, and in the end credits). It also features English (a "do not disturb" sign at 2:36), and 'Bavarian English' on a comic strip sign that reads "pardy ends" (i.e. 'party ends', 1:23), the spelling *pardy* reflecting the voicing of the alveolar plosive in Bavarian. Rather than being neatly separated from the linguistic text, these images contribute to the overall linguistic make-up of the video; and, while the lyrics of AP come in a homogenous dialectal voice, its footage constructs the entire video as a heteroglossic ensemble.

Commenting on *YouTube* is, by default, open to anyone. However, the comments to these two videos come entirely in German and, as the page's audience statistics indicate, they originate in the German-speaking countries. Many comments index a relation to the Bavarian region and/or dialect, through propositional content, intertextual reference or dialect choice.[22] I focus here on the way local language ideologies are brought to bear on the evaluation of the videos. Metalinguistic commentary is most pronounced in the local freestyle, where 40 percent of all comments counter the clip's claim to being Bavarian and suggest another dialect label, namely Franconian (*fränkisch*). Users draw on specific examples to illustrate differences between the two dialects, in a manner reminiscent of dialect norming debates online (Johnstone and Baumgardt 2004). For example it is pointed out that the video uses *kuh* – monophthongal [kʰuː] – instead of *kuah* – diphthongal [kʰuaː], which is the Bavarian pronunciation for 'cow.' Commentators also debate the regional boundaries between Bavarian and Franconian dialect (both are spoken in the federal state of Bavaria), thereby evoking distinct regional histories and traditions. The link between dialectal and regional identity is paramount, whereas the clip's relation to the original fast-food freestyle is hardly addressed in the comments.

In the comments to AP, metalinguistic discourse hardly occurs. Instead, statements of the type "that's how we Bavarians/we in Bavaria are" express regional pride and ratify the clip's claims. These comments tend to be cast in dialect, displaying an alliance to the clip's dialect voice. The relation of AP to its original is evoked frequently, and in an antagonistic way. In my sample I identified some fifteen comparisons to the original, all expressing praise for the parody and/or criticism of the original, some alluding to being fed up with the heavy rotation of "Umbrella" in mainstream media (see Excerpt 3).

Excerpt 3   Selection of comments to "An Preller" with reference to its pretext:

- *so sehr wie ich das original hasse, liebe ich diese version*
  "as much as I hate the original, so do I love this version"
- *Also des is die viel bessere Version von Umbrella*
  "Well this is a much better version of Umbrella"
- *von wegen parodie das hier is das original; umbrella is eh en scheiß lied aber das hier wird bald kult sein*
  "by no means a parody, this is the original; umbrella is a crap song anyway but this one will be cult soon"

A further technique by which comments give local grounding to this video consists in referencing its local circulation (Excerpt 4). Some commentators ask how to download the song, implying a wish to use it in other contexts; others want to play it at the next party, others report such usage or its circulation on mobile phones at schools, or discuss its perceived suitability for wider circulation. Some comments set the song prospectively and retrospectively in the context of the *Wiesn*, that is, Munich's *Oktoberfest*. Predictions such as *Wiesnhit 2007!* (that the song is bound to become a hit at the *Wiesn's* party tents) are expressed, then followed later on by reports that AP was indeed played by *Wiesn* DJs.

Excerpt 4   Selection of comments to "An Preller" with reference to its local circulation:

- *seit tagen singen wir den song an jeder party!*
  "for days now we're singing this song at every party"
- *in unsana niederbayerischen schui kursiert des scho lang wieder auf de handys...*
  [spelling includes dialect features]
  "in our lower bavarian school it's been circulating across mobiles"
- *will ich im Radio hören!*
  "I want to hear it on the radio!"

Using the spectacle page as unit of analysis, my analysis develops a view of localization as a discursive process carried out in a two-fold dialogue: between an antecedent text and its local recontextualization, as well as between the recontextualized spectacle and the publicly displayed reactions to it. Comments indicate whether a video is accepted by local spectators; how it speaks to local concerns; and what opportunities of identity negotiation it offers. I identified three ways in which comments contribute to the local grounding of recontextualized spectacles: by doing local 'folk linguistics'; by comparison (or even antagonism) to the original' and by offering hints to their local circulation.

Discussion: Vernacular Spectacles as 'Localization from Below'

Contemporary video-sharing platforms on the participatory web facilitate a culture of vernacular media productions, which circulate outside mainstream media yet interrelate with it in various ways. Spectacles that involve the appropriation and modification of mainstream antecedents can be markedly local in terms of their new indexical grounding, their circulation, and their discursive uptake; however, my examples and observations suggest that the delight people find in making and viewing vernacular spectacles is not limited to a particular country or region.

I suggest that recontextualized spectacles illustrate a distinct interplay between global media content and local responses that is broader, more fluid, and less predictable than other, more familiar types of interdependence between the global and the local. In order to contextualize this claim, consider how processes of globalization and localization have been discussed in sociolinguistics and discourse studies. These accounts often involve some kind of transnationally invariant backdrop, against which mechanisms of localization in discourse are examined. Well documented examples are local appropriations of global hip hop across the world (Alim, Ibrahim, and Pennycook 2009; Higgins 2009; Androutsopoulos and Scholz 2002; Pennycook, this volume). Despite cross-linguistic differences, some crucial aspects of cultural and linguistic practice are deemed to be relatively constant across local instantiations. Be it rap's rhyme principle, a thematic canon, a set of rhetorical resources, or the local anchoring of poetic discourse ("keeping it real") – certain creative principles constitute the global identity of rap as a genre system, and are at the same time available to variable local interpretation and appropriation, facilitating the relation of global and local in discursive practice as well as in analysis (see Pennycook 2007: 92–3).

This invariant backdrop is even more pronounced in practices of 'top-down globalization,' in which corporate media are launched in a series of national versions that operate independently of each other, yet under a common policy, format, and agenda (Machin and van Leeuwen 2007; Fairclough 2006: 108–11). In *Cosmopolitan* magazine, the image of the 'fun fearless female' is globally constant, yet each national version is adapted to local influences and references. The publishing corporation sets style principles, and the local editors "must somehow translate the *Cosmo* style into their own languages" (Machin and van Leeuwen 2007: 139). As a result, "although local versions adopt it in their own specific ways, overall it is a *global* style" (ibid., p. 48).

Cosmopolitan is not the only instance of what I would call 'localization from above' – a corporatively driven tailoring of global patterns to local conditions and audiences (Fiske 1997). In the field of technical translation, localization is the issuing of products (interface design, software, reference manuals) by global corporations in the languages of their target markets (Cronin 2003). In media marketing, localization signifies the strategies by which international media companies adapt their programming to local audiences. Discussing such strategies in India, Pathania-Jain (2008: 132–3) distinguishes between localization of content and "cosmetic localization." In the latter, local vernacular speech is one element – alongside local cultural iconography and humor – through which a program's local orientation is constituted.

Against that backdrop, vernacular spectacles appear to be a practice that is *unregulated, individualized,* and *in control of recontextualization*. The label 'localization from below,' coined here in analogy to the notion of "globalization from below" (Fairclough 2006, ch. 6), emphasizes the difference from corporative, top-down localization or 'localization from above.' Vernacular spectacle producers are no doubt influenced by transnational trends in digital vernacular culture. But there is no single blueprint behind their multimedia practices, no binding institutional guideline or common generic framework. Vernacular spectacles are the outcome of individual activity with regard to their resources and outcomes. Their circuit – that is, the selection of globally circulating materials, their modification, the local resources they draw on, and the ways they are interpreted in the comments – might be similar across different spectacles, but is not preconfigured by a common antecedent. Recontextualized spectacles obviously differ from top-down corporate localization (of the *Cosmopolitan* type) by the lack of an overarching policy, and from the local appropriation of pop music culture (the global hip hop type) by the lack of guiding generic traditions and principles. Recontextualization in vernacular spectacles is driven by playful, creative activity rather than by corporate planning or collective fan productivity, and it maintains control over the recontextualization process. Consider the four factors of control and power over recontextualization – *access, legitimacy, competence, values* – as postulated by Bauman and Briggs (1990). Vernacular spectacle makers have access to the web mediascape, a vast repository of semiotic materials that can be recycled and endlessly recombined; they obviously circumvent or ignore institutional regulations of legitimate usage, such as copyright; they are competent in using digital technologies to sample, modify, and publish their productions; and, by publishing them, they invite valuation by web audiences. Responses by these audiences are not always positive, but they often indicate an intense local circulation of the recontextualized spectacles and little interest in the globally available antecedent text. Taking these responses seriously would invite us to reverse the directionality of the global to local relationship: here the global diffusion and availability of digital content are a given. What is at stake is their recontextualization and subsequent responses – in other words, the local end of the globalization process.

Of course there are limits to this lack of regulation. *YouTube* and the commercial field in which it operates impose certain limitations in terms of content and copyright on the kind of video material that may be uploaded. Moreover, some types of global material seem more likely to be appropriated than others, in particular film and music – and indeed sometimes film music. The reasons for this presumably include the traditional role of film and music as sites of audience responses of echoing, modifying, and parodying, and the potential of these genres for popular circulation, which creates more opportunities of audience reaction to vernacular spectacles.

The examples suggest that the distinction between global antecedents and local versions must in principle be distinguished from the one between English and 'other' languages. Vernacular recontextualizations do not always appropriate English-language content; we just as well find Japanese songs given Greek, Bollywood 'misheard lyrics' given English phonetic subtitles. Such appropriated material is defined as 'global' through its corporate dissemination, which is often contextualized in the English-language media (as in the Greek case, where the Japanese song is part of the soundtrack to a Hollywood movie). While any *YouTube* video is potentially globally available, its factual global diffusion depends on a number of factors beside language choice. Being on *YouTube* makes the original fast-food freestyle globally accessible, and being in English facilitates its global consumption more than being in other languages. But its topic lends itself to local appropriation, and, as is evidenced by the regional breakdown of views, having reached a degree of international popularity increases the likelihood of such appropriation.

Moreover, multimodal localizing does not necessarily imply a critical position towards the antecedent text. The two examples represent two strikingly different responses to globally available material and the staging of localness. The distinction between two types of Bakhtinian double-voicing (as elaborated by Rampton 1995) seems useful here. The Bavarian fast food freestyle stands to the original US freestyle in a relation of *unidirectional double-voicing*: it is a response that agrees and aligns with that of the original and uses it as a backdrop to demonstrate the actors' own creative skills (regardless of the fact that these are contested by the commenting audience). With "An Preller," there is sufficient contrast between the narrative worlds and the aesthetic means of the song and of the video to view the local adaptation as an instance of *varidirectional double-voicing*: an appropriation that challenges the original voice by superimposing a different intention. To the professional, sensual, feminine, romantic image of "Umbrella," it juxtaposes a male, amateur, trash aesthetic.[23]

At the same time, the two recontextualizations differ in the way they constitute their own localness. Both feature a variety of local indices in the use of dialect and imagery and the design of bracketing sequences. But they do not stylize localness in equal terms. The fast food freestyle contextualizes itself as local (through dialect, a new title, a Bavarian hat worn by the rapper), but does not foreground localness in a reflexive, metapragmatic manner. By contrast, AP plays out 'Bavarian' stereotypes at many levels (in propositional content, imagery, linguistic choice), resulting in a kitsch celebration of local clichés. Linking these observations to the origin and status of the two antecedents, we see how scales of globalness tie in with a differential intensity of local responses. The original fast food freestyle, a rather obscure vernacular production with some degree of *YouTube* popularity, gives rise to a friendly imitation, whose receptive commentary unfolds around the legitimate use of local indexicality rather than around its appropriation of a global antecedent. By contrast, we can view the Bavarian binge drinking video as a voice of resistance to a globally popular, and therefore discursively powerful cultural commodity, and its exaggerated stylization of localness is part of that resistance. In any case, a generalizing assumption that items from "American" pop culture will receive similar intertextual responses due to their mere origin is clearly not supported by these examples.

Finally, the two examples show how the localization of globally circulating media material creates novel opportunities for the staging of vernaculars in the digital age. This is not to suggest an automatic, as it were, link between vernacular spectacles and vernacular speech, even though it can be observed that vernacular spectacles on *YouTube* are frequently sites of vernacular linguistic expression. Rather, the point is that recontextualization processes such as the ones discussed in this chapter offer a niche where, paraphrasing Coupland and colleagues (2003), vernaculars establish a presence in contemporary sociolinguistic ecologies. It is tempting to view spectacles, and web 2.0 environments generally, as extending the scope of vernaculars in computer-mediated discourse. On the internet, discourse spaces emerge where vernacular speech gains legitimacy and vernacular voices may be established as predominant and authoritative (Androutsopoulos 2006a, 2010). However, it remains to be seen whether video-sharing sites offer opportunities of public representation of vernacular speech that go beyond its staging in mainstream broadcasting, where vernaculars are often framed as non-institutional speech and turned into icons of traditional localness (Androutsopoulos 2010). One could argue that, even though dialects and other vernacular varieties may be established as dominant voices within spectacles, their surrounding web interfaces, which are available only in standard varieties, constitute an encasing frame of standardness that is roughly analogous to the framing of, say, a dialect show within the flow of broadcast program. Whether spectacles extend the restrictive positions allocated to vernaculars in mainstream media is open to further scrutiny.

ACKNOWLEDGMENTS

Writing this chapter has benefited from presentations in Mannheim, Jyväskylä, Cardiff and Seattle during 2009, and by research cooperation with Horst Simon. I am grateful to Nik Coupland and Adam Jaworski for their constructive and insightful feedback. The usual caveats apply.

NOTES

1   Following the practice by Markham and Baym 2009, I spell 'web' with lower case, to indicate that it is neither a proper noun nor a specific place.

2   I use the term 'environment' as a generic designation for websites which enable a range of user activities, and the term 'platform' for websites of a specific type; e.g. *facebook* is a web 2.0 environment and a platform for social networking.

3   The characteristics of social networking sites are profile pages and networks of 'friends' (Boyd and Ellison 2007; Boyd 2008). Media-sharing sites enable people to upload digital content such as photos, videos, and music.

4   For example a *MySpace* page can be thought of as composition of a number of 'modules,' some obligatory (such as the owner's 'calling card'), others optional (e.g. a testimonial, or embedding videos or photos). What is known as 'mash-up,' i.e. the individual composition of content from different sources on a personal webpage, is another instance of modularity.

5   The spectacle metaphor ties in with Goffman's distinction between "game" and "spectacle," i.e. "between a dramatic play or contest or wedding or trial and the social occasion or affair in which these proceedings are encased" (Goffman 1986: 261). On this analogy, a *YouTube* video could be likened to Goffman's "game," while the page hosting the video and the comments to it is the spectacle, i.e. the (virtual) social occasion in which the video is "encased." Note that this view presupposes a screen-based approach. From a user-based perspective, we can think of web pages in their entirety as 'game,' with a 'spectacle' constituted on each instance of reception.

6   Thanks to Adam Jaworski for insightful comments on this issue.

7   Even though this table was put together with web 2.0 in mind, the four dimensions bear similarities to typologies of the functions of language generally. Taking Halliday's "macro-functions" into consideration, my 'interaction' resembles the interpersonal, my 'organization,' the textual function, while 'self-presentation' and 'spectacle' carry ideational as well as interpersonal ones. Thanks to Nik Coupland for drawing my attention to these parallels.

8   On language variation and other facets of linguistic heterogeneity in CMC, see Paolillo 1999, Androutsopoulos 2006a, Siebenhaar 2006, Tagliamonte and Denis 2008, Tsiplakou (2009); on the limits of variationism, see Coupland (2001).

9   A *YouTube* search for that phrase yielded "about 6,270" results in August 2009. The most popular (and apparently the first) of these goes by the title *Buffalaxed*, a stretch of Bollywood musical with English phonetic subtitles that had over 13 million views during that period.

10 Dialect dubbing is sometimes screened in southern German public television, which might have served as a model to *YouTube* practices; thanks to Jana Tereick for bringing this to my attention.

11 An antecedent of these practices is the tradition of 'fansubbing' in grass-roots cultural productions (discussed by Jenkins 2006: 161–4).

12 This section draws on ideas developed in collaboration with Horst Simon (King's College London).

13 As of 24/07/2009, this copy (as quoted in sources) has 5,864,682 views, 4 video responses and 14,039 comments.

14 The relevant German tags (with counts as of June 12, 2009) are *bairisch* (206 items), *bayrisch* (912) and *boarisch* (262). The variant *bairisch* refers specifically to the Austro-Bavarian group of dialects; *bayrisch* refers to the region, but *de facto* to the dialect as well; *boarisch* is a phonetic spelling indexing a broader dialect.

15 See http://en.wikipedia.org/wiki/Umbrella_(song).

16 As of 12/06/2009, "An Preller" had 1,362,584 views, 1,235 comments and 2 video responses; the local freestyle had 85,275 views, 163 comments and no video responses.

17   For all examples, the lyrics are quoted as seen in subtitles, channel information boxes, or comments; all English glosses are translated by the author.

18   I follow Goffman's understanding of brackets as a process by which social activity "is often marked off from the ongoing flow of surrounding events by a special set of boundary markers or brackets of a conventionalized kind" (Goffman 1986: 251).

19   I use time stamps to refer to screen positions of the *YouTube* video. Readers may move the video's time shifter up and down in order to access a specific screen position.

20   These include former German chancellor Kohl, shown on a reference to his corpulent size (2: 29); comic strip figure *Sandmännchen*, shown on the line "now I'm going to sleep" (3: 44); and a banner on German beer, shown on a line praising its taste (2: 33).

21   These display a wide range of dialect features (see Excerpt 2), but not all dialect features are orthographically represented, and there are a few instances of eye dialect.

22   I have analyzed all 163 comments to Bavarian fast-food freestyle (as of 12/6/2009) and a sample of 500 comments to "An Preller" (approximately 40% of the grand total of comments at the time of sampling).

23   Significantly, "An Preller" is labelled a 'parody' by some commentators, even though it lacks an overt element of parody on the semantic or formal plane. Without knowledge of the original, it appears to be a bland parody of local beer culture.

APPENDIX: SOURCES OF EXCERPTS (ALL ACCESSED ON JANUARY 24, 2010)

- "Fast food freestyle" or "Mc Donalds rap" is available in different copies. The earliest attested version, called "Fast food freestyle at the drive thru", is no longer available on YouTube. The one with most views is "Mcdonald's rap" (http://www.youtube.com/watch?v=5sw2OvIgoO8).
- "Mc Donalds rap (bayerisch)": http://www.youtube.com/watch?v=DQP5QShpDR8
- "Umbrella" (one of several amateur clips): http://www.youtube.com/watch?v=UGT5BuKkAPc
- "Schwappe Productions – An Preller": http://www.youtube.com/watch?v=icmraBAN4ZE
- "To krasaki tou Tsou": http://www.youtube.com/watch?v=y-wF3pHpEt8

REFERENCES

Alim, H. S., Ibrahim, A., and Pennycook, A. (eds) (2009) *Global Linguistic Flows. Hip Hop Cultures, Youth Identities, and the Politics of Language*, 43–62. Abingdon and New York: Routledge.

Androutsopoulos, J. (2006a) Introduction: Sociolinguistics and computer-mediated communication. *Journal of Sociolinguistics* 10(4): 419–38.

Androutsopoulos, J. (2006b) Multilingualism, diaspora, and the internet: Codes and identities on German-based diaspora websites. *Journal of Sociolinguistics* 10(4): 520–47.

Androutsopoulos, J. (2007) Style online: Doing hip-hop on the German-speaking Web. In P. Auer (ed.). *Style and Social*

Identities, 279–320. Berlin, NY: Mouton de Gruyter.

Androutsopoulos, J. (2008) Potentials and limitations of discourse-centered online ethnography. *Language@Internet* 5, article 8. Available at: http://www.languageatinternet.de/articles/2008 (accessed on January 24, 2010).

Androutsopoulos, J. (2009) «Το κρασάκι του Τσου»: Πολυτροπικότητα, διακειμενικότητα και ετερογλωσσία στο «δεύτερο ιστό» ["To krasaki tou tsou": Multimodality, intertextuality and heteroglossia in Web 2.0.]. *Zitimata Epikoinonias [Communiction issues]* 3(9): 49–61.

Androutsopoulos, J. (2010) The study of language and space in media discourse. In P. Auer and J. E. Schmidt (eds), *Language and Space: An International Handbook of Linguistic Variation. Vol. 1: Theory and Methods*, 740–58. Berlin and New York: Mouton de Gruyter.

Androutsopoulos, J., and Scholz, A. (2002) On the recontextualization of hip-hop in European speech communities, In *PhiN – Philologie im Netz* 19: 1–42. Available at: www.fu-berlin.de/phin/phin19/p19t1.htm (accessed on January 24, 2010).

Appadurai, A. (1996) *Modernity at Large: Cultural Dimensions of Globalization*. Minneapolis: University of Minnesota Press.

Bailey, B. (2007) Heteroglossia and boundaries. In M. Heller (ed.), *Bilingualism: A Social Approach*, 257–74. New York: Palgrave.

Bakhtin, M. (1981) Discourse in the novel. In M. Bakhtin, *The Dialogic Imagination*, translated by C.l Emerson and M. Holquist, 259–422. Austin: University of Texas Press.

Baron, N. S. 2008. *Always On: Language in an Online and Mobile World*. Oxford: Oxford University Press.

Barton, D., and Hamilton, M. (1998) *Local Literacies. Reading and Writing in One Community*. London and New York: Routledge.

Bauman, R., and Briggs, C. L. (1990) Poetics and performance as critical perspectives on language and social life. *Annual Review of Anthropology* 19: 59–88.

Blommaert, J. (2003) Commentary: A sociolinguistics of globalization. *Journal of Sociolinguistics* 7(4): 607–23.

Blommaert, J. (2005) In and out of class, codes and control: Globalisation, discourse and mobility. In M. Baynham and A. De Fina (eds), *Dislocations/ Relocations: Narratives of Displacement*, 127–42. Manchester: St Jerome.

Boyd, D. M. (2008) Why youth (heart) social network sites: The role of networked publics in teenage social life. In D. Buckingham (ed.), *Youth, Identity, and Digital Media*, 119–142. Cambridge, MA: MIT Press.

Boyd, D. M., and Ellison, N. B. (2007) Social network sites: Definition, history, and scholarship. *Journal of Computer-Mediated Communication* 13(1). Abailable at: http://jcmc.indiana.edu/vol13/issue1/boyd.ellison.html (accessed on January 24, 2010).

Boyd-Barrett, O. (ed.) (2008) *Communications Media, Globalization and Empire*. Eastleigh: John Libbey.

Castells, M. (2000) *The Rise of the Network Society*, 2nd edn. Oxford: Blackwell.

Chandler, D. (1998) Personal home pages and the construction of identities on the web. WWW document. Available at: http://www.aber.ac.uk/media/Documents/short/webident.html (accessed on January 24, 2010).

Chouliaraki, L., and Fairclough, N. (1999) *Discourse in Late Modernity. Rethinking Critical Discourse Analysis*. Edinburgh: Edinburgh University Press.

Coupland, N. (2001) Dialect stylization in radio talk. *Language in Society* 30: 345–75.

Coupland, N. (2003) Introduction: Sociolinguistics and globalisation. *Journal of Sociolinguistics* 7(4): 465–72.

Coupland, N. (2007) *Style. Language Variation and Identity*. Cambridge: Cambridge University Press.

Coupland, N., (2009) The mediated performance of vernaculars. *Journal of English Linguistics* 37(3): 284–300.

Coupland, N., Bishop, H., and Garrett, P. (2003) Home truths: Globalization and the iconising of Welsh in a Welsh–American newspaper. *Journal of Multilingual and Multicultural Development* 24(3): 153–77.

Crane, D. (2002) Culture and globalization. Theoretical models and emerging trends. In D. Crane, N. Kawashima, and K. Kawasaki (eds), *Global Culture. Media, Arts, Policy, and Globalization*, 1–25. New York and London: Routledge.

Cronin, M. (2003) *Translation and Globalisation*. London: Routledge.

Döring, N. (2002) Personal home pages on the web: A review of research. *Journal of Computer-Mediated Communication* 7(3). Available at: jcmc.indiana.edu/vol7/issue3/doering.html (accessed on January 11, 2010).

Fairclough, N. (2006) *Language and Globalization*. London and New York: Routledge.

Fiske, J. (1987) *Television Culture*. London and New York: Routledge.

Fiske, J. (1997) Global, national, local? Some problems of culture in a postmodern world. *The Velvet Light Trap* 40, 56–66.

Goffman, E. (1986) *Frame Analysis: An Essay on the Organization of Experience* [1974]. London: Harper and Row.

Herring, S. C. (2004) Computer-mediated discourse analysis: An approach to researching online communities. In S. A. Barab, R. Kling, and J. H. Gray (eds), *Designing for Virtual Communities in the Service of Learning*, 338–76. Cambridge and New York: Cambridge University Press.

Herring, S. C. (2007) A faceted classification scheme for computer-mediated discourse. *Language@Internet*, 4, article 1. Available at: http://www.languageatinternet.de/articles/2007/761 (accessed on January 11, 2010).

Higgins, C. (2009) *English as a Local Language. Post-Colonial Identities and Multilingual Practices*. Bristol: Multilingual Matters.

Hinchcliffe, D. (2006) The state of Web 2.0. *Web Services Journal*. Available at: http://web2.socialcomputingjournal.com/the_state_of_web_20.htm (accessed on January 24, 2010).

Hutchby, I. (2001) *Conversation and Technology: From the Telephone to the Internet*. Cambridge: Polity.

Jenkins, Henry (2006): *Convergence Culture: Where Old and New Media Collide*. New York: New York University Press.

Johnstone, B., and Baumgardt, D. (2004) 'Pittsburghese' online: Vernacular norming in conversation. *American Speech* 79: 115–45.

Johnstone, B., Andrus, J., and Danielson, A. E. (2006) Mobility, indexicality, and the enregisterment of 'Pittsburghese.' *Journal of English Linguistics* 34: 77–104.

Jones, R. (2004) The problem of context in computer-mediated communication. In LeVine and Scollon (eds), 20–33.

Kelly Holmes, H. (2006) Multilingualism and commercial language practices on the Internet. *Journal of Sociolinguistics* 10(4): 510–23.

Kress, G., and van Leeuwen, T. (1996) *Reading Images. The Grammar of Visual Design*. London: Routledge.

Kress, G., and van Leeuwen, T. (2001) *Multimodal Discourse: The Modes and Media of Contemporary Communication*. London: Arnold.

Lee, C. K. M., and Barton, D. (in press) Constructing glocal identities through multilingual writing practices on Flickr.com. Fortchcoming in *International Multilingual Research Journal*.

LeVine, P., and Scollon, R. (eds) (2004) *Discourse and Technology: Multimodal Discourse Analysis*. Washington, DC: Georgetown University Press.

Machin, D., and van Leeuwen, T. (2007) *Global Media Discourse: A Critical Introduction*. Abingdon: Routledge.

Markham, A. N., and Baym, N. (eds) (2009) *Internet Inquiry: Conversations about Method*. Thousand Oaks, CA: Sage.

O'Reilly, T. (2005) What is Web 2.0? Design Patterns and Business Models for the Next Generation of Software. Available at: http://oreilly.com/web2/archive/what-is-web-20.html (accessed on January 24, 2010).

Paolillo, J. (1999) The virtual speech community: Social network and language variation on IRC. *Journal of Computer-Mediated Communication* 4(4). Available at: jcmc.indiana.edu/vol4/issue4/paolillo.html (accessed on January 24, 2010).

Pathania-Jain, G. (2008) *Localization strategies of international media companies entering India in the 1990s*. In Boyd-Barrett (ed.), 129–46.

Pennycook, A. (2007) *Global Englishes and Transcultural Flows*. Abingdon and New York: Routledge.

Rampton, B. (1995) *Crossing. Language and Ethnicity among Adolescents*. London: Longman.

Rowe, C., and Wyss, E. L. (eds) (2009) *Language and New Media: Linguistic, Cultural, and Technical Evolutions*. Cresskill, NJ: Hampton Press.

Scholz, T. (2008) Market ideology and the myths of Web 2.0. *First Monday* 13(3). Available at: http://www.uic.edu/htbin/cgiwrap/bin/ojs/index.php/fm/article/ viewArticle/2138/1945 (accessed on January 24, 2010).

Siebenhaar, B. (2006) Code choice and code-switching in Swiss–German Internet Relay Chat rooms. *Journal of Sociolinguistics* 10(4): 481–509.

Snyder, I. (ed.) (2002) *Silicon Literacies. Communication, Innovation and Education in the Electronic Age*. London and New York: Routledge.

Tagliamonte, S. A., and Denis, D. (2008) Linguistic ruin? LOL! Instant messaging and teen language. *American Speech* 83(1): 3–34.

Thimm, C. (2008) Technically-mediated interpersonal communication. In G. Antos and E. Ventola (eds), *Handbook of Interpersonal Communication*, 331–54. Berlin: Mouton de Gruyter.

Tsiplakou, S. (2009) Doing bilingualism: Language alternation as performative construction of online identities. *Pragmatics* 19(3): 361–91.

Van Leeuwen, T. (2004) Ten reasons why linguists should pay attention to visual communication. In LeVine and Scollon (eds), 7–19.

Wikipedia (2009) Web 2.0. Available at: http://en.wikipedia.org/wiki/Web_2.0 (accessed on January 24, 2010).

10 Globalizing the Local: The Case of an Egyptian Superhero Comic

THEO VAN LEEUWEN AND USAMA SULEIMAN

Introduction

Much of the literature on global media has sought either to critique (American) 'cultural imperialism,' or to minimize its impact by arguing that American (and other) global cultural imports are localized and indigenized, so that there is no need to fear increasing cultural and linguistic 'McDonaldization' (Ritzer 2000). In our view, the relation between the global and the local is more complex and more diverse. Case studies are needed rather than sweeping generalizations, studies of just what is global and what local in the media of countries and regions with different recent histories – in the northern European countries, which have been so wide open to globalization while at the same time seeking to become exporters of global media themselves; in the ex-communist countries of eastern Europe and the still communist countries that are now engaging in market reform; in those developing countries that are increasingly prosperous – and in those that are not. In the past few years we have published a number of such case studies.[1] In our studies of *Cosmopolitan* magazine, for instance, we looked at "top down localization" (Machin and Van Leeuwen 2003, 2004, 2005a, 2007). This magazine appears in forty-three different languages and is produced by local editors, but remains under tight control from the Hearst Corporation in New York. We translated and analyzed articles on sexuality and women's careers; we interviewed local editors and readers in ten countries; and we found that the local versions of the magazine followed much the same agenda – all propagate the independent, freedom-loving 'fun, fearless' Cosmo woman. The visual style and generic structure of the articles (and of the magazine as a whole) were also near-identical in all the versions we studied (only the Japanese version had a different format). There were nevertheless local differences – for instance in the way editors sought to bend their 'local' languages to the informal and tongue-in-cheek style prescribed by the magazine or to resist that informality; or in the solutions suggested in advice columns to what, in essence, was a set of problems of very much the same kind – related to

The Handbook of Language and Globalization, First Edition. Edited by Nikolas Coupland.
© 2013 Blackwell Publishing Ltd except for editorial material and organization © 2013 Nikolas Coupland.
Published 2013 by Blackwell Publishing Ltd.

'relationships,' sex, and work. In another study (Machin and Van Leeuwen 2007: 30ff.) we tracked the history of women's magazines in the Netherlands, where such magazines were initially local, though influenced by American models, and local versions of American magazines entered the market only much later. This contrasted with our studies of computer war games and comic strips in the Middle East (Machin and Suleiman 2006; Machin and Van Leeuwen 2007: 36ff.), where markets were initially flooded by American products, whereas local products emerged only later, being motivated by political or religious considerations. We also looked at local media produced by less developed countries not – or not only – for local consumption, but also in order for them to have a voice in the wider world: for instance the *Vietnam News*, an English-language newspaper produced in Vietnam (Van Leeuwen 2006), and the comic strips we will discuss in this paper. In all these studies we focused on specific cases, combining linguistically informed text analysis with interviews and/or focus groups with producers and readers (or, in the case of computer games, players) and with close attention to the relevant social, historical, and political contexts.

Just as in these earlier papers we looked at particular computer war games, newspapers, and magazines, we will, in this paper, analyze a particular Egyptian superhero comic. This comic, *Zein*, is one out of four superhero comics produced by AK Comics in Cairo. It is published in Arabic as well as in English, and the two versions have distinct purposes. The Arab version has a 'local' purpose: according to the inside cover of the magazine, it seeks to create a "genuine Middle Eastern superhero," a role model for young people in the Middle East that will give them "pride and optimism." The English version has a 'global' purpose, seeking to act as a "global ambassador, spreading peace and good will" (again, according to the inside cover of the magazine) – and seeking also, of course, to be globally marketable, especially in the US, and also in the UK (where it is mostly read by learners of Arabic). This is the reverse of the process of localization which we investigated in our studies of *Cosmopolitan* magazine. The 'local' is globalized here, rather than that the global being localized.

To realize these different purposes, the English translation is not literal, but an adaptation rather than a translation (see Van Leeuwen 2006). As is often the case in global media, the same visuals are used in the two Arabic and English versions, and only the linguistic elements and the 'sound effects,' the onomatopoeic words, are translated. However, these 'sound effects' (which include human and animal sounds such as menacing growls and cries of fear or pain as well as non-human sounds such as gun shots, punches, and so on) make extensive use of the synaesthetic potential of typography, and so they introduce a visual element in the translation, as we will discuss below at some length. In this paper we will therefore attempt a detailed analysis of the differences between the Arabic text and its English translation, and we will seek to relate these differences, interpretatively, to the different purposes of the two versions and to the views of the 'local' and the 'global' that underlie them.[2] Supplementary evidence for our interpretations comes from interviews we conducted with comic strip publishers, writers, and artists in Cairo, Beirut, Abu Dhabi, and Kuwait.[3]

Comic strips are not new to the Middle East. Some of the Egyptian artists we spoke to referred to the scrolls of the Pharaonic era as a distant predecessor. Superheroes have a long history too, as is discussed in Eco's celebrated essay on Superman (1976). But, whatever its antecedents and whatever has happened to them since antiquity, it is perhaps fair to say that the modern superhero comic strip is an American invention. As Jeremy Tunstall (1977: 17) has said, the most important influence of American imported media has been in "the styles and patterns which most other countries in the world have adopted and copied. This influence includes the very definition of what a *newspaper*, or a *feature film*, or a *television set* is." This undoubtedly applies to superhero comics as well.

America began to export comic strips to the Middle East in the late 1930s. From 1937 on Micky Mouse ('Miki') was published, in a fairly literal translation, in the Cairo magazine *Samir*, which also published *Tarzan*, *The Phantom*, *Tin Tin*, and others, as well as some locally produced content. *Superman* began publication in 1964, also in Cairo, under license from Diamond Comic Distributors (DC). Later both magazines moved to Beirut, where conditions were a little more liberal, and *Superman* continued there until 1995. Leila Shaheen Da Cruz, former managing director of the Lebanese *Superman* from shortly after its inception till 1995, told us that she replaced the Egyptian dialect with high Arabic and employed a teacher of Arabic as translator in order to increase the educational value of the comic. While she found the older *Superman* comics educationally valuable because of the scientific and technical knowledge they contained, later *Superman* comics had become too violent, she said, and therefore she often resorted to reprinting old material until DC ordered her to print the newer, more violent material; after this she decided to pull out.

Initially, then, Middle Eastern comics were American (and French) imports, translated literally, though with some censorship (such as ensuring that dogs are only seen in the garden and not in the house), but recontextualized as educational publications, modeling 'proper' Arabic and omitting content that was considered too violent or lacking in educational value. Even *Zein* still includes "Challenge your mind" and "Fun facts" educational features.

As the Arab world became oil-rich, locally produced comics emerged. They were produced by highly respected visual artists and serious writers and journalists, who traveled across the Arab world and had a pan-Arabic outlook, and they were published (and censored) by governments as educational material for children. These comics had themes of pan-Arab solidarity, anti-imperialism, anti-Zionism, and the glory of Arab history and heritage, and they frequently dealt with political–historical themes. The mission statement of Lebanon's *Samer* magazine proclaimed itself to be "proud of Arab values," to "raise the child proud with his homeland and Pan-Arab belonging," and to "bring the proper Arabic closer to children." Some Cairo comic strip artists mourn the passing of this period. Golo, a French comic strip artist who has lived and worked in Cairo for thirteen years, resents AK Comics' commercial approach and contrasts it to that of the revolutionary artists of the 1960s. Many of the comic strips of the earlier period are discussed in Douglas and Malti-Douglas' excellent book about comics in the Middle East (1994).

Most recently, two new trends emerged. On the one hand, more and more Islamic comic strips were produced, in the beginning mostly by the religious wings of government ministries, for example by the Egyptian Council of Islamic Affairs, but from the late 1980s onwards also by non-governmental organizations, some with connections to Islamic oppositional groups, for instance the Egyptian Al-Muslim al-Saghîr ('The Little Muslim'). As Douglas and Malti-Douglas (1994) document, some of these Islamicized comics are quite political. In one, a group of children are heroes in the Intifada, collecting dynamite to be used against the Israelis; in another, morality and patriotism go hand in hand as a little girl finds a box with a letter from a soldier to his mother and takes the box to the mother. At the same time commercial ventures such as AK Comics began to 'globalize the local' instead of 'localizing the global,' and to translate from Arabic into English instead of doing it the other way round. Started in 2002 by Ayman Kandeel, a graduate of the American University Cairo with an American PhD in economics and finance, the company is global also in the sense that the artwork is outsourced to Brazil's PopArt Comics Studio. The verbal elements and the sound effects are then added in Cairo, for both the Arabic and the English version, and the color is also adjusted in Cairo, where it is made more 'Egyptian,' with dusky desert-like yellows and browns dominating. Another similar venture, Teshkeel Comics, started in 2006 in Kuwait. It partnered with Marvel Comics in order to publish the Marvel Comics titles in Arabic, but it also published its own action comic, *The 99*, both in English and in Arabic. At Teshkeel, production is even more globalized than at AK Comics, penciling and inking being outsourced to the UK and coloring to the US, while writing is divided between the US and Kuwait. The company's 'chief operations officer' is Canadian.

In short, the situation is complex. The importing and translation of the globally most dominant Marvel and DC superhero comics continue, as does the production of comic strips for purely local consumption – often in the much less realistic, much more cartoon-like style which many in the Middle East prefer. At the same time local products are now recontextualized for global consumption. The story premises of AK Comics' superhero series reveal some of the adaptations that this process requires. Almost all the plots are set in the future, in a time when the 'fifty-five-year war' in the Middle East has finally come to an end and all the inhabitants live peacefully together. But while, as Eco has observed, in *Superman* "civil conscience" becomes completely separated from "political conscience" (Eco 1976: 38), in the AK Comics politics has only gone underground. In *Jalila*, for instance, the action takes place in "the City of All Faiths" (Jerusalem?), where both the "Zios Army" (Zionist?) and the "United Liberation Force" (Palestine Liberation Organization?) fight sinister terrorists with names like Jose Darion (Moshe Dayan?) and Aton (Ariel Sharon?).

Narrative Adaptation

Zein is a superhero in the mould of Superman, with hints of Batman and Zorro thrown in (see Figure 10.1). But he is also the last descendant of the Pharaohs. His

Figure 10.1   Zein, the last pharaoh. From AK Comics (2005) *The Year of the Beast*, *Zein* 4, Cairo

parents had put him in a special capsule that allowed him to live forever, and now he is the protector of "the Ancient Land of the River" and "Origin City," seeking to rebuild the ancient civilization, aided by the "Jewel of the River" (Zein's equivalent of Superman's "kryptonite"; AK Comics 2005: 2).

Like Superman, Zein takes on the guise of a modest, unassuming citizen. In *The Year of the Beast* (AK Comics 2005), the story on which we will focus in this chapter, he is a medical assistant, Ashraf Kabil, working in the colonial army hospital with a British doctor, Dr Livingstone, "observing his enemies and learning from them." There is a mysterious monster about, an "Adamic Beast," as the Arabic has it ("the Beast" in the English translation), whose victims have strange wounds for which there is no easy medical explanation.

After another attack by this Beast has been reported, Doctor Livingstone cursorily dismisses the possibility of a mythical beast and burns the report. There must be a scientific explanation, he says. But, while he is not in the lab, Ashraf examines the victims' bodies and suspects an "animal like no other animal," as the Arabic version describes it. Suddenly an alarm sounds. Zein quickly dons his superhero outfit and attacks the Beast, being helped by the British soldiers. With a gunshot wound in his arm, the Beast retreats. Afterwards Ashraf finds Livingstone in the hospital with a bandaged arm. He is suspicious now: *"There was uneasiness in the air, but it had not come to the surface, because we did not want to express it. On the face a smile, but inside suspicion"*[4] (p. 19, Arabic version; in English this becomes: "There was a strange tension in the air. Though our conscious minds did not want to admit it, something was subliminally wrong. Call it a sneaking suspicion"):

"كانت سحب التوتر تملأ سماء الحوار بيننا. ولكنها لم تسقط أمطارها بعد.. فلم نكن نود

الإفصاح عن شيء."

In the next scene, Ashraf and Dr Livingstone, his arm still in a sling, attend a reception by the colonial Secretary-General. Ashraf watches Livingstone leave the room, ostensibly to go to the toilet. He follows him and finds a syringe. Quickly he transforms himself into Zein and is only just in time to save the Secretary-General from the Beast's deadly grip by injecting it with the syringe, which "overloads the creature's tissues" and "reaches toxic levels," causing the Beast to flee. Ashraf now confronts Livingstone, who confesses that he is the Beast. He had "experimented with cell generation" to help the victims of war, but, after injecting himself with the serum he had developed, had turned into a monster.

What is, at first sight, peculiar about this story is that Zein, the noble superhero who seeks to revive the glory of Pharaonic Egypt, protects the British soldiers and the Secretary-General, while Dr Livingstone, the evil Beast, *attacks* the colonizers, his own people. This at least is what unfolds in the pictures, and the question is now whether, and if so how, the verbal text puts this in perspective, or, perhaps, in two different perspectives, one for local and one for global consumption. Comparing the Arabic and the English introductions, some changes became immediately obvious: '*colonizers*' become 'imperialists from the continent beyond our own'; '*the land of my ancestors*' becomes 'the sacred homeland of my forefathers'; '*their largest colonies*' become 'their most cherished of imperial possessions.' These are relatively small changes, but there is a difference between being a colony and being part of an empire. The latter, at least in principle, leaves open the possibility of equality between the parts of the empire and of a *pax romana*, a "peaceful coexistence," while the former always involves subjugation and exploitation. Yet later the "imperialists" become "occupiers," whose "burdens we bore."

The English translation also adds new material. The "imperialists" become "a people as different in way of life as the animal must have been to primitive man," which (though very obliquely) suggests that the invaders were less civilized than the Egyptians, but they also become "a permanent and familiar fixture," with which Egyptians can "peacefully coexist" and from which they gain "valuable insights." In other words, there is an ambivalence in the English text which does not exist in the original Arabic. The British are imperialists as well as occupiers, motivated by greed and less civilized, yet also advanced. In the Arabic version, on the other hand, they are simply "colonizers" and "the enemy."

The translation also adds some 'local color' (the camels). Such touches of local color for global consumption can be found in other Zein stories as well. In *The Game*, for instance, a character exclaims: "Praise Allah! Could this be a treasure?!! Is it finally my lucky day out here in this dry barren land?" – and later on an armed robber shouts: "Everybody complies or they end up as fertilizer for my date palms" (AK Comics 2004).

In table 10.1 below we show a literal translation of the Arabic text of the introduction to *The Year of the Beast* (AK Comics 2005) side by side with the English translation produced by AK Comics:

On the next two pages, the relationship between Dr Livingstone and Ashraf/ Zein is introduced – a relationship which, in this story, personifies the relation between colonizer and colonized. The Arabic version uses footnotes to introduce

Table 10.1 Introducing *The Year of the Beast*

Arabic	English
In the second half of the nineteenth century, colonizers from the continent beyond our own began to occupy the land of my ancestors. خلال النصف الثاني من القرن التاسع عشر جاء المستعمرون من قارة بعيدة عن قارتنا ومن حياة مختلفة عن حياتنا ليحتلوا أرض أجدادى.	Through the second half of the nineteenth century, Imperialists from the continent beyond our own, a people as different in way of life as the animal must have been to primitive man, began to occupy the sacred homeland of my forefathers.
Their major motivation was greed ... and control of the canal that would open trade to the largest colonies in the East. جاءوا بدافع الجشع والرغبة في السيطرة على القناة التى ستفتح لهم الطريق إلى أكبر مستعمراتهم في الشرق.	Their major motivation was greed ... and control of the canal that would open trade routes to their most cherished of imperial possessions in the East.
We are in the year 1889, the year when many frightening events took place that no-one understood. This was the year of the appearance of the Adamic Beast. نحن في سنة 1889 تلك السنة التي حدث فيها ما أثار الرعب والفزع ولم يعرف سره أحد. كان ذلك عندما ظهر الوحش الآدمي.	The year was 1889, the year the Beast struck.
The colonizers stayed for a long time in our land ... and their presence was imposed on us night and day. طال بقاء المستعمرين في أرضنا وصار وجودهم مفروضاً علينا نراهم صباحاً ومساء.	The Imperialists were firmly entrenched in our land ... a fixture as permanent and familiar as the camels which bore our burdens.
	We bore theirs ...
People resisted and rejected their presence. And I worked in a medical department of the Army barracks to observe them closely, and convinced of my father's wisdom, "Keep your friends close so they can know you and your enemies closer, so you can know them." كان الشعب يقاومهم ويرفض وجودهم، وكنت أعمل في القسم الطبى بمعسكرهم لأراقب عن كثب كل ما يفعلون اقتناعاً بحكمة أبى: "اقترب من أصدقائك ليعرفوك .. واقترب أكثر من أعدائك لتعرفهم".	Though many resented their presence I decided early on that peaceful coexistence was the best course of action ... causing the least friction while learning what valuable insights I could from our occupiers. "Keep your friends close and your enemies closer," as my father would say.

Table 10.2 Introducing Dr Livingstone

Arabic	English
I spoke with Dr Livingstone about politics, philosophy and medicine. He is a knowledgeable doctor and he was interested when I told him about ancient Pharaonic medicine and revealed some of its secrets to him. تحدثت مع د. لفنجستون في السياسة والفلسفة والطب وهو طبيب عالم وقد بدا مهتماً عندما حدثته عن أسرار الطب الفرعونى العريق وكشفت له بعض غموضها.	Dr Livingstone was considered a pioneer in his field and a pillar of imperial society. During his time here we had established mutual respect and rapport […] more than just a professional courtesy. We shared beliefs and ideas, debated philosophy and politics. From Dr Livingstone I learned the special knowledge of Western medicine. And from me, he discovered the secrets of our culture's traditional practice. We were colleagues, yes, but more than that, we were friends.

the two formally, in the one case "*Dr Livingstone, the Head of the Medical Department of the Occupying Army*," in the other "*Dr Ashraf Kabil is Zein's name in this story*." In the English version, 'Ashraf Kabil' is not revealed as Zein until much later, when, during his first fight with the Beast, he muses: "I was a doctor, yes. But that was just a façade. Truly I am son of Greatest Pharaoh, the last of my bloodline," and Dr Livingstone is introduced as follows.

The "secrets of "ancient Pharaonic medicine" here become "the secrets of our culture's traditional medicine," and Livingstone's knowledgeability becomes "the special knowledge of Western medicine." Although both versions leave it open to what extent Dr Livingstone's 'serum,' with its healing as well as its destructive powers, is of Egyptian origin or a product of western science, in the English version the balance shifts towards the latter. Dr Livingstone also becomes more than just "knowledgeable": he is "a pioneer in his field and a pillar of imperial society," and the relationship between him and Ashraf becomes one of "mutual respect" and friendship, in which Ashraf learns "special knowledge" from the good doctor.

Ashraf's friendly attitude to the colonizers also extends to the British soldiers, as shown, for instance, in the following dialogue, which appears only in the English version:

SOLDIER: We'd be dead if it hadn't been for you. Who are you?
ZEIN: A friend …
SOLDIER: Well, friend, it went that way.

In the Arabic version, Zein helps the soldiers not out of friendship, but out of compassion: *"The screams and entreaties of the soldiers compelled me to protect them. Despite the fact that they were occupying my country I felt sorry for them"*

"دفعتني صرخات الجنود وتوسلاتهم إلى التدخل لحمايتهم ورغم أنهم يحتلون بلادى إلا أننى أشفقت عليهم."

Clearly, in the 'local' version, the West can remain an enemy, protected, if necessary, by a noble local hero, while in the 'global' version West and East co-exist peacefully, with the East 'learning' from the West.

How are these ambivalences resolved in the two versions? In table 10.3 below we reproduce the final scene in full.

In the Arabic version, the western colonizers' intentions to "help" the colonized are unmasked and lead to self-destruction. Dr Livingstone has to pay the price and Zein shows no compassion, even though the doctor begs his forgiveness. His only question is why Livingstone kept repeating the experiment. At most we can say that Livingstone is recognized as a worthy opponent, an opponent who "is able to face the truth."

The English version first of all needs to make explicit what needs no explanation in the Arabic version: the exploitative nature of colonization and the ultimate duplicity of the colonial missionaries and good doctors. It also makes much more of the doctor's good work, expanding the story of how he cured a "native boy" (in Arabic he is just a "little boy") and allowing him to retain his conscience to the end. Even his "madness," "subconsciously," had the good intention of avenging "your people." And in the end he is willing to face the consequences of his deeds and to "give himself up." Zein acknowledges all this: "You've always meant well doctor," and in the end he "doesn't know what to say."

Translating Narrative and Dialogue

In a sense, the pictures are also a translation – the translation, or rather adaptation, from a verbal script to a visual story. As we have no access to the script of *The Year of the Beast*, we cannot study it in detail here, but it is clear that mistakes have occurred. The 'visual language' of Brazil clearly has not provided the artists with adequate cognitive schemata for drawing camels, as the camels in the Zein stories look more like llamas than like camels (this is particularly evident in *The Game*). They also seem unaware of the significance of various aspects of dress and grooming as markers of identity. Ashraf's fez is a mixture of Middle Eastern and Chinese headwear, and at the colonial Secretary-General's gala reception he wears the costume of a hotel doorman. Given that the story is set in the late nineteenth century, it is inappropriate that the hero should *not* have a moustache (which would have been shameful for Arab men of the period) while Dr Livingstone has one. However, as we are focusing here on differences between the Arabic and English versions, we will leave these interesting issues for another occasion.

Table 10.3 Final scene of *The Year of the Beast*

Arabic	English
"I beg you, all I want is for you to listen to me one last time.	
أرجوك .. كل ما أريده منك أن تسمعني .. للمرة الأخيرة!	
I came here motivated by noble intentions. I wanted to help humanity and not just my nation's army, but your people too. I beg you, my friend.	"Oh! I came here with such high ideals, Ashraf! I thought that the work we were doing would advance not only the empire, but your people too!"
لقد جئت إلى هنا تدفعني غاية نبيلة.. كنت أتمنى أن أخدم	"You've always meant well, doctor."
البشرية وليس فقط جيش بلادي بل وشعبك أيضاً..	"Ah! Meaning well and doing well are two entirely different things. We invaded your land, Ashraf! We exploited your resources and oppressed your people! We rationalized that our own needs were superior to your own! Those actions have more meaning than a lifetime of good intentions.
أرجوك صدقني!	
I have been working with the army for a long time. I have seen a lot of wars and victims. The screams of the victims used to shake me up. I stood there unable to help them. I began doing some research experiments with a new treatment, I took some genes from an Egyptian lizard that renews its limbs. I experimented on people, I began with a little boy who had an atrophied arm. I injected him with the genetic serum. Immediately his arm began to develop quickly.	I felt helpless, like I should be doing more. As a doctor of science I wanted to heal the people who were brutalized by this occupation. Somehow I felt responsible. So I forged ahead with my research. I sampled materials from countless sources, experimenting on cell regeneration wit the indigenous spiny-tailed lizards. They possess the uncanny ability to regenerate their limb once amputated. I isolated a chemical from their very unique biology, and was able to synthesize it in the lab. It was the equivalent of a growth hormone, or so I thought. The first human trial was on a native boy whose arm had been severed by an imperial shell. There was little I could do surgically for him, so I made an ethical decision, risk his life through conventional means, or … take a chance on the serum. I took the chance, Ashraf and it worked! The boy's arm regenerated literally before my eyes!!!
أنا أعمل مع الجيش منذ فترة طويلة، رأيت حروباً كثيرة	
وضحايا أكثر.. كانت صرخات الجرحى تزلزل كياني	
وأنا أقف عاجزاً عن مساعدتهم.. بدأت بعض التجارب	
بحثًا عن علاج جديد وأخذت بعض الجينات من زواحف	
مصرية تجدد ما تفقده من أعضائها! وجربتها مع البشر	
فبدأت بصبي يعاني من ضمور في ذراعه وحقنته	
بالمصل الجيني! وفوجئت بذراعه تنمو من جديد بشكل	
هائل!!	

Table 10.3   *(Cont'd)*

Arabic	English
I began to think, what if I used the medicine on someone in good health? And in a moment of madness I injected myself, There was an amazing transformation. I became bigger, broader and stronger, until I became an uncompassionate beast. ثم تساءلت ماذا لو حقنت شخصاً سليم الأعضاء؟ وفي لحظة جنون حقنت نفسي!! وحدث لى تحول عجيب فصرت أكبر.. وأضخم.. وأقوى! حتى صرت وحشاً لا يرحم!	Imagine the serum's reaction to an intact body ... I introduced it to my own bloodstream. My cells replicated insanely, as if they couldn't grown fast enough. My body was transforming into something more than human. In each trial I lost consciousness, but the monster within me emerged with the ferocity you saw today, as if my subconscious rage adopted such a shape that I might make a change ... that I might avenge your people.
"When you were transformed into this violent beast for the first time, why did you keep repeating it?" عندما تحولت إلى وحش قاتل في المرة الأولى.. ما الذي دعاك إلى تكرار الحقن؟	"I don't know what to say."
"I was behaving unconsciously. I was blinded by the madness and the control of the beast inside me over my thinking soundly. I was his prisoner. I would do what he wanted without wanting to. Take these, my friend. They are my experimental notes and the formula. Destroy them or keep them. Do whatever you want with them. كنت أتصرف بشكل لا إرادي.. أعماني جنون القوة وسيطر الوحش في داخلي على إدراكي! كنت أسيراً له أفعل ما يمليه عليّ بلا إرادة مني!! خذ يا صديقي.. هذه كل أدواتي وأوراق التركيب! كل شيء.. كل شيء دمرها، احفظها، افعل بها ما تشاء!	"Don't say anything. I've betrayed your trust, Ashraf. I truly am a Monster. Here, here, take them ... burn them ... Do what you want with them. Just take them! I've caused enough destruction already. "Where are you going, Dr Livingstone"

Table 10.3   (*Cont'd*)

Arabic	English
Do you think this is enough? *I haven't told you the rest of the story.* *Because you injected me with the* *excess dose, my circulation will keep* *increasing, and I will explode in a few* *hours. I am going to drink from the* *same cup that I made others drink* *from. Goodbye my friend, I beg you to* *forgive me."*	"To give myself up ... I have to pay for my crimes, faithful friend ..."
وهل تظن هذا كافياً؟	
لم أخبرك بقية القصة بعد. إن الجرعات الزائدة التي	
حقنتني بها ستجعل أوعيتي الدموية تنفجر بعد ساعات!	
سأرحل بنفس الكأس التي أذقتها للآخرين.. وداعاً يا	
صديقي.. وأرجو أن تسامحني!	
A lot of people know the truth but only *a few are able to face it.*	The doctor might have become the deadly giant of his inner mind, but in the end, he succumbed to the greatest giant of them all [...] his own conscience ...
كثيرون منا يعرفون الحقيقة.. قليلون منا قادرون على	
مواجهتها.	

Three kinds of visual containers frame the verbal text: narrative boxes, which take the form of faded documents with frayed edges (see Figure 10.2); speech balloons; and thought bubbles.

It is immediately obvious that the Arabic and English versions distribute content differently across these different types of container, as for instance on page 7, where most of the Arabic thought bubbles become narrative boxes in the English text (see table 10.4).

The English also adds colloquialisms such as "Hmmm" and emotive terms such as "ghastly." Lebanese comic strip artist Jad Khoury told us that he would like to abolish the use of high Arabic and imitate the liveliness of American comic strip dialogue by using local dialects in speech balloons. However, the English version also uses formal language, especially in the narrative boxes, for instance to introduce medical 'technicality' and to give the boxes the flavor of an 'objective' historical document, a detached and truthful 'report.'

Figure 10.2   Narrative box. From AK Comics (2005) *The Year of the Beast*, *Zein* 4, Cairo

Narrative boxes

Narrative boxes are used a great deal more in the English version, where there are forty-nine of them, as opposed to nineteen in the Arabic version. There is also more text in the English boxes: 4.5 lines on average – whereas the Arabic boxes contain on average 3 lines. It is primarily through these boxes that the English version adds the explanations which the Arabic version takes for granted, the kind of 'orientalisms' we have already mentioned (camels, date palms, and so on), and the 'export' version of the history of colonialism.

Thought bubbles (see tables 10.5 and 10.6)

Thought bubbles, on the other hand, are more frequent in the Arabic version – there are twenty-two of them, as opposed to fourteen in the English text. Occasionally they also contain the thoughts of characters other than Zein, which is not the case in the English version. Although some reveal *reactions* of the characters ("My God, it is worse than I imagined"; "Unbelievable!"), most of them function as 'suspense devices,' throwing seeds of suspicion ("Where is this man going?") or uncertainty ("The emergency alarm?!"), or prompting readers to anticipate further events on the basis of what they have seen ("What? A syringe?!"). Sometimes they combine the two functions. "Hmm … most peculiar," for instance, is at once a reaction and a clue which tells readers that there is a mystery attached to the wounds of the victims which will keep them in suspense until it is solved.

Dialogue

The English version contains more speech balloon dialogue than the Arabic version (113, as opposed to 74 in the Arabic version), but most of the additional

Table 10.4   Distribution of content into different types of container in the Arabic and in the (original) English version

Frame	Arabic	English
1	Thought bubble *My God, it is worse than I imagined* يا إلهى إنها أبشع مما كنت أتصور!	Narrative box The Officer was right …
2	Thought bubble *These wounds are deep and the internal organs are ruptured* الإصابات غائرة في الجسد كله والأحشاء ممزقة!	Narrative box The bodies were a ghastly sight.
3	Thought bubble *It is the work of some wild animal, but not of any known animal* إنها من فعل حيوان مفترس ولكنه ليس من الأنواع المعروفة لنا!	Thought bubble Hmmm … most peculiar
4	Thought bubble *It appears as though what has befallen these victims is some sort of explosion, yet there is no gunpowder residue and there are no burns on their bodies* إن ما حدث لهؤلاء الضحايا يبدو كأنه انفجار قنبلة ولكن لا أثر للبارود ولا توجد حروق على أجسادهم!!	Narrative boxes It appeared as if they were torn apart by some tremendous blunt force. I instantly ruled out animal attack, due to the absence of puncture wounds from fangs or claw! And for the life of me I could not locate any powder burns from explosive devices, though it seemed only such a force could have produced the trauma

dialogue does not contain much narrative information and serves merely to add realism, to have people speak where you might expect them to 'in reality' – as in this scene, which in the Arabic version has no dialogue at all:

SOLDIER:	Eh-?!
EGYPTIAN WORKER:	Look! Do you see it?!

Table 10.5 Thought bubbles, example 1

English	I don't know what you're up to, Dr Livingstone, but your actions lately have been out of character
Arabic	*Where is this man going? Indeed, all his actions are frightening* أين يذهب هذا الرجل؟ إن كل تصرفاته مريبة!!

Table 10.6 Thought bubbles, example 2

English	Wha-?! A syringe?! In the General's Estate?!
Arabic	*What is this? The same syringe we use in the hospital? What is inside?* هه.. إنها نفس أداة الحقن التي نستخدمها في المستشفى!!

Table 10.7 Dialogue, example 1

English	Ungh!!
Arabic	*Oh how terrible*

Table 10.8 Dialogue, example 2

English	Noooooo!! Help me!!
Arabic	*Salvation!*

Table 10.9 Dialogue, example 3

English	Got him!
Arabic	*Indeed, I got him.*

Soldier:	In the name of the Queen, what is that –?!
Other soldier:	Ohhhh!!
Third soldier:	Aggggh!!!

In the Arabic version this kind of dialogue is mostly restricted to the action scenes, and even there it is a good deal more formal than in the English version, as the following examples show (tables 10.7–10.10).

Table 10.10   Dialogue, example 4

English	Please … Gasp!
Arabic	*I beg you, please help me*

Figure 10.3   Graphic prosody substitutes (English version). From AK Comics (2005) *The Year of the Beast*, *Zein* 4, Cairo

Figure 10.4   Graphic prosody substitutes (Arabic version). From AK Comics (2005) *The Year of the Beast*, *Zein* 4, Cairo

Both the Arabic and the English version use graphic devices to indicate prosodic elements such as intonation, loudness, and voice quality. Dialogue balloons may have jagged edges (for loudness), wavy edges (for pain), red edges (for fear), and letters may vary in size or color (see Figures 10.3 and 10.4). Different as the two versions may be in the use of language, in the use of these graphic devices they are not very different. However, the typical comic strip use of bold and cursive font for emphasis ("THE OFFICER WAS **RIGHT** ... THE BODIES WERE

A *GHASTLY* SIGHT!") does not have an equivalent in the Arabic speech balloons.

Multi-modality

Non-human 'sound effect' words, such as 'clack clack' for horse's hooves, 'bang bang' for guns, and so on are relatively rare in *Zein*, though they occur somewhat more in the English text (sixteen times) than in the Arabic text (eleven times), where they are mainly confined to the attacks of the Beast. It has long been a commonplace in linguistic literature on onomatopoeia (see Ullman 1982: 82 ff.) that the same meanings have somewhat different onomatopoeic signifiers in different languages – which demonstrates that even relatively 'motivated' signs still have a significant element of arbitrariness. A gun goes 'bang' or 'crack' in English, but 'pum' or 'paf' in Spanish. Dogs go 'bow-wow' in English, 'gnaf-gnaf' in French, 'guau-guau' in Spanish, and 'won-won' in Japanese. In *Zein*, however, some of the Arabic 'sound effect' words are anglicisms transposed into Arabic script ("*scratch*," "*crack*"), and other onomatopoeic words, too, are quite similar in the two languages. Onomatopoeic words signifying speed, for instance, have an extended vowel ending in '-sh' in both languages, for example "Whoosh!" in English and "*Wooooooosh!*" in Arabic. Of course, examples can be found in which the onomatopoeic words are quite different in the two languages; thus a kick of the foot is "Takh" in English and "*Deeb!*" in Arabic. But this may stem, not so much from the difference between the two phonological systems (as 'Takh' would be quite possible in Arabic), but from the fact that sound effects are complex, so that different onomatopoeic signifiers may be motivated by different aspects of the sound they stand for (or of the way in which that sound is produced): in the one case, the sharpness of the foot that kicks ("Takh") – in the other, the softness of the flesh on which it makes its impact ("*Deeb*"); in the one case, the speed of the thump ("Fooooosh"), in the other, the impact it makes ("Pooow"). The following table (10.11) shows some comparisons between the Arabic original and the English translation.

The amount of 'sound effects' produced by humans – threatening roars of the Beast, cries of fear or pain, and so on – is more or less the same in the two versions. We counted thirty in English and twenty-nine in Arabic. Yet there are some subtle differences. Vocalizations of puzzlement ("Hmmm") or surprise ("Eh") are absent from the Arabic original, and the English Beast more often wails of pain than the Arab Beast. When the his claw grips the throat of a soldier in the Arabic version, the Beast utters a muffled "*Ummmm.*" In English, this becomes a loud "Aghghgh!"

All these 'sound effects' are synaesthetically enhanced through color and typographic expression. The temporal unfolding of a word may be shown by a gradual increase in the size of the letters and a widening of the space between them (see Figures 10.5 and 10.6); loudness may be suggested through size, through high color saturation, and through the use of salient colors such as red and yellow;

Table 10.11   Onomatopoeic sounds in the Arabic and in the (original) English version

Sound effect	English	Arabic
Kick from Zein's foot	Takh!	*Deeb!*
	Dip!	*Dush!*
Beast's claw	Scratch!	*Scratch!*
Thump	Krack!	*Crash!*
Gunshots	Bam bam!	*Bam! Bam!*
Speed of Beast's arm	Whoosh!	*Woooooosh!*
	Flousssh!	*Slaaaaaaash!*
Gunshot hitting Beast's arm	Thwank!	*Tashak!*
Structures breaking as Beast crashes through them (?)	Crash!	*Craaaack! Traaaakh!*
Thump from Zein	Trakh!	*Trakh!*
	Pooow!	*Foooosh!*

Table 10.12   The sounds of menace and pain in the Arabic and in the (original) English version

Sound	English	Arabic
The Beast's menacing growls	Graaaowr!!! Graaamph!!!	*Graaaaaaaa!!!*
The Beast's cry as it is hit by a bullet	Graaaaaaaa!!!	*Graaooww!!!*
The Beast in pain	Grmmph!	*Grmmmph!*
The Beast when it is injected with the serum	Arghghgh?!	*Grrrrrr!*
The Beast as it flees after having been injected with the serum	Orghghghhhhh!!!!	*Graaaaaaaa!!!*
Soldiers as the Beast grabs them by the throat	Aghghgh!	*Ummmm*
Soldiers as the Beast punches them	Aieee!!	*Ayyyy!*

intonation, through rising, falling, and undulating baselines (see Figures 10.7 and 10.8) – not unlike those used by the intonation theorist Bolinger (1972) in his representations of intonation contours.

The illustrations show that the graphic representation of intonation, loudness, and temporal structure does not differ much in the two versions. Both make use of the international language of comic strips developed in the 1930s by American

Figure 10.5   Temporal structure of exclamations in English. From AK Comics (2005) *The Year of the Beast*, *Zein* 4, Cairo

Figure 10.6   Temporal structure of exclamations in Arabic. From AK Comics (2005) *The Year of the Beast*, *Zein* 4, Cairo

Figure 10.7   Graphic representation of intonation and loudness in English. From AK Comics (2005) *The Year of the Beast*, *Zein* 4, Cairo

Figure 10.8   Graphic representation of intonation and loudness in Arabic. From AK Comics (2005) *The Year of the Beast, Zein* 4, Cairo

comic strip artists and well described by the French semiotician René Lindekens, who compiled a lexicon of 120 *onomatopées* that demonstrates that French comics, too, contain many anglicisms ('crunch,' 'crackle,' 'knock knock,' 'ouch,' 'sniff,' to mention just a few), as well as many of the *onomatopées* we encountered in *Zein* – for instance 'Arrgrr' for the sound of a 'savage beast,' 'tak' for 'dry impact,' and 'woossh' for the "explosive departure of a missile" (Lindekens 1976: 173–6). But there are subtle differences. The typography emphasizes fear, pain, and agony more strongly in the English version, humanizing the Beast to some extent, while in the Arabic version the Beast is unambiguously evil to the very end. The threatening growl of the Beast ('Graaaaowr!!') is large, colored in yellow with red edges (hence loud and intense), and has a rise–fall intonation contour in both versions. But, while in Arabic the Beast's howl of pain looks much the same as his threatening roar (Figure 10.10), in English the typography changes: as the Beast flees after having been injected with the 'serum,' his cry is blue and decreases in size (Figure 10.9).

Conclusion

For a time, AK Comics seemed to get a foothold in the US market, selling some 5,000 copies of each issue. But the reactions of critics and readers in American web magazines such as *Comic Bulletin* and *Comic World News* were critical:

> A strong concept is underlined by mediocre writing, the art is stiff with a dull ink line. Unfortunately the creators have chosen the path of least resistance and served up what amounts to another brain-dead superhero book that's not even visually appealing. (Watson 2009)

Figure 10.9   The graphic representation of agony in English. From AK Comics (2005) *The Year of the Beast*, Zein 4, Cairo

Figure 10.10   The graphic representation of agony in Arabic. From AK Comics (2005) *The Year of the Beast*, Zein 4, Cairo

And their critique was not restricted to technical issues. Above all, they lambasted *Zein* for the very thing which AK Comics had hoped would sell it, its global orientation:

> Lacking details to distinguish the environment of Egypt and Algeria from Metropolis and Gotham, the heroes and their adventures come off as near clones of their American counterparts. (Manning 2008)

> I am greatly disappointed that the titles do not reflect the diversity of the Middle Eastern people [...] There is not enough suggestion of local culture [...] It does not feel genuine. [...] These books were a great letdown. I'm convinced we do not need more superhero comics in general, but if we have to have more, then they need to blow Marvel and DC out of the water, or at least be able to provide a new twist to the superhero genre. If AK Comics were to embrace its cultural heritage more fully,

they might have a chance. As it is now, they're poised to get dumped in the quarter bins with *Malibu*, *Defiant*, *Tekno* and a dozen other wanna-bees. (Watson 2008)

The same critique played out in Cairo as well. Golo, a French comic strip artist living in Cairo, told us of a workshop he co-organized at Cairo's American University. The sixteen participants were encouraged to develop a *local* story, the traditional story of Saif bin Zi Yazin, a Yemeni prince, and to make it "contemporary" while "keeping the local spirit." Yet, he reported, the participants wanted to master the American style. They "only wanted to imitate," and they "could not see their surroundings."

Clearly, in the matter of superhero comics, the Middle East in supposed to remain 'local.' Trying to become global is crossing a line that should not be crossed. Not long after we started this research, AK Comics announced they were giving up comic strips and moving into graphic novels. It will not have surprised the comic strip artists we interviewed. Jad Khoury, a comic strip artist from Beirut, saw no way out of this dilemma. Defeated nations cannot produce superheroes, he said, this requires a nation on the offensive. In defeated nations, people turn back to heritage and history. We will leave it to our readers to consider whether this is an all-too pessimistic view, but it seems clear that some locals are more local than other and experience global pressure to 'act local,' to stick to local heritage, and to desist from aspiring to more.

NOTES

1 The research for all these publications, including the present one, formed part of the research programme Language and Global Communication, conducted at Cardiff University's Centre for Language and Communication Research, and funded by the Leverhulme Trust.
2 Literal translations of the Arabic version were provided by Kais Al-Momani and Nour Dados.
3 All in all, thirty-eight interviews were conducted by Usama Suleiman in May–June 2006.
4 Literal translations of the Arab text will be italicized throughout.

REFERENCES

AK Comics (2004) *The Game, Zein 2*, Cairo: AK Comics.

AK Comics (2005) *The Year of the Beast, Zein 4*, Cairo: AK Comics.

Bolinger, D. (1972) *Intonation*. Harmondsworth: Penguin.

Douglas, A. and Malti-Douglas, F. (1994) *Arab Comic Strips: Politics of an Emerging Mass Culture*. Bloomington, IN: Indiana University Press.

Eco, U. (1976) Le Mythe de Superman. *Communications* 24: 24–40.

Lindekens, R. (1976) Analyse structurale de la Stripsody de Cathy Berberian. *Communications* 24: 140–76.

Machin, D. (2004) Building the world's visual language: The increasing global importance of image banks. *Visual Communications* 3: 316–36.

Machin, D., and Suleiman, U. (2006) Arab and American computer war games: The influence of a global technology on discourse. *Critical Discourse Studies* 3(1): 1–22.

Machin, D., and Van Leeuwen, T. (2003) Global schemas and local discourses in *Cosmopolitan*. *Journal of Sociolinguistics* 7(4): 493–513.

Machin, D., and Van Leeuwen, T. (2004) Global media: Generic homogeneity and discursive diversity. *Continuum* 18(1): 99–120.

Machin, D., and Van Leeuwen, T. (2005a) Language style and lifestyle: The case of a global magazine. *Media, Culture and Society* 27(4): 577–600.

Machin, D., and Van Leeuwen, T. (2005b) Computer games as political discourse: The case of *Blackhawk Down*. *Journal of Language and Politics* 4: 119–41.

Machin, D., and Van Leeuwen, T. (2007) *Global Media Discourse: A Critical Introduction*. London: Routledge.

Manning, S. (2008) Special AK: AK Comics and heroes of the Middle East. Available at: http://www.comicsbulletin.com/sopabox/114895569441667.htm (accessed on January 20, 2010).

Ritzer, G. (2000) *The McDonaldization of Society*. Thousand Oaks, CA: Pine Forge Press.

Tunstall, J. (1977) *The Media Are American*. London: Constable.

Ullman, S. (1982) *Semantics: An Introduction to the Science of Meaning*. Oxford: Blackwell.

Van Leeuwen, T. (2006) Translation, adaptation, globalization: The Vietnam news. *Journalism* 7(2): 217–37.

Watson, Rich (2009) Review spotlight: AK Comics. Available at: http://www.comicworldnews.com/cgi-bin/index.cgi?column=chick (accessed on January 29, 2010).

11 Language and the Globalizing Habitus of Tourism: Toward a Sociolinguistics of Fleeting Relationships

ADAM JAWORSKI AND CRISPIN THURLOW

In contrast to imperialism, Empire establishes no territorial center of power and does not rely on fixed boundaries or barriers. It is a decentered *and* deterritorializing *apparatus of rule that progressively incorporates the entire global realm within its open, expanding frontiers. Empire manages hybrid identities, flexible hierarchies, and plural exchanges through modulating networks of command.*

Hardt and Negri 2000: xiii

We start this chapter from the premise that sociolinguistics is on the move. This is partly in response to the reorderings of contemporary social life under global capitalism, partly in keeping with the reconceptualizing of key ideas in social theory – both of which are exemplified in the work of Michael Hardt and Antonio Negri quoted above. We are living and researching at a time when power is no longer so neatly centered or easily tracked (see also Deleuze and Guattari 2000; Harvey 2006) and when people's lives and identities are no longer so neatly bounded or easily located (cf. also Sheller and Urry 2006; Urry 2007; Bauman 2000). As scholars of language-in-society, we are therefore necessarily obliged to review the bread-and-butter material of our work. Specifically, we need to rethink – and, in some cases, to ditch altogether – some of the central tropes of our field such as 'community,' 'authenticity,' 'identity' – and indeed 'language' and 'society' themselves. In this regard, Jan Blommaert (2005), Nikolas Coupland (2007), and Ben Rampton (2009) – among others – have written about the need for a sociolinguistics or discourse analysis that is better able to account for the hybrid, the trans-local, the spectacular, the idiosyncratic, the creative, and the multi-modal (on this last point, see Kress and van Leeuwen 2001). Following the lead of Richard

The Handbook of Language and Globalization, First Edition. Edited by Nikolas Coupland.
© 2013 Blackwell Publishing Ltd except for editorial material and organization © 2013 Nikolas Coupland.
Published 2013 by Blackwell Publishing Ltd.

Bauman and Charles Briggs (1990), Blommaert, Coupland, and Rampton make a special point of promoting the importance nowadays of attending to processes of *entextualization* and *recontextualization*, as well as to situated, local practices and to the linguistic reflexivity and metapragmatic awareness of language users (compare Jaworski, Coupland and Galasiński 2004).

Tourism, we think, offers itself as an ideal – and surprisingly overlooked – context for studying precisely the kinds of theoretical issues and social processes Blommaert, Coupland, Rampton, Hardt, Negri, and others address. In its pursuit and endless production of difference, tourism is a past master at recontextualiza-tion, lifting the everyday into the realm of the fantastical, transforming the banal into the exotic, and converting use-value into exchange-value. Tourism, however, not only demands a rethinking of certain sociolinguistic truisms; it also helps to moderate any tendency to throw out the baby with the bathwater. Not all of our old notions are defunct, just as contemporary life continues to be shaped by many of the disciplining, colonizing, determining habits of the past (Hardt and Negri 2000; Deleuze and Guattari 2000). We have shown this to be the case in our own work, for example with regards the tenacious influence of nationality and national identity in tourism discourse (Thurlow and Jaworski 2003; Jaworski and Thurlow 2004; for a broader discussion, see also Heller 2008). In the current chapter we want to explore this old–new tension a little further, with particular reference to some of the ways in which we see language and other semiotic material to be commonly moved and exchanged in tourism. (It is by no means only the English language that is on the move under global capitalism, but also a wide range of genres, discourses, styles, and so on.) We start by reconsidering the general sig-nificance of tourism for sociolinguistics, and then we look at two fundamental principles shaping language in tourism: its *commodification* and its *dislocation* under global capitalism. We turn next to several examples of what we take to be common language exchanges in tourism, which we illustrate with data collected as part of our larger programme of work on language and tourism as a global cultural industry (see Jaworski and Pritchard 2005; Thurlow and Jaworski 2010a; Jaworski, Thurlow, and Ylänne, in preparation). We see these habituating, normative prac-tices as instantiating, together, an often playful *performance of contact* which, in turn, establishes a globalizing habitus, both for tourists and for their hosts.[1]

Tourism under/as Global Capitalism

Whether one thinks of people privileged enough to tour or people who are 'toured,' there is no one whose life remains unaffected by tourism – the single largest international trade in the world and a hallmark of globalization (Appadurai 1996; Bauman 1998). Indeed, social theorists argue that tourism not only reflects socioeconomic relations but is actually instrumental in organizing them (see Lash and Urry 1994). Nor is tourism simply an economic activity. A large body of work in anthropology, sociology, and cultural studies has produced detailed analyses of the social and cultural practices by which tourism is realized, demonstrating its role in establishing ideologies of difference and relations of inequality. This view is consistent with Hardt and Negri's (2000) observation that, in the world order organized by global capitalism, economic power and social power have come to coincide increasingly.

As a once quintessentially modernist project of 'organized' or industrial capitalism (Lash and Urry 1994), tourism continues unabated as a powerful agent of, and channel for, capital. In the age of "liquid modernity," argues Zygmunt Bauman (in Franklin 2003), tourism is both a vast movement of specific people (the tourists) and a metaphor for much of contemporary (Western) life: the "tourist syndrome," which is characterized by temporariness, a looseness of attachment to places and people, and an endless "grazing" (or consumption) of sensations and interactions. Although tourism is not something Hardt and Negri address, it is surely one of the "national and supranational organisms united under a single logic of rule" (ibid., p. xii) by which sovereignty and power are networked and sustained under global capitalism. In many respects tourism is the ideal industry for global capitalism, because it is highly flexible, deeply semiotic, and constantly reflexive (compare Urry 2002). Tourism exemplifies a semiotically embedded service because, like advertising and marketing, a key part of what is actually produced and consumed in tourism is the semiotic context of the service. Not only does tourism involve face-to-face (or more mediated) forms of visitor–host interaction, like in many other types of service encounters, but the ultimate goods purchased by tourists during their travels are images, lifestyles, memories, and their narrative enactments. Material goods such as souvenirs and other artefacts, not unlike snippets of language formulae brought back from foreign trips, are themselves (re-)packaged and promoted as useful props in the enactment of these performances, and they serve as an extension of the *tourist gaze* – the socially organized, systematized and 'disciplining' ways in which tourism is structured and learned (Urry 2002; after Foucault 1976).

Especially given this global or, more accurately, *globalizing* context, it seems obvious that sociolinguists and discourse analysts would want to engage with tourism and mobility more broadly. It is here that the encounter between host and tourist (and between tourist and tourist) manifests itself as one key site articulating the "human consequences" (Bauman 1998) of globalization, with all its concomitant privileges and inequalities. Indeed, tourism discourse reveals nicely what we call 'banal globalization,' the everyday textual realization and interactional enactment of global capitalism (Thurlow and Jaworski 2010a; see Billig 1995 and Beck 2002). If the functioning of Empire is dependent on the agentic subjectivities of its 'citizens,' as Hardt and Negri propose, then tourists, with their desire to consume movement, places, bodies, images, and information (Urry 2007) are the perfect exponents of Empire and the perfect agents for its assertion and reproduction. And it is in the singular interpersonal, intercultural exchanges between the touring and the toured that we find the most forceful manifestations of the internalized, global order. This is where language and communication become both commodities and the vehicle for their exchange. It is also where the traditional places of language are dislocated.

Language as Commodity

The expansion of tourism as a dominant cultural industry is one of the major areas of economic activity under globalization which have highlighted the significance of language commodification in the study of shifting identities, interpersonal relations, and group structures. The political economy of language has long been recognized (Bourdieu 1991; Irvine 1989; Tan and Rubdy 2008), and so have the general processes of commodification and appropriation of language in the new economic order of flexible accumulation and of time–space compression (Harvey 1989; Lash and Urry 1994; Cameron 2000). For example, in her work on bilingual areas of francophone Canada, Heller (2003; see also her chapter in the present volume and Budach, Roy, and Heller 2003) demonstrates how the collapse of traditional industries (cod-fishing, mining, logging, and so on) in the second half of the twentieth century and their substitution with new, information and service-based industries (most notably, call centers and tourism), have led to the commodification of language (understood as a measurable skill) and identity (especially in relation to other forms of cultural practice such as dance and music in tourism). In these domains of economic practice based on contact between different linguistic markets through advances in communication technology (call centers) or mobility (tourism), linguistic and other symbolic resources become highly marketable commodities. Deregulation of national economies and welfare provision, for example privatization and outsourcing of large segments of education, healthcare, penitentiary services, or warfare (a process arguably being halted or even reversed as witnessed by the nationalization of significant parts of the banking system in the global economic downturn begun in 2008) has led to a shifting of national and regional points of reference among ethnolinguistic majority and minority groups globally. Often re-orientating to tourism as their main economic activity, these groups engender a new sense of community and authenticity, invoke new place-identities predicated on the (re)invention of tradition, heritage, and heavy policing of language boundaries (as in francophone Canada and Catalonia, for example, see Heller 2003; Pujolar, 2006; Pujolar and Heller, in press). However, due to the new conditions for its commodification, language and other forms of cultural practice can now be more easily detached from 'identity,' used as strategic styling resources (Bell 2009; Cameron 2000; Coupland 2007; Thurlow and Jaworski 2006), and marketed and traded as metonyms of places to be consumed by tourists (Urry 2007).

Of course, in Bourdieu's (1991) terms, all linguistic exchanges are also economic exchanges; however, under the new economic conditions of globalization, existing language forms and configurations (for example bilingualism) are put to new uses, gain new values, and become objects of intense scrutiny as well as vehicles and sites of ideological struggle, contestation, legitimation, and authentication of ethnic, national, and other subject positions. In the context of tourism this is especially clear in the proliferation of theme parks, open-air museums, festivals, and spectacles laying out displays of ethnicity, nationality, culture, and urban or industrial heritage through the (re-)invented narratives of group origins, history, and present-day lives (see Kirshenblatt-Gimblett 1998; Bruner 2005; Coupland, Garrett, and Bishop, 2005; Heller 2008, 2010). These are also the most obvious areas of tourism-driven activity, where language and other semiotic codes become vehicles of explicit staging (Edensor 2001) or of "high performance" (Coupland 2007); in them, gathered (rather than simply co-present) participants overtly orient themselves to the formal properties of the code, through metapragmatic commentary and evaluation, translation, and labelling of linguistic items. Such performances are heavily marked by claims to ownership, belonging, and authenticity; or, conversely, by pragmatic instrumentalism, playfulness, and appropriation; and, not infrequently, by a mixture of all these positions, dynamically and dialectically negotiated in the process of staged, ritualized enactments and interactions. The role of language in identity formation is crucial, then, but not as straightforward and clear-cut as might be assumed – there is no one-to-one correspondence between linguistic units and ethnic, social, or cultural formations (Le Page and Tabouret-Keller 1985; for discussion, see Coupland 2006). Sociolinguistic items, be they language codes or subtle phonological variants, may be strategically deployed as indexes of specific identities, but their projection and interpretations are always filtered through a plethora of objective and subjective dimensions of self- and other-perception, uptake, interpretive frames and communicative goals (Coupland 2006), and the political economy of difference (Heller 2008). For example, as observed by Rampton (1995), traditional conceptions of what it is to be a *native speaker* break down when instrumental language use is separated from the symbolic value of language as a means of manifesting and asserting one's ethnic or national allegiances or loyalties, or when language inheritance is separated from language allegiance and from the degree of linguistic expertise. As David Block also notes in the context of the discourses surrounding language shift within specific communities, "what ultimately galvanizes people around a language is probably not a question of either/or: *either* the more emotive cultural/ national identification with the language *or* the more practical instrumental uses of language" (Block 2008: 201; and see his chapter in this volume). Likewise, in the context of tourism, we see speakers deploying 'old' linguistic resources in novel forms, styling self and other in new, often surprising ways, playing with social norms and establishing new *regimes of truth*, and unexpectedly conflating instrumental and emotive uses of language, or shifting between use-value and exchange-value.

All of these sociolinguistic processes have a profound effect on the reordering of space, creating new senses of place, be it in private, public, commercial, or media contexts. Blommaert, Collins, and Slembrouck (2005) develop the idea of space as organized along different hierarchically ordered scales of social structures (local, national, transnational, global, ethnic, political, and so on). These spaces are filled with various sorts of material and symbolic attributes and constitute an active, contextualizing (Gumperz 1982; Duranti and Goodwin 1992) semiotic source of indexical meaning; while people move between differently ordered spaces, their linguistic repertoires give rise to new indexicalities. The movement through space of linguistic and communicative resources affects the value of the linguistic skills and repertoires of speakers such that, for example, a bilingual migrant from eastern to western Europe (that is, from the 'periphery' to one of the 'centers' of the continent) who cannot communicate in one of the 'host' languages may be described as having 'no language.' (As some of our examples below demonstrate, similar, if more subtle and superficially innocuous 'play' with linguistic repertoires is present in tourist–host interactions.) In consequence, Blommaert and colleagues (2005: 203) argue that:

> [e]ntering such spaces involves the imposition of the sets of norms and rules as well as the invoking of potentially meaningful relations between one scale and another (e.g., the local versus the national or the global). This has effect on
>
> (a)   what people can or cannot do (it legitimizes some forms of behavior while disqualifying or constraining other forms);
> (b)   the value and function of their sociolinguistic repertoires;
> (c)   their identities, both self-constructed (inhabited) and ascribed by others.

Certainly space is also modified by people's semiotic behavior (Jaworski and Thurlow 2010), and linguistic signs will also bear indexical values involving scalar relations (Blommaert and colleagues link these ideas with Goffman 1974 and his frame analysis). For example shifts in accent, topic, or communicative event may invoke (or index) different scales: local, national, private, public, and so on. In sum,

> people have varying language abilities – repertoires and skills with languages – but [...] *the function and value of those repertoires and skills can change as the space of language contact changes.* (Blommaert et al. 2005: 211, original emphasis)

It is with these general remarks in mind that we turn to present some of our data from the domain of tourism, in which borrowing, appropriation, and re-valuing of language are part and parcel of face-to-face interactions. In doing so we want to tease out some of the key sociolinguistic processes typical of the fleeting relationships that characterize the language exchanges of those people who are privileged enough to criss-cross the planet by choice – those who ordinarily get to come home at the end of their travels.

Turning to Tourism: Language on the Move

One of the inevitable consequences of tourism is that language in the shape of codes, discourses, styles, genres, voices, or repertoires participates in the global flows of tourists and of their hosts – those people who are the recipients and/or targets of the stream of tourists. The language that accompanies, facilitates, or results in these flows is also 'on the move,' as people bring into new spaces their ways of speaking, singing (see Excerpt 1 below), and writing, alongside their clothes, accessories (again, see Excerpt 1), and bodies, which are unavoidably recontextualized and resemioticized in the process and often breed scorn and resentment from hosts and other tourists (Boissevain 1996; Jaworski and Thurlow 2009) – notwithstanding numerous rewarding, enriching, and hospitable encounters between friendly locals and courteous tourists. To stay with somewhat more problematic instances of tourists' insertions of semiotic repertoires and skills into their destinations, let us quote just one example – random but illustrative – of a metapragmatic comment on (from a rather middle-class perspective) non-normative behavior in a fleeting encounter between British tourists on an apparently up-market, family-oriented camping holiday. After the first day of blissful rural idyll, just as advertised in the camp's brochure, the unsuspecting author could not imagine anything going 'wrong.' But, as it turned out, something did – and, according to the report, in no small measure:

> Excerpt 1   Inflatable penis and that godawful Umber-ella song (Source: Stephen Bleach, Don't believe the hype. *The Sunday Times Travel*, May 3, 2009, p. 4)

> They'd booked out two of the tents to a hen party: the first giveaway was the huge inflatable penis being carried across the site, which certainly wasn't in the brochure. Nice enough girls, but tent walls did nothing to muffle the racket of that godawful Umber-ella song at 11.30 p.m.

As the above example demonstrates, when people travel, their semiotic worlds clash in uncontrollable ways. Silence and quietude rather than loud singing are commonly associated with 'up-market' or 'luxury' holidays (Thurlow and Jaworski 2010b; see also Clifford 1997: 233), and huge inflatable toys are certainly common signifiers of the presence of children on the beach, or even on a camping site – as long as they are not penis-shaped. Excerpt 1 makes it plain that forced or accidental contact does not always lead to understanding, so, rather than thinking of globalization generally and of tourism in particular as introducing markedly or necessarily *new* ways of speaking and writing into people's repertoires, we prefer to focus our attention on how the 'meaning' or symbolic and economic value of what is said (or sung or written) changes (or not) when tourists (or any other travelers, including migrants, business people, politicians, or academics) move around the globe (see Blommaert 2003, 2005, 2009), or when space is re-scaled and re-imagined, say, from 'national' to 'local'/'regional' (as has been the case in parts of francophone Ontario; see Heller 2003, 2010).

As we suggested above, tourist–host interactions embody core globalizing processes. It is in communication with each other, in every instant of contact, that hosts and tourists negotiate the nature of their experience, the meanings of culture and place, as well as their own relationships and identities. It is here, too, that many of the meanings of globalization are realized. Shaped by a mythology of contact (the encounter with the exotic Other) and by an ideology of leisure, pleasure, and entertainment, the kind of linguistic exchanges that take place between tourists and hosts are also often very playful. And, to be sure, the fun usually starts at home, as tourists are first schooled (or disciplined) into a global tourist habitus, learning the dispositions and ways of touring. In the excerpts which follow, however, we focus on the actual moment of contact and on some of the exchanges of linguistic material which, performatively, establish the host–tourist encounter and, in large part, the *raison d'être* of tourism (at least among the more 'ambitious' tourists), alongside other tourist pursuits such as authenticity, adventure, self-discovery, education (the Grand Tour) – or plain, unadulterated pleasure (MacCannell 1999; Löfgren 1999; McCabe 2005).

The tourist linguascape

Like any other landscape, the tourist landscape is *a way of seeing* (Cosgrove 1984; Favero 2007). Expressed through the powerful metaphor of the tourist gaze, tourist consumption is organized around the recognition and interpretation of various signs – symbols, icons, and metonyms of place – emplaced and displayed for tourists, noticed, objectified, appropriated, and discarded by them (see Culler 1981; Urry 2002). These signs are frequently linguistic. In search of picture post-card views, breathtaking landscapes and cityscapes, exotic peoples and artefacts, the tourist also consumes textualized histories, mythologies, facts, and information. Embedded in tour guides' narratives of place, for example, are jokes, personal anecdotes, and trivia of all sorts. While wandering round foreign cities, tourists gaze with more or less understanding at linguistic inscriptions. At times, the linguistic inscription itself becomes the object of tourist gaze and consumption.

In Excerpt 2, which comes from a guided tour in the Maori village of Whakarewarewa, Rotorua, New Zealand, the guide stops with a group of tourists in front of a sign explaining the name of the village. This is one of many such stops, which include accounts of local customs, traditions, way of life, nature, and material culture. The guide stands next to the sign, facing a small group of tourists (Figure 11.1) and occasionally turning toward the sign and pointing to various parts of the name of the village as he speaks (Figure 11.2).

Excerpt 2   Whakarewarewa. From Adam's fieldwork, April 2003

G = Guide
A = Audience, a small group of tourists

1   G   but firstly folk can you all say <u>Whaka</u>?
2   A   (different voices) Whaka
3   G   Whaka yeah that is the name of this valley (.) and the
4   village (.) and that's been the name for a long long
5   time the common name [drop out] true name folks (.)
6   is a <u>lot longer</u> (1.5) (Guide points to name on the sign
7   with tip of his umbrella) Te Whakarewarewa-tanga-o-
8   te-ope-taua-a-<u>Wa</u>hiao

Figure 11.1   'can you all say Whaka?' (Extract 2, line 1); April 2003. Photo © A. Jaworski

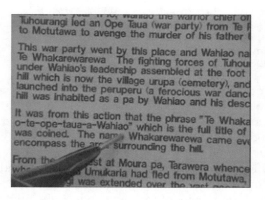

Figure 11.2   'Te Whakarewarewa-tanga-o-te-ope-taua-a-Wahiao' (Extract 2, lines 12–13); April 2003. Photo © A. Jaworski

```
 9   A   (laughter)
10   G   very very long name, isn't it folks? (.) Whaka W-H-A-
11       K-A (.) (uses hands to frame the first five letters) is the
12       shortened version (.) but folks the long version (.) Te
13       Whakarewarewa-tanga-o-te-ope-taua-a-Wahiao (.)
14       Wahiao the great chief (.) Ope-taua war party (.)
15       Te Whakarewarewa-tanga the uprising of the war
16       party of Wahiao (.) and uh folks (.) how you get that
17       name actually comes about by the actions of a haka and
18       the surrounding activities so you saw the haka on
19       stage?
20   A   yes=
21   G   =three or four men on there just imagine three or
22       four hundred? doing a haka folks (.) when kicking their
23       feet up and making all the dust rise around the place (.)
```

```
24        an:d the dust rising was likened to the steam all over the
25        valley (.) now out of the dust rising the men would leap
26        as high as they could (.) and the men leaping all over
27        the place folks was likened (.) to the steam (.) oh sorry
28        to the geysers shooting out of the ground (.) up to
29        two hundred years ago thirty-six geysers in this valley
30        so that would've been [drop out] so folks by the
31        action of that haka (.) the rising dust (.) jumping men
32        (.) likened to the rising steam (.) geysers shooting out
33        (.) and all the action over the valley that is how you get
34        the name the uprising war party of Wahiao (.)
35        shortened to Te Whakarewarewa (.) shortened even
36        more folks to W-H-A-K-A (.) when we shorten it to this
37        version we try not to pronounce the W-H as F (2.0)
38        (smiles and looks across the crowd) for obvious reasons
                                                    [
39     A                                       (laughter)
40     G   we don't want anyone getting the wrong ideas (.)
41        especially (unclear) so um that's why we just say
42        (unclear) anyway let's go and have a look at these
43        geysers folks
```

What is offered for tourist consumption here is the place name of the destination itself. This act of consumption is couched in terms of a multi-modal and interactive performance. The place name is displayed and described on a written sign, it is repeatedly produced by the guide (lines 7–8, 12–13, 15, 35), and the tourists are invited to say it as well (lines 1–2), albeit in a shortened version. The significance of the name lies partly in its length. The tourists respond to the guide's fast rendition of the name in lines 7–8 with laughter. No doubt the source of humor is the 'unimaginable' complexity of the name, which the guide confirms with his rhetorical question 'very, very long name, isn't it folks' in line 10.

Long place names are not infrequently turned into tourist attractions in other parts of the world, especially if they happen to belong to lesser spoken languages and thus they help to 'exoticize' the destination. Figure 11.3 reproduces a postcard from North Wales with a photograph of "The railway station with the longest name in Great Britain": 'Llanfairpwllgwyngyllgogerychwyrndrobwllllanty siliogogogoch.' (This name was apparently fabricated in the nineteenth century precisely in order to draw attention to the village – an act of pure "tourism reflexivity" in itself: Urry 2002). The Welsh place name on the station's sign is clearly framed as a tourist attraction by appearing in white block letters against the red background (which is rather unusual for other railway signs in Britain). A guide to the name's 'pronunciation' appears underneath, and a separate sign to the left provides the 'translation' of its constituent parts. The iconizing of the place name is completed through the act of recontextualizing that name on the postcard – one out of many that can be bought in the area.

Returning to Excerpt 2, the guide explains the meaning of the name of the village by weaving into it the military past of Maori people, the actions of the ritu-

Figure 11.3 Postcard from Llanfairpwllgwyngyllgogerychwyrndrobwllllanty siliogogogoch. John Hinde (UK) Ltd. Photo © C. Underhill

alistic dance of Maori men (the haka), and evocative scenery – the rising steam of the geysers (lines 12–36). This long section, which introduces profound imagery based on Maori heroic history, old heritage, and unique landscape, is delivered in a rather solemn, even poetic tone. The text in lines 31–3, in particular, is marked by slower tempo, level intonation throughout, and pauses reminiscent of poetry recitation. There is also frequent lexical and phonological repetition introducing internal rhyme and creating coherence – for example "dust rise" (l. 23), "dust rising" (ll. 24, 25), "the rising dust" (l. 31), "rising steam" (l. 32), "uprising" (ll. 15, 34); "men would leap" (l. 25), "men leaping" (l. 26), "jumping men" (l. 31); and the repetition of "likened" (ll. 24, 27, 32). These are formal features of "public oral poetry" (Tannen 1989: 82; see Bauman 2001), used in conversational discourse to communicate ideas in a vivid and moving manner. Clearly the guide engages here in more than a bit of metalinguistic translation and explanation; he puts on a poetic performance of place to create an aesthetically pleasing and emotionally involving performance.

The use of visual repetition, or visual rhyming, to create a verse-like effect can also be found in our postcard example (Figure 11.3). The four key linguistic elements seen on the postcard – the place name, its 'pronunciation,' the 'translation,' and the English gloss at the bottom of the card – are roughly equal in length and can be seen as four verses in a stanza. The composition of the post-card, with some visual, phonological, and semantic repetition, aspires then to the status of a poetic text rather than being simply the image of a sign emplaced at a railway station.

Considering Excerpt 2 again, in line 36 the key (Hymes 1974) of the guide's speech changes. After a short pause, the guide says in fast tempo, "when we shorten it to this version we try not to pronounce the W-H as F," and then he pauses for about two seconds, looking at the tourists with a broad smile. However, it seems to take a while for the tourists to realize that the guide has now shifted from a serious to a playful key, jokingly suggesting a possible obscene version of the name 'Whaka.' He even finds himself in need of filling up the ensuing pause with the comment "for obvious reasons" (l. 38), by which time the tourists finally get the joke and respond with some laughter.

The funniness of the joke is not the main issue here. What we find more inter-esting is that the guide shifts so freely and rapidly from the lofty and poetic key to a ribald, frivolous one. Although the two performances seemingly occupy opposite sides of the rhetorical spectrum, they are both unmistakably deliberate, scripted with the aim of creating a degree of spectacle, drama, and audience par-ticipation. And in both examples referred to in this section, the source and object of the tourist gaze is the place name of the tourist destination, used not as an index of place but as part of the place's *linguascape*. As we shall see in the next excerpt, this commodification and strategic–playful deployment of language is prevalent in a number of other types of exchange.

Tourist small talk

For all its mythologies and ideologies, visiting a tourist destination is, at core, a business transaction – or series of transactions – in which tourists consume (or graze on: see Bauman 2001) performances of local scenery, heritage, customs, stories, and so on, alongside the purchases of even more tangible goods and serv-ices such as meals, souvenirs, and postcards. Not unlike in other types of service encounters, business transactions in tourism are replete with instances of small talk, or relationally oriented acts of verbal sociability (see J. Coupland 2000). We explore some relational aspects of specifically 'selling and buying' discourse elsewhere (see Jaworski et al. in preparation). Here we focus on just one instance of phatic talk (Malinowski 1923) taking place between a tour guide and tourists visiting the PheZulu 'cultural village' in the province of KwaZulu-Natal, South Africa.

In Excerpt 3, a group of tourists gather at a 'cooking hut,' where a demonstra-tion of traditional Zulu food preparation is about to take place. The tourists and the guide (Patrick) are sitting in a circle and, while waiting for the demonstration to start, Patrick feels compelled to fill the time by initiating a phatic sequence with the tourists. This is a typical example of a group of relative strangers gathered temporarily in close proximity in a small, confined space – a 'with,' to use

Goffman's terms (1971) – where substantial stretches of time are filled with talk aimed at avoiding silence (McCarthy 2000 refers to such participants as "each others' captive audience"). Relying on the repertoire of stock formulaic phrases typically used in small talk sequences, the guide settles on the question "Where are you from?" – found in a wide range of similar contexts in our data, as well as in many other conversational encounters (see Myers 2006).

> Excerpt 3 The cooking hut – "Where are you from?" (The personnel listed below is common to Excerpts 3, 5, and 6 which all derive from the same episode in the cooking hut). From Crispin's fieldwork, April 2003

Patrick = Guide
TZW = 'Traditional Zulu Woman'
PT1 = Tourist from Poland (mother)
PT2 = Tourist from Poland (son)
PT3 = Tourist from Poland (father)
ET1 = Tourist from England (father, husband)
ET2 = Tourist from England (son)
ET3 = Tourist from England (son)
ET4 = Tourist from England (wife, mother)
HT = Tourist from Hilcrest (grandmother of ET5)
ET5 = Tourist from England (grandson of HT)
ZT1 = Tourist from KwaZulu (1, female)
ZT2 = Tourist from KwaZulu (2, female)
ZT3 = Tourist from KwaZulu (3, female)
CT = Tourist from Cape Town (female)
RT = Researcher/tourist (male)

Patrick is sitting at the entrance to the hut while the tourists enter and settle down. As the cooking demonstration is getting delayed due to one of the performers' absence, he has just initiated a series of getting-to-know-you questions amidst general laughter. TZW, visibly uninterested in what's going on around her, sits among the tourists waiting for her colleague to come in and start the show.

1	PATRICK	(to PT1 and PT2) niphumaphi? phuma kuyiphi icountry?
		where are you from? from which country?
2	PT1	(2) (looks quizzically)
3	ZT1	(translating) where have you come from?
4	PT1	ah Poland
5	PATRICK	ah: now (points at ET1) wena?
		and you?
6	ET1	UK England
7	PATRICK	OK (points at ET1's sons) nina bafana?
		what about you boys?
8	ET1	all of us

9	PATRICK	UK (.) nalomfazi? UK?
		and this woman? [is she from the UK?]
10	ET4	England as well
11	PATRICK	OK umfazi wkhe
		this is his woman
12	ET1	we are all together
13	PATRICK	wena ma? (.) niqhamukapi?
		and you, mother? where do you come from?
14	HT	er Hilcrest [=a town nearby]
15	PATRICK	ah (.) just around the corner
16	HT	ja (general laughter) yena (indicating her grandson)
17		yena England (1)
		yes he comes he comes from [England]
18	PATRICK	five minutes from here driving (general laughter)
19	HT	(laughing) you see you lucky
20	PATRICK	(looking at PT4) wena ughamukaphi mfowethu?
		where do you come from brother?
21	PT1	from Poland
22	PATRICK	ah: OK wena?
		and you?
23	ZT1	KwaZulu (laughs loudly and with others laughing too)
24	PATRICK	ah khona la (turning to ZT2) nawe futhi?
		just here and you too?
25	ZT2	ja Maritzburg
		yes Maritzburg ['Pietermaritzburg']
26	PATRICK	OK eMugungundlovu? [Zulu name for Pietermaritzburg]
27	ZT2	eMugungundlovu ja
28	PATRICK	wean? (.) nawe futhi eMugungundlovu?
29		*and you? are you also from eMugungundlovu?*
30	ZT2	ja
31	PATRICK	u: gogo ke yena
		a:nd the granny here?
32	CT	from Cape Town
33	PATRICK	ah so uyapraata Afrikaans
		you speak Afrikaans?

Although the working language of the guide is English, he unexpectedly starts the conversation in Excerpt 3 by asking two of the Polish tourists the 'Where are you from?' question in Zulu. This clearly baffles PT1 (PT2 looks rather worried throughout the entire episode; see Excerpt 5, line 9, below), and her quizzical facial expression and a two-second silence in response to Patrick's question elicit a translation from ZT1 ("where have you come from?" in l. 3). Visibly relieved, PT1 responds "Poland" (l. 4), and this is preceded by the discourse marker "ah," which indicates a change in the state of knowledge (see Heritage 1984; Schiffrin 1987). Setting the tone for the tourists' self-identification through their country of origin, Patrick moves on to the next person (ET1), who infers (correctly) that Patrick's turn in line 5 is a request for the same information from him. This pattern of code-switched interrogation of the tourists continues throughout, until Patrick addresses tourists from South Africa, who speak Zulu partially (HT) or as their first language (ZT1, ZT2, ZT3). The self-identification of these tourists as 'locals' creates much laughter and further banter, which partly suggests the non-normativity of the local residents' visiting tourist attractions in 'their' area. Interestingly, Patrick ignores RT (Crispin), to whom he had talked to before entering the cooking hut; he already knows that Crispin is British but had lived in South Africa for twelve years.

What is interesting for us here, however, is not the nature of the ostensibly sociable talk initiated by Patrick to kill the time. As we said earlier, small talk generally and "Where are you from?" questions specifically are unremarkable in the context of tourist–host encounters – albeit the latter is often organized around a common repertoire of topics ("Is this your first time here?"; "How are you liking it here?"; "Where else have you been?"). What is remarkable and noteworthy is Patrick's use of Zulu with the tourists whom he knew (or whom he should expect) would not to be able to understand him. We suggest that, as a sequence outside of the transactional part of Patrick's performance in the cooking hut (which is to explain the meal preparation), his code-switching to Zulu is a playful, if somewhat teasing act of language (dis)play. Because of its relational rather than instrumental focus, the "Where are you from?" question in Zulu does not carry much propositional weight. However, it visibly unsettles PT1, who may have felt marginalized by Patrick's use of Zulu, having her entire linguistic repertoire disqualified (see Blommaert et al. 2005, quoted above). PT1 is positioned almost as an intruder toward the local space, which requires at least a rudimentary knowledge of Zulu to claim legitimacy. She is then 'rescued' from sociolinguistic oblivion by ZT1 and responds in English – the lingua franca of international guides and tourists in many destinations – redefining the cooking hut as part of a global, transnational tourist playground.

The fact that Patrick may expect some of the tourists not to understand the propositional contents and pragmatic force of his questioning in Zulu is compounded by his apparently impertinent – or at least cheeky – forms of address and reference used throughout: "nalomfazi" ("this woman") in line 9, "umfazi wkhe" ("this is his woman") in line 11, and "gogo" ("granny") in line 30. Such usage of (or even insult in) a local language by guides/performers in addressing foreign tourists is not uncommon (see for instance Senft 1999). It appears to be an effective strategy for disempowering tourists who may be perceived as disproportionally wealthy, privileged, and disrespectful to their hosts (Abbink 2000), while being relatively harmless if the tourists, through their linguistic ignorance, remain oblivious to such verbal attacks (see, again, Senft quoted above; also Löfgren 1999: 124–8 on 'meeting the locals'). What makes Patrick's behavior even more 'daring' is that some of his addressees are fluent Zulu speakers. Just the same, the sequence in Excerpt 3 demonstrates that social banter and verbal play in the context of tourism appear to assume positions of familiarity (teasing, mild insults) normally reserved for intimates, for whom the safety of their close relationship overrides the threatening nature of such verbal attacks (such baneter and play constitute positive politeness acts according to Brown and Levinson 1987).

Figure 11.4   Hongi photographic studio, Tamaki Maori Village; April 2003. Photo © A. Jaworski

In part, these exchanges merely add to the linguascape; they are, however, also instances of quintessential tourist talk – banal, familiar exchanges which can be easily transposed and exotically reframed for the 'safe adventure' of tourism. Another such example is the 'greeting game.'

Tourist greetings

Jaworski (2009) suggests that, viewed sociolinguistically, the speech act of the greeting has become one of the most typical resources for the enactment and mediation of the tourist experience. Functioning in the liminal space of tourism, greetings are recontextualized and commodified in ways that violate their 'normal' felicity conditions (Duranti 1997). In New Zealand, for example, one of the key resources for packaging Maori heritage for tourists has been the commodification of the Maori greeting, the hongi, which involves two people pressing their noses against one another. In Tamaki Maori Village in Rotorua, tourists can have a picture of themselves taken in a makeshift photographic studio while they do a hongi with an actor against the photographic backdrop of an idyllic rural scenery and a wooden carved totem pole (Figure 11.4). Images of Maori people performing a hongi can be bought on postcards and posters in numerous souvenir shops across New Zealand. The blog NZ Tramping explains hongi as follows:

> Hongi is a traditional Maori greeting, which literally means 'to share breath.' Hongi is done by pressing one's nose to the other person when they meet each other. It is believed that when the two noses meet, people exchange their breath and the visitor becomes one of the local people (tangata whenua).

The beginning of this ceremony is believed to be in one of Maori legends, in which gods made a woman from earth, and god Tane (in translation from Maori Tane means Male) breathed life into her through the nostrils. She then sneezed and came to life. Her name was Hineahuone, which means 'earth formed woman.'

After the visitor is greeted, and for the remainder of his stay, he is obliged to share in all the responsibilities of the hosts.

What a beautiful and tender greeting! It says a lot about the whole Maori nation. (http://www.nztramping.com/new-zealand-history/hongi-in-new-zealand%E2% 80%99s-traditions/; last accessed September 12, 2009; used by kind permission of Steve Brave; <http://www.nztramping.com>)

However, despite what the tourist guides and websites may suggest, it is virtually impossible for a tourist to perform a hongi with a Maori person other than in the context of a paid performance. Our next example is in fact an instance of a com-modified greeting exchange (involving a hongi) between a Maori guide/coach driver and an American tourist en route for a night's entertainment at Tamaki Maori Village at Rotorua, New Zealand. The tourists are collected by several coaches from hotels in the area. Once all the tourists are on board their designated bus (*waka*, 'boat,' 'vessel'), the guide/driver welcomes everyone and announces that the tourists will not only experience Maori song, dance, food, and so on, but will also 'become' Maori for the night. Each busload of tourists is branded a 'tribe' (*iwi*), with a 'chief' (*rangatira*) 'elected' from among the tourists (the chief seems usually to end up being white, male, American), and the driver offers to 'teach' the tourists some Maori language – typically just one phrase: the greeting formula *Kia Ora*, 'Hello/ Good luck/ Good health/ Thank you' (see Auger 2002), which may be emically more significant than the category 'greeting' usually implies, although we surmise that more international tourists will not easily access all these possible meanings of the phrase in the short span of the night's performances.

Kia Ora is, then, to be repeated in unison by the tourists following a prompting from the guides and other performers. The 'chiefs' become privileged participants in representing their 'tribes' in the Village Welcome, 'gift' presentation, various speeches throughout the night, and so on. One such privilege includes the per-formance of a hongi with the guide/ driver in front of all the other tourists on the bus. The following excerpt presents one sequence of this kind of performance aboard the bus, before its departure for Tamaki Maori Village, some twelve kilo-metres away from town.

Excerpt 4   The Maori Greeting

G = Guide (Driver)
K = Kenny, the 'chief' tourist
T = Unidentified tourists

1   G   for you people from different tribes (.) this is how we the
2   Maori people will usually greet each other (.) grab my right
3   hand Kenny (.) (off mike) stand up stand up

```
4            (Kenny stands; he towers over the driver)
5       T    (light laughter) (1)
6       G    now go down on the step (Kenny goes one step down)
7       T    (laughter) (2)
8       G    ok we- (.) put your left hand on my shoulder Kenny (1) ok
9            (.) now what we do, we press our noses together twice (.)
10           and then we say kia ora ok (.) nice and gentle (.) don't go
11           (thrusts his head forward quickly towards Kenny's face;
12           Kenny tilts his head backwards in a reflex)
13      T    (light laughter) (2)
14      G    and whatever you do: (.) don't kiss me.
             [
15      K    (inaudible speech to Guide)
16      T    (continued laughter) (2)
17           (Guide and Kenny perform a hongi, cameras flash)
18      G    kia ora: didn't he do well (.) how-bout a big round=
19      T    (applause 4 sec.; loud female voice) yeeeahh
20      G    =of applause for Kenny (.) my people interpret the hongi
21           like this when the two noses come together (.) it's the
22           sharing of common breath creating a legion of friendship
23           (1) as a point of interest for you, we the Maori tribe here in
24           Te Arawa are familiar to all this area of Rotorua and Bay of
25           Plenty (.) we are the only Maori tribe in New Zealand that
26           hongi twice (.) all other tribes do it once (.) that's our
27           trade mark. (.) we're now gonna pull out rangatira our big
28           kahuna, the big chief Ken here to the entrance way (.) I'll
29           make the official welcome the challenge you're gonna
30           have a wonderful evening (.) kia ora
31      T    (loud voices) kia ora
```

Although the hongi is framed as a typical Maori greeting (lines 1–2) and as a way of establishing "a legion of friendship" (line 22) between two people, the guide's display and 'lesson' in Maori etiquette has an undercurrent of cultural subversion and resistance to dominant ideologies of tourism. The guide does not adopt unambiguously the stance of a friendly, deferential, and subservient host. Under the guise of humor – reminiscent of genres where mock-aggression and mild humiliation are part of the participation ritual (for example TV quiz-shows) – he positions Kenny, the archetypal powerful and wealthy westerner about to be exposed to "Pre-European lifestyle experience of customs and traditions" (http://www.maoriculture.co.nz/Maori%20Village/Home), as a relatively powerless and ignorant 'foreigner.' In order to 'teach' Kenny the hongi ritual, the guide instructs him to adopt the appropriate body posture. When Kenny comes to the front of the coach and faces the guide, the guide unceremoniously orders Kenny to go one step down, to reduce the difference in their height – having their faces at the same level is more amenable to hongi and symbolically maintains a proxemic equilibrium between the two men. The driver uses unmitigated directives, "stand up stand up" (l. 3), "now go down on the step" (l. 6), reminiscent of an adult disciplining a child, and his 'bossing' Kenny around elicits outbursts of laughter from the onlookers on the coach.

In lines 10–11 the guide teases Kenny, implying that he is likely to hongi inappropriately: "nice and gentle (.) don't go (thrusts his head forward …)." The guide's hyperbolic mock head-butt is clearly an exaggeration for comic effect, as he cannot realistically expect Kenny to act in such a foolish manner. The guide also seems to frighten Kenny intentionally with his head gesture, but only to elicit a reaction of slight panic from Kenny and more laughter from the other tourists. Another ridiculing turn at Kenny's expense is the guide's teasing, heteronormative joke "and whatever you do:? <u>don't</u> <u>kiss</u> me" (line 14). The guide then proceeds with the hongi (l. 17), and positions Kenny again as a child-like figure who deserves a round of applause as a reward for his performance (another game show-like feature). The guide then appears to be in total control of the situation – a knowledgeable expert as well as a mocking director–choreographer of the scene, blatantly 'othering' Kenny by adopting the key of teasing and ridicule. Indeed the guide's control over this intercultural exchange is also manifested in his artful management of the theme of tourists 'crossing' into Maori, which he achieves through his constant pronominal ingrouping/outgrouping; visitors are reminded that they ("you people") are outsiders who merely play at being Maori ("we"; see ll. 1–2).

Excerpt 5 demonstrates another example of the 'tourist greeting,' this time turning tourists into performers for other tourists and their guide (Edensor 2000, 2001). At the end of the "Where are you from?" sequence in Excerpt 3, the PheZulu group is threatened by another silence, and one of the tourists from South Africa (as if assuming the role of 'host') suggests that some of the other tourists show their foreignness through the verbal display of their native language.

Excerpt 5   The cooking hut – "Say hello in Polish" (this excerpt starts a few turns after the end of Excerpt 3).

1	CT	they (indicating Polish family) should say hello in Po:lish
		[
2	KT2	in Po:lish
3	PATRICK	that's just what I'm looking for
4	CT	ja (laugh)
5	PATRICK	(to Polish mother and son) how do you say hello in Polish?
6		(2)
7	PT1	(quietly to PT2) no powiedz (.) pan się (unclear) chce
8		żebyś powiedział cześć po polsku powiedz cześć=
		well say it (.) the gentleman (unclear) wants
		you to say hello in Polish say hello
9	PT2	(turns towards his mother and hides his face)
10	PATRICK	=how do you say hello in your language?=
11	PT1	(to Patrick, softly) =cześć
		hello

12	PATRICK	sorry?
13	PT1	cześć
14	PATRICK	(looks at other tourists, smiles) I can't say it
15		(general laughter)
16	PT3	nothing ((for)) easy
17		(general laughter)
18	RT	cześć
19	PATRICK	(to RT) can you say it?
20	RT	cześć
21	HT	cześć
22	PT1	cześć
23	PATRICK	(surprised tone) have you heard it before?
		[
24	RT	cześć I have a friend who is Polish I
25		know dziękuję and that's it
		thank you
26	PT1	(nods and smiles, outburst of general laughter)

In an instance of 'reverse crossing,' PT1 is made to demonstrate one of the Polish greeting formulae to the guide and the other tourists. This situation is a mirror image of that in Excerpt 4, where the guide was the one 'teaching' the tourists how to use local greetings. The initial move made by CT toward ethnotyping the Polish tourists as 'Polish' is premised on her request to hear a sample of the Polish language, and a greeting formula is chosen as a token Polish expression. The request appears to be unexpected and does not trigger immediate compliance. There is a pause of two seconds (l. 6), followed by PT1's request for her son (PT2) to say *cześć* ('hello') in Polish (ll. 7–8), rather than a spontaneous offer to demonstrate it herself. CT's and KT2's eliciting the Polish greeting seems like a childish game – it sounds more like requesting a small, pre-literate child at a family gathering to recite a poem, spell his or her name, or 'count to 100' than like requesting expert advice on the use of a second language (which is not known to CT and KT2).

The embarrassed boy struggles *not* to have to perform (l. 9), and finally his mother utters the first, soft instance of 'cześć' (l. 11). Patrick does not quite grasp the pronunciation of the word and asks for a repetition (l. 12), but even after he hears it again (l. 13) he still appears confused and uncertain as to how to pronounce the greeting. Two participants try to rescue Patrick from his embarrassment. The father (PT3) declares that the Polish greeting is rather hard to pronounce (l. 16), possibly in the hope of closing off further attempts for anyone to say it, and this is followed by RT's demonstration of his ability to do so (l. 18). This triggers four more repetitions of 'cześć' – by RT, HT, and PT1.

Most of the 'universal' criteria for identifying greetings (Duranti 1997) are violated here (see Jaworski 2009). The greeting crops up as part of an ongoing (though faltering) interaction, rather than in the liminal moment of the conversational opening; the perceptual field among the participants is already established, rather than in need of being established; there is no adjacency pair format (the greeting is *displayed* by various participants rather than inviting a response in kind); the form and content are not predictable to non-Polish language speakers (except for RT's snippets), which diminishes the 'safety' of its formulaicity; and so on. Thus the use of the greeting formula *cześć* does not constitute a greeting in terms of Duranti's criteria – a fact seemingly recognized and acted on through PT2's refusal to take part in the 'show.' In the fleeting context of tourism, the recontextualized greeting – or its performance, representation, learning, repetition, and metapragmatic commentary – may constitute the focal and exclusive orientation of talk, as is the case in Excerpts 4 and 5: a form of (dis-)play through which national and ethnic identities are elicited, enacted, and appropriated.

Tourist teasing

The light-hearted tenor of touristic encounters has been clearly manifested in Excerpts 2–5 above. Humor is, unsurprisingly, a common element of tourist texts and interactions, frequently with insulting overtones (see Pritchard and Morgan 2005) due to the preoccupation of tourism with hedonistc pleasure, unrestrained consumption, and the oxymorinic promise of 'safe adventures.' Excerpt 6 is the last episode in our PheZulu cooking hut sequence, leading up to the cooking demonstration everyone has gathered to watch.

Excerpt 6 The cooking hut: "You don't cook in UK do you?" (following on directly from Excerpt 5)

1	PATRICK	(laughs) OK well so (.) I'm- (3) I forgot my name
2		(everyone laughs) I'm stupid (3) (leans out of the entrance
3		way; to a group outside) come here guys tell me my name?
4	RT	(laughs) could be Patrick but- (laughs)
5	PATRICK	ja: ja: I'm Patrick er (.) Angigquize Qakala (= 'Mr Easy-
6		Go-Lucky'; pronounced with two loud clicks) is my
7		African name and (looks at his watch) this is now the
8		kitchen hut where you ladies (points at some of the female
9		tourists) do all the cooking because only ladies must cook
10		men just relax (1.0) (turns to ET1) you don't cook in UK
11		do you?
12	ET1	er (looking at other tourists) yeh I do (laughter from others)
13	PATRICK	hum (.) your wife's a lazy cook=
		[
14		ABEZE (to people outside)
		let them come
15	ET1	=yeh yeh I enjoy cooking=
16	PATRICK	=but you don't have to=
		[
17	PATRICK	ABEZE (even louder)
18	ET1	=no I do have to (.) (wife laughs loudly) she'll (pointing to
19		his wife and looking at everyone else with a smile) she'll

20		tell me off if I don't (laughs)
21	PATRICK	(2.0) (playfully) shame (pointing at ET4) you are <u>naughty</u>
22		(2.0) don't let your husband cook (general laughter)

When the 'Polish greeting' exchange fizzles out in fits of laughter, Patrick decides to start the core part of the event, focusing on the cooking demonstration. He begins by introducing himself, but after a three-second pause in line 1 he quips that he has forgotten his name. Whether he *really* forgot his name or not, his faltering start becomes a pretext for creating a humorous situation at his own expense when he positions himself as the butt of his joke (see "I'm stupid," l. 2). Once RT (who has met him already) reminds the guide that his name is "Patrick," Patrick recovers from his lapse and declares that he also has an African name, "Angigquize Qakala," which he over-pronounces with two loud clicks for 'qu' and 'q' (l. 5). In fact, Angigquize Qakala appears to be a nickname or a pseudonym, a type of self-naming behavior of tour guides we have observed on numerous other occasions (for example the guide/driver featured in Excerpt 4 introduced himself at the beginning of the tour as 'Dennis the Menace'). Angigquize Qakala, glossed in Excerpt 6 as "Mr Easy-Go-Lucky" (ll. 5–6), can be literally translated as 'I don't care type.' The nickname serves, then, as another display of an 'exotic' feature of the local language (the clicks), and it signals the relaxed, even irreverent disposition of Patrick toward tourists, or toward life more generally – whether the tourist gets this or not.

What is even more significant in this excerpt is Patrick's overtly sexist but, again, playful framing of the cooking hut as the female domain ("this is now the kitchen hut where you ladies [...] do all the cooking because only ladies must cook men just relax," ll. 8–10). We do not know whether Patrick here unreflexively perpetuates the entrenched patriarchal ideology permeating much of Zulu society, or whether he plays another trick on the unsuspecting tourists. The latter interpretation seems more plausible (despite the Zulu machismo underlying his gambit), as in line 10 he turns to ET1 in an act of male collusion and solidarity, asking him "you don't cook in UK do you?." Perplexed (by comparison with PT1 in l. 2 of Excerpt 2 and with PT2 in l. 9 of Excerpt 4), ET1 looks around as if in search of a bailout from answering an awkward question. With no help arriving, he confronts Patrick by admitting to taking on this 'unmanly' activity, which produces bursts of laughter from the group, as his shaky masculinity gets exposed. Continuing with his sexist jibe, Patrick mockingly insults ET1 (as well as ET4, by treating her as a non-present or, at best, as a ratified overhearer): he teases the husband about his lack of control over his 'lazy' wife ("your wife's a lazy cook," l. 13). This exchange continues for another four extended turns (line 15–16, 18–22), in which ET1 first tries to save face by maintaining that he enjoys cooking (l. 15), and then falls prey to Patrick and colludes in the sexist tenor of the banter by stating "she'll tell me off if I don't [do the cooking]" (ll. 19–20). Even when this sequence comes to an end, Patrick does not relent; he insists that ET1 does not "have to cook" (l. 16), that ET4 is "naughty" (l. 21), and that she should not allow her husband to cook (l. 22).

Throughout lines 10–22, when Patrick targets ET1 and ET4 as the butts of his jokes, there is much laughter and Patrick delivers his lines with a 'smiley' voice, although his tone is also ambiguously stern and reproachful. On the part of ET1, ET4, and the other tourists, laughter may then be a good-natured reaction to the perceived humor of Patrick's comments; but the loud laughter from ET1 and ET4 (especially in lines 18 and 20) may also be a display of their vulnerability to Patrick's ridicule and of their inability to defend themselves – two highly salient threats to their 'positive face' (Brown and Levinson 1987), as Patrick blatantly questions and rejects the value of sharing domestic chores in their marital arrangements, and they lose self-control, which is manifested by the outbursts of laughter. Finally, what also strikes us about this particular exchange is that, as with the heteronormative hongi jesting in Excerpt 3, a shared frame of reference is clearly assumed: specifically, the deployment of gendered cultural practices and interactional norms (or stereotypes) as a kind of global – or at least intercultural – common ground for play. This is what alerts us to the globalizing habitus of tourism.

Being a Tourist, Doing Tourism: The Performance of Contact

> Whenever discourses travel across the globe, what is carried with them is their shape, but their value, meaning, or function do not often travel along. Value, meaning, and function are a matter of uptake, they have to be *granted* by others on the basis of the prevailing orders of indexicality, and increasingly also on the basis of their real or potential 'market value' as a cultural commodity. (Blommaert 2005: 72)

Each of the exchanges presented here constitutes a series of language games, playful moments which help to realize the performance of contact between hosts and tourists (and elsewhere between tourists and tourists). Each demonstrates the particular – but not unique – ways in which language and other semiotic material are entextualized and recontextualized for touristic purposes. They also show how certain values, meanings, and functions are not necessarily reinvented or refashioned, as Blommaert (quoted above) suggests; often the values, meanings, and functions endure over time and extend across space – were it not for this, the staging of tourism and the stylizing of tourist or host identities would not be possible. Tourism demands a ritualized familiarity or recognizablity. In other words, each of these language games, while being specifically situated and locally meaningful, also has a transposable, *generic* significance, which plays out more generally. Each game is a stock-in-trade of tourism discourse; this is how we know that we are doing tourism and being tourists (or hosts). These language games are ubiquitous, although no doubt they vary across different sub-genres of tourism. Here we have dealt with individual tourists visiting cultural–ethnic villages (they are organized into groups for the purpose of specific guided tours). These 'mainstream' holiday-makers fall somewhere between the extremes: independent tourists and budget package holiday-makers, who may, respectively, either be sheltered from or not seek such staged encounters with the hosts. The encounters are also inherently normative, structuring (or determining) creative acts and/or acts of resistance. It is in this way that tourism discourse – the globalizing tourist gaze (Urry 2002) – still tends to flatten and homogenize other people's spaces.

The specifics of tourist–host interactions inevitably emerge from, and are dictated to a large extent by, the centers of power – often those at the 'global core.' Typically, tourists are the ones who set the agenda and hosts are the ones who must fashion themselves in the image (or imagination) of the tourists. Host dwelling places become place names, and these place names in turn become tongue-twisters (see Excerpt 1 and Figure 11.3); host languages become impenetrable codes and ciphers of local communities (Excerpt 2); greetings become trademarks of ethnic identity (Excerpt 3); names become nicknames (Excerpt 5) – and so on. The "global semioscape" (Thurlow and Aiello 2007) is clearly not an equal playing field; while there is always a huge potential for speakers or designers to rework semiotic repertoires in circulation (symbols, sign systems, and meaning-making practices), some people's ways of speaking, design practices, and aesthetic preferences dominate and set 'the standard.' In the context of tourism, this type of semiotic agenda setting is evidenced in, for example, the fashioning of traditional Zulu craftwork into 'curios' for touristic consumption, which must also be constantly refashioned in accordance with the changing tastes and, indeed, fashions of western consumers – as is the case with the Zulu beadwork, whose design nowadays reflects the utilitarian/lifestyle demands of a westernized market (key chains, place mats, napkin rings, mobile phone pockets).

One aspect of most tourist interactions is that they are also typically one-offs. While we were doing our fleeting ethnographies of Whakarewarewa and PheZulu, our repeated visits to these sites appeared quite inexplicable and rather amusing to the guides, who recognized us from previous days. Of course, tourists visiting theme parks and other attractions are not 'regulars.' In their global flow, they reappear as types, not tokens – which means that these encounters are also singular for the hosts, allowing each of their performances to maintain the aura of spontaneity and uniqueness – a paradox, given the meaning of performance as 'never for the first time' (Schechner 1985: 36, cited in Bauman 2004: 9). The inherent fleetingness of tourist–host encounters creates a further paradox of instant and short-lived 'friendships' – another, if extreme, example of Zygmunt Bauman's (2000) "liquid" (as opposed to lasting) and "adiaphoric" (exempt from moral judgement or moral significance) relationships (Bauman 1995), of human life being driven predominantly by enjoyment and seeking aesthetic pleasure rather than responsibility and commitment. In this vein, identities become fragmented and somewhat schizophrenic, as blending them into cohesive lifestyles poses an obstacle. One of the obstacles, certainly, must be the short duration of some of these relationships – especially when they last for no longer than a day or a one-hour guided walk around a 'cultural village.' This is why the performance of a hongi between the guide and Kenny in Excerpt 4 may be glossed as "the sharing of common breath creating a legion of friendship" (l. 22); but, however good-willed and meaningful it may be, its chances of establishing between the two men, in the liminal space of the tourist encounter, anything more enduring than a passing, spontaneous "communitas" (Turner 1974) are destined to be terminated once the evening is over. In this sense, therefore, a transient experience or feeling of togetherness is produced which, as Eade (2000: xiii) explains, expresses itself as "an ideological programme that is only partially and fleetingly realized in practice." In this sense, too, *communitas* is akin to Bourdieu's (1977) notion of habitus, mediating between structured, hegemonic 'givens' of tourism and the everyday, agentful actions of individual tourists (and hosts).

So, however one-off and however fleeting, these reiterated performances of contact also work *performatively* (Butler 1990), to secure the mythologies of interpersonal and intercultural exchange that run central to tourism discourse (Thurlow and Jaworski 2010a). Much tourism is, for example, premised on the idea of tourists being instantly welcomed by the hosting community as 'friends' (see Jaworski et al. 2003; Jaworski and Lawson 2005; Lawson and Jaworski 2007), and even finding romance (on sexualizing travel spaces and sex tourism, see Piller 2010; Ryan and Hall 2001). The fact of the matter is that most of these relationships, at least the ones exemplified in our data here, terminate as rapidly as they begin. Sociolinguistically, they manifest a number of familiar but recontextualized strategies, typical of intimate behavior. While many of these strategies are commonly associated with threats to the social actors' positive face (Brown and Levinson 1987), Sifianou (1992) suggests that what may be perceived as a positive threat of this kind in one community or context may constitute a positive politeness strategy (one which assumes closeness and intimacy) in another:

- nicknames, terms of endearment, and downright derogatory terms of address (see Patrick's "mfowethu" ('brother'), "ma" (short for 'mama' 'mother'), and "gogo" ('granny') in Excerpt 2; "Angigquize Qakala" ("Mr Easy-Go-Lucky") in Excerpt 5);
- bald-on-the-record, unmitigated directives and personal questions (see Patrick's eliciting the tourists' place of origin in Zulu; the inquiry about CT's ability to speak Afrikaans in Excerpt 2; the question about the 'Polish hello' in Excerpt 4; the guide's 'bossing around' of Kenny in Excerpt 3; the inference about ET1's undertaking of the domestic chores in Excerpt 5);
- risqué humor and (suggestion of) obscenities (see Patrick's heteronormative 'jokes' in Excerpt 6 and the guide's homophobic tease in Excerpt 4; also, the guide's play with the pronunciation of 'Whaka' in Excerpt 2);
- teasing, ridicule, and insults (see Excerpts 4 and 6).

Tourists' behavior often displays ambivalence in such situations. Kenny, in Extract 4, appears not only obedient but quite meek, and not particularly amused (unlike his host and fellow tourists) in following the guide's instructions; PT1 draws a blank when addressed in Zulu by Patrick in Extract 3; PT2 refuses to "say hello in Polish" in Extract 5; and ET1 shifts from claiming to draw pleasure from cooking to complaining that his wife would "tell him off" if he did not cook in

Extract 6. Perhaps such hesitation, tentativeness, or inconsistency in behavior is partly due to tourists' uncertainty of their roles in moments when they are drawn from the relative safety of 'gazing onlookers' to being 'speaking participants,' singled out, put on the spot as *individuals*, unable to 'hide' in the safety of a group and group response, lacking a clear script or not knowing the language in which they are being addressed. These are examples of Jaquemet's (2005) *transidiomatic practices*, instances of deterritorialized and reterritorialized sociolinguistic disorder, possibly well rehearsed and strategically deployed by hosts as part of their routine encounters with tourists, while they are completely novel, hence disorienting and disempowering for the latter.

Nearly a billion people a year engage in international tourism of one sort of another, and many will face encounters of the type described above, out of countless other interactions which we may never gain access to. Many tourists joining daily guided tours will remain strangers, maintaining a convenient silence and avoiding eye contact (Löfgren 1999). In their fleeting encounters with guides, they will be largely addressed *en masse* and talked at rather than talked to. They may end up being photographed with their guides or other local performers, or they may ask each other personal questions; but ultimately they will only do so having bought their holidays, having paid for their guided tours, meals and souvenirs, and having left their tips. The more the tourists pay, the more service and interaction their money will buy (Sherman 2007). In such cases, then, any sense of 'community' or 'friendship' is often a function and a result of economic exchange. Which is not to dismiss these exchanges as simply 'synthetic' or without basis (compare Fairclough 1989 on synthetic personalization). Within tourism's theatrical framework of 'suspended disbelief,' the apparently "inauthentic" or "fake" are not necessarily obstacles to exchange; indeed they invariably become the substance of exchange, in a discourse which readily entertains the notions of "safe adventures," "planned spontaneity," "exotic familiarity," "contemporary tradition," and "genuine fakes" (Thurlow and Jaworski 2010a; see also Brown 1996). It is this quality of the oxymoronic/paradoxical that often makes the moments and meanings of contact in tourism so hard to read or predict. Our intention is certainly not to dismiss touristic *communitas* as necessarily shallow or disingenuous; the tourist experience is invariably pleasurable and always meaningful (Gottlieb 1982; Harrison 2003). This does not, however, absolve tourism (or tourists) of its ideological and political consequence.

The sociolinguistic characteristics of the discursive practices described in this chapter – the commodified framing of the interactions; the recontextualized displays of poetic language, stories, place names, formulaic expressions, and other snippets of verbal banter; instances of addressing interlocutors in languages they may not understand; code-crossing; language learning; reliance on the competence of others (interpreters); explicit evaluation of linguistic and non-verbal performances (namely the applause for Kenny in Excerpt 3, l. 19) – all point to an increasing need to theorize encounters occasioned by global mobility in terms of spatially heterogeneous, transcultural contact zones between people with distinctive, often conflicting social, geographic, historical, and economic trajectories

(Pratt 1992). These are Rampton's (2009) "communities of contact" operating in re-scaled, hybrid spaces, where familiar repertoires, styles of speaking, and genres often – but, as we have seen, not always – change their meaning and value. Where languages are intermixed, hybridized and syncretized, recontextualized words and expressions acquire indexical functions independent of their denotational meanings, transforming identities and becoming emblematic of spatial stratification in the political and economic local–global order (Silverstein 1998). Tourists go 'native' by mastering only minimal amounts of the 'native' language; tourists become interpreters for other tourists; speakers lose their confidence (Blommaert et al. 2005: 203) or claim power by subverting the dominant patterns of authority and privilege – as in 'playful' moments when wealthy tourists in former colonial spaces have their self-assured status put into question and undermined. Echoing Heller (2008), we find these discursive formations to be part of the processes and practices which establish fleeting identities, relationships, and communities existing *in the moment*, working across national and ethnic boundaries, refocusing social difference and social inequality, and redefining power relations through the negotiation and definition of meaning.

ACKNOWLEDGMENTS

We are grateful to Nik Coupland for his very useful comments on an earlier draft of this chapter, to Smangele Mkhwanazi for her help with translating our PheZulu data, and to Lauren Wagner and Ody Constantinou for their help with transcribing our Maori data. Research for this paper was supported by funding from the Leverhulme Trust (Grant No. F/00407/D) made to the Centre for Language and Communication Research, Cardiff University.

TRANSCRIPTION CONVENTIONS

[	= start of overlapping talk
(word)	= nonverbal, paralinguistic and other contextual information
((word))	= best approximation of talk
<u>word</u>	= perceptible additional emphasis
wo:rd	= perceptible lengthening
wo-	= truncated word/utterance
(.)	= pause shorter than one second
(1)	= length of pause in seconds
?	= utterance interpreted as carrying the pragmatic force of a question
=	= contiguous, latched talk
hello	= translation/gloss
[drop out]	= temporary loss of audio track
[word]	= additional explanation of non-English material

NOTES

1   We tend to use the term 'hosts' in an effort to avoid the disparaging connotation of 'locals.' We do recognize, however, that 'hosts' risks making assumptions about the relative power status of local people, about their motivation to entertain, and about the homogeneity of inhabitants who may or may not be native/local and whose role-identities will inevitably vary.

REFERENCES

Abbink, J. (2000) Tourism and its discontents: Suri–tourist encounters in southern Ethiopia. *Social Anthropology* 8: 1–17.

Appadurai, A. (1996) *Modernity at Large: Cultural Dimensions of Globalization.* Minneapolis: University of Minnesota Press.

Auger, T. (ed.) (2002) *DK Eyewitness Travel Guides: New Zealand.* London: Dorling Kindersley Limited.

Bauman, R. (2001) Verbal art as performance. In A. Duranti (ed.), *Linguistic Anthropology: A Reader [1975],* 165–88. Oxford: Blackwell.

Bauman, R. (2004) *A World of Others' Words: Cross-Cultural Perspectives on Intertextuality.* Oxford: Blackwell Publishing.

Bauman, R., and Briggs, C. (1990) Poetics and performance as critical perspectives on language and social life. *Annual Review of Anthropology* 19: 59–88.

Bauman, Z. (1995) *Life in Fragments.* Oxford: Blackwell.

Bauman, Z. (1998) *Globalization: The Human Consequences.* Cambridge: Polity.

Bauman, Z. (2000) *Liquid Modernity.* Cambridge: Polity.

Beck, U. (2002) The cosmopolitan society and its enemies. *Theory, Culture and Society* 19: 17–44.

Bell, A. (2009) *Language style as audience design.* In Coupland and Jaworski (eds),

265–75. Basingstoke: Palgrave Macmillan.

Billig, M. (1995) *Banal Nationalism.* London: Sage.

Block, D. (2008) *On the appropriateness of the metaphor of LOSS.* In Tan and Rubdy (eds), 187–203.

Blommaert, J. (2003). Globalisation and sociolinguistics. *Journal of Sociolinguistics* 7: 607–23.

Blommaert, J. (2005) *Discourse: A Critical Introduction.* Cambridge: Cambridge University Press.

Blommaert, J. (2009). *A sociolinguistics of globalization.* In Coupland and Jaworski (eds), 560–73.

Blommaert, J. (2010). *A Sociolinguistics of Globalization.* Cambridge: Cambridge University Press.

Blommaert, J., Collins, J., and Slembrouck, S. (2005) Spaces of multilingualism. *Language and Communication* 25: 197–216.

Boissevain, J. (ed.) (1996). *Coping with Tourists: European Reactions to Mass Tourism.* Oxford: Berghahn Books.

Bourdieu, P. (1977) *Outline of a Theory of Practice,* translated by R. Nice. Cambridge: Cambridge University Press.

Bourdieu, P. (1991) *Language and Symbolic Power,* edited and introduced by J. B. Thompson, translated by G. Raymond and M. Adamson. Cambridge: Polity.

Brown, D. (1996) Genuine fakes. In T. Selwyn (ed.), *The Tourist Image: Myths and Myth Making in Tourism*, 33–47. Chichester: John Wiley and Sons.

Brown, P., and Levinson, S. C. (1987) *Politeness: Some Universals in Language Usage*. Cambridge: Cambridge University Press.

Bruner, E. M. (2005) The Maasai and the Lion King: Authenticity, nationalism, and globalization in African tourism. In E. M. Bruner, *Culture on Tour*, 71–100. Chicago: The University of Chicago Press.

Budach, G., Roy, S., and Heller, M. (2003) Community and commodity in French Ontario. *Language in Society* 32: 603–27.

Butler, J. (1990) *Gender Trouble: Feminism and the Subversion of Identity*. London: Routledge.

Cameron, D. (2000) Styling the worker: Gender and the commodification of language in the globalized service economy. *Journal of Sociolinguistics* 4: 323–47.

Clifford, J. (1997) *Routes: Travel and Translation in the Late Twentieth Century*. Cambridge, MA: Harvard University Press.

Cosgrove, D. (1984) Prospect, perspective and the evolution of the landscape idea. *Transactions of the Institute of British Geographers* 10: 45–62.

Coupland, J. (ed.) (2000) *Small Talk*. London: Longman.

Coupland, N. (2006) The discursive framing of phonological acts of identity: Welshness through English. In J. Brutt-Griffler and C. Evans Davies (eds), *English and Ethnicity*, 19–48. Basingstoke: Palgrave Macmillan.

Coupland, N. (2007) *Style: Language Variation and Identity*. Cambridge: Cambridge University Press.

Coupland, N., Garrett, P., and Bishop, H. (2005) Wales underground: Discursive frames and authenticities in Welsh mining heritage tourism events. In A. Jaworski and A. Pritchard (eds), *Discourse, Communication and Tourism*, 199–222. Clevedon: Channel View.

Coupland, N., and Jaworski, A. (eds) (2009) *The New Sociolinguistics Reader*. Basingstoke: Palgrave Macmillan.

Culler, J. (1981) Semiotics of tourism. *American Journal of Semiotics* 1: 127–40.

Deleuze, G., and Guattari, F. (1987) *A Thousand Plateaus*, translated by B. Massumi. Minneapolis: University of Minnesota Press.

Deleuze, G., and Guattari, F. (2000). *Anti-Oedipus: Capitalism and Schizophrenia*. Minneapolis: University of Minnesota Press.

Duranti, A. (1997) Universal and culture-specific properties of greetings. *Journal of Linguistic Anthropology* 7: 63–97.

Duranti, A., and Goodwin, C. (eds) (1992) *Rethinking Context: Language as an Interactive Phenomenon*. Cambridge: Cambridge University Press.

Eade, J. (2000) Introduction to the Illinois paperback. In J. Eade and M. J. Sallnow (eds), *Contesting the Sacred: The Anthropology of Christian Pilgrimage*, ix–xxviii. Champaign, IL: University of Illinois Press.

Edensor, T. (2000) Staging tourism: Tourists as performers. *Annals of Tourism Research* 27: 322–44.

Edensor, T. (2001) Performing tourism, staging tourism: (Re)producing tourist space and practice. *Tourist Studies* 1: 59–81.

Fairclough, N. (1989) *Language and Power*. Harlow: Longman.

Favero, P. (2007) "What a wonderful world!": On the "touristic ways of seeing," the knowledge and the politics of the "culture industries of otherness." *Tourist Studies* 7: 51–81.

Foucault, M. (1976) *The Birth of the Clinic*, translated by A. M. Sheridan. London: Tavistock.

Franklin, A. (2003) The tourist syndrome: An interview with Zygmunt Bauman. *Tourist Studies* 3: 205–17.

Friedrich, P. (1989) Language, ideology, and political economy. *American Anthropologist* 91: 295–312.

Goffman, E. (1971). *Relations in Public: Microstudies of the Public Order*. New York: Basic Books.

Goffman, E. (1974) *Frame Analysis: An Essay on the Organization of Experience*. New York: Harper and Row.

Gottlieb, A. (1982) American vacations. *Annals of Tourism Research* 9: 165–87.

Gumperz, J. J. (1982) *Discourse Strategies*. Cambridge: Cambridge University Press.

Hardt, M., and Negri, A. (2000) *Empire*. Cambridge, MA: Harvard University Press.

Harrison, J. (2003) *Being a Tourist: Finding Meaning in Pleasure Travel*. Vancouver: University of British Columbia Press.

Harvey, D. (1989) *The Condition of Postmodernity: An Enquiry into the Origins of Cultural Change*. Oxford: Blackwell.

Harvey, D. (2006) *Spaces of Global Capitalism: Towards a Theory of Uneven Geographical Development*. London: Verso.

Heller, M. (2003) Globalization, the new economy and the commodification of language and identity. *Journal of Sociolinguistics* 7: 473–98.

Heller, M. (2008) Language and the nation–state: Challenges to sociolinguistic theory and practice. *Journal of Sociolinguistics* 14: 504–24.

Heller, M. (2010) *Paths to Post-Nationalism: A Critical Ethnography of Language and Identity*. New York: Oxford University Press.

Heritage, J. (1984) A change-of-state token and aspects of its sequential placement. In J. M. Atkinson and J. Heritage (eds), *Structures of Social Action*, 299–345. Cambridge: Cambridge University Press.

Hymes, D. (1974) *Foundations in Sociolinguistics: An Ethnographic Approach*. Philadelphia: Pennsylvania University Press.

Irvine, J. (1989) When talk isn't cheap: Language and political economy. *American Ethnologist* 16: 248–67.

Jaquemet, M. (2005) Transidiomatic practices: Language and power in the age of globalization. *Language and Communication* 25: 257–77.

Jaworski, A. (2009) *Greetings in tourist–host encounters*. In Coupland and Jaworski (eds), 662–79.

Jaworski, A., Coupland, N., and Galasiński, D. (eds) (2004) *Metalanguage: Social and Ideological Perspectives*. Berlin: Mouton de Gruyter.

Jaworski, A., and Lawson, S. (2005) Discourses of Polish agritourism: Global, local, pragmatic. In A. Jaworski and A. Pritchard (eds) *Discourse, Communication and Tourism*, 123–49. Clevedon: Channel View Publications.

Jaworski, A., and Pritchard A. (eds) (2005) *Discourse, Communication and Tourism*. Clevedon: Channel View Publications.

Jaworski, A., and Thurlow, C. (2004) Language, tourism and globalization: Mapping new international identities. In S. Hung Ng, C. N. Candlin, and Chi Yue Chiu (eds), *Language Matters: Communication, Identity, and Culture*, 297–321. Hong Kong: City University of Hong Kong Press.

Jaworski, A., and Thurlow, C. (2009) Taking an elitist stance: Ideology and the discursive production of social distinction. In A. Jaffe (ed.), *Stance: Sociolinguistic Perspectives*, 195–226. New York: Oxford University Press.

Jaworski, A., and Thurlow C. (eds) (2010). *Semiotic Landscapes: Text, Image, Space*. London: Continuum.

Jaworski, A., Thurlow, C., and Ylänne, V. (in preparation) *Language, Tourism and Globalization: The Sociolingusitics of Fleeting Relationships*. London: Routledge.

Jaworski, A., Ylänne-McEwen, V., Thurlow, C., and Lawson, S. (2003) Social roles and negotiation of status in host–tourist interaction: A view from British TV holiday programmes. *Journal of Sociolinguistics* 7: 135–63.

Kirshenblatt-Gimblett, B. (1998) *Destination Culture: Tourism, Museums, and Heritage.* Berkeley: University of California Press.

Kirshenblatt-Gimblett, B., and Bruner, E. M. (1992) Tourism. In R. Bauman (ed.), *Folklore, Cultural Performances, and Popular Entertainments: A Communications-Centred Handbook,* 300–307. New York: Oxford University Press.

Kress, G., and van Leeuwen, T. (2001) *Multimodal Discourse: The Modes and Media of Contemporary Communication.* London: Arnold.

Lash, S., and Urry, J. (1994) *Economies of Signs and Spaces.* London: Sage.

Lawson, S., and Jaworski, A. (2007) Shopping and chatting: Reports of tourist–host interactions in The Gambia. *Multilingua* 26: 67–93.

Le Page, R. B., and Tabouret-Keller, A. (1985) *Acts of Identity: Creole-Based Approaches to Language and Ethnicity.* Cambridge: Cambridge University Press.

Löfgren, O. (1999) *On Holiday: A History of Vacationing.* Berkeley: University of California Press.

Malinowski, B. (1923) The problem of meaning in primitive languages. Supplement to C. K. Ogden and I. A. Richards, *The Meaning of Meaning,* 146–52. London: Routledge and Kegan Paul.

MacCannell, D. (1999) *The Tourist: A New Theory of the Leisure Class [1976].* Berkeley: University of California Press.

McCabe, S. (2005) "Who is a tourist?" A critical review. *Tourist Studies* 5: 85–106.

McCarthy, M. (2000) Mutually captive audiences: Small talk and the genre of close-contact service encounters. In J. Coupland (ed.), *Small Talk,* 183–207. London: Longman.

Myers, G. (2006) "Where are you from?": Identifying place. *Journal of Sociolinguistics* 10: 320–43.

Piller, I. (2007) Cross-cultural communication in intimate relationships.

In H. Kotthoff and H. Spencer-Oatey (eds), *Intercultural Communication* (Handbook of Applied Linguistics 7), 341–59. Berlin: Mouton de Gruyter.

Piller, I. (2010) Sex in the city: On making space and identity in travel spaces. In A. Jaworski and C. Thurlow (eds), *Semiotic Landscapes: Text, Image, Space,* 123–36. London: Continuum.

Pratt, M. L. (1992) *Imperial Eyes: Travel Writing and Transculturation.* London: Routledge.

Pritchard, A., and Morgan, N. (2005) Representations of 'ethnographic knowledge': Early comic postcards of Wales. In A. Jaworski and A. Pritchard (eds), *Discourse, Communication and Tourism,* 53–75. Clevedon: Channel View Publications.

Pujolar Cos, J. (2006) *Language, Culture and Tourism: Perspectives in Barcelona and Catalonia.* Barcelona: Universitat Oberta de Catalunya.

Pujolar, J., and Heller, M. (in press) The political economy of texts: A case study in the structuration of tourism. *Studies in Sociolinguistics.*

Rampton, B. (1995) *Crossing: Language and Ethnicity among Adolescents.* London: Longman.

Rampton, B. (2009) Speech community and beyond. In Coupland and Jaworski (eds), 694–713.

Ryan, C., and Hall, M. (2001) *Sex Tourism: Marginal People and Liminalities.* London: Routledge.

Schechner, R. (1985) *Between Theater and Anthropology.* Philadelphia: University of Pennsylvania Press.

Schiffrin, D. (1987) *Discourse Markers.* Cambridge: Cambridge University Press.

Scollon, R., and Wong Scollon, S. (2003) *Discourse in Place: Language in the Material World.* London: Routledge.

Senft, G. (1999) The presentation of self in touristic encounters: A case study from the Trobriand Islands. *Anthropos* 94: 21–33.

Sheller, M., and Urry, J. (2006) The new mobilities paradigm. *Environment and Planning A* 38: 207–26.

Sherman, R. (2007) *Class Acts: Service and Inequality in Luxury Hotels.* Berkeley: University of California Press.

Sifianou, M. (1992) *Politeness Phenomena in England and Greece.* Oxford: Clarendon Press.

Silverstein, M. (1998) Contemporary transformations of local linguistic communities. *Annual Review of Anthropology* 27: 401–26.

Tan, P. K. W., and Rubdy R. (eds) (2008) *Language as Commodity: Global Structures, Local Marketplaces.* London: Continuum.

Tannen, D. (1989) *Talking Voices: Repetition, Dialogue, and Imagery in Conversational Discourse.* Cambridge: Cambridge University Press.

Thurlow, C., and Aiello, G. (2007) National pride, global capital: A social semiotic analysis of transnational visual branding in the airline industry. *Visual Communication* 6: 305–44.

Thurlow, C., and Jaworski, A. (2003) Communicating a global reach: Inflight magazines as a globalising genre in tourism. *Journal of Sociolinguistics* 7: 581–608.

Thurlow, C., and Jaworski, A. (2006) The alchemy of the upwardly mobile: Symbolic capital and the stylization of elites in frequent-flyer programs. *Discourse and Society* 17: 131–67.

Thurlow, C., and Jaworski, A. (2010a) Silence is golden: Elitism, linguascaping and 'anti-communication' in luxury tourism discourse. In A. Jaworski and C. Thurlow (eds) *Semiotic Landscapes: Text, Space, Globalization,* 187–218. London: Continuum.

Thurlow, C. and A. Jaworski. (2010b) *Tourism Discourse: Language and Global Mobility.* Basingstoke: Palgrave Macmillan.

Turner, V. (1974) *Dramas, Fields, and Metaphors: Symbolic Action in Human Society.* Ithaca: Cornell University Press.

Urry, J. (2002) *The Tourist Gaze,* 2nd edn [1990]. London: Sage.

Urry, J. (2007) *Mobilities.* Cambridge: Polity.

12 Globalization and Language Teaching

DAVID BLOCK

Introduction

In 1981 I began a one-year RSA (Royal Society of Arts) diploma course in teaching English as a foreign language at the British Council Institute in Barcelona. Having spent some two years as an unqualified teacher struggling to do my job in none-too-prestigious language teaching academies, I was seeking professional development or, in simpler terms, looking for someone to tell me how to teach. The course did not disappoint me, as I finished it with very clear ideas about how to plan and deliver English lessons. What I did not really think about at the time, however, was how I had been trained as a mediator and spreader of the emergent official approach to language teaching – communicative language teaching (CLT). I was a convert, a zealous proponent of all things CLT, and I was these things independently of whether or not CLT was appropriate to my context or consistent with local language and language teaching ideologies. There was not at this time a fully developed public discourse around globalization in Spain (or anywhere else in the world, for that matter), but, looking back, it is easy to see how I was mediating what today might be understood as an "ideoscape" (Appadurai 1990) or a global flow of ideas about language teaching pedagogy. I also now realize that I was entering the profession of language teaching at a key and pivotal point when CLT had begun to gather force on its way to becoming the globalized approach to language teaching that it is today. This chapter is my personal reflection on CLT as a global approach to language teaching.

Although CLT applies to the teaching of all languages, I will focus here almost exclusively on the teaching of English as an international language (hereafter TEIL). I do so for three reasons. First, English is the most globally taught language today, as David Crystal has argued (Crystal 2003; see also McKay and Bokhorst-Heng 2008), and it is the one accorded privileged status in the national curricula of countries around the world (see for instance Kubota 2002 on Japan; McKay 2003 on Chile; Tupas 2008 on the Phillipines; Phillipson 2003 on European Union member states). In effect, English is the prime mediator of the economic, political,

The Handbook of Language and Globalization, First Edition. Edited by Nikolas Coupland.

cultural, and social relations and flows that constitute globalization. Secondly, it is the language which I have taught in my lifetime, and therefore the language with reference to which I can discuss globalization and language teaching with the greatest authority. Thirdly and finally, space does not allow a broader consideration, which would include the teaching of other languages taught extensively – such as French, Spanish, Mandarin, and Arabic.

I begin in the next section with an examination of the rise of CLT as well as with an examination of the approach it has evolved into in recent years – task based language teaching (TBLT) – as global methods. I then briefly discuss the ongoing struggle in English language teaching as regards attempts to reconcile the global and the local, the center and the periphery, and the western and non-western. This done, I move on to consider the global TEIL textbook as the mediator of CLT in English language teaching. In particular, I focus on how publishers in recent years have come to position learners as cosmopolitan consumers and have set up branded identities for them to aspire to.

The Rise of CLT/TBLT

As authors such as Richards and Rodgers (2001) and Howatt (2004) argue, there has been a shift in many (if not most) parts of the world over the past three to four decades, from well established approaches to language teaching such as audiolingualism and grammar translation, to communicative language teaching (CLT) and its more recent incarnation, task-based language teaching. This shift has not been sudden, and it has not by any means been the same where it has taken place. However, a perusal of the current national curricula for language teaching in North and South America, Europe and East Asia reveals that official discourses on language teaching are remarkably similar, based as they are on an assemblage of ideas originating for the most part in the work carried out in the late 1960s and early 1970s the by Council of Europe.[1] In this work there were recommendations for changes in language teaching which involved radical breaks with the past, calling into question the basic premises of approaches such as audiolingualism and grammar translation. These recommendations concerned views on education in general, in an era of cooperation across nation-state borders in post-World War II Europe; what constituted language as the goal of language teaching; what was to be the organizing principle of language teaching as regards its content; and, finally, the methodology to be employed in language teaching.

First, CLT was very much about new ways of viewing language education in modern societies. It was a development of its time, as it emerged out of the socially tumultuous 1960s, during which the respective roles of institutions and of the individual in society had begun to be questioned and reformulated in many parts of the world, most notably in western Europe and in the anglophone world. Legutke and Thomas (1991) discuss changes in approaches to education during this period which contributed to what they believe to have been a move towards "humanistic language teaching":

> In the aftermath of anti-establishment movements with explicit anti-institutional implications [...] educational approaches which called for the de-schooling of society [...] or, in its less radical forms, for a basic humanizing of technocratic and de-humanizing schools, had gained ground. To humanize schools would require an orientation towards 'holistic' education, which aimed to promote growth in intrapersonal awareness and interpersonal sharing as well as intellectual development. (Legutke and Thomas 1991: 36)

This humanist side of language teaching was not generally articulated in an overt manner in early discussions of CLT, although it was arguably fundamental to understanding the new attitudes toward language and communication which were incorporated into discussions about education. In addition, over the past three decades this humanist aspect has dropped out of discussions somewhat, particularly in cases where language educators have moved in the direction of more technical task-based approaches (more on these below).

A second component of the Council of Europe work on language teaching was a change in the way language was conceived. The object of language teaching – the competence to be developed in learners – shifted from an exclusive focus on grammar (syntax, morphology, and phonology) and lexis to communicative competence (Hymes 1971). Language user competence was conceptualized not only in relation to grammar and lexis, but also in relation to the way a language is used by members of a speech community to accomplish their purposes (in terms of culturally bound discursive organization and function) and in relation to the interactional skills necessary to communicate effectively and appropriately in that language (in terms of culturally shaped pragmatic knowledge). In addition, Michael Halliday's (1973) early form of functional linguistics was influential at the time. In particular, Council of Europe scholars were interested in his outline of the basic functions of language for children during the early period of development, when these begin to engage in the acquisition of their first language; in short, scholars were interested in how children use language to obtain things, to acquire control over the behavior of others, to initiate and maintain interaction, to express personal feelings and meanings, to learn and discover, to create imaginary worlds, and to convey information. Finally, there was an interest in the work of John Austin (1962) and John Searle (1965) and the development of 'speech act theory.' Speech act theory moved beyond an exclusive focus on the meaning of the words uttered by speakers, to a consideration of the constituents of communicative events; and these included the social contexts in which the events take place as well as the intentions of speakers. Intentions in effect give life to utterances, making them 'illocutionary acts' – for instance offering, refusing, asserting, describing, promising, suggesting, or complaining.

It was speech act theory that most directly informed what Council of Europe scholars recommended as regards the organization of the content of language teaching (Wilkins 1976; Munby 1978). In particular, functions – which derived directly from speech act theory and from the concept of illocutionary acts – became by the early 1980s the staple of language teaching syllabuses and the backbone of commercially produced materials in Europe and North America. It became hard to conceive of the contents page of a syllabus or coursebook which was not, first and foremost, a list of functions – such as asking for information, asking to receive directions, making and responding to suggestions, or making and responding to requests. On the RSA course which I attended in 1981 in Barcelona, functions formed the basis of all the activities designed by teachers, as they were easily convertible into behavioral goals to work toward (for example, by the end of the lesson students will be able to request information in a shop).

In terms of the actual practices adopted by teachers, CLT involved an emphasis on interaction-based activities carried out exclusively in the target language. These activities were often conducted on the principle of the information gap, whereby students working in pairs or groups ask for and provide information which is needed for the completion of a task. However, in CLT there was also room for more student-focused work which involves the sharing of personal experiences, for instance exchange of opinions about real or imagined events or talking about one's job or holidays. Above all, two interrelated notions became axiomatic to CLT: (a) that it is necessarily and inherently good to speak, and to do so as frequently as possible; and (b) that one learns to speak by speaking.

In recent years CLT has been transformed in different ways; currently, as a label for language teaching practices, it is used synonymously with – or in any case alongside – task-based language teaching (hereafter TBLT), an approach which, as the name suggests, puts tasks at its center. Much has been written about different ways of defining tasks, and there has been an evolution of sorts, from an insistence on tasks being replicas of real world activities to a broadened view, which includes classroom activities that resemble more traditional exercises, focusing explicitly on form and lexis, for example. At present, there seems to be a general consensus around the idea that that tasks are goal-directed pedagogical activities involving a primary focus on meaning (although a focus on linguistic form is also important), during which participants choose and implement the linguistic resources they need as they work towards a clearly defined outcome (Ellis 2003).

Task, defined in Ellis's goal-oriented, instrumental terms, has served as a key construct both in language teaching and in second-language acquisition research (SLA), which has come to support it (Block 2003). Over the past thirty years, SLA researchers have built a considerable body of findings, an important one being that tasks act as triggers for language learning due to the way in which their meaning-centeredness and goal-directedness activate the type of language-processing cognition that leads to learning (see Gass and Selinker 2008 and Ellis 2008 for a thorough account of current SLA research). This cognitive activity is thought to begin with the process of negotiation for meaning, whereby, "in an effort to communicate, learners and competent speakers provide and interpret signals of their own and their interlocutor's perceived comprehension, thus provoking adjustments to linguistic form, conversational structure, message content, or all three, until an acceptable level of understanding is achieved" (Long 1996: 418). For Long and many other researchers (see for instance the contributions to

Doughty and Long 2003), negotiation for meaning "facilitates acquisition because it connects input, internal learner capacities, particularly selective attention, and output in productive ways" (Long 1996: 451–2). Because cognitive processes are theorized, as is characteristic of the human mind, and hence they are not idiosyncratic to each individual, tasks and the negotiation for meaning that they elicit are deemed to be applicable to all language learners in all contexts, even if their exact and specific content and focus would depend on locally executed needs analyses (Long 2005). And this notion, universalist as regards learning, has become a global notion as regards how teaching should take place in all the parts of the world – as I explain in the next section.

CLT/TBLT as a Globalized Phenomenon

Arjun Appadurai (1990) has famously described globalization as a "complex, overlapping and disjunctive order" made up of five types of forces and flows, which he calls "scapes." These five scapes are:

1 ethnoscapes or flows of people (e.g. migrants, asylum seekers, exiles, tourists);
2 technoscapes or flows of technology (e.g. hardware components, technical know-how);
3 financescapes or flows of money (e.g. national stock exchanges, commodity speculations);
4 mediascapes or flows of information (e.g. newspapers, magazines, satellite television channels, websites); and
5 ideoscapes or flows of ideas (e.g. human rights, environmentalism, free trade movements, fear of terrorism).

CLT/TBLT, as discussed thus far, seems to be an *ideoscape*, that is, a global flow of ideas about language teaching and learning.

At first glance, this description of CLT/TBLT might seem relatively innocuous and devoid of negative connotations. However, ideoscapes are not freestanding sets of ideas that just emerge in one context and then flow freely around the world. Rather, as authors such as Pennycook (1994) and Canagarajah (1999) have noted, they are ideologically loaded, in that they are related to sets of values, beliefs, and feelings about the best way to conceptualize particular domains – in the present case language, communication, and language teaching and learning. As for ideologies, it is worth noting that they are, always and necessarily, constructed in the interest of a particular group or groups (here, the academic and educational communities propagating CLT/TBLT) and that they serve both as shapers of larger discourses (here, discourses about communication and language teaching and learning) and as justifications for practices adopted (here, pedagogical practices).

Numerous authors have noted clashes of ideologies, as the spread of communicative approaches to language teaching has not been as smooth as many in the language teaching profession might have hoped. For example, Canagarajah (1999 and 2002) has criticized the spread of CLT, lamenting that, "[j]ust as the technologically and economically developed nations of the West (or center) hold an unfair monopoly over less developed (or periphery) communities in industrial products, similar relations characterize the marketing of language teaching methods" (Canagarajah 2002: 135). For Canagarajah, both the academic and the educational practitioners of CLT are able to take advantage of the prestige and power associated with all things 'western' as they export new methods, CLT being the most recent example. While methodological novelties tend be accepted with "awe," they are also met with "bewilderment" (ibid.), and the latter is due to several factors. First, new approaches to language teaching are disembedded – that is, lifted out from the context of their sources, for example the US or UK – and then taken up elsewhere in the world, as if their form and content transcended spatio-temporal contexts (Giddens 1990). Secondly, there is seldom (if ever) any dialogue between the exporters of new approaches and those who import them; and there is no discussion of the form and content of approaches, or even of their ideological underpinnings.

For those local teachers who follow pedagogical practices imported from the West or center in a relatively unquestioning manner, lessons may be of limited use to their students, who are asked to conform to procedures and practices toward which neither they nor their teachers feel any sense of ownership. By contrast, where teachers appropriate and reconfigure imported pedagogical practices, combining the global with the local, the results are far more optimal (Canagarajah 1999). Such a process may be conceptualized in terms of what many globalization theorists refer to as 'glocalization' – a word taken from the world of business in Japan, where it means marketing goods and services on a global basis by catering to local particularities. For globalization theorists, however, it conveys the idea that the global does not merely overwhelm or swallow the local; rather, syntheses emerge from contacts between the global and the local via a processes involving the "interpenetrating" of the "particular" and the "universal" (Robertson 1995: 30).

In the spread of CLT, *glocalizing* processes have emerged due to the need to develop approaches to language teaching at the crossroads between western/center practices and local knowledge. In addition, a good number of applied linguists have made proposals for the resolution of conflicts arising when the global meets the local and educational ideologies come into conflict (Kumaravadivelu 2003, 2008; Holliday 1994, 2005; Canagarajah 1999, 2005). While the proposals of these authors vary considerably, they all involve a call for local teachers to work out their own solutions, appropriating from globally circulating ideas about language education, what they deem to be suitable in the development of locally generated pedagogical practices. However, in books where concrete examples are provided (Hall and Eggington 2000; Norton and Toohey 2004), there seems to be a near-exclusive focus on anglophone countries or on English-dominant educational environments.

An exception of sorts – that is, an example of *glocalized* TEIL – is Cheiron McMahill's account of how she set up and ran "grass-roots feminist English classes," which were organized by the learners themselves and taught via a "feminist second language pedagogy" (1997: 612; see also McMahill 2001). This pedagogy was a combination of explicit teaching of morphology, syntax, phonology, and pragmatics and so on, and feminist concerns such as women's rights in Japan and elsewhere. Activities organized by McMahill included

> preparing to give presentations in English at, for example, the United Nations conference for women, […] working on a translation of a feminist book from English into Japanese while seeking help from native-speaking English feminists, […] simply taking part in a discussion of women's issues with women from other countries. (McMahill 1997: 613)

The chief aim of such classes was to create an English-medium alternative "female discourse community of resistance to sexism" in Japan and in the world. In McMahill (2001), the author focuses on one particular course theme, "Colors of English," which is aimed to empower Japanese women through the learning of English as a means of communication with women around the world. Sessions are generally organized around topics such as ethnic identities, discrimination in employment, problems with the learning of English, personal histories, and so on. McMahill argues that, through their discussions of such topics, the women came to be more confident as users of English, since they positioned themselves as global feminists.

Impressive as it is, McMahill's teaching comes across as a unique example of resistance to the global hegemony of CLT/TBLT in TEIL. Among other things, McMahill seemed to have *carte blanche* as regards the selection and implementation of teaching materials, and apparently she did not have to use a standard text. This situation seems to make an exception of sorts in the world of TEIL, given the dominance of global textbooks as mediators of most TEIL around the world (Gray 2002). It is to the topic of the global TEIL textbook that I now turn.

The Global TEIL Textbook and Commodified Identities

At the heart of debates about TEIL methodology are the language teaching materials which mediate them. And one key question that arises in the market of global language teaching materials concerns the cultural content of textbooks, normally published in the US or the UK, for export around the world. On the one hand, there has been a growing awareness among publishers in recent years that content which is appropriate in one part of the world might not be appropriate in another.

One example, cited by John Gray (in preparation), is the inclusion of homosexuality, either as a topic of discussion or as the lifestyle option of individuals portrayed in textbooks. When he interviewed publishers about the cultural content of the books they published, Gray was told that it was easier to leave out references to homosexuality, and indeed to sexual practices in general. Elsewhere Gray (2002) talks about lists of taboo topics, which can assist publishers in their attempt to avoid anything that might offend local sensitivities and lead to cancelled contracts or low sales:

> Some publishers provide lists of proscribed topics, while others rely informally on the acronym PARSNIP (politics, alcohol, religion, sex, narcotics, isms, and pork) as a rule of thumb. One publisher's list I saw contained some thirty items to be avoided or handled only with extreme care. This included alcohol, anarchy, Aids, Israel and six pointed stars, politics, religion, racism, sex, science when it involves altering nature, e.g. genetic engineering, terrorism, and violence. (Gray 2002: 159)

By contrast, what does seem to be allowed, as regards content, is the sanitized presentation of various aspects of national cultures (their geography, social norms, history, iconography, and so on) – in effect the traditional content of foreign language textbooks. However, as Gray notes, in recent years there has been a shift in content, as new textbooks and new editions of older textbooks include more and more references to an emergent global culture. Thus, if in the past the idea of culture in the global TEIL textbook was linked to nation–states such as Britain and the US, in more recent books an altogether different kind of culture – cosmopolitan and consumerist – is the glue that holds together the language concerns. Foundational to this shift in emphasis has been the commodification of the English language and – as I will argue – the concomitant branding of English-speaking identities, which learners can aspire to as cosmopolitan consumers on the global stage.

In Marxist economic theory (Marx 1990), commodities are objects which have two types of value. They have exchange-value in a market, which means that they can be exchanged for other objects or for money. The framing of objects in terms of their exchange-value was essential to the development of early capitalist economies, which arose as part of the industrial revolution in Europe beginning in the early part of the nineteenth century, and this framing remains fundamental in capitalism today. However, it is worth remembering that the move to commodities seen in terms of exchange-value represented a major historical shift, away from the centrality of the use-value of objects – that is, the more utilitarian and qualitative valuing of objects according to their ability to satisfy basic human needs. In the work of Monica Heller (for instance Heller 2003) and other sociolinguists, the commodification of language has been a focal theme for some time. For Heller, the commodification of language means a shift from a valuing of language for its basic communicative function and more emotive associations – national identity, cultural identity, the authentic spirit of a people and so on – to valuing it for what it means in the globalized, deregulated, hyper-competitive, post-industrial "new work order" in which we now live (see also Gee, Hull and Lankshear 1996; Cameron 2002). In other words, it means a shift from language as use-value to language as exchange-value.

However, as Lash and Lury (2007: 6) note, commodities "have no relationships" and "they only have value in the way that they resemble every other commodity." Thus English, as the consumer good called 'global English,' is understood to be vaguely the same thing in different educational contexts around the world. It is the language for communication in business and leisure settings that everyone needs to know in the age of globalization. This implies, among other things, that the English offered as a skill by a language school or global textbook in one context is fundamentally the same as the English offered as a skill by a language school or global textbook in another context. And the English required as a job qualification in one context is pretty much the same as the English required in another context. There arises therefore a need to bring English alive, to make it more attractive and ultimately more saleable. In short, it needs to be presented and wrapped in some form of content which in effect carries it to learners. To understand how this process works, it is useful to frame matters in terms of 'brand.' In order to inject commodities with life, advertisers brand them; that is, they link them to particular world views, behaviors, and artefacts, developing narratives in the process and what Banet-Weiser and Lapansky (2008: 1249) call "whole environments of meaning," which over time become recognizable to the public as ways of life and lifestyle options that can be opted into or abandoned, depending on circumstances.

To understand how branding works, one need only look as far as television commercials, which run in series over months and sometimes years. One such example is the series of BT (British Telephone) commercials which began to run in the UK in 2007. Actors Kris Marshall and Esther Hall play a couple in the process of negotiating each partner's degree of commitment to the relationship, and each commercial provides a piece of this ongoing story. Thus, for example, the selling of a service commodity such as broadband service is packaged in an argument between the two protagonists which is being resolved at a distance, via e-mail.

A broadband service is obviously very different from a language. And a television commercial is a very different medium from a global textbook. However, in both cases there occurs the branding of a commodity. The issue here is how the global textbook links the English language into particular world views, behaviors, and artefacts – in short, into lifestyle options that learners can aspire to. One lifestyle option which has become prevalent in recent years revolves around the idea of cosmopolitan global citizens who embody an ideology of global capitalism and consumerism in the different activities that textbooks show them engaging in.

Cosmopolitanism has been written about a great deal over the years (Hannerz 1996; Tomlinson 1999; Vertovec and Cohen 2002; Beck 2006), and one finds a kind of sliding scale at work, in discussions. At one extreme, there is cosmopolitanism as the very superficial contact and engagement with cultures encountered via physical movement from one place to another (or, progressively in recent years, via electronically mediated experiences). This cosmopolitanism is usually associated with tourist travel, and it is often what Hannerz (1996) has called "home plus": the individual wants the place he/she is visiting to have one or two exotic attractions, yet for the most part he/she wants everything else – the standard of accommodation, the transportation facilities, the nature and quality of services, and in some cases even the food – to be the same as it would be at home. At the other extreme is a higher-minded cosmopolitanism, construed as the positive disposition to engage and mix with other cultures. David Held describes what he calls "cultural cosmopolitanism" as follows:

> Cultural cosmopolitanism should be understood as the capacity to mediate between national cultures, communities of [faith] and alternative styles of life. It encompasses the possibility of dialogue with traditions and discourses of others with the aim of expanding horizons of one's own framework of meaning and prejudice. (Held 2002: 57–8)

The global citizens envisaged by TEIL textbooks today are cultural cosmopolitans to the extent that they are willing to engage with and embrace the ever-increasing interconnectedness, time–space compression, and multiple forces and flows (for instance Appadurai's scapes), which are both constitutive of globalization and consequences of it. They are not afraid of the brave new world of the global age, and they revel in the diversity and hybridity that characterize it. As a result, they manifest solidarity toward those who are in effect their fellow global citizens above and beyond nation-state loyalties. In the world of TEIL, these global citizens need English as the mediator of communications with the peoples of the world and not, as might have been the case until recently in some contexts, as the mediator of American culture, or British culture, or Australian culture, and so on.

However, there is an aspect to this cultural cosmopolitanism which is probably not what Held and others have in mind, one which appears to fall somewhere between the tourist and cultural types outlined above. Urry (1995) uses the phrase "aesthetic cosmopolitanism" to describe an engagement with the 'Other' which goes deeper than the superficiality of Hannerz's home-plus, but does not attain the moral high ground implied in Held's "cultural cosmopolitanism." This cosmopolitanism is driven by a desire to consume the 'Other' – cuisine, sight-seeing, music, cinema, and so on – and it is the domain of those members of society with sufficient economic capital to afford to act on it. While the current era of cheap air travel has brought this type of aesthetic cosmopolitanism to a larger proportion of the population, particularly in wealthier European countries, it nevertheless remains primarily a middle-class enterprise. This is the case not least because being an aesthetic cosmopolitan requires sustained and relatively high levels of economic, social, and cultural capital (Bourdieu 1984, 1991). In short, one needs money, social networks, knowledge, and taste to be a consistent aesthetic cosmopolitan. In addition, aesthetic cosmopolitans may be seen to affiliate to what

Garcia Canclini (2001) describes as a global consumer citizenship, built around common tastes and commodity consumption.

In the global textbook, this primarily middle-class global consumer–citizen is presented as a competent individual who is either successful or on the way to becoming successful. In this context, success may be defined in different ways. First, there is success associated with celebrity and with being famous, and text-books now include a good number of activities with photos of highly recognizable global figures, past and present, such as Mahatma Ghandi or Bill Gates. Thus, if I examine a current fairly typical global textbook, *Cutting Edge Intermediate* (Cunningham and Moor 2005; hereafter *CEI*), I find an activity entitled "Talk about someone you admire" (pp. 42–3), in which learners are shown photographs of figures deemed to be global celebrities from different domains of activities: from sport, David Beckham and Serena Williams; from politics, Nelson Mandela; from literature, J. K. Rowling; from art, Pablo Picasso. Learners are asked to "work in small groups" and answer the following questions: "How many of the people in the photos do you recognize?" and "What do you think people admire in them?" (p. 42). In fairness to the authors, it should be noted that this initial activity leads eventually to others, which allow learners the option of talking about non-celebrities whom they admire, for example family members. It is nevertheless interesting that their way into this more personalized activity involves a kind of recognition based above all on the global flow of information via globalized media (cinema, magazines, websites, and so on). There is therefore an appeal to a certain cult of the celebrity, to an affiliation to individuals who "provide a sort of glue that brings and holds together otherwise diffuse and scattered aggregates of people" (Bauman 2005: 50).

As regards the functioning of non-celebrities as examples of successful people, it is important to examine how these are presented. In *CEI* there is a procession of physically attractive young men and women from a range of national, racial, and ethnic backgrounds, engaging with a world of work, technology, the media, and leisure (travel, eating, socializing, and so on). Thus in the opening unit, enti-tled "All about you," there are photographs of no fewer than seventeen different people in the first three pages (Cunningham and Moor 2005: 6–8). The people span a broad range of ages, racial phenotypes, and dress, and they are engaged in an array of encounters and activities in different physical settings, such as "a busi-nesswoman meeting a colleague from abroad for the first time" or "some students on an English course getting to know each other during a break" (p. 6). In a unit entitled "Success," the topic is dealt with via the ambitions of young graduates, the theme of having the right profile for a job – there is for instance a question-naire headed "Have you got what it takes?" (pp. 48–9) – and the details of getting a job (including initial contacts and eventually a job interview).

Zygmunt Bauman's assessment of the current state of work is that "[a] steady, durable and continuous, logically coherent and tightly structured working career is [...] no longer a widely available option" (Bauman 2005: 27). In what is perhaps a nod towards this view, there is a listening activity in which young men and women explain how they have abandoned more traditional employment and now feel more fulfilled in their new means of employment. Thus we are introduced to people like "Clare Davis, 26, [who] resigned from her job as a geography teacher in secondary school and started retraining as plumber" and "Lorna Whitwort, 29, and husband Ian [who] gave up their jobs in the city of London [...] and moved to the country to run a small hotel ..." (Cunningham and Moor 2005: 52). These individuals represent the spirit of a global age of flexible employment: they have what is known as 'low drag time,' that is, they are not tied down by narrow career aspirations or limitations on their ability to move from one geographical location to another. Thus they can change careers and/or move freely, as the dictates of the job market change. In addition, they embody the spirit of the individual consumer pursuing and attaining what he/she wants (Bauman 2007).

Apart from the success motif, there is another important current running throughout *CEI* as well as throughout other global textbooks: the conflation of the private and the public – such that what was once private and personal is now deemed to be public and treatable in public. Frank Furedi (2004) has noted how in countries like the US and the UK it has become acceptable, far more than was the case in the past, for individuals to 'emote' in public, to display their inner feelings, and to disclose what are often very private matters in public fora. Somewhat following this trend, textbooks now contain a good number of activities which involve personal disclosure, thus affording learners of English greater opportunities to talk about their families, their relationships, and every detail of the activities that they engage in every day (Kullman 2003). Here are some examples of *CEI* activities in which learners are asked to talk about themselves:

> Work in pairs. Have you got any brothers or sisters? In what ways are you similar/ different? Which of your parents/grandparents do you take after? [...] (Cunningham and Moor 2005: 36, under the heading "Life stories")

> You go out to a restaurant for dinner. Do you: a. dress up? b. wear smart casual clothes? c. wear traditional dress of your country? d. wear whatever you feel like? (Ibid., p. 74, under the heading "Social behaviour")

> Would you [...] hand in a wallet that you found in the street? [...] park in a disabled parking space? [...] drop litter? [...] (Ibid., p. 96, under the heading "How socially responsible are you?")

Lastly, running through TEIL textbooks today are representations of cosmopolitan capital: this is a variation on Bourdieusian cultural capital (Bourdieu 1984), which may be defined as the behavioral patterns, value systems, and cultural knowledge of the well educated and well travelled, offered up as resources or assets to which the English language learner can aspire. The behavioral patterns in question are about activities such as doing sport, reading, and going to the cinema, and they include the two most common ones: shopping and travelling. The value systems conveyed are eminently capitalist, consumerist, and ultimately conformist as regards the current version of demand-led capitalism, which dominates in most parts of the world today. Finally, the cultural knowledge of cosmopolitan capital is about technological skills – with reference to the internet, the worldwide web, and emailing – and includes an appreciation of cinema, literature, music, art and so on.

The positioning of learners as possessors of cosmopolitan capital is, at a minimum, a flattering entry point, and it could be argued that it has the advantage of lifting English from the mundaneness of the low-level service encounter to the status of a potential mediator in meaningful communication. Following Bauman (2007), one can easily see these global textbooks in Althusserian terms (see also Althusser 2001), as 'interpellating' (hailing, recruiting) individuals to become English speakers in the global consumerist culture, even if, as Gray (in preparation) suggests, teachers and students are not always heeding such interpellation, as they adapt and reshape published material according to local contexts. One needs to examine, however, whether in such cases the consumer culture is being resisted in form or in substance. Thus to replace the American film stars and other globally recognizable celebrities with local ones, in a textbook, is merely to engage in superficial substitution, since the change does not alter the substantial affiliation to celebrity and success. And to move shopping venues from generic international scenes such as airports or from concrete geographical locations such as New York to more local environments is, once again, merely a superficial change, as long as the centrality of the consumerist activity of shopping is still retained.

McMahill's feminist TEIL class in Japan, cited above, offers perhaps a way forward in this regard, as it does mean an abandonment of mainstream textbooks in favor of materials catering directly for the interests of students. However, there is also scope for transnational alternatives to global ELT, as is witnessed by the establishment of the website *TESOL Islamia* (http://www.tesolislamia.org/). This site presents itself as an alternative source of language teaching materials for Muslim teachers and students around the world. According to its 'About us' section, *TESOL Islamia* is, among other things, "committed to promoting and safeguarding Islamic precepts and values in the teaching of English as a second or foreign language in the Muslim World," as well as to "'empowering' Muslim learners to use the English language in ways that best serve the socio-cultural, socio-political and socio-economic interests of Muslim communities worldwide." It is difficult to know how influential, or even how effective this website has been since its establishment in 2003. In addition, some of the teaching ideas made available thus far (for example straightforward readings of religious texts translated into English) show the website to be somewhat conservative in its political aims, as it wishes to safeguard essentialized views of culture and identity on the basis of strong religious views instead of challenging the current state of global capitalism, or even taking on more specific issues in Muslim and non-Muslim countries, such as workers' rights and feminism.

Nevertheless, the website does provide an extra dimension to debates about the complexities and problematicities of TEIL; and the attempt to create an alternative to the hegemony of the global textbook is, in general, to be applauded. Otherwise life goes on in the world of TEIL. CLT, in its various permutations, continues to dominate as a default approach to teaching, and so does the global TEIL textbook, albeit often with local adaptations (Gray 2002; Gray in preparation). And, in the midst of the global imperative toward making consumption the dominant ideology, both in general and in more specifically TEIL, there is a continued need for the critical approaches outlined by the authors cited above to be taken up in the multitude of TEIL contexts around the world.

Conclusion

I began this chapter with an anecdote about my first contact with the approach to language teaching known as 'communicative language teaching' (CLT) and about my experience as an unwitting mediator and spreader of this approach to all parts of the world, or at least to the part in which I was living in the 1980s. I then went on to discuss the origins of CLT and how it is an 'ideoscape' – that is, a global flow of ideas about language teaching. Here I made the point that CLT is ideologically loaded, like all ideoscapes, and that there is at present an ongoing struggle in TEIL, as local educators adopt, adapt, and resist CLT in an attempt to reconcile global flows with local cultures and educational traditions. However, I noted that most of the literature which deals with resistance to currently dominant discourses of global capitalism has been situated in contexts where English is the official language. An exception I cited is McMahill (1997, 2001), who points to the possibility of developing a grassroots pedagogy in Japan around international feminist discourses. Of course, language teaching methodology is but one part of language education, and it is often language teaching materials that are the most salient mediators of what goes on in classrooms – including TEIL classrooms. Thus, after considering CLT as an approach to language teaching, I shifted my attention to the 'global textbook.' I examined how, through TEIL textbooks currently used around the world, CLT is wrapped up in processes of language commodification. Specifically, these processes are the commodification of English as a necessary skill in the global age and the positioning of learners as global citizens/cosmopolitan consumers. I concluded, once again, with a call for more critical approaches to TEIL, in particular in relation to the language teaching materials used.

The ever-increasing interconnectedness of the world – one of the most cited characteristics of globalization – means that the uptake of CLT/TBLT, the commodification of English as a necessary skill, and the positioning of learners as cosmopolitan global citizens/consumers are likely to continue, and even increase, in coming years. Or, at any rate, one would come to this conclusion if one made two key assumptions: first, that English will remain *the* global language; and, secondly, that the anglophone countries, the United States in particular, will continue to exercise a considerable (though by no means complete) dominance over the global flows of technology, the media, and finance – that is, over Appadurai's *technoscapes*, *mediascapes*, and *financescapes*, respectively. However, as authors such as David Harvey (2005) and Samir Amin (2006) have noted, American cultural, economic, and political hegemony in the world could be on the wane, along with many of the assumptions which people around the world have made over the past sixty years. On the one hand, at the nation-state level, the new neo-liberal economy has led the US to ever greater budget deficits, and US citizens are the most indebted in the world today. At the same time, in geopolitical terms, the power of the US in the world – above all, its capacity to influence events – may well be declining. Among other things, China has emerged as a rival for oil and other commodities; Russia has recently re-surfaced as a world player, through the dependence of many European powers on its energy resources; and, finally, Brazil and India are developing as economic powers. In addition, the current crisis of capitalism, in which we are all immersed, may yet have a great effect on any directorship of the world economy that the US might wish to assume.

As a result of such real and emergent developments, there is now the prospect of a multi-polar new world order, along the lines of what Hardt and Negri (2000) envisaged a decade ago (though it is by no means identical to what they envisaged). Such a new order would replace the US-dominated 'new world order' of George Bush Sr and might lead to changes in language teaching worldwide, such as the following:

1 **What languages are most studied globally** English may no longer be *the* global language; it could be supplanted in many contexts by Mandarin, Arabic, or Spanish.

2 **How languages are taught** As authors like Shi-xu (2005) have suggested, there are different ways of conceptualizing and framing any number of socio-cultural phenomena; and, as seen in Phan Le Ha (2008) and Sharifian (2009), approaches to language teaching must follow such different ways.

3 **The kinds of teaching materials employed in instruction, including the carrier content of these materials** There could be, for example, changes in the carrier content, as we enter a post-neo-liberal era.

On the other hand, it may well be that no such changes will occur, at least not to a significant degree, and that someone writing a chapter like this one in twenty-five years time will still be discussing the teaching of English as a global language, according to the latest permutation of CLT and via consumerist-driven global textbooks. After all, as Harvey (2005) and Callinicos (2009) argue convincingly, economic and political imperialism, as practiced and enforced by the US over the last century, shows itself to be amazingly resilient and adaptable to circumstances. Far more likely, however, is a future falling somewhere in-between these alternatives: a more recognizably multi-polar world than exists at present, but one in which the English language and the influence of anglophone nation–states will continue to be important. And in that case grassroots language teaching methodologies such McMahill's "feminist second language pedagogy," and transnational materials in the spirit of *TESOL Islamia*, may well be more common than they are at present.

NOTES

1   The Council of Europe is an organization of European states established in May 1949 with the purpose of developing social, cultural, and economic ties among the member states.

REFERENCES

Althusser, L. (2001) *Ideology and Ideological State Apparatuses. Lenin and Philosophy and Other Essays [1971]*. New York: Monthly Review.

Amin, S. (2006) *Beyond US Hegemony? Assessing the Prospects for a Multipolar World*. London: Zed Books.

Austin, J. L. (1962) *How to Do Things With Words*. Oxford: Oxford University Press.

Appadurai, A. (1990) Disjuncture and difference in the global cultural economy. In M. Featherstone (ed.), *Global culture: Nationalism, Globalization and Modernity*, 295–310. London: Sage.

Banet-Weiser, S., and Lapansky, C. (2008) RED is the new black: Brand culture, consumer citizenship and political possibility. *International Journal of Communication* 2: 1248–68.

Bauman, Z. (2005) *Liquid Life*. Oxford: Polity.

Bauman, Z. (2007) *Consuming Life*. Oxford: Polity.

Beck, U. (2006) *Cosmopolitan Vision*. Oxford: Polity.

Block, D. (2003) *The Social Turn in Second Language Acquisition*. Edinburgh: Edinburgh University Press.

Block, D., and Cameron, D. (eds) (2002) *Globalization and Language Teaching*. London: Routledge.

Bourdieu, P. (1984) *Distinction: A Social Critique of the Judgment of Taste*. London: Routledge.

Bourdieu, P. (1991) *Language and Symbolic Power*. Cambridge, MA: Harvard University Press.

Callinicos, A. (2009) *Imperialism and Global Political Economy*. Cambridge: Polity.

Cameron, D. (2002) *Globalization and the teaching of 'communication skills.'* In Block and Cameron (eds), 67–82.

Canagarajah, S. A. (1999) *Resisting Linguistic Imperialism in English Teaching*. Oxford: Oxford University Press.

Canagarajah, S. A. (2002) *Globalization, methods, and practice in periphery classrooms*. In Block and Cameron (eds), 134–50.

Canagarajah, S. A. (2005) Introduction. In S. Canagarajah (ed.), *Reclaiming the Local in Language Policy and Practice*. Mahwah, NJ: Lawrence Erlbaum, xiii–xxx.

Crystal, D. (2003) *English as a Global Language*, 2nd edn. Cambridge: Cambridge University Press.

Cunningham, S., and Moor, P. (2005) *New Cutting Edge Intermediate*. Harlow, UK: Longman.

Doughty, C., and Long, M. (eds) (2003) *The Handbook of Second Language Acquisition*. Oxford: Blackwell.

Ellis, R. (2003) *Task-Based Language Learning and Teaching*. Oxford: Oxford University Press.

Ellis, R. (2008) *The Study of Second Language Acquisition*, 2nd edn. Oxford: Oxford University Press.

Featherstone, M. (1995) *Undoing Culture: Globalization, Postmodernism and Identity*. London: Sage.

Furedi, F. (2004) *Therapy Culture*. London: Routledge.

Garcia Canclini, N. (1999) *La globalización imaginada*. México: Paidós.

Garcia Canclini, N. (2001) *Consumers and Citizens: Globalization and Multicultural Conflicts*. Minneapolis, MN: University of Minnesota.

Gass, S., and Selinker, L. (2008) *Second Language Acquisition: An Introductory Course* 3rd edn. Mahwah, NJ: Lawrence Erlbaum Associates.

Gee, J. P., Hull, G., and Lankshear, C. (1996) *The New Work Order: Behind the Language of the New Capitalism*. Boulder, CO: Westview Press.

Giddens, A. (1990) *The Consequences of Modernity*. Cambridge: Polity.

Gray, J. (2002) The global coursebook in English language teaching. In Block and Cameron (eds), 151–67.

Gray, J. (in preparation) *The Construction of English*. London: Palgrave.

Hall, J. K., and Eggington, W. G. (eds) (2000) *The Sociopolitics of English Language Teaching*. Clevedon, UK: Multilingual Matters.

Halliday, M. A. K. (1973) *Explorations in the Functions of Language*. London: Edward Arnold.

Hannerz, U. (1996) *Transnational Connections*. London: Routledge.

Hardt, M., and Negri, A. (2000) *Empire*. Cambridge, MA: Harvard University Press.

Harvey, D. (2005) *The New Imperialism*. Oxford: Oxford University Press.

Held, D. (2002) Culture and political community: National, global, and cosmopolitan. In S. Vertovec and R. Cohen (eds), *Conceiving Cosmopolitanism: Theory, Context and Practice*, 48–58. Oxford: Oxford University Press.

Heller, M. (2003) Globalization, the new economy, and the commodification of language and identity. *Journal of Sociolinguistics* 7(4): 473–92.

Holliday, A. (1994) *Appropriate Methodology and Social Context*. Cambridge: Cambridge University Press.

Holliday, A. (2005) *The Struggle to Teach English as an International Language*. Oxford: Oxford University Press.

Howatt, A. (2004) *A History of English Language Teaching*, 2nd edn. Oxford: Oxford University Press.

Hymes, D. (1971) *On Communicative Competence*. Philadelphia: University of Pennsylvania Press.

Kubota, R. (2002) The impact of globalization on language teaching in Japan. In Block and Cameron (eds), 13–28.

Kullman, J. (2003) The Social Construction of Learner Identity in the UK–Published ELT Coursebook. Unpublished PhD thesis, Canterbury, Christ Church University College.

Kumaravadivelu, B. (2003) *Macrostrategies for Language Teaching*. New Haven, CT: Yale University Press.

Kumaravadivelu, B. (2008) *Cultural Globalization and Language Education*. New Haven, CT: Yale University Press.

Lash, S., and Lury, C. (2007) *Global Culture Industry*. Cambridge: Polity.

Legutke, M., and Thomas, H. (1991) Process and experience in the language classroom. London: Longman.

Long, M. (1996) The role of linguistic environment in second language acquisition.' In W. Ritchie and T. Bhatia (eds), *Approaches to Second Language Acquisition*, 413–68. London: Academic Press.

Long, M. (ed.) (2005) *Second Language Needs Analysis*. Cambridge: Cambridge University Press.

McKay, S. (2003) Teaching English as an international language: The Chilean context. *ELT. Journal* 57(2): 139–48.

McKay, S. L., and Bokhorst-Heng, W. D. (2008) *International English in Its Sociolinguistic Contexts: Towards a Socially Sensitive EIL Pedagogy*. London: Routledge.

McMahill, C. (1997) Communities of resistance: A case study of two feminist

English classes in Japan. *TESOL Quarterly* 31(4), 612–22.

McMahill, C. (2001) Self-expression, gender, and community: A Japanese feminist English class. In A. Pavlenko, A. Blackledge, I. Piller, and M. Teutsch-Dwyer (eds), *Multilingualism, Second Language Learning and Gender*, 307–44. New York: Mouton de Gruyter.

Marx, K. (1990) *Capital: Critique of Political Economy* [1867], Vol. 1. Hammondsworth: Penguin.

Munby, H. (1978) *Communicative Syllabus Design: A Sociolinguistic Model for Designing the Content of Purpose-Specific Language Programmes*. Cambridge: Cambridge University Press.

Norton, B., and Toohey, K. (eds) (2004) *Critical Pedagogies and Language Learning*. Cambridge: Cambridge University Press.

Pennycook, A. (1994) *The Cultural Politics of English as an International Language*. London: Longman.

Phan Le Ha (2008) *Teaching English as an International Language: Identity, Resistance and Negotiation*. Clevedon, UK: Multilingual Matters.

Phillipson, R. (1992) *Linguistic Imperialism*. Oxford: Oxford University Press.

Phillipson, R. (2003) *English-Only Europe? Challenging Language Policy*. London: Routledge.

Richards, J., and Rodgers, T. (2001) *Approaches and Methods in Language Teaching*. 3rd edn. Cambridge: Cambridge University Press.

Robertson, R. (1995) Glocalization: Time–space and homogeniety–heterogenity. In M. Featherstone, S. Lash, and R. Robertson (eds), *Global Modernities*, 25–44. London: Sage Publications.

Searle, J. (1965) *Speech Acts: An Essay in the Philosophy of Language*. Cambridge: Cambridge University Press.

Sharifian, F. (ed.) (2009) *English as an International Language: Perspectives and Pedagogical Issues*. Clevedon, UK: Multilingual Matters.

Shi-Xu (2005) *A Cultural Approach to Discourse*. London: Palgrave.

Tomlinson, J. (1999) *Globalization and Culture*. Oxford: Polity.

Tupas, T. R. F. (2008) Anatomies of linguistic commodification: The case of English in the Philippines vis-à-vis other languages in the multilingual marketplace. In R. Rubdy and P. Tan (eds), *Language as Commodity: Global Structures and Local Market Places*, 89–105. London: Continuum.

Urry, J. (1995) *Consuming Places*. London: Routledge.

Van Ek, J. (1975) *The Threshold Level*. Strasbourg: Council of Europe.

Vertovec, S. and R. Cohen (eds) (2002) *Conceiving Cosmopolitanism: Theory, Context and Practice*. Oxford: Oxford University Press.

Wilkins, D. (1976) *Notional Syllabuses*. Oxford: Oxford University Press.

13 Discursive Constructions of Global War and Terror

ADAM HODGES

Introduction

As globalization scholars widely acknowledge, we live in a world of cultural flows (Appadurai 1996). National borders no longer tightly constrain the movement of "ideas and ideologies, people and goods, images and messages" (Appadurai 2001: 5). Of particular importance for discourse scholars is the "flows of representations, narratives and *discourses*," as Fairclough (2006: 3) emphasizes (emphasis in the original). In his discussion of "mediascapes," Appadurai (1990) points out how the interconnectedness of the world's media plays an important role in disseminating messages and discourses around the world. As these representations enter local contexts, they may be reworked and reshaped in line with local assumptions and conventions. In the study of language and globalization, we therefore need to pay close attention to the way discourse travels around the world and is taken up and reshaped by actors in local situations.

To these ends, the Bakhtinian perspective on language provides a useful framework for exploring the global interconnectedness of discourse. Bakhtin (1981, 1986) emphasizes that language use does not take place in a vacuum; rather, all language use is fundamentally dialogic in nature. In their examination of political discourse in the media, Leudar and colleagues (2004) adapt these ideas in their notion of a "dialogical network." As they explain, "media events, such as television and radio programs, press conferences and newspaper articles are networked: connected interactively, thematically and argumentatively" (Leudar et al. 2004: 245; see also Nekvapil and Leudar 2002). At the global level, we can observe how political discourse that emanates from Washington shapes and is shaped by discussions that take place in Europe, in the Middle East, and elsewhere. Against the backdrop of the Bush administration's 'war on terror,' to what extent does such a dialogical network impact on the way war is justified and understood around the world?

In this chapter I examine the dialogic connections involved in the global interchange of ideas about terrorism and the 'war on terror.' Discourse moves across

The Handbook of Language and Globalization, First Edition. Edited by Nikolas Coupland.
© 2013 Blackwell Publishing Ltd except for editorial material and organization © 2013 Nikolas Coupland. Published 2013 by Blackwell Publishing Ltd.

national boundaries in a manner that shapes global relations and actions, and reshapes the dialogue that takes place within local contexts. To explore these processes, I discuss three contexts in detail. In the first, I examine recent work by Zala Volcic and Karmen Erjavec on the appropriation of the Bush administration's 'war on terror' discourse by Serbian intellectuals (Volcic and Erjavec 2007, Erjavec and Volcic 2007). These young Serbs incorporate this discourse into their own project of imagining and shaping contemporary war and politics, as well as geography and history. The second context discusses research undertaken by Becky Schulthies and Aomar Boum on the recontextualization of terrorism discourses on Al-Jazeera (Schulthies and Boum 2007). Their work underscores both the importance of discourse emanating from Washington and the way in which Middle Eastern commentators rework its language in light of their own cultural assumptions. For the third context, I provide my own analysis of the dialogic connections found in George W. Bush's speeches where he uses reported speech frames to recontextualize the words of Osama bin Laden as part of his discursive construction of the 'enemy' in the 'war on terror.' As Bush provides his own preferred reading of bin Laden's words, he reshapes these words in a way that works to justify his administration's 'war on terror' and war in Iraq. Before exploring each of these contexts, however, I begin with a theoretical overview of the Bakhtinian concept of dialogism, contextualized within the framework of global cultural flows.

Dialogism and Global Interchange

Bakhtin's (1981, 1986) notion of dialogism, which Kristeva (1980) rearticulates with the notion of intertextuality, is useful in the analysis of global discursive interchange because it emphasizes the connections across multiple discursive encounters where issues are contested. Intertextual relations are implicated in a process whereby the discourse is lifted from one setting – in other words, decontextualized – and brought into another discursive encounter, or recontextualized (Bauman and Briggs 1990; Briggs and Bauman 1992). Entextualization, the act of turning a piece of discourse into a text and of moving it from one context to another, allows social actors to bring with the text, to varying degrees, its earlier context, while also transforming the text in the new setting.

The interconnectivity of discourse appears in different guises. The incorporation of previously uttered quotations into a current context is one way in which discourse connects across situations of use. Yet the concept of dialogism, as expressed by Bakhtin (1981, 1986), holds that any use of language is effectively implicated in a wider dialogue. Within the context of a political speech, for example, where the role of the audience is limited to non-verbal responses (applause, cheers, jeers), the speaker must account both for the immediate audience and for "an indefinite, unconcretized *other*" (Bakhtin 1986: 95), or for what Bakhtin calls "a higher *superaddressee*" (ibid., p. 126). Such political speeches build upon what has already been said (perhaps in a previous speech or media commentary), anticipate potential responses (both from the present audience and from a wider public), and formulate arguments in an attempt to overcome possible objections (which may follow at a subsequent time and in another place). In this way discourse enters into a speech chain (Agha 2003) where "the utterance is related not only to preceding, but also to subsequent links in the chain of speech communion" (Bakhtin 1986: 94).

In the "natural histories of discourse" (the title of Silverstein and Urban 1996), the repetition of texts across discursive encounters inevitably involves reshaping those texts to some degree. As it was expressed by Becker, any use of language – what he calls *languaging* – consists in "taking old language [...] and pushing [...] it into new contexts" (Becker 1995: 185). In this process, prior text is not just repeated but reworked. The reshaping of prior text may occur with varying degrees of fidelity toward its meaning in the 'original' context. As Kristeva points out, repetition may be done "seriously, claiming and appropriating it [prior text] without relativizing it" – or the process of recontextualization may introduce "a signification opposed to that of the other's word" (Kristeva 1980: 73). Bakhtin (1981) speaks of a "double-voiced discourse," which "serves two speakers at the same time and expresses simultaneously two different intentions: the direct intention of the character who is speaking, and the refracted intention of the author" (p. 324). Double-voiced discourse may be uni-directional when another voice is sympathetically represented, or vari-directional when the representing voice is critical toward the one represented (Morson and Emerson 1990: 149ff.; see also Rampton 1995 and 2006 on stylization). In its extreme form, resignification may move into the realm of parody (Bakhtin 1981: 340; Coupland 2007: 175; Álvarez-Cáccamo 1996: 38).

Previously uttered discourse commonly enters new contexts as reported speech. The importance of reported speech in the Bakhtinian perspective is underscored by the significant discussion of the phenomenon by Voloshinov, who characterizes reported speech as "speech within speech, utterance within utterance, and at the same time also *speech about speech, utterance about utterance*" (Voloshinov 1973: 115; original emphasis). Voloshinov's comments highlight the capacity of reported speech not just to represent pieces of previously uttered discourse, but to *re-present* what has been said elsewhere by others – that is, to recontextualize a prior utterance with different shades of meaning (Voloshinov 1971). As Buttny reminds us, "Reporting speech is not a neutral, disinterested activity" (Buttny 1997: 484). The contextualization of prior words within the reporting context imbues them with new connotations and interpretations, as will be illustrated later in the chapter.

Dialogic interchange at the global level can be seen operating in recent sociolinguistic research that examines the impact of global linguistic flows on local communities of interaction. As the language of hip-hop spreads, for example, it is taken up in local contexts, where it is refashioned or 'glocalized' (Alim and Pennycook 2007; Pennycook 2003, 2007; Sarkar and Allen 2007). The forms of language associated with English and hip-hop therefore become hybridized (Bakhtin 1981) or indigenized (Appadurai 1990) as they mix with local languages.

As a result, hip-hop language may not only act as an index of transnational identity, but it becomes a fluid resource for shaping new local identities. In the realm of media advertising, Piller (2001) shows how the insertion of English into German advertisements does symbolic work by constructing a cosmopolitan identity for the product's targeted consumers. While the advertisements often draw upon the hegemonic influence of English as a global language to achieve an authoritative voice, Piller (2001) notes that, "as people appropriate the discourses of multilingual consumerism for their own ends, the ways in which they do so are no longer controlled by the original advertisers" (p. 181). English is symbolically reworked by local actors in such instances. Also looking at the symbolics of global English in local interaction, Bucholtz and Hall illustrate the use of the English language by self-identified lesbians in New Delhi, India, where these women view English "as the appropriate medium for the expression of a progressive sexuality, rejecting Hindi as indexical of backwards and discriminatory attitudes about sex" (Bucholtz and Hall 2008: 419). In this setting, English possesses what the authors call "sociosexual capital" in the construction of local sexual identities. These examples provide glimpses into the way transnational linguistic flows enter new contexts. As Blommaert (2008) summarizes in his own work on transnational flows of English and literacy skills, 'glocalization' involves the flow of resources into a local symbolic economy, where those global resources are transformed accordingly.

At bottom, global discourse flows are enabled by the global media landscape, which connects myriad texts and voices together in a dialogical network. It is against this backdrop that I examine the global circulation of discourse about war and terror. Even widely circulated discourses, like those associated with the Bush administration's representation of the 'war on terror,' are subject to reshaping as they enter new settings; and the discourse of the Bush administration is itself embedded within the global dialogic connections that exist on the global level. I now turn to three case studies that examine these issues in more detail.

The 'War on Terror' Discourse in Serbia

Zala Volcic and Karmen Erjavec's examination of the discourse of young Serbian intellectuals offers a glimpse into how a widely recognized global discourse may be taken up and reshaped within a local context (Volcic and Erjavec 2007, Erjavec and Volcic 2007). In their studies, Volcic and Erjavec conducted ethnographic interviews with Serbian intellectuals aged 23 to 40. Their pool of interviewees included journalists, writers, artists, and politicians; and the interviews took place between October 2001 and the end of 2002, with follow-ups conducted in 2003 and 2004. Questions focused on the Yugoslav wars of the prior decade, as well as on the events of 9/11. As Volcic and Erjavec illustrate, the "anti-terrorism discourse" emanating from the George W. Bush administration in Washington after the events of 9/11 becomes the basis for the articulation of a "Serbian war on terrorism" in the accounts of these young intellectuals.

Volcic and Erjavec summarize the Bush administration's 'war on terror' discourse as follows: "War has been proclaimed; the enemy is Islamic terrorism, personified by bin Laden; and the West has to unite in a war against terrorism" (Volcic and Erjavec 2007: 187). In the renegotiation of Serbian intellectuals' global cultural and political position after the collapse of the Milošević regime, Serbian intellectuals adapt this discourse within their own national context, in order to redefine the conflict in the former Yugoslavia. In effect, the 'war on terror' discourse provides a ready-made template for young Serbians to re-imagine their identity on the world stage, as well as the identity of the 'enemy' they faced at home. Volcic and Erjavec (2007) note: "In the light of the global 'war on terror' discourse, the enthusiastic attempts of the Balkan countries themselves to borrow and exploit the global 'war on terror' in order to remain in the center of global attention are significant and remarkable" (p. 190). Volcic and Erjavec's role as scholars positioned them as representatives of the West in the eyes of many of the interviewees. Accordingly, the Serbian intellectuals couched their political claims in a language that would be likely to resonate with a Western audience – the language of the 'war on terror' – and to allow them to position their situation "in the center of global [or at least Western] attention." In Bakhtinian terms, the Serbians were speaking to multiple audiences at once: the interviewers in particular, and the West in general.

As Volcic and Erjavec illustrate, the young Serbians discursively equate the terrorism of 9/11 with the violence perpetrated by Muslims in the former Yugoslav wars. As summarized in the subtitle to Volcic and Erjavec's article, the sentiment conveyed by these Serbians is that "we were fighting the terrorists already in Bosnia." Notably, the Serbians do not merely refer here to terrorists in a general sense; rather they specifically point to the antagonists of the Bush administration's 'war on terror' to define the enemy they faced. This point is underscored by one informant, who remarks: "It is very tragic, what has happened in the former Yugoslav republics [...] we were fighting the Osama terrorists by ourselves already then" (Volcic and Erjavec 2007: 196). Here the name of al Qaeda's leader is used as an adjective, to personify the concept of 'terrorists' within the Serbian's characterization of his nation's 'enemy.' This allows the informants to paint a picture of themselves as astutely aware of, and involved in, the 'war on terror' long before the USA woke up to the reality of Islamic terrorism on 9/11. As noted by another informant, Serbia's fight in the 'war on terror' stretches back to the 1980s: "Just see what is going on around the world today [...] Some people in Serbia recognized the danger of fundamentalism and terrorism in the 1980s [...]" (ibid.). As the authors explain, "The analogy, 'Serbia is to Muslims as USA is to terrorists,' starts to serve as a strategy of legitimizing the Serbian war against Muslims in the former Yugoslavia" (ibid.). As the young Serbians describe their own experience, they adopt the language of the 'war on terror' to do so.

As the Bush administration uses the term "terrorism" to describe not just the actions of the perpetrators of 9/11 but also those of the enemy faced in Iraq, in the Serbians' accounts the term "terrorism" has also become a catch-all label for any acts carried out by their enemy. That is, the term "terrorism" extends "to all the violent acts – historical and contemporary – committed against them, the Serbs" (ibid.). In this way Serbian intellectuals rework the 'war on terror' discourse so as to represent themselves as positive figures, on the right side of the line drawn by President Bush in the 'war on terror.' In the "with us or against us" binary formulated by Bush in his speeches after 9/11, the Serbians discursively position themselves in the former category. They opt into one side of the highly contested ideological divide represented in Bush's vision of the world. Thus, "in contemporary Serbian discourse, expressions such as 'war on terror' or 'fighting Muslim terrorists' are turned into legitimate terms designating political wishes of belonging and even legitimizing the violent former-Yugoslav wars" (ibid., p. 187).

Notably, the 'war on terror' discourse becomes an important element for the accomplishment of identity work. The 'us' versus 'them' binary in the Bush administration's 'war on terror' plays upon geographical, racial, and religious differences to distinguish the United States and its allies from Islamic terrorists. The negative images of Islam that underlie this discourse are easily exploited in the Serbians' own discourse. "By denoting Bosnian and Kosovar Muslims as terrorists, Islamic fundamentalists, and Islamic radicals, the informants reduce all Muslims to a monolithic and irrationally violent 'Other,' and in that sense, recycle the Western stereotype about Muslims and Islam (Karim 1997; Said 1978, 1997)" (ibid., p. 193). The Serbians position themselves as the "victims" of actions perpetrated by what they term the "terrorist religion." Through the use of 'commonsense' markers such as "everybody knows" or "we all know," Volcic and Erjavec's informants formulate essentialist claims about Muslims – for instance that they are "violent by nature" (p. 194). Another informant remarks: "They do not share the European manners, they are not developed in such a way" (p. 195). The authors note that their informants use the descriptors 'terrorists' and 'Muslims' interchangeably in talking about the 'enemy.' In contrast, in talking about themselves, they use 'Serbs' and 'Europeans' synonymously.

The global identity categories that underlie the 'war on terror' discourse provide a type of template to be applied to the local context of Serbia. Irvine and Gal's (2000) concept of "fractal recursivity" is useful for thinking through this application of a global discourse to a local context. As these authors explain, "*Fractal recursivity* involves the projection of an opposition, salient at some level of relationship, onto some other level" (p. 38). In the case of the Serbian intellectuals, the dichotomy between the West/Europe/Christianity and the East/non-Europe/Islam is applied within Serbia itself. This allows the Serbians to draw from the negative conceptions of the Muslim 'Other' and to align themselves with the West. In this way the Serbians "present themselves as those (misunderstood and betrayed) heroes that have been long fighting the terrorists in Kosovo and Bosnia, which are Muslim countries, in order to defend the Christian West" (Volcic and Erjavec 2007: 187). The mimetic oppositions provide the Serbians with cultural resources to use in the discursive construction of identities in their regional landscape.

Volcic and Erjavec argue that the use of the 'war on terror' discourse by Serbian intellectuals works to naturalize and reproduce "a hegemonic global order of discourse" (p. 197). They illustrate this reproduction by pointing to the overlap of key words used both by Bush and by the Serbian intellectuals in their talk about 'terrorism.' As Bush describes the events of 9/11 so do the Serbians describe their war against Muslims in the former Yugoslavia. In particular, Erjavec and Volcic highlight descriptors that refer to "a crusade against Muslim terrorists" and to "a fight for our freedom and civilization" (Erjavec and Volcic 2007: 129). Volcic and Erjavec therefore argue that the language of the 'war on terror' put forth by the Bush administration becomes further entrenched as a dominant discourse in world affairs. To be sure, although it may be considered 'dominant' in the sense of being widely circulated and recognized, it has also been highly resisted. Nevertheless, where accepted and taken up, as in the case highlighted by Volcic and Erjavec, it provides local actors with a ready-made framework for articulating their own political and militaristic struggles.

Serbia is not the only context in which the 'war on terror' has become reconfigured. Russia provides another interesting example (Volcic and Erjavec 2007: 199; Tishkov 2004). Where convenient, the Russians' war against Muslim separatists in Chechnya has discursively morphed into a fight against terrorism. The connection between Russia's actions in Chechnya and the 'war on terror' has been embraced and reified by President Bush. In speeches delivered in October 2005, for example, Bush cites the school hostage crisis that took place in Beslan in 2004 as evidence of a widespread global 'war on terror' situated on numerous "fronts," including Chechnya. Bush states:

> Some have argued that extremism has been strengthened by the actions of our coalition in Iraq, claiming that our presence in that country has somehow caused or triggered the rage of radicals. I would remind them that we were not in Iraq on September 11th, 2001, and al Qaeda attacked us anyway. The hatred of the radicals existed before Iraq was an issue, and it will exist after Iraq is no longer an excuse. ((applause)) The government of Russia did not support Operation Iraqi Freedom, and yet the militants killed more than 150 Russian schoolchildren in Beslan. (Bush 2005)

Here Bush responds to critics who argue that the war in Iraq has nothing to do with 9/11 and the 'war on terror.' In his retort, the president lumps together all acts of violence waged by Muslims as instances of actions of the 'enemy' in the 'war on terror.' Like with the Serbian intellectuals' recontextualization of the 'war on terror' discourse, which is made in order to explain the former Yugoslav wars, Bush applies the 'war on terror' rubric to the Russians' fight in Chechnya. Not surprisingly, in the 2008 conflict between Russia and Georgia, where the United States adopted a decidedly anti-Russian and pro-Georgian stance, the language of the 'war on terror' was conspicuously absent from the Bush administration's descriptions of the situation. The adoption and adaptation of the 'war on terror' discourse has little to do with socio-political realities and everything to do with the discursive framing of those realities. Global actors constantly position themselves in a world marked by widely circulating discourses – like the one about the 'war on terror,' which acts "as a common reservoir and reference point"

(Spitulnik 2001: 112) for interpreting socio-political realities. As Volcic and Erjavec (2007: 199) summarize, "[w]hat one sees globally is the ongoing appropriation of this discourse into local contexts."

Recontextualization of Terrorism Discourses on Al-Jazeera

Discourse, according to Bakhtin, "cannot fail to be oriented toward the 'already uttered,' the 'already known,' the 'common opinion' and so forth" (1981: 279). Becky Schulthies and Aomar Boum (2007) illustrate this point in their work on the recontextualization of western terrorism discourses on the Arab media station Al Jazeera. As in the Serbian context described earlier, political discourse on Al Jazeera television is in a dialogical network (Leudar et al. 2004) with the Bush administration's representation of the 'war on terror.' Al Jazeera was established in 1996, with the help of Sheik Hamad bin Khalifa Al Thani, Qatar's British-trained emir. Hamad, interested in introducing democratic reforms in Qatar, provided the financial backing for Al Jazeera throughout the first five years of its existence. Both popular and controversial, Al Jazeera provides an Arab–Islamic perspective on regional and world events, much as CNN provides an American perspective (Schulthies and Boum 2007: 147). Al Jazeera's importance in the global media's dialogical network is underscored by its launching of an English-language website, and, more recently, by the affiliated Al Jazeera English broadcast station. Although Al Jazeera's primary audience consists of Arabic speakers in the Middle East, the broadcast station engages directly with discourse emanating from American and European contexts, often by providing direct responses to, or discussion on, statements made by President Bush in the American media.

In their study, Schulthies and Boum (2007) draw from two programs featured on Al Jazeera: *min washington* ("From Washington") and *al-sharī'a wa al-hayāt* ("Islamic Law and Life"). In particular, *min washington* offers an important glimpse on the way the Bush administration's discourse about terrorism is taken up and reshaped by social actors in the Middle East. This Arabic-language program, which broadcasts from Washington, DC, focuses on American policy that impacts the Middle East. Discussions are often framed with clips from President Bush's speeches. Thus the insertion of the American president's words into the show is part of the global speech chain that amplifies and multiplies the Bush administration's discourse worldwide (Leudar et al. 2004: 245, 251). Although Bush himself has never appeared on the show, his words "are appropriated and then debated by third party representatives or critics" (Schulthies and Boum 2007: 147). As the show's participants recontextualize these words, the discourse from Washington is refracted and reshaped through the lens of a cultural position decidedly different from the American perspective. As Schulthies and Boum (2007) emphasize in discussing the global dialogic context, "Al-Jazeera, and specifically *min washington*, is an intersecting node of ideas, images, people, and voices that is constantly being negotiated and reshaped in the dialogic interchange between circulating cultures: Western, Arab, Islamic, American, Arab Nationalist, Secularist, Qatari, Israeli" (p. 154).

Notably, the key phrase forwarded by Bush in the wake of 9/11 to characterize America's response to terrorism, 'war on terror,' is represented on *min washington* not as *harb al-irhab*, 'war on terror,' but rather as *mukafaha al-irhab*, 'terrorism battle' or 'struggle' (Schulthies and Boum 2007: 154). As critical linguists have widely pointed out, language use is never neutral. The metaphorical characterization of the struggle against terrorism as a war carries certain ideological attachments. As Fairclough notes, "Different metaphors imply different ways of dealing with things: one does not arrive at a negotiated settlement with cancer, though one might with an opponent in an argument. Cancer has to be eliminated, cut out" (Fairclough 1989: 120). The Bush administration's conceptualization of America's response to terrorism as a 'war on terror' is a discursive achievement that forwards a set of assumptions on how to deal with terrorism – namely by engaging in real wars in Afghanistan and Iraq (Hodges 2008). The alternative designation on *min washington* reshapes the Bush administration's metaphor for Middle Eastern discussants. It lessens the militaristic connotations associated with a war and characterizes the situation as a struggle.

Also on *min Washington*, the word 'terrorist' is qualified as the 'so-called terrorist,' *'ma yusama bil-irhab*. Schulthies and Boum (2007) explain that this tactic provides distance "from the meaning this term has accrued in Western contexts by visualizing it in quotes, while at the same time indicating [the speaker's] epistemic stance toward the truth-value of its usage by others" (p. 154). In my own focus group interviews with politically involved college students in the USA about terrorism and war, I have found similar tactics used by critics of the Bush administration when they cannot help but use a phrase in widespread circulation (for instance the 'war on terror') despite their non-acceptance of its validity (Hodges 2008). In these discussions, several critics of the Bush administration's policy put the 'war on terror' in verbal quote marks. One participant, for example, remarked for my audio-recorder that he was using (in his own words) "the little finger quotes thing" to qualify the phrase. These verbal scare quotes achieve the same effect as the marker 'so-called.' Critical voices within American media discourse, such as Anderson Cooper on CNN or Amy Goodman on the independent radio program Democracy Now, also use the 'so-called' marker to qualify the Bush administration's phrase and challenge the 'war on terror' designation. In contrast to these discursive contestations of what might be termed the dominant discourse, the website of Fox News – a media outlet that is generally supportive of the Bush administration's ideological position – represents the 'war on terror' in its reportage, orthographically, with capital letters, as the War on Terror. The turning of the 'war on terror' into a proper name through the stylistics of capitalization legitimizes the concept. Whereas this capitalization of the War on Terror on FoxNews.com represents one end of the ideological spectrum, the use of the phrase 'the so-called war on terror' by critical voices like Amy Goodman represents the other end. As discourse is recontextualized in different milieux, it can be reshaped in ways such as these to challenge dominant understandings (Hodges 2008).

As Schulthies and Boum point out, the participants on *min washington* "use words that reflect the meanings of previous uses and contexts and yet each new use alters the meaning" (2007: 154). The concept of indexicality is useful for understanding this ongoing dialogic process of meaning-making. As developed by Charles Peirce (1932) and further refined by Silverstein (1976, 1985, inter alia), Ochs (1992, inter alia), and others, indexicality "is the semiotic operation of juxtaposition" (Bucholtz and Hall 2004: 378) whereby contiguity is established between a sign and its meaning. Bauman (2005: 145) reminds us that "Bakhtin's abiding concern was with dimensions and dynamics of speech indexicality – ways that the now-said reaches back to and somehow incorporates or resonates with the already-said and reaches ahead to, anticipates, and somehow incorporates the to-be-said." While the indexical associations between words and their contextual significance may draw on already established meanings – what Silverstein (2003) terms "presupposed indexicality" – new indexical links may also be created – what Silverstein calls "creative or entailed indexicality." In other words, the non-denotational social meanings associated with a text are both partly pre-established and partly recalibrated when that text is brought into a new setting. In this way, as words – for example the key phrase 'war on terror,' or the label 'terrorists' – are presented and re-presented across differing contexts, social actors draw upon the use of those words in prior contexts as well as on their refraction in the current context, to arrive at larger social meanings. As Schulthies and Boum (2007) illustrate, the struggle over the meaning of words used to discuss political issues is subject to this ongoing dialogic revision.

The negotiation of meaning sometimes takes place at a metadiscursive level. For example, Schulthies and Boum (2007) point to the discursive struggle over the definitions and meanings of *al-irhab* ('terrorism') and *al-jihad* ('jihad') on Al Jazeera. The designation *'ma yusama bil-irhab*, 'so-called terrorist,' discussed earlier, points to the problematic nature of characterizing the concept of terrorism and of establishing who constitutes a terrorist. In debating the distinction between 'terrorism,' 'martyrdom,' and 'resistance,' the guests on *min washington* call into question the manner of applying 'terrorism' in the global discourse dominated by the American 'war on terror.' In one exchange, reproduced below, the host (Al-Mirazi) and a guest (Musa) extend the notion of terrorism to actions conducted by state actors. That is, whereas the concept of terrorism has traditionally been used to refer to actions carried out by non-state organizations (for instance al Qaeda or Hamas), they agree to expand the term so as to make it include similarly destructive actions carried out by the governments of nation–states.

AL-MIRAZI: In other words, then, if a bombing of a bus occurs, whether a Palestinian or non-Palestinian blows it up, or civilians and innocents are killed in a residence, whether with an F16 plane or even a hand grenade, this is terrorism. Is there agreement on this?

MUSA: Everything that harms civilians and targets civilians is terrorism, [whether] it is undertaken by a state or an organization, this … (*min washington* episode aired on July 22, 2004, cited in Schulthies and Boum 2007: 155)

As Schulthies and Boum point out, exchanges such as this one illustrate the collaborative nature of meaning construction. The show's participants jointly endeavor to "move away from unequivocal designations" and bring more nuanced understandings to the meaning of terrorism (2007: 155). As participants on these Al Jazeera programs dialogically respond to the discourse about terrorism emanating from Washington, they revise the meanings found in the Bush administration's representation of the issue. In short, they reshape the discourse to give it meaning within their own cultural context.

Construction of the Terrorist 'Enemy' through Their Own Words

As Leudar and colleagues (2004: 245) note in their discussion of dialogical networks, "even the talk of enemies is intricately networked." Notably, the words of an 'enemy' can be integral to the construction of the binary relation between 'us' and 'them' in times of war. In this way, the global circulation of discourse plays into the tactic of distinction involved in the construction of identities (Bucholtz and Hall 2004). In the 'war on terror' discourse, Bush builds a narrative that details the terrorist threat embodied in the personage of Osama bin Laden and in his al Qaeda network. In the narrative, Bush often draws upon the words of bin Laden himself to construct a representation of the 'enemy.' The numerous tapes released by bin Laden, which are broadcast on Al Jazeera and translated into English for global consumption, provide not only a dialogic retort to Bush's discourse, but also fodder for Bush's representation of bin Laden. Therefore the dialogic connections between Bush and bin Laden through the global media produce what Stocchetti (2007) refers to as mutually constitutive identities. That is, "each of the antagonists depends on the other for the legitimacy of its [*sic*] own actions" (Stocchetti 2007: 237). Bush depends upon bin Laden and bin Laden depends upon Bush as they weave their narratives about the 'war on terror.'

As Buttny (1997) and Buttny and Williams (2000) point out, reporting the words of others is often done in order to construct representations of those who are quoted. In his speeches, Bush makes good use of quotations to build a picture of the terrorists against which the United States is fighting in the 'war on terror.' The examples that follow are taken from a speech delivered by Bush on September 5, 2006. In the speech, he focuses on, as he describes, "the terrorists' own words, what they believe, what they hope to accomplish, and how they intend to accomplish it" (Bush 2006). Through the use of reported speech frames, he contextualizes and metapragmatically evaluates the prior discourse attributed to the 'enemy,' to remind Americans: "Five years after our nation was attacked, the terrorist danger remains. We're a nation at war" (ibid.). Bush's discursive construction of this "terrorist danger" squares firmly with his administration's aims in the 'war on terror' and provides justification for his administration's militarized foreign policy.

A great deal of discursive work in Bush's speech is dedicated to building a case for the seriousness of the terrorist threat and to backing up that case with strong evidence. Knowledge must be distinguished from mere belief or opinion in presenting this case. Bush therefore works to present 'facts' to back up the truth claims he forwards. As seen in the extracts that follow, he emphasizes the source of this evidence, which validates what "we know."

> We know what the terrorists intend to do because they've told us, and we need to take their words seriously. (Bush 2006)

> We know this because al Qaeda has told us. (Ibid.)

Reported speech works toward providing evidence and corroborating accounts (Hill and Irvine 1993). The belief in the objectivity of quoted words lends much of the corroborative power of reported speech. In his analysis of courtroom discourse, for example, Matoesian (2000) shows how the referential function of language (on which see Silverstein 1976 and 1979) is privileged. As a result, reported speech is treated as the transparent conveyor of the meaning of prior words (see also Blommaert 2005: 185ff. on the "ideology of a fixed text," and Álvarez-Cáccamo 1996: 55 on the verisimilitude of reported speech). By repeatedly emphasizing that the information he lays out is known "because al Qaeda has told us," Bush sets up an authoritative source, to offer outside corroboration for his depiction of the 'enemy.' In the courtroom, the words of a defendant can be the most damning evidence against him. Likewise, one need not merely believe Bush, the implied reasoning goes, but "hear the words of Osama bin Laden," as Bush emphasizes in the extracts that follow.

> They reject the possibility of peaceful coexistence with the free world. Again, *hear the words of Osama bin Laden* earlier this year, "Death is better than living on this Earth with the unbelievers among us." (Bush 2006)

> Despite these strategic setbacks, the enemy will continue to fight freedom's advance in Iraq, because they understand the stakes in this war. Again, *hear the words of bin Laden*, in a message to the American people earlier this year. He says, "The war is for you or for us to win. If we win it, it means your defeat and disgrace forever." (Ibid.)

> But they've made clear that the most important front in their struggle against America is Iraq, the nation bin Laden has declared the "capital of the Caliphate." *Hear the words of bin Laden*, "I now address the whole Islamic nation. Listen and understand. The most serious issue today for the whole world is this Third World War that is raging in Iraq." He calls it "a war of destiny between infidelity and Islam." He says, "The whole world is watching this war," and that it will end in "victory and glory, or misery and humiliation." For al Qaeda, Iraq is not a distraction from their war on

America. It is the central battlefield where the outcome of this struggle will be decided. (Ibid.)

In these extracts, the reported speech attributed to bin Laden does more to convey Bush's perspective on the world than anything else. The "words of bin Laden" effectively forward several key tenets of Bush's own narrative about the 'war on terror.' Namely, Bush reinforces the notion that Iraq is "the central battlefield" of the 'war on terror.' In other speeches, Bush makes ubiquitous reference to Iraq as the "central front in the war on terror" (Hodges 2008). The conflation of the war in Iraq with the struggle against al Qaeda has perhaps become one of the most contested elements of Bush's 'war on terror' narrative. Under dialogic pressure from administration critics and from the American public, Bush attempts here to solidify the notion that the war in Iraq is part and parcel of the 'war on terror.' Rather than mere belief or opinion, Bush discursively positions his claims about the connection between Iraq and al Qaeda as an objectively verifiable 'truth.' The direct quotations of bin Laden's words provide evidence to back up Bush's assertion. Bin Laden's words therefore work to authenticate Bush's perspective from a position seemingly untainted by his own ideological bias.

As Sacks (1992) points out, the reported speech frame works to convey to listeners "how to read what they're being told" (p. 274). Through metapragmatic comments that accompany the direct quotations from bin Laden, Bush works to "assimilate, rework, and re-accentuate" those words (Bakhtin 1986: 89). In short, he reshapes the words through his own interpretive lens. In introducing the enemy's words, Bush notes that "they've made clear that the most important front in their struggle against America is Iraq." After he cites several direct quotations from bin Laden, Bush concludes with another evaluation of the quoted words, "For al Qaeda, Iraq is not a distraction from their war on America. It is the central battlefield where the outcome of this struggle will be decided." Not surprisingly, the evaluations that frame the reported speech mirror directly Bush's own claims. Where Bush recognizes Iraq as the "central front in the war on terror," we are told that bin Laden affirms this vision of reality. This view, however, is not presented as Bush's personal belief, but as a view that holds "for al Qaeda." Through the words of bin Laden, Bush therefore provides his own dialogical retort to administration critics who see the war in Iraq as a 'distraction' from the struggle against al Qaeda.

Bush reinforces the notion of objectivity in his depiction of the 'enemy' in the extract that follows.

Now, I know some of our country hear the terrorists' words, and hope that they will not, or cannot, do what they say. History teaches that underestimating the words of evil and ambitious men is a terrible mistake. In the early 1900s, an exiled lawyer in Europe published a pamphlet called "What Is To Be Done?" in which he laid out his plan to launch a communist revolution in Russia. The world did not heed Lenin's words, and paid a terrible price. The Soviet Empire he established killed tens of millions, and brought the world to the brink of thermonuclear war. In the 1920s, a failed Austrian painter published a book in which he explained his intention to build an

Aryan super-state in Germany and take revenge on Europe and eradicate the Jews. The world ignored Hitler's words, and paid a terrible price. His Nazi regime killed millions in the gas chambers, and set the world aflame in war, before it was finally defeated at a terrible cost in lives. Bin Laden and his terrorist allies have made their intentions as clear as Lenin and Hitler before them. The question is will we listen? Will we pay attention to what these evil men say? (Bush 2006)

The comparisons in this extract are represented not as interpretations provided by the narrator but as lessons that "history teaches," and as events that were foretold in the "words" of the protagonists named in those lessons (Lenin, Hitler, and bin Laden). In his examination of the discursive construction of reality, Potter discusses how the personification of facts in descriptions obscures "the work of interpretation and construction done by the description's producer" (Potter 1996: 158). Here the personification of history gives history an agency its own, to "teach" us lessons. Rather than Bush discursively positioning himself as the teacher, "history teaches," and the historical facts that follow "do their own showing" (ibid.). The expression "history teaches" works to remove the narrator's own subject position as a historical interpreter. Bush, as a politician, could be accused of drawing biased interpretations; but the lessons that "history teaches" provide an air of objectivity.

As Bush builds an image of the terrorists as "evil men," he juxtaposes the "terrorists' words" with those of the nation's historical enemies – namely Lenin and Hitler. Bush sets up an historical analogy, so that the current threat posed by bin Laden's al Qaeda appears to be analogous to the threat posed by Lenin's Communist Russia and Hitler's Nazi Germany. In what Bucholtz and Hall (2004) would term the "adequation" of these disparate figures from the canon of American history, "potentially salient differences are set aside in favor of perceived or asserted similarities that are taken to be more situationally relevant" (383). Bush constructs a rogues gallery of personages who are linked together through their embodiment of "evil." Importantly, Bush does not merely present this depiction as his own interpretation; he constructs it rather through "what these evil men say" – through their own words. In a rhetorical question posed to the American people, Bush implores, "Will we pay attention to what these evil men say?"

As Bakhtin (1986) notes, others' "utterances can be repeated with varying degrees of reinterpretation" (p. 91). In constructing the 'Other' in the 'war on terror,' Bush draws on bin Laden's words, but replaces the accounts and motives behind those words with his own interpretations. The recontextualization of bin Laden's words within the framework of Bush's speech allows Bush to supply his own preferred reading of those words and to reshape them so as to help justify his administration's 'war on terror' and war in Iraq.

Conclusion

In this chapter I have presented three case studies that illustrate the dialogic connections involved in the global interchange of ideas about terrorism and about the 'war on terror.' An underlying premise of much of the chapter has been the prominent position of the Bush administration's representation of terrorism in the global media's dialogical network. In a sense, the Bush administration's voice from Washington establishes a dominant, hegemonic discourse in global talk about war and terror. Yet, as Williams (1977: 133) notes, "[t]he reality of any hegemony, in the extended political and cultural sense, is that, while by definition it is always dominant, it is never either total or exclusive." The examination of the 'war on terror' discourse in this chapter has therefore focused on the fluidity and malleability of this discourse as it enters into a web of dialogic interconnections. Rather than being a matter of cultural hegemony and imposition in a world of global discourse flows, the 'war on terror' discourse is subject to what Appadurai (1990) terms "indigenization," as it enters into different cultural milieux, where it is adapted according to local experiences and aims. While the power of the Bush administration's voice in world affairs may be to establish an agenda and to provide a macro-level discourse for talking about war and terror, how that discourse is taken up and rearticulated can only be understood by examining the way it enters local contexts of interaction.

As Bakhtin (1981) notes, "in real life people talk most of all about what others talk about – they transmit, recall, weigh and pass judgment on other people's words, opinions, assertions, information; people are upset by others' words, or agree with them, contest them, refer to them and so forth" (p. 338). In global talk of war and terror, it is difficult even for critics and opponents of the Bush administration's foreign policy to avoid the language of the 'war on terror.' As seen in the case study of Al Jazeera, resistance to the terms and actions associated with the American 'war on terror' begins by reanimating its language. As Al Jazeera commentators respond to the discourse from Washington, they reshape it. As seen in the case study from Serbia, more sympathetic voices can also be seen reworking an influential discourse in line with their own aims. Insofar as the young Serbs interviewed by Volcic and Erjavec side with the Bush administration's vision of the world, they still rework the language of the 'war on terror' in line with their own nationalistic aims. And, as seen in the analysis of Bush's own speech, even the 'dominant' perspective is itself stitched together from the words of other actors involved in the global interchange about war and terror. The dialogic connections in the global interchange about war and terror provide a common framework that allows social actors to discuss and debate the topic. Even as social actors resist the discourse or put it to different aims, they must appropriate its language if they are to be listened to and understood. It is through this agentive act of speaking that social actors make a discourse "vulnerable to unpredictable futures" and open to "the possibility of resignification" (Inoue 2006: 21). As they speak within the 'war on terror' discourse, the possibilities for reshaping it are not always foreseen or consciously pursued. Nevertheless, the possibilities are there.

As was posed in the introduction: to what extent do the dialogic connections involved in global interchange about war and terror impact the way war is justified and understood around the world? This chapter has suggested that the answer lies in the close examination of global discourse flows as they are taken up and reshaped in local contexts, since it is in these contexts that meanings are ultimately worked out.

ACKNOWLEDGMENTS

I owe special thanks to Chad Nilep for feedback on earlier versions of this chapter. Moreover, this chapter could not have taken shape without the thoughtful input of Nikolas Coupland. Any shortcomings that remain are my sole responsibility.

REFERENCES

Agha, A. (2003) The social life of cultural value. *Language and Communication* 23: 231–73.

Alim, H. S., and Pennycook, A. (2007) Glocal linguistic flows: Hip-hop culture(s), identities, and the politics of language education. *Journal of Language, Identity, and Education* 6(2): 80–100.

Álvarez-Cáccamo, C. (1996) The power of reflexive language(s): Code displacement in reported speech. *Journal of Pragmatics* 25: 33–59.

Appadurai, A. (1990) Disjuncture and difference in the global cultural economy. *Theory, Culture and Society* 7: 295–310.

Appadurai, A. (1996) *Modernity at Large: Cultural Dimensions of Globalization*. Minneapolis: University of Minnesota Press.

Appadurai, A. (2001) Grassroots globalization and the research imagination. In A. Appadurai (ed.), *Globalization*, 1–21. Durham, NC: Duke University Press.

Bakhtin, M. (1981) *The Dialogic Imagination: Four Essays*, edited by M. Holquist, translated by C. Emerson and M. Holquist. Austin: University of Texas Press.

Bakhtin, M. (1986) *Speech Genres and Other Late Essays*, edited by C. Emerson and

M. Holquist, translated by V. W. McGee. Austin: University of Texas Press.

Bauman, R. (2005) Commentary: Indirect indexicality, identity, performance: Dialogic observations. *Journal of Linguistic Anthropology* 15(1): 145–50.

Bauman, R., and Briggs, C. L. (1990) Poetics and performance as critical perspectives on language and social life. *Annual Review of Anthropology* 19: 59–88.

Becker, A. L. (1995) *Beyond Translation: Essays Towards a Modern Philology*. Ann Arbor: University of Michigan Press.

Blommaert, J. (2005) *Discourse: A Critical Introduction*. Cambridge: Cambridge University Press.

Blommaert, J. (2008) Bernstein and poetics revisited: Voice, globalization and education. *Discourse and Society* 19(4): 425–52.

Briggs, C., and Bauman, R. (1992) Genre, intertextuality, and social power. *Journal of Linguistic Anthropology* 2(2): 131–72.

Bucholtz, M., and Hall, K. (2004) Language and identity. In A. Duranti (ed.), *A Companion to Linguistic Anthropology*, 369–94. Malden, MA: Blackwell.

Bucholtz, M., and Hall, K. (2008) All of the above: New coalitions in sociocultural linguistics. *Journal of Sociolinguistics* 12(4): 401–31.

Bush, G. W. (2005) Speech at Bolling Air Force Base, Washington, DC. October 25. Available at: http://www.whitehouse.gov/news/releases/2005/10/20051025.html.

Bush, G. W. (2006) Speech at Capital Hilton Hotel, Washington, DC. September 5. Available at: http://www.whitehouse.gov/news/releases/2006/09/20060905-4.html.

Buttny, R. (1997) Reported speech in talking race on campus. *Human Communication Research* 23(4): 477–506.

Buttny, R., and Williams, P. L. (2000) Demanding respect: The uses of reported speech in discursive constructions of interracial contact. *Discourse and Society* 11(1): 109–33.

Coupland, N. (2007) *Style: Language Variation and Identity*. Cambridge, UK: Cambridge University Press.

Erjavec, K., and Volcic, Z. (2007) 'War on terrorism' as a discursive battleground: Serbian recontextualization of G. W. Bush's discourse. *Discourse and Society* 18(2): 123–37.

Fairclough, N. (1989) *Language and Power*. London: Longman.

Fairclough, N. (2006) *Language and Globalization*. London: Routledge.

Hill, J., and Irvine, J. (1993) *Responsibility and Evidence in Oral Discourse*. Cambridge: Cambridge University Press.

Hodges, A. (2008) *The 'War on Terror' Discourse: The (Inter)Textual Construction and Contestation of Sociopolitical Reality*. Unpublished PhD Dissertation, University of Colorado at Boulder.

Hodges, A., and Nilep, C. (eds) (2007), *Discourse, War and Terrorism*. Amsterdam: John Benjamins.

Inoue, M. (2006) *Vicarious Language: Gender and Linguistic Modernity in Japan*. Berkeley: University of California Press.

Irvine, J., and Gal, S. (2000) Language ideology and linguistic differentiation. In P. Kroskrity (ed.), *Regimes of Language*,

35–84. Santa Fe: School of American Research.

Karim, K. H. (1997) The historical resilience of primary stereotypes: Core images of the muslim other. In S. H. Riggins (ed.), *The Language and Politics of Exclusion: Others in Discourse*, 153–82. Thousand Oaks, CA: Sage.

Kristeva, J. (1980) *Desire in Language: A Semiotic Approach to Literature and Art*, edited by L. S. Roudiez, translated by T. Gora, A. Jardine, and L. S. Roudie. New York: Columbia University Press.

Leudar, I., Marsland, V., and Nekvapil, J. (2004) On membership categorization: 'Us,' 'them' and 'doing violence' in political discourse. *Discourse and Society* 15(2–3): 243–66.

Matoesian, G. (2000) Intertextual authority in reported speech: Production media in the Kennedy Smith rape trial. *Journal of Pragmatics* 32: 879–914.

Morson, G. S., and Emerson, C. (1990) *Mikhail Bakhtin: Creation of Proaics*. Palo Alto, CA: Stanford University Press.

Nekvapil, J., and Leudar, I. (2002) On dialogical networks: Arguments about the migration law in Czech mass media in 1993. In *Language, Interaction and National Identity*, Stephen Hester and William Housley (eds), 60–101. Burlington, VT: Ashgate Publishing Company.

Ochs, E. (1992) Indexing gender. In A. Duranti and C. Goodwin (eds), *Rethinking Context: Language as Interactive Phenomenon*, 335–8. Cambridge: Cambridge University Press.

Peirce, C. (1932) *Collected papers of Charles Sanders Peirce*, edited by C. Hartshorne and P. Weiss. Cambridge, MA: Harvard University Press.

Pennycook, A. (2003) Global englishes, rip slyme, and peformativity. *Journal of Sociolinguistics* 7: 513–33.

Pennycook, A. (2007) *Global Englishes and Transcultural Flows*. London: Routledge.

Piller, I. (2001) Identity constructions in multilingual advertising. *Language in Society* 30(2): 153–86.

Potter, J. (1996) *Representing Reality: Discourse, Rhetoric and Social Construction.* London: Sage.

Rampton, B. (1995) *Crossing: Language and Ethnicity among Adolescents.* London and New York: Longman.

Rampton, B. (2006) *Language in Late Modernity.* Cambridge: Cambridge University Press.

Sacks, H. (1992) *Lectures on Conversation.* Cambridge: Blackwell.

Sarkar, M., and Allen, D. (2007) Hybrid identities in Quebec hip-hop: Language, territory, and ethnicity in the mix. *Journal of Language, Identity, and Education* 6(2): 117–30.

Said, E. (1978) *Orientalism.* New York: Pantheon.

Said, E. (1997) *Covering Islam.* New York: Vintage Books.

Schulthies, B., and Boum, A. (2007) 'Martyrs and terrorists, resistance and insurgency': Contextualizing the exchange of terrorism discourses on Al-Jazeera. In Hodges and Nilep (eds), 143–60.

Silverstein, M. (1976) Shifters, linguistic categories, and cultural description. In K. Basso and H. Selby (eds), *Meaning in Anthropology*, 11–55. Albuquerque: University of New Mexico Press.

Silverstein, M. (1979) Language structure and linguistic ideology. In P. R. Clyne, W. F. Hanks, and C. L. Hofbauer (eds), *The Elements: A Parasession on Linguistic Units and Levels*, 193–247. Chicago: Chicago Linguistic Society.

Silverstein, M. (1985) Language and the culture of gender: At the intersection of structure, usage, and ideology. In *Semiotic Mediation: Sociocultural and Psychological Perspectives*, E. Mertz and R. J. Parmentier (eds), 219–59. Orlando: Academic Press.

Silverstein, M. (2003) Indexical order and the dialectics of sociolinguistic life. *Language and Communication* 23: 193–229.

Silverstein, M., and Urban, G. (eds) (1996) *Natural Histories of Discourse.* Chicago: University of Chicago Press.

Spitulnik, D. (2001) The social circulation of media discourse and the mediation of communities. In A. Duranti (ed.), *Linguistic Anthropology: A Reader*, 95–118. Malden, MA: Blackwell.

Stocchetti, M. (2007) The politics of fear: A critical inquiry into the role of violence in 21st century politics. In Hodges and Nilep (eds), 223–41.

Tannen, D. (1989) *Talking Voices: Repetition, Dialogue, and Imagery in Conversational Discourse.* New York: Cambridge University Press.

Tishkov, V. (2004) *Chechnya: Life in a War-Torn Society.* San Francisco: University of California Press.

Volcic, Z., and Erjavec, K. (2007) Discourse of war and terrorism in Serbia: 'We were fighting the terrorists already in Bosnia …' " In Hodges and Nilep (eds), 185–204.

Voloshinov, V. N. (1971) Reported speech. In L. Matejka and K. Promorska (eds), *Readings in Russian Poetics: Formalist and Structuralist Views*, 149–75. Cambridge, MA: MIT Press.

Voloshinov, V. N. (1973) *Marxism and the Philosophy of Language*, translated by L. Matejka and I. R. Titunik. New York: Seminar Press.

Williams, R. (1977) *Marxism and Literature.* Oxford: Oxford University Press.

14 Has God Gone Global? Religion, Language, and Globalization

ANNABELLE MOONEY

In the beginning was the Word, and the Word was with God, and the Word was God.

John 1:1 (King James' Bible)

Placing the study of religion within the context of language and globalization is a multi-faceted task. The body of relevant work is diverse and comes from a variety of areas. There has been significant work in the field of linguistics and religion, for example on sociolinguistic engagement (Webster 1988; Szuchewycz 1994), on the ethnography of language (Bauman 1989), on theo-linguistics (Crystal 1965, 1966; van Noppen 1995, 2006), and on the sociology of language and religion (Omoniyi and Fishman 2006). However, it is only in other disciplines that there has been an explicit engagement with globalization. The attention given to this area in the media (Mitchell and Marriage 2003), mass communication (Stout and Buddenbaum 1996), and sociology (Kurtz 1995) is valuable in that it may help to guide and frame future work in linguistics by providing context, organization information, and theoretical schemata. In this chapter I suggest and outline four emerging areas which may be of particular interest to linguists.

The importance of linguistics in understanding religion has long been recognized. Crystal's early work (1965) can be seen as the starting point for theo-linguistics, a field which did not have a name until more than ten years later. Research in the field covered the stylistics – in its full linguistic sense – of religious language, as well as the social situatedness of language in religion – which included context, register, and genre and extended to debates about language in particular religions, especially with respect to sacred texts, their translation, and altering their register to bring it 'up to date.' Moreover, dealing with religious texts (spoken and written) will always have to address the status of particular languages in particular religions. Thus the status of Arabic in Islam (on which see Suleiman 2004 and Miller 2008), or that of Hebrew in Judaism, are examples of the sacred relationships between language and religion. Not all denominations have singular relationships with language, and this will naturally have an effect

The Handbook of Language and Globalization, First Edition. Edited by Nikolas Coupland.

on the spread of both. These relationships are also subject to shift. Fishman notes that "in premodern times […] there was no 'commandment' to speak or safeguard (or even pray in) Hebrew" (2001: 179). Some changes are more recent; Turner for instance notes: "While Arabic retains its orthodox authority, the Islamic masses are encountering religion in their native languages often for the first time" (2007: 133; see also Eickelman and Piscatori 1996).

The spread of religion is intimately bound up with the spread of language. As is well known, the move to the vernacular in Christianity opened up sacred texts to lay populations and "ended the interpretative monopoly of the institutional church" (O'Leary 1996: 785). Thus the link between religion and language contact is important (Spolsky 2003). Missionaries, for example, are able to convert the linguistic and religious 'Other,' and often also to influence local language development (through the development of orthographies, for example). Close connections between language and liturgy persist, and may be found not only in religions with a particular language allegiance, but also where language and religion are used as central tools in the construction and maintenance of ethnicity and national identity (Omoniyi and Fishman 2006; Rosowsky 2008). This may occur in many ways, from preserving community languages through religion (Woods 2004) to constructing and projecting identity by retaining traditional practices in the choice of personal names (Jayaraman 2005: 476).

Despite the importance of the local, religion has always had an international – or even global – face, if only because religion pre-exists the very concept of nation (see Yates 2002: 70). If we take the global face of religion as a prompt, it is possible to see economic globalization in terms of what, traditionally, counts as theological or religious categories. On such a reading, neo-liberalism becomes the religion; discourses of economic free trade, democratization, and human rights become the dogma; and the developed world becomes the missionary force, which sends institutional representatives to spread the good global word.

> In the words of Salomon Nahmad of the National Indigenist Institute of Mexico, "Those [mobile] Americans are the Franciscans and the Dominicans of our time. They may not see it that way, but they are the religious arm of an economic, political, and cultural system." (Yates 2002: 89)

At the same time it is important to remember that flows in the global world do not move in only one way. Crucially, religion is also an important resource for the oppressed (Hatem 2006). In all cases, 'traditional' identity categories should also be explored. It is essential, for example, for gender to be central in analysis (see Jule 2005), especially because this feature can be linked (either in a theoretical or in an activist mode) to feminism, which is an important and positive global force (Walby 2002).

In the same way in which 'globalization' is a contested or, at least, polysemic term, 'religion' is multifaceted. In what follows I conceive of religion broadly, so as to include: self-identifying communities already recognized as 'religions' (for example Christianity, Islam, or Judaism) as well as less accepted ones (new religious movements or New Age groups); religion as cultural practice, distinct from formal membership and worship; religion as ideology, especially of the kind deployed in political contexts; and commitment to religion as a central element in conceptions of identity. Certainly these aspects are not mutually exclusive; and, in order to take proper account of the existing work and the emerging opportunities in the field, it is necessary to have a broad conception of religion. This means, of course, that the present chapter cannot be exhaustive.

The forthcoming linguistic analysis is largely discourse analysis. This is not to suggest that other kinds of analysis are impossible or unproductive. Rather, in trying to describe the four strands I identify below, uncovering ideology through discourse analysis is an economic way forward. As well as being amenable to analysis, each piece of data presented here will serve to provide material from the area under discussion and thus to furnish context. Further, the field of globalization invites an ideological examination of discourses. Regarding religion, Heather argues that "Christ sometimes in effect practises CDA [critical discourse analysis]" (2008: 472). Moreover, in general, religious affiliation is directly related to textual affiliation. The texts, practices, interpretations, and hermeneutic systems that are considered sacred are determined by the religious group one belongs to. Naturally, the syntactic and phonetic levels of these texts are amenable to linguistic and hermeneutic analysis. However, the shibboleth is more often at the level of discourse and ideology than at the level of the phoneme.

Arguments that globalization is merely a new phase of imperialism and colonization are common in globalization literature and in popular opinion. This position is based on evidence to the effect that the flow of cultural and material goods runs largely from the North to the South – which is positive for the North but not always for the South. While flows of religion from the East to the West have received attention, especially because of fears of fundamentalism, little attention has been paid to the influence of the global South, notably on Christian denominations. The influence of the global South will be addressed first, and particular arguments, both from the North and from the South, will be examined concerning this influence. In the next section I turn to one of the richest areas of research: that of hybridity, relocalization and re-territorialization. This strand is most apparent in the attention accorded by researchers to popular music and to its transformation and use by religious groups. Hybridity is also evident in the dual spread of language and religion. Here communicative function, genre, and speech act theory are directly relevant. Given the wide variety of texts that are hybridized, multi-modal analysis is also appropriate. The values which language, genres, and styles signal are important here, especially in the 'missionary' TESOL material examined in this section. The third section examines the opportunities that technology, especially the internet, has provided for religion. Just as the internet and television are used by established religions to connect with their members and to recruit new ones, virtual spaces create new possibilities for ways of thinking and communicating about religion, as well as new ways of practicing and creating it. Thus, the speech community needs to be considered in this new context. This area also offers a rich scope for concepts such as communities of practice, ethnography of communication, and conversation analysis. As for the fourth section, given that one of the paradigmatic emblems of globalization is neo-liberal capitalism, it is important to track some of the incorporation of consumer discourses and practices into religious doctrine and activity. Here Bourdieu's concept of social capital is useful – and most appropriate, in view of the real capital involved. Some well known new religious movements are particularly adept at fusing these domains; however, such practices are not linked only to 'newcomers.' Ideology is central here, as is argument theory, especially when warrants are required for behavior related to wealth accumulation – something which is not normally considered in the religious frame. By way of conclusion, I briefly address the fundamentalism of the new atheism and link it to the challenges that the field holds for linguistics. What needs to be considered, specifically, is the kind of text and identity to which religious experience is often connected.

The Southern Shift

As mentioned, those who understand globalization as a second period of imperialism stake their claims on directionality of flow. Neo-imperialism, neo-colonialisim, McDonaldization (Ritzer 1997) and coca-colonization (Wagnleitner 1994), Westoxification (Juergensmeyer 2005: 136), and even globalatinization (Derrida 1998) are some of the terms used in this broad and diverse area. These views are more nuanced than might first be apparent, and the focus they can give to inequality, poverty, patterns of trade, and ethical dimensions of the global order should not be dismissed. That is to say, 'imperialism' is always locally imposed, realized and resisted. Thus Beyer argues for the importance of glocalization in understanding contemporary religion, while recognizing that a core/periphery, "great tradition"/"little tradition" prevailed in the past (Beyer 2003: 363). He argues that the existence of "globalized localizations at the same time as localized globalizations" means that there is only a "symbolic priority of authenticity or authority" (p. 376): in other words, because of the multiplicity of origins and flows, there can be no prioritization of a singular authority. At the same time authenticity and authority are important concepts, and they are nevertheless deployed.

Far from threatening to colonize religions, localization has often provided new impetus and productive resources for religions colonizing from the North. Perhaps ironically, resistance and reinvention are possible in part because of the "semantic slippage entailed in translation" – namely the translation of sacred texts (where translation is allowed, as some sacred texts are only considered sacred/correct in the original language: Cole 2001: 485) and because of the religions' symbolic vocabulary (Meyer 1999; Rey 2004). This means that religious flows are never unidirectional; rather,

> today continued missionary activity contains important cross-flows and reverse-flows, from previously missionized areas to the European heartlands and to other previously missionized areas. (Beyer 2003: 367–8)

More specifically, James and Shoesmith argue that "the centre of gravity of Christianity is moving from the North to the South and from the West to the East" (2008: 5; see also Yates 2002 and Jenkins 2002). Religious commitment, in global demographic terms, is clearly located in the South. While the Pew Research Centre (2001) reports that religion is more important to people in the US than to people in other "wealthy nations," religion there is still only rated as very important by 59 percent. In African countries, by contrast, values range from 80 percent (Angola) to 97 percent (Senegal). In Asia, too, Indonesia and India rate the importance of religion at over 90 percent (95 and 92 respectively), and the Philippines and Bangladesh follow closely (88 percent for both). It would seem that patterns of conversion and allegiance in world religions such as Christianity and Islam mean that the global 'South' has religious significance, if only in terms of numbers.

I suggest that there is more than a demographic religious influence flowing from the South. Here I take Anglicanism as an example of this shift in flow. While to my knowledge there has not been any recent linguistic work on the topic, an examination of current press material in terms of argument, stylistic choices, and discourse suggests that the importance of the religious South has been recognized, but not always in geographic terms. A comment column in one newspaper conceives of the distinction as between liberal Anglicanism and evangelical orthodoxy. The issue was construed as a game of numbers: "Surely most British Anglicans were committed to gay rights and would not compromise? It seemed axiomatic that the evangelicals were a minority movement – a pushy and growing one, but still a minority" (Hobson 2008: 27). The Pew report figures suggest that, globally, the evangelicals are probably not a minority; but only the British congregation is considered here when the author makes the 'commonsense' claim ("Surely"). Nevertheless, there is a realization that something has changed and that power is involved. "The nature of liberal Anglicanism quietly shifted. It became meek before the rise of evangelical orthodoxy" (ibid.). Here the numerical majority of liberal Anglicans appears to be taken for granted, even though the global picture questions this assumption. Moreover, the distinction made between liberalism and orthodoxy maps onto a North/South distinction.

While Hobson's comment frames the issue largely in terms of a political spectrum, other members of the Anglican church are explicitly religious in their language, adopting traditional militant tropes in areas of conflict. A pressing issue for the church is the discord created by the admission of homosexual clergy. One senior English bishop compares "the consecration of a gay bishop in America to the invasion of Iraq" (quoted in Gledhill and Combe 2008). He then deploys an argument recently used by Bush: "Either the rest of the world caves in or someone has to stand up to them" (ibid.), returning this figure of speech to its original religious field. The argument is conceived of as a holy war (Lakoff and Johnson 1980) with mutually exclusive sides – a clear and false polarization of argument positions. Others, from the South, interpret liberal attitudes in the church as selfish "personal dissent" (rather than theological diversity), which "severs" "the grace of Christ from his moral commandments" (quoted in Gledhill 2005: 16). Thus the global South claims orthodoxy for its collective self, stressing historical continuity, unity, and faithfulness to the Word of God (see Vanguard 2003). This orthodoxy is opposed to personal opinion, taken in isolation from the group and from tradition. The position of the South is, however, consistent with national laws in countries of the global South, where homosexuality is illegal.

The Primates of the Global South are clear in their condemnation of the liberalization of the Anglican church. "The overwhelming majority of the Primates of the Global South cannot and will not recognize the office or ministry of Canon Gene Robinson [American homosexual] as a bishop" (Akinola 2003). This is articulated not as a choice, but as the only possible option; they 'cannot' recognize the decision. Further, they "deplore the act of those bishops who have taken part in the consecration which has now divided the Church in violation of their obligation to guard the faith and unity of the church" (ibid.). This is the voice of southern orthodoxy making claims to truth, unity, and authenticity. The split has left the bishops of the Anglican North in a precarious position. However, the influence of the South is such that the North does not overrule them, but rather becomes "meek before the rise of evangelical orthodoxy" (Hobson 2008: 27). Authenticity is a central concern here. It is one of the recurring themes and core challenges in the field, and I return to it in my conclusion.

Mixing It Up: Hybridity in Form and Function

One of the central analytic terms in language and globalization is hybridity. This is not an altogether new concept in linguistics (see Coupland 2003: 423); however, the specific term which conveys it may offer new opportunities for analyzing language as well as associated visual and material culture (Omoniyi 2006; Shinhee Lee 2007; Pennycook 2003). Certainly hybridity in religion is nothing new. As Stewart (1999) points out, syncretism has always been a part of religion, though distinguishing between the syncretic and the heretic is not straightforward. While some will accept innovative hybrid forms as syncretic, for others, the introduction of new elements will take the hybrid texts and practices outside orthodoxy and into the domain of heresy.

In the field of music, for example, separating the sacred from the secular is a difficult task. From the religious music of the Renaissance to the spiritual lyrics of the later Beatles' work, there has always been exchange, colonization, and communication between the two. In a contemporary frame, James and Shoesmith refer to the "'rock concert' flavour of Hillsong," an Australian Charismatic group attempting to break into Asian popular music markets (2008: 33). Across the globe, Jelbert (2003) reports on the cross-over of Christian pop groups to the mainstream, from "the American rock quartet Evanescence" topping the UK charts to "[t]he Arkansas band's 'Bring Me Life,' a polite slab of heaven metal" appealing to an older demographic. While the British band "Delirious?" was "originally" made up of "the house musicians at a Sussex 'worship session'" (Jelbert 2003), not all music with religious underpinnings originates from formal religious organizations; Nick Cave, Belle and Sebastian, U2, Johnny Cash are, argues Jelbert, not identified as religious, since "such seriousness [of belief] just doesn't go with their image" (ibid.). That is not to say that such seriousness is not retrieved by listeners. U2's Bono has long enjoyed enthusiastic support in Christian circles.

This hybrid religious music is far from conservative; it may even be heard as radical. Howard argues that Contemporary Christian Music (CCM) is committed to "pointing out the contradictions of modern society and rejecting its values and norms" and to challenging "the Church itself to resist conformity to modern society" (1992: 125). Similarly, rap music has been used especially to reach the young, with lucid meta-arguments made about the connections of the music and the lyrical content to scripture (Gooch 1996: 234). These "hybrid" forms, whether hybridized by author or audience, "call into question the artificial boundaries that historically have separated religious and secular styles, their performers, and their audiences" (Maultsby 1992: 32, cited in Gooch 1996: 231; see also Pennycook and Coutand-Marin 2003). This signals, I suggest, a hybridity of communicative function as well as of musical form. While the latter is more or less obvious, in that two musical traditions are brought together and fused, the former depends more on audience and uptake. Naturally, the two are related, although in complex ways. This is clear from Pennycook's discussion of hip hop with Koranic lyrics (2006: 124–5). Thus "British band Fun-Da-Mental's engagement with Islam is 'central to its *multipronged* intervention [...]'" (ibid., p. 124, citing Swedenburg 2001: 62; my emphasis). The multiplicity can be seen in the band's punning name, fusing as it does recreation and entertainment ('Fun-', retrievable most easily in the written form of the name) with religious values, indexed by the full name (and linked with the oral/aural realization of the name). Hybridity is not just about innovation of form, but also about joining traditionally separate communicative domains, so that more than one illocutionary effect is produced.

It is not only in music that such hybridity of form and function occurs. While literacy development and practice is often bound closely to religious instruction (especially where religious institutions are among the few opportunities for literacy), there has also been some concern about the relationship between TESOL and Christianity, the former being portrayed as a missionary arm of the latter – as well as of neo-liberal western values generally (Pennycook and Makoni 2005). While Purgason (2004) rightly cautions against homogenizing either the TESOL or the Christian community, particular texts that can be understood in this frame are worthy of analysis. Indeed there has already been discussion about the cultural and religious values that may accompany English-language teaching, especially in Muslim contexts (Mohd-Asraf 2005). Thus Karmani notes the "astonishing formula that has emerged [...] to promote 'more English, less Islam'" (2005: 263) – a formula which understands English as vehicle for a set of religious and cultural values (see Phillipson 1992). This is clearly a zero-sum game, as Karmani draws attention to imperatives issued by the US government to fight terrorism with English (2005: 263; see also Karmani and Pennycook 2005), thus pointing to an explicit framing of linguistic export as soft power and hybridity in the domain of function as well as in that of form. Such texts and practices need not come from governments, or even from large organizations, as the following example demonstrates.

Soon! is a printed pamphlet/magazine with an online version (www.soon.org. uk), which is formatted differently, although it has similar content. Produced by an evangelical Christian group in Derby, England, it claims to be inter-denominational and not interested in recruiting for any particular religious group (http://www.soon.org.uk/info/who.htm). The magazine is listed on various English-language learning resource websites, and it presents itself as a tool for students of English. But, as its name and explanatory phrases placed next to it indicate, *Soon!* is also a text for a Christian movement. The phrase above the name, at the top of the pamphlet – "things that must happen" – and the phrase beneath it – "helping to make sense of life" – pick up clearly two meanings of 'soon.' It refers both to the advancement in the world facilitated by learning English and to the second coming of the Lord. The cultural capital that may accrue on account of the former meaning is clear when one considers the international audience and circulation network of the pamphlet, which has offices in Asia, eastern Europe, and Africa.

The pamphlet contains explicit tools for learning English – tools in the form of glossaries entitled "Words for English learners" and placed at the end of short news-style stories, or in the form of "Easy English exercise(s)" dealing with homophones and tackling English spelling. While the stories report current events, they are framed in terms of Christian faith and experience. Thus a story entitled "Boris Yeltsin pardons murderer" is in fact an account of how the imprisoned man found God by listening to Russian Christian Radio while he was in prison (*Soon Magazine* 163, n.d.). In addition, a slip that can be returned in exchange for "Free papers and study course" is printed with instructions for "Filling in the coupon" and with samples of letters and numbers, showing clearly how these should be constructed with a single pen stroke and thus providing literacy instruction in a functional domain.

This fusion of the pedagogic with the religious is not uncommon. However, the opportunities that the internet provides for *Soon!* in terms of dissemination are significant. Further, the implications for the spread of English are also worth considering. If English comes to be used in the religious domain, there are consequences for identity construction, for the allegiance to cultural and linguistic values, and for the influence of English as a global language (Crystal 1997; Graddol 1997). Offering valuable cultural capital (in the form of English tuition) in tandem with enculturation into a religious group may be problematic in a number of ways. That is not to say that the internet is an evil force; the virtual world is at least as complex as the real.

Virtually Everywhere

Multi-modality, visual semiotics, and work in computer-mediated communication provide a firm base for linguistics to explore the nuances of religion as it is present in the technology associated with globalization (Herring 1996; LeVine and Scollon 2004). While television has had religious programs for a long time, audiences in the past were confined to countries of origin or nations in which there was linguistic commonality and/or a strong diaspora. Thus US television evangelists (televangelists) had access to markets in the UK, Australia, and North America for the past few decades.

More recently, satellite and cable television, access to programs via the internet, and the advent of virtual reality (VR) spaces such as Second Life have provided a readily accessible global audience. As will be discussed, the religious 'marketplace,' with its commercial and consumerist connotations, is an appropriate label, if only because it captures "the economic logic at the structural heart of the religious field" (Rey 2004: 341). The relationship of religion with commerce and consumption has historical precedent (see McDannell 1995: 12), but continues in different forms. James and Shoesmith, for example, describe the influence of Charismatic evangelism in India. They argue that colonial models of ministry are being displaced by an American model, which thus constitutes a second phase of colonization. In language terms, "[s]eventy-five percent of all programmes are produced in the English language" (James and Shoesmith 2008: 25), which arguably competes with local and national languages in this important domain. Meanwhile other televangelists localize their product. American Joyce Meyer "is heard in seven Indian languages several times a day on Indian television" (ibid., p. 42). Even though the product is adapted, it nevertheless originates in the North.

There is ample evidence of localization for such ministries, especially in respect of mega-churches. The "Fountain of Wisdom Ministries" began in Kano, Nigeria, and now has churches in Ghana, the United States, and the United Kingdom – each with its own presence on the web. The Nigerian homepage is dominated by a large photograph of the founders, "Rev. Kola and Rev. (Mrs) Funke Ewosho" (http://www.wofcc.org/). The British site (http://www.fowm.org/), on the other hand, foregrounds its virtual presence, providing direct links to video on demand, an online shop, an online donation site, as well as a link to the archive of cyber messages. The contrast between the domestic and the digital is clear. Further, on the British site, Rev. Mrs Ewosho is given no title at all, which suggests independence from the marital and religious units. The self-description of the church also differs: the Nigerian site provides a page on "Identity," with an historical account of the church's development, while the British site's equivalent is "Our statement of faith" – a numbered list of doctrinal statements. The kind of community these two sites evoke may thus be conceptualized in terms of prioritizing corporeal versus digital community and narrative versus propositional meaning. Global organizations have local faces, influenced by the direction of flow.

The configuration of flows made possible by the internet means that, while the internet is itself a religious marketplace, it is also "a place rather than just a tool for communication" (Helland 2002: 298). This does not mean that the "tool" itself, the technology, is uninteresting. Karaflogka reports a rumor that monks from the technologically isolated Monastery of Christ in New Mexico (a community with no electricity or phone) designed the Vatican's web page (2002: 281). This suggests possible rich comparisons with writing technology that pre-dates Gutenberg, such as illuminated manuscripts (see O'Leary 1996).

The internet provides even more varied opportunities for religious communication and experience than have hitherto been possible (Wertheim 2000). MacWilliams argues that, unlike radio and television, "the Internet is interactive" and "provides a dynamic multimedia environment for communing with the sacred" (2002: 319). Where exactly the sacred is to be found, and what kind of communion occurs, varies. A distinction which may be useful in coming to terms with this variation is the one between religion online and online religion (Helland 2002; Karaflogka 2002; Maxwell 2002). While religions with a centralized hierarchy and power structure use the internet to disseminate and confirm doctrinal information – religion online, in Helland's terms (2002: 294) – the internet also allows for more active and fluid religious activity (online religion). The former creates a "controlled environment" as it communicates "in a one-to-many" fashion (ibid.). As for the latter, the "form of participation closely mirrors the ideal interactive environment of the web itself and allows for many to many communication" (ibid., p. 294).

When "many to many communication" takes place, it may also be controlled by conventions borrowed from the non-virtual world. Second Life, the largest of the virtual reality domains, gestures towards the religious in its very name (see Hill 2008). Though not limited to religious communities, it does host them. Schroeder, Heather, and Lee (1998) provide important insight into how traditional religious genres are accommodated in the virtual reality environment. The liturgical structure, prayer genres, openings and closings familiar from 'real' services are all transposed into the E-church investigated (one of the first of its kind). One of the services examined "contains much more joking around than real world services [–] not only verbal clowning but also chasing each other around after the service or 'flying' and going through walls and the like" (Schroeder, Heather, and Lee 1998). However, during the service proper "a serious tone is generally maintained," and indeed enforced (ibid.). The conventions of actual churches, in this case at least, are thus translated into the virtual space.

Exciting as it is, and even democratic in the case of online religion, the 'virtual' nature of such spaces is problematic for some. Buchanan compares the efficacy of a virtual church in "provid[ing] nourishment for the soul" to "relying on a wax banana to provide nourishment for your body" (Buchanan 1996). This binary division between the 'real' and the 'virtual' is difficult to maintain, however, given the available evidence on how people 'do religion' on the internet. O'Leary reports that, even though religious gathering spaces may be virtual, members can use "real" objects in their online worship (O'Leary 1996: 799). Further, the 'virtual' may not be as distant from the 'transcendent' as Buchanan's wax banana analogy suggests. Indeed a "virtual prayer" (Karaflogka 2002: 283) may be difficult for a non-believer to distinguish from an "authentic one," inasmuch as prayers are quintessentially personal, interior communications with the divine. The only difference appears to be that the virtual prayer is mediated by technology, and thus more material than an 'ordinary' prayer. It is important to note that some exclude sacraments from the virtual world, as they are considered "personal, even physical, encounters" (Hill 2008).

One might have thought that virtual worship space was typical only of new religious movements, such as the First Church of Cyberspace (Buchanan 1996). This is clearly not the case, as Karaflogka notes the existence of

> cyber-churches, cyber-sanghas, cyber-synagogues, and cyber-mosques, each giving the opportunity to its followers to be part of the 'community' when physical contact, for whatever reason, is not possible or desirable. (Karaflogka 2002: 283)

This proliferation is not surprising, as such spaces may be particularly useful to the new breed of mobile elite and the digital nomads that the globalized economy produces. While these new ways of connecting and building 'local' communities provide continuity for dispersed individuals, they do not always lead to continuity of the religious tradition. Turner, commenting on Islam, argues that the "intellectual elites [have] come to depart radically from tradition, building up their own internal notions of authority, authenticity and community" (2007: 127). The internet, in the same way as any communication technology, provides opportunities but does not dictate outcomes.

Certainly the concept of a 'speech community,' or indeed of a 'community' of any sort, is radically refigured in the global age (see Rampton 2000). As Silverstein reminds us, " '[l]ocality' of language community is only a relationally produced state in a cultural–ideological order" (1998: 404). It is, however, possible to deal with this shifting order because of "the power of language to bring about wish fulfilment through the verbal act of declaring the wish within the ritual circle" (O'Leary 1996: 803), whether that is the virtual religious space or the internet generally. Further, given that the internet is "organized laterally rather than vertically or radially, with no central authority and no chain of command" (Zalenski 1997: 111), it seems particularly suited to social network analysis (Paolillo 2001). (Indeed, intelligence gathering in cyberspace by government intelligence agencies works on exactly such principles.) That the "Internet was designed to allow for one-to-many communication as well as many-to-many communication" (Helland 2002: 293) means that existing linguistic models of bystanders, eavesdroppers and the "several varieties of overhearers in between" (Clark 1996: 14) are particularly suitable for analyzing the different kinds of communicative relationships the internet allows. The transfer of liturgical structures and frames in the VR religious environment has been mentioned (Schroeder et al. 1998). While it might not be the same as a corporeal encounter, "[a] prayer meeting in the virtual world [...] certainly reproduces some of the essential features" of traditional worship (ibid.).

The internet not only provides places for communicating religiously with others, it also allows individuals to 'do religion' by taking complex journeys – specifically, virtual pilgrimages (MacWilliams 2002). While this might again be thought to be limited to new 'technology-friendly' religions, the late Pope John Paul II embarked on a virtual journey when an actual visit to Iraq became

impossible (ibid., p. 319). As a response to the geopolitical realities of the globalized world, traveling virtually was in this instance a logical solution in an
unstable world. Moreover, understanding these virtual journeys (whether the
trajectory is geographic or spiritual) can be analyzed in terms of mythscapes
(along Appadurai's lines). Work in the field of tourism and globalization is also
useful, reminding us that even "physical travel is largely an imaginative act"
(ibid., p. 321). Thus religious and secular journeys follow the same theoretical
trajectories, in that the same tools and theories can be used to understand them.

These examples may suggest a permissive and radical freedom, which is not
always tolerated by central religious authorities. The medium provides constraints
and affordance to messages, but authors position themselves differently in relation to policing such freedoms. While O' Leary argues that "[i]n computer networks the global village has found its public square" (1996: 786), the public square
is often subject to controls and surveillance. The best example is perhaps that of
the Church of Scientology (Kent 1999). This organization (recognized legally as a
religion by some nations, but prohibited by others) has a significant official internet presence (http://www.scientology.org/home.html). However, the organization has been vigilant in policing access to its official texts, invoking copyright
regimes to prosecute individuals who disseminate material intended only for
members. Because of the cost sometimes involved in membership and thus in
access to these materials, one might draw an analogy with systems of protection
against pirated articles devised by prestige brands and global media organizations. Analyzed in this way, a religion starts to look like a corporation. However,
it is also possible to see the protection of texts as being related to a hermeneutic
strategy, similar to that of any religious organization with non-negotiable articles
of faith.

Given broad conceptions of 'religion,' it is also possible to see the internet itself
in a different light. The mundane experience of technology (mundane because of
the opaqueness of the systems driving it) can itself be transposed to a religious
mode. Thus the internet becomes a metaphor for, or even a new mode of presence
of, the divine (Henderson 2000). Indeed, such a conception of technology – as
creating, rather than merely mediating or allowing, the religious experience – is
captured by Arthur C. Clarke's third "law" of prediction: "Any sufficiently
advanced technology is indistinguishable from magic" (1962: 36). The line between
religion and magic (or superstition) is arguably an ideological one (Chidester 1996:
748).

Seeing the internet and the technology required to access it as objects of worship
can be explained in terms of fetishes (ibid., p. 749), and linked to identity construction. A small lexical shift, coupled with an intense commitment, transforms these
technological objects, from mere 'fetishes,' into objects of *religious* devotion. As a
specific example at the level of brand and identity, many people see a clear distinction between the Mac and the PC as objects and as sites of identity construction. Recent Apple advertising campaigns in the UK and US (with similarly
dubbed and localized versions across the world) personified the brands explicitly:
in one of the series the PC 'nerd' sneezes and has a 'virus,' while the Apple

'hipster' claims never to get sick. The British version of the virus advertisement differed from the one used in the American campaign with respect to two lexemes. Whereas the former described the virus as a "humdinger," the American version used "doozy"; and when the PC sneezes the British Mac says "bless you," while the American offers "gesundheit." Some of the advertisements do not lend themselves to direct UK/US comparison; while the messages are broadly similar, their realization differs greatly. The most significant difference is that the comedians in the American version, not generally known in the UK, are replaced with a more recognizable British comic 'couple.'

Cultural commentator Charlie Brooker, in a scathing commentary of the British campaign, writes: "Ultimately the campaign's biggest flaw is that it perpetuates the notion that consumers somehow 'define themselves' with the technology they choose" (Brooker 2007: 262). In this way he ironically describes the self-reflexive, postmodern, social constructionist identity project as "essentially" empty. Brooker portrays the Mac user as fundamentally alienated, with a "dark fear haunting their feeble quivering soul – that in some sense, they are a superficial semi-person assembled from packaging …" (ibid.). But this idea – that consumer habits construct, and are constructed by, identity projects and membership of a tribe – clearly has some currency in advertising discourse, as it is used so frequently; and certainly it enjoys a level of academic respect in the postmodern climate (see Thomas 2002: 60). In this mode, but subverting this underlying premise, Think Christian (2006) has created a series of spoof advertisements, contrasting "Christians" (PCs) with "Christ Followers" (Macs). The "Christian" places emphasis on external markings of religious affiliation (books, smart clothes, explicitly Christian music, bumper stickers), while a "Christ Follower" demonstrates his faith with a calm, "laid back" claim to authenticity. If nothing else, the virtual world and the tools it provides allow such rewriting of texts, and question the possibility of pinning down both authenticity and origin-ality.

Seeing religion, whether online worship or veneration of technology itself, as an identity project linked to consumption behavior leads to consideration of other capitalist discourses that have been adopted by and incorporated into the practice and understanding of religion.

Show Me the Money

Cutting across all of the areas mentioned, and central to globalization itself, is the specter of money. This is most obvious in the case of 'mega-churches,' which have large local congregations, often in more than one country. The financial resources necessary to maintain such groups are considerable; however, the number of members means that income can be correspondingly large. Hillsong, an Australian church, preaches to a local Sydney congregation as large as 40,000 each week. Like similar organizations, it has established churches in London, Kiev, and Capetown and uses internet technology in a sophisticated way, to build community and orient new members (http://www2.hillsong.com/; see also www.willowcreek.

org). Such mega-churches originate not only in the developed world. The Kingsway International Christian Centre, founded in 1992 by a former Muslim Nigerian, now has around 12,000 attendees every Sunday (www.kicc.org.uk). The challenge for such large organizations is to maintain a sense of community. One shared value that is often exploited is the value of money. One of Hillsong's stated beliefs links divine love to material wealth: "We believe that God wants to heal and transform us so that we can live healthy and prosperous lives in order to help others more effectively."

While the prototypical idea of 'religion' may be antithetical to market-driven capitalism, at an elementary level, global religions would struggle to thrive without a secure financial base. Religion, politics, and money have always formed an unholy triumvirate. Methodism, for example, has been accused of acting "as the handmaid of industrial capitalism, in that it advocated diligence and application in people's vocational life" (van Noppen 2006). The very existence of mega-churches requires considerable business expertise; this can then be fused with religious teaching and used for the benefit of the congregation. At the same time, capitalism itself can be understood as a religion, as Benjamin (1996) has argued.

Consumption requires wealth of an appropriate kind. Possessing capital (of the literal kind) has been interpreted in the past as evidence of divine favor. Jones observes that in Pentecostalism "[e]ven a meagre increase in social status or arrangement is taken as evidence of God's blessing on the faithful" (2002: 111). While praying for consumer goods may chafe with many orthodox religious adherents, The "Faith Movement" – "Health and Wealth" or "Prosperity Christians" (Coleman 1998: 245) – is thriving in many parts of the world. To take one group as an example, Kong Hee from Singapore "represents the new pattern of Christian media flows from Asia" (James and Shoesmith 2008: 23), with sermons like "You can be a millionaire" going out on the Indian TV networks (God TV). The theme is not limited to Christian denominations. Aldred documents the same ideology in New Age discourses. Shakti Gawain, for example, "claims that money is merely a symbol of our creative energy" (Aldred 2002: 62–3). In the same area, the aptly named "Prosperity Now" appeared in the 1980s, and is described by Aldred as "an entire subdivision of the New Age movement" (ibid., p. 63).

One way of understanding the current use of prosperity discourse is to see it as an example of a more general eclectic approach to religion; bricolage spirituality (Aupers and Houtman 2006: 201). As is already clear, the incorporation of such values is not limited to specific denominations or modes of religion. Nevertheless, this bricolage is not without complications, as this approach may undermine any meaningful sense of the 'sacred' – not only because of the nature of elements incorporated (such as prosperity discourse), but because it may radically disturb the very notion of religion. O'Leary describes audiences of online bricolage as having a "postmodern sensibility" which "floats like a hummingbird over the flowers of the world's historical archive, extracting nectar from the offerings of folk culture and high culture like without distinction" (O'Leary 1996: 803–4). It may be that "one defining aspect of the postmodern era is that it is an age when *literally* nothing is sacred" (ibid., p. 804); however, this is not quite as catastrophic for religion as it may at first appear. If *nothing* is sacred, it is in fact possible for *anything* to be sacred. The particular religious relations that individuals create and maintain are not necessarily threatened. Postmodernity has not led to the end of religion; rather, the globalizing world has provided new ways of doing religion and being religious. Alongside the virtual and the bricolage, we find also a return to 'tradition.'

Fundamentally Speaking

The discourses of terrorism and fundamentalism are intimately related to the construction of identity, which, in religious, political, and ideological terms, is "often formed at least in part by dialectical exclusion ('We're not like that other lot') ..." (Heather 2005: 167). Thus dedication to religious values (to a 'we') can be explained in terms of a "'loss of faith' in the ideological form of [...] secular nationalism" (the corresponding 'they') (Juergensmeyer 2003: 231). In this way religious fundamentalists create notional enemies. Whatever the precise configurations of fundamentalism, it can be understood as a reaction *to* a postmodern world, as it is generally phrased in binary oppositional terms and draws on semiotic resources and discourses from a more 'traditional' period. There has been a deal of incisive work in the field of fundamentalism, terrorism, identity, and language (Simkins 2007; Mandaville 2007; Turner 2007). Here I want to mention a different kind of fundamentalism: the recent resurgence of atheism.

Lull echoes Dawkins (2006) when he writes: "Religious fundamentalists of all denominations willingly, even proudly, refuse to make use of the one ability that separates human beings from all other living organisms – the capacity to reason" (2007: 101). As Beattie (2007) persuasively argues, the situation is not quite so simple. I suggest that to make a single distinction between the 'rational' and the 'irrational' here misunderstands the human experience of religion, and is blind to the fact that faith has little to do with 'rationality.' As Beattie explains,

> If we are to understand the role that religion plays in people's lives, then we need to pay more attention to the many different ways in which religious and cultural narratives act as vehicles of meaning for those who inhabit them. (2007: 2)

Narrative, symbols, and the enacting of symbols through ritual, are central to human life. Their significance is not only propositional; examining them in terms of truth and falsity is inadequate. It is not so much that these symbols and practices are irrational as that the lens provided by the rational/irrational bifurcation blinds us to their meaning, especially as part of authentic experience. The authenticity of such experience is of a different order from, for example, textual authenticity.

In Christianity, as in many religions, texts are central and, to varying extents, true, inviolable, and authentic. This is one kind of authenticity that needs to be grappled with. However, "Faith is undeniably more a matter of how people live than how they talk" (van Noppen 2006). In order to understand what religion means to people, we must take account of the fundamental, even disjunctive, difference between living religion and speaking religion. St Augustine writes (in Joseph's 2006 translation): "Here is an inner word, conceived in the heart – it is trying to get out, it wants to be spoken [...] [but] the inner word itself, as conceived in the heart" is not in any language (Joseph 2006: 43, with a reference to Augustine 1863: 1304–5). Speaking the "inner word" is desirable, but judging the truth, or even authenticity, of such a speech cannot be done with Dawkin's mode of rationality. This is the first challenge to linguistics that I want to raise, and it relates specifically to our understanding of authenticity. In one sense, the authenticity of speaking the inner word comes from mastery of the genres provided by a particular religious group; such speech acts, performed correctly, are self-certifying. At the same time, the admittedly sophisticated understandings of authenticity in sociolinguistics are concerned with a different kind of authenticity from that which sustains the religious adherent.

The criteria by which authenticity of language is judged in sociolinguistics are framed increasingly in terms of performance (Coupland 2003). Our current models for dealing with discourse tend to follow Barthes: we agree that the author is dead. "We know now that a text is not a line of words releasing a single 'theological' meaning (the 'message' of the Author-God) but a multi-dimensional space in which a variety of writings, none of them original, blend and clash" (Barthes 1977: 147).

The inner word St Augustine refers to is the single 'theological' meaning that guarantees the authenticity of the religious *experience*. In short, the terms of our discipline may well be received as an insult to certain religions, if only because 'performance' suggests artifice in its normal usage. This raises ethical questions which will need to be addressed in certain research contexts. A way of describing religious affiliation that does not represent it solely as an identity project, but rather as an authentic experience, will need to be found. This can be done by sectioning off intention, of both text author and religious member, and by accepting that trying to evaluate the truth of religion, even by describing it as performance, may be inappropriate. For some research questions, it may be more appropriate to excavate, articulate, and deploy the hermeneutic tools of the particular religion, in order to account for these texts in members' terms. Heather's concept of the "invisible noticeboard" as a metaphor for religious communities' ideologies is an excellent example of such an approach (Heather 2005, 2007). However it is done, walking these fine semantic lines is a journey that must be taken.

Apart from challenges *for* linguistics, there are two specific challenges *to* this discipline. The first relates to the globalization element of the religion and globalization dyad. Particularly in relation to religion, Crystal notes that the linguist

> is first of all concerned with language studied as an end in itself [...] only secondarily
> is he concerned with applying the results of his knowledge to specific situations and

to elucidating and suggesting solutions for the main language problems that are inherent in all social linguistic situations. (1966: 12)

The fast pace of the global age means that there is little opportunity for the linguist to do the former and a great deal of pressure to offer the latter. The kind of linguistic 'expert' that this situation may create is, I suggest, potentially very damaging to the public face and the actual practice of linguistics. This is not a phenomenon with a singular cause. The changing nature of universities, especially in Britain, is producing entrepreneurial institutions and professionals (see Mautner 2005). At the same time, popular interest in language creates 'celebrity' experts who, once familiar to audiences, may be called upon to comment on areas outside their direct expertise. It has, for example, become generally accepted that the appearance of 'high rising intonation' or 'uptalk' in British English was caused by exposure to Australian soap operas like *Neighbours* (Bathurst 1996). Well known 'intellectual' personalities in Britain, such as Stephen Fry and Kathy Lette, have lent their voices to this 'truism.' Finally, one needs to consider the ownership that language speakers feel for their own language, and the perennial return to prescriptivism (see Truss 2003). The idea that native competence is enough for its possessor to comment on language and that languages have 'correct' forms works toward marginalizing real linguistic expertise.

The second challenge is found in the religious mode of commitment to globalization as a discourse and a phenomenon (Hopkins 2001: 112). It seems to me that linguistics risks being colonized by analytical tools and theories from other disciplines, with a corresponding danger that 'traditional' linguistic tools will be considered obsolete. Because globalization takes in the whole world, the detail of the local and rigorous description of linguistic detail is often lost. As mentioned in the introduction, there has been in linguistics a great deal of research relevant to the field of globalization and religion (see for example Omoniyi and Fishman 2006). However, the kind of focus that linguistics necessarily requires means that particular research is not usually framed in terms of globalization. In short, the purview of linguistics is often in conflict with that of globalization, notwithstanding the importance of localization in the area. Ironically, globalization as a field lends itself to the overview or to the grand narrative, where the particular instance is deployed as an illustration rather than an example, in Perelman and Olbrechts-Tyteca's terms (1969: 357). That is, the contours of the field of globalization tend to encourage the illustration in support of the general thesis, rather than the generation of the thesis from a collection of examples through the rigorous analysis of a carefully constructed data set. This is not intended as a criticism of other disciplines; rather I mean to identify a tendency which all disciplines contend with. Linguistics is, perhaps, more vulnerable than others.

Moreover, the vocabulary and levels of analysis in sociology and critical theory are both more accessible and more attractive to many people. I do not want to suggest that other disciplines neglect rigorous detailed research. The problem relates rather to how difficult it is to communicate research to the media and to the public generally. For example, 'trend' stories, of which the popular press are so fond, integrate more easily concepts like 'the network society' and 'bricolage' than concepts like 'code-switching' and 'syntactic structure.' Thus this danger is exacerbated by media interest in globalization, especially in respect of language change. In fact, linguistics is well equipped to deal with the changing face of religion in globalization, as previous illustrations have suggested. Academic practices, rites, and rituals are just as open to flows as any other part of life. It is important that we understand the influence of these flows in our own academic 'global village.'

Heather notes: "today the understanding of religious forces is perhaps rather higher on the agenda of the international community than for many years" (2005: 166). This understanding needs also to be translated for various audiences (Crystal 1966: 11). An agenda of understanding and translation is inevitably an agenda for linguistics. No matter how globalization is changing the world, and no matter how much religion is changing in this world, language will still be central to religious practice. New forms of religion may develop; communication technology will change and interlocutory relationships will shift; but, because of the kind of attention that linguistics pays to detail, interaction, and consequence, linguistics will always have an important role to play.

ACKNOWLEDGMENTS

Special thanks to Dr Noel Heather for careful reading and invaluable ideas and sources.

REFERENCES

Augustine, St (1863) Sermo CCLXXXVIII (alias 23 inter sermones cotidianos) in natali Joannis Baptistae. In *Sancti Aurelii Augustini, Hipponensis Episcopi, Opera Omnia*, edited by J.–P. Migne, Vol. 5, 1302–8. Paris (= *Patrologiae cursus completus*, Series Latina, Vol. 38).

Akinola, P. J. (2003) Statement of the Primates of the Global South in the Anglican Communion, November 2, 2003. Available at: www. globalsouthanglican.org (accessed on August 14, 2008).

Aldred, L. (2002) 'Money is just spiritual energy': Incorporating the New Age. *The Journal of Popular Culture* 35(4): 61–74.

Aupers, S., and Houtman, D. (2006) Beyond the spiritual supermarket: The social and public significance of New Age spirituality. *Journal of Contemporary Religion* 21(2): 201–22.

Barthes, R. (1977) *Image Music Text*, translated by S. Heath. New York: Hill and Wang.

Bathurst, B. (1996) A cute accent? *The Observer*, March 24, p. 9.

Bauman, R. (1989) Speaking in the light: The role of the Quaker minister. In R. Bauman and J. Sherzer (eds), *Explorations in the Ethnography of Speaking*, 2nd edn, 144–60. Cambridge: Cambridge University Press.

Beattie, T. (2007) *The New Atheists: The Twilight of Reason and the War on Religion*. London: Dartman, Longman and Todd.

Benjamin, W. (1996) Capitalism as Religion. In M. Bullock and M. Jennings (eds), *Selected Writings*, Vol. 1, 288–91. Cambridge, MA: Harvard University Press.

Beyer, P. (2003) De-centring religious singularity: The globalization of Christianity as a case in point. *Numen* 50: 357–86.

Brooker, C. (2007) *Dawn of the Dumb: Dispatches from the Idiotic Frontline*. London: Faber and Faber.

Buchanan, T. S. (1996) *A view from the keyboard*. *Touchstone* (Winter). Available at: www.touchstonemag.com (accessed on August 3, 2008).

Chidester, D. (1996) 'The church of baseball, the fetish of coca-cola, and the potlatch of rock 'n' roll: Theoretical models for the study of religion in American popular culture. *Journal of the American Academy of Religion* 64(4): 743–65.

Clark, H. H. (1996) *Using Language*. Chicago: Cambridge University Press.

Clarke, A. C. (1962) *Profiles of the Future, An Inquiry into the Limits of the Possible*, New York: Harper and Row.

Cole, J. (2001) Review: *Translating the Devil: Religion and Modernity among the Ewe in Ghana*. *Journal of Religion in Africa* 31(4): 484–7.

Coleman, S. (1998) Charismatic Christianity and the dilemmas of globalization. *Religion* 28: 245–56.

Coupland, N. (2003) Sociolinguistic authenticities. *Journal of Sociolinguistics* 7(3): 417–31.

Crystal, D. (1965) *Linguistics, Language and Religion*, London and New York: Burns Oates/Hawthorn Books.

Crystal, D. (1966) Language and religion. In L. Sheppard (ed), *Twentieth Century Catholicism*, 11–28. New York: Hawthorn Books.

Crystal, D. (1997) *English as a Global Language*. Cambridge: Cambridge University Press.

Dawkins, R. (2006) *The God Delusion*. London: Bantam Press.

Derrida, J. (1998) Faith and knowledge: The two sources of religion within the limits of pure reason. In J. Derrida and G. Vattimo (eds), *Religion*, 1–78. Cambridge: Polity.

Eickelman, D. F., and Piscatori, J. (1996) *Muslim Politics*. Princeton, NJ: Princeton University Press.

Fishman, J. (2001) Interwar eastern European Jewish parties and the language issue. *International Journal of the Sociology of Language* 151: 175–89.

Giddens, A. (1990) *The Consequences of Modernity*. Cambridge: Polity.

Gledhill, R. (2005) Church of England evil, say archbishops. *The Times*, November 17. Available at: www.lexisnexis.com (accessed on August 10, 2008).

Gledhill, R., and Combe, V. (2008) Gay bishop's row "like Iraq war."' *The Sunday Times*, July 20. Available at: www.timesonline.co.uk (accessed on August 10, 2008).

Gooch, C. R. (1996) Rappin' for the Lord: The uses of Gospel music in black religious communities. In D. A. Stout and J. M. Buddenbaum (eds), *Religion and Mass Media: Audiences and Adaptations*, 228–42. London: Sage.

Graddol, D. (1997) *The Future of English? A Guide to Forecasting the Popularity of the English Language in the 21st Century*. London: British Council.

Hatem, M. F. (2006) In the eye of the storm: Islamic societies and Muslim women in globalization discourse. *Comparative Studies of South Asia, Africa and the Middle East* 26(1): 22–35.

Heather, N. (2005) Critical postliberalism: Critical discourse analysis as the basis for new theology. *Critical Discourse Studies* 2(2): 165–87.

Heather, N. (2007) What the linguist saw: Approaches to church discourse from contemporary critical sociolinguistics. *Theology* 110(857): 340–50.

Heather, N. (2008) Critical postliberalism: Lindbeck's cultural–linguistic system and the socially extrasystemic. *Scottish Journal of Theology*. 61 (4): 462–76.

Helland, C. (2002) Surfing for salvation. *Religion* 32: 293–302.

Henderson, C. (2000) The internet as a metaphor for God. *Cross Currents* 50(1/2): 77–83.

Herring, S. C. (1996) *Computer-Mediated Communication: Linguistic, Social, and Cross-Cultural Perspectives*. Amsterdam: John Benjamins.

Hill, C. (2008) One way of growing a global mission. *Church Times* 7584, July 25 www.churchtimes.co.uk (accessed on September 5, 2008).

Hobson, T. (2008) Williams has enabled a schism: Anglican v liberal. *Guardian*, August 5, p. 27.

Hopkins, D. (2001) The religion of globalization. In D. Hopkins, L. A. Lorentzen, E. Mendieta, and D. Batsone (eds), *Religions/Globalizations: Theories and Cases*, 7–32. Durham, NC: Duke University Press.

Howard, J. R. (1992) Contemporary Christian music: Where rock meets religion. *Journal of Popular Culture* 26(1): 123–30.

James, J. D., and Shoesmith, B. P. (2008) The anointing of the airwaves: Charismatic televangelism's impact on the church and community in urban India. *Journal of Religion and Popular Culture* 18. Available at: http://www.usask.ca/relst/jrpc/ (accessed on August 10, 2008).

Jayaraman, R. (2005) Personal identity in a globalized world: Cultural roots of Hindu personal names and surnames. *Journal of Popular Culture* 38(3): 476–90.

Jelbert, S. (2003) God is in the retail. *The Independent*, June 11. Available at: http://www.independent.co.uk/arts-entertainment/music/features/

god-is-in-the-retail-540363.html (accessed on August 4, 2008).

Jenkins, P. (2002) *The Next Christendom: The Coming of Global Christianity*. Oxford: Oxford University Press.

Jones, S. L. (2002) Religious landscapes of globalization: A review. *Hedgehog Review* 4(2): 109–15.

Joseph, J. E. (2006) *Language and Politics*. Edinburgh: Edinburgh University Press.

Juergensmeyer, M. (2003) *Terror in the Mind of God*, 3rd edn. London: University of California Press.

Juergensmeyer, M. (2005) Religious antiglobalism. In M. Juergensmeyer (ed.), 135–48.

Juergensmeyer, M. (ed.) (2005) *Religion in Global Civil Society*. Oxford: Oxford University Press.

Jule, A. (ed.) (2005) *Gender and the Language of Religion*. Basingstoke: Palgrave.

Karaflogka, A. (2002) Religious discourse and cyberspace. *Religion* 32: 279–91.

Karmani, S. (2005) English, 'terror,' and Islam. *Applied Linguistics* 26(2): 262–7.

Karmani, S., and Pennycook, A. (2005) Islam, English and 9/11. *Journal of Language, Identity, And Education*, 4(2): 157–72.

Kent, S. A. (1999) The globalization of Scientology: Influence, control and opposition in transnational markets. *Religion* 29: 147–69.

Kurtz, L. (1995) *Gods in the Global Village: The World's Religions in Sociological Perspective*. London: Pine Forge Press.

Lakoff, G., and Johnson, M. (1980) *Metaphors We Live By*. Chicago: University of Chicago Press.

LeVine, P., and Scollon, R. (2004) *Discourse and Technology: Multimodal Discourse Analysis*. Washington DC: Georgetown University Press.

Lull, J. (2007) Television and communicational space: The clash of global hegemonies. *New Review of Film and Television Studies* 5(1): 97–110.

MacWilliams, M. W. (2002) Virtual pilgrimages on the internet. *Religion* 32: 315–55.

Mandaville, P. (2007) Globalization and the politics of religious knowledge: Pluralizing authority in the Muslim world. *Theory, Culture and Society*, 24(2): 101–15.

Maultsby, P. K. (1992) The influence of Gospel music on the secular music industry. In B. J. Reagon (ed.), *We'll Understand It Better by and by: African American Pioneering Gospel Composers*, 19–33. Washington, DC: Smithsonian Institution Press.

Mautner, G. (2005) The entrepreneurial university: A discursive profile of a higher education buzzword. *Critical Discourse Studies* 2(2): 95–120.

Maxwell, P. (2002) Virtual religion in context. *Religion* 32: 343–54.

McDannell, C. (1995) *Material Christianity: Religion and Popular Culture in America*. New Haven: Yale University Press.

Meyer, B. (1999) *Translating the Devil: Religion and Modernity among the Ewe in Ghana*. Edinburgh: Edinburgh University Press.

Miller, F. (2008) Al-Qāida as a "pragmatic base": Contributions of area studies to sociolinguistics. *Language and Communication* 28: 386–408.

Mitchell, J., and Marriage, S. (eds) (2003) *Mediating Religion: Conversations in Media, Religion and Culture*. London: T&T Clark.

Mohd-Asraf, R. (2005) English and Islam: A clash of civilizations? *Journal of Language, Identity, and Education* 4(2): 103–18.

O'Leary, S. D. (1996) Cyberspace as sacred space: Communicating religion on computer networks. *Journal of the American Academy of Religion* 64(4): 781–808.

Omoniyi, T. (2006) Hip-hop through the world English lens. *World Englishes* 25(2): 195–208.

Omoniyi, T., and Fishman, J. (eds) (2006) *Explorations in the Sociology of Language and Religion*. Amsterdam: John Benjamins.

Paolillo, J. C. (2001) Language variation on Internet Relay Chat: A social network approach. *Journal of Sociolinguistics* 5(2): 180–213.

Pennycook, A. (2003) Global Englishes, Rip Slyme, and performativity. *Journal of Sociolinguistics* 7(4): 513–33.

Pennycook, A., and Coutand-Marin, S. (2003) Teaching English as a missionary language. *Discourse: Studies in the Cultural Politics of Education* 24/3: 337–53.

Pennycook, A., and Makoni, S. (2005) The modern mission: The language effects of Christianity. *Journal of Language, Identity, and Education* 4(2): 137–55.

Pennycook, A. (2006) *Global Englishes and Transcultural Flows*. London: Routledge.

Perelman, C., and Olbrechts-Tyteca, L. (1969) *The New Rhetoric: A Treatise on Argumentation*, translated by J. Wilkinson and P. Weave. Notre Dame: University of Notre Dame Press.

Pew Research Centre for the People and the Press (2001) Among wealthy nations … US stands alone in its embrace of religion. Available at: http://people-press.org/report/167/among-wealthy-nations- … (accessed on August 12, 2008).

Phillipson, R. (1992) *Linguistic Imperialism*. Oxford: Oxford University Press.

Purgason, K. B. (2004) Readers respond to Julian Edge's "Imperial troopers and the Servants of the Lord": A clearer picture of the "Servants of the Lord."' *TESOL Quarterly* 38(4): 711–13.

Rampton, B. (2000) Speech community. In J. Verschueren, J-O. Östman, J. Blommaert and C. Bulcaen (eds), *Handbook of Pragmatics 1998*, 1–34. Amsterdam: John Benjamins.

Rey, T. (2004) Marketing the goods of salvation: Bourdieu on religion. *Religion* 34: 331–43.

Ritzer, G. (1997) *The McDonalization Thesis.* London: Sage.

Rosowsky, A. (2008) *Heavenly Readings: Liturgical Literacy in a Multilingual Context.* Clevedon: Multilingual Matters.

Schroeder, R., Heather, N., and Lee, R. (1998) The sacred and the virtual: Religion in multi-user virtual reality. *Journal of Computer Mediated Communication* 4(2). Available at: http://jcmc.indiana.edu (accessed on September 5, 2008).

Shinhee Lee, J. (2007) I'm the illest fucka. *English Today* 23: 54–60.

Silverstein, M. (1998) Transformation of local linguistic communities. *Annual Review of Anthropology,* 27: 401–26.

Simkins, R. A. (2007) Al-Qaeda, specter of globalization. *Journal of Religion and Society* 2 (suppl.): 103–9.

Soon Educational Publications, England (nd) Boris Yeltsin pardons murderer. *Soon!* 163.

Spolsky, B. (2003) Religion as a site of language contact. *Annual Review of Applied Linguistics* 23: 81–94.

Stewart, C. (1999) Syncretism and its synonyms: Reflections on cultural mixture. *Diacritics* 29(3): 40–62.

Stout, D. A., and J. M. Buddenbaum (eds) (1996) *Religion and Mass Media: Audiences and Adaptations.* London: Sage.

Suleiman, Y. (2004) *A War of Words: Language and Conflict in the Middle East.* Cambridge: Cambridge University Press.

Swedenburg, T. (2001) Islamic hip-hop vs Islamophobia. In T. Mitchell (ed.), *Global Noise: Rap and Hip-hop Outside the USA,* 57–85. Middletown, CT: Wesleyan University Press.

Szuchewycz, B. (1994) Evidentiality in ritual discourse. *Language in Society* 23: 389–410.

Think Christian (2006). Available at: http://www.thinkchristian.net/index.php/2006/11/01/christian-vs-christ-follower/ (accessed on August 15, 2008).

Thomas, G. M. (2002) Religious movements, world civil society and social theory. *Hedgehog Review* 4(2): 50–65.

Truss, L. (2003) *Eats, Shoots and Leaves: The Zero Tolerance Approach to Punctuation.* London: Profile.

Turner, B. S. (2007) Religious authority and the new media. *Theory, Culture and Society,* 24(2): 117–34.

Van Noppen, J. P. (1995) The English of religion: At the edges of language. In J. P. van Noppen: *Developing Pragmastylistic Competence,* Université Libre de Bruxelles, Senior year coursebook. Available at: http://homepages.ulb.ac.be/~jpvannop/Theoling.doc (accessed on August 15, 2008).

Van Noppen, J. P. (2006) From theolinguistics to critical theolinguistics: The case for communicative probity. *ARC, The Journal of the Faculty of Religious Studies, McGill University* 34: 47–65. Available at: http://homepages.ulb.ac.be/~jpvannop/CommProb.doc (accessed on August 15, 2008).

Vanguard (2003) Gay priest: African Anglicans denounce US diocese. *Africa News* 4 (November). Available at: www.lexisnexis.com (accessed on August 20, 2008).

Wagnleitner, R. (1994) *Coca-Colonization and the Cold War: The Cultural Mission of the US in Austria after the Second World War.* Chapel Hill: The University of North Carolina Press.

Walby, S. (2002) Feminism in a global era. *Economy and Society* 31(4): 533–57.

Webster, J. (1988) The language of religion: A sociolinguistic perspective. In M. Ghadessy (ed.), *Registers of Written English: Situational Factors and Linguistic Features,* 85–107. London: Pinter.

Wertheim, M. (2000) *The Pearly Gates of Cyberspace: A History of Space from Dante to the Internet.* London: Virago.

Woods, A. (2004) *Medium or Message? Language and Faith in Ethnic Churches.* Clevedon: Multilingual Matters.

Yates, J. J. (2002) American Evangelicals: The overlooked globalizers and their unintended gospel of modernity. *The Hedgehog Review* 4(2): 66–90.

Zalenski, J. P. (1997) *The Soul of Cyberspace: How New Technology is Changing our Lives.* New York: Harper Collins.

Part III   Language, Values, and Markets under Globalization

15 Language as Resource in the Globalized New Economy

MONICA HELLER

What Is Global? What Is New?

This chapter focusses on some of the ways in which historically emerging conditions shape both how we think about language and what we do with it. The premise behind the title of the present volume is that there is something about globalization which is tied to language in some way worth remarking on. In this chapter I will take the position that it is not globalization alone that is so new and different in its relevance to language, but rather the emergence of the globalized new economy, which has, among its consequences, new conditions for the production of language practices and forms and new challenges to current ways of thinking about language.

The central argument here is that we are in a period of capital expansion which allows the movement of basic primary resource extraction and manufacturing production into hitherto peripheral zones of the First World (such as the Arctic), or even out of it altogether (notably to China and India); the development of new consumer markets (again, notably in China and India); and an increase in the importance of symbolic capital in the development of niche and value-added products (which is why Giddens refers to this period as *late* modern rather than *post*modern; Giddens 1990). Currently, then, we are seeing the expansion of capital happening simultaneously in two ways: through seeking out new markets for mass production, and through developing niche markets and symbolic forms of added value where existing markets are saturated. This has four consequences for language.

The first consequence is that many more social actors than ever before are now involved in economic activities that have to deal with globalized forms of exchange; more markets involve wider networks. Some authors, notably David Harvey and Manuel Castells (Harvey 1989; Castells 2000) agree (in spite of their differences) that these exchanges are now more rapid, so that both time and space seem, in Harvey's words, "compressed." Even more important, to my mind, is the fact that this experience is socially more widespread – that it involves more people in

The Handbook of Language and Globalization, First Edition. Edited by Nikolas Coupland.
© 2013 Blackwell Publishing Ltd except for editorial material and organization © 2013 Nikolas Coupland.
Published 2013 by Blackwell Publishing Ltd.

dealing more often with communication across social, cultural, and linguistic differences.

The second consequence is that the management of these exchanges and these networks involves a wider repertoire of forms of communication, and hence of language use. Earlier forms of globalization were mediated through the writing of accounts, which was undertaken by the few literate members of small social groups (many of these members were missionaries) and through oral reports delivered in face-to-face settings, albeit sometimes to fairly large audiences. Today's technology, of course, affords a broader range of forms of mediation, which are used by a broader set of social actors, and arguably more often.

The third consequence is that a tension emerges between relatively anonymous, agentless, and transferrable forms of *standardization* on the one hand and situated and identifiable forms of *authenticity* on the other. Industrial management practices – generally referred to as 'Taylorist,' after Frederick Winslow Taylor (1856–1915), who first developed them for the early twentieth-century industrial production of the US – have historically favored assembly-line production, which uses rigidly controlled and uniformized acts of physical labor; and the general preference for Taylorism has persisted even when labor became less physical and more verbal. Companies tend to favor the use of one language, one set of practices, and one set of forms (Boutet 2001; Cameron 2001; Boutet 2008), although now they function across all the kinds of linguistic and cultural differences which markets encompass. At the same time, the saturation of industrial markets for standardized products has led to an increasing focus on niche markets and on adding value to standardized goods, often in the form of symbolic value. Niche markets can best be reached by appealing to their specificity (and sense of distinction: see Bourdieu 1979), often through use of their own linguistic varieties and through reference to, or incorporation of, their cultural preferences. Standardized goods can be made special by being marketed as local, authentic, and in some ways unique products with limited distribution. Whether by appealing to exoticism, familiarity, or rarity, language and culture can be mobilized to counterbalance Taylorism with the value they place on authenticity and artisanal production.

The final consequence has to do with what Josiane Boutet (2001) calls "*la part langagière du travail*" ("the language dimension of work"). She points out that industrial workplaces used to control communication among workers severely, considering it a distraction from the physical work involved in production. Today much of that work is already computer-mediated, requiring literacy and numeracy skills which would have been irrelevant to the workplaces of the past. More importantly, in much contemporary work, language is not only an integral, if not the only, part of the work *process*; it is also frequently the work *product*. I can perhaps best illustrate this through contrasting vignettes from my own fieldwork, which I will then also use as a basis for discussing how these shifts are tied to ethnolinguistic divisions of labor.

In 1979 I did fieldwork in a large manufacturing company in Montreal (Canada). This English-speaking and family-owned company had a classic profile for the Quebec private sector: an anglophone management and francophone labor, mediated through the linguistic brokerage offices of four Irish bilingual superintendents. The job descriptions of these four people had nothing to do with their linguistic skills, which were none the less crucial to the smooth operation of the company hierarchy. The overlap between hierarchy and ethnolinguistic categorization has long been one way in which the Canadian labor market legitimates the reproduction of class hierarchies (Porter 1965). In companies such as this one, the trope of 'family' also opened up opportunities for constructing labor loyalty, as the real family members who owned and ran the company encouraged their workers to recruit new workers from their own kinship and community networks. But the language differences were mainly used to organize relations of power, and interfered little in the conduct of actual work. On the factory floor, the noise of the machinery was so loud that the workers, all francophone men, had to wear earplugs. Together with the foremen, they developed a small repertoire of gestures for those occasions when communication was essential; they had neither the time nor the possibility to move off the line and into the glassed-in, sound-proofed foreman's office to talk, if, for example, it looked as if some kind of mechanical problem was developing. All the talking was carried out in French and only occurred at breaks, or just before or after work. Managers, of course, used language much more; but they were only able to do so in English. In that respect, language differences served to reinforce the impossibility of social mobility.

In the late 1990s I conducted an interview with a group of francophone men in Welland, a steel, textile, and automobile town in southern Ontario which had fallen on hard times as a result of the rapid restructuring, downsizing, and off-shoring of its industries at that time (at one point in the late 1980s, the town had the highest unemployment rate in Canada). These men had all been workers in anglophone-owned and run factories; they were members of an ethnic community which had been recruited from Quebec, along with immigrant labor from outside Canada, to work in the mills during the boom years between the 1920s and the 1940s. They had all been laid off or forced to take early retirement. In their workplaces, they said, it was also too noisy to talk on the floor. But there were lots of talk at lunch, as workers sat at ethnolinguistically homogeneous tables, among which they might temporarily circulate to chat, typically in English, with a buddy. Here linguistic difference served not only to maintain the hierarchical divisions, but also to make it quite difficult for workers to build solidarity across ethnolinguistic lines. This group represents, then, a kind of transition, the last of its kind to occupy the traditional slot for non-anglophones in an industrial economy.

In 2002 I accompanied colleagues to collect data in a call center in Moncton (in eastern Canada). Moncton had been a town like many others in eastern and central Canada, with a largely francophone industrial workforce and an anglophone elite. When the industrial basis of the economy collapsed there as well, the province invested in attracting the call center industry, which it did by building infrastructure, by providing tax and other breaks, and by marketing the bilingual skills of a workforce badly in need of jobs. The call center we were in was similar to others we had seen in Ontario. It had about 100 bilingual Acadian women, most of them young, sitting at work stations and talking on the phone while simultaneously reading off a computer screen or entering text onto it, and often also jotting down handwritten reminders as a side-job – all this in French, in English, or in both. As I sat in a side-office waiting to talk with a manager, I could hear the noise of the new factory floor: the low hum of a hundred voices. Since management was still anglophone and monolingual, language was still a basis for maintaining hierarchy; now, however, managing the work necessitated a linguistically more sophisticated set of techniques than the hiring of four bilingual superintendents.

The point I wish to make with these vignettes is that one major result of a shift in economy is to make language central, both as a process and as a product of work: what the call center sells is mainly information (although at the end of the line there may be something more concrete which is exchanged for money, like a car, a hotel reservation, or a replacement part for a broken machine). More generally, we are indeed seeing the emergence of what has been called the 'language industries' – that is, those types of work in which language is either the product or an important dimension of it, for example translation, speech recognition, or language teaching. At the same time this shift seems to be gendered (Cameron 2001; Mirchandani 2004); it is certainly ethnicized or racialized; and it is more likely to reinscribe class relations on a new territory than to transform them. In the section below, which deals with the management of linguistic resources, I will return to the question of language as process of labor and, in particular, to how this plays out for people who are differentially situated in the class hierarchy. In the next section, which deals with the production, distribution, and attribution of value to linguistic resources, I will turn to consider the struggles over what value to ascribe to what linguistic resources, and how to measure that value. In the final section (on nation–states and post-nationalism) I will discuss what the commodification of language in the globalized new economy means for how we think about language.

For the moment, I simply want to underscore the ways in which the new economy highlights language as a resource, and indeed as a commodity (Heller 2003), as part of a general commodification of knowledge and semiosis (Fairclough 2002; Fairclough 2006). Some authors have remarked that contemporary debates about the economic value of language and culture – as seen for example in education, in discussions about what languages to teach, when, how, and to whom, as a matter of preparing little entrepreneurs for the global marketplace – is not a matter of concretely changing conditions as much as a new form of legitimation for neo-liberal regimes of regulation, and one worthy of independent scrutiny (Tsing 2000). While I certainly support the argument that one characteristic of the political–economic changes related to the specific forms of capital expansion we are undergoing is the increasing importance of economic rather than political modes of authorization and legitimation, I take the position that there are empirically observable shifts in the organization of the capitalist economy which help us to understand why this is the case. In particular, I think that we need to foreground through neo-liberal and symbolic capital modes of regulation the relationship between the emergence of the globalized new economy and the manner in which the state manages it – that is, the manner in which the globalized new economy is materially tied to the state's (not always smooth) shift from welfarism to neo-liberalism – as the private sector has sought greater freedom for the global circulation of (often symbolic) goods and workers. In other words there is a political–economic reason why economic arguments are now more authoritative than political ones, although the state still has a role to play in the advancement of the economic interests of its producers and consumers. The state and the private sector, however, have to figure out how to manage the new communication-oriented forms of production, as well as the circulation and value of its communicative products.

The Management of Linguistic Resources

There are few empirical studies of how this management happens (although there are many new how-to or best-practices manuals for managers), either from the perspective of workers or (in fact, even less frequently) from the perspective of managers. Cameron, Boutet, and others have argued that the growing linguistic dimension of work has not changed the fundamentally Taylorist practices of management. They show how standardized scripts are associated with control over the quality of the mass-produced product and over the production of workers as interchangeable producing bodies (or, more accurately in this case, voices). Following Alexandre Duchêne's adoption of the phrase *parole d'œuvre* to replace the idea of the *main d'œuvre* (Duchêne 2009), we might think of a transformation of the 'workforce' into a 'wordforce,' retaining the idea that what counts is not the individual as a whole, but his or her ability to produce certain kinds of standardized products. Already in the mid-1990s, Gee and colleagues (1996) argued that the new economy, despite its rhetoric about empowering the individual worker to take control over his or her working life, actually heightened Taylorist practices by forcing workers to acquire the ability to occupy multiple functions in the chain of production, as was needed at different moments, without any concomitant rewards, while removing job security (this is known as 'flexibility'); many of those practices are now related to increased abilities to manipulate language.

Much of the work that has been done focuses on the call center industry, especially the call center industry in India and the work produced by my collaborators in francophone Canada (Cameron 2001; Larner 2002; Budach et al. 2003; Chassey and Case 2003; Roy 2003; Mulholland 2004; Dubois et al. 2006; Sonntag 2006; Cowie 2007; Poster 2007). This body of work includes, interestingly, a cluster of documentaries (Stitt 2002; Addelman 2005; Golati 2005; Belkhodja 2006). Their emergence may have something to do with the iconic status of call centers as symbols of the new economy (consisting, as they apparently do, mainly of deterritorialized, or at least distant, disembodied voices), and possibly also with the relative easy affordance to access to data which such sites provide (in a similar way, much early sociolinguistic work on institutions focussed on schools). There is, however, also a body of work on other sites, where language-as-work and language-as-product is important – for example multilingual public service offices, environmentalist NGOs, multimedia companies, tourism information offices, or airports. Much of this work was conducted by team members in Canada; by those involved in research directed by Alexandre Duchêne and Ingrid Piller in Switzerland; and by those involved in the more established French network *Langage et travail* (see for example the cases reported in Kergoat et al. 1999; Heller and Boutet 2006; Boutet 2008; McLaughlin et al. 2009; Duchêne 2009). Translation and interpretation are beginning to receive ethnographic attention as sites of production (Sturge 2007), although this tends to be limited to those activities which mainly involve humans, without much attention to what goes on in the area of speech technology. The final area we can draw on is the language teaching industry – an increasingly competitive arena (Block and Cameron 2002; Yarymowich 2005; Liddicoat 2007).

Most of this work points to a series of contradictions – or perhaps we can think of them as obstacles to Taylorist practices, or as difficulties in implementing such practices when the process and product (communication) is not easily treated as a machine or an object and when the conditions of the market require both large-scale standardization and local flexibility. This flexibility is not only a requirement of the ways in which the new economy is organized, as Gee and colleagues argued; it is also a product of the ways in which local authenticities play into the production of added value, into the construction of niche markets, and into the remaining traces of both capital and labor drawing on older ideologies of nationhood (and on the ideologies of language and culture, which are part and parcel of them) in order to continue to struggle over privileged access to resources and over the production and distribution of those resources. In other words, language and culture were initially mobilized in the development of national markets to allow national bourgeoisies privileged access to material and human resources and to consumer markets (Hobsbawm 1990); the globalized new economy sometimes stretches the limits of that mode of political economic organization, but sometimes draws on it, notably in constructing niche markets and in adding symbolic value to products. As I will discuss in this section, contemporary modes of managing communicative production and communicative products have to balance contradictions or tensions between:

- the *standardization* of communicative practices and forms, and the appropriation of *variability* in the service of meeting consumer expectations across a range of diverse markets, especially where these are constituted as niche markets, and in the service of *flexibility*;
- the constitution of language as a standardizable and measurable *skill*, and the treatment of language:
  1 as an individual *talent*;
  2 as an *authentic* and socially situated *cultural commodity*;
  3 as a set of situated *practices*.

Indeed, in order to function, Taylorist management practices such as the ones which tend to dominate spaces like call centers must turn language into a job skill, measurable the same way as any other job skill. This has the advantage not only of not disrupting the general management system, but also of conforming to ideologies of transparency – that is, to ideologies which legitimate power by taking it to rely on the kind of knowledge that is equally accessible to all, and measured the same way for everyone.

In the call center studied by Sylvie Roy (2003), for example, knowledge of a language other than English (typically French) was slotted into the broader system of 'knowledge blocks,' which mainly included mastery of information about specific sets of products or services. Staff could ask for, or be invited to receive, training in one of these areas in order to gain certified recognition of their mastery, which would translate into a certain degree of job mobility – or at least shift choice and some additional pay for individual employees, as well as an increasing flexibility of the entire employee pool.

Evaluation of such skills, whether at the recruitment stage or during in-service training of this kind, becomes an issue. Within the language-as-skill framework, the process of evaluating usually results in reliance upon standardized tests. A spin-off of this process is a market for those tests, and some competition over who produces the best ones. The Canadian government, having long grappled with such issues in its attempts to construct a largely bilingual civil service, began in the early 2000s to think about exploiting its expertise as an industry to be developed and marketed (Canada 2003). One result of this plan has been the establishment of the Canadian Language Benchmarks agency (www.language.ca), whose job is to develop and standardize procedures and tools for the evaluation of linguistic proficiency, principally for French and English. A further spin-off is the growth in language industry companies in general, which provide specialized services not only in testing, but also for example in interpretation and translation (while we wait for machine translation to work better than it currently does).

Two major disadvantages to this approach have emerged. One is that it has met with stiff resistance from Canadian francophones, who consider that such a move devalues a form of linguistic capital to which they had privileged access because of oppression and marginalization; now that the value of that capital has changed in the new market conditions, it is difficult for them to stomach competition from their former oppressors on the very terrain which those groups used to disdain. They argue that their prior investment deserves special recognition. This is particularly evident in the federal civil service, where most francophones come to the job being already bilingual, while anglophones are provided resources to acquire French while they are on the job. This also leads some people to fall back on older nationalist ideologies of sociolinguistic authenticity (Coupland 2003) – that is, to argue that knowledge of a language gained through participation in ethnic or national social networks is necessarily of higher value than knowledge gained through language classes and a six-week home-stay in a Quebec village.

The second disadvantage, of course, is that such an approach is considerably heavier and more expensive than one which devalues language as a talent or a characteristic that people may happen to have, like having a good singing voice or being double-jointed, which may come in handy from time to time, but which really remains in the realm of the individual. This allows many companies to rely on the good offices of employees whose job descriptions have nothing to do with language skills per se. This is not a new story; we have already seen, for example, the unrecognized translation and interpretation work done by superintendents in the Montreal company where I studied in the 1970s. In addition, secretaries often acted as translators, and employees unsure of a term would come to them for access to their dictionaries (to my regret, I never asked, but I like to think those dictionaries were paid for out of company funds). I suspect that this case was not unusual, and that in companies like this such free labor was often provided precisely by secretaries and involved both the management of multilingualism and that of language norms. Today I hear a different kind of report: usually someone in the company would receive a text or phone call in a language they don't speak, and put out an email request to all employees to see if someone can help out. Alexandre Duchêne (forthcoming) reports that a version of this practice has been institutionalized, in the airport he studied, through polling all employees for their knowledge of different languages: the results, together with contact information, are kept on a database that any airport employee can access in case of need. Presumably orthographic norms are enforced these days by spell-check.

But, in addition to these disadvantages, the new economy has also created spaces where the nature of the product tends to contradict the Taylorist skilling of language as a commodity, disconnected from communication as social practice. Symbolic added value, and the importance of niche markets, position language also as an emblem of the authenticity which is sold in such domains as tourism, as well as in the circulation of artistic and cultural artefacts. Finally, language as authenticity is crucial in dealing with local markets, which develop to construct some privileged position in the global economy; that is, authenticity is one way to assert consumer power in a world where producers are competing for markets, and for producers it offers a way to add value to their product.

Drawing on language as a way to authenticate a commodity, whether an object, an experience or a service, draws on still dominant ideologies of language, on (mainly national or nation-like) identities, and on their constitutive myths. In our 2005 fieldwork, which covered the selling of Canada in France (selling consumer goods, or dreams of vacations, even of immigration), we mainly saw stereotyped renditions of francophone Canada, identical to those developed in the nationalist movement of the 1960s (images of nature, the *voyageur*, the lumberjack, the raftsman, the log cabin, and the sugar shack), consciously presented in a Canadian accent for consumers who reportedly would ask vendors to talk to them before they would look at the goods for sale. Organizers dealt with this aspect of the demand by recruiting 'real' Canadian francophones – mainly from among young people studying or living in Europe, but, if necessary, also importing them for the season. At the Rennes Christmas market in 2002, I was approached to buy 'real' Canadian polar fleece jackets with red maple leaves embroidered over the heart by a man who tried very hard to produce a Canadian accent, but couldn't keep it up after the first minute of conversation. (The only other place where I have ever seen such jackets is China. In Canada we buy ours with the logo of the Vancouver-based Mountain Equipment Coop.) But I also chatted with a youth from eastern Quebec who had flown over to do the rounds of French Christmas markets with cans of maple syrup, identified as having come from a specific site (which of course may or may not be true, but the identifying form – the kind of labelling – and practice are entirely recognizable to eastern Canadians. If it was fake, it was a fake based on excellent cultural knowledge).

Similar authentifying practices are used in tourism, as locales compete for an increasingly lucrative market and use heritage as a major means to distinguish one site from another and to add value to experiences of leisure, recreation, environmentalism, or whatever else people pay for when they travel (Craik 1997; Urry 2002; Roy and Gélinas 2004; Coupland et al. 2005; White 2005; Moïse et al. 2006; Pujolar 2006; Heller and Pujolar 2009). The problem that arises however, as many of the cited authors point out, is that it is difficult to balance authenticity with intelligibility, given that tourists of one's own group, however interested they may be in their own heritage, are not likely to constitute a big enough market for such heritage tourism activities to survive without drawing on a consumer pool from outside. Where linguistic minorities are concerned, this may require turning back to the bilingual practices that much ethnolinguistic nationalism eschews as a mark of oppression.

While there are clearly good reasons for commodifying 'authentic' (and almost by definition non-standardized) linguistic practices, doing so does present a management challenge, since it requires a flexible and variable approach to management, an approach not consistent with Taylorist ones. The dilemma is similar to the ones experienced by service workers such as those in call centers, who have to be able to respond to a wide variety of consumer expectations, ideologies, values, and competencies while being expected simultaneously to stick to a standardized script. The commodification of language, whether as a technical skill or as an authentic artefact, makes plain some central dilemmas of the new economy, notably how to be flexible and uniform at the same time – that is, how to ensure control over wide-flung markets while attending to locally variable market conditions, including those that produce different ideas about what added value is, or what constitutes specific niche markets.

The commodification of language also renews the importance of some questions long familiar to sociolinguists, such as what norms are for, what they might look like, and who gets to decide. In the next section I will discuss some contemporary debates about the relative merits of monolingualism and multilingualism, and of specific forms of monolingualism and multilingualism. These topics – relative merits and specific forms – are two key dimensions of the tension between standardization and variability characteristic of this field, and as a salient manifestation of the problem of norms as forms of social control and as modes of social reproduction. Here the two dimensions will be treated as a problem in the social organization and regulation of linguistic resources. Linguistic commodification also raises questions as to the extent to which language can be treated as a commodity in this way at all, or as to whether the aspects of language which are not about autonomous forms, but rather about social practices, necessarily escape the strict confines of marketization; and I will return to this question in the final section, on nation–states and post-nationalism.

The Production, Distribution, and Attribution of Value to Linguistic Resources

The commodification of language in the globalized new economy has a direct impact on the organization of the production, distribution, and attribution of value to linguistic resources. The nation-state economy harnessed the state bureaucracy and the establishment of state-run educational institutions (themselves bureaucratized, of course) to establish linguistic norms and to mask their use in social reproduction (Bourdieu and Passeron 1977), thereby protecting the interests of the bourgeoisie who built and ran the state. If anything, the globalized new economy has stiffened competition over linguistic resources at all points in the process of their marketization. It has also changed the grounds of how they are produced and valued, since they are linked to access to the new forms of economic activity characteristic of the new economy. The competition can include bones of contention in the form of all kinds of linguistic varieties (from standardized to authentically variable; from 'international' to authentically local; from 'monolingual' to 'multilingual'). It is apparent in the development of the language teaching industry, and in the multiplication of strategies social actors use to gain access to valuable linguistic resources.

We can begin with the obvious debates about whether English is taking over the world, and, if so, which English, and to what effect (Phillipson 1992; Bhatt 2001; Melchers and Shaw 2003; Phillipson 2003; Rubdy and Saraceni 2006; Duchêne and Heller 2007; Pennycook 2007). Here we have a general concern about whether the globalized new economy is really a form of neo-colonialism, and one in which the 'native speaker,' especially the native speaker of English, will have an unfair advantage, that is, one in which the old ideologies of how to evaluate linguistic proficiency will remain – because essentially we are dealing with an old familiar phenomenon (colonialism), dressed up and legitimized through new discourses (we see similar debates in other former colonialist spheres, such as those dominated by European French and Spanish; see contributions to Duchêne and Heller 2007; Del Valle 2006; Del Valle and Villa 2006; Mar-Molinero and Stewart 2006). We may talk about language as a technical skill available to anyone persevering enough to learn one, but really we will continue to use older ideas about language and identity to exclude any newcomers who want to get in on the act.

The idea that English in particular, and also other languages which are potentially important on the world market (notably Mandarin, in addition to former colonial languages like French and Spanish), are crucial to access to global markets has, of course, led to competition over their production and distribution. Language schools (both private and state-supported) are a growing industry; speakers of valuable languages are recruited, or recruit themselves, to the language teaching industry in major markets in Asia and Latin America, which has spin-offs for producers of teaching materials and organizers of what Yarymowich (2005) calls "edutourism" – that is, language learning activities connected to tourism. Potential learners invest time and money in language learning, usually valuing learning in an 'authentic' milieu over language classes at home. Emerging scholars, for example, are documenting class divisions in Korea between those whose search for English leads them to emigrate, to spend time in English-speaking countries, to have their tongues surgically altered, to attend language camps, or to consume English-language mass media (Shin 2009; Park 2009). Similar arguments can be made about growing interest in individual multilingualism among the middle class in the First World, as manifested in debates in countries such as Switzerland and Canada over the organization of second and third-language teaching through state-sponsored schooling. Individuals worry about what kind of linguistic repertoire they need in order for them or their children to profit from current conditions, and states worry about whether their citizens have the language skills they need in order to function under those conditions.

This set of market conditions is contested in multiple ways. One way has been to contest the very idea of the native speaker as the gold standard of linguistic proficiency (Singh 1998; Shin 2006) in favor of legitimizing multiple paths to linguistic proficiency and linguistic authority, and indeed in favor of delegitimizing ethnonational identity as even relevant to the question of how people should use language. Another way has been to argue for the legitimacy of multiple linguistic varieties; this amounts to a rejection of centralized norms of world languages like English, French, and Spanish in favor of something resembling what Marcellesi (1989) called "polynomia": the legitimation of multiple centers of definition of norms. These approaches also have their critics, who find in them an only slightly attenuated acceptance of neo-colonialist processes.

A final approach has been to resist the dominance of those languages altogether, sometimes on overtly political grounds, sometimes on the basis of other, but equally universalist, arguments. The political grounds are framed as struggles for language rights, building on the gains made by linguistic minorities in the past few decades; the best known proponent – from a sociolinguistic perspective – of the universalist movement, which casts language as a human right, is Tove Skutnabb-Kangas (2000), although political philosophers explore what the limits might be of linguistic diversity and of language rights in liberal democracies (Taylor 1994; Kymlicka and Patten 2003; May et al. 2004; May 2005). At the same time, arguments are also being made about the importance of maintaining linguistic diversity and of increasing the numbers of speakers of languages other than those which currently dominate the market, which goes under the rubric of what is generally known as the 'language endangerment' movement (Grenoble and Whaley 1998; Nettles and Romaine 2000; Hinton and Hale 2001). This movement tends to draw on environmentalist arguments, contending that linguistic diversity is like biodiversity, and similarly good for the planet. Linguistic diversity is important, they argue, because linguistic knowledge contains cultural knowledge which is untranslatable; because studying the diversity of linguistic forms allows us to capture the nature of language as a human phenomenon; and because communities of speakers should be able to control their own space through control of their own language (this last, of course, rejoins the language rights arguments cited above).

Critiques of these discourses in Duchêne and Heller (2007) argue that the latter cannot account for social, cultural, and linguistic change; that they assume ease of identification of boundaries of languages and of communities of speakers; that they assume the possibility of erasing variability within what is posited as a 'language,' to be protected and revitalized; and that they have no means of dealing with the ways in which linguistic variation is connected to relations of power, other than the simplified binary, hierarchical relationship of "dominated" and "dominant" languages – in other words, they suffer from all the flaws developed and practiced in linguistics within nation-state regimes. In addition, the contributors to Duchêne and Heller's volume note that an identical discourse is found in spaces where putatively powerful, dominant languages hold sway, including Swedish, French, Spanish, and even English itself. Following Cameron (1995), these authors argue that it is more effective to ask why this discourse is appearing so widely at this historical point; and they hypothesize that it represents a means for the existing elites – including those involved in the current state structures – to retain control over local or national markets, which may be threatened by capitalist expansion and by the consequent mobility of goods, information, and people.

Put differently, we can see the various strategies adopted by individuals, groups, or institutions to gain or retain control over linguistic resources, or simply access to them, as well as the discursive means for legitimating those strategies, as manifestations of changing market conditions (Bourdieu 1977). Bourdieu points out that, when the political–economic conditions underpinning markets shift, people generally have a predictable set of responses: they try to save the market (using old or new legitimating discourses) and to maintain or improve their position with respect to it; they try to gain a good position with respect to what might be emerging new markets; or they try to develop alternative markets. In the various positionings around the value and distribution of linguistic resources in the globalized new economy, we can see evidence of the first two kinds of strategies; alternative visions seem to be thin on the ground.

Language as Resource, Language as System: Nation–States and Post-Nationalism?

The emergence of the idea of language as a resource and of the new forms of its production and circulation in current market conditions does challenge dominant ideologies of language in important ways. Notably, it challenges the idea of language as a system, which has been the foundation of academic disciplines as well as of methods and programmes of teaching, learning, and evaluating language

– all of them implicated in the production and reproduction of ideologies of the nation–state.

We find ourselves instead looking for a framework and a methodology which free us from the constraints of thinking in terms of bounded homogeneous units. Contributors to Heller (2007) argue that we can draw on Bakhtinian notions of heteroglossia, on Foucauldian ideas of discourse, and on Bourdieuan ideas of markets to reimagine languages as communicative resources, socially constructed in uneven, unequal, distributed social spaces. These circulate – also unevenly and unequally – through social networks and communicative archipelagos, in ways which make them more or less accessible to speakers, as the latter have greater or lesser interest in mobilizing them in their own communicative action.

Heller (2007) argues that one consequence of this view is that we also have to focus, not on communities and identities, but rather on communicative processes and practices. This is not to say that social categories are not relevant, but rather that our focus has to shift away from taking dominant ideas about categories as not just socially but also somehow objectively real, or at least as units of analysis which can be presupposed, rather than problematized. The question then becomes one of discovering which forms of categorization are relevant to specific fields or areas of inquiry, how they are constituted, what makes their constitution possible and desirable (or not), and how looking at the communicative practices and resources involved helps us to understand the construction of relations of social difference and social inequality under certain historical conditions. Pujolar (2007) argues that a move in this direction constitutes a kind of post-national sociolinguistics: not in the sense that we are actually free of, or need not pay attention to, nation–states (which are clearly still present and highly functional), but rather in the sense that we need to be able to use the lens of language to understand how current social change reshapes it and constructs other potential forms of social, political, and economic organization. Put differently, this is an argument for reframing sociolinguistics at a distance from the essentially nationalist ideologies out of which it grew, as well as from the emerging forms of social organization we are currently involved in.

It is also an argument for analyzing linguistic forms and practices as situated in specific political–economic conditions, from which arise regimes of regulation and their legitimating discourses; and in both of these language may play a greater or a lesser role, or a role of different shapes, depending on what counts as authoritative or convincing under those conditions. Here I have argued that the globalized new economy places language in a particularly salient role, both as process and as product of work. As a result, language may also become a particularly salient site of contestation of high modern regimes of regulation, as is perhaps evidenced in movements for subverting state control of communicative technologies.

There remain a few further questions in this vein. One is: In whose interest does it lie to treat language as resource? Who benefits – and how – and who does not from understanding and doing language in this way? Another question is: Do the two main management practices in sight – that of standardizing as a skill and that of leaving it unregulated, as a talent – actually achieve management goals, or is it the case that the availability of communicative resources outside the ability of any institution to control them will undermine the only forms of control we know? And then, what will we invent?

REFERENCES

Addelman, B. (2005) Bombay calling: Life on the other end of the line. Thornhill, Ontario: Mongrel Media.

Belkhodja, C. (2006) *Au bout du fil*. Canada: Office national du film.

Bhatt, R. (2001) World Englishes. *Annual Review of Anthropology* 30: 527–50.

Block, D., and Cameron, D. (eds) (2002) *Globalization and Language Teaching*. London: Routledge.

Bourdieu, P. (1977) The economics of linguistic exchanges. *Social Science Information* 16(6): 645–68.

Bourdieu, P. (1979) *La Distinction: Critique sociale du jugement*. Paris: Editions de Minuit.

Bourdieu, P., and Passeron, J.-C. (1977) *Reproduction in Education, Society and Culture*. London: Sage.

Boutet, J. (2001) Le Travail devient-il intellectuel? *Travailler. Revue internationale de psychopathologie et de psychodynamique du travail* 6: 55–70.

Boutet, J. (2008) *La Vie verbale au travail. Des manufactures aux centres d'appels*. Toulouse: Octares.

Budach, G., Roy, S., and Heller, M. (2003) Community and commodity in French Ontario. *Language in Society* 32(5): 603–28.

Cameron, D. (1995) *Verbal Hygiene*. London: Routledge.

Cameron, D. (2001) *Good to Talk?* London: Sage.

Canada, Gouvernement du (2003) Le prochain acte: Un nouvel élan pour la dualité linguistique canadienne. Le plan d'action pour les langues officielles. Ottawa: Bureau du Conseil privé.

Castells, M. (2000) *The Information Age: Economy, Society and Culture*, 3 vols. Oxford: Blackwell.

Chassey, C., and Case, P. (2003) Talking shop: Contact centres and dimensions of 'social exclusion.' *Telematics and Informatics* 20: 275–96.

Coupland, N. (2003) Sociolinguistic authenticities. *Journal of Sociolinguistics* 7(3): 417–31.

Coupland, N., Garrett, P., and Bishop, H. (2005) Wales underground: Discursive frames and authenticities in Welsh mining heritage tourism events. In A. Jaworski and A. Pritchard (eds), *Discourse, Communication and Tourism*, 199–221. Clevedon, UK: Channel View Publications.

Cowie, C. (2007) The accents of outsourcing: The meanings of 'neutral' in the Indian call centre industry. *World Englishes* 26(3): 316–30.

Craik, J. (1997) The culture of tourism. In C. Rojek and J. Urry (eds), *Touring Cultures: Transformations of Travel and Theory*, 113–36. London: Routledge.

Del Valle, J. (2006) US Latinos, la hispanofonia, and the language ideologies of high modernity. In C. Mar-Molinero and M. Stewart (eds), *Globalization and Language in the Spanish-Speaking World*, 27–46. London: Palgrave Macmillan.

Del Valle, J., and L. Villa (2006) Spanish in Brazil: Language policy, business and cultural propaganda. *Language Policy* 5: 369–92.

Dubois, L., LeBlanc, M., and Beaudin, M. (2006) La Langue comme ressource productive et les rapports de pouvoir entre communautés linguistiques. *Langage et société* 118: 17–42.

Duchêne, A. (forthcoming) *Plurilinguisme, mobilité et nouvelle économie globalizée. Pratiques et idéologies langagières dans l'industrie aéroportuaire*. Bern: Peter Lang.

Duchêne, A. (2009) Marketing, management and performance: Multilingualism as a commodity in a tourism call center. *Language Policy* 8(1): 27–50.

Duchêne, A., and Heller, M. (eds) (2007) *Discourses of Endangerment: Ideology and Interest in the Defense of Languages*. London: Continuum.

Fairclough, N. (2002) Language in new capitalism. *Discourse and Society* 13(2): 163–6.

Fairclough, N. (2006) *Language and Globalization*. London: Routledge.

Gee, J., Hull, G., and Lankshear, C. (1996) *The New Work Order: Behind the Language of the New Capitalism*. Boulder, CO: Westview Press.

Giddens, A. (1990) *The Consequences of Modernity*. Berkeley, LA: University of California Press.

Golati, S. (2005) *Nalini by Day, Nancy by Night: A Film*. New York: Women Make Movies.

Grenoble, L., and Whaley, L. (eds) (1998) *Endangered Languages: Language Loss and Community Response*. Cambridge: Cambridge University Press.

Harvey, D. (1989) *The Condition of Postmodernity*. Oxford: Blackwell.

Heller, M. (2003) Globalization, the new economy and the commodification of language and identity. *Journal of Sociolinguistics* 7(4): 473–92.

Heller, M. (ed.) (2007) *Bilingualism: A Social Approach*. London: Palgrave Macmillan.

Heller, M., and Boutet, J. (2006) Vers de nouvelles formes de pouvoir langagier? Langue(s) et économie dans la nouvelle économie. *Langage et société* 118: 5–16.

Heller, M., and Pujolar, J. (2009) The political economy of texts: A case study

in the structuration of tourism. *Sociolinguistic Studies* 3(2): 177–202.

Hinton, L., and Hale, K. (eds) (2001) *The Green Book of Language Revitalization in Practice*. San Diego: Academic Press.

Hobsbawm, E. (1990) *Nations and Nationalism since 1760*. Cambridge: Cambridge University Press.

Kergoat, J., Boutet, J., Jacot, H., and Linhart, D. (eds) (1999) *Le Monde du travail*. Paris: La découverte.

Kymlicka, W., and Patten, A. (2003) Language rights and political theory. *Annual Review of Applied Linguistics* 23: 3–21.

Larner, W. (2002) Calling capital: Call centre strategies in New Brunswick and New Zealand. *Global Networks* 2: 133–52.

Liddicoat, A. (2007) Internationalising Japan: Nihonjinron and the intercultural in Japanese language-in-education policy. *Journal of Multicultural Discourses* 2(1): 32–46.

Mar-Molinero, C., and Stewart, M. (eds) (2006) *Globalization and Language in the Spanish-Speaking World*. London: Palgrave Macmillan.

Marcellesi, J.-B. (1989) Corse et théorie sociolinguistique: Reflets croisés. In G. Ravis-Giordani (ed.), *L'Ile miroir*, 165–74. Ajaccio: La Marge.

May, E. S. (2005) Debating language rights. Theme issue. *Journal of Sociolinguistics* 9(3): 319–460.

May, S., Modood, T., and Squires, J. (eds) (2004) *Ethnicity, Nationalism and Minority Rights*. Cambridge: Cambridge University Press.

McLaughlin, M., LeBlanc, M., Heller, M., and Lamarre, P. (2009) Les Mots du marché: L'inscription de la francophonie canadienne dans la nouvelle économie. *Francophonies d'Amérique* 27 (special issue).

Melchers, G., and Shaw, P. (2003) *World Englishes: An Introduction*. London: Arnold.

Mirchandani, K. (2004) Practices of global capital: Gaps, cracks and ironies in transnational call centres in India. *Global Networks* 4(4): 355–73.

Moïse, C., McLaughlin, M., Roy, S., and White, C. (2006) Le Tourisme patrimonial: La commercialisation de l'identité franco-canadienne et ses enjeux langagiers. *Langage et société* 118: 85–108.

Mulholland, K. (2004) Workplace resistance in an Irish call centre: slammin', scammin', smokin' and leavin.' *Work, Employment and Society* 18(4): 709–24.

Nettles, D., and Romaine, S. (2000) *Vanishing Voices: The Extinction of the World's Languages*. Oxford: Oxford University Press.

Park, J. (2009) *The Local Construction of a Global Language: Ideologies of English in South Korea*. Berlin: Mouton de Gruyter.

Pennycook, A. (2007) *Global Englishes and Transcultural Flows*. London: Routledge.

Phillipson, R. (1992) *Linguistic Imperialism*. Oxford: Oxford University Press.

Phillipson, R. (2003) *English-Only Europe? Challenging Language Policy*. London: New York, Routledge.

Porter, J. (1965) *The Vertical Mosaic: An Analysis of Class and Power*. Toronto: University of Toronto Press.

Poster, W. (2007) Who's on the line? Indian call centre agents pose as Americans for U.S.-outsourced forms. *Industrial Relations* 46(2): 271–304.

Pujolar, J. (2006) *Language, Culture and Tourism: Perspectives in Barcelona and Catalonia*. Barcelona: Turisme de Barcelona.

Pujolar, J. (2007) Bilingualism and the nation-state in the post-national era. In M. Heller (ed.), *Bilingualism: A Social Approach*, 71–95. London: Palgrave.

Roy, S. (2003) Bilingualism and standardization in a Canadian call center: Challenges for a linguistic minority community. In R. Bayley and S. Schecter (eds), *Language Socialization in Multilingual Societies*, 269–87. Clevedon, UK, Multilingual Matters.

Roy, S., and Gélinas, C. (2004) Le Tourisme pour les Franco-Albertains: Une porte d'entrée au monde. *Francophonies d'Amérique* 17(1): 131–40.

Rubdy, R., and Saraceni, M. (eds) (2006) *English in the World: Global Rules, Global Roles*. London: Continuum.

Shin, H. (2006) Rethinking TESOL from a SOL's perspective: Indigenous epîstemology and decolonizing praxis in TESOL. *Critical Inquiry in Language Studies* 3(2–3): 147–67.

Shin, H. (2009) 'Girogi Gajok': Transnationalism and language learning. *Curriculum, Teaching and Learning*. PhD thesis, Toronto, OISE/University of Toronto.

Singh, R. (ed.) (1998) *The Native Speaker: Multilingual Perspectives*. New Dehli: Sage.

Skutnabb-Kangas, T. (2000) *Linguistic Genocide in Education or Wolrdwide Diversity and Human Rights?* London: Lawrence Erlbaum.

Sonntag, S. (2006) Appropriating identity or cultivating capital? Global English in offshoring service industries. *Anthropology of Work Review* 26(1): 13–19.

Stitt, G. (2002) *Diverted to Delhi*. Australia: Filmakers Library, NY. [Documentary made in Australia and distributed by Filmakers Library, NY; running time 55 minutes.]

Sturge, K. (2007) *Representing Others: Translation, Ethnography and the Museum*. Manchester: St Jerome.

Taylor, C. (ed.) (1994) *Multiculturalism: Examining the Politics of Recognition*. Princeton, NJ: Princeton University Press.

Tsing, A. (2000) The global situation. *Cultural Anthropology* 15(3): 327–60.

Urry, J. (2002) *The Tourist Gaze*, 2nd edn. London: Sage.

White, C. (2005) L'Affirmation ou la négation de la différence: Pratiques et représentations linguistiques de francophones de Chéticamp dans le contexte du tourisme patrimonial. MA thesis, Moncton: Université de Moncton, Département d'études françaises.

Yarymowich, M. (2005) 'Language tourism' in Canada: A mixed discourse. In F. Baider, M. Burger, and D. Goutsos (eds), *La Communication touristique. Approches discursives de l'identité et de l'alterité*, 257–73. Paris: L'Harmattan.

16 Language and Movement in Space

JAN BLOMMAERT AND JIE DONG

Two Paradigms

Commenting on the way in which globalization processes are currently represented, Immanuel Wallerstein cautions:

> If we look at globalization and terrorism as phenomena that are defined in limited time and scope, we tend to arrive at conclusions that are as ephemeral as the newspapers. By and large, we are not then able to understand the meaning of these phenomena, their origins, their trajectory, and most importantly where they fit in the larger scheme of things. (Wallerstein 2004: ix)

Part of the problem, Wallerstein adds, is "that we have studied these phenomena in separate boxes to which we have given special names": the social sciences as currently constituted. He thus outlines the challenge of coming to terms with contemporary globalization processes: to understand them by means of theoretical frames that transcend the currently established ones. This means that we all have to move to more holistic objects of analysis, and that we continually have to re-examine critically the conceptual and methodological toolkits we use (Blommaert 2009).

The current wave of globalization is best understood as a development *within* globalization. The fact that we now use the term 'globalization' to describe the current developments should not trick us into believing that what we observe is fundamentally new. We just have a better word for it – a word that triggers a range of metaphors and images of intensified flows and movements across space and time of people, goods, messages, objects. These flows have been there for quite a while; we are now in a position to examine them more accurately.[1] The advent of the internet has given many of us a sense that we live in an age of revolutionary change. It is good to remember that the development of the telegraph, telephone, radio, and television caused the same buzz among contemporary observers. And what to think of the development, centuries earlier, of book

The Handbook of Language and Globalization, First Edition. Edited by Nikolas Coupland.

printing?[2] These earlier developments, too, had an impact on the way in which people used and circulated language, and on the way in which language varieties penetrated societies. Only, contemporary observers sought to understand linguistic phenomena very much with reference to language, not to society, and very much from within a frame in which the temporal and spatial conditions of language occurrence were seen as accidental and not very important. The descriptive and comparative tradition in linguistics in the late nineteenth and early twentieth century was an 'artefactual' tradition, according to which languages were connected to timeless peoples, who were topographically plotted on a particular area of distribution (Irvine 2001; Blommaert 2006). When time was at stake, linguistics tended to use *genealogical* models; when space was at stake, it tended to use *horizontal* models of space, expressed in stock metaphors such as those of the 'spread' or 'distribution' of languages or linguistic features.

Modern sociolinguistics drew this artefactualized image of language into real time and space. Studies of language variation focused strongly on diffusion – the spread of linguistic variables over a horizontal space – as in the work of Trudgill, Labov, and others (see Britain and Cheshire 2003). The conceptual development of space and time in such studies is superficial: there is attention to generational transmission (time) and to the distribution of variables in one locality, or across localities such as cities, regions, or countries (space). Labov's famous studies of New York City (1966) and of Martha's Vineyard (Labov 1972) are classics in this trend. Contact linguistics, in the meantime, focused on the sociolinguistic and linguistic patterns resulting from migration (Clyne 2003); and patterns of multilingualism resulting from migrations also caught the attention of scholars (Extra and Verhoeven 1998). One widespread problem with such studies is that the people whose language repertoires are studied, even if they are migrants, are 'fixed,' so to speak, in space and time. The phenomenology of migration and diaspora became an object of theoretical elaboration in cultural studies, sociology, and anthropology; and surely, in the context of recent globalization processes, notions such as transcultural flows, transidiomaticity and deterritorialization made their way into mainstream social science (Appadurai 1996; see also Jacquemet 2005). We now see that the mobility of people also involves the mobility of linguistic and sociolinguistic resources, that 'sedentary' patterns of language use are complemented by 'trans-local' forms of language use, and that the combination of both often accounts for unexpected sociolinguistic effects. The possibility of frequent electronic contact with the country of origin, for instance, can generate new forms of language innovation (and thus contribute to language maintenance) in diasporic communities (Blommaert 2009); small and marginal languages can, in the context of tourism, acquire new and unexpected forms of prestige (Heller 2003); popular culture such as hip hop or reggae can be a vehicle for the worldwide dissemination of particular language forms (Pennycook 2007), including new forms of literacy and message design (Kress and van Leeuwen 1996). All of these dimensions of mobility still collapse in concrete spaces where actual people live and interact with one another; the structure of people's repertoires and the patterns of multilingual language use, however, become less predictable and significantly more complex (Blommaert, Collins, and Slembrouck 2005a, 2005b; Collins 2007).

The upshot of these developments is that we see two paradigms developing: one is established, the other is just emerging. The established paradigm is the sociolinguistics of distribution as sketched above, in which movement of language resources is seen as movement in a horizontal and stable space; within such spaces, vertical stratification can occur along lines of class, gender, age, social status, and so on. The object of study, however, remains a 'snapshot,' in which things are in place, so to speak. The second paradigm can be called a sociolinguistics of mobility, and it focuses not on language-in-place but on language-in-motion, with various spatio-temporal frames interacting with one another. Such spatio-temporal frames have been described as 'scales,' and the assumption is that, in an age of globalization, language patterns must be understood as patterns that are organized at different, layered scale-levels (Blommaert 2005, 2007; Collins 2007). Access to, and control over, scales is unevenly distributed; it is a matter of power and inequality – as becomes clear when we consider typical resources for access to higher scales (that is, non-local and non-situationally specific ones) such as a sophisticated standard language variety, or advanced multi-modal and multilingual literacy skills.

This second paradigm, of course, faces the challenge of incorporating a more profound theoretical understanding of space. Space here is metaphorically seen as *vertical* space, as layered and stratified space. Every *horizontal* space (for instance a neighborhood, a region, a country) is also a *vertical* space, in which all sorts of socially, culturally, and politically salient distinctions occur. Such distinctions, as we shall see later, are *indexical* distinctions: distinctions that project minute linguistic differences onto stratified patterns of social, cultural, and political value-attribution; they convert linguistic differences into social inequalities, and thus they represent the 'normative' dimensions of situated language use (Silverstein 2006; Agha 2007). The stratified and ordered nature of such indexical processes we can call, by analogy with Foucault's 'order of discourse,' *orders of indexicality* (Blommaert 2005); and every horizontal space is filled with such orders of indexicality – with normative complexes that organize distinctions between 'good,' 'normal,' 'appropriate,' 'acceptable' language use and 'deviant,' 'abnormal,' and so on language use. Orders of indexicality define the dominant lines for senses of belonging, for identities and roles in society; and thus they underlie what Goffman called the "interaction order" – which is an *indexical* order (Silverstein 2003; Agha 2007; Collins and Slembrouck 2007).

The movement of people across space is therefore never a move across empty spaces. The spaces are always someone's space, and they are filled with norms, expectations, conceptions of what counts as proper and normal (indexical) language use and what does not. Mobility, sociolinguistically speaking, is therefore a trajectory through different spaces – stratified, controlled, and monitored ones – in which language 'gives you away.' Big and small differences in language use locate the speaker in particular indexical ascriptive categories – that is, categories that ascribe an identity and a role; and, as we have learned from John Gumperz' work (see for example Gumperz 1982), this is rarely inconsequential. Let us now turn to such patterns of mobility.

Globalization, Super-Diversity, and Multilingualism

Super-diversity

As mentioned above, the current globalization processes are best seen as part of longer, wider, and deeper globalization processes, in which they represent a particular stage of development. That development is real, however, and especially the changes in economic and technological infrastructure have affected whatever we currently understand by mobility. Migration was long seen as people *emigrating* and *immigrating* – that is, an enduring change in the spatial organization of one's life. People left their country and settled in another. In that new country, they lived separated from their country of origin, perhaps (but not necessarily) in ethnic communities. They took their languages and other cultural belongings with them, but the separation from the land of origin and the permanent nature of migration were likely to put them under pressure to accommodate to the host society. A tradition of study emerged in western host societies which was dedicated to such immigrant groups – relatively isolated, stable, and residential, often also consisting of large communities from the same country or even region of origin: Turks in Germany, Algerians and West Africans in France, Caribbean and East or South Asian people in Britain.[3]

The 1990s brought a change in the nature and profile of migration to western host societies, and Steven Vertovec (2006: 1) summarizes that process as follows:

> Over the past ten years, the nature of immigration to Britain has brought with it a transformative 'diversification of diversity' not just in terms of ethnicities and countries of origin, but also with respect to a variety of significant variables that affect where, how, and with whom people live.

These variables, Vertovec continues,

> include a differentiation in immigration statuses and their concomitant entitlements and restrictions of rights, labour market experiences, gender and age profiles, spatial factors, and local area responses by service providers and residents. [...] The interplay of these factors is what is meant here, in summary fashion, by the notion of 'super-diversity.'

The new migrants typically settle in older immigrant neighborhoods, which thus develop into a layered immigrant space, where resident ('old') immigrants often rent spaces to newer, more temporary or transient groups, and where new seg-ments of the labor market are developed. Many of the new immigrants live in economically and legally precarious circumstances, and many of them are strongly dependent upon informal employment and solidarity networks such as churches (Blommaert et al. 2005c; also Blommaert et al. 2005a, 2005b). The extreme linguistic diversity of such neighborhoods generates complex multilingual repertoires, in which often several (fragments of) 'migrant' languages and of lingua franca are combined.[4] And such neighborhoods often display a density of mediating institu-tions such as welfare and employment offices, as well as night shops and – sig-nificantly – telephone shops where international calls and internet access are offered at bargain prices.

Super-diversity poses descriptive as well as theoretical challenges. Descriptively, these globalized neighborhoods appear chaotic, and common assumptions about the national, regional, ethnic, cultural, or linguistic status of the inhabitants often prove to be useless. The presuppositions of common integration policies – that immigrants were known, and that they would have a shared language and culture – can no longer be upheld. In addition, the telephone shops show that, even if new migrants reside in one particular place, they are capable of maintaining intensive contacts with networks elsewhere, often including in their countries of origin. A burgeoning network of satellite and internet providers also allows them to follow (and be involved in) events in their country of origin and to consume its media and cultural products. Their spatial organization, consequently, is local as well as trans-local, real as well as virtual – and all of this has effects on the structure and development of language repertoires and patterns of language use. Theoretically, this stretches the limits of existing frameworks for analyzing and understanding multilingualism and the dynamics of language change. We can illustrate the complexity of these phenomena and theoretical issues by looking at a globalized neighborhood in Berchem: Antwerp.

Multilingual repertoires and super-diversity

The repertoires of new migrants often appear to be "truncated" (Blommaert et al. 2005a): highly specific 'bits' of language and varieties of literacy combine in a repertoire that reflects the fragmented and highly diverse life trajectories and environments of such people. Thus recent West African immigrants in Berchem, Antwerp can combine one or more African languages with a heavily accented vernacular variety of West African English, which can be used with some inter-locutors in the neighborhood and would be the medium of communication during weekly worship sessions in a new evangelical church in the neighborhood (Figure 16.1). English, however, is not part of the repertoire of most other immigrants in the neighborhood. Most of the shops, for instance, would be owned by Turkish or Moroccan people, who would often use vernacular forms of German or French as a lingua franca. Thus, when a Nigerian woman goes to buy bread in a Turkish-owned bakery, the code for conducting the transaction would be, for both, a strongly accented and very limited variety of local vernacular Dutch, mixed with

Figure 16.1   Posters at an Evangelical church. © Jan Blommaert

some English or German words. In the phone shops vernacular English would have slightly more currency, because the phone shops would typically be run by people from India or Pakistan. Note, however, that the particular varieties of English spoken in such transactions would be very different: none would be 'standard,' each variety would reflect informal patterns of acquisition and an uneasiness in use.

The Dutch used in the bakery is a minimal, informally acquired 'bit' of language – a specialized language skill that has its limits. It is insufficient for navigating institutional encounters: bureaucratic procedures are in standard and literate varieties of Dutch – typically, varieties that result from efforts at formal acquisition. Thus, when the Nigerian woman goes to her daughter's school for consultation on the child's progress, she would have to revert to her vernacular English. This would then be met by a heavily accented Belgian–Flemish variety of English from the teachers, and the interaction is typically less than smooth. The medium of communication between mother and child would be a mixed code, often blending unevenly distributed chunks of Dutch and English. The child, of course, would have access to more elaborate varieties of Standard and local vernacular Dutch and would often have to assist the mother and the teacher in accomplishing the communication tasks. This, importantly, points towards another feature of language that one encounters in such neighborhoods: the fact that communicative tasks often involve *collaborative work*. People would call on others, or others would volunteer, to translate and assist in communication. This is not only the case for tasks that involve literacy; it can also be found in face-to-face encounters. People very often pool their competences and skills in language when they have to accomplish demanding communication tasks.

At home the Nigerian family would have access to television, and the choice would be for English channels such as BBC World or MTV, with an occasional foray, often initiated by the children, into Dutch children's programmes. The level of consumption of local printed mass media would be very low, and access to printed sources from Nigeria would be limited. At the same time, telephone contacts would be maintained with people back home and with fellow migrants from the same area of origin, now living in Brussels, London, or Paris. Occasionally there would be mutual visits during which the African regional language could be the medium of communication among adults, while the children would revert to vernacular forms of English to interact with each other. Their exposure to education environments in which different languages are the medium of instruction – Dutch and French, for instance – precludes the use of any other language.

Thus we see very fragmented and 'incomplete' – 'truncated' – language repertoires, most of which consists of spoken, vernacular, and accented varieties of different languages, with an overlay of differentially developed literacy skills in one or some languages (depending on the level of literacy at the time of migration). We also see how many communication tasks are accomplished collaboratively, by combining the resources and skills of several people. The particular patterns of such repertoires are difficult to establish in detail – here is the descriptive challenge. The sociolinguistic world of these people is strictly local (the neighborhood) as well as widely trans-local (the network of fellow migrants elsewhere, the communication with people back home, the media). And, internally, we find differentiation in language repertoires: adults have different repertoires from children, and fellow migrants from the same region, now living elsewhere, have different repertoires as well.

The local environment of these people is abundantly multilingual. Since Nigerians are a very small minority, their languages are invisible in the public space. The older, resident communities – Turks and Moroccans – do publicly display the formal, literate aspects of their multilingualism (Figure 16.2).

We see Arabic and Turkish displayed in shops and on posters announcing cultural or political events. Such public language displays can index the size and the degree of solidification of particular immigrant communities. Thus Albanian posters have recently begun to appear, indicating the existence of a well-organized and resident Albanian migrant community in Belgium (Figure 16.3).

Groups that have not yet achieved this level of stability and visibility revert to highly unstable forms of written language, mixing English and Dutch and betraying a vernacular pronunciation of words, as the display of tariffs in phone shops

Figure 16.2 Moroccan bakery. © Jan Blommaert

Figure 16.3 Albanian poster. © Jan Blommaert

Figure 16.4   Rates at a phone shop. © Jan Blommaert

illustrate (Figure 16.4). They are also addressed by fully globalized signs in Standard English – advertising products that cater to the specific needs of recent and economically vulnerable immigrants (needs such as money transfer operations; see Figure 16.5).

The uneven distribution of language resources, of degrees of public legitimacy of languages, and of patterns of access to language resources becomes clear when we consider examples such as the one displayed in Figure 16.6, where we see how someone changed the name 'Clear Channel' to 'Liar Channel' on a billboard.

This is a playful language act, revealing advanced competence in English and in literacy, as well as a particular critical political stance. When we compare Figure 16.6 with Figure 16.4, we see how strongly the levels of literacy and command of language varieties differ within one community. The reason is the particular social and cultural mix of the neighborhood. Of late, the neighborhood has also seen an influx of educated, middle-class native Belgians, attracted by the affordable housing prices and (like the other immigrants) by the presence of a big railway station. These people typically have access to prestige varieties of language and prestige forms of multilingualism – Standard Dutch and Standard English. In this

Figure 16.5   Advertisements for money transfer services at a phone shop. © Jan Blommaert

way highly advanced multilingual repertoires can be displayed alongside very incomplete ones, and the general picture is one of extreme mixedness. It is hard to identify the 'dominant' language in the neighborhood. Vernacular forms of Dutch would probably have the widest local currency; at the same time various languages point inwards, to local communities and small networks in the neighborhood, as well as outwards, to trans-local and transnational networks that have their 'hub' in the neighborhood. Languages and language varieties operate and have validity at particular scale levels, from the strictly local to the strictly global, with all sorts of intermediate scale levels in between. In our example, the weekly worship session gathers several hundreds of people and so creates a trans-local, but locally anchored scale-level. And the occasional visits from and to fellow immigrants also create a local–trans-local scale level. Each time, elements of the repertoires will have to be mobilized, because the different criss-crossing scales answer to different orders of indexicality. A language variety that is good enough for performing adequately during the worship session is not necessarily good enough for buying bread in the bakery or for talking to the schoolteacher.

Figure 16.6   'Liar Channel.' © Jan Blommaert

Stratified distribution

If we now try to summarize some of the elements discussed so far, we see that a sociolinguistic analysis of such globalization phenomena cannot proceed on the basis of common notions of distribution. First, *what* is distributed is not easily defined, for we are never just talking about languages, but always about highly specific language resources (the 'little bits' of language we referred to earlier). Second, *how* these resources are distributed also requires a lexicon and imagery of considerable complexity, for there is no 'flat' distribution, no juxtaposition of particular resources. We see a range of densely layered, *stratified distribution patterns*, in which the particular, specific language resources are deployed (and deployable) on particular scale levels and not on others; what is valid in one situation is not valid in another. Some resources will allow mobility across situations and scale levels. Prestige varieties of language, Standard Dutch for instance, would have currency across a wide variety of situations; the same goes for prestige and literate varieties of English, be it in a very different set of situations. These are highly mobile resources. Others – think of the African languages spoken by our Nigerian subjects – have very little in the way of mobility potential. Their range is largely confined to the adults in the family and the wider network, and to some restricted use with the children. Outside these situations, such languages have no potential for use. Institutionally they are often not even recognized as languages.[5]

The key to understanding this complex pattern is *what counts as language* in particular contexts: what is ratified and recognized as a valid code for making oneself understood. The key is, in other words, the indexical value that particular linguistic resources have. In highly complex neighborhoods such as the one we discussed here, complex and truncated repertoires can have such validity, at least to the extent that particular ingredients of the repertoires are mapped onto particular microenvironments, networks, or situations. Migrants, consequently, are often confronted with situations in which the language and the communicative requirements stretch their repertoires and in which complex patterns of shifting and mixing occur. It is in such moments that we see delicate articulations of subject position that index migrant identities and life trajectories. Let us now examine such patterns.

Accents, Shifting, and Microvariation

Accent at a street corner

Human trajectories leave traces in speech repertoires, and whenever people produce language, they produce complex packages of accents: various regional accents, social status accents, age accents, and gender accents. Such accent packages index identities, and the organization of this indexical work is non-random. In order to illustrate the complexities as well as the systematic nature of such work, we will look at an excerpt from a fieldwork interview recorded in a migrant neighborhood in Beijing, China, in late 2006. China has known a massive internal migration over the last decades, from rural areas to the cities and the special economic regions, as an effect of the country's economic boom. In the multi-ethnic and multilingual context of China, this phenomenon has involved a reordering of the sociolinguistic landscape of immigrant areas. While Standard Chinese – Putonghua – is known by an overwhelming majority of citizens, regional accents do occur, and, as elsewhere, they are ordered hierarchically. Certain accents mark a metropolitan, sophisticated identity, while others mark rural origins, low levels of education, and marginal social–economic status.

In this excerpt, the fieldworker (R) goes out in the morning to buy dumplings from a street corner dumpling seller (X), whose origins lie in the South. The fieldworker has been a regular customer of the dumpling seller's breakfast business. She (R) has a Beijing accent, and during the interaction with the dumpling seller a delicate play of topic, accent, and identity develops.

Excerpt   From authors' own data

Transcript.
{traffic noise, people talk unintelligibly}

1   **X.** ni <u>yao</u> *shen me [shrən² mə] de (baozi)*? {weak slow voice, noticeably trying to pronounce in local Beijing accent}

   R. ni zhe er dou you shen me de ya?

   X. you...

5   ...{conversations about the kinds of steamed dumplings he offers}

   R. nimen zhe er de shengyi tinghao de, zheme duo ren dou mai nimen de baozi.

   X. {laughing voice}*jiushi* zaoshang hao, daole xiawu jiu <u>mei ren</u> chi baozi le {still making efforts to mimicking Beijing accent}.

   R. zaoshang shengyi hao jiu xingle. Neige xia de ni fang jin (dai er li) qu le ma?

10   **X.** {nod with smile}nei tinghao de – women cong <u>laojia</u> dailai de.

   R. zhende?! Shi na er ya?

   X. {proud, smile} women de xia doushi <u>changjiang</u> li de xia... **tebie haochi** [t'ə⁴ xo³k'e¹] {his voice is noticeably higher and faster, and with clearer southern accent}.

   ...{conversations about how they brought the shrimps from that far away place}

15   **R.** ni Putonghua shuo de ting hao de, zai xuexiao li xuede?

   X. *hai xing ba*. You de (gu ke) ye buzhidao wo shuo shenme {end with laughing   voice, Indicating this is a humble response}

   R. wo juede ni de Putonghua zhen tinghao de, wo tingde ting qingchu de ya.

   X. en, zai xuexiao li xuede. Wo du <u>dao</u> **gao zhong** [kau¹ chrɔŋ¹] ne {switches from

20   noticeable southern accent to near-Putonghua}.

   Ni jiu shi [ni³ chyiu̜⁴ shrɪ̜⁴] Beijing ren? {smile, and switch to certain characteristics of Beijing accent}

   R. ai. Wo jiushi zhe er de.

   X. *jiushi zhe er de* [chyiu̜⁴ shrɪ̜⁴ chreɻ⁴ de]{repeat in a low voice, still in a effort of producing Beijing accent}

25   **R.** nimen zai xuexiao <u>quan</u> yong Putonghua?

   X. women xue (Putonghua in school), ye shuo nei zhong fangyan.

   R. na ni zenme lian de ya {smile}?

   X. wo... wo zai zhe er **dai guo** [tai¹ kuɔ]{switch to his Beijing accent with a higher, prolonged and jolly voice, indicating he was pleased by my comment on his Putonghua, and was proud

30   that he was not a stranger to the city of Beijing}

   R. na ni dou ting de dong zhe er ren shuo hua ma?

   X. ting de dong, jiu shi bie ren **shuo <u>fangyan</u>** [fɒŋ¹ ien²] wo ting bu dong {switches back to Putonghua}.

   R. = nashi. Bie ren shuo fangyan wo ye ting bu dong.

35   **X.** = youde shuo <u>fangyan</u>, wo bantian buzhidao shenme ne {end with laughing voice, amused}

   R. jiu shi; erqie zhe di er ba, na er de ren dou you, suoyi na er de fangyan dou you...

Translation
{traffic noise, people talk unintelligibly}

1   X.   *which ones* (of the steamed dumplings) would you <u>like</u>? {weak slow voice, noticeably trying to pronounce in local Beijing accent}

    R.   what kinds do you offer?

    X.   here we have …

5   … {conversations about the kinds of steamed dumplings he offers}

    R.   you are doing a good business: so many people get their breakfast from you.

    X.   {laughing voice} *only* good in the morning; <u>no one</u> comes in the afternoon {still making efforts at mimicking Beijing accent}.

    R.   the morning business is good enough. Have you put the shrimp one in (the bag)?

10   X.   {nod with smile} that's a good one – we brought the shrimps from our <u>hometown</u>.

    R.   seriously?! Where is it?

    X.   {proud, smile} they are shrimps from the <u>Yangtze river</u> … **good shrimps** {his voice is noticeably higher and faster, and with clearer southern accent} … {conversations about how they brought the shrimps from that far away place}

15   R.   you speak good Putonghua, did you learn that from school?

    X.   *just so-so*. Some (customers) couldn't figure out what I said {end with laughing voice, indicating this is a humble response}

    R.   I found your Putonghua is really good, I have no problem understand you.

    X.   well, we <u>learnt</u> Putonghua in school. I studied **up to high school** {switches from

20   noticeable southern accent to near-Putonghua}.

    are you a Beijing person? {smile, and switch to certain characteristics of Beijing accent}

    R.   yeah, I am from here.

    X.   *from here* {repeat in a low voice, still in a effort of producing Beijing accent'}

25   R.   did you <u>all</u> use Putonghua in school?

    X.   we learnt (Putonghua in school) but also talk in our own dialect.

    R.   then how comes your Putonghua is so good {smile}?

    X.   I… I **was here** before {switch to his Beijing accent with a higher, prolonged and jolly voice, indicating he was pleased by my comment on his Putonghua, and

30   was proud that he was not a stranger to the city of Beijing}

    R.   Do you (always) understand what people speak here in Beijing?

    X.   usually I can, when people **talk in their dialects**, I can't {switches back to Putonghua}.

    R.   = sure. I can't if they use dialects.

35   X.   = they use <u>dialects</u> when order steamed dumplings, for a few minutes I don't know what they are telling me {end with laughing voice, amused}

    R.   that's right; also there is very mixed, you can find people from everywhere (of the country), and many dialects …

We see in this brief, friendly, and informal interaction a series of shifts that are hardly noticeable when we use 'language' as our only diacritic. The whole of the conversation is in Chinese; but different varieties of Chinese are used, and the use of these differences is not random. This becomes clear when we look at the distribution of regionally marked, accented utterances made by X. They start occurring from line 12 on, each time in a mix with an approximate Beijing accent, and they stop occurring in line 31. The fragments before and after that section are spoken respectively in an approximate Beijing accent (ll. 1–11) and in a rather neutral variety of Putonghua (ll. 32–7). This summary of accent shifts does not intend to suggest that the shifts occur across clearly defined boundaries; rather, several closely related language varieties are creatively and delicately played out in the episode.

These shifts in accent are part of a bigger series of shifts in the conversation. The three units are topical as well. In the first unit (ll. 1–11), R and X initiate a business transaction and the talk is about what is on offer, what exactly will be bought by R, and how business is these days. This topic ends when X mentions the fact that the shrimps he uses come from his home town; R picks it up and asks in line 11 where X's home town is. This initiates a second topic: the migration trajectory of X and his knowledge of Putonghua. The topic shifts again in line 30, when R inquires about the comprehensibility of the speech of other immigrants in the area. The topical shifts correlate with the accent shifts. Latter they also correlate with shifts in 'footing': X speaks differently and enacts different personae in each of the units. In the first unit, his role can best be described as that of a dumpling seller (a clear commercial identity) and, stylistically, he talks in a slow and neutral tone. In the second topical unit he speaks as an immigrant who comes from the South and has acquired Putonghua at school; stylistically, he appears more excited and enthusiastic. The shift to the topic of the other, more recent, immigrants in the area triggers again another role. He now aligns with R and appears to define himself as an inhabitant of the local Beijing neighborhood. The migrant identity has been overlaid by a local identity, and he expresses a sense of belonging in and entitlement to a place in an engaged and enthusiastic style. He is from an earlier generation of migrants and in contrast with newer immigrants; he is a local man.

The shifts in accents thus come in a package in which topic and role, or identity, correlate with accent and style. And orientations to space shoot through these packages. In the first unit, the space is neutral: it is a commercial transactional space, in which R and X have clear roles. In the second unit, the space is that of the South versus Beijing, or the periphery versus the center, and in the third unit the space is the particular area in Beijing. Spatial orientations frame the interaction, and shifts in such orientations again correlate with the other shifts we already mentioned. Let us try to summarize these packaged shifts in X's speech in a table.

Micro-variation

The shifts we have seen in the example above are microscopic; they are shifts within one language, shifts in accents that are often only perceivable and

Table 16.1 Summary of the shifts

	Space	Accent	Style	Identity
Unit 1 (1–11)	commercial	Putonghua, Beijing accent	neutral	dumpling seller
Unit 2 (12–31)	the South and Beijing	Southern accent, Beijing accent	engaged, enthusiastic	immigrant from the South
Unit 3 (32–38)	neighborhood	Putonghua	engaged	local resident

distinct to insiders (for an overview of variationism in sociolinguistics, see Coupland 2007). Their distribution and correlation with other discourse features – topic, style, identity – and the correlation we see with particular spatial orientations show, however, that they provide rich indexical meanings to these insiders, who pick up the shifts and project meanings onto them. In the context of migration, accents – always a plural phenomenon – become very much a part of the speech repertoires of people, and they reflect the spatial and social mobility that is a central feature of the experience of migration.[7] They also become part of indexical repertoires, as accents 'give off' rich meanings about who one is and how one talks. Accents betray life trajectories, and in a real social world, where people have mental maps and images of reality, such trajectories are meaningful: spaces are never neutral, as we said earlier, they are always someone's space and always contain orders of indexicality that provide frames for inferring social meanings. X's attempted Beijing accent, consequently, has a very different indexical value in Beijing from the one it has in his home town in the South. In both places the accent produces different images of identity, different interactional orders, and different effects on interlocutors. Indexical judgments are primarily local, and when indexical elements move through space they change value and meaning.

In the context of globalization, consequently – and perhaps paradoxically – analytic attention should go to microvariation. Increased mobility of people means increased mobility across markets of accents and speech varieties. And what works well in one place can backfire elsewhere. This, no doubt, has implications for the study of language contact. Often what comes into contact is not languages but regionally (and hence socially, culturally, politically) marked varieties. As we have seen in the example above, the result of such contacts is a layered, multi-accented repertoire that can be mobilized by speakers to produce particular meanings, but can also be mobilized by their interlocutors, who ascribe particular meanings to them. If we go back to our Nigerian woman for a moment: the heavily accented variety of vernacular Dutch she masters can, for her, be an index of successful integration into the host society; for the schoolteacher, however, or for the welfare worker or local politician, that same accent can index a lack of integration, even a resistance to integration – exactly the opposite.

Conclusion: The Unfinished Story

The study of language and space requires a new conceptual apparatus and vocabulary, one in which mobility is central and in which the effects of mobility on repertoires and interactional practices can be addressed in their full complexity. Language is traditionally seen as something that anchors people in a local context: it is described as something that belongs to a particular environment, is locked into local meanings and interactional dynamics. This insight is too important to be dismissed, and research on it has yielded important results. But it is a partial view, for language is also something trans-local: it moves along with people across space and time, and it is being deployed locally in ways that reveal the trans-local histories of the speaker's resources. Language is not just a tool for the construction of locality, it is also a tool for mobility (Blommaert 2009).

This assumption moves several theoretical issues to the forefront. The effect on concepts such as 'speech community' should be evident (Rampton 1998): in a context of mobility, the connection between a speech community and a set of established, and shared, forms of knowledge of languages and of language norms must be questioned. The one who speaks may belong to the same speech community as the one who listens, but only temporarily and without the shared understandings we assume in members of a speech community, traditionally defined. This, then, locks into another issue: we need to have a closer look at the dialogical nature of social interactions as foundations for sociolinguistic research. When common ground between interlocutors can no longer be taken for granted, it is the interactional dynamics and the uptake of each other's words that will inform us about the sociolinguistic contexts of interactions. A fully developed interactional sociolinguistics is therefore something of a priority.

Another issue that awaits focused attention is that of function. Hymes (1996) already warned against the lack of theoretical concern for language functions, observing that the same language form may (and does) have very different functions, depending on where, how, and why it is used and on how it fits into speakers' repertoires. This functional relativity is of crucial importance for understanding processes of mobility and language (Blommaert 2003). As was repeatedly mentioned earlier, what works well in one place may not work at all elsewhere; highly articulate people in one place may be very inarticulate in other places. Spatial trajectories are also trajectories that affect the function and value of linguistic resources; examining this issue is a critical task for a sociolinguistics of mobility. All of this, and much more, will be on the agenda of the current and future generations of scholars. We have only begun to spot the challenges, and some we have been able to identify. But the story is, as yet, very much unfinished.

NOTES

1   In the opening chapter of his *Age of Empire*, Eric Hobsbawm asks how the world of the 1880s could be compared with that of the 1790s; his answer is: "[i]n the first place, it was now genuinely global" (Hobsbawm 1987: 13). In effect the nineteenth century was the era of globalization, and Hobsbawm actually uses the term globalization for the processes of capitalist expansion in the nineteenth century (ibid., p. 14n).

2   Hobsbawm's oeuvre is, again, instructive on this point. What we see, in effect, is how every step in the development of modern capitalism was accompanied by political transitions – from oligarchic to democratic states – and by changes in the educational and communication infrastructure of societies that underwent such political and economic transformations. Mass politics (an effect of the labor movement, in turn an effect of the growth of industrial capitalism) required mass media. Globalized business required globalized communication systems such as the telegraph. Observers from each period noted and commented upon such changes as fundamental, deep, and lasting changes in society.

3   We must note here the very restricted gaze of such studies. The typical 'host' society since the 1970s is not a late modern west European state, but a Third-World country adjacent to another Third-World country, who is torn by civil war or by natural disaster. To give one illustration: during the genocide in Rwanda in 1994, an estimated 700,000 Rwandan people entered Tanzania. The refugee camp where most of them were harbored was, for all practical purposes, the second largest 'city' in the country.

4   The observations in this and the next subsection are the result of fieldwork carried out by Jan Blommaert and associates – in 2004, in migrant neighborhoods in Ghent (Blommaert et al. 2005a, 2005b), and in 2006–7, in a similar neighborhood in Berchem, Antwerp. (The latter is Jan Blommaert's home neighborhood.)

5   Turkish, Arabic, Spanish, Portuguese, Russian, and Chinese, on the other hand, would occur in the multilingual flyers of welfare or socio-cultural organizations in the neighborhood. Blommaert and colleagues (2006) examined processes of linguistic disqualification in a Dutch immersion class in Antwerp. It appeared that teachers often did not even know the linguistic repertoires of their pupils. The attitude was that only one language counted as a language: Dutch.

6   Fieldwork was conducted by Jie Dong. Transcription conventions:

_ (underline)	stress
=	interruption or next utterance following immediately
{ }	transcriber's comment
**	segment quieter than surrounding talk, or weaker than the rest of the sentence
( )	omitted part in the utterance
italics	the shifts among accents (Beijing accent – provincial accent – Putonghua – Beijing accent – Putonghua).

7   Similar phenomena, also revealing the close connections between spatial orientations and packaged micro-shifts, were described by Maryns and Blommaert (2001) and by Blommaert (2005, chapter 8). Attention to phonetic detail – the usual clue to microvariation – is also strongly emphasized by Rampton (2006), whose analyses of multi-ethnic British classrooms reveal very similar patterns of salience for microscopic accent differences.

REFERENCES

Agha, A. (2007) *Language and Social Relations*. Cambridge: Cambridge University Press.

Appadurai, A. (1996) *Modernity at Large*. Minneapolis: University of Minnesota Press.

Blommaert, J. (2003) Commentary: A sociolinguistics of globalization. *Journal of Sociolinguistics* 7(4): 607–23.

Blommaert, J. (2005) *Discourse: A Critical Introduction*. Cambridge: Cambridge University Press.

Blommaert, J. (2006) From fieldnotes to grammar: Artefactual ideologies and the textual production of languages in Africa. In G. Sica (ed.), *Open Problems in Linguistics and Lexicography*, 13–59. Milan: Polimetrica.

Blommaert, J. (2007) Sociolinguistic scales. *Intercultural Pragmatics* 4(1): 1–19.

Blommaert, J. (2009) *A Sociolinguistics of Globalization*. Cambridge: Cambridge University Press.

Blommaert, J., Collins, J., and Slembrouck, S. (2005a) Spaces of Multilingualism. *Language and Communication* 25(3): 197–216.

Blommaert, J., Collins, J., and Slembrouck, S. (2005b) Polycentricity and interaction regimes in 'global neighborhoods.' *Ethnography* 6(2): 205–35.

Blommaert, J., Creve, L., and Willaert, E. (2006) On being declared illiterate: Language-ideological disqualification in Dutch classes for immigrants in Belgium. *Language and Communication* 26: 34–54.

Blommaert, J., Beyens, K., Meert, H., Hillewaert, S., Verfaillie, K., Stuyck, K., and Dewilde, A. (2005c) *Grenzen aan de Solidariteit: Formele en informele patronen van solidariteit in het domein van migratie, huisvesting en veiligheid*. Brussel and Ghent: Federaal Wetenschapsbeleid/ Academia Press.

Britain, D., and Cheshire, J. (eds) (2003) *Social Dialectology: In Honour of Peter Trudgill*. Amsterdam: John Benjamins

Clyne, M. (2003) *Dynamics of Language Contact*. Cambridge: Cambridge University Press.

Collins, J. (2007) *Migration and Multilingualism: Implications for Linguistic Anthropology and Education Research*. London, Ghent, Albany: Working Papers in Urban Language and Literacies 47.

Collins, J., and Slembrouck, S. (2007) *Goffman and Globalization: Participation Frames and the Spatial and Temporal Scaling of Migration-Related Multilingualism*. London, Ghent, Albany: Working Papers in Urban Language and Literacies 46.

Coupland, N. (2007) *Style: Language Variation and Identity*. Cambridge: Cambridge University Press.

Extra, G., and Verhoeven, L. (eds) (1998) *Bilingualism and Migration*. Berlin: Mouton de Gruyter.

Gumperz, J. (1982) *Discourse Strategies*. Cambridge: Cambridge University Press.

Heller, M. (2003) Globalization, the new economy, and the commodification of language and identity. *Journal of Sociolinguistics* 7(4): 473–92.

Hobsbawm, E. (1987) *The Age of Empire: 1875–1914*. London: Abacus.

Hymes, D. (1996) *Ethnography, Linguistics, Narrative Inequality: Toward an Understanding of Voice*. London: Taylor and Francis.

Irvine, J. (2001) The family romance of colonial linguistics: Gender and family in nineteenth-century representations of African languages. In S. Gal and K. Woolard (eds), *Languages and Publics: The Making of Authority*, 30–45. Manchester: St Jerome.

Jacquemet, M. (2005) Transidiomatic Practices: Language and power in the age of globalization. *Language and Communication* 25(3): 257–77.

Kress, G., and van Leeuwen, T. (1996) *Reading Images: The Grammar of Virtual Design*. London: Routledge.

Labov, W. (1966) *The Social Stratification of English in New York City*. Washington, DC: Center for Applied Linguistics.

Labov, W. (1972) *Sociolinguistic Patterns*. Philadelphia: University of Pennsylvania Press.

Maryns, K., and Blommaert, J. (2001) Stylistic and thematic shifting as a narrative resource: Assessing asylum seekers' repertoires. *Multilingua* 20(1): 61–84.

Pennycook, A. (2007) *Global Englishes and Transcultural Flows*. London: Routledge.

Rampton, B. (1998) Speech community. In J. Verschueren, J.-O. Östman, J. Blommaert, and C. Bulcaen (eds), *Handbook of Pragmatics 1998*, 1–30. Amsterdam: John Benjamins.

Rampton, B. (2006) *Language in Late Modernity*. Cambridge: Cambridge University Press.

Silverstein, M. (2003) Indexical order and the dialectics of sociolinguistic life. *Language and Communication* 23: 193–229.

Silverstein, M. (2006) Pragmatic Indexing. In K. Brown (ed.), *Encyclopaedia of Language and Linguistics*, 2nd edn, Vol. 6, 14–17. Amsterdam: Elsevier.

Vertovec, S. (2006) *The Emergence of Super-Diversity in Britain*. Centre on Migration, Policy and Society, Working Paper 25: Oxford University.

Wallerstein, I. (2004) *World-Systems Analysis: An Introduction*. Durham, NC: Duke University Press.

17 Indexing the Local

BARBARA JOHNSTONE

Globalization divides as much as it unites; it divides as it unites – the causes of division being identical with those which promote the uniformity of the globe. Alongside the emerging planetary dimensions of business, finance, trade and information flow, a 'localizing,' space-fixing process is set in motion.

Bauman 1998: 2

Attention to linguistic variation world-wide is evidenced in efforts to document or revive dying languages; in political struggles over language and dialect rights, national languages, and language in education; and in the commodification of languages and language varieties in film, on TV, radio, and the internet, in folk dictionaries and on other tourist artefacts. New attention to regional variation has been part of this trend. As speech in Newcastle (England) levels to a regional standard in the wake of outmigration (Watt 2002), people start to refer to the Newcastle football club as *The Toon*, spelling the local pronunciation of 'town' (Beal 1999). As island-dwellers in the eastern US encounter more and more outsiders and their dialects die, they cling to one or two local forms (Schilling-Estes 1998, 2002). This is not the first time that regional linguistic variation has become salient in political and popular culture. But it seems paradoxical that regional variation should be so noticeable in the early twenty-first century, in the context of the globalizing trends that are leading people to speak more like people from other places. What are we to make of such apparent returns to the local in the context of globalization? Why does discourse about linguistic variety arise even as the differences between dialects and languages threaten to disappear? Why is this happening now, and when and why has it happened in the past? I hope to show in this chapter that dialect leveling and dialect awareness in fact have exactly the same origins – namely in social and geographical mobility and in the discursive practices that arise in its wake. The noticing of linguistic difference that can lead to celebrations of, or conflicts over, linguistic localness can also lead to the eradication of difference, and the conditions that make dialect awareness possible are the same as those that make leveling possible.

The Handbook of Language and Globalization, First Edition. Edited by Nikolas Coupland.
© 2013 Blackwell Publishing Ltd except for editorial material and organization © 2013 Nikolas Coupland.
Published 2013 by Blackwell Publishing Ltd.

According to globalization theorist Stuart Hall, "[t]he return to the local is often a response to globalization" (Hall 1991: 34). "It is a respect for local roots," says Hall, "which is brought to bear against the anonymous, impersonal world of the globalized forces which we do not understand" (ibid.). I argue that such accounts oversimplify the situation when it comes to the current resurgence of interest in regional dialects. After summarizing research on dialect contact and dialect awareness, I show that, at least when it comes to language, renewed attention to the local is not a nostalgic or desperate *response* to globalization but an inevitable *result* of globalization. While such attention can, as Hall suggests, involve renewed "respect" for people's local roots, it does not arise from respect. Rather, changes attendant upon globalization – geographic mobility, the increased heterogeneity of local demography, and economic change that forces people to re-imagine themselves – are precisely the conditions that most effectively foster dialect and language awareness. To illustrate this claim I draw on work that I and my colleagues have done in Pittsburgh, PA, a deindustrializing city in northeastern US (Johnstone et al. 2002; Johnstone and Baumgardt 2004; Johnstone et al. 2006). I use the concept of indexical order (Silverstein 2003) to model how social and economic change over the course of the latter half of the twentieth century has made local speech forms hearable, first as "markers" (Labov 1972: 178–80) of correctness, care, and the like, and later as examples of 'Pittsburghese,' an (imagined) dialect associated with local identity.

Regional Dialects in Contact

Peter Trudgill's *Dialects in Contact* (1986) set off a wave of work leading to a more and more nuanced understanding of 'dialect leveling' – that is, the ways in which dialects can lose aspects of their distinctiveness when their speakers come into contact with speakers of other dialects. According to Trudgill's influential model, contact among speakers who use different linguistic forms might be expected to lead to linguistic accommodation (Giles et al. 1973) on the part of speakers who need to express solidarity or avoid miscommunication with others. Over the long run, this process might be expected to lead to the leveling of varieties – a reduction, that is, in the number of differences between them. In the US as in Europe, industrialization, which began in the eighteenth century, made people move from the countryside to the cities. Subsequent developments included the emergence of suburbs and of 'new towns' during the twentieth century and a current urban revival trend that, in some cases, is shifting poorer people outwards from city centers as wealthier people move back in. The sociolinguistic consequences of these historical developments have included dialect leveling and the formation of *koine*-ized 'new dialects' when sets of simplified, mixed, and leveled forms were no longer identified with the source dialects (Kerswill 2005).

Dialect leveling has been documented in many geographic settings, including England (Kerswill and Williams 2000; Britain 2002; Watt 2002), the US (Thomas

1997), and Europe (Auer et al. 2005), and in a number of colonial varieties of English (Trudgill 1986) and other languages (Trudgill 2008). The sociolinguistic consequences of early twenty-first-century urbanization in India, China, and elsewhere have yet to be studied in detail, but it would not be surprising to find there the same processes leading to similar results.

However, according to Auer and colleagues, "it is too early yet to tell if the internationalization of economic and administrative structures and the increase in international communication in present-day Europe will strengthen or weaken the traditional dialects" (Auer et al. 2005: 36). For one thing, when no other variety is part of a speaker's environment, accommodation is not an option. If urbanization is accompanied by the formation of ethnic or working-class enclave neighborhoods, traditional distinctions may be enforced through dense, multiple social networks (Milroy 1987). Similar processes in the context of residential and educational segregation are responsible for the maintenance of substantial differences between the English of some African Americans and that of nearby whites. Furthermore, speech accommodation theory, as well as more recent adaptations of it (Bell 1984, 2001), also allow for the possibility of divergence as well as convergence.

And leveling is not the only consequence of dialect contact. Research in the US (Labov et al. 2005) and in the UK (Watt 2002, Watt and Milroy 1999) suggests that leveling at the subregional level has been accompanied by the maintenance and even increase of dialect differentiation among larger 'supralocal' dialects – such as midland versus northern speech in the US or northern versus southern speech in England. At more local levels, too, the linguistic effects of dialect contact are unpredictable. Schilling-Estes (2002) compares two islands off the east coast of the US whose residents are now in massive contact with outsiders. While the pronunciation of /ay/ (as in 'tide') in one of the two post-insular dialects is becoming more similar to that of the dominant outside dialect, the pronunciation of /ay/ in the other of the two is becoming more dissimilar to that of the outside. Schilling-Estes suggests that there are linguistic, social, and attitudinal factors at work to differentiate the behavior of the two island dialects in the face of contact. The details of the sound's function in the linguistic system, how the local-sounding form is socially marked, and what kind of population shift is taking place all affect the outcome of dialect contact in these two places.

The fact that the social meanings of linguistic forms can change means that forms that once sounded non-local can be preserved if they come to function as part of the local semiotic repertoire. Dyer (2002) shows for example that forms brought to Corby (an English steel town) from Scotland have come to index Corby identity in opposition to a nearby English town. In Glasgow, Stuart-Smith and colleagues (2007) show that the people with the loosest social networks and the most ties to speakers of English English are maintaining distinctive Scottish features in their speech, while less mobile working-class adolescents are adopting non-local forms, which distinguish them from other Glaswegians.

Dialect Awareness

Further complicating the picture of dialect contact are attitudes about regional varieties vis-à-vis other varieties, which are enacted in various practices that invoke dialect difference. Auer and colleagues (2005) discuss "sociolinguistic polarisation," which they describe as the counterpart of dialect borrowing. Sociolinguistic polarization can be defensive, if people refuse to adopt new forms from elsewhere (in which case it hinders dialect borrowing); or offensive, if people aggressively adopt outside forms (in which case it can lead to new developments such as hyperdialectalism). According to Auer and colleagues, "it would seem that a precondition for sociolinguistic polarisation, be it defensive or offensive in nature, is a certain level of awareness of the spreading feature in the consciousness of speakers of the 'threatened' dialect" (2005: 9).

An important strand of research about awareness of regional dialects is the work of Dennis Preston and his colleagues (Preston 1989; Niedzielski and Preston 1999; Long and Preston 2000), who use mapping and other experimental tasks to explore folk ideas about dialect boundaries and the social meanings of dialects. This work describes attitudes in considerable depth, and in some cases it explores the consequences of 'folk linguistics' for people's sociolinguistic perceptions (Niedzielski 1999; Fridland et al. 2004). Preston (1996) also explores the issue of what it is about dialects that can become the focus of awareness. On the whole, however, this body of work tends to hypostatize dialect awareness, treating it as a mental condition that pre-exists discourse rather than as the emergent discursive phenomenon it is. The kinds of talk and other behavior that Preston and his colleagues use as evidence of dialect awareness not only point to pre-existing ideology but also help create it. Thus it is important to explore not just the consequences of dialect awareness but the processes through which dialect awareness is enacted in discourse.

To do this, we have started to ask new questions about representations of regional variation in writing and in other media, about performances of regional-sounding speech linking localized linguistic forms to localized identities, about metalinguistic talk concerning dialects and their speakers, and about discursive practices involving the commodification of regional varieties. We have begun to view regional speech not just as an automatic consequence of where a person was born or raised but as a resource for social action (Johnstone 2004). Work on 'style' (Coupland 2001, 2007; Eckert 2000; Eckert and Rickford 2001) has showed how social identities can be evoked or created through the use of particular linguistic forms and has suggested that, at least for some people and in some ways, regional forms could serve such purposes.

Awareness of regional dialects, and the evaluative attitudes that accompany dialect awareness, are often enacted in stylized performances of localness. On one of the islands studied by Schilling-Estes (1998), the pronunciation of /ay/ (as in 'tide'), often in the context of the phrase *hoi toid on the Sound soid* ('high tide on the

Sound side') has come to serve as the key element in self-conscious performances of the receding island dialect. Coupland (1985, 2001, 2007, 2008) has explored the way in which radio and television personalities use features of Welsh English to project particular local personae. Beal (1999) has described how 'Geordie,' historically associated with the Northumbrian gentry, has come to be overtly linked with the city of Newcastle, and especially with its working class. Beal contrasts the situation in Newcastle with the situation in Sheffield, where local speech is linked less with the city than with the county it is in, Yorkshire. She shows that the difference between how the two dialects are imagined results from different histories of metadiscourse, or talk about talk (Beal 2009). In both cases, a particular subset of locally hearable forms, often represented in particular lexical items, has come to stand in for the variety as a whole – as when the word *mardy* stands in for Sheffield speech, or when the Geordie words *Broon* (Newcastle Brown Ale) and *Toon* (referring to the Newcastle football club) stand in for the northern long /u/. Hilliard and Wolfram (2003), Johnstone (2005), and others have studied how regional dialects are represented as stylized sets of words in folk dictionaries, and Johnstone has explored the dialect stylization process with reference to other artefacts such as newspaper articles (Johnstone et al. 2006) and t-shirts (Johnstone 2009).

Scholars and laypeople alike pay attention to regional variation when they think it is under threat. Beal (2009) shows how current scholarly discourse about dialect leveling echoes the discourse of the late eighteenth and early nineteenth centuries, when "the enclosure of common land, the mechanization of agriculture, and the Industrial Revolution [...] caused people to move from the countryside into rapidly expanding industrial towns and cities" (p. 139). Beal points out that many of the English dialects now considered endangered were themselves the result of leveling processes sparked by geographical mobility. In England, dialect dictionaries in the nineteenth and early twentieth centuries were accompanied by a boom in dialect literature and by the development of regional dialect societies. In the US, nineteenth-century 'local color' fiction featured re-spelled representations of regional dialects, and actors performing stereotypical regional characters were popular on the entertainment circuit. The American Dialect Society was founded in 1889, at the height of the 'gilded age' of industrialization and of the accompanying immigration from Europe and geographical mobility in the US.

A similar burst of regional dialect awareness appears to characterize popular culture at the beginning of the twenty-first century. A British rock band, The Arctic Monkeys, who might once have wanted to sound American (Trudgill 1983: 141–60), now features words associated with Sheffield, their city of origin (Beal 2008). Advertisements feature representations of the dialects of their target audiences, even if these are non-standard or minority ones (King and Wicks 2008). Internet sites now supplement folk dictionaries; one called Slanguage (http://www.slanguage.com/) offers to help viewers "talk like the locals in cities around the world." Coffee mugs inscribed 'Bawlmer' are on sale in Baltimore, as are mugs featuring 'Pittsburghese' in Pittsburgh. Groups on social networking sites emerge around regional identities, and membership often requires knowing – or acting as if one knows – the correct regional words for things.

Place, Indexical Order, and the Resemioticization of Regional Forms

To summarize, economic and cultural globalization and the attending social and geographical mobility and dialect contact seem to result in two contradictory trends: increased dialect leveling and increased talk about dialect. To put in another way, globalization erases objectively visible linguistic difference through leveling and dialect loss and at the same time creates ideological difference among imagined language varieties through increased popular attention to variation. This is because people's noticing of difference – something which occurs as a consequence of dialect contact – may lead to semiotic change at two levels. At one level, dialect contact may produce accommodation, which may in turn favor dialect leveling. At another level, dialect contact may spark the kinds of metapragmatic activities that lead to ideological differentiation among dialects (Gal and Irvine 1995). To account for this phenomenon, several claims about place, language, and semiotic change can usefully be brought together.

Localities are products of experience and discourse. As cultural and humanistic geographers have pointed out, physical spaces are transformed into meaningful places as humans interact with them, imbuing them with value (Lefebvre 1991, Entrikin 1991, Tuan 1991; see Johnstone 2010). Different ways of interacting with space lead to different ways of delimiting and describing places. Political boundaries represent one way in which spaces can be made meaningful. Space can be acted upon and made valuable through agriculture, landscaping, or building. Physical spaces can be imbued with meaning by how they are experienced, how humans navigate through them, the angles from which they are viewed, what they smell like, feel like, or sound like. Individuals' experiences of the world are necessarily disparate (no two people have precisely the same set of experiences), so in order for intersubjectivity to be possible, different impressions and evaluations of these impressions must be coordinated in interaction. We come to share ideas about boundaries through activities like mapping; about a place's history, through books, lectures, and tourist representations; about the meanings of farms or buildings, by working in them, touring them, interacting with the things produced there.

One of the activities through which the meaning of a place can be articulated and coordinated is talk about talk (Johnstone 2004). If the conditions are right – if there is at least one linguistic form that people can notice which is heard in one city or region and not in others, if linguistic difference is ideologically associated with social difference in the socio-cultural milieu at hand, and if reasons to notice and to talk about such differences arise – then people may link the identity of a place with particular forms of speech.

Languages and dialects are likewise products of experience and discourse. As linguists in the humanistic and integrationist traditions have argued (Harris 1981, Hopper 1988, Johnstone 1996), relations between form and meaning do not pre-exist discourse but are rather evoked and created in discourse, as particular forms coincide with particular semiotic effects in individuals' experience. As Michael Silverstein puts it (with respect to a somewhat more restricted domain of language), linguistic forms *index* meanings rather than *having* meanings (Silverstein 1993, 2003).[1] This is to say that, when a form comes to be observably correlated with a semantic or pragmatic function (referential or 'social'), the form becomes usable to evoke or create that meaning.

Humans may be born with the tendency to pay attention to talk and to make certain kinds of generalizations – and not others – about order and form. This means that people who have similar linguistic experiences are likely to make the same generalizations about them, or to re-use the same words and phrases. Such people can be said to speak 'the same' language or variety, or to 'share' a way of talking. But such sharing is never complete, and thus it must be renegotiated in every interaction. Just as we continually calibrate our senses of the meaning of a place by talking about it, we continually calibrate our language and our explicit ideas about language as we speak, write, or sign. Languages and dialects, like localities, are 'imagined,' to use Benedict Anderson's (1991) term. They exist as useful, even necessary ideas, not as things objectively observable by a socio-cultural outsider. Associations between particular features of pronunciation, grammar, and vocabulary, on the one hand, and imagined 'languages,' 'dialects,' and 'speech communities,' on the other, arise in local social and discursive practices that are enabled and constrained by larger-scale political and economic conditions. According to Silverstein (1993: 408), "users of languages in essence construct culturally particular concepts of [linguistic] normativity that bind subsets of them into 'language'-bearing groups." This is to say that 'languages' and 'dialects' are cultural constructs, produced by a group of people using, orienting to, and/or talking about a particular set of linguistic features, in a process that also constructs the group itself (Gal and Irvine 1995).

In a study of the history of Received Pronunciation (RP) in Britain, Asif Agha (2006) describes some of the mechanisms involved in the mutual calibration of sets of ideas about form–meaning relations. Agha uses "enregisterment" to label the identification of a set of linguistic forms as a "linguistic repertoire differentiable within a language as a socially recognized register," which has come to index "speaker status linked to a specific scheme of cultural values" (p. 231). What became RP was once a regional variety, used by socially privileged speakers in a geographically bounded area in southeastern England; it was neither associated with correctness more generally nor advocated as a national model for pronunciation. Since the eighteenth century, however, as a result of a variety of prescriptivist ideas and 'metapragmatic' activities that circulated these ideas – activities, that is, which point to a feature's appropriate context of use – a set of features of this regional variety has been enregistered as a supralocal standard accent. This set of features has been represented collectively in the public imagination as a stable variety and maintained across time and region, through metapragmatic practices that reiterate the value of this variety and its link to social status and correctness.

Because not all metapragmatic practices involve explicit metadiscourse, or talk about talk, people are not always conscious of links between linguistic forms and social meanings, even when they use the forms appropriately in their own speech. Once the links are somewhat stabilized, however, people can in some circumstances respond reflexively to the social meanings of linguistic forms, explicitly talking about appropriate usage in handbooks, representing users of the forms in cartoons, and so on.

Particular forms can index multiple meanings at the same level and at multiple levels of abstraction. This is a consequence of the fact that language is never completely shared and that different individuals experience the linguistic and sociolinguistic environment in different ways, depending on the context (who is talking, in what circumstances) and the co-text (what else is being said or done at the same time), and meaning can change. For example, the same linguistic form can potentially index a referential meaning, social class, and/or place. In Pittsburgh, Pennsylvania, the form *yinz* /yɪnz/ can simply be a second-person plural pronoun; or it can sound sloppy, uneducated, and low class; or it can sound like 'a Pittsburgh thing,' an index of local identity. In order to understand the distribution of meaning of variant forms, we need to take a phenomenological approach – an approach, that is, which attends to the multiplicity and indeterminacy of indexical relations and to the question of how such relations arise historically and in lived experience (Johnstone and Kiesling 2008).

Michael Silverstein provides a model of semiotic variability that captures the relationship between dialect leveling and dialect awareness. According to Silverstein (2003), relationships between linguistic form and social meaning can emerge, and sometimes stabilize, at various levels of abstraction. An indexical is a feature whose use can be associated with a sociodemographic identity (for instance region or class) or with a semantic or pragmatic function (for instance number-marking or formality). An nth-order indexical is one that has reached a stage in its semiotic development at which, for a particular person or group, its use *presupposes* the existence of an identity or pragmatic function. N^{th}-order accounts can be generated by cultural outsiders, if the phenomena being accounted for are 'objectively' visible through the ideological grid a particular outsider brings to bear. To say that a feature's indexicality is presupposing something is to say that the occurrence of the feature can only be accounted for with reference to a pre-existing grid: a presupposed or pre-chosen way of partitioning social or semantic space, such as a system for dividing people up by region, gender, or class, or a preconceived understanding of what constitutes number or formality in language. At this stage an indexical form is not yet *creative*: neither outsiders nor members of the speech community use the form in question to do semantic or social work, because the form is not variable in individuals' speech. A dialectologist who notices that people in the midwestern US say things like "the car needs washed" (rather than "the car needs to be washed"), while people in the Northeast do not, comes to the situation with a presupposed way of dividing up the social world (by region); to the linguist, the forms are n^{th}-order indexes of region. However, if the linguist were to use the form in question in speaking to a fellow linguist, as an inside joke or a demonstration of expertise – for example, if a linguist from the Northeast were to enumerate to a fellow linguist from the Northeast questions about midwestern speech that "need answered"– the form is being used creatively, to proffer a claim about identity or expertise. The form is now being used at the $n+1^{th}$-order of indexicality.

If the right historical, geographical, and ideological conditions are in place, members of the speech community may come to notice that different forms are used by different people, or in different contexts. They may then begin to vary the usage of these forms in their own speech, depending on whether they are trying to sound more local or more supralocal, more careful or more relaxed, more working-class or less so. When this happens, the features are functioning as $n+1^{th}$-order indexicals. An $n+1^{th}$-order indexical is an nth-order indexical feature that has been assigned "an ethno-metapragmatically driven native interpretation" (Silverstein 1998: 212) – that is, a meaning in terms of one or more native ideologies (the idea that certain people speak more correctly than others, for example, or that some people are due greater respect than others). The dimensions along which indexical meanings vary (locality, carefulness, class, gender, respect, and so on) depend on local (not linguists') ideas about what linguistic variation can mean. At this stage, the feature has been 'enregistered,' in other words it has become associated with a style of speech and can be used to evoke a context for that style. For example, a person can make use of a feature that he or she has noticed to be correlated with being working class in order to create rapport with a working-class speaker or annoy an English teacher. The indexicality of the form is thus creative. As this example suggests, a form can index meaning along a variety of dimensions: the same form can create solidarity or distinction. Different members of a community, differently placed through class, education, gender, mobility, and the like, can use locally available features to do different kinds of social work and can hear these features as doing different kinds of work. (In Pittsburgh, women are more likely to hear local features as sloppy, ugly, and uneducated, lining them up with one end of an ideological cline of correctness; men are more likely to hear local features as suggesting localness, solidarity, friendliness, or masculinity, and thus to line them up with one end of an ideological cline that goes from self to other.)

The same process can recur: a feature with $n+1^{th}$-order meaning for some people may, for them or for others, come to be reinterpreted in terms of yet another ideological scheme. For example, because in some Pittsburghers' experience particular variants are correlated with being working class and male, a subset of these features has come to be identified with being an 'authentic' Pittsburgher.[2] The ideological schemata in play here include the idea that places have dialects associated with them and that prototypical Pittsburghers are working-class men. People who want to create the perception that they are authentic Pittsburghers (in this ideological sense) can use this cluster of features to set the scene, and people whose perceptions are shaped by the ideological cline of authenticity may hear those who use these features as authentic or real Pittsburghers whether the people they hear are using the features for this purpose or not (see Johnstone and Kiesling 2008). From an analyst's perspective, the forms that have been resemioticized (given new meaning) in this way are now $(n+1) +1^{th}$-order indexicals.

The process of resemioticization can recur indefinitely. For example, if it is noticed that Pittsburghers are people who talk about 'Pittsburghese' (as intense media coverage of the topic has made it increasingly likely), and if people associate cities that have dialects with the post-industrial 'rust belt' and cities that do not have dialects (or are thought not to have them) with the new economy, then the forms hearable in Pittsburgh have come to have indexical meaning at yet another level.

Historically, but not inevitably, in Pittsburgh and elsewhere the resemioticization process has tended to loosen the semiotic ties between locally hearable forms and social class; instead (or in addition), it links these forms with place. Forms that once sounded working class only have come to sound local as well for some speakers, or local only for others;[3] and these forms become useful resources in the discursive calibration of people's sense of place. We have described this history in detail elsewhere (Johnstone et al. 2006). Pittsburghers began to hear local forms as indexes of place only relatively recently. One telling bit of evidence for this claim – that the linkage of geographically local forms with place is a relatively recent development – is the fact that the term 'Pittsburghese,' which explicitly links dialect and place, was apparently coined during the 1960s. (By 'geographically local' I mean forms that are in fact local, in a geographic sense, rather than forms thought to be local, which may or may not actually be restricted to the Pittsburgh area.) Self-conscious performances of dialect can also serve to explicitly link speech forms that people think of as local with local places. Ocracokers, who encapsulate the local 'brogue' in the phrase *high tide on the Sound side* (of the island) are doing this (Schilling-Estes 1998). Coupland's Welsh stylizers use phrases that both refer to places and provide "phono-opportunities" (Coupland 2007: 124) for the performance of local-sounding forms, such as *Cardiff Arms Park* with its repeated opportunities for the local pronunciation of long /a:/ as [ae:]. In Pittsburgh, the phonological feature most often identified with local speech in the print media is the monophthongization of /aw/, and more often than not the word it appears in is *dahntahn* ('downtown'; see Johnstone et al. 2002).

Mobility and Resemioticization

The historical contexts that give rise to the kinds of change in the meaning of regionally variable linguistic forms I have just described are ones that foster social and geographical mobility. This can be illustrated with a sketch of the sociolinguistic history of Pittsburgh (presented in more detail in Johnstone et al. 2006).

The fact that Pittsburgh is located at the edges of the North and South Midland and Appalachia means that there is a large number of non-standard sounds, words, and structures that can be heard in the area. Simply by virtue of distributional facts, these features are potential n^{th}-order indexes (in Silverstein's sense) of geographic location. A dialectologist using a word list to elicit regional pronunciations could describe for example the link between the speakers' location or place of origin and the occurrence of these features in people's speech. Although all of these features are limited in geographical distribution one way or another, none is heard only in Pittsburgh or in the Pittsburgh metropolitan area. Most features of pronunciation that sound local to Pittsburghers are widespread in central and western Pennsylvania, if not throughout the United States, and some of the lexical and morpho-syntactic features thought of as local can be heard throughout the Ohio Valley or the midland, southern, and/or Appalachian dialect areas.

Along with the availability of non-standard features that could potentially be heard as local, local social and economic history created additional preconditions for the emergence of 'Pittsburghese' (Oestreicher 1989; Lubove 1996; Hays 1989). Until World War II, Pittsburgh was relatively isolated. Many European immigrant languages were spoken in the city, but working-class Pittsburghers had little contact with anyone who spoke English differently from them. Dense, multiple social networks strengthened local dialect norms (Milroy 1987), and the fact that Pittsburghers had inherited a Scots–Irish-influenced dialect that could be heard as distinctive was almost never brought to their attention.

Historical and sociolinguistic evidence suggests that, before the 1960s, the use of regional speech forms could have been correlated with social class and with localness, if anyone had done the sociolinguistic fieldwork necessary to establish such correlations. But the nth-order indexicality of these forms was rarely brought into higher-order local play. While regional speech features could index class identity for some people (and to some people), many others sounded like working-class Pittsburghers because they had no other way to sound. People growing up in working-class families lived in insular neighborhoods, within walking distance of the steel mills and other factories where the adults worked, and children went to school and church with their neighbors. These dense, multiplex sociolinguistic networks gave them access to regional dialect features and little opportunity to become aware that they spoke differently from people elsewhere, that others would consider their way of talking to be non-standard, or that the use of non-standard features varied with socioeconomic class. Because in some Pittsburghers' experience the usage of regional forms was correlated with class, adopting an attitudinal or affiliative stance toward or against working-class identity could involve adopting or not adopting regional forms; but this option was open only to those whose repertoires included both regional and supraregional variants, and the kinds of social and geographical mobility that would give rise to varied linguistic repertoires were available to relatively few people.

As features that could be heard in the speech of working-class Pittsburghers were taken up as sociolinguistic resources, n^{th}-order geographically regional features acquired social meaning, coming to do $n+1^{th}$-order sociolinguistic work connected with correctness, class, and place. This became possible in the context of social mobility, which gave Pittsburghers access to new variants of forms that had been relatively invariable in their speech or in that of their neighbors. Once forms became variable, the choice among variants could, for some people, be invested with n^{th}-order indexical meaning such as class or correctness.

In the post-World War II decades, the $n+1^{th}$-order indexicality of certain features (their potential to index correctness, class, and locality) became itself usable. While the $n+1^{th}$-order indexicality of these forms continued to make them hearable and usable as markers of social class, education, and local life experience, the fact that they could be used in these ways became more and more salient. This occurred through metapragmatic practices, which selected a subset of the forms that can do $n+1^{th}$-order indexical work, linking this subset to a more stabilized social identity and making these forms available for self-conscious, performed identity work. The raw material for $n+1^{th}$-order indexicality is the existence of nth-order correlations, which, filtered through ideologies about connections between correctness and class, become resources for hearing other people's class and education level and for projecting one's own. The raw material for $(n+1)+1^{th}$-order identity work is $n+1^{th}$-order stylistic variability, which is filtered through more abstract ideologies about what dialects are and how they are linked to identities. At this stage people notice that those with more stereotypical Pittsburgh identities have less variable and more regional-sounding accents, and they attribute this to an essential connection between place and language. In the process, the subset of nonstandard forms has come increasingly to index localness and much less (or more indirectly) class. While they continue to do $n+1^{th}$-order work as well, regional forms are now increasingly heard as signals of local identity and can be used to project localness. Many of the metapragmatic practices that have made this possible are metadiscursive, involving explicit talk about talk.

During World War II, many working-class Pittsburgh men were geographically mobile, traveling in the military; and the industrial workers of the post-World War II years, who were mostly unionized, were paid enough to be able to take holidays at East Coast beaches and other places, where they interacted with people who sounded different and noticed how different the Pittsburghers sounded. Demographic change at home also helped to create the conditions for talk about local speech. During the 1960s and 1970s, the 'baby-boom' grandchildren of the immigrant industrial laborers (who had arrived between 1880 and 1920) began to come of age; they were no longer speaking the homeland language, and their ties to the immigrant religions had weakened (Oestreicher 1989 and personal communication). While their parents and grandparents thought of themselves mainly in ethnic or religious terms (as Polish, for example, or as eastern Orthodox), these Pittsburghers began to develop class and regional consciousness. Their increased reflexivity about social identity was arguably enhanced also by the increased speed with which popular culture circulated on television.[4] The ground was fertile for imagining what it meant to be a working-class Pittsburgher, and the existence of variable regional pronunciations that could index class and place – forms that people elsewhere heard as different and Pittsburghers elsewhere identified with home – provided an easily available resource for doing this.

Economic upheaval in the 1970s and 1980s meant vastly increased geographical mobility and resulted in new opportunities for interaction with non-Pittsburghers, which led to dialect leveling; at the same time it made people link dialect and social identity more explicitly. When local steel production was moved to areas where labor was cheaper, people whose families had lived in Pittsburgh for generations were forced to relocate in order to find work. Displaced Pittsburghers who visited, or eventually moved back, brought back with them stories in which they were told that they sounded funny (Johnstone 2007a), and nostalgic talk about Pittsburgh and Pittsburgh speech became common in diasporic communities of Pittsburghers (Johnstone and Baumgardt 2004). New opportunities for talk about talk meant that Pittsburghers became increasingly aware that features of their speech were local in geographic distribution and noticeable to others, and the potential for indexical linkages between local forms and social identities was increasingly made explicit.

Working-class Pittsburgh neighborhoods and schools are less homogeneous than they once were, so young Pittsburghers now come into contact at a much earlier age with people who are unlike them. Thus even among people who have not (or not yet) left the city, conditions are conducive to discursive practices that give rise to explicit talk about the indexicality of certain forms. The medical and university sectors of the economy have also grown, attracting students and professionals from elsewhere. The availability of inexpensive housing, studio, and office space in former industrial neighborhoods means that young 'creatives' can stay in the city after graduating from local universities. Now these people notice regional speech features in mass media representations like folk dictionaries and websites, which metapragmatically link regional speech and local identity, as often as they do it by actually interacting with locals. They use these features in self-conscious performances of 'Pittsburghese.' Such performances are invariably reflexive, indirectly commenting on local speech and local speakers; but they can make various kinds of comments, not all of which are seen as derogatory. Performances of 'Pittsburghese' can enter into attempts to claim local identity by displaying local knowledge (Johnstone and Baumgardt 2004; Johnstone 2007b). People can win arguments about what Pittsburgh and Pittsburghers are like, or they can claim to be long-time residents or urban hipsters in the know, by showing that they can speak the dialect. Performances of 'Pittsburghese' can be intended as, and/or taken up as, gentle teases or degrading insults, depending on whether the performer is an insider or not (Wisnosky 2003). Thus, on the stage set by the nth-order indexicality of certain local speech features, discursive practices and artefacts have emerged that have enregistered local speech in the local imagination as unique and unchanging and have strengthened and stabilized the ideological links between local speech and place, making other indexicalities less and less available for identity work.

Discussion

We have seen that the conditions which foster dialect leveling are also those which foster the production of locality through the ideological differentiation of imagined dialects. Some variants index supra-locality, and can thus be used in the accommodative speech that leads to leveling. Other forms index locality, and can be used in discourses that shape people's sense of place and the social identities associated with place. Pittsburgh, where semiotic change of the sort I have been describing is ongoing, offers a synchronic apparent-time view of mobility-induced resemioticization. Some Pittsburghers still live in a sociolinguistic world in which linguistic variation does little or no social work. These are people who do not notice local accents because they have had relatively little opportunity to hear anything else and because linguistic difference has rarely been called to their attention. There are Pittsburghers who use local forms in everyday speech but who cannot mimic 'Pittsburghese.' There are, conversely, people who *can* perform 'Pittsburghese' but who do *not* use local forms in more unselfconscious speech. Additionally, there are people who know about local speech only from seeing it on t-shirts and bumper stickers. Furthermore, various sets of indexical relations can characterize the same speaker's sociolinguistic competence. Shifting from supraregional forms to performances of local-sounding forms can index both a nostalgic sense of belonging and a youthful sense of urban hipness. While metadiscourse about 'Pittsburghese' arises in speech situations that involve people of all ages, those who participate most often are middle-aged people who left the city several decades ago, because of economic change, and younger people who are staying in or moving to the city because of new economic opportunities.

The model I have sketched explains the well-known fact that "stereotyped" linguistic forms (Labov 1972: 178–80) often recede and disappear. It is commonly thought that this happens because, once people know that a form is socially stigmatized, they stop using it. But, while this may be true at the level of the community as a whole, it is not necessarily true for individuals, who may know that a form is negatively evaluated yet use it nonetheless, either because they cannot hear it in their own speech or because they do not have productive control both over the stigmatized and over the newer, non-stigmatized form (Johnstone and Kiesling 2008). Rather, stereotyping in Labov's sense and the recession of locally marked forms coincide because they both result from the same set of socioeconomic changes, which lead on one hand to dialect awareness and on the other to dialect leveling.

I have focused mainly on one of globalization's effects: economic change resulting in human mobility. I touch, in conclusion, on what the sociolinguistic process I have described suggests with reference to more specific claims about cultural production in the interdisciplinary literature on globalization. I organize this necessarily brief discussion around several concepts that recur in this body of work: *rupture*; *deterritorialization and the production of locality*; and *virtual places and diasporic public spheres*. Finally, I turn to a brief discussion of the idea of *returning to the local* in the context of globalization.

'Rupture' labels the idea that contemporary economic and cultural change is fundamentally unlike anything that has happened before. Versions of this claim are made by Appadurai (1996) and Bauman (1998), who hold that communications media that have vastly increased the speed of communication, and/or the extent and ease of geographic mobility, have resulted in "a general break with all sorts of pasts" (Appadurai 1996: 3). This is because the decline of the nation-state in the face of global economic forces means that people are no longer associated with territories automatically, from birth, and identities are no longer first and foremost national ones. In general, as people move around the globe, identities assigned at birth and assumed to be primordial become less relevant, or relevant in different ways. Social effort is required to produce the identities that were once thought to be inherent. Among these are identities associated with places. "Deterritorialized" people and institutions work to produce locality (Appadurai 1996: 178–95).

The processes of semiotic change I have described have clearly happened before, as Beal's (1999, 2009) work makes clear. 'Rupture' is thus too strong a term to describe the contemporary situation with regard to regional forms of speech. But we do appear to be in a moment – though it may not be the first one – when the production of locality is hard to miss. As we have seen, when material conditions are conducive, regional speech forms (or forms imagined to characterize regional speech) are being taken up in higher-order indexical performances of localness, even as people become less likely to use these forms in less performance-inducing contexts. Through activities like online and face-to-face talk about 'Pittsburghese' and the consumption of 'Pittsburghese' t-shirts, folk dictionaries, talking dolls, and websites, Pittsburghers make sense of what it means to be a Pittsburgher in an era when the answer to that question is no longer as obvious as it once was. It should be noted, though, that this is almost entirely grassroots, bottom-up cultural production work. Institutions of economic development seeking to 'brand' Pittsburgh's identity do not emphasize – or even mention – the local dialect, thinking it to be an embarrassing relic of the past.[5] Thus the focus of globalization theory on the role of powerful political institutions and industries in the production of locality needs to be supplemented with a look at the role of individuals outside of institutions and at the kind of grassroots economy represented by people who sell t-shirts on the sidewalk or dolls and refrigerator magnets over the internet.

A great deal of the work of locality production is done online, in email, through websites, and on blogs. This is because many of the people who do locality producing work about Pittsburgh and Pittsburghers do not live in Pittsburgh. In an analysis of an online discussion of Pittsburgh speech (Johnstone and Baumgardt 2004), we found that at least half the participants were ex-Pittsburghers. Active members of the Pittsburgh diaspora (often called the 'Steeler Nation' because of their fanatical relationship with the city's American football franchise, the Pittsburgh Steelers) are often people in later middle age who left the city in the 1980s, and members of their families. The Steeler Nation could be said to constitute a diasporic public sphere of the sort that globalization theorists argue to have replaced the traditional, physically based public spheres such as the eighteenth-century coffee houses (Habermas 1989). From a normative, Habermasian perspective like that of Eco (1986), the Steeler Nation could be said to be a simulacrum of Pittsburgh in which serious discourse about ethics and politics is replaced by football statistics and arguments about whether Pittsburgh speech is charming or embarrassing. From a sociolinguistic point of view, however, this mostly virtual community is engaged in the work of dialect construal. While they may not increase the number of people who speak the dialect un-self-consciously in their daily life, such activities help to make people aware of the dialect's existence and, ultimately, to preserve its memory. Metalinguistic activities such as these are only now being added to the set of phenomena sociolinguists are interested in, and it is not yet clear how they interact with our primary object of study: language variation and its role in language change. But, whether or not performances of and talk about dialect help in the revitalization of dialects in everyday life (where and when this is seen as a good thing), they have come to be part of people's sociolinguistic world and cannot be dismissed as 'inauthentic' or evaluated as only second-best.[6]

The fact that leveling and dialect awareness go hand in hand also provides support for some theorists' claim that the effects of globalization are hard to resist. Under globalization, as Appadurai puts it (1996: 187), "[t]he capacity of neighborhoods to produce contexts [...] and local subjects is profoundly affected by the locality-producing capabilities of larger-scale social formations." Nothing seems more local than discursive practices like the production and consumption of folk dictionaries (Johnstone 2005) or t-shirts (Johnstone 2009), or the broadcasting of radio programs (Coupland 2001) that circulate dialect awareness and celebrate locality by inscribing dialects imagined as unique onto people and locations thought to be unique. In fact, however, these practices become possible only in the context of larger-scale social forces and formations such as the globalizing economy, changing communication technology, and the mass media.

NOTES

1 Although this is never entirely clear from his writing, Silverstein appears to intend the concept of indexicality to describe "non-denotational" meaning only, seeing denotational meaning as arising from other mechanisms. He objects to the claim that meaning is "indexicality all the way down" (personal communication, November 2007).

2 As noted by Bucholtz (2003) and others, 'authentic' is an ideologically shaped characterization, in sociolinguistics and elsewhere. There are no (objectively) authentic speakers of any variety. Authenticity is, however, locally relevant in the ethnographic setting at hand. There are t-shirts that list the characteristics of the 'authentic Pittsburgher,' and people use this phrase in conversation to describe someone who is close to the prototype of the local persona. ('Authentic' Pittsburghers are often referred to as 'Yinzers.')

3 Speakers who link these forms with place but not with class include people who experience local speech entirely through mediated contexts, in which the forms are linked with place, but not with class. Such contexts include t-shirts and postcards that superimpose local forms on the city skyline; and they include no "characterological" cues (Agha 2006: 165) such as references to working-class practices or sketches of stereotypical Pittsburghers. In the US, the fact that language forms are non-standard is not sufficient to enregister them as lower-class. People notice politicians' regional accents, for

example, and talk about them in regional terms rather than in terms of class. (Americans hear former President George W. Bush as having a Texas accent, but not as coming from the lower classes, for example.)

4   I have no evidence that this was in fact the case in Pittsburgh, but theorists have proposed the idea. I am grateful to Nik Coupland for suggesting it.

5   In the UK, vernacular speech is sometimes involved in attempts to brand cities for tourist purposes (Nik Coupland, personal communication, July 2008).

6   Whether or not reflexive and performative activities of the sort I have described do play any role in regenerating the use of local speech forms in Pittsburgh is not yet known. Like most (if not all) Pittsburghers, I would not want children or grandchildren of mine to grow up with no other option but to speak a stigmatized dialect, which is celebrated mainly by people who do not use it (Johnstone and Kiesling 2008). My work is motivated not by the goal of dialect revitalization but by the wish to preserve the evidence of, and to promote pride in, Pittsburgh speech as an element of the Pittsburghers' cultural heritage.

REFERENCES

Agha, A. (2006) *Language and Social Relations*. Cambridge: Cambridge University Press.

Anderson, B. (1991) *Imagined Communities: Reflections on the Origin and Spread of Nationalism*. London and New York: Verso.

Appadurai, A. (1996) *Modernity at Large: Cultural Dimensions of Globalization*. Minneapolis: University of Minnesota Press.

Auer, P., Hinskens, F., and Kerswill, P. (2005) The study of dialect convergence and divergence: Conceptual and methodological considerations. In P., Auer, F. Hinskens, and P. Kerswill (eds.), *Dialect Change: Convergence and divergence in European languages*, 1–48. Cambridge: Cambridge University Press.

Bauman, Z. (1998) *Globalization: The Human Consequences*. New York: Columbia University Press.

Beal, J. C. (1999) 'Geordie Nation': Language and regional identity in the north–east of England. *Lore and Language* 17: 33–48.

Beal, J. C. (2008) "You're not from New York City, you're from Rotherham":

Dialect and identity in UK 'indie' music. Paper presented at the Sociolinguistics Symposium 18, Amsterdam.

Beal, J. C. (2009) Enregisterment, commodification, and historical context: 'Geordie' versus 'Sheffieldish.' *American Speech* 84: 138–56.

Bell, A. (1984) Language style as audience design. *Lanuage in Society* 13: 145–204.

Bell, A. (2001) Back in style: Reworking audience design. In P. Eckert and J. R. Rickford (eds.), *Style and Sociolinguistic Variation*, 139–69. Cambridge: Cambridge University Press.

Britain, D. (2002) Diffusion, levelling, simplification and reallocation in past tense BE in the English Fens. *Journal of Sociolinguistics* 6(1): 16–63.

Bucholtz, M. (2003) Sociolinguistic nostalgia and the authentication of identity. *Journal of Sociolinguistics* 7: 398–416.

Coupland, N. (1985) 'Hark, hark the lark': Social motivations for phonological style-shifting. *Language and communication* 5: 153–72.

Coupland, N. (2001) Dialect stylization in radio talk. *Language in Society* 30: 345–75.

Coupland, N. (2007) *Style: Language Variation and Identity*. Cambridge: Cambridge University Press.

Coupland, N. (2008) Post-industrial voice in Wales. Paper presented at the Sociolinguistics Symposium 16, Amsterdam.

Dyer, J. (2002) "We all speak the same round here": Dialect levelling in a Scottish–English community. *Journal of Sociolinguistics* 6: 99–116.

Eckert, P. (2000) *Linguistic Variation as Social Practice*. Oxford: Blackwell.

Eckert, P., and Rickford, J. (eds.) (2001) *Style and Sociolinguistic Variation*. Cambridge and New York: Cambridge University Press.

Eco, U. (1986) *Travels in Hyperreality*. New York: Harcourt Brace Jovanovich Inc.

Entrikin, J. N. (1991) *The Betweenness of Place: Towards a Geography of Modernity*. Baltimore: Johns Hopkins University Press.

Fridland, V., Bartlett, K., and Kreuz, R. (2004) Do you hear what I hear? Experimental measurement of the perceptual salience of acoustically manipulated vowel variants by Southern speakers in Memphis, TN. *Language Variation and Change* 16: 1–16.

Gal, S., and Irvine, J. (1995) The boundaries of languages and disciplines: How ideologies construct difference. *Social Research* 62: 967–1001.

Giles, H., Taylor, D., and Bourhis, R. (1973) Towards a theory of interpersonal accommodation through speech: Some Canadian data. *Language in Society* 23: 177–92.

Giles, H., and Powesland, P. F. (1975) *Speech Style and Social Evaluation*. London: Academic Press.

Habermas, J. (1989) *The Structural Transformation of the Public Sphere*. Cambridge, MA: MIT Press.

Hall, S. (1991) The local and the global: Globalization and ethnicity. In A. D. King (ed.), *Culture, Globalization, and the World-System*, 19–39. Basingstoke: MacMillan.

Harris, R. (1981) *The Language Myth*. London: Duckworth.

Hays, S. P. (ed.) (1989) *City at the Point: Essays on the Social History of Pittsburgh*.

Hilliard, S., and Wolfram, W. (2003) The sociolinguistic significance of folk dictionaries. Paper presented at the Southeastern Conference on Linguistics (SECOL) 68, Washington, DC.

Hopper, P. J. (1988) Emergent grammar and the a priori grammar postulate. In D. Tannen (ed.), *Linguistics in Context: Connecting Observation and Understanding*, 117–34. Norwood, NJ: Ablex.

Johnstone, B. (1996) *The Linguistic Individual: Self-Expression in Language and Linguistics*. New York: Oxford University Press.

Johnstone, B. (2004) Place, globalization, and linguistic variation. In C. Fought (ed.), *Sociolinguistic Variation: Critical Reflections*, 65–83. New York: Oxford University Press.

Johnstone, B. (2005) How to speak like a Pittsburgher: Exploring the role of a folk dictionary in the production of a dialect. Paper presented at the Sociolinguistics Symposium 16, Limerick, Ireland.

Johnstone, B. (2007a) A new role for narrative in variationist sociolinguistics. In M. Bamberg (ed.), *Narrative: State of the Art*, 57–67. Amsterdam and Philadelphia: John Benjamins.

Johnstone, B. (2007b) Linking identity and dialect though stancetaking. In R. Englebretson (ed.), *Stancetaking in Discourse: Subjectivity in Interaction*, 49–68. Amsterdam and Philadelphia: John Benjamins.

Johnstone, B., (2009) Pittsburghese shirts: Commodification and the enregistration of an urban dialect. *American Speech* 84: 157–75.

Johnstone, B. (2010) Language and geographical space. In P. Auer and

J. Erich Schmidt (eds.), *Language and Space: An international handbook of linguistic variation*, 1–18. Berlin and New York: Walter de Gruyter.

Johnstone, B., and Baumgardt, D. (2004) 'Pittsburghese' online: Vernacular norming in conversation. *American speech* 79: 115–45.

Johnstone, B., and Kiesling, S. F. (2008) Indexicality and experience: Exploring the meanings of /aw/-monophthongization in Pittsburgh. *Journal of Sociolinguistics* 12(1): 5–33.

Johnstone, B., Andrus, J., and Danielson, A. (2006) Mobility, indexicality, and the enregisterment of 'Pittsburghese.' *Journal of English Linguistics* 34(2): 77–104.

Johnstone, B., Bhasin, N., and Wittkofski, D. (2002) 'Dahntahn Pittsburgh': Monophthongal /aw/ and representations of localness in southwestern Pennsylvania. *American Speech* 77: 148–66.

Kerswill, P. (2005) Migration and language. In K. Mattheier, U. Ammon, and P. Trudgill (eds.), *Sociolinuistics/ Soziolinguistik: An International Handbook of the Science of Language and Society*, 2nd edn, 2271–85. Berlin: Mouton de Gruyter.

Kerswill, P., and Williams, A. (2000) Creating a new town koine: Children and language change in Milton Keynes. *Language in Society* 29: 65–115.

King, R., and Wicks, J. (2008) "Aren't we proud of our language": Commodification and the Nissan Bonavista TV Commercial. Paper presented at the Sociolinguistics Symposium 18, Amsterdam.

Kurath, H. (1949) *A Word Geography of the Eastern United States*. Ann Arbor: University of Michigan Press.

Labov, W. (1972) *Sociolinguistic Patterns*. Philadelphia: University of Pennsylvania Press.

Labov, W., Ash, S., and Boberg, C. (2005) *Atlas of North American English*. Berlin and New York: Mouton de Gruyter.

Lefebvre, H. (1991) *The Production of Space*, translated by D. Nicholson-Smith [1974]. Malden, MA: Blackwell.

Long, Da., and Preston, D. R. (eds.) (2000) *Handbook of Perceptual Dialectolog*, 2 vols. Amsterdam: John Benjamins.

Lubove, R. (1996) *Twentieth Century Pittsburgh. Vol. 1: Government, Business and Environmental Change*. Pittsburgh, PA: University of Pittsburgh Press.

Milroy, L. (1987) *Language and Social Networks*, 2nd edn. Oxford: Basil Blackwell.

Niedzielski, N. (1999) The effect of social information on the perception of sociolinguistic variables. *Journal of Language and Social Psychology* 18: 62–85.

Niedzielski, N., and Preston, D. (1999) *Folk Linguistics*. Berlin: Mouton de Gruyter.

Oestreicher, R. (1989) Working-class formation, development, and consciousness in Pittsburgh, 1790–1960. In S. P. Hayes (ed.), *City at the Point: Essays on the Social History of Pittsburgh*, 111–50. Pittsburgh: University of Pittsburgh Press.

Preston, D. R. (1989) *Perceptual Dialectology*. Dordrecht: Foris.

Preston, D. R. (1996) Whaddayaknow? The modes of folk linguistic awareness. *Language Awareness* 5: 40–74.

Schilling-Estes, N. (1998) Investigating 'self-conscious' speech: The performance register in Ocracoke English. *Language in Society* 27: 53–83.

Schilling-Estes, N. (2002) On the nature of isolated and post-isolated dialects: Innovation, variation, and differentiation. *Journal of Sociolinguistics* 6: 64–85.

Silverstein, M. (1993) Metapragmatic discourse and metapragmatic function. In J. A. Lucy (ed.) *Reflexive language*, 33–58. Cambridge: Cambridge University Press.

Silverstein, M. (1998) Contemporary transformations of local linguistic communities. *Annual Review of Anthropology* 27: 401–26.

Silverstein, M. (2003) Indexical order and the dialectics of sociolinguistic life. *Language and Communication* 23: 193–229.

Stuart-Smith, J., Timmins, C., and Tweedie, F. (2007) 'Talkin' Jockney?' Variation and change in Glaswegian accent. *Journal of Sociolinguistics* 11(2): 221–60.

Thomas, E. (1997) A rural/metropolitan split in the speech of Texas Anglos. *Language Variation and Change* 9: 309–32.

Trudgill, P. (1983) *On Dialect: Social and Geographical Perspectives*. Oxford and New York: Basil Blackwell/New York University Press.

Trudgill, P. (1986) *Dialects in Contact*. Oxford and New York: Basil Blackwell.

Trudgill, P. (2008) Colonial dialect contact in the history of European languages: On the irrelevance of identity to new-dialect formation. *Language in Society* 37(2): 241–54.

Tuan, Y.-F. (1991) Language and the making of place: A narrative–descriptive approach. *Annals of the Association of American Geographers* 81: 684–96.

Watt, D. (2002) "I don't speak with a Geordie accent, I speak, like, the Northern accent": Contact-induced levelling in the Tyneside vowel system. *Journal of Sociolinguistics* 6: 44–63.

Watt, D., and Milroy, L. (1999) Phonetic variation in three Tyneside vowels: Is this dialect levelling? In P. Foulkes and G. J. Docherty (eds.), *Urban Voices: Accent Studies in the British Isles*, 25–46. London: Arnold.

Wisnosky, M. (2003) *'Pittsburghese' in Pittsburgh Humor*. MA thesis, Department of Linguistics, University of Pittsburgh.

18 Ecolinguistics and Globalization

ARRAN STIBBE

Introduction

Ecolinguistics provides an important dimension for studies of language and globalization because it encompasses the physical globe, or rather the biosphere – the thin outer layer of the planet Earth and its atmosphere, which supports all known life. The need for an ecolinguistics arises only to supplement a discipline, linguistics, which rarely acknowledges the ecological embedding of the animal it investigates, treating humans as existing in isolation rather than in relationship with the rest of the biosphere and the diversity of lifeforms within it. This applies to structuralist linguistics, with its emphasis on language as an isolated system; to sociolinguistics, with its focus on human society; as well as to critical linguistics, with its focus on unequal power relationships among humans. In fact, without their interconnections with the biosphere, humans would be extremely transient beings, lasting only a few minutes without drawing in air, a few weeks without water, or a few months without feeding on a diversity of other species.

Few would dispute that language is informed by the physical and biological world that humans find themselves in and by the practical business of surviving in that world. Also, few would dispute that language has an impact on the physical and biological world through all those phenomena that could not exist without it – such as environmental legislation, trade agreements, advertising, market regulation, scientific predictions, or international institutions. Yet only recently have linguists begun to view language as something beyond an isolated system, beyond a socially embedded and socially constructive phenomenon, something which both reflects and has an impact on the larger ecosystems that societies are embedded in and depend on for their continuing existence.

Although there were, of course, precursors such as Haugen (1972), ecolinguistics in its current form emerged in the early 1990s following Halliday's (1990) seminal address at the AILA conference, and since then there has been an exponential increase in interest and publications (such as Chalwa 1991, Fill 1993,

The Handbook of Language and Globalization, First Edition. Edited by Nikolas Coupland.
© 2013 Blackwell Publishing Ltd except for editorial material and organization © 2013 Nikolas Coupland.
Published 2013 by Blackwell Publishing Ltd.

Abram 1996, Myerson and Rydin 1996, Harré et al. 1999, Fill and Mühlhäusler 2001, Mühlhäusler 2003a, Stibbe 2006, 2008). The emergence of ecolingustics at this point in history is partly a result of advances in human ecology, where inter-connections and interdependencies between all kinds of systems (including eco-nomic systems, social systems, religious systems, cultural systems, linguistic systems, and ecosystems) are being highlighted and explored rather than being sidelined for disciplinary convenience. More importantly, though, ecolingusitics is generating intense interest because the consequences of ignoring the ecological embedding of humans are becoming starkly clear, as climate change, resource depletion, and ecosystem degradation reduce the ability of the Earth to support humans and many other species. All kinds of disciplines are broadening them-selves to engage with the reality of the ecological dependence of humanity, from ecological economics to ecofeminism, ecopsychology, ecopoetics, ecocriticism, ecosociology, social ecology, and political ecology, and it is within this general 'ecological turn' that ecolingusitics finds its place.

One of the unique facets of the human species is, of course, the possession of a sophisticated written and oral language. Another is the ability to alter the global conditions of the Earth single-handedly, as a species, so as to make it less hospi-table for our species and for others. What unites the majority of ecolinguists is the suspicion that these two facets of humanity are connected. Halliday (2001: 103), for instance, claims that "[t]here is a syndrome of grammatical features which conspire […] to construe reality in a certain way; and it is a way that is no longer good for our health as a species." Mühlhäusler (2003a: 91) similarly writes that "grammatical constructions have developed in the more recent past that might encourage language habits which have contributed to our present environmental crisis." Abram (1996: 267) claims that "our organic atonement to the local earth is thwarted by our ever-increasing intercourse with our own signs," which makes us "so oblivious to the presence of other animals and the earth, that our current lifestyles and activities contribute daily to the destruction of whole ecosystems" (p. 137). Nettle and Romaine (2000: 204), in discussing the hegemonic spread of monolingualism, write that "our global village must be truly multicultural and multilingual, or it will not exist at all." The discovery that emerges from ecolin-gusitics is not only that language and ecological destruction are linked, but that globalization of various kinds plays a central role in linking the two. This chapter attempts to bring together some of the diverse (and sometimes contradictory) perspectives and voices of ecolingusitics to help contextualize the study of lan-guage and globalization within the threatened ecosystems that humans, and hence human language, exist.

Movement of Peoples: The First Wave

The starting point of ecolinguistic consideration occurs before the invention of writing, when all cultures were oral cultures. Abram's *The Spell of the Sensuous* (1996) describes how, with settled oral cultures, languages remain intensely localized, and their vocabulary and grammar respond to, and reflect, the local environment and the human needs for survival within that environment: "the linguistic patterns of an oral culture remain uniquely responsive, and responsible, to the more-than-human life-world, or bioregion, in which that culture is embedded" (p. 78). While subpopulations of any species can eventually adapt genetically to suit the environments they find themselves in, the flexibility of human language permits new lexical distinctions, discursive models, and narratives to be created and quickly transmitted within a group, allowing humans to adapt culturally to a great diversity of environments, in a way that is much faster than genetic adaptation. Well adapted populations can live in the same place sustainably for hundreds of generations, while populations who cannot adapt will die out – a phenomenon which leads to natural selection toward the sustainability of settled oral cultures. However, that is not the end of the story, because for many reasons, including sudden environmental change, populations move.

When populations move physically, the new bio-region they find themselves in may be quite different from the one they have left – the one that their language is attuned to. Therefore their language may not have the lexical, discursive, and narrative resources necessary for living sustainably in the new region (Mühlhäusler 1996). Mühlhäusler (2003a: 46) uses the metaphor of invasive species to describe this situation: "Such languages are exotic in the sense of introducing and not adapting [...] exotic discourse can contribute significantly to environmental degradation." And we do see a pattern of environmental degradation when populations move; this pattern includes waves of extinction in large animals, in the wake of human arrival in new regions as long ago as 46,000 years ago, in Australia, North America, South America, and the Pacific Islands (Diamond 2005: 9, Flannery 1994). Abram (1996: 269) writes that the extinctions in the Americas may have been precipitated by "a lack of cultural and linguistic patterns tuned to the diverse ecologies of this continent." In the case of extinctions of large animals, however, it was not just human language and cultures that were badly adapted to the environment. The animals in the new regions were themselves not adapted to humans, and so, lacking defences, they were far more open to overexploitation (Diamond 2005: 9). Mühlhäusler (2003a: 37) puts the timing for languages to adapt to new locations (and for the locations to adapt to the people) at about three hundred years: this span would allow for settled groups living sustainably in one place to emerge.

The movement of oral peoples to regions that their language is not attuned to, and the consequent ecological destruction and slow process of re-attunement, can be considered the first wave of ecolinguistically significant globalization. However, the central concept, that of the ecological attunement of language, is controversial. Pennycook (2004) starkly puts forward the opposing view that "languages do not adapt to the world: they are part of human endeavours to create new worlds" (p. 213) and that ecolinguistics "reduces languages to reflections of the environment rather than a key locus of human creativity" (p. 222). In taking this somewhat overstated position, however, Pennycook is merely attempting to combat any tendency that ecolinguistics may have toward biological or environmental determinism. In fact Pennycook's view is more sophisticated, conceiving of language "as a set of semiotic relations dynamically integrated across physical, social, mental, and moral worlds" (p. 236).

Key to moving beyond the dualism of environmental determinism and social construction is a conception of language which is broader than its lexical, syntactic, and semantic resources, including in addition the ways in which these building blocks are put together to create social worlds. It is highly unlikely that there is a deterministic relationship between regions which have a river and the particular morphology of the local language. However, the features of the environment may well be infused into the local stories, songs, proverbs, poems, metaphors, ceremonial expressions, discourses, and ways of referring to particular animals, plants, and geographic features of salience to people's lives. In this way the features of the environment are not deterministically 'reflected' in the 'language,' but they participate instead in larger, constructed narratives, which structure peoples lives in ways that allow them to live sustainability within that environment.

Movement of Written Materials: The Second Wave

The second wave of ecolinguistically significant globalization occurred with the invention of writing and the enormous changes that take place when oral cultures become transformed into literate cultures. Abram (1996: 100) describes how, "[w]ith the invention of the *aleph-beth*, a new distance opens between human culture and the rest of nature [...] a concerted shift of attention [...] away from the sensible phenomenon that previously called forth the spoken utterance." With writing, discourses, stories, and models of reality from one bio-region can travel with great ease to another, without the need for whole populations to uproot themselves and physically move. The narratives become fixed by the writing system, being unable to change according to changing conditions, as orally transmitted narratives can, and the semantic distinctions and values contained in the itinerant written narratives may be entirely inappropriate or irrelevant for sustainable living within the local environmental conditions.

The ease of movement that writing facilitates has allowed the languages of a few dominant populations to spread across the world and replace countless local languages (Nettle and Romaine 2000). In this way languages which encode relationships with local environments die out, and cultures which have lived sustainability in the same place for hundreds of years are lost. The loss of local cultures and the important ecological knowledge contained within their languages has led to a significant movement, within ecolingusitics, to protect both cultural diversity and the linguistic diversity that supports it (Terralingua 2008, Nettle and Romaine 2000, Harmon 1996, Mühlhaüsler 1995). This movement is in tune with the United Nations Environment Program's position that "[b]iodiversity also incorporates human cultural diversity, which can be affected by the same drivers as biodiversity, and which has impacts on the diversity of genes, other species, and ecosystems" (UNEP 2007). Mühlhaüsler (2003a: 60) describes how "[t]he rapid decline in the world's linguistic diversity thus must be regarded with apprehension by those who perceive the interconnection between linguistic and biological diversity." Nettle and Romaine (2000: 166) write:

> Delicate tropical environments in particular must be managed with care and skill. It is indigenous peoples who have the relevant practical knowledge, since they have been successfully making a living in them for hundreds of generations. Much of this detailed knowledge about local ecosystems is encoded in indigenous language and rapidly being lost.

This does not deny that large, globalized languages are adaptable – capable of being used to create new stories, metaphors, identities, and cultural norms in adaptation to new locations. There is, however, the crucial dimension of time, as Mühlhaüsler (2003b: 77) points out:

> English in many places has been an exotic language, in the sense of ill-adapted to the new environments to which it was transported [...] those who argue that English can be nativized and adapt to new conditions tend to underestimate the time it takes – and that in the meantime considerable collateral damage may be caused.

For Abram (1996), written language comes under suspicion not just because it is easily put out of place by being read in a different physical bio-region from the one it was written in, but because of the process of abstraction, or movement away from the concrete, that itinerant forms of language tend toward. Halliday (2001: 181) examines the nature of written language in detail, describing how its grammar is very different from the grammar of oral languages. With writing, "[s]ocial relations are transformed into institutions [...] the main source of *abstract* meaning seems to shift from the interpersonal to the ideational [...] from processes to things." This leads to a situation where "the nominalising, metaphorical grammar of late twentieth century prestige varieties of English has become dysfunctional [...] it construes the world after a fashion which [...] has now become excessively abstract, objectifying and determinate" (p. 191).

Abstraction occurs not only in generalizing away from specific aspects of reality, but also in the creation of symbolic realities, which exist primarily within the world of words and have little or no connection with the larger reality. Suspicion of a mismatch between language and the world is certainly not something new – Grigg (1994) describes the belief, both in Taoism and in Zen Buddhism, that "[t]he world of suchness does not correspond to any conceptual model expressed or invented by words" (p. 191) and that "[l]anguage, like pure intellect, moves experience inexorably into the abstract, away from the finality of grounded reality" (p. 196). The question for ecolingusitics is: What, specifically, is it about the abstraction of language and the realities it creates that is implicated in ecological destruction?

Halliday (2001: 103) investigates aspects of the grammar of English which, he claims, construct reality in ways which are "no longer good for our health as a species." The first aspect he describes is that mass nouns like 'soil' and 'water' are unbounded and do not therefore reflect the limited supply of such essential resources. The second is that antonymic pairs have a positive (unmarked) pole, which means that 'bigger' is aligned with 'better'. The third is that, in grammar, humans tend to be given more agency than other species. The fourth is that pronoun use and mental processes divide the world falsely into conscious beings (humans – and to some extent their pets) and non-conscious beings (other species). Chalwa (1991: 262) likewise claims that "the language habits of fragmenting the mass, quantifying intangibles and imaginary nouns, and perceiving time in terms of past, present and future are factors in our inability to perceive the natural environment holistically." Halliday is also concerned that, as the unmarked pole of the pair *growth–shrinkage*, the word 'growth' is intrinsically positive, and the idea that the economy must shrink, or that "economic shrinkage is good" is just not going to catch on. He considers terms such as "negative shrinkage" or "elephantiasis" (instead of growth), and "zero growth" or "negative growth" (as a goal), but rejects these unpromising alternatives (p. 193). Clearly, these claims are not empirically based or testable, and it is uncertain that a different configuration of linguistic resources would help to build a more sustainable society, even if they could be found. For instance, it seems unlikely that people would suddenly realize the importance of soil for sustaining life if the term was suddenly replaced universally with a count noun like 'clumps' or 'sods.'

Goatly (1996) also focuses on the level of grammar and argues that modern scientific theory demands a grammar which does not simplistically separate out agentive participants, affected participants and circumstances, since this is out of step with the radical interconnectedness of the world that modern science reveals. For instance he rejects the simplistic cause-and-effect patterning of agent and patient (the affected), because agents, too, are also affected by their actions. So in driving a car the driver is not only the agentive participant, but also the affected participant – affected by the pollution and climate change he or she is contributing to. Goatly therefore argues against Halliday and others, who criticize nominalizations such as 'pollution' on the grounds that they disguise the agent. Clearly agency *is* more complex than can be expressed in language: does sulphur dioxide pollute? or do factories which produce sulphur dioxide pollute? or do consumers who buy the products pollute? or do the social systems which manufacture demand for the products pollute? Schleppegrell (2001: 228) correctly argues that "[d]iffusing agency to all individuals or people in general is a misrepresentation of the real causes of environmental problems," but clearly language cannot represent the deep complexity of the "real causes" within its basic grammatical structure. Language can, however, represent causality in units which go beyond single grammatical features – discourses which combine together various features to produce particular representations of reality (van Dijk 1993).

Movement of Discourses: The Third Wave

Discourses are central to the third wave of ecolinguistically significant globalization. The first wave consisted of the physical movement of oral peoples; the second, of the movement of written texts and of the spread of dominant languages it occasioned. The third wave consists of the more recent large-scale translinguistic spread of particular discourses. Fairclough provides an excellent example of this phenomenon when he looks at a statement made by a Romanian minister and notices the use of the terms *outsourcingul* ('the outsourcing'), *competitia* ('the competition'), *satul global* ('the global village'); *strategie* ('strategy'), *marketing* ('marketing'), *branding* ('branding'), *competitie globala* ('global competition'). The minister in question is using the same neo-liberal discourse as senators in Washington and MPs in the UK, even though he speaks in a different language. The discourse of neo-liberalism represented here is hegemonic in the sense of being associated with powerful transnational institutions which have unequal access to forms of mass dissemination such as the media and educational institutions. The discourses can therefore spread across the world, although this is not an entirely one-way process. As Fairclough (2006: 4) points out, not only are discourses influenced on arrival by the local social and historical context; counter-discourses also arise and compete with the hegemonic discourses.

The hegemonic spread of discourses is problematic from an ecolinguistic perspective, partly because the environmentally attuned discourses which form the basis of local cultures are not represented in the educational system or in the media, and so they may be displaced by the more powerful incoming discourses. More importantly, however, there may be aspects to particular hegemonic discourses which contribute directly to ecologically destructive behavior. The discourse of neo-liberalism, for example, has been criticized for representing globalization, trade liberalization, and international competitiveness as inevitable and unstoppable phenomena, to which other things (such as workers' rights and the environment) must be sacrificed (Fairclough 2006). The following extract provides an example of how neo-liberal discourse is used to justify the sacrifice of the environment. In the extract, a pilot (Chalk) gives his opinion on why the controversial plans of the UK government to build a third runway at Heathrow are justifiable:

> As an environmentalist, I believe that we will solve nothing by asking the majority of people to suffer the loss of a leisure activity they enjoy, and business will not curtail an activity vital for it to succeed in a progressively more globalised marketplace. (Chalk 2008)

In this passage, the inevitability and unavoidability of the "progressively globalised marketplace" is simply presupposed, and "succeed" clearly fits the neo-liberal representation of success in purely financial terms. The agent of the process of 'curtailing' is the businesses themselves, as if there was no possibility of government stepping in and curtailing the excesses of business.

A series of discourses which have been criticized for their potential negative impact on ecosystems when they are spread on a global scale, including the following: discursive constructions of neo-classical economics (Stibbe 2005b); consumerism (Slater 2007); development (Sachs 1992); progress (Mühlhäusler 2003a: 110); intensive agriculture (Stibbe 2003); masculinity (Stibbe 2004); and advertising (Williams 2007, Gargan 2007). Slater (2007) looks at the discursive construction of the new masculine identity of the 'Gadgeteer' in Stuff Magazine, noting the environmental impact that overconsumption of 'gadgets' can have. Stibbe (2003) describes how the language of the pork industry redefines pigs as machines, objects, and resources, leading to intensive forms of farming which are out of touch with natural cycles and extremely destructive environmentally.

Coupland and Coupland (1997: 7) suggest a "competing discourses" formulation for ecolinguistics, noting how environmental discourses on ozone depletion are reformulated in media texts in terms of hedonistic summer leisure or ascetic body culture. Gössling and Peeters (2007) show how a range of discourses are employed by airlines to justify expansion in flying; these include discourses centered around the energy efficiency of the airline sector as a whole, social and economic benefits, and technological progress. Goatly (2000) proposes an "ecological critical discourse analysis," and provides an example by conducting an analysis of the discursive construction of nature in a typical broadsheet newspaper, by comparison with that of Wordsworth. His conclusion is that "the view of the natural world represented by Wordsworth, along with aspects of his grammar, provides a much better model for our survival than that represented by *The Times*" (p. 201). In particular, he finds as praiseworthy Wordsworth's placing of mountains and landscapes in the role of Actor, of rivers in the role of Sayer, of nature as 'doing' rather than 'being,' and the way ergative verbs are used to show landscape as possessing its own energy.

Usefully, Fairclough (2006: 5) analyzes discourses in terms of "practical adequacy," which he specifies as "whether they are reliable guides to action, whether what they suggest or imply about what will happen if we act in certain ways actually *does* happen." He states that

> Certain discourses (which arguably include [...] neo-liberal economic discourse) which can be shown to be *not* adequate for real processes, which lack 'practical adequacy,' can also be shown to be used to create and sustain unjust or undemocratic positions and relations of power. (Fairclough 2006: 5)

One problem with Fairclough's work is that it is based on a form of neo-Marxist social theory which has traditionally "ignored nature and the environment" (Biersack 2006), focusing on relationships of inequality, without consideration for the ecological conditions which support or undermine people's lives, and on which (and through which) power operates. From an ecolinguistic perspective, then, it would be possible to add to Fairclough's statement above that certain discourses which lack practical adequacy also undermine the ecological basis of society, oppressed groups being the first ones to suffer the consequences. A typical example would be consumerist discourses which imply that happiness or spiritual wellbeing will arise out of the materialist accumulation of unnecessary goods. Such discourses are in practice inadequate, since long-lasting spiritual wellbeing is unlikely to occur from excessive material consumption. In addition, the discourses sustain unjust relations of power *and* undermine the ecological basis of society by encouraging the overconsumption of natural resources and the overproduction of waste. This has negative consequences for all, the greatest impact being on groups who have the least power.

Although it is, arguably, discourses such as those of progress, consumerism, neo-liberalism, and classical economics that have the greatest potential impact on ecological systems, the discourse which has received most attention from ecolinguistics is that of environmentalism (see Nygren 1998, Haig 2001, Väliverronen 1998, Väliverronen and Hellsten 2002, Stibbe 2005a, 2005c, Pickett and Cadenasso 2002, Stott and Sullivan 2000, Stamou and Paraskevopoulus 2004, Mühlhaüsler 2003a, Penman 2001). An early attempt at analyzing environmental discourse is the book *Greenspeak: A Study of Environmental Discourse* by Harré and colleagues (1999), which described both the internal and the external aspects of the globalization of environmental discourse – or the "globalisation of Greenspeak," as they put it (p. 12).

The first aspect – internal – consists of a shift, within environmental discourse itself, toward representing environmental problems as global ones rather than as visible issues related to people's immediate environment. This shift involves changes to "linguistic expressions and photographic, cinematic and graphic representations" (ibid.), for instance the lexicalizations "global thinking," "spaceship Earth," "One World," or the iconic "blue planet" photograph. The internal construction of the emergent discourse on the environment has been criticized from a variety of perspectives.

Harré and colleagues claim that "[t]here is a fundamental mismatch between the problems to be tackled and the linguistic resources for dealing with them" (p. 178). They describe this mismatch in terms of *referential adequacy* (for instance the lack of a word meaning "not biodegradable," p. 31), *systematic adequacy* (e.g. English does not encode time-related changes in its grammar, p. 34), *social adequacy* (reflected, say, in the undesirable proximity of "population control" to "pest control," p. 35), *semantic vagueness* (as illustrated by terms like pollution or progress, p. 29), *semantic underdifferentiation* (for example 'growth' refers to natural growth, exponential growth, and other forms of growth, p. 29), and *misleading encoding* (for example fertilizers can render soils infertile, p. 29). Others who have taken up this approach include Penman (2001: 148), who has analyzed the term 'sustainability' using the notion of referential adequacy and concluded that it is "semantically vague and semantically undifferentiated, meaning many different things to many different people."

There has been a number of analyses of the use of metaphors in environmental discourse (Väliverronen 1998, Pickett and Cadenasso 2002, Väliverronen and Hellsten 2002, Stibbe 2008) – both as 'boundary objects' necessary for rapidly explaining complex issues among diverse groups and across languages, and as oversimplified models of reality, which highlight some aspects while hiding others. Stibbe (2008), for instance, criticizes the metaphor of biodiversity as *a library of species which is burning down* on the grounds that it promotes a tokenistic approach, whereby only one or two specimens of a species (copies of a book) need to be preserved, and also because it places humans outside the library, as unharmed spectators. On the other hand, the metaphor of biodiversity loss as *the unravelling of the web of life* places humans within the web, emphasizing that disintegration of the web (loss of biodiversity) has an impact on human survival. In a different direction, Carolan (2006) describes metaphors within environmental sciences – such as *ecosystem health, ecosystem integrity, restoration, invasive species, alien species,* and *fragmentation* – as problematic because with them "we find values creeping into our discussions of ecology" (p. 925), whereas "science does not (or at least should not) prescribe" (p. 929).

In contrast to Carolan (2006), mainstream environmental discourse has been criticized precisely for its lack of values – in particular, its tendency to discuss the great diversity of lifeforms that inhabit the Earth as resources of value only for human exploitation. Stibbe (2006) describes how the influential Millennium Ecosystem Assessment (MEA) officially "recognizes that the actions people take that influence ecosystems result not just from concern about human wellbeing but also from considerations of the intrinsic value of species and ecosystems," while at the same time species and ecosystems are represented, within the same report, as if they were entirely worthless in and of themselves. Looking at the representation of fish in particular, Stibbe (2006) presents a syndrome of features in the discourse of the MEA which conspire together in denying them intrinsic worth. The syndrome includes the following features:

(a) the affected participant of processes of *harming* is exclusively human or human related;
(b) the word 'fishery' appears more often than 'fish';
(c) metaphors of harvesting and stock depletion are applied to fish;
(d) euphemisms such as *removed, caught, captured, landed* or *eliminated* are used instead of *killed* or *died*;
(e) there is complete lack of agency in the representation of fish across processes in all clauses;
(f) there is frequent embedding of the word 'fish' in noun phrases such as *fish stocks, fish supplies* or *quantity of fish* rather than as direct participants in processes.

This is contrasted with the influential writing of Rachel Carson, which generated tremendous support for the environment movement in the 1960s (Waddell 2000). Carson (1962: 122), for instance, writes, "[f]or thousands upon thousands of years the salmon have known and followed these threads of fresh water that lead them back to the rivers," representing fish as agents of material and mental processes, and "[d]ead and dying fish, including many young salmon, were found along the banks of the stream [...] All the life of the stream was stilled," which avoids euphemisms and represents the death of the fish as something negative in itself. If fish are depicted as living beings leading lives, rather than as objects, this would not ethically preclude killing them for food; but it might discourage the unnecessary suffering and loss of life that occur in polluted rivers and lakes or through by-catch. Stibbe (2005a, 2005c) provides further evidence that current mainstream environmental discourse, unlike Carson's writings, often fails to tap into the motivating power of people's concern to protect ecosystems for the sake of all the life supported by them.

The second, external, aspect of the globalization of environmental discourse described by Harré and colleagues (1993: 16) relates to the way in which the discourse as a whole spreads across the world through transnational documents like the MEA described above and through high-profile events such as the Earth Summit in Rio, which led to unprecedented levels of "global attention, perception and affirmation [...] in other words the globalization of the discourse." The hegemonic spread of environmental discourse across the world is problematized within a strand of the recently emerging transdisciplinary *Political Ecology* associated primarily with Phillip Stott. Although Stott is a controversial figure associated with the discredited *Great Global Warming Scandal* (a documentary presenting false 'evidence' that global warming is not caused by humans), the general approach put forward in the edited collection *Political Ecology: Science, Myth and Power* (Stott and Sullivan 2000) is a form of ecolinguistic study of globalization. Stott and Sullivan bring together "a collection of observations and analyses regarding the creation, legitimization and contestation of environmental narratives that draw their power by using the 'Big Talk' of a reified science" (p. 1). By 'Big Talk' the authors mean "important, male, metonymic, serious, official, correct, objective and emphatic" (p. 1), echoing some of Halliday's criticisms of the reifing scientific discourse. Sullivan looks at how the concept of "desertification," used in and about Namibia, is part of a global discourse which clashes with actual local facts on the ground. According to Sullivan (2000:15), the global discourse "occluded local narratives and wider ecological theorising," blamed local "misuse of resources" for ecological problems (p. 17) and socialized "young Namibians to view the land-use practices of their communal area country-folk as environmentally degrading" (p. 20). Overall, Stott and Sullivan (2000) ask "What is the potential for challenging the status quo, particularly in light of the processes of globalisation?" and attempt to challenge the status quo by enabling "alternative voices to be heard; that is, to release the 'excluded voices' of Michael Foucault" (p. 5).

One of the most influential channels through which environmental discourse spreads around the world is environmental education. While environmental education plays an essential role in bringing attention to global environmental issues which are not locally discernible, it tends to be heavily based on written materials supplied from the centers of power and distributed outwards to local communities. This means that it lacks the power to inspire specific solutions, which may be in tune with the local bio-region and the culture within it. And, even worse, environmental education has the potential to be a Trojan horse for spreading the values which lead to environmental destruction in the first place. Bowers (2001: 141) argues that,

> in many instances, environmental education contributes to the double bind of helping to address environmental problems while at the same time reinforcing the use of the language/thought patterns that underlie the digital phase of the Industrial Revolution we are now entering on a global scale.

In a case study of this phenomenon, Stibbe (2005c) analyzes twenty-six environmental education textbooks written in English by UK and US authors and used in Japanese universities. The analysis reveals that, while ostensibly teaching about environmental issues, the discourses conveyed consumerist attitudes, anthropocentricism, and reductionist views of natural systems; placed the blame for environmental problems such as deforestation with the local populations rather than with First-World overconsumption; and presented technological fixes as the primary or only solution to environmental problems. In other words, while attempting to solve environmental problems, the textbooks were exporting values and ideas which have been implicated in causing the problems in the first place. As an example, a textbook entitled *Make It or Break It: The Future of our Environment* describes the problem of car pollution using discourse which could have come from a car advertisement:

> Simply stated, cars offer fun and freedom. When we get behind the wheel and get on the road, we can flee the monotony of daily life [...] even if we are forced to spend most of our time sitting in traffic jams, the allure of the automobile is its promise of escape. (Evanoff et al. 1999)

Similarly, another textbook on global issues states:

> Cars [...] are expressions of a person's individuality [...] An office worker may go to work in sombre clothes, but on weekends he or she drives a dashing sports car [...]: the car has released that person's inner self, which is obviously hidden during the week! (Randle et al. 1997)

As with advertising discourses, these passages work to make everyday life seem monotonous, sombre, and constrictive, while an environmentally damaging product is represented as a positive, liberating alternative that will provide a new you. Ironically, it is the overconsumption of unnecessary products that forces people into stressful, monotonous jobs in the first place. By encouraging consumerism and opening up markets (Phillipson 1992, Pennycook 1998) rather than genuinely educating students about the environment, these textbooks, along with many of the other environmentally themed textbooks analyzed in Stibbe (2005c), seem to be fulfilling a traditional imperialist function of English-language text-books written for use abroad.

In many of these textbooks language is used to represent lifeforms other than human in ways which deny them intrinsic value. The following example is from the textbook *Ten Minute Ecologist:*

> Much of what humans do with their biological resources – including […] species harvested from natural populations – depends on our having an accurate inventory of life on Earth. (Janovy 1997: 13)

This example uses pronouns in ways which make all species in the world appear to be human possessions. It uses instrumental metaphors which represent other lifeforms as resources, wild animals and plants as crops, and species as inventory items. This is in sharp contrast with discourses of traditional Japanese culture such as the discourse of Haiku, which conveys positive regard, empathy, and a sense of identity with even the most ordinary of animals and plants (Stibbe 2007). While not all discourses of traditional Japanese culture necessary contribute to sustainability, there are some which encourage a deep respect for nature, construe modesty and simplicity as virtues, represent wasting food as a waste of life, and express gratitude to other species for giving up their lives for humans. It is therefore conceivable to have an environmental education where students draw on discourses from their traditional culture and put them in dialogue with western environmental discourse for the benefit of both.

Toward Sustainability

In summary, then, the world is currently on an unsustainable path leading to ecological collapse on an unknown scale (Diamond 2005), and ecolinguists have investigated a number of language-related factors which are claimed to have contributed to this unsustainable trajectory. These include the mismatch between language and environment that occurs when oral peoples move to new locations, the easy circulation of written language to bio-regions and localities it was not created in, the abstract nature of written language, grammar's general manner of obscuring complex relations of causality by simplifying the world into discrete participants, and specific features of grammar such as the concealment of agency that occurs in nominalization. Also, certain discourses were implicated in ecological destruction: hegemonic discourses of consumerism, neo-liberalism, progress, and intensive farming, all of which model reality in ways that disregard natural limits. The discourse of environmentalism itself has been criticized as being important, but ultimately an inadequate response to the global situation.

The question is, what can ecolinguistics – as a subdiscipline, metadiscipline, or part of the larger ecological 'turn' both in academia and in society – do to contribute toward the quest for a more sustainable world? The question arises from the nature of ecolingusitics, which, like medical science, is a goal-orientated activity rather than a purely exploratory science.

Halliday (2001) makes a pessimistic comment on the power of ecolinguistics to address issues of sustainability, primarily because his analysis focuses on the level of the general grammar of languages. He writes: "I do not think even the language professionals of AILA can plan the inner layers of grammar" (167). Indeed, the feminist struggles to change even the most superficial aspects of grammar (generic 'he,' Mr/Mrs, the -ess morpheme, and the like) have met with only limited success and have created an atmosphere where grammatical tinkering is strongly resisted (Cameron 1995).

There is, however, an alternative to attempting to change something as funda-mental as the grammar of English. Rather than trying to modify the unmarked (and hence positive) status of the word 'growth,' for instance, it would be possible simply to look for an entirely different way of talking about the economy, which does not include the idea of 'growth', and to stop using the term *growth* at all. The New Economics Foundation, for example, points out that growth in GDP beyond a certain level does not correspond with increases in wellbeing, and hence it replaces the inadequate proxy, growth, with the end itself, wellbeing. This leads to a discourse where the maximization of wellbeing, rather than of growth, is presented as the goal and which includes terms such as *wellbeing indicators, Gross National Happiness* and *Happy Planet Index*. David Cameron, leader of the Conservative Party, already seems to have taken up this discourse, stating for example that "[w]ell-being can't be measured by money or traded in markets. It's about the beauty of our surroundings, the quality of our culture, and, above all, the strength of our relationships" (quoted in Brown 2007).

Harré and colleagues (1999) suggest intervention at a variety of levels, in a process they call "language planning." At a lexical level, the language planning advocated here consists in the replacement of lists of terms in order to give greater referential adequacy. For instance, their "proposed alternative" to the term *clear-ing* is *native vegetation removal*, and their proposed alternative to *greenhouse effect* is *human induced climatic dislocation* (p. 28). The project also consists in inventing new words – for instance one meaning "not biodegradable," one meaning "a special refuse container for recyclable goods," and one meaning "the needless transhipping of commodities to places where they are freely available," for which they suggest "to Newcastle" (p. 31). In general, Harré and colleagues believe that, if, through language planning, language can be made "referentially, systemati-cally and socially adequate, it is […] likely to be environmentally adequate" (p. 42). Carolan (2006: 928) takes a similar approach, arguing: "Language planning would thus involve taking words that invite vague associations and/or that are laden with normative assumptions and replacing them with terms that more closely capture their nonlinguistic correlate."

Needless to say, the language planning approach leaves itself open to accusa-tions of 'ecological correctness.' In reviewing the work of Harré and colleagues,

Smith (1999) points out: "There is something rather Orwellian about the concept of 'language planning' which sometimes imparts a managerial overtone to their agenda. Just who is to determine what language is appropriate [...]?" It does seem somewhat naïve to assume that phrases like "human induced climatic dislocation" are likely to inspire people to take action just because some linguists have declared that they are at the correct level of semantic differentiation and are not misleadingly encoded. In fact, the influential *Ecolinguistics Reader* (Fill and Mühlhaüsler 2001) later contained the clear statement that "[t]he idea of an 'ecological correctness' is rejected by all authors" (p. 45), and, in general, piecemeal and obvious attempts to replace individual terms with more correct ones have been abandoned.

A more holistic approach is to make available the critiques of influential discourses to those who produce them, showing what features are suspected to encourage unsustainability and providing examples of actual alternative discourses – discourse which represent reality in other ways. As an example, the ecolinguistic analysis of the Millennium Ecosystem Assessment discussed above was presented to its authors, and received the following response from one of the leaders of the project:

> [this ecolinguistic research] is extremely interesting. I very much appreciate this type of analysis and also think that your conclusions are quite correct. There is no question but that we framed the assessment in extremely anthropocentric terms [and this] [...] has costs in devaluing the intrinsic worth of species as you note. For the audience we were aiming at, that cost was worth paying in my view but ideally in the future assessments might be able to provide a better balance here.

And, in terms of providing a better balance, the ecolinguistic report sent to the MEA included analysis of the linguistic features of Rachel Carson's discourse, giving ideas for effectively conveying the value of the natural world without using clumsy expressions such as 'intrinsic worth.' This is just one small example; but there are whole subdisciplines such as environmental rhetoric, environmental communication, and ecocomposition which (among other things) analyze entire discourses in the search for effective ways of inspiring people to lead their lives, businesses, and societies in more sustainable ways (Coppola and Karis 2000, Dobrin and Weisser 2002, Herndl and Brown 1996, Owens 2001, Killingsworth 2005, Waddell 2000).

Perhaps the clearest example of an effective application of ecolinguistic analysis can be found in the work of someone who would not claim to be a ecolinguist at all. Vandana Shiva is a physicist, an environmental activist, and one of the leading voices in resisting the socially and ecologically destructive aspects of globalization. Shiva's work is based on the following position:

> The global free trade economy has become a threat to sustainability and the very survival of the poor [...] in a systematic way through a restructuring of our worldview at the most fundamental level. (Shiva, quoted in Alexander 2003: 6)

In looking at the influence of the forces of globalization on restructuring world-views, Shiva is operating at the level of discourse. Alexander (2003: 9) writes that

> in Shiva's work we encounter semantic analysis as well as objective political and scientific reasoning [...] [she] manifests a critical capacity to see through language employed in industrial and commercial agriculture [uncovering] the ideologies and values which specific terminological or lexical choices make.

Shiva's goal is to expose and criticize hegemonic global discourses and to replace them with others, which serve the agenda of "sustainability, sharing and survival." To give just one example, she states that, "[w]hen patents are granted for seeds and plants, as in the case of basmati, theft is defined as creation, and saving and sharing seed is defined as theft of intellectual property" (Shiva in Alexander 2003: 12). In this way Shiva undermines western discourses which represent the discovery, engineering, and patenting of genes as a form of "creation," and renames it instead as a crime, namely "theft," since it deprives local people of the right to products based on genes which evolved naturally in the area they live in.

Shiva stays directly in touch with the reality of the social and environmental impact that neo-liberal discursive constructions of reality have on the most exploited people and environments in the third world. She challenges those constructions in the First-World countries they originate from, and she offers alternatives that are in tune with the values and practices of the people who are being exploited. Although Shiva's actual analysis of discourse is limited, her work shows the potential for an engaged form of ecolinguistics in a global context, which could use detailed and systematic analyses of hegemonic discourses and of their alternatives as a basis for effective environmental communication.

A final point to make about ecolinguistic analysis is that, as Harris puts it, "[a]ny linguistic critique of environmental discourse will ultimately lack force unless it is clear on what theoretical assumptions the critique itself is based. Otherwise, the objections will appear *ad hoc* [...]" (Harris 2001: 154). While the broader area of ecology itself involves a philosophical struggle among the perspectives of social ecology, deep ecology, political ecology, human ecology, ecofeminism, and environmentalism, ecolinguists often remain sheltered from the storm, making judgments about what kind of language contributes to ecological destruction on linguistic grounds such as 'semantic vagueness,' without being clear what model of ecology, model of the world, or actual aspects of the world the judgments in question relate to. Nettle and Romaine feel that ecolinguistics could do harm, if

> putting our current environmental and human crisis down to the way of discourse works means we end up [...] picking away self-referentially at discourse, and not thinking about important material factors like land ownership, pollution, population growth [...] which are the factors indigenous peoples on the ground experience. (Nettle and Romaine 2000: 465)

Conclusion

This chapter has looked at the role of globalization of various forms in linking two of the unique characteristics of humanity: its ability to use language and its ability to make the world less hospitable for itself and for other species. Ecolinguistics is in an interesting position, being predominantly an abstract, written form of discourse which is diffused from the 'center': this makes it one of the discourses that it itself criticizes. There is something ironic about Halliday's claim that the "grammar of late twentieth century prestige varieties of English has become dysfunctional [...] excessively abstract, objectifying and determinate" (Halliday 2001: 191), since Halliday's own writing is a prime example of what he criticizes. David Abram, perhaps more than any other ecolinguist, goes beyond critiquing the abstraction and rootlessness of written language, to incorporate an alterative form of discourse into his own writing. The following quotation both explains why and illustrates how Abram uses language to bring his writing literally 'back to Earth':

> there can be no question of simply abandoning literacy, of turning away from all writing. Our task, rather, is that of *taking up* the written word, with all of its potency, and patiently, carefully, writing language back into the land. Our craft is that of releasing the budded, earthy intelligence of our words, freeing them to respond to the speech of the things themselves – to the green uttering-forth of leaves from the spring branches. (Abram 1996: 273)

Few ecolinguists have followed, or can follow, Abram, partly due to their own inability to write in alterative styles, and partly because the majority of academic forums will only accept writing that is dry and technical and keeps its values suppressed. The redeeming feature of ecolinguistics, however, is its self-reflection, since this discipline is well aware of the dangers of overabstraction and rootlessness, so it is in a position to use the authority of abstract academic language in order to expose the dangers of hegemonic discourses such as its own. It can then point beyond itself so as to call for a revaluing of local languages, oral communication, and discourses which are more responsive to and responsible to the ecosystems that support life.

REFERENCES

Abram, D. (1996) *The Spell of the Sensuous*. New York: Vintage.

Alexander, R. (2003) Resisting imposed metaphors of value: Vandana Shiva's role in supporting Third World agriculture. *metaphorik.de* 04. Available at: www.metaphorik.de/04/alexander. pdf (accessed on January 9, 2008).

Biersack, A. (2006) Reimagining political ecology: Culture/power/history/nature.

In A. Biersack and J. Greenberg (eds), *Reimagining Political Ecology*, 3–42. Durham: Duke University Press.

Bonnett, M. (1997) Environmental education and beyond. *Journal of Philosophy of Education* 31(2): 249–66.

Bowers, C. (2001) *Educating for Eco-Justice and Community*. Georgia: University of Georgia Press.

Brown, C. (2007) Blair challenges Cameron on his 'happiness' agenda. *Independent*, March 31.

Cameron, D. (1995) *Verbal Hygiene*. London: Routledge.

Carolan, M. (2006) The values and vulnerabilities of metaphors within the environmental sciences. *Society and Natural Resources* 19: 921–30.

Carson, R. (1962) *Silent Spring*. Harmondworth: Penguin.

Chalk, M. (2008) Blue-sky thinking. *Guardian* on-line. Available at: http://commentisfree.guardian.co.uk/martin_chalk/2008/03/blue_sky_thinking_1.html (accessed on January 9, 2008).

Chalwa, S. (1991) Linguistic and philosophical roots of our environmental crisis. *Environmental Ethics* 13(3): 253–62.

Coppola, N., and Karis, B. (eds) (2000) *Technical Communication, Deliberative Rhetoric, and Environmental Discourse*. Stamford, CT: Ablex.

Coupland, N., and Coupland, J. (1997) Bodies, beaches and burn-times: 'Environmentalism' and its discursive competitors. *Discourse and Society* 8(1): 7–25.

Diamond, J. (2005) *Collapse: How Societies Choose to Fail or Survive*. Harmondsworth: Penguin.

Dobrin, S., and Weisser, C. R. (2002) *Natural Discourse: Toward Ecocomposition*. Albany: State University of New York.

Evanoff, R., Paxton, C., and Paxton, H. (1999) *Make It or Break It: The Future of Our Environment*. Tokyo: Sanshusha.

Fairclough, N. (2006) *Language and Globalisation*. New York: Routledge.

Fill, A. (1993) *Ökolinguistik: Eine Einführung*. Tübingen: Gunter narr.

Fill, A., and Mühlhäusler, P. (eds) (2001) *The Ecolinguistic Reader*. London: Continuum.

Flannery, T. (1994) *The Future Eaters: An Ecological History of the Australasian Lands and People*. New York: Grove Press.

Gargan, M. (2007) Magic Romance: On perfume, language and the environment. *Language and Ecology* 2(1). Available at: www.ecoling.net/journal.html (accessed on January 9, 2008).

Goatly, A. (1996) Green grammar and grammatical metaphor, or language and the myth of power, or metaphors we die by. *Journal of Pragmatics* 25: 537–60.

Goatly, A. (2000) *Critical Reading and Writing: An Introductory Coursebook*. London: Routledge.

Gössling, S., and Peeters, P. (2007) "If it does not harm the environment!" An analysis of industry discourses on tourism, air travel and the environment. *Journal of Sustainable Tourism* 15(4): 402–17.

Grigg, R. (1994) *The Tao of Zen*. New Jersey: Alva Press.

Haig, E. (2001) A study of the application of Critical Discourse Analysis to ecolinguistics and the teaching of eco-theory. *Studies in Language and Culture (Nagoya University)* 22(2): 205–26.

Halliday, M. (1990) New ways of meaning: The challenge to applied linguistics. *Journal of Applied Linguistics* 6: 7–36.

Halliday, M. (2001) New ways of meaning: The challenge to applied linguistics. In A. Fill and P. Mühlhäusler (eds), *The Ecolingusitics Reader*, 175–202. London: Continuum. [Originally published as Halliday (1990).]

Harmon, D. (1996) Losing species, losing languages: Connections between biological and linguistic diversity. *Southwest Journal of Linguistics* 15: 89–108.

Harré, R., Brockmeier, J., and Mühlhäusler, P. (1999) *Greenspeak: A Study of Environmental Discourse.* London: Sage.

Harris, R. (2001) *A note on the linguistics of environmentalism.* In Fill and Mühlhäusler (eds), 154–9.

Haugen, E. (1972) *The Ecology of Language.* Palo Alto: Stanford University Press.

Herndl, C., and Brown, S. (eds) (1996) *Green Culture: Environmental Rhetoric in Contemporary America.* Madison: University of Wisconsin.

Janovy, John (1997) *Ten Minute Ecologist.* Tokyo: Kinseido.

Killingsworth, J. (2005) From environmental rhetoric to ecocomposition and ecopoetics: Finding a place for professional communication. *Technical Communication Quarterly* 14(4): 359–73.

Mühlhaüsler, P. (1995) The interdependence of linguistic and biological diversity. In D. Myers (ed.), *The Politics of Multiculturalism in Oceania and Polynesia*, 154–61. Darwin: University of the Northern Territory Press.

Mühlhäusler, P. (1996) Linguistic adaptations to changed environmental conditions: Some lessons from the past. In Alwin Fill (ed.), *Sprachökologie und ökolinguistik*, 105–30. Tübingen: Staffenburg.

Mühlhaüsler, P. (2003a) *Language of Environment, Environment of Language: A Course in Ecolinguistics.* London: Battlebridge.

Mühlhaüsler, P. (2003b) English as an exotic language. In Christian Mair (ed.), *The Politics of English as a World Language: New Horizons in Postcolonial Studies*, 67–86. Amsterdam: Rodopi.

Murata, K. (2007) Pro- and anti-whaling discourses in British and Japanese newspaper reports in comparison: A cross-cultural perspective. *Discourse and Society* 18(6): 741–64.

Myerson, G., and Rydin, Y. (1996) *The Language of Environment: A New Rhetoric.* London: UCL Press.

Nettle, D., and Romaine, S. (2000) *Vanishing Voices: The Extinction of the World's Languages.* Oxford: Oxford University Press.

Nygren, A. (1998) Environment as discourse: Searching for sustainable development in Costa Rica. *Environmental Values* 7: 201–22.

Owens, D. (2001) *Composition and Sustainability: Teaching for a Threatened Generation.* Urbana, IL: NCTE.

Penman, R. (2001) *Environmental matters and communication challenges.* In Fill and Mühlhäusler (eds), 143–53.

Pennycook, A. (1998) *English and the Discourses of Colonialism.* London: Routledge.

Pennycook, A. (2004) Language policy and the ecological turn. *Language Policy* 3(3): 213–39.

Phillipson, R. (1992) *Linguistic Imperialism.* Oxford: Oxford University Press.

Pickett, S., and Cadenasso, M. (2002) The ecosystem as a multidimensional concept: Meaning, model and metaphor. *Ecosystems* 5: 1–10.

Randle, J., Gerard-Sharp, L., and Yagi, Y. (1997) *Global Issues Today.* Tokyo: Seibido.

Evanoff, R., Paxton, C., and Paxton, H. (1999) *Make It or Break It: The Future of Our Environment.* Tokyo: Sanshusha.

Sachs, Wolfgang (ed.) (1992) *The Development Dictionary: A Guide to Knowledge as Power.* London: Zed Press.

Schleppegrell, M. (2001) What makes a grammar green? A reply to Goatly. In Fill and Mühlhäusler (eds), 226–8.

Slater, P. (2007) The gadgeteer: Sex, self and consumerism in Stuff magazine. *Language and Ecology* 2(1). Available at: www.ecoling.net/journal.html (accessed on January 9, 2008).

Smith, M. (1999) Review of Greenspeak: A study of environmental discourse. *Environmental Politics* 8(4): 231–3.

Stamou, A., and Paraskevopoulus, S. (2004) Images of nature by tourism and environmentalist discourses in visitors books: A critical discourse analysis of ecotourism. *Discourse and Society* 15(1): 105–29.

Stibbe, A. (2003) As charming as a pig: The discursive construction of the relationship between pigs and humans. *Society and Animals* 11(4): 375–92.

Stibbe, A. (2004) Real men do shop: Images of masculinity and consumerism in Men's Health magazine. *Language and Ecology* 1(2). Available at: www.ecoling. net/journal.html (accessed on January 9, 2008).

Stibbe, A. (2005a) Counter-discourses and harmonious relationships between humans and other animals. *Anthrozoös* 18(1): 3–17.

Stibbe, A. (2005b) Ecology and the magic of economics. *Language and Ecology* 1(4). Available at: www.ecoling.net/journal. html (accessed on January 9, 2008).

Stibbe, A. (2005c) Environmental education across cultures: Beyond the discourse of shallow environmentalism. *Language and Intercultural Communication* 4(4): 242–60.

Stibbe, A. (2006) Deep ecology and language: The curtailed journey of the Atlantic salmon. *Society and Animals* 14(1): 61–77.

Stibbe, A. (2007) Haiku and beyond: Language, ecology and reconnection with the natural world. *Anthrozoös* 20(2): 101–12.

Stibbe, A. (2008) The discursive construction of biodiversity. In M. Döring, H. Penz, and W. Trampe (eds) (2008) *Language, Signs and Nature:* *Ecolinguistic Dimensions of Environmental Discourse*, 165–82. Berlin: Verlag.

Stott, P., and Sullivan, S. (eds) (2000) *Political Ecology: Science, Myth and Power*. London: Arnold.

Sullivan, S. (2000) Getting the science right, or introducing science in the first place? Local 'facts,' global discourse – 'desertification' in north-west Namibia. In Stott and Sullivan (eds), 15–44.

Terralingua (2008) *Terralingua: Unity in Biocultural Diversity*. Homepage. Available at: http://www.terralingua. org/ (accessed on January 9, 2008).

UNEP (2007) *Global Environment Outlook 4*. United Nations Environment Program. Available at: www.unep.org/GEO/ geo4/ (accessed on January 9, 2008).

Väliverronen, E. (1998) Biodiversity and the power of metaphor in environmental discourse. *Science Studies* 11(1): 19–34.

Väliverronen, E., and Hellsten, I. (2002) From 'burning library' to 'green medicine': The role of metaphors in communicating biodiversity. *Science Communication* 24(2): 229–45.

van Dijk, T. (1993) Principles of critical discourse analysis. *Discourse and Society* 4(2): 249–83.

Waddell, C. (ed.) (2000) *"And No Birds Sing": The Rhetoric of Rachel Carson*. Carbondale: Southern Illinois University Press.

Williams, R. (2007) On voit grand. Très grand: Language and the construction of nature across cultures. *Language and Ecology* 2(1). Available at: www.ecoling. net/journal.html (accessed on January 9, 2008).

19 The Chinese Discourse of Human Rights and Glocalization

SHI-XU

Introduction

On November 19, 2008 – the fifth anniversary of the founding of the Chinese journal *Human Rights*, *Guangming Daily* – one of the three official Communist Party newspapers oriented toward Chinese intellectuals and teaching professionals carried a public contest transcript of 100 questions on human rights. The contest was jointly organized by the Chinese Society for Human Rights, the journal's management, and the newspaper itself. There were to be 500 winners, with a top prize of 2,000 RMB for five of them – the equivalent of a month's salary for an ordinary middle-school teacher. Just ten years earlier, the topic and the notion of human rights had been beyond the knowledge and concerns of ordinary Chinese people and was merely the object of occasional discussions by a few government institutions. And ten years earlier than that, any talk of human rights was an extremely sensitive political issue.

And yet such a vast and deep change in Chinese political communication in general and in the discourse of human rights in particular does not seem to have been recognized and understood by international scholars. The mainstream model and theory of (Chinese) political discourse remain entrenched in a framework of political economy based on the nation–state: the Chinese political discourse of human rights is determined by its political ideologies.

In this chapter I shall argue, however, for a historically conscious, culturally specific, and globally minded understanding of Chinese political discourse; proceeding from this conception, I shall present a dynamic picture of the Chinese discourse of human rights, both localizing and globalizing. In other words, the Chinese political discourse (of human rights) can be seen from the perspective of glocalization (Robertson 1992, 1995), and hence as creative and developing out of globalization and localization in addition to tradition. This view implies that we should approach Chinese political discourse not merely as a product of the Chinese Communist Party and government (or rather of their ideology), as so

The Handbook of Language and Globalization, First Edition. Edited by Nikolas Coupland.
© 2013 Blackwell Publishing Ltd except for editorial material and organization © 2013 Nikolas Coupland.
Published 2013 by Blackwell Publishing Ltd.

much of the western research has assumed, but also in relation and in response to past and present, local and global dynamics.

From another perspective, it may be said that I am interested in the human rights situation in China as part of its wider contemporary culture. I shall not be concerned with it in terms of the wellbeing of individuals or groups in the conventional sense, although this is a subject worth studying. Nor shall I try to judge it according to some such national or international standard, or attempt to account for it in terms of some causal, socio-political reasons. I take instead a different – *discursive* – perspective; in other words I treat the Chinese human rights situation as a form of discourse.

By *discourse* I do not mean text and talk as verbal products alone. Rather, I refer to text and con-text in some strategic relation. That is, it is considered a cultural event, or a class of such events, in which Speaker and Hearer manage Text/Talk in strategic relation to the evolving Situation, thereby co-constructing Meaning. So discourse is not simply a string of words organized according to some principle, but, from our more holistic point of view, a scenario involving several constituent elements and factors in complex and dialectic relationships.

This implies that, in *doing discourse research*, I shall be looking not just at what people say or write, and not just how they do it, but also, crucially – and this has usually been neglected – at who is (not) speaking, how text or talk is related to the surrounding situation, how text or talk is received, how otherwise, or in future, text and talk of human rights could be better produced and understood.

I assume that one cannot understand the human rights situation, at least not fully, unless one also sees whether in their ordinary life people actually speak about it or not, and how they speak about it – the discourse of human rights. In this sense, it should be noted first of all that 'human rights,' translated into Chinese as *Ren-quan*, has not been a native notion there. In traditional China, ordinary people did not have rights; only the emperor had rights, which were endowed by his God and which he could use to rule the people. There had never been a functional concept of human rights in Chinese culture and hence virtually no discourse of such.[1] Secondly, the new discourses of human rights reflect and are part of a wider culture. The discourse of human rights in China, for instance, is an indication and reflection of the cultural and political condition itself. For the former is constitutive of the latter. It is my contention therefore that answers to questions such as when and where the phrase 'human rights' was first used in China, how it has been defined and evaluated, who talked about it, how it is used (in what form, to what effect, and so on), or how it was received, will contribute significantly to our *understanding of the situation of human rights in China itself*.

Research questions

Discourse studies, from a Chinese holistic and dialectic perspective, must not be restricted to a 'neutral/objective' analysis of (aspects/fragments of) observable

texts, but should draw on a diversity of integrated methods (Shi-xu 2005). But, given the aims and scope of the present case study, I shall not cover them all, but restrict myself to aspects or dimensions of the following types of question:

Historical context   When and where did the technical notion of 'human rights' – that is, the Chinese term *Ren-quan* – and its official use originally come from? How have the discourses of human rights evolved with special reference to China? How has the West, in particular, spoken about human rights in relation to China?

Trajectory of the Chinese discourse of human rights [CDHR]   Under what circumstances did the term appear in China, and how was it interpreted? How have the uses of this notion evolved from the past to the present day? Are there any changes in meaning through time?

Concepts and evaluation of human rights in China: Core question   How do people define the notion of a human right? How do people evaluate the human rights situation in China?

Speakers/hearers   Who are the main producers of this discourse? How do they represent contemporary Chinese society? Are there any internal differences in terms of understanding and uses, say, between the discourse in Hong Kong and the one on mainland, or between the official and the semi-official media? What would the discourse in question signify from the viewpoint of the relevant hearer?

Uses   How is the notion of human rights used in contemporary Chinese communication – to whom, on what occasions, for what purposes? How is the notion of human rights related to other social affairs in discourse?

Cultural comparison   If one were to take the 'same' topic of human rights and its related affairs, how does the Chinese discourse fare, compared with that of the international community, especially in western countries?

Analytic concepts

Depending on the nature of the data at hand, one or the other of the following analytic concepts may be employed, or a combination of them. These concepts may be organized under four headings:

1   textual strategies – for instance topics, descriptions (definitions, narratives), evaluations, categorization, classification, argumentation, explanation, comparison, contrast (historical and cross-cultural), presuppositions, implications, speech acts, metaphor, narrative/story-telling;

2   contextual strategies – for instance the contextual management of time, space, settings, topics, turn-taking, speaker, hearer, use of forms of media;
3   statistics – that is, the quantitative side of discourse phenomena (for example the rate at which the number of speakers on human rights is increased);
4   cross-cultural comparison (along all the above categories).

Contextualizing Chinese Discourse

In relation to, and consistent with, the general, global framework of intercultural communication outlined above, I must now proceed to sketching out a particular, local – that is, Chinese – perspective, which may guide the study of contemporary mainland China's communications with the West. While the local perspective that I shall present is informed by the global one and will in this sense be multi-culturalist in nature, it will, more importantly, focus on the concrete properties of Chinese intercultural communication in the global, historical, and contemporary context. Further, it will concern more the hitherto neglected area of communication in the public, mass-mediated, and political sphere, as research has generally concentrated on private, commercial, or other institutional settings (Shi-xu 2005).

In order to construct such an account, we can draw upon a number of important arguments. Firstly, there is the Chinese *philosophical* tradition on language and society, which can provide vital information about the nature of Chinese intercultural communication, for a culture's philosophy provides information not just about the contents, values, and methods of its communication, but also about its own world-view, from which one can make sense of its communications (Cheng 1987). Secondly, it would be helpful to draw on traditional *indigenous scholarship* on language and communication. This is because it is the most direct way to obtain general understanding. Not to pay attention to the indigenous intellectual heritage would be ethnocentric on the part of the observer and would risk losing important insights. Thirdly, it will obviously be necessary to take into account the *textual context* or intertexts of contemporary discourse – the relevant past and the surrounding discourses. The discursive background is a resource for theorizing about discourse, because it provides reference points for sense-making. Fourthly, we must of course take seriously the past and current conditions or the *historical context* of Chinese intercultural communication, seen both locally and globally. For, as an integral part of discourse, this context, just like any textual context, enlightens our understanding of the language and communication in question. Finally, knowledge about the *global order of power* or especially about the hegemonic West in it will be instructive, too. In the globalized world, domination and resistance are relational and interactive; any dualistic, bipolar, and individualistic understanding will be biased. The outcome of such reconsideration will be a basis for reinventing a new perspective on contemporary mainland China's public communications with the West.

Chinese philosophy

To begin with, according to classic Chinese epistemology, the world is to be understood holistically, relationally and dialectically, which contrasts with the western dualistic, bipolar, and hence fragmentary world-view (see for instance Zhuangzi's 天人合一 (Universe as Oneness)). The best symbolic representation of this way of looking at the world is *Yin-Yang* (阴阳, as found in *I Ching* (易经)) – a dialectic wholeness or oneness consisting of two opposites, where for example self and other, form and meaning, East and West, domination and resistance, good and bad, right and wrong, co-exist and reproduce or overcome each other. For theorizing Chinese intercultural communication, then, this means that we must understand it in relational and dynamic, rather than decontextualized and fixed, terms.

Another relevant aspect of Chinese philosophy is its view of language (Cheng 1987): people use language and communication in order to achieve or maintain good social relationships, and to do so one must position oneself to others and to society, in language and in communication, in certain ways (see for example Confucius' *knowing speech*). For a theory of Chinese (intercultural) communication, this implies that people are to be seen in relational terms and that a balanced human relationship is to be interpreted as a highly regarded value.

Indigenous intellectual heritage

There has not been much theoretical work on Chinese communication and discourse, for the reasons mentioned at the outset. A prominent tradition, though, has characterized Chinese communication as oriented toward harmony as its highest ideal (see for instance Chen 2001, 2004). That is, according to Chinese intellectual tradition from Confucius and Zhuangzhi to Liu Xie, language and communication are not a form of representing the world, but essentially a mode of activity for the sake of establishing and maintaining a harmonious relationship with social others. In other words the ideal state or ultimate goal is the harmonious relationship between participants rather than personal, group, or community purposes or functions (note that the Chinese word 仁 (*ren*), 'humanity,' is etymologically composed of two radicals indicating 'person' and 'two'). This would mean that a theory of Chinese communication should reflect a dialogical or interactive property and a harmonious orientedness, which goes beyond, and is different from, the western representationalist and individualistic position (see Shi-xu 2005).

Local historical context

Inclusive culture   Chinese culture since its recorded history has generally been receptive and inclusive with regard to foreign cultures, often unreservedly. We only have to recall the co-existence of various kingdoms in the pre-Qing period, the Silk Road and consequently the influx of Islamic culture, the introduction of Buddhism from India, of western science and democracy since the New Culture Movement. This intrinsic force of cultural openness explains the contemporary Chinese engagement with the West.

Colonial experience   The past and the recent historical context of Chinese communication, intercultural communication included, must be considered. We need not go very far. Chinese history from the middle of the nineteenth century until the end of World War II had been one of western imperial domination and brutalization. During this long period, China has been repeatedly pillaged, conquered, and divided up by European and American colonial powers and by Japanese fascists. Chinese people understand that this fate of their country had also to do with the declining Chinese feudalist system and the corrupt Chinese governments of the time. This tragic and humiliating history is engraved in the minds of the Chinese people. After the end of World War II, China's international relations and standing were somewhat changed, but they continued to be dogged in particular by American political and military policies toward Taiwan, which China regards as an inalienable part of it, and more generally – like with most other non-western countries – by western domination in politics, economy, military, diplomacy, science, education, and virtually every other area. Given this past of brutal western aggression and exploitation and its regained international standing, mainland China is particularly conscious of, and sensitive to, foreign subjugation and cultural hegemony; a theory of its communication must take into consideration this colonial experience.

Economic and political rise   Real changes have started to occur in mainland China only since the late 1980s, after the country embarked on an open-door policy and economic reform. Since then, China has achieved and enjoyed unprecedented and internationally extraordinary economic success, with a GDP in 2004 of over RMB 13 milliard (or billion), or $1.6 milliard, and with an annual GDP growth rate of over 8 percent since 2001; and owing to this it has gained increasing international recognition and position. During this time, too, Hong Kong and Macao became decolonized. Along with its economic success, China has also achieved international political ascendancy as one of the major players in the world, whether on the Korean nuclear issue, on international terrorism, or on UN reform.[2] No theorizing over Chinese media communications can ignore this dramatic historical change in economic and political ascendancy.

Current intercultural practice   While China's media communication about and with the non-western world (or, strictly speaking, countries with diplomatic relations with China) has always been friendly and peaceful, until the late 1980s China was rather uniformly oppositional toward the West, as well as toward the eastern bloc countries in the broader context of the Cold War, where China had generally been a weak international player. A prominent and typical example of its discourse throughout that period is "Jiu Ping" ("The nine responses"), offered by the

Chinese Communist Party's official publication, *Hongqi* (the *Red Flag*), in response to the Soviet Communist Party. To America and the West, China had been perhaps more confrontational on nearly all issues. This provides a reference point for characterizing contemporary media discourse.

It seems that present-day Chinese interaction with the West, especially America, has not been merely oppositional but rather more complex. In years past, while persistently trying to produce a more distinct, positive, and assertive voice in the international arena, China has on the one hand increased its friendly exchanges with the West and on the other hand strengthened its opposition to it. So, while maintaining good bilateral relations with Europe, China insists that Europe should lift its ban on arms sales to China, which it sees as representing a "political prejudice" against it (see "EU moves to lift arms embargo," *China Daily*, Dec. 9, 2004). Over European pressure on Chinese textile exports in 2005, again, the Chinese government and its media consistently defended the country's rights and demanded fairness. In a similar vein, China has only this year started "high-level strategic talk" and naval exchanges with the USA and received visits from the secretary of state, the secretary of defence, and the president himself; but at the same time it continues to oppose American actions and positions on a range of other issues such as trade, arms sales, and security in Taiwan.

The American–western global hegemony

Our earlier account of the Chinese philosophical stance (in epistemology and ethics) indicates that a theory of Chinese intercultural communication cannot be correct unless it pays due attention to the interlocutor (and its actions) and to the wider interactional context. Chinese contemporary intercultural communication must not be seen as separated from the international communication order – an order which has continued to be one of inequality, the West (especially America) being the dominant meaning-maker and the rest being marginalized, discredited, or silenced. Those who can and do resist, and challenge the status quo through modern media, are still in the minority and have limited effect.

Theoretical reformulation

So, finally, let me try to attempt a general theoretical statement based on what has been advanced so far. Provisionally and suggestively, *contemporary Chinese media communication to the West can be understood as being geared toward achieving a cultural power balance or equilibrium with the West*. This orientation may be achieved through a variety of means, but at this point in time it appears that China accommodates the West on some issues and challenges it on others, accomplishing an enhanced level of resistance to the dominant West and hence a balance of power.

Data selection as part of the analysis

Given the types of question described above, it is possible to imagine that the following kinds of data would be relevant, or even ideal, to the job of offering a comprehensive picture of the contemporary Chinese discourse of human rights:

1   international, and especially American, documents on human rights (general information and systematic data);
2   Chinese political documents (government and party documents, the constitution, documents typically published in the official newspapers);
3   Chinese media publications (radio, TV, newspapers, internet articles, websites);
4   text/talk by Chinese associations and societies (typically published in the media);
5   systematic, face-to-face and on-line interviews with a set of Chinese rural workers and well-educated ordinary citizens.

But my current analysis will be based on data of the first four types.

Analytic questions

The questions below are intended as tools or guidelines in discourse analysis, having been selected and designed on the basis of our theoretical–conceptual framework, as set out in the beginning. Subject to data characteristics and research objectives, the following questions are possible guidelines:

1   How is the notion of 'human rights' defined and redefined?
2   How is the human rights situation described and evaluated?
3   How is the phrase 'human rights' used:
    (a)   in what circumstances (time and place)?
    (b)   in relation to what issues?
    (c)   in relation to whom?
    (d)   in what ways:
        • in what medium?
        • in what genre?
        • to what purposes?
        • with what consequences?
4   How is talk or text concerning human rights responded to?
5   Who is (not) speaking about human rights?
6   How does text or talk evolve historically?
7   How does the text or talk of human rights compare cross-culturally?

Growing Discourses of Human Rights

In the reminder of the chapter I shall focus on the Chinese discourse of human rights in order to highlight the structure, the historical change, and the local and global meanings of this discourse. It will be useful to describe from the outset the local – global and cultural – interactive context. This has to do mainly with the American State Department's annual report on human rights violations or infringements in about 190 countries in the world – usually non-western, Third World countries. For many consecutive years this report has included China. This practice, oriented toward non-western and Third-World cultures, of (negatively) evaluating their human rights situation is not intended for genuine intercultural communication and critique, because it is concluded officially and unilaterally, and internationally publicized. The United States has linked the alleged issues of human rights violations in China, as in other countries, to bilateral matters of trade, diplomacy, international politics, and the like. Therefore the reports are also motivated by these concerns. Further, the concepts, values, and standards employed in the American reports are all self-righteously presented as universal, and the issues are raised as a matter of course. It may be claimed from these facts that the American State Department's human rights reports explicitly form a class of acts that are directed at cultural others, and that these acts constitute a culturally high-handed practice that effectively creates cultural domination, control, and discrimination. Recently there was also the publication of "Country reports on human rights practices" by the US Department of State, which was submitted to its Congress.[3]

China as a re-emerging international speaker on human rights

As was mentioned at the start of the chapter, 'human rights' as a functional concept is, strictly speaking, foreign to Chinese traditional culture, although notions of social equality have been registered and calls for the removal of differences between social classes have been made by leaders of peasant uprisings in modern Chinese history. The main idea is European; the concept originated in the European context of struggles against monarchies, religious authorities, and feudal hierarchies in the seventeenth and eighteenth centuries. In 1948 the United Nations passed the *Universal Declaration of Human Rights*; China had been an initiator (Zhang Pengchun represented China as vice-chairman of the UN Human Rights Commission) and participated in drafting the declaration.

Since then, China has only gradually gained a voice on the topic in the international arena, by being involved in a number of international organizations concerned with human rights. At the first regular session of the UN Economic and Social Council in April 1981, China was elected as a member state of the UN Human Rights Commission (established in 1946 as one of the nine ECOSOC functional commissions). Further, since resuming its lawful seat in the United Nations in 1971, China has begun to participate in discussions on human rights held by the UN General Assembly and by the ECOSOC, and the Chinese delegation attended the sessions of the UN Human Rights Commission as an observer, in 1979, 1980, and 1981. However, until recently China was rather passive and silent in the international hierarchy of communications, usually responding only to criticisms and attacks from the US and Europe. I shall have occasion to return to this point in what follows.

Increasing number of domestic speakers

Domestically, China did not speak about 'human rights' as such until about ten years ago. It had relatively few organs dealing with the issue of human rights, or public spokesmen on the topic. Consequently human rights also appeared to be a politically sensitive topic. However, since the publication of the US record of human rights by the Information Office of the State Council of China in 2000, which systematically confronts the US government on its imputations of human rights problems in China, there has been a steady growth in the number and variety of organizations and institutions speaking about human rights, as may be seen from table 19.1.[4]

It is particularly noteworthy that, since the early 1990s, the number of research centers on human rights at major Chinese universities has increased; there are now eight of them. In addition, the Society for Human Rights in China was very active in organizing international conferences on the topic in 2008. The point is not so much to show what kinds of practical consequences these institutions might have on human rights, but rather to suggest that in China there are now more speakers on the theme of human rights, as part of a change in contemporary Chinese culture in general and in the moral climate on human rights in particular.

Redefining human rights

After directly confrontational discourses in the late twentieth century and earlier this century, there have been recent attempts at redefining the very concept of human rights. In particular, culturally different versions of the concept and value of human rights have been put forward by means of different historical accounts and different social explanations. (In the next section I shall also show that this diversity is held as a reason for correspondingly different approaches to human rights protection and development.)

On November 1, 1991, the Information Office of the State Council published *The Human Rights in China*. It was the first white paper on human rights in China published by the government, and also the first official document on human rights. In this paper human rights are actively defined as "the rights of subsistence and development" and "as primary human rights." (In all following quotations, the spaces between paragraphs have been bridged for the sake of space.)

Table 19.1 List of organizations, institutions, and media speaking on human rights. Compiled by the author from information gathered from various sources

AGENTS	TIME
Foundation	
China Human Rights Development Foundation	1994
Non-governmental research institution	
Society of Human Rights of China	1993
University research institute	
Human Rights Research Centre of Peking University	1991
Human Rights Research Centre of People's University	1991
Human Rights Research Centre of Central Chinese Communist Party University	1994
Human Rights Research Centre of Shandong University	1990
Human Rights and Humanitarianism Research Centre of the Chinese University of Politics and Law	2002
Human Rights Research Centre of Fudan University	2002
Human Rights Research Centre of Nankai University	2005
Human Rights Research Centre of Guangzhou University	2004
Website	
China Human Rights: http://www.humanrights.cn/	1998
Human Rights: http://www.humanrights.com.cn/	1994
Tibet Human Rights: http://www.tibet328.cn/	2009
China Human Rights Protection: http://www.cnrqbz.com/	2005
Conference	
Forum on the 60th Anniversary of the Universal Declaration of Human Rights, organized by the Society for Human Rights of China	Dec. 10, 2008
Forum of Human Rights in Beijing, organized by the Society for Human Rights of China	April 21, 2008
International Forum: Respecting and Promoting Human Rights and Building a Harmonious World, organized by the Society for Human Rights of China	Nov. 22, 2008
Conference on China's 30 Years of Reform and Human Rights Development, organized by the Society for Human Rights of China	Dec. 2, 2008
Conference on Scientific Development and Human Rights, organized jointly by the Society for Human Rights of China and the Society of Anthropology of China	Dec. 9, 2005
Journal	
Human Rights	2002

BEIJING, Dec. 9, 2008   China's human rights development still had "quite a few things less than satisfactory," but would see progress as the modernization drive went on, a top official said here on Tuesday. "Due to natural, historical, cultural and economic and social factors, there are still many problems and difficulties in the development of human rights," said Wang Chen, minister in charge of the State Council Information Office. […] He admitted that the country's economic and social development was uneven and the enlarging gaps between the urban and rural areas, between different regions, and between the rich and the poor had not been brought under control. Problems and difficulties were quite outstanding in areas such as employment, social security, income distribution, education, medical service, housing and production safety. "All these will affect the immediate interests and rights of the people. It is, therefore, a long-term and arduous task of the Chinese government and people to continue and strengthen their efforts to promote and protect human rights," said Wang. (China acknowledges human rights problems, but confident of prospect, Xinhuanet; accessed on December 20, 2008)

Chinese officials on Wednesday called for international support for the country's efforts to ensure human rights for its citizens, stressing that different modes of rights development should be respected. "With varied social systems, levels of development and historical and cultural backgrounds, different nations have varied modes of human rights development, and we should respect such diversity," said Cai Wu, director of Information Office of State Council, at an ongoing international human rights protection forum in Beijing. […] Chinese officials and rights experts have repeatedly stated China's concept of human rights focuses on the collective, specifically, state sovereignty, rights of subsistence and development of the people as a whole, while Western concepts give priority to the rights of the individual. Dong Yunhu, vice chairman of the China Society for Human Rights Studies said the differences largely stemmed from different historical backgrounds. Western human rights concepts developed in the wake of calls to confront monarchies, religious authorities and feudal hierarchies after the Renaissance. "Therefore individual and political rights came at the top of the human rights agenda," he added. "China's recent history, however, involves cruel imperial invasion," Dong said. "Imperialism caused a humanitarian crisis in China so human rights calls came with the liberation of Chinese people and the founding of a people's republic. (Xinhua News Agency, November 23, 2006; accessed on December 20, 2008)

Redefining approaches to human rights

On top of arguing for diversity and providing alternative versions and explanations of human rights, there is a corresponding pattern of advocating appropriate methods of enhancing human rights.

BEIJING, Dec. 9, 2008   The international community should deal with human rights issues through dialogues and cooperation, a senior Chinese official said here on Tuesday. "In promoting human rights, only by carrying out constructive dialogues, exchange and cooperation on the basis of equality and mutual respect, […] can all countries in the world achieve common progress and development," said Wang Chen, minister in charge of the State Council Information Office. In an interview with the Human Rights journal, affiliated to the China society for Human Rights Studies,

Wang said countries in the world should enhance mutual understanding, and learn from each other's experiences, instead of confronting each other. Wang said some countries and regional groups had "politicized and ideologized human rights by practicing double standards, flying the 'human rights' flag to negate the sovereignty of other countries and carry out power politics." (China calls for dialogue, cooperation in human rights, Xinhuanet; accessed on December 20, 2008)

BEIJING, Nov. 23, 2006   China stands for dialogue and is opposed to antagonism in human rights area, said Zhou Jue, president of China Society for Human Rights Studies, here Thursday. At the ongoing Symposium on Respecting and Promoting Human Rights and Constructing a Harmonious World, Zhou said adherence to dialogue on an equal footing and opposition to power politics and antagonism are becoming a unanimous call from people of all countries and all individuals who stand for justice. (Xinhuanet; accessed on December 20, 2008)

BEIJING, Nov. 24, 2006   What's the new catchphrase for human rights development in China? Well, it's Harmony, or peace, security and a happy co-existence between different people, communities and nations. With top leaders tirelessly calling for the building of a "harmonious society" in China, as well as a "harmonious Asia" and "harmonious world," Chinese officials and human rights experts now take pride in their creative adding of "harmony" as a key conception of human rights promotion and guarantee. Peace and security are invariably interlinked with human rights, they preach, finding both echoes and questioning at an international symposium held in Beijing from Nov. 22 to 24. With the theme of Respecting and Promoting Human Rights and Constructing the Harmonious World, the symposium attracted experts on human rights from 18 countries and regions including the United States, Switzerland, South Africa and Vietnam. "Only in the regions of East Asia can it (human rights) be connected to harmony," says Makarim Wibisono, Indonesian Ambassador and Permanent Representative to the United Nations. "The idea of harmony being connected to human rights is significant and relevant to Asian cultures, which are largely rooted in Confucianism, he said. It certainly can render the concept of human rights more approachable to many who are not familiar with the notion," he said, noting many remain suspicious of human rights as an ideology foisted upon developing countries by a hypocritical western world. (Wen Chihua, Xinhuanet; accessed on December 20, 2008)

Creating constitutional discourse

The concept of human rights saw a significant change of nature and status when it was adopted in the Constitution of the People's Republic of China in 2004 and in the Constitution of the Chinese Communist Party in 2007. The relevant information may be found in the following extracts:

Amendment to the Constitution of the People's Republic of China (Approved on March 14, 2004, by the 10th NPC at its 2nd Session): Section 8, Article 33 has a third paragraph added: The State respects and preserves human rights.

Constitution of the Commmunist Party of China (Amended and adopted at the Seventeenth National Congress of the Communist Party of China on Oct. 21, 2007):

It takes effective measures to protect the people's right to manage state and social affairs as well as economic and cultural programs. It respects and safeguards human rights. It encourages the free airing of views and works to establish sound systems and procedures of democratic election, decision-making, administration and oversight.

Timing counter-discourses

Beginning in 2000, the Information Office of the State Council of China has published annually an extensive record of human rights violations in the US (this record is detailed in full in the major Chinese newspapers, and more recently also on websites). What is particularly noteworthy about the Chinese discourse on human rights is the way it *times* its response to the US counterpart. That is, for the past ten years, the report is always published *a couple of days after* the US government's publication (see tables 19.2 and 19.3).

In order to see the details of the accusations and counter-accusations between the US government on one side and the Chinese government on the other, let us focus on the time-line of one particular year in which the two governments interacted with each other on the topic: 2005. Here I shall register not only the timing of the texts produced by the two sides but also the textual strategies employed by the Chinese government in opposition to the US repressive discourse. It is hoped that both the close timing and the resistant language on the part of the Chinese media (and of the Chinese government behind them) will show that the Chinese did not see eye to eye with the US at a time of cultural repression imposed by the latter.

Table 19.2 US's country reports and China's record of US human rights in a time line. Compiled by the author from information gathered from various sources

Period Covered	Country Reports on Human Rights Practices (by US)	Human Rights Record of the US (by China)
1999	February 2, 2000	February 27, 2000
2000	February 23, 2001	February 27, 2001
2001	March 4, 2002	March 11, 2002
2002	March 31, 2003	April 3, 2003
2003	February 25, 2004	March 1, 2004
2004	February 28, 2005	March 3, 2005
2005	March 8, 2006	March 9, 2006
2006	March 6, 2007	March 8, 2007
2007	March 11, 2008	March 13, 2008
2008	February 25, 2009	February 26, 2009

Table 19.3   China's White Papers on the progress of human rights. Compiled by the author from information gathered from various sources

Time	Titles
04/2005	China's Progress in Human Rights in 2004
03/2004	China's Progress in Human Rights in 2003
04/2001	Progress in China's Human Rights Cause in 2000
06/2000	Fifty Years of Progress in China's Human Rights
04/1999	Progress in China's Human Rights Cause in 1998
03/1997	Progress in China's Human Rights Cause in 1996
12/1995	The Progress of Human Rights in China
11/1991	Human Rights in China

On March 3, 2005, *Guangming Daily* carried a small news item, which reported that on February 28 the US State Department had issued *Country Reports on Human Rights Practices* involving various other countries for the year of 2004. The news item in question was entitled "China resolutely opposes America's unfounded accusations of our human rights situation." This piece contained a set of features that rebuffed the US report; further, it advised the US to take a different stance on the communication between the US and China on human rights. These admonitions included the use of verbs and verbal phrases ("oppose" and "express strong dissatisfaction"), disqualifying definitions of the other's actions ("unfounded accusations," "so-called"), claims to authority ("the Chinese people have the most authority"), positive evidence ("holds the principles of [...]" and "enjoying a higher level of human rights in various areas") and recommendations ("pay more attention").

On the following day (March 4), *Guangming Daily* filed another report on the same issue of human rights, but with additional developments and information. This second report was harsher in dealing with the US. In addition to the devices we saw in the first item, more space was devoted to wrong-doing in the matter of human rights by the US itself. The report revealed the double standard and rude behavior of the US. And it provided a justification for its own current practice, legitimating its own oppositional activity.

On March 3, the day of the publication of the previous news report, and in the same newspaper, the Chinese State Council Information Office published a large report with the title of "America's Human Rights Record 2004," which occupied a little over one page and enumerated America's human rights abuses, both at home and abroad (see also *People's Daily Online*: Full text of Human Rights Record of the US in 2004).[5] A set of features of the report is worth noting. First, the report detailed human rights mishaps in six different areas of American social and cultural life – 1. Life, freedom and safety; 2. Political rights and freedom; 3. Economic, social and cultural rights; 4. Racial discrimination; 5. Women and children's rights; 6. Violating other countries' human rights – and did this by using a large space – a whole page. It opened with mimicry, humor, and revelation. What is particularly unusual about this article is that it included a list of eighty-two endnotes, offering the sources of the information used in the article – an extraordinary practice for just an ordinary newspaper. This shows effectively the documentary foundations of the report and the care taken compiling it, and therefore the credibility of the negative report on the US human rights situation. All three discursive features discussed above serve to undermine the trustworthiness and respectfulness of the 'Other,' and hence of the report produced by the 'Other.'

Then, according to *Guangming Daily* (April 1), the American State Department issued another human rights report, *Supporting Human Right and Democracy: The US Record 2004–2005* (March 28), accusing China of human rights abuses. This constituted an immediate, important contextual circumstance[6] in which China had to act. Thus this very piece of Chinese news report, entitled "China opposes American unfounded accusations on China's state of human rights" *Guangming Daily*, April 1) put up a form of resistance. It presented an opposition similar to the two actions reproduced above but employed a stronger term for what the State Department had done, namely 'abhorrent practice' (*erlie zuofa*).

Following that, over two weeks later, on April 14, the Chinese State Council Information Office published, again in the same newspaper, a one-and-a-quarter-page report bearing the title "China's progress in human rights in 2004."[7] It included seven sections: Foreword; 1. People's rights to subsistence and development; 2. Civil and political rights; 3. Judicial guarantee for human rights; 4. Economic, social and cultural rights; 5. Equal rights and special protection for ethnic minorities; 6. The rights and interests of the disabled; 7. International exchanges and cooperation in the field of human rights. The opening section is particularly interesting in that it clearly displays an intercultural orientation when it says: "To help the international community toward a better understanding of the human rights situation in China, we hereby present an overview of the developments in the field of human rights in China in 2004."[8]

This newspaper presentation offered a wide-ranging and detailed account of the achievements made by China in 2004. It presented a completely positive picture of the human rights situation in China. Thus the official, public, and explicitly intercultural display of these accomplishments is in direct opposition with the preceding, other-negating American act and undermines it.

Multiplying official discourse

The Chinese government has published thirty-eight white papers on human rights since 1991. According to statistics, it has published fifty-five white papers in total since the beginning of the reform and opening-up of the country, and 70 percent of them are on human rights (www.chinahumanrights.org; accessed on February 20, 2009).

Similarly, up to the end of June 2008, China had ratified twenty-three international conventions and protocols on human rights in total. While four were ratified in the 1950s, nineteen have been ratified since the reform and opening-up policy begun in 1978, registering a swift change in a short space of time (www.chinahumanrights.org; accessed on February 25, 2009).

Let the 'Other' Speak/Act, Listen, Be Informed, and Critique

Last but not least, culturally critical intellectuals should not merely rely on their own perspective and model, impose their own definitions, categories, and values on the researched, tell or instruct the researched 'Other' or negate it. Our research could well be enriched and rendered more useful for the researched if we let the 'Other' speak and act, if we listen to the 'Other,' choose to be informed by the 'Other,' and engage in critical conversation with the 'Other.' If we hold this attitude and sympathize with the 'Other,' there will be much to learn:

> On March 14th, 2004, an amendment to the constitution was adopted by China's 10th National People's Congress (NPC) on its second session. The concept of 'human rights' was written in China's constitution for the first time. The amendment stipulated clearly that "the state respects and safeguards human rights." This is a major event in the development of China's democratic constitutionalism and political civilization, and an important milestone in human rights progress in China. The Constitutions of China had always attached considerable weight to human rights. Civil rights were clearly stated from the first constitution of 1954 to the constitution of 1982, though the concept of human rights was not included in them. Confirmation of political and legal status of human rights concept is an outcome of gradual deepening of understanding of human rights issues by the CPC and the state after the beginning of the reform and opening-up cause. In the late 1980s and early 1990s, the Central Committee of the CPC began to reconsider the human rights issue by summarizing the practice of the human rights development in contemporary China and the rest of the world, and made it clear, for the first time ever, that socialist China should hold the banner of human rights in her hands. On November 1st, 1991, a White Paper titled "Human Rights in China" was issued by the Information Office of the State Council. This was the first time that the status of the human rights concept in China's socialist political development had been positively confirmed in the form of a governmental document. When the 15th National Congress of the CPC was convened in September 1997, the human rights concept was for the first time included in the major report to the Congress, making human rights one of the subjects of national construction under the leadership of the Party. By adding "the state respects and safeguards human rights" to the Constitution, the present amendment had promoted 'human rights' from a political concept to a legal one for the first time, and the main body in respecting and safeguarding human rights had been upgraded from the Party and government to the state. Therefore, respecting and safeguarding human rights had been raised from the will of the Party and the government to that of the people and the state. The enshrinement of human rights in the Constitution is a major development of people's democratic constitutionalism. Firstly, it established the principle of human rights and improved the country's democratic constitutionalism;

secondly, it highlighted the value and concept of human rights and gave new meanings to the Constitution's stipulations concerning civil rights; thirdly, it improved [principal] prescriptions of the guarantee of civil rights and reinforced [the] human rights spirit of the Constitution. The enshrinement of human rights in the Constitution initiated a new era of guaranteeing human rights with the Constitution. It established a legal base for respect and guarantee of human rights in China. It brings good fortune for both the people and the country. ("The state respects and safeguards human rights" enshrined in the Constitution, *chinahumanrights.org*; accessed on February 25, 2009)

BEIJING, Dec. 9, 2008   The international community should deal with human rights issues through dialogues and cooperation, a senior Chinese official said here on Tuesday. "In promoting human rights, only by carrying out constructive dialogues, exchange and cooperation on the basis of equality and mutual respect, [...] can all countries in the world achieve common progress and development," said Wang Chen, minister in charge of the State Council Information Office. In an interview with the Human Rights journal, affiliated to the China society for Human Rights Studies, Wang said countries in the world should enhance mutual understanding, and learn from each other's experiences, instead of confronting each other. Wang said some countries and regional groups had "politicized and ideologized human rights by practicing double standards, flying the 'human rights' flag to negate the sovereignty of other countries and carry out power politics." This would seriously spoil the atmosphere of international cooperation and obstruct the healthy development of human rights in the world, Wang said. The minister said people in different countries have different understandings and demands with regard to human rights and their human rights problems that need priority solution also vary. "Under the precondition of recognizing the universality of human rights, all governments and people have the right to adopt different policy measures according to their respective national conditions to seek human rights development best suited to their country," he said. He called on the nations to focus on the "prominent problems in the present-day" world, such as armed conflicts, terrorism, environmental pollution, hunger, poverty, uneven economic development and the growing South–North gap, all seriously threatening human rights in the world, the minister said. "Dialogue and cooperation are conducive not only to human rights progress in all countries, but also to the harmonious and healthy development of human rights in the world," Wang said. Power politics, on the other hand, contributes nothing to human rights development, and would poison the international relations and harm the healthy growth of the cause of human rights in the world," he said. (China calls for dialogue, cooperation in human rights, Xinhuanet; accessed on February 25, 2009)

BEIJING, Dec. 9, 2008   In an interview with the Human Rights journal, Wang said China's political and economic structural systems were yet to be improved, democracy and the legal system remained to be perfected, and governments at all levels had to heighten their awareness about protecting human rights and about exercising administration according to law. He admitted that the country's economic and social development was uneven and the enlarging gaps between the urban and rural areas, between different regions, and between the rich and the poor had not been brought under control. (China acknowledges human rights problems, but confident of prospect, Xinhuanet; accessed on February 25, 2009)

Conclusions

I hope it has become clear by now that, first of all, the human rights discourse in China has changed dramatically, from being relatively weak and simple to becoming a voluminous and multifarious one in the short space of two decades or so. The transformation is manifest, specifically, in the increasing numbers and kinds of people and organizations who speak for it, in the enhanced legal and political status of the discourse, in the modified conception of human rights and approach to it in relation to those of the western counterpart, in the amplified official production of the discourse, and in the forceful opposition to the US discursive domination on the issue of human rights. Arguably, the discursive enhancement of the topic in China reflects a development in, and an improvement of, the human rights situation itself.

Secondly, it should become clear, too, that the present historical and historic change of discourse is closely linked with the Chinese past. For one thing, Chinese traditional culture values the balance of power, reciprocality, moderation, unity in diversity – 'the middle way,' or what I call 'the Chinese equilibrium' – and the increasingly systematic discursive opposition to American–western domination is precisely the evidence of that. For another, the oppositional counter-discourse of human rights can also be interpreted as linked to the more recent modern history of subjugation to the imperial and colonial powers and so to a natural aversion toward cultural hegemony and oppression.

Thirdly, the Chinese discourse on human rights is also inextricably linked with global discourse and with the US political discourse on human rights regarding China in particular. From the above historical and cultural account and analysis, it should have become evident that, had the US not been so high-handed in its own presentation of China's human rights, China would not have developed its oppositional and vociferous discourse. But, without the American–western discourse on the Chinese human rights situation, there might have been no expansion of this kind of discourse in China at all.

It may be suggested, then, that because the Chinese discourse of human rights is ever shifting and resistant to cultural hegemony, continued egalitarian intercultural communication on the topic must be conducted for the sake of improvement in human relations in general and in the human rights situation in particular.

ACKNOWLEDGMENTS

The author gratefully acknowledges the help and support received from the Centre of Contemporary Chinese Discourse Studies, Zhejiang University, during the research on this project.

NOTES

1   During the Taiping Tianguo period (1851–64), the constitutional State Regulations on Agricultural Land stipulated that all land be divided evenly amongst all countrymen/ women. Later, Sun Yehsien (1866–1925) proposed the principles of national sovereignty, democracy, and livelihood, which gave further, extended rights to ordinary people. It may be that said these proclamations were the first ever statements and policies made in Chinese history on the rights of ordinary people. It should be observed, too, that they are different in content from the European notion of human rights in that they concern social rights (e.g. equal share of the land, political democracy).
2   See http://english.people.com.cn/200506/08/eng20050608_189000.html.
3   See http://www.state.gov/g/drl/rls/hrrpt/2004/.
4   All the information here has been gathered from various websites.
5   See http://english.people.com.cn/200503/03/eng20050303_175406.html.
6   See http://www.state.gov/g/drl/rls/shrd/2004/.
7   See http://english.people.com.cn/200504/13/eng20050413_180786.html.
8   See http://english.people.com.cn/200504/13/eng20050413_180786.html.

REFERENCES AND FURTHER READING

Chen, G. M. (2001) Towards transcultural understanding: A harmony theory of Chinese communication. In V. H. Milhouse, M. K. Asante, and P. O. Nwosu (eds), *Transculture: Interdisciplinary Perspectives on Cross-Cultural Relations*, 55–70. Thousand Oaks, CA: Sage.

Chen, G. M. (2004) The two faces of Chinese communication. *Human Communication* 7: 25–36.

Cheng, C. Y. (1987) Chinese philosophy and contemporary human communication theory. In D. L. Kincaid (eds), *Communication Theory: Eastern and Western Perspectives*, 23–43. New York: Academic Press.

Chou, C. C. (2008) Bridging the global and the local: China's effort at linking human rights discourse and neo-Confucianism. *China Report* 44(2): 139–52.

Healy, P. (2006) Human rights and intercultural relations: A hermeneutico-dialogical approach. *Philosophy and Social Criticism* 32(4): 513–41.

Robertson, R. (1992) *Globalization: Social Theory and Global Culture*. London: Sage Publications.

Robertson, R. (1995) Globalization: Time–space and homogeneity–heterogeneity. In M. Featherstone, S. Lash, and R. Robertson (eds), *Global Modernities*, 25–44. Thousand Oaks, CA: Sage.

Shi-xu, M. (2005) *A Cultural Approach to Discourse*. Houndmills: Palgrave Macmillan.

Shi-xu, M., Kienpointner, M., and Servaes, J. (eds) (2005) *Read the Cultural Other*. Berlin: Mouton de Gruyter.

Steiner, H. J., and Alston, P. (2006) *International Human Rights in Context:*

Law, Politics, Morals. Oxford: Oxford University Press.

Tu, W. M. (1994) Cultural China: The periphery as the center. In Tu W. M. (ed.), *The Living Tree: The Changing Meaning of Being Chinese Today*, 1–34. Stanford, CA: Stanford University Press.

Yin, J. (2007) The clash of rights: A critical analysis of news discourse on human rights in the United States and China. *Critical Discourse Studies*. 4(1): 75–94.

Zhang, Y.-w., and Huang, R.-w. [张幼文、黄仁伟] (2005) *China's International Status Report 2005* [2005 中国国际地位报告] Beijing: People's Publisher.

20 Meanings of 'Globalization': East and West

PETER GARRETT

Introduction

This chapter reports public perceptions of globalization across a range of countries. Data were collected from respondents in Australia, China, Japan, New Zealand, the UK, and the USA – contexts in which public experiences and perceptions of globalization are likely to differ considerably. The study was prompted by the fact that 'globalization' is often viewed as a "catchword" (Yamashita and Eades 2003: 4), whose meaning is vague and elusive, and which is consequently open to variable interpretations.

Perspectives on globalization

Academic and professional debate on globalization is generally summarized under three schools of thought: the hyperglobalizers, the skeptics, and the transformationalists. Within each group there is considerable diversity (for a comprehensive account, see Held et al. 1999), but the three nevertheless represent very distinct sets of understandings and arguments around globalization and provide useful reference points. To exemplify, the hyperglobalizers regard contemporary globalization as a new epoch in human history, which marks the end of the nation–state and in which people everywhere are subjected to the disciplines of the global marketplace. The skeptics counter this view, maintaining that the international economy is increasingly divided into three major geographical blocs: North America, Europe, and Asia–Pacific. The skeptics see national governments as being still powerful in these groupings and as engaging in various ways with the processes of internationalization. The transformationalists (for instance Giddens 1991, 2002) see contemporary globalization as an "historically unprecedented" world order (Held et al. 1999: 2). Unlike the other two perspectives, however, transformationalism does not regard the market, or the economy, as the single cause of globalization, but sees instead a greater range of influences. In addition, transformationalists regard the outcomes of globalization as much less

The Handbook of Language and Globalization, First Edition. Edited by Nikolas Coupland.
© 2013 Blackwell Publishing Ltd except for editorial material and organization © 2013 Nikolas Coupland.
Published 2013 by Blackwell Publishing Ltd.

certain. For them, societies around the world are involved in a process of profound change and have to find ways to adapt to a far more interconnected and uncertain world than the previous one was. Arguably, academics engaging with the overall prospects of globalization (rather than, say, with the specifically economic ones) tend to work from a transformationalist perspective (Zimmerling 2005).

Domains

Globalization can be considered in terms of economic, political, and cultural domains. The economic domain is privileged by the hyperglobalist school of thought (see Ohmae 1995), and controversies around global institutions such as the World Trade Organization (WTO) have been a main focus in this domain, along with effects on job security and employment. And while hyperglobalizers tend to see the emergence of a borderless global economy and marketplace that reduces the state to a mere conduit for the transnational flows of capital and trade, skeptics such as Hirst and Thompson (1996) view the current global marketplace as not fundamentally dissimilar from the one existing a hundred years ago. Indeed they see today's economy as less global than it was then, since economic power is now concentrated in fewer spheres and is less integrated throughout the world. In the words of Hamelink, this view claims that, if the world were a global village with a population of 100, six of these would be Americans, and those six would account for half of the village's entire income (Hamelink 2003: 250). Hence Scholte (2000) points to important differences in the economic power of the northern hemisphere, to the deepening of global income inequality, and to North–South worker migrations.

Political factors also feature in the globalization debates. The growth of transnational organizations and networks such as intergovernmental organizations and international non-governmental organizations means that governance increasingly transcends national boundaries. Giddens (1990) and other transformationalists argue that countries must engage with this profound change toward expanded interconnectivity, while Hirst and Thompson (1996) hold that nation–states should continue to exist unaltered – although these authors prioritize financial matters, especially regarding national and foreign policies. Ohmae (1995: 5) argues from the hyperglobalist perspective that national governments are so subjected to the global economy that by now they must be regarded as "unnatural."

Cultural issues also have a strong presence in globalization literature. In particular, many concerns arise from the generally widespread recognition of inequality associated with globalization (although inequality is not only a cultural matter, of course). Homogenization is one of these concerns, and it is often referred to also as cultural imperialism, westernization, or Americanization (Giddens 2002). Some of the discussion centers on the global distribution of goods such as television programs and other media, cinema, or company franchises created by western, especially US, businesses. Hannerz (1991), for example, argues that these products carry and spread the ideology and values of their creators and will ultimately replace the cultures in which they are distributed. Opposed to this is the view that such commodities become localized or hybridized, and adapt to local tastes. (See for example Pennycook 2007 on hip hop as a global code demonstrating a sense of locality.) The claimed outcome is that only the genre of the original is ultimately disseminated, whereas the ideology and the cultural value system of its source culture are ignored, or at least perceived differently in their new contexts (Howes 1996).

Also at the cultural level, discourses on globalization focus on the "compression of space and time" (Giddens 1990; Massey 1994). Discussions point to the dramatically increased velocity of movement of people, objects, ideas, and information around the world. Technological developments, increased interdependence between countries, supraterritoriality and transnationalism are all flagged both as contributing factors and as symptomatic factors. Interaction across large distances enters into a complex relationship with local activity. Compressed time and space is also seen as relating to homogenization through the impression of living in a global village. Further, the compression of time and space is related to risk, as dependence on and confidence in technology entails potentially drastic consequences affecting the entire world, and binds us together in "communities of fate" (Marske 1991).

Diversity of views on the nature and scope of globalization

Potential for polarization exists within all of these domains and perspectives; each of them can be seen as heterogeneous or homogenous, global or local, empowering or disempowering, regardless of whether they are perceived as good rather than bad or as threats rather than opportunities. Within the hyperglobalist perspective, orientations range from that of the neo-liberal hyperglobalizers, who are well disposed toward "the triumph of individual autonomy and the market principle over state power," to that of the neo-Marxist hyperglobalizers, who view contemporary globalization as "the triumph of oppressive capitalism" (Held et al. 1999: 3). "'Going global' can be seen as attractive or pernicious" (Massey 2000).

In setting the scene for reporting the study on public perceptions of globalization across many countries, it is important to capture the diversity of views about the concept of globalization that is expressed in the academic literature. We will see to what extent the public perceptions studied mirror these distinctions or reveal others.

Before moving on to consider the study itself, it is useful (for the same reason) to summarize globalization from an angle which is slightly different from (although inevitably overlapping with) that reviewed above. Eriksen (2007: 8f) sets out several salient characteristics of contemporary globalization that cut across discussions of many of its aspects, from global communication to consumer behavior, transnational migration, and so on. These include:

1   **Disembedding**   Driven by economic and technological changes, capital, labor, ideas, social life, and so on are less anchored in a local and fixed space and tend to travel faster than ever before.

2   **Standardization**   A continuation and expansion of the processes of standardization imposed by nation states, this process extends to such phenomena as international agreements, international hotel chains and shopping centers, and the increased use of English.

3   **Interconnectedness**   The increasing density, speed, and extensiveness of transcontinental connecting networks require more international agreements and new foreign policies, creating new opportunities at some times, new constraints at other times.

4   **Movement**   Increasing migration, leisure, and business travel carry implications for local economies, politics, and community life.

5   **Mixing**   The meeting of different cultures is increasing, both in terms of physical mixing and in terms of instantaneous message exchange over vast distances.

6   **Vulnerability**   The weakening or disappearance of borders means that territorial political units have difficulties protecting themselves against unwanted flows – from epidemics to terrorism, climate change, or credit crunches.

7   **Re-embedding**   Globalization can be seen as a dual process, on the one hand of 'shrinking' and homogenizing the world and on the other hand of expanding and heterogenizing the world by making people more aware of difference and thus by leading to new forms of diversity. Re-embedding is a counter-action to disembedding. Eriksen (2007: 143) writes:

> The more abstract the power, the sources of personal identity, the media flows and the commodities on the market become, the greater will the perceived need be to strengthen and sometimes recreate (or even invent) local foundations for political action and personal identity, locally produced books and songs, products with the smell, the sound, the taste of home.

Motivations for the Study

Why should we be interested in finding out about common understandings of globalization? To begin with, such subjectivities can provide insights into how people respond to what they feel globalization might imply for them, and into how this affects their lives in terms of priorities, aspirations, and futures. Most conspicuously, anti-globalization events have shown that there certainly are some sections of the global population who hold fiercely negative perceptions. But other groups too, in a much less overt manner, will have impacts on societies in various ways through their beliefs, attitudes and behaviors. Examining these basic perceptions also provides material, understandings, and directions for those working with globalization in their various fields. In his weighing-up of conflicting definitions of globalization, Scholte (2002: 7) argues:

Definitions fundamentally shape descriptions, explanations, evaluation, prescriptions and actions. If a definition of a core concept is slippery, then the knowledge built upon it is likely to be similarly shaky, and in turn the policies constructed on the basis of that knowledge can very well be misguided.

Most obviously, those working in political and professional spheres cannot afford to overlook public understandings and orientations. And in this regard the International Labour Organization (ILO) has argued that the "current impasse" in the public debate on globalization means that it is of timely importance to focus on the concerns and aspirations of people in general (2004: 12).

The study reported here, then, takes up this important focus. Surprisingly, to date, not a great deal of work has been published on such public perceptions. One exception is a study by the ILO itself, which looked at the perceptions of decision-makers and social actors with considerable involvement in globalization issues. Although reporting in terms of regional groupings of countries (such as 'Latin America' or 'Europe'), the ILO study captured a diversity of perspectives. The present study also explores how globalization looks different from different cultural positions, but this time through data collected from a number of specific countries spread around the world: Australia, China, Japan, New Zealand, the UK, and the USA. Globalization is likely to have been experienced quite differently in these countries over the past fifteen to twenty years, not least in the cases of China and the USA (see the discussion later in this chapter). In addition, the study seeks an emic view of globalization, gathering perspectives from people with no great direct involvement in globalization issues at the professional level. Its approach is sociolinguistic, in the sense that it studies the sociolinguistic resources that such people draw upon as they seek to represent their perceptions of globalization. It is such discourses that give globalization its shape. While we have seen earlier, in the literature review, the shapes of globalization that emanate from the discourses of academics, we know little about those of non-academics and non-professionals.

Methodological Issues

The perceptions of people who can reasonably be regarded as 'non-experts' in an area under investigation can be termed 'folk perceptions.' Globalization touches all of our lives to some extent – and indeed this is why studying folk perceptions is informative – but the respondents in this study can be seen as 'folk' because they are not engaged in any in-depth theorizing about globalization at an academic or professional level. The study of folk perceptions has been conducted in a range of fields. In sociolinguistics, for example, the analysis of folk-linguistic data has allowed significant insights into how people perceive and how they stereotypically evaluate language variation; and it has added to our understanding of, for example, the various social and cultural forces promoting and resisting language maintenance, change, decay, or revival (see Preston 1996; Williams et al. 1996; Niedzielski and Preston 2000; Garrett et al. 2003, 2004). Various techniques are employed, depending in part upon research questions and disciplines. To illustrate, in some perceptual dialectological studies respondents are asked to draw lines on blank maps in order to show where they believe dialect boundaries lie, and then to jot down their own labels for the dialects they indicate. Such labels are often highly evaluative rather than purely descriptive.

The present study sought the respondents' perceptions by eliciting and analyzing their spontaneous associations of the word 'globalization.' The technique employed was essentially a free-response word association task – "a framework and method for the comparative study of perceptions, attitudes and cultural frames of reference shared by groups of people" (Szalay and Deese 1978: vii), intended to provide researchers with the concepts that are the most salient to the informants and to show how the informants orient toward them.

There is a range of designs to word association tasks: 'discrete association,' 'continuous association,' and 'continued response.' The first of these asks respondents to give just one response to a word. The second is the design employed by Freud, in which respondents produce as many responses as they can manage. 'Continued response,' by contrast, imposes a limit – either in terms of the time allowed for making responses or in terms of requesting a specific number of them – and this is the design employed in this study. Szalay and Deese (1978: 11) note that one advantage of this third design for cross-cultural work (of the kind reported in this chapter) is that it can elicit an informative distribution of responses without the need for very large samples of respondents.

A further advantage of these approaches is that relatively rapid responses can be gathered, which gives less chance for monitoring and bias to occur (see Garrett et al. 2005a). Szalay and Deese (1978: 151) compared data gathered in the form of short essays with data where whole sentences were requested and with data gathered from free word association tasks. They found that short essay data tended to be very brief and dominated by a single theme. In contrast, word associations captured more themes than the short essays and contained more attitudinal information than the sentences – which tended to provide comparatively descriptive data. However, against the advantages of word association tasks, including their immediacy and simplicity, one has to set the tendency of the resulting data toward vagueness, ambiguity, and incompleteness – a situation which requires some care in their interpretation.

This same method was employed, then, in data collection in Australia, China, Japan, New Zealand, the UK, and the USA. While some findings from Australia, New Zealand, the UK, and the USA have been reported previously (Garrett et al. 2006), this chapter extends the earlier analysis and discussion so as to incorporate the two significant Asian contexts for further comparison. For this reason the earlier findings have not been reviewed in this introduction, but they are revisited and integrated into the results and discussion section, alongside the China and Japan findings.

Table 20.1   Comparative overview of respondent samples. Compiled by author from his own data

Origin	Sample size	% female	% male	Mean age
Australia	103	78%	22%	21
China	135	70%	30%	20
Japan	93	85%	15%	20
New Zealand	70	76%	24%	21
UK	99	86%	14%	20
USA	100	50%	50%	20

Method

Respondents

Data were gathered from convenience samples of student respondents attending public universities in Australia, China, Japan, New Zealand, the UK, and the USA. While differences are inevitable among convenience samples spread across such diverse contexts and educational systems, the respondent groups were broadly comparable in terms of their all being students of about the same age, taking degrees in arts and social studies fields. The main details of the six respondent groups are shown in table 20.1.

In China, questionnaires were originally completed by 247 respondents studying a much broader range of subjects than the other respondent groups. Accordingly, those in the Chinese sample who were studying for more technical and scientific degrees, such as Chemistry, Automation, Engineering, and Computer Science, were removed from the database. This left a sample that compared more easily with those of the other national groups, both academically and in terms of sample-size.

In terms of respondents, the design aligns well with the recommendations of Szalay and Deese (1978), who hold that, rather than attempting representative sampling at a more general level (for example national), there are overall advantages to trying to match samples of particular groups (in this case, comparable age groups of students following similar fields of study), and that such samples, containing around 50 to 100 respondents, are sufficient to provide stable and adequate data in this kind of word association study.

Procedure

The data collection procedure was also well aligned with Szalay and Deese's (1978: 24) conclusion that the most effective mode of data collection in such studies is to elicit written (rather than oral) responses in group sessions (but with respondents working alone), giving the respondents an assurance of anonymity. Respondents were asked quickly to write down, individually and without discussion, the first five things that came to mind when they saw or heard the word 'globalization.' In the USA, the UK, New Zealand, and Australia, questionnaires were issued and completed in English. In Japan and China, respondents received and completed questionnaires in their own languages, and their responses were subsequently translated into English. They were encouraged to write down their instantaneous reactions without spending long to reflect on this task. The aim was to elicit immediate cognitive responses, as opposed to 'worked on' answers that involved a greater level of information processing. Hence the respondents were not informed about the purpose of the study prior to the data gathering task. In addition, the data gathering took place at the end of their normal lectures, a fact which imposed some degree of time restriction on completing the task. Apart from helping to eliminate possible biases in these ways, it is also assumed that the respondents' quick responses indicated their most immediate affective associations. Colleagues at universities in the various countries assisted with data collection.

Data processing and analysis

Data analysis aimed at a balance between reflecting the varied character of the responses on the one hand, and, on the other hand, reducing the data to reasonably manageable proportions in order to allow some broad quantitative comparisons. In previous work it has been more illuminating to regard this kind of data as a sort of "discursive shorthand" (Garrett et al. 2003, 2004, 2005a, 2005b; Williams et al. 1996) and to retain some of its qualitative value, rather than to prioritize data reduction for statistical analysis. To this end, procedures of content analysis (see Krippendorf 2004) were employed to organize the data into groupings. To begin with, the relatively discrete ideas expressed in each answer ('referential units') were identified. Given the generally short responses obtained from asking respondents to write down the first five 'things' they thought of, rather than longer comments, this stage in analysis was, in the main at least, unproblematic. These 'referential units' were then clustered into broader thematic categories ('thematic units'), and thereafter percentages were used as a basis of comparison. Responses were not weighted in any way according to whether they were written first, second, and so on.

A common quality of this type of data, and indeed of folk comment generally, is that, in terms of detail, they range along a continuum of general to specific (see Preston 1996). Some items such as 'business' and 'trade' were easily gathered up into broader themes. But other comments, while more elaborate, contained less specific detail, as in 'the world taken over,' and the placing of such data into discrete, mutually exclusive categories was less straightforward. Some items remained therefore unclassified into thematic categories, and, where this is of interest, they are raised in the discussion section below. As Potter and

Wetherell (1987: 41) have emphasized, there is a risk that interesting differences become obscured by attempts to "over-fit" the data into categories. For all this warning, however, it was not feasible or of value to pursue individually and exhaustively all of the 2,600 items gathered in the data from our six groups of respondents.

To orient readers to the tables and discussion in the remainder of this paper, I list below the broad categories arrived at and their contents.

1 **Culture, unity, cooperation and diversity** This is a broad category that includes comments about "global" or "world" and mentions unity; comments about expansion, cooperation ("acceptance of other cultures," "world working together"), opportunity ("we get to learn about foreign cultures and to understand them better"), cultural convergence ("sharing of culture") and cultural assimilation ("some people losing their culture"), diversity ("multiculturalism") and change ("new cultures").

2 **Economy** Comments in this category fall into two broad spheres. The 'corporate' sphere comprises comments about companies and businesses generally, about multinational companies (MNCs) and big businesses, including the names of some; comments about corporate expansion, the world being taken over, monopoly, lack of competition, and the demise of small businesses. The 'economy' sphere includes comments relating to money, currency, banking and trade, as well as comments about capitalism, markets, economic links, the reduction of economic barriers, and about wealth creation, prosperity, the availability of products.

3 **Politics and power** This category comprises comments relating to politics, power, domination, westernization, Americanization, exploitation and inequality.

4 **Communication/technology** This category comprises comments about language, English, communication (including the media), technology (including computers and mobile phones), and the internet.

5 **Ecology and health** This category comprises comments about the environment and climate, and thematically related issues such as pollution or health.

6 **Anti-globalization** This category comprises references to anti-globalization protests and opposition.

7 **War/peace** This category comprises references to war, conflict, peace, and the like.

The above categories account for a good proportion of the data. Items that could not be thematically categorized amounted to 5 percent of the total data for the USA, 6 percent for the UK and New Zealand, 4 percent for Australia, and 8 percent for China and Japan. "Don't know" responses were 1 percent for the UK and Australia, 4 percent for Japan, and zero for China, the USA, and New Zealand. In the larger categories above (1–4), separate percentages of subcategories are recorded so as not to conceal important detail, and in order to enable fuller discussion of the data.

Table 20.2 Proportion of total globalization comments by each national group that were positive or negative. Compiled by author from his own data

	CHINA	USA	JAPAN	UK	NZ	AUS
Total comments	649	460	314	455	281	477
Positive	22%	16%	8%	8%	7%	4%
Negative	10%	9%	5%	15%	30%	27%

Results and Discussion

Positive and negative orientations

To gain an initial general impression of the different groups' orientations, an estimate was made of the overall positivity and negativity in the perceptions of the respondents. Often items such as "business" or "global village" do not exhibit enough cues to allow much certainty as to whether the respondents' attitudes to these features are positive, negative, or neutral. Some, however, can be reasonably assumed to carry positive connotations (for instance "education," "better understanding") or negative ones ("too much power," "fancy way of saying they are massing us into one group"). Identifying such inferable items for each respondent group and then calculating them in terms of proportions of each group's total of keyword items gave what could be interpreted as a rough index of overall evaluative stances toward globalization. These are set out in Table 20.2. (As in all the remaining tables in this paper, percentages are rounded up or down to the nearest whole.)

The table shows some polarization. Relative to the other groups, the New Zealand and Australian respondents display a strong leaning toward negativity, in contrast to the Chinese respondents, who show a more positive inclination. Taken together, these three are also the groups with the highest proportion of inferably evaluative comments. The USA and the UK also differ from each other, although to a lesser extent, the USA holding an overall positive rather than negative view, whereas the UK's general orientation is negative more than positive. Comments inferable as positive or negative account for a much smaller proportion in the case of the Japanese respondents and are more evenly balanced, with a slight leaning toward the positive.

Broad patterns across the categories

Table 20.3 sets out the distribution of comments for each respondent group in each of the seven broad categories summarized earlier. The percentages represent the number of items mentioned by each group in each category, and are calculated as a percentage of their total number of comments (shown in table 20.2), including

Table 20.3   Overall percentages of comments by each group in each of the broad categories. Compiled by author from his own data

	Category	AUS	CHINA	JAPAN	NZ	UK	USA
1	**Culture**	26%	36%	58%	25%	33%	52%
2	**Economy**	34%	31%	7%	33%	29%	20%
3	**Politics/Power**	18%	8%	4%	15%	12%	4%
4	**Communication**	6%	13%	15%	11%	15%	11%
5	**Ecology/Health**	2%	1%	2%	5%	3%	2%
6	**Antiglobalization**	7%	0%	0%	2%	0%	1%
7	**War/peace**	1%	3%	2%	2%	1%	4%

those which could not be categorized. The same practice is followed in the remaining tables. This section looks at the relative salience of the categories for each of the groups and at the comparative profiles of the groups across these broad categories. In subsequent sections, closer consideration is given to the thematic groupings within each of these categories in turn. Some of the groupings are rather small, so discussion of them is necessarily selective.

Table 20.3 show that, across all respondents, the most salient associations generated by the term 'globalization' concern cultural aspects, economic matters, political and power issues, and communication and technology. Beyond these, environmental issues, possibilities for peace and war, and anti-globalization protests received comparatively little comment.

Overall, it is the culture category that is the most salient. To some extent, it is possible to identify a hierarchy of paired groups. In terms of the relative proportions of comments for each category (as displayed in table 20.3), the Japanese and US respondents comment on culture the most, being followed first by the Chinese and UK respondents, and next by the Australians and New Zealanders. The pattern is reversed in the 'economy' category, which attracts the second most comments. The 'politics and power' category shows, again, a quantitative similarity between Japan and the USA. One could argue that Australia and New Zealand make the most comments in this category, while China takes the middle ground again, perhaps with the UK. For all other categories – communication, ecology/health, anti-globalization, war/peace – the respondent groups are all broadly similar, apart from the Australians, for whom globalization activates a stronger association with anti-globalization protests than it does for the others, and for whom the communication category is less salient. Comparing table 20.3 with table 20.2, it is noteworthy that the two highly evaluative and most negative groups regarding globalization (Australia and New Zealand) are those that have the most to say on economic issues – as well as on politics and power rather than culture. Interestingly, too, the Japanese respondents, who have the most to say about

Table 20.4   Percentages of total comments of each group in culture subcategories. Compiled by author from his own data

Subcategory	AUS	CHINA	JAPAN	NZ	UK	USA
Global/unity	9%	8%	31%	11%	17%	21%
Expansion	1%	0%	1%	1%	1%	3%
Co-operation	2%	5%	6%	1%	1%	9%
Opportunity	2%	15%	5%	1%	2%	4%
Assimilation	6%	2%	2%	6%	7%	6%
Convergence	1%	1%	0%	1%	2%	2%
Diversity	2%	0%	4%	2%	1%	5%
Change	1%	4%	0%	1%	2%	3%

culture and the least about economic issues, appear to be by far the least evaluative of the groups.

Culture, unity, cooperation, and diversity

As a whole, this category accounts for a good half of the comments made by the US and Japanese respondents, compared to about a third of those from the UK and China and to about a quarter of those from New Zealand and China. Table 20.4 shows that these differentiations are evident across several subcategories.

To construct an initially simplified picture, it is possible to take in turn the relative salience of items of the subcategories for each of the respondent groups, to arrive at the following hierarchies of what might be reasonably seen to be the main frequencies (taking 4 percent as a threshold).

USA: global/unity – cooperation – assimilation – diversity – opportunity
Japan: global/unity – cooperation – opportunity – diversity
UK: global/unity – assimilation
New Zealand: global/unity – assimilation
Australia: global/unity – assimilation
China: opportunity – global/unity – co-operation – change

It is notable that the global/unity subcategory holds a position of strong salience, albeit differentially, across most of the groups. Under this heading items are grouped which refer to global scope – for instance "world" or "earth" – and also to unity – for instance "unified" or "the world becomes united."[1] One view of globalization that the hyperglobalizers and transformationalists share is the recognition that there is an intensification of global interconnectedness (for an overview, see Held et al. 1999), and doubtlessly this overarching perspective is what these comments reflect. The perspective is continually reinforced in our everyday lives – for example when the person answering a customer services telephone line dialled on a freephone or national number is found to be speaking from the other side of the world; or when people realize that places they had regarded as too remote to travel to for vacations are now within striking distance; or when bank lending policies in one nation jeopardize the employment and financial security of populations all over the world. In addition, especially with the development of the global media and increased accessibility to it (even if this is partly linked with a controversial concentration of ownership), people in most parts of the world are recognized to have an enhanced awareness of issues and events else-where (ILO 2004: 48). Leaving this aside, though, there is a broad patterning here. In China, Australia, and New Zealand the subcategory global/unity has less sali-ence than the others (although in general 8 percent, 9 percent, and 11 percent are still quite high figures for subcategories and reflect that they are important). While the UK and the USA have more comment to give on such issues than these three groups, it is clearly the Japanese respondents who stand out, with an average of 31 percent: for them, global/unity is by far the most salient subcategory across the board.

Looking now at the qualitative nature of the comments themselves made under "global/unity," there are no marked differences among the groups. These are overwhelmingly neutral comments in all the cases. People's associations can be activated by two routes. One is the similarity in meanings between two cognitive representations; the other is the association established between two representa-tions, although they are not semantically linked in any obvious way, only because they are repeatedly thought about together (Smith and Mackie 2000). These global/unity comments seem to arise by the former route more than by the latter; they can almost be viewed in terms of attempts to find approximate synonyms for globalization. In any event, the associations of globalization that are upper-most in the minds of the Japanese and US respondents are just these sorts of neutrally descriptive items focusing on global scope and interconnectedness. Their prominence for the Japanese respondents doubtlessly explains their low proportions of inferably positive and negative comments in table 20.2.

Assimilation is another subcategory that divides the respondent groups. It is strongest among the UK respondents, the Australians, and the New Zealanders. The US figure, too, comes close, although for these respondents assimilation has less prominence than other items in the category of culture – as if notions of same-ness, uniformity, and melting-pots hold less salience among the various aspects of culture. Assimilation is also a less negative subcategory for the US than for the UK, Australia, and New Zealand in terms of items that refer to notions of restric-tion and loss (if one takes them as expressing negativity). Remarkably, assimila-tion does not seem to produce strong associations for the Chinese and Japanese respondents. Perhaps in the case of Japan this is partly attributable to the fact that traditional culture and religion continue to play an important role in everyday life (Cvetkovich and Kellner 1997: 11), and globalization is seen as having little influence over such a strong national identity (Inoguchi 2000: 231).

The subcategory of cooperation contains few comments from the UK, New Zealand, and Australian respondents, but more from the Japanese and Chinese, and especially from the US respondents. While there are some seemingly neutral comments in this subcategory, for instance "big meetings" and "networking," cooperation is marked by a proportion of positive comments such as "more and deeper contact with people from other countries." The US data include comments on "helping" and "togetherness," which seems to underline a view of globalization as a force of good for the world from their standpoint.

Opportunity is the culture subcategory which holds the most salience for the Chinese respondents (15 percent of all their comments are on it), but also the one which differentiates Japan and the US from the UK, Australia, and New Zealand in this study. In fact for the UK, Australia, and New Zealand respondents, globalization activates almost no associations with opportunity. Within this Chinese subcategory there are three qualitative groupings. One contains comments making a general reference to "opportunity," "challenge," "citizens will benefit." This accounts for about a third of all the comments in this subcategory. A second subgroup, accounting for about a quarter of the comments, refers to cultural exchange and knowledge. But the largest of the three groupings is one about "people on the move" (Held et al. 1999): namely opportunities for travel abroad and tourism. There is some qualitative contrast here. While the Japanese comments (which are numerically small due to the smaller sample size) are varied, but with some focus on international exchange, the strongest theme in the US comments is increased understanding, learning, and awareness from exchange, with no comments about the more practical dimension of travel opportunities. In all cases, this is an overwhelmingly positive subcategory, and suggests a powerfully optimistic climate, in particular among these young Chinese adults.

Diversity does not attract a great deal of comment from any of the groups, but nevertheless it reveals some difference insofar as it is a link with globalization that is more marked for the US and Japanese respondents than for the others, and indeed not at all for the Chinese. Qualitatively, the comments do not differ among any of the groups: they refer to "differences," "many cultures," "several ethnicities," "bringing diversity out into the open." There are no clear clues in the data through which one might safely infer either a generally negative or positive viewpoint in the groups. On the other hand, at least in the case of foreigners in Japan, there is evidence in Sasaki (2004: 81) that younger age groups (15 to 29 in that study), compared to older age groups, had generally more favorable attitudes toward cultural benefits.

Taking just the two groups (the US and the Chinese), change is a relatively neutral subcategory for the US respondents ("change," "new"), whereas it has a far more positive feel in the case of the Chinese ("the world will become better," "China will play an important role in the world"). Alongside this, the Chinese respondents link globalization explicitly with change in the sense of development ("China will develop more rapidly," "human beings develop and advance together"). Indeed, if this grouping of comments on development within the change subcategory is combined with those in the economy category referring to

Table 20.5   Percentages of total comments by each group in the subcategories of the economy category. Compiled by author from his own data

	Subcategory	AUS	CHINA	JAPAN	NZ	UK	USA
1	Corporations	5%	1%	1%	0%	3%	2%
2	MNCs	3%	0%	0%	0%	2%	0%
3	Names of MNCs	5%	0%	1%	7%	7%	1%
4	Big business	4%	0%	0%	3%	4%	0%
5	Corp expansion	1%	0%	1%	4%	2%	1%
1–5	**Corporate sphere**	**18%**	**1%**	**2%**	**15%**	**18%**	**4%**
6	Economy	3%	7%	1%	4%	3%	5%
7	Capitalism	3%	0%	0%	0%	2%	1%
8	Money/currency	4%	1%	1%	3%	2%	1%
9	Global trade	4%	4%	0%	5%	1%	4%
10	Economic links	0%	6%	2%	0%	1%	1%
11	No borders	1%	0%	0%	1%	0%	0%
12	Market economy	0%	4%	1%	0%	0%	0%
13	Availability/prosperity	0%	8%	0%	6%	2%	3%
6–13	**Economy sphere**	**16%**	**31%**	**5%**	**5%**	**12%**	**16%**

economic development, development emerges as a significant theme in its own right for the Chinese respondents, accounting for 5 percent of their total of 649 comments, and, again, it expresses an overall optimistic orientation toward globalization, to an extent that differentiates them from the other respondent groups in this study.

Economy

Notwithstanding the relatively small proportion of comments from the Japanese respondents on the associations of economy, the relative salience of this category mirrors the focus on economic matters in the globalization literature generally, and in the hyperglobalist and skeptical perspectives in particular. Many of the groupings in table 20.5 are small, but nevertheless allow a glimpse into the breadth of comment around economic issues. Below, the focus is limited to one or two main trends. Table 20.5 is organized into two main spheres. Rows 1–5 are concerned with references to corporations and MNCs (the corporate sphere), and rows 6–13 are concerned with more varied economic issues (the economic sphere).

The corporate sphere is a strikingly stronger association for the New Zealand, UK, and Australian respondents (15 percent, 18 percent, and 18 percent respectively) than for the US respondents (4 percent), and even more so than for the Chinese (1 percent) and Japanese (2 percent) respondents. MNCs tend usually to be connected in people's minds with American companies (Jones and Galvez-Muños 2001), and it may be that their presence in some foreign contexts is more marked, especially if they are perceived as a threat, as happened often in New Zealand, Australia, and, perhaps to a lesser extent, the UK. The Chinese economy is very different; it enjoys far more control and protection from the state and has its own strong and large state-owned companies, along with a market which is not nearly as consumer-oriented as that of all the other respondent groups; so there may have been far less experience there of the threatening presence of western multinationals. While the western respondents name some multinationals as seemingly iconic representations of globalization (for instance Starbucks or McDonalds), the Chinese respondents do not do this. In the case of the Japanese respondents, it is possible that, with so many Japanese companies with a global presence and familiarity (Sony, Mitsubushi, and the like), and perhaps given a certain loyalty to Japanese products (Chang 1995), they, too, may feel less threatened by western multinationals and hence do not connect them instantaneously with their most prominent globalization issues. However, the Japanese respondents have fewer associations in the entire category of economy, rather than only in the corporation sphere, whereas the Chinese respondents have a great deal to say about the other economic issues too (rows 6–13). So other differences must be at work. These will be considered in the later part of this chapter.

In the economic sphere (rows 6–13), the most striking results come from the Chinese and Japanese respondents, who occupy the two extremes. For the Japanese, globalization triggers only a few associations with economic issues, by comparison both with results in the cultural and political category and with responses from the other groups. But the Chinese respondents make very strong links between globalization and economic matters. Their comments stand out in terms of the higher frequency of broad references to "economy," accounting for 7 percent of the total number of comments; to economic links (references to economic exchange), accounting for 6 percent of the total number of comments; and to the availability of goods and prosperity, accounting for 8 percent of the total number of comments.

Within these quantitative patterns there are some marked qualitative features in the Chinese data. In particular, three generalizations emerge. First, while many comments on market economies are general ("market," "market globalization," "competition"), more than half arguably show some specific affective loading ("fiercer competition," "cruel competition"). Secondly, the relatively large subcategory "economic links" contains items across the whole spectrum running from optimism to concern. The majority of the comments in this subcategory are seemingly neutral ("economic unity") or positive ("equal economic cooperation," "easier for countries to have economic exchanges"). Nevertheless, echoing the concern shown in the market economies subcategory, some 28 percent of the comments here express disquiet ("economic invasion"). Looking for patterns that cut across these subcategories, we might surmise from these data that such Chinese concerns are equivalent to those shown by some other national groups, especially those from New Zealand and Australia, about the power and encroachment of

MNCs. The effects are comparable (ruthless competition, economies being invaded), even if the Chinese respondents do not attribute them explicitly to MNCs. MNCs have perhaps had a more visible and long-standing presence in the lives of our western respondents, whereas China's exposure to the global economy is relatively recent. These Chinese comments need to be set in the context of China's recent entry into the World Trade Organization.

The third trend in the economic category concerns the large availability/prosperity subcategory. These are overwhelmingly positive comments and actually amount to 26 percent of all the Chinese comments regarding economic matters. Of these comments referring to availability/prosperity, some 40 percent refer to the anticipated drop in prices and increased availability of imported goods in China ("easier and cheaper for citizens to buy goods"; "able to buy foreign goods in the Chinese market"; "prices will drop"). Interestingly, too, a third of the comments in this subcategory refer to better resource-sharing and resource availability. As a rule, comments about resources do not feature at all in the data from the USA, UK, New Zealand, Australia, and Japan. I will is return to this in the discussion section below.

Economic matters, then, undoubtedly evoke powerful associations with globalization in the minds of the Chinese respondents. Overall these respondents demonstrate a strong optimism, albeit tempered somewhat, perhaps, by the uncertainties of recent WTO membership. For the Australians and New Zealanders, the salience of economic issues is more negatively motivated. We return to this when we look at the power subcategory below, as we deal with issues of inequality.

Politics and power

Although many items in this category cannot be labelled as unambiguously negative for instance "politics," "power," "westernization," "Americanization"), it is nevertheless a negative category overall, particularly the rich/poor subcategory. Given the findings reported earlier regarding the relatively low presence of economic associations for the Japanese and, to some extent, for the US respondents too, along with a greater focus on cooperation and opportunity, it is perhaps not surprising to find that the politics/power category carries little salience for the US and Japanese respondents in comparison with the other groups (see table 20.6). In fact, the rich/poor subcategory receives barely a mention from either of these respondent groups. The UK respondents, too, make fewer such comments. And, although in this politics/power category many UK comments are negative, most have a more general tone (or feel less clearly negative) – for instance "dominance." The Chinese comments in this politics/power category are more evenly spread. About two thirds of them are relatively general ("politics," "mutual influence on world politics," "political stability") and have no overall positive or negative flavor coming from the respondents as a group. Interestingly, globalization activates virtually no associations with western domination or Americanization. The other third are mainly comments about rich/poor exploitation and inequality

Table 20.6   Percentages of total comments of each group in politics/power subcategories. Compiled by author from his own data

Subcategory	AUS	CHINA	JAPAN	NZ	UK	USA
Politics/power	5%	5%	0%	4%	7%	2%
Western domination	0%	0%	0%	2%	1%	0%
Americanization	4%	0%	4%	3%	2%	1%
Rich/poor	8%	3%	0%	6%	2%	0%

("great distance between rich and poor," "more difficult for the weak to survive"), and constitute a pocket of negativity in the Chinese responses. In the cases of New Zealand and Australia, though, rich/poor is the most significant grouping in this category, with many references to poor nations getting poorer, to "sweatshops," and to "people getting oppressed."

Many inequality and exploitation comments tend to have an economic character to them, and therefore could also be considered in the economy category. This would make no difference, though, to the overall patterns of positivity and negativity across the whole data-set (see table 20.2); it would only further confirm other patterns in the data: the comparative tendency for the US respondents to focus more on positive cultural issues than on explicitly economic ones, and the overwhelmingly negative orientation to the economic aspects of globalization which comes from the Australian and New Zealand respondents.

Communication and technology

Looking back at this category as a whole in table 20.3, the quantitative pattern across the respondent groups is fairly level, varying between 11 percent and 15 percent, except for the Australians at 6 percent. Subcategories in table 20.7 are grouped in order to show comments concerning language on the one hand, communication and technology on the other (see the two bold rows of percentages); and for all groups communication and technology trigger a stronger association with globalization than language does. Numbers are generally small in this category.

The grouping into comments about language and comments about communication and technology reveals that the difference in the Australian proportion is due to their having less to say about language than the other groups. Interestingly, too, the Australian respondents are the only group to make no comments at all about English. Language clearly provokes much stronger associations to the Japanese respondents than to the others, although the comments do not differ much in content from those of the rest. Most of their comments are about English, either just as 'English' or in its role of principal lingua franca ("we can"t do without English," "everybody gets to know English"). It is possible that the

Table 20.7   Percentages of total comments of each group on communication and technology. Compiled by author from his own data

	Subcategory	AUS	CHINA	JAPAN	NZ	UK	USA
1	Languages	1%	2%	3%	1%	3%	2%
2	English	0%	0%	5%	1%	1%	0%
3	English domination	0%	1%	0%	0%	1%	2%
4	One language	0%	1%	0%	1%	1%	0%
1–4	Language combined	1%	4%	9%	4%	5%	4%
5	Communication	2%	5%	3%	0%	4%	3%
6	Technology	2%	2%	0%	4%	2%	3%
7	Internet	1%	3%	3%	3%	3%	0%
5–7	Communication combined	5%	9%	6%	7%	9%	7%

English-dominant groups do not see the sociolinguistic position of English 'from the other side,' that the Chinese respondents do not see global English as a threat to them, and that the Japanese respondents value the associations of English with modernity. It is not easy to place an interpretation on these findings, however, and further study may be required.

The main qualitative point of interest in this category is that, for the Chinese respondents, information technology and the sharing of science and technology is more strongly associated with globalization than it is for the others.[2] In contrast to this, the Chinese respondents do not link globalization significantly with the global media, TV, film, and newspapers, which are not mentioned at all in their data (perhaps an effect of controls on access to some overseas sources in China).

Across all the respondents, the evaluative tone in this category is neutral or positive ("communication getting better," "it will be good to learn some foreign languages"). The communication–technological aspects, which are so central to the time–space compression identified in globalization, seem not to arouse any substantially negative reactions in these young respondents, and some features such as the internet doubtlessly play irreplaceable roles in their everyday lives. Negative aspects of such technology do not eclipse these positive associations. The ILO report (2004: 48) refers to widespread concern at the dominance of western culture and values through the global media and entertainment industries; but, from the respondents who mention the global media in the present study, there are no accompanying negative references to such dominance.

Ecology, health, anti-globalization, war and peace

Categories 5, 6, and 7 from table 20.3 are gathered together here in table 20.8. These are self-explanatory headings, apart perhaps from "concerns," which

Table 20.8   Percentages of total comments of each group on ecology, health, antiglobalization, and war and peace. Compiled by author from his own data

Subcategory	AUS	CHINA	JAPAN	NZ	UK	USA
Environment	1%	1%	2%	1%	2%	2%
Concerns	1%	0%	0%	3%	1%	1%
Health	0%	0%	0%	1%	0%	0%
Anti-globalization	7%	0%	0%	2%	0%	1%
War/peace	1%	3%	2%	2%	1%	4%

includes other issues than environment and health, for instance overpopulation. Perhaps the most remarkable feature in table 20.8 is that globalization does not link strongly to such matters in the minds of the respondents. Notwithstanding the small numbers of comments, then, content in all groups generally focuses on the environment and on global warming, with some mention of other concerns such as overpopulation. In the case of China, all the comments (apart from those on war and peace) are about the environment and pollution. The association with anti-globalization protests is mainly significant for the Australians. Associations with war and peace feature little too. For the New Zealanders, the association is more with terrorism than with peace. The balance is fairly even between conflict and peace for the Japanese respondents. Overall, the associations of the US and Chinese respondents are more with peace than with war, which further implies a more overtly optimistic view of globalization than is manifest in the other groups.

Further discussion

The findings in this study support a number of the findings of the ILO (2004) study. Some negative perceptions emerge from both studies, in terms of bias toward the rich and the powerful, increased income disparities emanating from exposure to greater economic competition, and feelings of vulnerability due to a perception of things being out of control. The ILO also found that, while the reports from the US showed a strong awareness of the US being the main driver of globalization, they were also more optimistic than others (although not without acknowledging adverse effects too). For US respondents, the present study finds relatively little preoccupation with economic issues and power and exploitation, and more focus on cooperation and opportunity than in most other groups.

Held and colleagues (1999), who differ both from the hyperglobalizers' and from the skeptics' perspectives on the position of the nation–state, emphasize that states are now locked into overlapping and diverse structures, which have a range of impacts on them. Cumulatively, these impacts are not uniform across all the states; they are mediated by such things as a state's position in the political, economic, and military global hierarchies, and also by specific governments. The US obviously ranks high in these hierarchies, and this is likely to lead to a different experience of globalization by comparison with many other countries. It might be reasonable to assume that this position enables some US respondents to feel less threatened by MNCs and by unequal international wealth distribution than some other groups.

Japan is also highly positioned in these global hierarchies – as a member of G8, for example, and as the world's second largest economy, with a strong international presence as regards MNCs.[3] In some aspects, the perceptions of the Japanese respondents are not dissimilar to those coming from the US. Both groups have little to say about MNCs, and the salience of economic associations is on the whole lower for both. They make more associations with global scope and unity than the other groups do, and they make almost no connections with issues of inequality and exploitation. And the Japanese tend to share a view of globalization in terms of cooperation and opportunity, at least more so than the UK, Australia, and New Zealand. Again, the US and Japanese respondents (together with the Chinese) do not share the negative balance of feeling toward globalization displayed by the other groups. However, if the 1990s are seen as the decade of globalization for Japan (and for others, of course), then the economic stagnation in Japan during those and subsequent years has made globalization a very different experience for the Japanese compared to the other groups in this study. The comparative weakness of the association made by these respondents between globalization and economic matters is certainly hard to explain and merits further research, perhaps with different age groups.

The perceptual and evaluative profile of the Australians is different from that emanating from Japan and the USA. Worthington (2001) points to some specific characteristics of Australia that might explain their different perspective. To begin with, Australia is territorially a vast country, rich in natural resources. But with a small population relative to its size, it has depended on foreign capital for developing these resources, and this has in fact led some to point to the risk of Australia becoming a "branch office country" (Kitney 2001). As a result, there can be a great deal of noise and resistance when there are foreign take-over bids for what have become "iconic" Australian brands (Worthington 2001). Correspondingly, there has been much public condemnation of companies moving business offshore. Indeed Worthington refers to a perceived threat to Australian national identity. Although Australia shares a colonial history with the USA, its population is much smaller, and it experiences a much stronger sense of geographical separation, being an island of predominantly European culture. Ryan (1999: 92) points to a view of globalization as primarily a "ruthless tyranny" in Australia. In addition, Wiseman (1998) considers issues of nationalism and identity in Australia during globalization, and how the state and inherited national identity might still seek a role to play for individual Australians. The primary and differentiating salience of economy, power, and exploitation in the Australian responses, their more strongly negative than positive orientation, and their associations with anti-globalization protests seem at least partly attributable to these sorts of factors.

The New Zealanders' profile comes closest to that of the Australians. It has been ranked as the most transnationalized of all the OECD economies, with substantial foreign direct investment into and control over its infrastructure (Kelsey 2004). While New Zealand workers enjoyed one of the highest standards of living in the world in the 1950s and 1960s, by end of the 1960s "there was a big increase in the number of transnational companies entering the economy, and many homegrown corporates had become large enough to go out onto the world stage" (Lusk 2001). With the UK strengthening its ties to Europe, economic growth in New Zealand fell to one of the lowest levels in the OECD (well below that of Australia), and this inevitably affected health, education, housing, and poverty in general (Kelsey 2004). So some key characteristics of globalization, such as increased capital flows, are likely to have associations with detriment and steep decline more than with gain or prosperity for the New Zealand respondents.

Overall the UK profile tends to occupy a middle ground, both quantitatively and qualitatively. MNCs have a similar salience for these respondents as they do for Australians and New Zealanders, and this may well reflect take-overs of some high-profile names in recent years, including famous car marques, and even football clubs. Alongside this, people in this group are used to seeing all the ubiquitous iconic global chains such as Starbucks and McDonalds. In the more positive areas of opportunity and cooperation they are, again, closer to the Australians and New Zealanders through their lack of comment. But this alignment is less close for issues of power and exploitation, where the UK respondents' associations are less explicitly negative. In general, they make less unfavorable and more secure associations with globalization than the Australians and New Zealanders, but they do not match the Chinese, the Japanese, and the US respondents for confidence and optimism.

The Chinese context is of course quite different from all the others included in this study. After 100 years of imperialism, war, and famine, production campaigns such as the Great Leap Forward in the 1950s were far from successful, and somewhere between 30 and 50 million people are estimated to have died in the famine of 1960–3 (Pringle 2001). Centrally directed allocation of resources through administrative means was increasingly seen as untenable and as working against economic development (Prasad and Rumbaugh 2004: 2). Since the 'Open Door' reforms at the end of the 1970s and with more radical reforms unfolding from the early 1990s, China has moved from a "hermetically sealed economy" toward economic integration into the global market (Sally 2007: 82). By 2002, China was attracting an amount of foreign direct investment second only to that of the US. According to the ILO (2004), the number of people living in poverty in China declined from 361 million to 241 million in the 1990s. Bello (2004) underlines the fact that China did not follow the kind of anti-state liberalization policies that worked badly in other developing countries, but maintained strong capital controls and protected its market. In addition, the priority has not been to develop a strong consumer society. About half of China's imports are for processing, which then accounts for about 40 percent of China's exports (Rumbaugh and Blancher

2004). This has helped China to meet its challenges of economic growth, industrial productivity, and employment.

This background makes it easier to understand the Chinese respondents' perceptions of globalization, and how theirs compare with those of the other respondent groups. The improvement in living standards during the 1990s had already laid the ground for an overall positive orientation toward globalization. China's accession to the WTO at the end of 2001, which involved for example the lowering of many tariffs (see Bhattasali and Kawai 2002), was seen as "the media event of the year" by the Chinese press (Pringle 2001). The dialogue in China emphasized that the opportunities and benefits of globalization were greater than the risks (ILO 2004: 16), and that, although there would be "growing pains," there would also be "exciting opportunities" (*People's Daily*, February 20, 2002). In the wake of such discourse, as China feels its way forward into new territory, there are two other qualities of the Chinese comments that are noteworthy. Firstly, a number of comments specifically referred to China: for instance "Chinese people must travel to the world," "China will develop more rapidly." Spread across the categories, these accounted for about 5 percent of China's comments. The other respondent groups referred to themselves in such terms minimally, or not at all. In the same anticipatory vein, another distinctive grouping of comments (this time not included in the categories discussed in this paper) comprised open questions, such as "Is China ready for it?" "Can Chinese enterprises and rural areas get used to globalization?" This was a small but conspicuous grouping, accounting for approximately 3 percent of the total comments, but it was of a kind quite absent from the comments of the other respondent groups.

The Chinese respondents' comments in the economic category, then, although quantitatively close to Australia's and New Zealand's, qualitatively tell a quite different story, in which predatory MNCs are absent and an opening-up is foregrounded, with greater links and exchange, greater availability of goods and services, and increased prosperity. Their comments about resources – the only group to mention them – are interpretable against the background of the earlier experiences of resource allocation in China mentioned above. The Chinese connection between globalization and links, cooperation, change, and opportunity also extends beyond the economic domain, into the cultural one. Opportunities for cultural exchange and for foreign travel are salient to a degree that far exceeds even the positive views of the US respondents.

Looking at the data as a whole, across all the respondent groups, it is noticeable that some themes, which one might have expected to be activated in the associations of the respondents, have little presence in the data. Some topics commonly prefixed by 'global' appear very little, if at all: for instance "global warming," "global terrorism," or "global epidemics" (such as HIV/AIDS). Such topics certainly feature commonly in many academic and media discussions of globalization. In these respects, the data appear to show a significant gap between the perceptions of expert commentators and folk-perceptions. On the other hand, it is important to be mindful of the fact that respondents were asked only for their first five associations. It may be that the data do indeed capture everything that is of significance to the respondents, but it is not impossible that they only capture the most salient of many topics that are all salient to them. We can only work within the parameters of the data.

The study has drawn data from groups of young adults studying at university in six countries with considerable geographical, economic, historical, and socio-cultural differences. Differences have been found in their perceptual and evaluative profiles of globalization, and these display much about how their perceptions appear to be influenced by local experiences and developments. If such perceptions are affected at the level of experiences and developments that are even more local, it is important to be mindful of sample characteristics. Perceptions may be different in different age groups. Sasaki (2004), for example, concludes that globalization is probably more welcomed in Japan by the younger generation than by the older ones. In addition, the perceptions of these young adults may change as they pursue their careers after their university studies. Besides, university students are also arguably a relatively privileged social group. Scheve and Slaughter (2001) for example, in their study of working-class perceptions in the US, found that those social groups who see themselves as more vulnerable are the more likely ones to be negative about globalization. Given that the phenomenon of globalization can have very diverse consequences, which are not uniformly good or bad (Schaeffer 2003: 11), social groups within national contexts may well differ in their perceptions; and, despite Szalay and Deese's (1978) methodological view that matched samples of particular groups provide sufficient data, the findings of the present study, with its focus on globalization, do not claim to be securely generalizable to other sections of the societies under investigation.[3]

Relatedly, there is the question of what makes some things rather than others more salient associations with globalization. The discussion above has tried to address this issue in part. At the general level, two main influences are recency and frequency (Smith and Mackie 2000). Examining the recency and frequency with which different issues are experienced in people's everyday social interactions, and the various reasons for them, may give us a deeper understanding; such experiences include for instance people losing their jobs, local pollution, applications of new scientific inventions, or strong media coverage of particular national issues such as joining the WTO. Media research, alongside the kind of perceptual survey work reported here, might help us to see how such issues impact on how people perceive globalization. It is also of value to examine to what extent the media set the perceptual agenda through their coverage of specific types of stories over time (stories about migrant workers one week, melting icecaps another) and convey explicit links with globalization. At different times, and for different social groups, globalization is likely to take on different values, as different arrays of factors achieve salience. Nevertheless, the present study has shown that academic and professional discourses of globalization do not constitute the whole picture, and has sought to demonstrate, through a linguistic approach, how 'vernacular' data on globalization across a range of cultural contexts can reveal other 'shapes' of the concept.

ACKNOWLEDGMENTS

The research for this paper is part of a larger project on Language and Global Communication, funded by The Leverhulme Trust (Grant No. F/00 407/D) and conducted at the Centre for Language and Communication Research, Cardiff University (see www.cardiff.ac.uk/encap/global/). Thanks are due to Michelle Aldridge, Cindy Gallois, Janet Holmes, Ian McCall, Susan McKay, Kazuhiko Namba, Dennis Preston, and Sally Zhao for their kind assistance with data collection. With regard to the Japanese and Chinese data, thanks are due to Kazuhiko Namba and Sally Zhao for their data translation and their helpful comments on an earlier draft of this paper, as well as to Angie Williams and Betsy Evans for their part in the research design, data collection, and processing. I am also grateful to Professor Jonathan Morris (Cardiff Business School) for valuable comments on an earlier draft.

NOTES

1   Initially such items were grouped separately into two subcategories: "global" and "unity," but too many of the items were too close in meaning to maintain or reveal any meaningful differentiation. For example, "countries' borders disappear" and "global village" could be seen as suggesting unity or global scope, or both.
2   The data from the Chinese science students who were removed from the sample did differ from the arts and social science students' data. The former made more comments in the communication category than the latter, specifically on communication and technology (comments about language were about the same). Qualitatively, though, there were no clear differences.
3   *Forbes* magazine 2008 listed 33% of the world's largest 2000 companies as US-owned, 15% as Japanese-owned, 6% as UK-owned, 2% China-owned (4% including Hong Kong), and 2% owned by Australia and New Zealand combined. (Source: http://www.forbes.com.)

REFERENCES

Bhattasali, D., and Kawai, M. (2002) Implications of China's accession to the WTO. In H. G. Hilpert (ed.), *Japan and China: Cooperation, Competition and Conflict*, 72–102. Basingstoke: Palgrave Macmillan.

Bello, W. (2004) Globalisation in Asia and China: Assessing costs and benefits. In *Linking Alternative Regionalism for Equitable and Sustainable Development*. TNI Briefing Series 5. September. Available at: http://www.tni.org/detail_page.phtml?act_id=567andusername=guest@tni.organdpassword=9999andpublish=Y (accessed on March 20, 08).

Chang, H.-J. (1995) Explaining 'flexible rigidities' in East Asia. In T. Killick (ed.), *Causes and Consequences of the Adaptability of National Economies*, 197–221. London: Routledge.

Cvetkovich, A., and Kellner, D. (1997) *Articulating the Global and the Local: Globalization and Cultural Studies*. Boulder, CO: Westview.

Eriksen, T. (2007) *Globalization: The Key Concepts*. Oxford: Berg.

Garrett, P., Coupland, N., and Williams, A. (2003) *Investigating Language Attitudes*. Cardiff: University of Wales Press.

Garrett, P., Coupland, N., and Williams, A. (2004) Adolescents' lexical repertoires of peer evaluation: *Boring prats* and *English snobs*. In A. Jaworski, N. Coupland, and D. Galasinski (eds), *Metalanguage: Social and Ideological Perspectives*, 193–226. Berlin: Mouton de Gruyter.

Garrett, P., Williams, A., and Evans, B. (2005a) Accessing social meanings: Values *of* keywords, values *in* keywords. In T. Kristiansen, P. Garrett, and N. Coupland (eds), *Subjective Processes in Language Variation and Change* (= *Acta Linguistica Hafniensia* 37, special issue), 37–54. Copenhagen: Reitzel.

Garrett, P., Williams, A., and Evans, B. (2005b) Attitudinal data from New Zealand, Australia, the USA and UK about each other's Englishes: Recent changes or consequences of methodologies? *Multilingua* 24: 211–36.

Garrett, P., Evans, B., and Williams, A. (2006) What does the word 'globalisation' mean to you? Comparative perceptions and evaluations in Australia, New Zealand, the USA and the UK. *Journal of Multilingual and Multicultural Development* 27: 392–412.

Giddens, A. (1990) *The Consequences of Modernity*. Cambridge: Polity.

Giddens, A. (1991) *Modernity and Self-Identity: Self and Society in the Modern Age*. Cambridge: Polity.

Giddens, A. (2002) *Runaway World: How Globalization is Reshaping our Lives*. London: Profile Books.

Hamelink, C. (2003) The elusive concept of globalisation. In R. Robertson and K. White (eds), *Globalization: Critical Concepts in Sociology*, 249–58. London: Routledge.

Hannerz, U. (1991) Scenarios for peripheral cultures. In A. King (ed.), *Culture, Globalization, and the World System*. Basingstoke: Macmillan.

Held, D., and McGrew, A. (2000) The great globalization debate: An introduction. In D. Held and A. McGrew (eds), *The Global Transformations Reader*, 1–50. Cambridge: Cambridge University Press.

Held, D., McGrew, A., Goldblatt, D., and Perraton, J. (1999) *Global Transformations: Politics, Economics and Culture*. Cambridge: Polity.

Hirst, P., and Thompson, G. (1996) *Globalization in Question*. Cambridge: Polity.

Howes, D. (1996) Commodities and cultural borders. In D. Howes (ed.), *Cross Cultural Consumption: Global Markets, Local Realities*, 1–18. London: Routledge.

ILO [International Labour Organisation] (2004) *A Fair Globalisation: Creating Opportunities for All*. Geneva: International Labour Office.

Inoguchi, T. (2000) National identity and adapting to integration: Nationalism and globalization in Japan. In L. Suryadinata (ed.), *Nationalism and Globalization: East and West*. Singapore: Institute of Southeast Asian Studies.

Jones, G., and Galvez-Muños, L. (eds) (2001) *Foreign Multinationals in the United States*. London: Routledge.

Kelsey, J. (2004) *At the Crossroads*. Wellington: Bridget Williams Books.

Kitney, D. (2001) Woodside: The verdict. Branch office shuts up shop. *Australian Financial Review*, April 24.

Krippendorf, K. (2004) *Content Analysis: An Introduction and Its Methodology.* Thousand Oaks, CA: Sage.

Lusk, P. (2001) Globalisation: The New Zealand Experience. *Asian Labour Update* 41: 1–3.

Marske, C. (1991) *Communities of Fate: Readings in the Social Organisation of Risk.* Lanham, MD: University Press of America.

Massey, D. (1994) *Space, Place and Gender.* Cambridge: Polity.

Massey, D. (2000) The geography of power. In B. Gunnell and D. Timms (eds), *After Seattle: Globalization and Its Discontents.* London: Catalyst.

Niedzielski, N., and Preston, D. (2000) *Folk Linguistics.* New York: Mouton de Gruyter.

Ohmae, K. (1995) *The End of the Nation State: The Rise of Regional Economies.* New York: Free Press.

Pennycook, A. (2007) *Global Englishes and Transcultural Flows.* London and New York: Routledge.

Potter, J., and Wetherell, M. (1987) *Discourse and Social Psychology.* London: Sage.

Prasad, E., and Rumbaugh, T. (2004) Overview. In E. Prasad (ed.), *China's Growth and Integration into the World Economy: Prospects and Challenges,* 1–4. Washington, DC: International Monetary Fund.

Preston, D. (1996) Whaddyaknow? The modes of folk linguistic awareness. *Language Awareness* 5: 40–74.

Pringle, T. (2001) The path of globalisation: Implications for Chinese workers. *Asian Labour Update* 41 (no page numbers).

Rumbaugh, T., and Blancher, N. (2004) International trade and the challenges of WTO accession. In E. Prasad (ed.), *China's Growth and Integration into the World Economy: Prospects and Challenges,* 5–13. Washington, DC: International Monetary Fund.

Ryan, J. (1999) Australia's globalisation: Cultural annihilation or cultural understanding? *Australian Folklore* 124: 86–97.

Sally, R. (2007) China and globalization. *Economic Affairs* 27: 82.

Sasaki, M. (2004) Globalization and national identity in Japan. *International Journal of Japanese Sociology* 13: 69–87.

Schaeffer, R. (2003) *Understanding Globalization: The Social Consequences of Political, Economic, and Environmental Change.* Lanham, MD: Rowman and Littlefield.

Scheve, K., and Slaughter, M. (2001) *Globalization and the Perceptions of American Workers.* Washington, DC: Institute for International Economics.

Scholte, J. (2000) *Globalisation: A Critical Introduction.* Basingstoke: Palgrave.

Scholte, J. (2002) What is globalization? The definitional issue – again. Centre for the Study of Globalisation and Regionalisation, Working Paper No. 109/02.

Sklair, L. (1999) Competing conceptions of globalization. *Journal of World-Systems Research* 2: 143–63.

Smith, E., and Mackie, D. (2000) *Social Psychology.* New York: Worth.

Szalay, L., and Deese, J. (1978) *Subjective Meaning and Culture: An Assessment through Word Associations.* Hillsdale, NJ: Erlbaum.

Rumbaugh, T., and Blancher, N. (2004) International trade and the challenges of WTO accession. In E. Prasad (ed.), *China's Growth and Integration into the World Economy: Prospects and Challenges,* 5–13. Washington, DC: International Monetary Fund.

Williams, A., Garrett, P., and Coupland, N. (1996) Perceptual dialectology, folklinguistics, and regional stereoptypes: Teachers' perceptions of variation in Welsh English. *Multilingua* 15: 171–97.

Wiseman, J. (1998) *Global Nation? Australia and the Politics of Globalisation.* Cambridge: Cambridge University Press.

Woodward, K. (2002) *Understanding Identity*. London: Arnold.

Worthington, G. (2001) *Globalisation: Perceptions and Threats to National Government in Australia*. Canberra: Department of the Parliamentary Library.

Yamashita, S., and Eades, J. (2003) *Globalization and Southeast Asia: Local,* *National and Transnational Perspectives*. New York: Berghahn Books.

Zimmerling, R. (2005) *Globalization and Democracy*. Tampere, Finland: Tampere University Press (The Tampere Club Series, Vol. 1).

21 Languages and Global Marketing

HELEN KELLY-HOLMES

Introduction

While McDonald's is widely regarded as an agent of global linguistic and cultural homogenization and as complicit in globalization processes of the worst kind, it was only in 2003 that the brand launched what it claimed to be its first global advertising theme: "i'm lovin' it" (Ives 2004). The decision to present the campaign as global had its genesis in an attempt to respond to exactly this type of positioning of McDonald's, by critics, as a negative agent of globalization, and also to respond to a feeling that the brand "has been rapidly becoming the international poster-brand for the costs and tragedy of people, especially children, getting fatter and sicker" (Kiley 2005). A global approach was deemed necessary to counteract the brand's image as "an exporter of sickness" and "the lead messenger of everything that is wrong with America" (ibid.). The launch of the integrated campaign in 2003 under the theme "It's what I eat and what I do [...] I'm lovin' it" was seen as "the beginning of the de-stinking process" (ibid.), and the global scale of the campaign was intended to match (or drown out) the increasing resonance of critics. "The 'i'm lovin' it' theme was designed to be integrated into every aspect of the business, from crew training and the overall restaurant experience to national sponsorships, promotions, television, Internet, merchandizing, and new local street marketing" (Rowley 2004: 230).

The message of the campaign is "connection with the customer" and it seeks to depict universal images of "how people live, what they love about life and what they love about McDonald's," promoting the brand's "core values" of "fun, family, community and social responsibility" (ibid.). At the center of the campaign, which has spearheaded McDonald's marketing and advertising for the last five years, is the "i'm lovin' it" slogan and graphic.

In this chapter I would like to explore the relationship between language(s) and global marketing practices, principally by using the "i'm lovin' it" campaign. There are three interconnected areas that I would like to focus on as having particular relevance for the sociolinguistic inputs and outcomes of the marketing

The Handbook of Language and Globalization, First Edition. Edited by Nikolas Coupland.
© 2013 Blackwell Publishing Ltd except for editorial material and organization © 2013 Nikolas Coupland. Published 2013 by Blackwell Publishing Ltd.

practices of global brands such as McDonald's: first of all, the issue of what constitutes 'global' marketing, which involves attempting to assess what makes something global, what the role of language is in this, and why/how McDonald's can claim "i'm lovin' it" as its first global slogan and integrated campaign; secondly, the issue of differentiation, and in particular of how global brands such as McDonald's seek to create a unique identity for themselves through particular linguistic choices; finally, the issue of segmentation in global marketing, and of how language is used as a means to segment markets.

Global Marketing

Generally, in exporting, the same product that is sold domestically is simply sold in the same format overseas, without great thought being given to adapatation of advertising and marketing. In international marketing, the export market is considered to have different needs from those of the domestic one (linguistic needs being among them), needs which call for a differentiated and localized strategy. Global marketing may, in practical terms, be very similar to old-fashioned export selling, in that the same product is sold at home and abroad in more or less the same way. However, the crucial difference is that the marketing strategy is conceived from the beginning as a global one, and all the decisions – including decisions about language – are supposed or deemed to be influenced by this factor. So, for example, the export of a German car to France with German slogans on the packaging and marketing material may simply be an oversight or the result of a non-decision in export sales, whereas in a global marketing strategy we might assume that this is the result of careful deliberation over how to differentiate this particular German brand from rivals and how to cash in on a German-language fetish associated with engineering and cars (see Kelly-Holmes 2005).

Consensus among marketing theorists is that exporting preceded international marketing (just as selling preceded marketing), and that global marketing is another advance on international marketing (for an overview, see for example de Mooij 2005). However, even though the development can be understood as a chronological one, 'straightforward' exporting still happens, as does international marketing. In fact, it is conceivable that one and the same brand or company could be involved in all three processes at the same time. Similarly, being involved in global or international marketing and advertising does not mean that domestic marketing and advertising are abandoned by strong domestic brands. For example, Guinness has managed to maintain a complex advertising portfolio on the Irish market, combining a number of levels: local, national, and global – all of which are experienced by the domestic consumer and all of which could be seen to present a hybrid identity.

A further feature of global marketing is that segmentation of the market (on which see below) is not supposed to take place primarily along geographic lines

– particularly not along the traditional delineators of national borders. Instead, it is Levitt's global village that is segmented, for example by age (Disney), by lifestyle or lifestyle aspiration (Nike), by sexuality and gender (Chanel perfumes), by income (Rolex watches), and by a whole host of other so-called psychographic features.

However, to what extent do these processes, beyond their discursive construction and packaging as 'global,' actually constitute universal, common, interconnected practices and processes? Yeung identifies "the discursive dimension of globalization" as one precondition for globalization and for legitimizing aspects of globalization "activities." Key to this discursive construction is the "mobilization of spatial metaphors and geographic imaginations," which "in turn shape social practices and empirical outcomes" (Yeung 2002: 287). The discourses of actors such as global marketers are "capable of producing significant material effects" and "fundamental in improving the political and social acceptance of economic globalization" (p. 292; see also Fairclough 2006 on this aspect). In this discursive construction three common features emerge, which are, again, common to 'global marketing' discourse. First of all, the notion that globalization is an external force. This has the result of constructing localities or internal relations (including domestic sociolinguistic conditions) as harmonious and comprehensible, in contrast to global or external relations, which are negative, incomprehensible, unaccountable, and uncontrollable. Secondly, globalization is constructed as natural, inevitable, irreversible, and historically determined. Thirdly, globalization is constructed as universal, a force with planetary reach, even though economic globalization as it is understood and practised requires the persistence of different conditions around the planet, and language is no exception here.

We can then validly posit the question as to whether brands such as McDonald's are creating or responding to globalization. Not surprisingly, the question is impossible to answer dichotomously, since, as Yeung points out, it is the actions of key agents – given the existence of specific preconditions – that shape praxis and constitute scalar relations. In his words, "their action – not economic globalization – accounts for empirical outcomes" (Yeung 2002: 291). In relation to language, we can see this perhaps most clearly with English, which has been anthropomorphized as an actor in and of itself, which is "out there," in some abstract sense, acting as "the killer language" (Skutnabb-Kangas 2000; Phillipson and Skutnabb-Kangas, this volume). However, if we look at the actions of agents who use English-language slogans because of the perception of the role of English as a global lingua franca and who are able to do so because of existing linguistic preconditions – many of which date from previous eras of globalization, for example the spread of English through colonization by the British Empire (for a particular perspective on the link between cultural, linguistic, and economic globalization in the context of India, see Pennycook 1994 and Robins 2006) – we can see that their actions effect sociolinguistic change and contribute to creating more favorable linguistic preconditions for other actors to use English in marketing, thus continuing the cycle.

Differentiation and Segmentation in Global Marketing

At the core of contemporary marketing practice lie two concepts, both of which are fundamentally linked to language. The first is differentiation, which involves the creation of a "unique selling proposition" for a brand or product, something that differentiates it from competitors. The second is segmentation, which involves dividing up global markets and consumers in order to create smaller markets that are loyal to this differentiated product or brand. Both differentiation and segmentation are driven by the contemporary market model of monopolistic competition. Monopolistic competition is a feature of late consumer society, whereby there are many producers of virtually the same product (say, running shoes). In order for consumers to differentiate between the many rows of running shoes they are faced with in shoe and sports shops, and in order for one particular type of running shoe to stand out, differentiation is necessary. Through marketing, a "unique selling proposition" (USP) is created for one particular product, encapsulated in the brand, packaging materials, advertising, and the like.

The USP can be seen as a fetish, something wholly symbolic, which is communicated by image, music, endorsement, celebrity, association, and language among many other elements. Through the creation of a USP and through differentiation, the marketer is seeking to create a small monopoly for the particular product or brand, a sub-market of the general market for running shoes, and the monopoly is then sustained by loyalty to the differentiated product. So, for a brand like Nike, the unique selling proposition is composed of, among many other things, the trademark "tick" or "swoosh," the slogan "just do it," and the association with tennis star Roger Federer, who wears the label, and with football teams such as Manchester United and Barcelona. All of these carefully chosen aspects – and many more – combine to create Nike's unique selling proposition.

Furthermore, marketers decide on a particular segment of the market at which to direct this differentiated product, since the entire market is simply too large. The segmentation can be based on any number of factors or combination of them – for instance age, gender, lifestyle, education, and language. Segmentation is also analogous to categorization in that it makes the market manageable for the marketer. It enables people to be categorized into groups, and these groups can be targeted with differentiated products, brands, messages, and so on through marketing of a USP. In this way marketers can create, through differentiation and segmentation, their own small monopoly, which they can then attempt to defend and exploit. The contemporary market is made up of many such small monopolies, each competing alongside rather than directly with each other, hence the phrase 'monopolistic competition.'

Language can be used in a variety of ways to differentiate a product and to become part of its USP (see Cook 2001; Myers 1994) – for example through the creation of a neologism as the product or brand name (like the 'iPod,' or the 'Wii'), or through the use of a word that has specific associations as a brand or product name (the 'O2' telecommunications brand, for instance, states a desire to be "a breath of fresh air" as part of its vision). In addition, brand names, slogans, and marketing texts such as advertisements can feature multilingual and heteroglossic play (see Martin 2006; Lee 2006; Bishop et al. 2005; Kelly-Holmes 2005; Ustinova and Bhatia 2005; Piller 2003; Haarmann 1989). Linguistic segmentation involves dividing up the market into speakers of different languages and creating glocalized marketing and advertising materials for these language groups. In practical terms, linguistic segmentation allows for communication with particular groups.

However, this practical concern may also have a symbolic input into the USP. For example, the need to speak the customer's language may not only be a marketing necessity, it may also be part of what differentiates a product or brand as being 'in touch with' and concerned about customers. Language, like lifestyle, can be an attractive differentiation and segmentation strategy, especially (though not exclusively) where speakers of a particular language are economically powerful, have activated language rights, and are protected by explicit language policies. For instance the provision, by a global brand, of advertising and product information in a peripheral rather than in a central language (De Swaan 2001, De Swaan this volume) may be motivated less by a desire to communicate a message that would not otherwise be understood, since speakers of peripheral languages tend by definition to be multilingual, than by a desire to be seen as sympathetic to speakers, to be supporting diversity, or simply to stand out as being different from other brands, particularly dominant national brands. For example two airlines, which specifically position themselves as 'European' (rather than national) and 'budget' – Ryanair and Easyjet – offer options in Catalan on their global websites, whereas the Spanish national carrier, Iberia, offers only Castilian/Spanish and English. So both the linguistic differentiation of the product or brand and the linguistic segmentation of markets and consumers can feed into the USP of the brand.

Linguistic differentiation and linguistic segmentation can be seen to contribute to and benefit from the competing forces of homogenization and heterogenization, which Appadurai (1996) sees as the defining feature of contemporary globalization. Linguistic differentiation is, on the surface and at the local level, a heterogenizing force: it introduces new linguistic elements into the local linguistic landscape (Landry and Bourhis 1997; Backhaus 2007; Gorter 2006; for a review and overview, see Coupland 2008) – elements which, in turn, index new associations. This process is perhaps best described by Haarmann's (1989) phrase "impersonal bilingualism," by which he means the practice of a type of multilingualism in advertising and marketing that has practically nothing to do with everyday lived multilingualism on the ground and everything to do with symbolic associations and a type of safely packaged and contained otherness (see Jaworski and Thurlow, this volume).

So, for instance, the use of French by a local coffee shop in Norway introduces more French into the linguistic landscape, thus diversifying it. Similarly, the use of French in advertising a perfume on a billboard in Australia interrupts the 'normal' linguistic landscape. However, linguistic differentiation is also homogenizing – in the first place because of the sheer reach and scale of global and international marketing efforts. If the same perfume ad is used not only in Australia, but also in Malaysia, the UK, Argentina, Finland, and so on, then what could be described as the global linguascape (Pennycook 2003) becomes more homogenized. This creates, for instance, a sameness about the commercial linguistic landscapes of cities across the world. Secondly, if the use of French in our Norwegian coffee shop is the result of a process of normativization, whereby French has become associated with coffee shops (over time, and not just in the last century), and this practice in turn influences other coffee shops to use French, then this normativization is also homogenizing. Coffee shops all over the worlds will adopt the same linguistic practices, using French in a "deterritorialised" (Tomlinson 1999) way.

Linguistic segmentation also contributes to the competing global currents of homogenization and heterogenizaion. On the one hand, speakers are categorized by different languages and addressed in an increasing variety of different languages – something which digital technology and associated media have made possible. For instance evidence shows that, in the provision of websites for marketing purposes, global brands are providing more sites, and text in more languages, and this is increasing (Kelly-Holmes 2006). In this way the global linguascape becomes more diverse. On the other hand, however, the role of English as a default lingua franca for global brands in many countries creates greater homogeneity in the same linguascape. These strategies of differentiation and segmentation become norms and commonsense practices, a type of normativity that inevitably results in and results from greater homogeneity and greater heterogeneity in the linguascape: more linguistic diversity is the result of more brands using linguistic diversity for segmentation and for differentiation; more linguistic homogeneity is the result of the homogenized and formulaic way in which this diversity is used, and of the normativity that develops around the use of certain languages as lingua francas in certain parts of the world, or around the use of English in large parts of the world. Put simply, there may be more languages – for example McDonald's and other global brands now provide websites in Arabic, a practice that has only become common in the last few years; and multilingual slogans are being used by a range of brands, for instance Kenzo perfumes and EDC clothing – but there is a sameness and predictability in the selection of languages and in their uses, alongside more English and more of the big supercentral languages, as De Swaan (2001 and this volume) has termed them.

Thus we can see a McDonaldization (Ritzer 1993) of the linguascape, whereby there is a samenesss and predictability in how we encounter different languages in commercial contexts, how they are used for differentiation, and how they are used for segmenting national and regional groups. These tensions also occur, of course, at the level of discourse: the global distribution of advertising slogans, formulaic, scripted marketing encounters (as work by Cameron 2000, Heller 2003, Heller this volume has shown), and the greater degree of manifest intertextuality

(Fairclough 1992), much of which has been spread by marketing practices, means on the one hand diversity in local discourse practices and on other greater homogenization at the national or international level.

Differentiation frequently involves heteroglossic play, code-switching and mixing, and non-standard usages, generally identified with individual language practices, which Shohamy (2006: 1) sees as "open, personal and dynamic." Segmentation, on the other hand, involves what Shohamy terms a "fixed" and "narrow" encoding of language for the purposes of "categorising group memberships, identities, hierarchies and a variety of other forms of imposition" (ibid.). On car manufacturer Seat's global site, we see multilingual play and a dynamic and open use of language for differentiation, in the form of a hand-written Spanish slogan "*auto emoçion*" on an otherwise English site. However, in segmentation and categorization – that is, in directing visitors to sites in other languages – we find a fairly rigid equation between language and country and a reinforcement of the principle of territoriality. A list of countries is provided on the Seat site, most of which lead to a linguistically localized site (thus the site for Lithuania is in Lithuanian; the site for Finland is in Finnish), and some of which lead to an English-language site (thus the site for Kuwait is in English). However, even where sites are offered in more than one language (for instance the Switzerland site is offered in German, French and Italian), these different language options are presented as parallel monolingual sites rather than as one mixed or multilingual site: there is an Italian Swiss site, a French Swiss site, and a German Swiss site, each of which excludes the other national languages. Thus, while linguistic differentiation and linguistic segmentation combine seemingly contradictory notions of language as being either "flexible" or "fixed" (Shohamy 2006), rather than leading to clashes (as she would predict), in global marketing these notions can co-exist easily, and actually they reinforce each other – something we shall see in particular in the "i'm lovin' it" example.

"i'm lovin' it"

In this section I would like to look at the McDonald's "i'm lovin' it" campaign in terms of its discursive construction of globalization; its use of linguistic differentiation; and its approach to linguistic segmentation.

Construction of globalization through "i'm lovin' it"

From the outset, as highlighted above, the "i'm lovin' it" campaign was constructed as global, the company describing it as McDonald's first global advertising theme. The description of the campaign as global and its publicizing as such can be seen to contribute to actually making it global. For the individual, there is no way of knowing if this campaign is happening and being experienced universally and equally. The use of the descriptor 'global' fetishizes and hides the actual piece-by-piece work of creating all of the advertising and packaging, picking the markets, deciding on the order of markets to launch in, transporting materials, producing and sourcing them locally, adhering to local language and trading regimes and regulations and so on – all of the minutiae that make an international or global presence possible and also comprehensible. Instead, "i'm lovin it" becomes something that is 'out there': universal, inevitable and uncontrollable, driven by an external force, not by many different and very tangible social actors. In this way, we can see the perlocutionary force of global marketing discourse: by declaring the campaign a 'global' one, the campaign becomes global, and if this becoming is perhaps in perception only, then that is sufficient, and indeed perfectly compatible with how globalization is understood or, more accurately, not understood. In this way the social actors who create the "i'm lovin' it" campaign also create globalization.

As Yeung (2002) has pointed out in relation to the discursive construction of globalization, the global is necessarily constructed as abstract and 'out there,' making the local, by default, harmonious and concrete. The abstract and global "i'm lovin' it" campaign enables the brand to reinforce the local as harmonious and 'straightforward.' The following quote from the McDonald's USA website illustrates this juxtaposition well:

> 'havin' fun: McDonald's is one of life's many small pleasures that millions of people around the world enjoy every day. Great food. Fun to eat. Casual environment. Local and familiar. And always something new. (www.mcdonalds.com/usa/fun.html)

We can see how the text manages to construct McDonald's as a global giant in the abstract sense ("millions of people around the world"), and at the same time as the opposite – even the antidote – to this and something that anchors the individual in what Giddens (2002) terms this "runaway world," for example through the use of colloquial American English ("havin' fun") and references to "small," "casual," and "local and familiar."

A second key element in the campaign's discursive construction of globalization is its utilization of spatial and geographical metaphors associated with globalization (see Yeung 2002). The central graphic image of the campaign, reproduced on packaging materials and so on, has been a sphere, colored in with the multilingual "i'm lovin' it" graphic (see below for discussion). The graphics within the campaign have exploited the combination of iconic metaphors of globalization, for example, mobile phones, sky scraper landscapes, boats, and other means of transport, with the multilingual wallpaper – multilingualism itself having become a metaphor of globalization. In this way, the multilingualism graphic is used to allude to geographical–spatial metaphors which are generally utilized in making globalization real and in legitimizing the activities of global actors.

Another element in the discursive construction of globalization is in the choice of the first person singular in the advertisement's slogan. Friedman (2006) has differentiated eras of globalization in relation to the key social actors, as follows: "globalization 1.0," as he terms it, was driven by states (in the colonial era), while in "globalization 2.0," the key actors were companies. The contemporary era of globalization ("globalization 3.0," which Friedman dates from around 2000) is for him driven by individuals, principally through new digital media:

> Globalization 3.0 is shrinking the world from a size small to a size tiny and flattening the playing field at the same time [...] the force that gives it its unique character is the newfound power for individuals to collaborate and compete globally. [...] Globalization 3.0 is going to be more and more driven not only by individuals but also by a much more diverse, non-Western, non-white – group of individuals. (Friedman 2006: 10–11)

Globalization in such a scheme is constructed as an individualistic process, a means of self-actualization, rather than a way for the individual to comprehend or gain mastery over the abstract 'out there' process. Rather than a call to universal brotherhood or to global solidarity, we can recall that the full slogan for this intentionally global campaign is: "It's what I eat and what I do: i'm lovin' it." This emphasis on the individual is enhanced by other aspects of the marketing; for instance in the linguistic segmentation on its global dot.com site, users pick the country site they wish to visit under the drop-down heading: "I'm going to McDonald's."

Linguistic differentiation and segmentation in "i'm lovin' it"

Language is a key tool for differentiating and segmenting in McDonald's most recent campaign, and both the segmenting and the differentiating strategies, although seeming to contradict each other, actually reinforce and complement each other and an existing order. The most obvious element in differentiation is the creation of the "i'm lovin' it" slogan itself. The slogan involves the linguistic choice of non-standard orthography and grammar – the first person 'I' is written with a small case 'i'; the 'g' is dropped from 'loving,' reflecting spoken speech; and 'love' is used in the continuous present tense ('I am loving') instead of its 'standard' usage in the simple present tense ('I love'). The slogan contains any number of allusions: first of all it alludes to spoken rather than written language, even though that spoken language is then codified in written form and conse-quently upscaled (Blommaert et al. 2005) by the brand; secondly, the slogan seems to allude to the "local and familiar," the comprehensible domestic sphere in a globalizing world, particularly for the domestic audience in the USA; thirdly, the slogan may index American English for other speakers of English around the world; in this way the local becomes scaled up (ibid.) to have global meaning – which is further reinforced by the choice of American singer and global pop star and 'heartthrob' Justin Timberlake to sing the "i'm lovin' it" song; fourthly, there also seems to be another allusion to the global, namely through hip hop language, albeit at the very anodyne end of the lyrics continuum (for a discussion of these issues, see Pennycook 2007). As pointed out earlier, the social actors who utilize global scales also, through their actions, create these global scales that enable 'deterritorialized' flows along the 'linguascape' – flows that both exploit and reinforce this linguascape. So McDonald's is on the one hand exploiting the upscaling of urban vernacular through the hip hop movement and industry, and on the other creating new scales for this type of language by using it in a global advertising campaign.

The second differentiating feature is the fetishizing of multilingualism through the creation of the multilingual graphic which features versions of the "i'm lovin' it" slogan in English and seven other languages – namely Arabic, Chinese, French, German, Tagalog, Turkish, and Ukrainian. Norman Fairclough and other discourse analysts urge us not to look just at what is in the text, but, sometimes more importantly, at what is missing, since this can provide the key to understanding the power relations and ideologies at work. The omission of other languages, it could be argued, amounts to their silencing (Butler 1997). The languages chosen are all official languages in one or many countries in the world. They are among the biggest languages in the world, all belonging to most estimations of the top ten languages in the world, the exceptions being Turkish, Tagalog/Filipino and Ukrainian; and again all, with the exception of these three, are considered by De Swaan in his "world language system" to be supercentral languages – so we would perhaps expect them to be chosen. However, a range of other languages, obviously large or supercentral, are missing, for example Hindi. The decision not to opt for Hindi, despite its being undisputably one of the world's largest languages and despite its having (on De Swaan's thesis) the greatest communicative value in the Indian language constellation, ties in with McDonald's linguistic segmentation strategy for India, which involves the use of English as a 'neutral' option (see Cheshire and Moser 1994 on the use of English as a neutral advertising option in Switzerland). Without input from McDonald's (which they decline to give), we can only remain at the level of speculation as to the choice of these four supercentral and three central languages (De Swaan 2001), and as to whether graphic considerations – the visual impression created by the particular combination – and/or domestic, international, or local, political or business concerns govern the inclusion or exclusion of certain languages.

A third feature of the campaign that contributes both to differentiating the brand and to segmenting the market along linguistic lines is the use of localized slogans for some markets and for some languages. Although I have been talking about the original English slogan, the global campaign was actually launched in Germany and used the German version, *"ich liebe es,"* the English version being launched a few weeks later. So segmentation was central to the campaign from the beginning and inherently it tied up with the brand's differentiating strategy. The original English slogan was used in most countries, but not in all, localized versions being developed for Latvian, Ukrainian, Polish, Spanish (with a slightly different version in Chile and Argentina), and Portuguese. It is also worth noting that the French slogan for Canada (*"c'est ça que j'm"* – and sometimes simply *"j'm"*) was different from the French slogan used in France and in the multilingual graphic (*c'est tout ce que j'aime*). There are a number of seeming anomalies worth pointing out in this 'glocalization' strategy: for example a German slogan was used in Germany, while the English version was used in Austria. Similarly, the Spanish version was used in South and Central America and also in certain parts of the USA, but the English version was used in Spain; and the Portuguese version was used in Brazil, but not in Portugal. The use of Spanish in the continental American campaign (north, center, and south), but not in the symbolic representation of global multilingualism, could perhaps signal a repositioning of the language, by the brand, as domestic rather than international – an important gesture in a contested situation, and evidence perhaps of an upscaling of Spanish in the USA. In some cases, the localized version was used on its own, while in others it was used in a parallel bilingual slogan, along with the English version.

Also, although the English slogan was used in a lot of countries which belong to Kachru's (1990) "inner circles" (for example the USA, Ireland, UK, Australia, New Zealand) and "outer circles" (for example India, Hong Kong, Indonesia, Malaysia, Singapore), it was equally widely used in expanding country circles (Denmark, Greece, Italy, Japan, South Korea). Likewise, there was no 'European' policy, some European countries getting a localized version and others having the English version. Furthermore, even though in Ireland, for example, the campaign was primarily presented via international or American English, radio advertisements featured a speaker of Dublin English, who rendered the slogan in her particular accent. In this way the abstract global and the familiar local can be simultaneously indexed, and homogenizing and heterogenizing effects can arise from one and the same campaign.

Multilingualism as depicted in the graphic is, however, I would argue, primarily associated with foreignness – with other countries, exotic places, and foreign languages spoken in foreign places. The day-to-day contact with these languages, and with multilingualism in general, in the individual's own country is not addressed or alluded to at all. As mentioned earlier, the campaign was launched in Germany under the German version of the slogan, 'localized' for that country. This effectively reinforces the Germany = German-speaking equation and silences or negates that country's extensive multilingualism. The Turkish 'spoken' in the multilingualism graphic is being spoken in Istanbul, not in Berlin. This visualization of multilingualism as parallel and neatly ordered monolingualisms avoids complex multilingualism and thus ultimately supports a monolingual ideology and the Herderian concept of one people speaking one language in one country.

Furthermore, this global campaign combines two seemingly opposing indexes of globalization: English as global lingua franca and multilingualism. If McDonald's were pursuing a straightforward globalization (one world = one market), then the brand might be expected to use only the English-language version in its advertising slogan. Likewise, a genuine belief in a type of commercial universalism would make the symbolic exploitation of multilingualism unlikely, since drawing attention to the multilingual nature of the globe also draws attention to difference and heterogeneity and to the fact that we might not all be one big happy family speaking the same language. If McDonald's were pursuing a true glocalization policy (Robertson 1992), then we might expect localized versions for all of the company's markets. We would also not expect a certain number of languages to be singled out for symbolizing global multilingualism. It would seem much more likely that the brand would either use every single language in the world in the graphic or only one – or none. A glocalized approach should, according to marketing and cultural theorists, respond to local sensitivities; a global one should disregard them. The "i'm lovin' it" campaign does neither to a complete extent, and the campaign, although described as global, like so many globalization processes, actually relies on different sociolinguistic conditions across the world (see Blommaert 2003, and this volume; Yeung 2002).

Finally, all of these practices can be seen to be homogenizing and heterogenizing. On the one hand, the use of English for the campaign in a large number of countries would seem to have a homogenizing effect on the global linguascape; however, in countries where English is not the main first or second language, the local linguistic landscape becomes more diverse through more English. The type of English used may be different, given its grammatical and orthographical deviations from written standards, and its reflection of 'spoken,' casual, vernacular language could also be seen to be heterogenizing; however, the spread of this spoken, casual, vernacular variety to different parts of the world creates a global homogenizing effect.

Discussion

In his critique of Ritzer's McDonaldization thesis, Kellner (1999) warns against dismissing the activities of McDonald's and of similar corporations as simply globalizing and homogenizing and points instead to the homogenization/heterogenization that lies at the heart of McDonald's practices. According to him, the McDonaldization thesis

> underplays the ways that McDonald's is an ideological and cultural phenomenon, as well as an economic and sociological set of practices […] Ritzer does not really engage the specifically cultural dimension of the operation. In Weberian terms, he neglects the charisma of the Golden Arches, Ronald McDonald and McDonaldland, the tie-ins and promotions, and the ubiquitous advertising, aimed at a variety of gender, race, class, and national subject positions. (Kellner 1999: 189)

If we want to avoid the danger of simply mystifying the social actors and processes at the heart of globalization even further, by dismissing them as a homogenizing force that is "out there," engaged in a "process of worldwide lingua-cultural homogenization" (Blommaert 2003: 611), what other insights can help us to move forward in our understanding of the linguistic dimensions of global marketing?

Coupland (2003) sees the foundational insight in globalization theory for sociolinguists as the "outgrowing" by private companies such as McDonald's of their domestic markets and their capacity "as new 'multinational' or 'transnational' or 'global' forces, reshaping community life" (Coupland 2003: 467). This outgrowing can be seen not only in terms of saturation (that is, of brands having to move on because the domestic market is saturated), but also (or even more so) in terms of an outgrowing of the confines of state jurisdiction and control – including language regimes. Coupland goes on to highlight the sociolinguistic consequences of this as follows:

> capital and investment can now be shifted unpredictably between sites in response to market forces, wrecking the stability of 'modernist' production-based economies and the social and sociolinguistic structures which they generated. (Coupland 2003: 467)

Just as flows of capital, investment, trade, and labor have the capacity "to both improve and destabilize an economy" (Sharma 2008: 13), so too do "deterritorialised" (Tomlinson 1999) flows of language have the capacity to both reinforce and simultaneously undermine existing language regimes and relationships, to heterogenize and homogenize, and to destabilize sociolinguistic structures.

Braj Kachru points out that "English comes through channels which bypass the strategies devised by language planners" (Kachru 1996: 137). However, this applies not just to English, but to all of the deterritorialized bits of language which travel through channels created by global brands. These deterritorialized bits of language in turn become part of new sociolinguistic contexts, which means for sociolinguists that the notion of impersonal bilingualism (Haarmann 1989) must be constantly revisited. As Blommaert points out, the key to understanding

> the processes of "globalised" insertion of varieties into newly stratified orders of indexicality, is to discover what such reorderings of repertoires actually mean, and represent, to people. (Blommaert 2003: 609).

A way of showing in more explicit terms the interdependence between these 'insertions,' 'deterritorializations,' and 'destabilizations' and economic and marketing processes, and of keeping a check on our own need to revisit them constantly, might be to borrow two concepts from economics in order to discuss these linguistic processes. The first is the notion of reflexivity and the second is internationalization.

As Bryant (2002) highlights, financier, philanthropist, and economist Soros is not the first to have used or derived the notion of reflexivity (for example Giddens, Beck, and others have found it useful in their work). However, Soros (1987, 1994) has used reflexivity to explain the workings of global markets, and for this reason his work seems to me to have particular potential for explaining the linguistic actions of global marketers. Soros has challenged ruling economic orthodoxy by arguing that demand and supply are not given or objective, and, far from determining how markets develop, it is the other way around – market developments determine demand and supply. Participants in economic processes inevitably and unavoidably shape and determine the outcome of those economic processes, and also create the conditions for the future development of those market processes. This particular insight, I would argue, can help us to understand and develop further the notion of normativity in global linguistic practices, particularly when these are linked to economic processes.

As mentioned earlier, the social actors involved in globalization not only use scales, which in turn create linguistic hierarchies; they, by their actions, also create these scales. As an example, a recent advertisement by global brand Carlsberg in Ireland used the Irish language. According to a source in Diageo, the global drinks company that owns Guinness, the marketing team, a very small group of individuals, felt that Irish is becoming 'trendy' and that an advertisement in Irish would work well (see Kelly-Holmes 2010). By using Irish in an advertisement for a global beer brand, these social actors have created a new scale for the language and have also created the conditions whereby more Irish can be used in future advertisements – they have started a trend. We can equate this decision to that of stock brokers, who largely act on their intuitions, but who in turn create conditions for those intuitions to be successful now and in the future.

Similarly, we can see in the linguistic choices made in the "i'm lovin' it campaign" how a social actor like Mcdonald's uses English because of a feeling that there is a demand for English in global advertising – despite the gap between this perception and actual reality in terms of knowledge of the language in many of the countries in which the English language slogan is used – something Soros calls a "fertile fallacy." These decisions then create the conditions for the success of this and future campaigns, and create scales which allow trends to flourish. The multilingualism graphic, for instance, was imitated by rival brand Burger King in its marketing, the English slogan "have it your way" being rendered into a number of languages and used in a similar way to the multilingual "i'm lovin' it" graphic.

Soros tells us that, in order to be successful, a financial hypothesis does not necessarily have to be true, real, or accurate – it just has to become accepted. We might usefully adapt this statement to the notion of a linguistic or sociolinguistic hypothesis, as formulated by global marketers. A linguistic hypothesis formulated by a small group of social actors that posits, for instance, that the insertion of German will help to differentiate their particular brand of car then becomes a trend, which is followed and becomes self-validating. It does not have to be true or real or accurate (the car may not even be made in Germany); but, if the association becomes accepted, then it can be successful. This type of acceptance and success leads to trends that are followed. More marketers uses German to differentiate their cars, so there is greater acceptance of German in the marketing of cars. In this way more competition (monopolistic competition, as discussed above) leads to more sameness: marketers imitate what is already being done linguistically by other marketers, with minute differences.

Turning to the second idea, namely internationalization, its main contribution is as an economic theory that challenges the globalization paradigm. According to the internationalization perspective, what we are actually experiencing is an increase in the volume and intensity of overall trade internationally, but without any change in underlying structures, hierarchies, and power relations – something globalization theorists would argue is happening. Most important from the point of view of the current analysis is the argument that economic internationalization does nothing to challenge the nation-state paradigm, and in fact takes it as its fundamental tenet.

Leaving aside its global marketing rhetoric and its positioning as a global force, McDonald's, far from being a 'born global' brand, conceived from the outset as having universal appeal, is instead an American brand that has been successfully exported. The brand's pattern of expansion overseas has been described as a process of internationalization, with the company treading carefully through more charted, familiar, and geographically proximal territory first (Vignalli 2001). While McDonald's has a number of iconic menu items and a standardized kitchen layout and processes, it also has a geographically differentiated pricing system and localized menus, which take cultural and religious differences into account. Training in its Chicago 'Hamburger University' is provided in twenty-two languages, not in English only, and advertising is localized to greater or lesser degrees in different markets – this being sometimes a local decision, sometimes a central one. Vignalli's analysis of McDonald's marketing mix found that it combined elements of globalization and internationalization, and could be adapted to local needs where this was sufficiently demanded (for instance by legislation, by pressure, and so on). "In a communications context, the maxim 'brand globally, advertise locally' […] is the McDonald's promotional strategy" (Vignalli 2001: 104). And language, both in differentiation and in segmentation, is a key factor in this negotiation and delicate balancing between global and 'local,' as the "i'm lovin' it" campaign shows. As Meyerhoff and Niedzielski (2003) point out in relation to globalization and language, "it is hard to think of clear linguistic examples of invariant transfer" (p. 538).

Rather than creating a brave new world of no borders, I would argue that the McDonald's "i'm lovin' it" campaign serves instead to reinforce borders drawn by linguistic differentiation and by languages afforded status particularly by national governments. On its corporate homepage, for example, which is intended as its world site, one is immediately directed to specific country homepages. There is no attempt to address individuals in a homogeneous or universal way. This desire to categorize individuals by country and to provide country-specific information is common to almost all of the largest brands in the world, and the World Wide Web has created greater opportunities for segmentation and localization, particularly in respect of national European languages (see Kelly-Holmes 2006). It could be argued that McDonald's is an inherently conservative company and it is not about to bring about a new world order – it needs nation–states and the stability and security which they afford, and strong national languages are a key part of this. The campaign reinforces the idea of monolingualism as norm, that one country equals one language, and that multilingualism is a deviation from this norm.

Conclusion

Language, as the "i'm lovin' it" campaign shows, represents a key preoccupation of the social actors involved in global marketing. Language is the main tool by which McDonald's creates the reality of its global campaign (mystifying the process and the painstaking steps involved in constructing a force that is 'out there' in international marketing), while at the same time keeping it familiar and comprehensible to domestic (the USA) and local audiences (its target markets). Through its linguistic differentiation and segmentation strategies, the campaign combines and balances the competing forces of homogenization and heterogenization, reflexively exploiting and creating the necessary conditions for future campaigns. Far from creating a new linguistic world order, the campaign, although on the one hand destabilizing linguistic orders that were the result of modernist projects, actually reconfirms these orders to a large extent, at least for economically prosperous countries, where the destabilization is safely confined. The "i'm lovin' it" campaign shows that we are only at the beginning in terms of trying to understand the sociolinguistic inputs and outcomes of global marketing and highlights the need for detailed examination of these activities on a case-by-case basis.

REFERENCES

Appadurai, A. (1996) *Modernity at Large: Cultural Dimensions of Globalization*. Minneapolis: University of Minnesota Press.

Backhaus, P. (2007) *Linguistic Landscapes: A Comparative Analysis of Urban Multilingualism in Tokyo*. Clevedon: Multilingual Matters.

Bishop, H., Coupland, N., and Garrett, P. (2005) Globalisation, advertising and shifting values for Welsh and Welshness: The case of Y Drych. *Multilingua* 24(4): 343–78.

Blommaert, J. (2003) Commentary: A sociolinguistics of globalization. *Journal of Sociolinguistics* 7(4): 607–23.

Blommaert, J., Collins, J., and Slembrouck, S. (2005) Spaces of multilingualism. *Language and Communication* 25: 107–216.

Bryant, C. G. A. (2002) George Soros's theory of reflexivity: A comparison with the theories of Giddens and Beck and a consideration of its practical value. *Economy and Society* 31(1): 112–31.

Butler, J. (1997) *Excitable Speech: A Politics of the Performative*. New York and London: Routledge.

Cameron, D. (2000) Styling the worker: Gender and the commodification of language in the globalized service economy. *Journal of Sociolinguistics* 4(3): 323–47.

Cheshire, J., and Moser, L.-M. (1994) English as a cultural symbol: The case of advertisements in French-speaking Switzerland. *Journal of Multilingual and Multicultural Development* 15(6): 451–69.

Cook, G. (2001) *The Discourse of Advertising*, 2nd edn. London: Routledge.

Coupland, N. (2003) Introduction: Sociolinguistics and globalization. *Journal of Sociolinguistics* 7(4): 465–72.

Coupland, N. (2008) Review of P. Bakhaus (2007), *Linguistic Landscapes: A*

Comparative Analysis of Urban Multilingualism in Tokyo, Clevedon: Multilingual Matters, and of D. Gorter (ed.) (2006), *Linguistic Landscape: A New Approach to Multilingualism*, Clevedon: Multilingual Matters. *Journal of Sociolinguistics* 12(2): 250–4.

De Mooij, M. (2005) *Global Marketing and Advertising: Understanding Cultural Paradoxes*. Thousand Oaks, CA: Sage.

De Swaan, A. (2001) *Words of the World: The Global Language System*. Cambridge: Polity.

Fairclough, N. (1992) *Discourse and Social Change*. Cambridge: Polity.

Fairclough, N. (2006) *Language and Globalization*. London and New York: Routledge.

Friedman, T. L. (2006) *The World is Flat: The Globalized World in the Twenty-First Century*. London and New York: Penguin.

Giddens, A. (2002) *Runaway World: How Globalization is Reshaping our Lives*. London: Routledge.

Gorter, D. (ed.) (2006) *Linguistic Landscape: A New Approach to Multilingualism*. Clevedon: Multilingual Matters.

Haarmann, H. (1989) *Symbolic Values of Foreign Language Use, From the Japanese Case to a General Sociolinguistic Perspective*. Berlin and New York: Mouton de Gruyter.

Heller, M. (2003) Globalization, the new economy and the commodification of language and identity. *Journal of Sociolinguistics* 7(4): 473–92.

Ives, N. (2004) For McDonald's, the "I'm lovin' it" phrase of its new campaign has crossed over into the mainstream. *New York Times*, May 13, 2004. Available at: http://query.nytimes.com/gst/fullpage.html?res=9A04E4D8113CF930A25756C0A9629C8B63andsec=andspon=andpagewanted=2 (accessed on July 8, 2009).

Kachru, B. (1990) World Englishes and applied linguistics. *World Englishes* 9(1): 3–20.

Kachru, B. (1996) World Englishes: Agony and ecstasy. *Journal of Aesthetic Education* 30(2): 135–55.

Kellner, D. (1999) Theorising/resisting McDonaldization: A Multi-perspectivist Approach. In B. Smart (ed.), *Resisting Mcdonaldization*, 186–206. Thousand Oaks, CA and London: Sage.

Kelly-Holmes, H. (2005) *Advertising as Multilingual Communication*. Basingstoke and New York: Palgrave Macmillan.

Kelly-Holmes, H. (2006) Multilingualism and commercial language practices on the internet. *Journal of Sociolinguistics* 10(4): 507–19.

Kelly-Holmes, H. (2010) Rethinking the macro–micro relationship: Some insights from the marketing domain. *International Journal of the Sociology of Language* 202: 25–40.

Kiley, D. (2005) McDonald's new campaign is the appearance of a good start. *Business Week*, March 9, 2005. Available at: http://www.businessweek.com/the_thread/brandnewday/archives/2005/03/mcdonalds_new_c.html (accessed on July 8, 2009).

Landry, R., and Bourhis, R. Y. (1997) Linguistic landscape and ethnolinguistic vitality: An empirical study. *Journal of Language and Social Psychology* 16(1): 23–49.

Lee, J. S. (2006) Linguistic constructions of modernity: English mixing in Korean television commercials. *Language in Society* 35(1): 59–91.

Martin, E. (2006) *Marketing Identities through Language: English and Global Imagery in French Advertising*. Basingstoke and New York: Palgrave Macmillan.

Meyerhoff, M., and Niedzielski, N. (2003) The globalization of vernacular variation. *Journal of Sociolinguistics* 7(4): 534–55.

Myers, G. (1994) *Words in Ads*. London: Edward Arnold.

Pennycook, A. (2003) Global Englishes, Rip Slyme and performativity. *Journal of Sociolinguistics* 7(4): 513–33.

Pennycook, A. (1994) *The Cultural Politics of English as an International Language*. London: Longman.

Pennycook, A. (2007) *Global Englishes and Transcultural Flows*. London and New York: Routledge.

Piller, I. (2003) Advertising as a site of language contact. *Annual Review of Applied Linguistics* 23: 170–83.

Ritzer, G. (1993) *The McDonaldization of Society: An Investigation into the Changing Character of Contemporary Social Life*. Thousand Oaks, CA: Pine Forge Press.

Robertson, R. (1992) *Globalization: Social Theory and Global Culture*. London: Sage.

Robins, N. (2006) *The Corporation That Changed the World: How the East India Company Shaped the Modern Multinational*. London: Pluto Press.

Rowley, J. (2004) Online branding: The case of McDonalds. *British Food Journal*. 106(3): 228–37.

Sharma, S. D. (2008) The many faces of today's globalization: A survey of recent literature. *New Global Studies* 2(2): Article 4.

Shohamy, E. (2006) *Language Policy: Hidden Agendas and New Approaches*. London and New York: Routledge.

Skutnabb-Kangas, T. (2000) *Linguistic Genocide in Education – Or Worldwide Diversity and Human Rights?* New York: Lawrence Erlbaum.

Soros, G. (1987) *The Alchemy of Finance: Reading the Mind of the Market*. New York: John Wiley.

Soros, G. (1994) The theory of reflexivity. Lecture delivered to the MIT Department of Economics World Economy Laboratory Conference, Washington, DC. Available at: http://www.geocities.com/ecocorner/intelarea/gs1.html (accessed on July 8, 2009).

Tomlinson, J. (1999) *Globalization and Culture*. Cambridge: Polity.

Ustinova, I., and Bhatia, T. K. (2005) Convergence of English in Russian TV commercials. *World Englishes* 24(4): 495–508.

Vignalli, C. (2001) McDonald's: "Think Global, Act Local" – The marketing mix. *British Food Journal* 103(2): 97–111.

Yeung, H. W. (2002) The limits to globalization theory: A geographic perspective on global economic change. *Economic Geography* 78(3): 285–305.

Part IV Language, Distance, and Identities

22 Shadows of Discourse: Intercultural Communication in Global Contexts

CLAIRE KRAMSCH AND ELIZABETH BONER

Introduction

In his recent book *Global Shadows. Africa in the Neo-Liberal World Order* (2006), anthropologist James Ferguson focuses our attention on the global areas of poverty that underlie the world's global networks, particularly in Africa: the invisible shadows of political–economic inequality, the discontinous hops rather than continuous flows of capital, the spatial and material disjunctures that globalization depends upon and in some ways helps to produce. A shadow, he notes, is not only darkness and invisibility but a kind of doubling, a copy of the original, like a parallel economy alongside the official one, or a private irregular army alongside the legitimate national army. Ferguson writes: "A shadow in this sense is not simply a negative space, a space of absence; it is a likeness, an inseparable other-who-is-also-oneself to whom one is bound" (Ferguson 2006: 17). He urges those who study the effects of globalization in places like Africa to center "less on transnational flows and images of unfettered connection than *on the social relations that selectively constitute global society*" (p. 23, our emphasis).

In the present chapter we examine how global society is selectively constituted through words and their shadows in intercultural discourse. The field of research in intercultural communication (IC) provides a good point of departure (see Kotthoff and Spencer-Oatey 2007). Putting aside the work done in cross-cultural psychology, intercultural management training, and intercultural learning, which deals with stable group memberships and pre-existing cultural characteristics (see Kramsch 2002a), many of the analytical tools developed in cross-cultural pragmatics and discourse studies (Blum-Kulka et al. 1989, Gumperz and Levinson 1996, Scollon and Scollon 2001) will be of use in studying the way interlocutors, in verbal exchanges, constitute the global world order. We will look for contextualization cues (Gumperz 1992), indexicality (Ochs 1996), and other discourse features

The Handbook of Language and Globalization, First Edition. Edited by Nikolas Coupland.
© 2013 Blackwell Publishing Ltd except for editorial material and organization © 2013 Nikolas Coupland.
Published 2013 by Blackwell Publishing Ltd.

that construct the context in which the interactions unfold among co-present interlocutors.

But to identify the shadows Ferguson refers to, we will need to draw on critical discourse studies that go beyond the speech event and co-presence. Researchers in this strand of IC research use concepts like intertextuality and interdiscursivity (Hanks 1996, Fairclough 2006: 168) to account for the fact that discourses refer to one another across contexts, and contexts themselves get transformed and resemi-oticized by one another across cultures. Researchers have focused on a variety of "intertexts" (Hanks 2000: 13) – that is, discourses whose meaning potential is realized in the context of other discourses, which we could call 'shadows': the instrumentalized, commodified discourse, which masquerades as genuine discourse in a communication culture (Cameron 2000); the technologized discourse of invisible ideology (Fairclough 1989); the naturalized discourse of the new fast capitalism, which mimicks the vernacular discourse of everyday life (Gee et al. 1997); the performative discourse, which empties words of their referential meanings and transforms utterances into ideologically correct performances (Yurchak 2006).

This work, however, does not necessarily apply to contexts in which local social actors engage in interactions that have global consequences and engage others on a global scale. What is the nature of intercultural communication when it constructs both local and global realities, and what is the best way to study it? Given the dual meaning Ferguson gives to the term 'shadow,' as both invisibile and inseparable double, we can expect discourse relations among global and local actors to be relations of power, where power is diffuse and an object of struggle across various scales of time and space. Such a Foucauldian view of discourse calls for a postmodern approach to intercultural communication, which takes into account the style shifts through which speakers perform a variety of identities so that they may deal with unequal and conflicting contexts on multiple timescales (Blommaert 2005: 232).

We first give a few operational definitions of globalization and examine what they mean for the relation between language and globalization. We then focus on a specific case of global intercultural communication, which took place in Tanzania between American representatives of a US-based NGO and Tanzanian representatives of local NGOs, working in partnership to develop environmentally friendly businesses. The contestation that took place around the neo-liberal discourse of globalization in these encounters can help us tease out the paradoxes of intercultural communication in global contexts.

Intercultural Communication in a Global Age

We start with three statements that capture some of the major aspects of the relation between language and intercultural communication in global contexts. They come respectively from an applied linguist, an historian, and a large American philanthropic organization that funds development projects around the world.

The first quotation is taken from Alastair Pennycook's *Global Englishes and Transcultural Flows* (2007):

> Globalization may be better understood as a compression of time and space, an intensification of social economic, cultural and political relations, a series of global linkages that render events in one location of potential and immediate importance in other, quite distant locations. [...] To view culture and language in terms only of reflections of the economic is to miss the point that new technologies and communications are enabling immense and complex flows of people, signs, sounds, images across multiple borders in multiple directions [...] resulting in changing practices in the new 'educational contact zones,' and new, appropriated knowledges traveling across borders. (Pennycook 2007: 25)

> The multidimensional nature of both dominating modes of globalization – corporatization, capitalization, conceptualization – and of resistant and localizing modes – transculturation, translocalization, transformation – leads to very different linguistic and cultural practices than international domination or national localization. (Ibid., p. 24)

This definition of globalization shows how the notion of context, essential to any analysis of discourse, has itself become problematic, since it is no longer bounded by the usual axes of space and time. Participants in conversation orient to events in quite distant locations, which are often invisible. Language loses its one-to-one correspondence between signs and referents as signs and sounds are resignified; knowledge is transformed as it gets translocalized and saturated with different contexts. In settings that involve global actors – that is, representatives of multinational institutions or individuals engaging with each other on a global scale, through internet technologies – linguistic and cultural practices might have to be seen as different from communication in national or international contexts – and different not just in degree, but also in kind.

The second quotation is taken from Tony Judt's (2007) summary of Robert Reich's argument in his book *Supercapitalism: The Transformation of Business, Democracy, and Everyday Life* (2007).

> Thanks to technologies initially supported by or spun off from cold-war research projects – such as computers, fiber optics, satellites, and the Internet – commodities, communications, and information now travel at a vastly accelerated pace. Regulatory structures set in place over the course of a century or more were superseded or dismantled within a few years. In their place came increased competition both for global markets and for the cataract of international funds chasing lucrative investments [...] Competition and innovation generated new opportunities for some and vast pools of wealth for a few; meanwhile they destroyed jobs, bankrupted firms, and impoverished communities [...] The notion of the 'common good' has disappeared. (Judt 2007: 22)

Judt focuses here on the social and political consequences of global capitalism: the speed of change, the exacerbated competition and constant innovation, the crucial importance of networking, fundraising, and the growing role of international funding agencies. Globalization, rather than lifting all boats, favors the few and leaves many communities behind. While it claims to encompass the globe, it does not seek the common good, but provides opportunities only for a global elite.

The third quotation is excerpted from the statement of mission of the Legacy Foundation, which can be found on its website.

> The mission of the Legacy [F]oundation is to promote sustainable human development and preserve our environment through the integration of technology innovation, media, and management [...] There is little doubt about the widening gap between rich and poor, about the increasingly crowded cities and the abandoned rural villages in the third world. At the same time there is a growing presence of telecommunications resources, including cell phones, internet and fiber optic networks. In taking advantage of these events, Legacy has embarked upon an ambitious and unique development program designed to give a self-sustaining voice to the rural areas [...] Under the direction of a locally trained three person communications team, the needs and resources of the rural poor can be organized more efficiently and cost effectively and allow them to better communicate with each other. (www.legacyfound.org)

This statement relates to the inequalities referred to in the previous quotation and to the destruction of our common good – the environment. It offers remedies through the use of telecommunication technologies that strive to counteract the fragmentation brought about by globalization. Better communication, it claims, will give the rural poor a voice in the global economy and will lead to sustained human development and environmental preservation.

Taken together, these quotations suggest that we might encounter some fundamental paradoxes when we study intercultural communication in global contexts. First, they show how inadequate our usual way of describing events has become when referring to global contexts: *flows, transculturation, trans-localization* are spatial metaphors that attempt to capture new phenomena through the traditional resources of the English lexicon. Secondly, these metaphors can easily become a kind of doublespeak that conceals impoverishment in the name of empowerment, inequalities in the name of equal opportunity (see Excerpt 3). The lucrative investments brought about by globalization cast long shadows of poverty and misery. Thirdly, the newspeak of a global economy – terms and phrases like *sustainability, resources*, and *cost effectiveness* – can elicit resistance and transformation at the local level. In global discourse the economic and the political form an uneasy alliance. Even though international foundations strive to give the rural poor a *voice*, there is no global parliament where this voice might be heard. Finally, given the isolation and fragmentation brought about by globalization, we can expect people often to communicate past one another, since they often lack ideological common ground, even as they like to imagine that communication technologies are politically neutral, socially beneficial, and culturally universal. We will seek to substantiate these claims in the rest of this chapter, but we can already expect IC in local contexts to be both similar to and different from IC in global contexts. It is similar because it brings together individual actors exchanging referential meanings and indexing stances and identities through linguistic and paralinguistic signs within local contexts of situation and culture. It is different because individuals, signs, and contexts have themselves been redefined by global communication technologies and by power struggles over the very discourse of globalization (see excerpt 4).

Global Intercultural Communication in a Tanzanian Eco-Partnership

Historical background

Tanzania's productive economy, which yields the agricultural products, natural resources, and minerals out of which the processes of global interconnection have been built, has been profoundly shaped and governed by the needs of colonial, international, and global capitalism (Cooper 2001; Shivji 2006). As the forms of global economic integration have changed, however, there have also been changes in the discourses articulating Tanzania's place in the global economy, the purpose of these global interactions, and the actors who both constitute and participate in such global conversations (Shivji 2007).

Discourses of development, which became hegemonic during the Cold War, have been instrumental in reorganizing global power while legitimizing continued intervention in the affairs of the Third World (Escobar 1995). The birth of development, with its corresponding practices and international development institutions,[1] is often cited in relation to the cold war and Truman's 1949 inaugural address, in which he appealed to the United States and to the entire world to solve the problems of the "underdeveloped areas," as their "poverty is a handicap and a threat both to them and to more prosperous areas" (Truman 1949). International development institutions created for the purpose of rebuilding a war-torn Europe responded to Truman's vision and set out to "make available the benefits of our technical knowledge in order to help them realize their aspirations for a better life" (ibid.).

It is within this framework – of development and of aspirations for eradicating poverty – that, after gaining independence from the British in 1961, Nyerere, the first president of Tanzania, severed economic relations with former colonizers and began to build a socialist nation according to principles of equality, freedom from exploitation, and self-reliance (Campbell and Stein 1991; Nyerere 1973). In the early 1980s Nyerere openly rejected aid from international development institutions, claiming that the conditional structural adjustment reforms – which opened up national markets, privatized government industries, and cut social services such as health care and education – served to undermine the socialist state and the corresponding core values of equality and non-exploitation. Nevertheless, by 1986, in conditions of growing economic crisis and increasing popular dissatisfaction with government-directed, 'top-down,' development, the new president

Mwinyi was forced to accept aid and structural adjustment reforms required by the International Monetary Fund, curtailing state intervention and opening up Tanzanian markets to 'free trade' (Campbell and Stein 1991; Kiondo 1994).

By the mid-1990s, however, with the recognition of growing poverty, falling literacy rates, and environmental destruction, market-directed development, which is characteristic of structural adjustment reforms, came under severe attack. As a result, while maintaining a critique of government and 'top-down' intervention, international development institutions shifted their focus toward strengthening 'civil society' as the site of social service provision (Mohan and Stokke 2000; World Bank 2001). Consequently numerous local and international non-governmental organizations (NGOs) were established and designed to take over the responsibilities once played by the government (Igoe and Kelsall 2005). Development discourse currently emphasizes the empowerment and participation of the local community in order for it to access the promised benefits of globalization, from which it has otherwise been excluded. In contrast to previous development interventions, which were envisioned and implemented by colonial administrations, development institutions, or the state, in current development discourse local knowledge and practices are valued and have become the foundation on which development priorities are built. Local people are encouraged to form diverse local and global partnerships in order to get access to the additional knowledge, technology, capital, and networks necessary for them to scale up current positions and resources and to participate more fully in global processes (Prahalad 2005; Sachs 2005).

The study

The data we analyze come from a larger study, conducted by Liz Boner in 2007 as part of her research on "The making of the entrepreneur in rural Tanzania" (Boner, 2011). Between January and July 2007, Boner recorded 100 hours of interviews, meetings, and training sessions related to one community's effort to promote environmental enterprise in partnership with an American NGO, Eco-Preneur.[2] Eco-Preneur's mission is to support sustainable communities and livelihoods through the development of green business. They came to Tanzania for the first time in 2004 and provided a three-month training in environmental business practices and in savings and credit for youth. It was from these efforts that the local Women's Savings and Credit Group (or Saccos; see Excerpt 1) was 'born.'[3] More recently, however, in line with current discourses of development, Eco-Preneur has shifted its focus from providing direct service (top-down) to building the capacity of local community organizations (bottom-up) – which, as Eco-Preneur feels, are better positioned to carry out the mission of environmental enterprise in ways that are sensitive to the particular needs and interests of the community. Accordingly, Eco-Preneur facilitated the initiation of an informal network called Tega, which brought together representatives from several local environmental and poverty-reduction NGOs, including two women from Saccos. The purposes of this network were to assess development priorities at the community level, to share technical knowledge among local and international stakeholders, and to collaborate on projects related to the promotion of environmental entrepreneurship.

Following principles of environmental enterprise that encourage the use of waste and sustainable resources in producing new beneficial products, Tega identified excess sawdust, left behind from numerous lumber mills, as a potential resource. Tega members drafted the proposal for a project intending to use sawdust and readily available agricultural residuals in order to produce fuel briquettes – which are used as alternatives to the more common but environment-taxing charcoal. While Eco-Preneur secured funding from the McNichols Foundation,[4] one Tega organization secured funding for the same project from the United Nations Development Program (UNDP).

The following data derive from two different and unrelated meetings.[5] The first excerpt comes from a two-hour meeting conducted in May 2007 between two Eco-Preneur representatives, David and Melissa, and two representatives from Saccos, Maria and Teresita, to discuss what they would need in order to set up a briquette business. The other three excerpts come from a three-hour Tega network meeting designed to discuss the same project; the meeting took place in March 2007 between David and Melissa and the eleven members of Tega, who represented ten organizations and two government departments. Liz Boner attended both meetings as a researcher; in the first one she also acted as an interpreter.

The data

Excerpt 1   Linguistic shadows: friend=*rafiki?*, *saidia*=help?

In this first excerpt from the May 2007 meeting, the Americans David and Melissa present themselves as facilitators of the briquette business which the Saccos members want to set up. Maria and Teresita don't speak English; David doesn't speak Swahili; Melissa knows a few words; Liz Boner has a good command of the language. This is already their third meeting. Maria and Teresita are not sure whether David and Melissa are really their friends and want to help them; but why would David and Melissa keep inviting them to meetings if they are not their friends? Although Maria and Teresita expect resources and clear directions for starting a business, Eco-Preneur wants to make sure that local groups don't expect them to be their cash cow and to provide all the answers. Their goal is instead to 'open up learning spaces' in which local Tanzanians can discover their own questions and give their own answers. In this excerpt Liz is called upon to translate both for the Americans and for the Tanzanians.

1   DAVID: how (2.5) how we want to help (1.) Saccos is- is by helping them
2   identify questions that need to be asked (2.) to start a business (3.)
3   because (1.5) before you start a new business (.) where there is risk

4		(1.0) involved (.5) you should make <u>sure</u> that you've asked every
5		question you can ask (.)
6	LIZ:	umhum
7	DAVID:	and (.) and <u>plan</u> for everything you can plan for (2.) so the reason why
8		we are asking questions <u>really</u> (2.) is to help <u>them</u> (.) identify
9		everything that they <u>need</u> to (.) if they'd like to start a business. (4)

For the next hour, Melissa and David ask the Tanzanians questions about how they 'envision' their business and what their 'thoughts' are. Maria keeps returning to the question of the briquette press, which they need in order to set up their briquette business. The following was said in Swahili, but is translated here into English.

10	MARIA:	we have this problem of the machine, still this is a big issue for us
		that =
11	TERESITA:	= we will get it where?
12	MARIA:	we will get it where?
13	TERESITA:	and also our group (.) we (.) help orphans (.) and those living
14		in difficult situations (.) so we can't help if we don't have
15		a <u>business</u> =
16	MARIA:	= if we don't have a business (.) yes
17	TERESITA:	so we're obliged to have a business for the group =
18	MARIA:	= in order [to help (*saidia*)
19	TERESITA:	[in order to help the orphan children

The question about the machine is ignored by the Americans, who continue to ask questions about the characteristics of potential customers. Also they want to know what the group sees as its next steps. At some point Melissa and David talk in English among themselves: they don't think the meeting is going well and they want Liz to translate their concerns.

20	DAVID:	one of our biggest troubles here (.)
21	LIZ:	um hm
22	DAVID:	in this meeting (.) is to make sure that (.) ↑they can mobilize the
23		↑resources (.) that they need (.) because we're not the resource that
24		they need (3.)
25	LIZ:	um hm
26	DAVID:	it's not sus↑tainable (1.5) to look (1.) for outside funding (2.) an
27		entrepre↑neur (.) can mobilize (.) resources through ↑friends (1)
28		resources through ↑loans (1) whatever (.) you ↑have um (.) so (.) so
29		basically they have some money (.) they might be able to buy a few
30		trainings along with a press and just <u>do</u> it (.) but (.) what happens
31		when the next thing comes up (.) that they don't know (1.) ↑<u>who</u> do
32		they turn to (.) <u>who</u> are their friends (.) and <u>who</u> are their <u>allies</u> (4)
33	LIZ:	um hm
34	DAVID:	and how can they get the things that they can't ↑afford (.) because
35		they <u>have</u> to be very very resourceful.

For the next six minutes, David and Melissa give examples of resourcefulness and descriptions of their organization's philosophy of sustainability. They ask Liz not to translate their views about the machine or give their concrete examples of resourcefulness because they want to provide the space for Maria and Teresita to give their own examples. Liz turns to Maria and Teresita and says in Swahili:

36	LIZ:	if you don't have money (.) are you able to call a friend (*rafiki*) or
37		whatever to get assistance ↑(*msaada*) your friends (*marafiki*) (.) are
38		↑who (.) your helpers (*wasaidizi*) (.) are ↑who (.) you – you will fail
39		↑completely (.) or do you have
40		thoughts or ways of getting assistance (*msaada*) (.) or advice
41	MARIA:	now (.) in other words (.) we have ideas (.) to do many things (.) but
42		we don't know (.) which people (.) are going to help us (.) but before
43		getting help (*msaada*) (.) we have already decided that if it's like ↑this[6]
44		(.) we will gather the group (.) and we will explain (.) to them and we
45		will decide what to do about the press.

This excerpt illustrates the tension between the discourse of global planning/ networking and the discourse of institutional patronage. For David, before you start a business, you have to plan. *Asking questions/finding answers* is the communicative bedrock of business planning. It will increase the social and economic bottom line and reduce the risk of failure. In Tanzania, where risk is a fact of life and failure is often independent of anyone's doing, you can't know, as Maria says, if a project is sustainable or non-sustainable before you have started.

For the Americans, the notion of *need* is related to *asking questions*. It has been technologized by a neo-liberal discourse that cloaks desire (making a profit) in the mantle of biological want (suffering from a need), and commercial practices (making money) in the mantle of philanthropy (responding to a need). Eco-Preneur's discourse of *need* collocates with identifying *resources* ("helping them identify the resources they need"), problem-solving ("questions need to be asked," "you need to find your own answers"), and accepting the imperatives of the market (not only what you need, but what you need to do: l. 2). The term 'need' here is both a euphemism and a naturalization of man-made market forces (Fairclough 1989).

For David, *getting help* is part of *mobilizing resources*. Resources can be money, things (machines), or people (friends and allies). Establishing a network of people likely to invest in your business is a prerequisite for setting up a business. David uses here the lexicon of economic entrepreneurship, of marketing research, which is the lexicon of communicative activism. He offers to help the Tanzanians to identify, in other words to set up a list of, potential stakeholders who can give advice when difficulties arise. Indeed, in lines 27–8, "friends" are put in parallel with "loans" and "outside funding" as a source of "sustainability." But Maria and

Teresita conceive of help (*msaada*) and helpers (*wasaidizi*) differently. Whereas social causes might require you to help (*saidia*) in a spontaneous and charitable way, as in helping orphaned children (l. 13), business, they argue, requires systematic capital infusion and technological investment (l. 10) – and not the verbal help given by David and Melissa, which Maria assesses as just blah blah (see n. 6).

The confusion created by words like 'help' and 'need' finds its expression in the multifunctional word 'friend.' For the Tanzanians, the word *rafiki* is used for intimate friends, but it can also be used ironically for powerful sponsors or *walezi* ('guardians'). Maria and Teresita certainly don't need lessons in how to call on their 'friends' in times of need, this is common practice in Tanzania, so why are David and Melissa returning to this question again and again? The problem lies in the differing timescales confronting each other here. On the one hand, the global timescale of communication technologies, community participation and activism, and marketing campaigns; on the other hand, the local timescale of family and friends and the hierarchical structures of institutional patronage. Both timescales overlap in what Blommaert calls "layered simultaneity" (Blommaert 2005: 136). The Americans, as if following a script from a global development handbook, expect the Tanzanians to fundraise and do market analyses freely, like global entrepreneurs, while the Tanzanians expect funds and technology to come from national or international institutions. The lexicon of euphemisms like 'friends,' 'help,' and 'need,' used by David, conceals the power struggles involved in both timescales. It also conceals the deinstitutionalized power of such NGOs as Eco-Preneur, whose entrepreneurial spirit can lead to a total lack of institutional accountability.

Maria and Teresita use local terms like *msaada/saidia* ('help') to refer to the assistance they want to give orphaned children through their briquette business (ll. 12–17). They know that many international visitors empty their pockets to save the world. It is poignant that they feel compelled to present themselves as caring philanthropists in order to impress the Americans, when what they really want is a machine to make briquettes. However, in this case, the Americans are not budging. They give the discourse of human caring a different meaning. 'Help' in their vocabulary means a business that creates job opportunities, not one that provides handouts.

We can see here how intercultural communication gets transformed in global contexts. While terms like 'help' (*msaada, saidia*), and 'friend' (*rafiki, marafiki*) index in local contexts the discourse of empathy and disinterested assistance to fellow human beings (for example orphans), in a global context this discourse gets instrumentalized in the interest of business entrepreneurs. One could say that it becomes part of an intertext that resemioticizes local discourse in the new context of global entrepreneurship. This intertext, which includes terms like 'help,' 'need,' and 'friend,' looks like the original text but is in fact a shadow, a double – hence the scarequotes in the next sentence. Networking and rallying financial support (making 'friends'), discovering market niches (meeting 'needs'), providing jobs (giving 'help'), is now called alternatively 'humanitarian aid' or 'global development.' In the same way as 'help' is the shadow of help, humanitarian aid is the shadow of global development.

The following three excerpts from the Tega meeting in March illuminate in dramatic detail the complexities of intercultural communication in global contexts. Now that the briquette project has been funded, the Tega members have come to this meeting expecting to decide who will be in charge of what project activities and who will take part in the training. In contrast, the Eco-Preneur representatives hope to discuss not just the training, but also how to support the briquette project in general, the spread of the technology, the development of the briquette market, and the creation of a briquette learning network, with briquette-makers in Uganda and Kenya who were also funded by the American foundation McNichols. Eco-Preneur informs the Tega members that participation has been limited to twenty-four villagers, which leaves only two spaces for Tega members.

At this meeting all but two Tega members (Maria and Teresita) were proficient in English. The meeting was conducted in English and not translated into Swahili. Although all were encouraged to speak, most of the speaking was done either by the Americans or by Kato, Kamu, and Earnest. These three Tanzanians hold key leadership positions in Tega. Kato is a well respected leader in the community and director of a local rural poverty alleviation organization. He holds a Master's degree from a university in the UK and is often contracted by international development agencies to provide training throughout the country. Earnest was instrumental in securing funding for the briquette project from UNDP. In addition to overseeing the implementation of this funded project, he is also chairman of the Tega network. Kamu is the director of yet a third organization, which promotes entrepreneurship for the youth.

Excerpt 2   Shadows of knowledge: skills versus capacity

This second excerpt illustrates the tension between the discourse of a global economy based on knowledge and that of a local economy based on manufacture. It is taken from the first five minutes of the meeting. While David doesn't think that all Tega members need to attend the training in order to support the briquette project, Earnest, Kato, and Kamu contest that. All Tega members must be trained, they argue, in order to be able to train others in the centers they have set up.

1	DAVID:	beyond being <u>trained</u> (.) how else can Tega <u>help</u> (.) the briquetting
2		↑project (.5) how can- how can the <u>Tega</u> support the groups of
3		entrepre↑neurs (.5) who are making the ↑briquettes (3)
4	EARNEST:	↑huh (.) what did you ↑say
5	DAVID:	is there-are there other ↑<u>ways</u> (.) for Tega to be involved (.) besides
6		↑train↓ing (4.0)
7	EARNEST:	of course, ah, ((clears throat)) Tega has the technical know-how (1.0)
8		these people-these people of course-we have established the centers
9		who will be following that (1) ↑↑if we <u>don't</u> have a:ny ↑<u>skills</u> (.)

10		↓ok (.) they are ↑taught (.) but you know you-you-you are teaching
11		village (.) ↑ people and they-they-they will forget ↑even how to
12		↑mix these ↑ashes and whatever (.) that's why they- we are saying
13		(.) we should be there (1.0) so that the-the-the skills is-is within Tega
14		members themselves (1.0) so that they can (.) propagate this (.5) all
15		over the-the-the-the-the ↑area (.) not just for this five groups (.) we
16		want this to-to- to=
17	KATO:	= to spread
18	EARNEST:	to ↑spread (.) not even in (the town) only (.) but in other areas
19		where there is sawdust and a lot of solid waste lying there (.) we
20		want to (.) -this is our ↑product=
21	KATO:	= this is our focus (.) this is our focus
22	EARNEST:	↑yeah! this is our focus

Melissa asks the group what should be done given the constraints. Kato
explains again that the purpose of the meeting is to harmonize these
differences, reiterating the importance of having Tega members participate.

23	DAVID:	I don't know what value (.5) you're going to get (.5) for every
24		member of Te:ga (.) knowing how to make ↑briquettes (.5) because
25		not e:very member of Tega (.) has the capacity to make briquettes (.)
26		but I think every member of Tega (.) has the capacity to ↑help
27		(.5) the people who know how to make briquettes (1.0) if you
28		↑need a briquette market (.) in ((the town)) (.) you don't need
29		everyone pro↑ducing briquettes. (.) but you need (.5) smart
30		entrepreneurs (.) to sell the briquettes (.) you need people to
31		support the briquette ↑market (.) and we need other ways to-to
32		support that ↑learning there's many ways (.) to spread (.) this
33		knowledge (.) besides having Tega know it and do this (.) because
34		as I under↑stand it (.) not (.) every member (.) can ↑produce
35		↓briquettes (1.0) does ↑everyone ↑want to ↑make their ↑own
36		↑briquettes?
37	KATO:	they can train (1.0) others to make briquettes everyone can have the
38		↑skill (1.0) and spread the skills to others
39	DAVID:	but not everybody needs (1) one skill (.)
40	KATO:	yes
41	OTHERS[7]:	hmmmmm?
42	DAVID:	every↑body ↓does

This excerpt illuminates the different understandings of how knowledge is spread.
In a product-based economy, formally trained experts have manufacturing skills
that they teach to individual villagers. In such an economy, the more people know
how to make briquettes the better, as they work to meet the demands of the local
market and thus raise the level of human development. In a knowledge-based
economy, all know different things: some know how to make briquettes, others
know how to market them, yet others how to fundraise. The term 'capacity'
captures the demands of this new economy. Unlike *"skill"* (ll. 9, 13) *"capacity"*

(ll. 24–5), or productive capacity, refers to the relationship between the actual output produced by an enterprise and the potential output that could be produced with installed equipment, business networks, and so on, when the capacity is fully used. When David says that "not every member has the capacity to make bri-quettes" but "every member has the capacity to help," he is using 'capacity' in this knowledge-based sense. In other words, knowing how to make briquettes is one thing, knowing how to manage a briquette business is another. What Tega members should focus on is not the skills but the capacities, not the product but the market.

Earnest and Kato contest both the lexicon and its underlying ideology. David's use of "involvement" (l. 5), "help" (l. 1), "support" (l. 2), to characterize Tega's role in the project only confuses Earnest, who had exclaimed in line 4 "What did you say?" Indeed, all three words refer to "the briquetting project," not to people. As Kamu will say in Excerpt 4, "Is this right for the people?" As we discussed in the previous excerpt, in the discourse of global development 'help' does not mean primarily giving assistance to individuals with money, tools, muscle, or any other physical means for the manufacturing of products; it means contacting potential donors, networking on behalf of others, talking to people for the promotion of the enterprise itself. In other words, help means using the 'resources' of a knowledge-based, not of a manufacture-based economy. It means using the tools of commu-nication technology to give the rural poor a 'voice' (see p. 498), and not only giving them the manufacturing technology to make briquettes. The Americans seem to distinguish between two groups: the managers and the manufacturers, the first being more prestigious than the second. This casts the shadow of a social hierar-chy in a purportedly egalitarian entrepreneurial culture.

Earnest's hesitations (ll. 10–13, 15, 16) might be significant in this regard. It seems that every time there is a hesitation, it might not be because of Earnest's limited English but because he is maneuvering his way between these two dis-courses: the discourse of manufacturing and the discourse of entrepreneurship. While both Kato and Earnest make prominent use of the entrepreneurial term *spread* (ll. 17–18), Earnest's use of *product* in "This is our product" (l. 20) is swiftly corrected by Kato into "This is our focus" (l. 21), a term typical of a knowledge-based economy that is all about vision, focus, and ideas and less about briquettes, sawdust, and ashes. Kato seems more attuned than Earnest to the newspeak of the global economy.

Excerpt 3   'Togetherness' and its doubles: We, you, they

Excerpt 3 continues where Excerpt 2 left off. While excerpt 2 focused on the importance of Tega members' gaining the knowledge taught in the training, Excerpt 3 assesses the limitations placed on the numbers of training partici-pants. Earnest explains: "for our environment, adding more people won't reduce the value of the training." Melissa rejects this 'local' assessment as she speaks on behalf of the absent trainers and enforces the number of participants they requested.[8] (Caps indicate increased loudness.)

43	MELISSA:	so (.) given the fact that you're interested in briquetting (1.0) given
44		the constra:ints_that we <u>have</u> (1.0) how can we <u>ma:ximize</u> this
45		(1.0) how can we really <u>u:se</u> this (1.0) we <u>have</u> (.) <u>constraints</u>(.)
46		there's <u>n:o</u> way around it (.) its <u>not</u> the ideal situation (.) how do
47		we work <u>together</u> to make this what we ↓want (4.0) I would
48		<u>RE:ALLY</u> like to know what you guys ↓think (.) because ↑<u>yes</u> (.)_we
49		ha::ve (.)_constraints (.5) <u>ideally</u> (.) it would be Tega members (.)
50		getting all the training (.) that's <u>not</u> (.) the way its working (.)
51		unfortunately (.5) we're <u>going</u> to work with the trainers (.) to <u>see</u>
52		what we can do (1.0) but giv-say for example (.5) o:nly (.) <u>two</u>
53		people (.) <u>can</u> (.) actually (.) take part in the technical training (1.)
54		w<u>hat</u> do yo:u think (.) would be the best wa:y (.) to maximize this (.)
55		for ↑Tega (5) ↑any↓body
56	KATO:	flexibility (2.)
57	MELISSA:	ok
58	KATO:	flexi↑bility (3.0) is ↓necessary (.) we <u>tell</u> these people (1.0)
59	MELISSA:	<u>yeah</u> (1.0) ((chuckling)) ↑good ↓luck ((laughter))
60	KATO:	↑this is one option (.) I'm proposing (1.0) we tell these people (.5)
61		they have to be eh flexible with the <u>numbers</u> (.) they are saying
62	DAVID:	ok (.) if they say ↑<u>no</u> (.5) what can we ↓<u>do</u>=
63	MELISSA:	= <u>yeah</u>
64	KATO:	yeah this is what we- [If they say no]
65	MELISSA:	[that's what- that's what the] question <u>is</u> (.) if they say <u>no</u>:: what do
66		we do=
67	KATO:	= yeah
68	MELISSA:	this is [what we ha:ve.]
69	KATO:	[I mean] ↑↑↑lead(.) ↑lead the way (.) ↑↑lead- ↑↑what do you
70		think
71	MELISSA:	↑↑↑↑n::o (.) I'm not- I wanna know what <u>yo:u</u> (.) think (.)=
72	KATO:	= ↑eh [that was]
73	MELISSA:	[because I'm the-]↑<u>you</u> guys are the ones that are going to ↑<u>be</u> here
74		for <u>years</u> and ↑<u>years</u>=
75	KATO:	= yeah yeah =
76	MELISSA:	= (.5) we're gonna be here for <u>five</u> ↑<u>months</u> (2.0) that's why- I mean
77		(.) what do ↑<u>I</u> ↓know (hhhhh) (3.5)
78	EARNEST:	th- th- that's was-wa your role (.) as-as Eco-Preneur (1.0) this they're
79		saying (.) -yah (2.0) this is an opportunity.

This excerpt brings to the fore the real and the imagined solidarities and exclusionary tactics of global discourse, in particular the discourse of togetherness and its opposite double: exclusion and put-downs.

As we described earlier (p. 500), in the 1990s development discourse in Tanzania shifted from interventions from above (the state and the international development agency) to participation, empowerment, and capacity building from below (the local and the civil society). But the first remains as the unacknowledged shadow of the second. The excerpt dramatically illustrates the tension between the discourse of empowerment/entrepreneurship ("we are all in this together, we are all entrepreneurs") and the discourse of expert trainer intervention, which seems to have replaced the old interventions from above.

The contextualization cues used by intercultural communication research make this tension visible. Melissa negotiates her role as a facilitator between the global *they* (funding and training organizations), the local *you* (the partnership of Tega) and the solidarity *we* that the Americans imagine themselves enacting, each pronoun indexing a different definition of the context. Her use of formal language ("given the fact that [...]; given the constraints [...] how can we maximize") confers a tone of factual inevitability to the dilemma they are in and underscores the fundamentally ambiguous position of Eco-Preneur at that meeting. Melissa not only asserts her helplessness vis-à-vis the constraints imposed by the funding agency (l. 44), but she throws the ball in the Tanzanians' court by using the distancing *you* (ll. 43, 48, l. 54), all the while affirming her solidarity with them through the use of the inclusive *we* (ll. 44–5, 47, 49). She then assumes her position as facilitator and, through the use of questions (ll. 44–7, 54), invites "local" solutions to the goal of "maximizing" briquetting (ll. 44, 54), skillfully avoiding the question of training. Each question uses the modal construction "can" (ll. 44, 52), which serves to focus on future possibility, juxtaposed with the "can't" implied by the constraints. With similar enthusiasm she uses discourses of solidarity in speaking of how "we can work together" and of the possibility of making this what "we want" (l. 47), which contrasts sharply with the inevitable and insurmountable constraints she identifies with. Melissa's discourse illustrates well the increased uncertainties of intercultural communication in global contexts, where the compression of time and space and the global linkages of individuals and institutions across large distances and radically different timescales create multiple allegiances and accountabilities that are often in conflict with one another. For the researcher, contextualization cues are useful but insufficient to explain the contextual complexities and ambiguities of communication on multiple timescales.

Kato immediately responds to her invitation to come up with solutions by using the very term used by entrepreneurs: *flexibility*. In contrast with the constraints that Melissa has delivered on behalf of the funding agency, Kato suggests that they tell the trainers they have to be "flexible" (ll. 56, 58, 61). His use of "we" in "we tell these people" (ll. 58, 61) is not only a response to Melissa's question ("what can we do?"), it is a claim to membership in a global society of equally empowered entrepreneurs, who globally seek to overcome barriers and constraints. Evoking the need for *flexibility* is "making implicit claims to the rights of a common membership in a global society" (Ferguson 2006: 173) and a "recognition of Africans as members of [this] new world society" (p. 174). However, this claim is met first with a two-second silence (l. 56) followed by a distinct lack of enthusiasm (l. 57), then with sarcasm (l. 59). Such sarcasm is uncommon in Tanzania, where offering solutions and advice is a highly respected practice,[9] and not one performed casually; but it also debunks the hypocrisy of the global discourse of empowerment and solidarity with the developing world.

To contest Kato's membership in a common global society even further, David raises the question "what if, " ("If they say no, what can we do?" l. 62), looking toward future possibilities rather than seriously discussing Kato's suggestion. Although such forward thinking is integral to the entrepreneurial problem-solving spirit, it is most likely read by the participants at the meeting as a rejection of the contribution made by a Tanzanian rather than as an effort to strengthen the strategy. Such a rejection suggests that the Americans don't really want the Tanzanians' ideas, but rather are 'performing' a relationship of solidarity, an orientation to the 'marginalized local,' which is so common in global discourses of development. Kato adamantly rejects further requests for input framed by Melissa's "what can we do?" and requires her instead to "lead the way." (l. 69). But, for the Americans, 'leading the way' indexes a discourse of power that runs counter to the kind of equal partnership they would like to forge, so Melissa forcefully refuses this leadership role (l. 71). This stands in stark contrast to her rejection of Kato's contribution. Her ambiguous reactions match the ambiguous discourse of the funding agencies, which she views as the uncontestable gatekeepers of the global market: on the one hand they are philanthropic organizations that want to empower the poor, on the other hand they serve profit-making institutions that want to foster global economic development. This fundamental ambiguity is of course one of the hallmarks of global capitalism. The paradoxical position of NGO representatives between the global market of funding agencies and the local demands on the ground finds its parallel in the paradoxical position of the Tega members between the international sources of funding and the local bureaucratic institutions to which they answer (see Excerpt 4). When tensions are high, these paradoxes can quickly get translated into an intercultural conflict of interests between 'Americans' and 'Tanzanians,' as we can see in the next excerpt.

Excerpt 4   Global and local shadows "the funding world," "the government," "the community"

This last excerpt begins just after Melissa has described the process of securing funding and the backhanded way in which Eco-Preneur was forced by the funder to accept these expensive trainers, who had in the process raised their training fees. She said the trainers did not want her to expose their training fees, but that she would do so anyway, thus once more showing evidence of her uncertain status as an intercultural communicator in this global context.

The excerpt highlights precisely these differences in accountability. In this context, giving a costly one-week training to only twenty-four participants flies in the face of the Tanzanians' conception of cost-effectiveness. In Tanzania such training could be easily given to 40–50 people.[10] Can the constraints imposed by the training and funding agencies (the global absent 'Other') be contested? How will they justify these costs to their government (the local absent 'Other')? How can this make sense within the global action plan that they are supposedly working toward, namely human development and environmental conservation?[11]

80   KATO: ↑look <u>here</u> (.) if (.) for a ↑<u>single</u> ticket (.) you could have trained a lot
81   of people ↑here (.)

82	MELISSA:	EX↑ACTLY (.) EX↑ACTLY
83	KATO:	the whole thing is just ↑bullshit (.)
84	MELISSA:	it ↑is (.5) complete bullshit (.) but (.) at the same ↑ti:me (.) this is
85		good fo::r the↑ community
86	KATO:	for WHICH ↑COMMUNITY (.) I MEAN (.) WHICH
87		↑COMMUNITY
88	MELISSA:	I mean you were the <u>ones</u> (.) that said you wanted to do this in
89		↑first place (.) we tried to make it happen (.) [and what we can
90		do <u>now</u>]
91	KATO:	[not in this way (.) not in this way] <u>WE</u> HAVE different ways, we
92		can do it in a better way we have these ↑<u>Kenyans</u> (.) we have ↑
93		<u>Ugandans</u> who've been <u>trained</u> (.) ↑↑↑↑we have some Tanzanians
94		from ↑↑<u>moshi</u> (.) we can use <u>them (.) </u>the issue here is to have this
95		technology ↑<u>spread</u> (.) if a ↑<u>single ticket</u> can train more than four
96		regions (.) why not using this-this at least (.) a single-at least a
97		single ticket for training even more ↑people (1.0) this is the
98		<u>planning</u> we're doing here(.) we ↑always (.) ↑try to mini↑mi:ze (.)
99		the use of <u>money</u> (.)
100	MELISSA:	yeah
101	KATO:	on un↑<u>necessary</u> thi:ngs (.)
102	MELISSA:	exactly, exactly
103	KATO:	such that we can reach, <u>mo::re</u> more- more people (.) but if you are
104		insisting on these kinds of things(.) I mean (.) it is all stupid we
105		shouldn't be <u>taken</u> for a ↑ride (.) I mean (3)
106	MELISSA:	↑well (hhhhh) =we were ↑basically (.) taken (.)for a ride.
107	KATO:	YEAH
108	MELISSA:	that's what happened (.) and so here's the thing (1.) the <u>training</u> is
109		going to start in a couple weeks
110	KATO:	forget about that (.)
111	MELISSA:	((nervous laughter))
112	KATO:	you can forget about that (.)
113	MELISSA:	and we can make what we can of it (.) we <u>have</u> the training (.) we
114		<u>have</u> some ↑excellent=
115	KATO:	((sigh))
116	MELISSA:	=international trainers that are ↑looking forward to working wi:th
117		(1.5) everybody (.) so <u>what </u>are we going to <u>do</u> with this (.) and how
118		are we going to make a success (.) given that (.) we went through
119		<u>sh:i:t (.)</u> to get here ((nervous laughter))
120	DAVID:	so the problem is (1) in the funding world (.) they have it backwards
121		(.) the way we ↑change that (.) is by working as a Tega (.) to
122		<u>maximize</u> this training (…) there is work that <u>each</u> member of the
123		Tega can do (.) to help ↑support (1.) the
124		briquetting project (…) and when we have (.) enterprises
125		(1) then we
126	KATO:	at ↑which costs (1) to have that at ↑which costs (.)

For fifteen minutes questions are raised by other Tega members about why the money that has been budgeted can't be used to pay for less expensive trainers from East Africa. David explains that this is not possible, but that in the future, if this training goes well, Tega can apply for better funding. David's enthusiasm about future possibilities is contested by Kamu's assessment of the sustainability of the current project.[12]

127	KAMU:	sustainability hm? of the project hm? and the environment? so
128		because McNichols and the trainers say please do this … but can the
129		government support this kind of thing? that one person coming
130		from USA paying a lot of money, staying here for
131		thre::e weeks eh? for maybe 25 people, can I guess this is right for
132		the ↑people?

This excerpt brings to the fore the invisible stakeholders in the project: large international funding agencies, David and Melissa's American NGO, the Tanzanian government and the Tanzanian NGOs, and the growing number of African networks evoked by Kato (ll. 91–4). The issue raised by the Tanzanians is: "Why do we have to accept the restriction on the number of participants imposed by the funding agency?" Opening up the training session to twice as many people would make a lot more sense to spread the entrepreneurial spirit around. The funding has been made conditional on hiring specific trainers, who are American and charge American rates, to give hands-on training which is more effective if the number of participants is small. But, even though the American funder is willing to pay these rates on this occasion, the Tanzanians argue that a project of such high costs cannot be mainstreamed into the local government action plans or replicated in other regions in the future. As such, this project would be considered unsustainable, as has been the case with so many such previous donor-initiated projects in the past. The paradox is that, while the American funders are keen on remaining in the background and on building the capacity of local Tanzanian NGOs, who admittedly know best how to do their own training, Tega is not listened to by the international funding agency, nor is Kato's suggestion in Excerpt 3 taken seriously by Eco-Preneur.

By insisting on having all Tega members attend the training sessions so that they can in turn train the villagers, Kato and Earnest in Excerpts 3 and 4 are asserting their advantage, as Tega members, over "those villagers who will soon forget how to mix the ashes " (Excerpt 2, l. 12). They are thereby implicitly contesting the official claim of global development that people are natural entrepreneurs, and that they will have a "self-sustaining voice" if only they are given the freedom and the communication tools to do so, that is, if they can be allowed to "better communicate with each other" (see p. 498). Under those circumstances it is difficult to interpret Kamu's concern for "the people" (l. 132): is this the discourse of moral responsibility? socialist solidarity? or the ventriloquation of a neo-liberal discourse of "empowerment"? The hierarchical structure encouraged by the global economy under the guise of equalizing relations and of making people believe that they can be and do anything they want if only they ask the right questions is one of the many contradictions of intercultural communication in global contexts.

Discussion

The question we posed at the beginning of this paper was both a descriptive and a methodological one: What is the nature of intercultural communication in global contexts, and what approaches to discourse are best suited to study it?

In these four excerpts we have identified some discourse features of global communication. We found in Excerpt 1 the newspeak of global capitalism and its mimicked 'Other,' the oldspeak of friendly business; the global lexicon of English and its counterpart, the local lexicon of Swahili, each with their own semantic fields. In Excerpt 2 we encountered the discourse of "free" knowledge and entrepreneurship and its double, the discourse of manufacture and its technical constraints. Excerpt 3 revealed the discourse of unfettered communication technology and its antonym, the discourse of the market's inflexible laws; the pronouns of solidarity and their twin deictics, the pronouns of exclusion. And in Excerpt 4 we found the rhetoric of the free sharing of ideas and its double, the subtle censorship placed on these ideas by international funding agencies; the economic discourse of efficiency and sustainability and its mirror image, the political discourse of the right to dissent, each with their internal contradictions; the language of economic inevitability and its counterpart, the language of political responsibility.

We have called these doubles, mirror-images and counterparts "shadows of discourse" because one discourse is entailed by the other – in other words it is indissociably associated with, or is the consequence of, the other. In the same manner in which 'friend' can be used to mean at once 'companion and patron' (Maria/Teresita) and 'stakeholder' (David), and 'knowledge' can mean both 'information' (David) and 'skill' (Maria/Teresita), 'entrepreneurship' can be resignified from economic (Melissa) to political resourcefulness (Kato), 'sustainability' can be reappropriated from markets (David) to people's livelihood (Kamu). A shadow can be visible or invisible, depending on the context and the position of the speaker. It bears the traces of various subjectivities and historicities, and of all the unsaid against which the said acquires its meaning. Many of the misunderstandings or disagreements between the participants in these exchanges were due to a disregard for the multiple shadows of words and their discourses in a global context of communication.

To what extent can one still speak of intercultural, or even of interdiscursive, communication in such global contexts? The compression of time and space, the circulation of decontextualized discourses such as the one seemingly transplanted by David from a global development textbook to a rural village in Tanzania, the illusory universality of technological benefits and the mirage of mutual understanding if only everyone speaks English – have drastically changed the parameters of human communication across national cultures. The power struggle between different versions of reality is concealed, as we have seen, by the a-political euphemisms of globalspeak. Intercultural communication is no longer a matter of understanding the different "discourse systems" (Scollon and Scollon

2001) – of westerners versus Africans, or of urban versus rural Tanzanians. Rather, it is a matter of recognizing which discourse is a simulacrum of other, past or present, discourses, which is a parody, a ventriloquation, an appropriation of the discourse of others. For example David's use of *friends* and *helpers* to mean funders and stakeholders in Excerpt 1, Kato's resignified use of the American term *flexibility* in Excerpt 3, and Kamu's ironical use of *sustainability* in Excerpt 4 all intend to appropriate for themselves conventional meanings or to rectify abused meanings. These tactics of appropriation are not just a question of semantics. *Friend,* for example, is not just a lexical entity, but a metaphor for larger discourses, for instance the discourse of global entrepreneurship (*friend-as-stakeholder*), the discourse of Tanzanian patronage (*friend-as-patron*), the discourse of local intimate human relations (*friend-as-companion*). In global contexts, when *friend* is used among interlocutors who belong to different discourse worlds and timescales, any one use bears the shadows of the others, thus increasing the zones of semiotic uncertainty and the opportunities for misunderstandings or for reappropriation.

Discourse wars are surrogates for political struggles that, as Blommaert (2005) has pointed out, have a stake in remaining in the shadows of factual information exchange. By multiplying the number of absent partners in conversation and the invisible constraints they place on what the actual/present partners say, globalization exponentially multiplies the possibility of animating the others' views, of dissociating speakers from responsibility for their utterances. International funding agencies each have their criteria for funding their particular interests and causes – for example environmental concerns, human development, women's rights, children orphanages – and for policing the discourse of funding proposals. They wield political power even as they purport to give only economic support. But local entrepreneurs, too, have their own, different ways of going about being an entrepreneur (see Excerpt 4). One of the ways, as we have seen, is to capitalize on the gray zones of contradiction in the discourse of global development and to draw political benefit from its vagueness.

The basic assumption that underlies the whole discourse of global entrepreneurship is that asking questions/finding answers, exploring market opportunities, identifying supporters, developing promotion and marketing strategies, and the like are all natural activities that anyone is able to engage in with a little determination and hard work. This discourse assumes that we are all potential entrepreneurs who only need to be socialized into behaving like entrepreneurs. But it is clear from the exchanges in Excerpt 1 that such behavioral training is misunderstood by the trainees as mere talk. If Maria and Teresita have difficulty "identifying their needs" and "asking the proper questions" (Excerpt 1), shouldn't they be explicitly trained to do so? It might be the case that, despite the lofty rhetoric of giving the rural poor a voice, neither the global nor the local elite are keen on teaching the rural poor how really to be entrepreneurs. In Excerpt 2 David saw Maria and Teresita's lack of entrepreneurial spirit as reflecting their "old mindset" of dependency. Eco-Preneur would rather support those like Kato, who already have the new entrepreneurial mindset, who – through education, innovation, and access to communication technology – can turn a simple idea or tool into something more far-reaching, and in doing so reach more people.

Discourse wars, as we have seen, also police the boundaries of the speakable and of who has the right to membership in a global society of speakers. Kato was apparently too entrepreneurial for David and Melissa's taste. It is not clear what role he will play as the project develops, but he is sure to establish his own boundaries of inclusion and exclusion. As Ferguson writes:

> In a world of non-serialized political economic statuses, the key questions are no longer temporal ones of societal becoming (development, modernization), but spatialized ones of guarding the edges of a status group – hence, the new prominence of walls, borders, and processes of social exclusion in an era that likes to imagine itself as characterized by an ever expanding connection and communication. (2006: 192)

What kind of analysis is called for when studying discourse practices in such global contexts? The data call for a multidimensional mode of analysis, proposed by postmodern sociolinguistics (Blommaert 2005, Coupland 2007) and ecological analyses of language use (Kramsch 2002b, Kramsch and Whiteside 2008). These approaches take into consideration the layers of historical simultaneity and the heteroglossia present in everyday utterances (Blommaert 2005: 130), the different timescales on which participants position themselves (ibid.; Lemke 2000), and the socially constructed categories on which they draw (Hacking 1999). But the notion of 'discourse shadow,' on which we have built our argument, also calls for taking into consideration aspects of discourse like stylization and ventriloquation, which have been studied in local contexts (see Rampton 1999, Hanks 1996), and in global cultural contexts (Pennycook 2007), but not in the contexts of global economic development. This is where work done in linguistic anthropology (Hanks 1996, Yurchak 2006) and performative linguistics (Robinson 2003) as well as performative theories of language (Bakhtin 1981, Butler 2008) can help to account for the reaccentuation (Bakhtin 1981), resignification (Butler 1997), and reappropriation (Pennycook 2007: 24) of discourses that we see at play here.

What we have witnessed here in these exchanges has larger significance for the relation of language and globalization. As Fairclough (2006) argues, while globalization in itself is a technological and economic reality, globalist discourses are discursive processes that constitute and attribute value to people and events and shape social relations and identities. These discourses are "strategically motivated" (ibid., p. 164) as they disseminate and reproduce ideologies that serve the interests both of the powerful and of those who seek to gain power. But in these discourse wars language becomes a double-edged sword. On the one hand it serves to minimize the uncertainties and fragmentations brought about by global communication technologies, through the use of euphemisms that appear to construct a familiar world of global friends and communities. On the other hand, as critics have noted (see Poster 1990), the speed and reach of global communication has given inordinate importance to signifiers; it risks reducing signs to what Roland Barthes called "myths" (Barthes 1972), and speak to doublespeak. Globalization has brought with it an increased reliance on, and at the same time an increased unreliability of, language and other symbolic systems for representing social and political realities. Ultimately globalization confronts linguists with the need to redefine the very basis of our "symbolic species" (Deacon 1997) and the power of language to guarantee our symbolic existence.

ACKNOWLEDGMENTS

Liz Boner wishes to thank Adam Mkarafu, her Tanzanian research assistant, a tour guide who was born and raised in a nearby village, and Antoni Keya, lecturer in the department of foreign language and linguistics at the University of Dar es Salaam, for their help with the understanding of the context in which our data unfold.

TRANSCRIPTION CONVENTIONS

(.)	pause of less than a second
(2)	two-second pause
<u>underline</u>	stress
[ ]	overlapping talk
=	continuous talk
↑↓	rising or falling intonation
↓	delete downward arrow
-	hesitation or rephrasing
italics	Swahili words which are the focus of analysis
↑ (underscore)	mis-start and rephrasing
(:)	extended vowel sound.

NOTES

1   Key International Development Institutions include the World Bank, United Nations Development Program, and the International Monetary Fund and have historically worked through government institutions. Non-Governmental Organizations (NGOs) are legally constituted organizations created by *private* persons with no government representation or participation. NGOs can be international, serving multiple countries, or 'local,' serving a particular area.

2   All names are pseudonyms.

3 The Tanzanian women (but not the American practitioners) use the term *kuzaliwa* ('to be born') to describe their relationship with this American NGO.

4 'McNichols' is a pseudonym for an American private philanthropic foundation whose mission is to improve the quality of life and to empower those whom it serves. The foundation provides grants for projects conducted in the US and internationally.

5 These two different meetings illustrate the different roles played by Eco-Preneur. In the first case they are working directly with one organization, Saccos, while in the second they are facilitating the activities of different organizations within the community-wide network – which, coincidently, includes these same Saccos representatives.

6 In an earlier turn, Maria has explained that "this" refers to the "blah blah" of the way that Melissa and David are explaining things, without giving advice.

7 Namely other Tega members.

8 The restrictions were imposed by the American trainers, who were themselves selected by the funding agency to train the Tanzanians; they were selected, namely, instead of the Kenyans or Ugandans, who had been taught and could have done the training. This is yet another example of multiple levels of global shadows. (See Excerpt 4.)

9 This disrespect for Kato's contribution is even more blatant when viewed as coming from a young woman like Melissa, a guest in the country, and as being directed toward a very prominent and older community member. It is, however, very unlikely that Kato understood the sarcasm. Other people present assumed that Melissa was trying to tell him to go and talk to the trainers and wishing him good luck.

10 In fact the Tanzanians' assessment of cost analysis has been taught to them by global monetary institutions like the IMF and the World Bank and reflects conditions created by them.

11 The global action plan referred to here covers the UN millennium development goals and the National Strategies for Development.

12 Assessing the sustainability of a project in relation to how it reflects the needs of the people and the potential future benefits became a widely accepted practice and discourse after critiques that international development often came up with projects that were damaging and/or irrelevant.

REFERENCES

Bakhtin, M. (1981) *The Dialogic Imagination*, edited by M. Holquist, translated by. C. Emerson and M. Holquist. Austin, TX: University of Texas Press.

Barthes, R. (1972) *Mythologies* [1957], translated by A. Lavers. New York: Hill and Wang.

Blommaert, J. (2005) *Discourse*. Cambridge: Cambridge University Press.

Blum-Kulka, S., House, J., and Kasper, G. (eds) (1989) Cross-Cultural Pragmatics: Requests and Apologies (= Vol. 31 in the series Advances in Discourse Processes, Roy O. Freedle general editor). Norwood, NJ: Ablex.

Boner, E. (2011) *The Making of the Entrepreneur in Rural Tanzania*. Unpublished PhD dissertation, University of California, Berkeley.

Butler, J. (1997) *Excitable Speech. A Politics of the Performative*. New York: Routledge.

Butler, J. (2008) *Critique, responsibility, and performative rights*. Maruyama Lecture on Political Responsibility in the Modern World, delivered at University of California, Berkeley, May 12.

Cameron, D. (2000) *Good to Talk? Living and Working in a Communication Culture.* London: Sage.

Campbell, H., and Stein, H. (1991) *The IMF and Tanzania: The Dynamics of Liberalisation.* Harare, Zimbabwe: Southern Africa Political Economy Series (SAPES) Trust.

Cooper, F. (2001) What is the concept of globalization good for? An African historian's perspective. *African Affairs* 100: 189–213.

Coupland, N. (2007) *Style.* Cambridge: Cambridge University Press.

Deacon, T. W. (1997) *The Symbolic Species. The Co-Evolution of Language and the Brain.* New York: Norton.

Escobar, A. (1995) *Encountering Development: The Making and Unmaking of the Third World.* Princeton, NJ: Princeton University Press.

Fairclough, N. (1989) *Language and Power.* London: Longman.

Fairclough, N. (2006) *Language and Globalization.* London: Routledge.

Ferguson, J. (2006) *Global Shadows. Africa in the Neoliberal World Order.* Durham, NC: Duke University Press.

Gee, J., Hull, G., and Lankshear, C. (1997) *The New Work Order. Behind the Language of the New Capitalism.* Boulder, CO: Westview Press.

Gumperz, J. J. (1992) Contextualization and understanding. In A. Duranti and C. Goodwin (eds), *Rethinking Context. Language as an Interactive Phenomenon,* 229–52. Cambridge: Cambridge University Press.

Gumperz, J. J., and Levinson, S. (1996) *Rethinking Linguistic Relativity.* Cambridge: Cambridge University Press.

Hacking, I. (1999) *The Social Construction of What?* Cambridge, MA: Harvard University Press.

Hanks, W. (1996) *Language and Communicative Practices.* Boulder, CO: Westview Press.

Hanks, W. (2000) *Intertexts. Writings on Language, Utterance, and Context.* Lanham, MD: Rowman and Littlefield.

Igoe, J., and Kelsall, T. (2005) *Between a Rock and a Hard Place.* Durham, NC: Carolina Academic Press.

Judt, T. (2007) The wrecking ball of innovation. Review of Robert Reich, *Supercapitalism: The Transformation of Business, Democracy, and Everyday Life. New York Review of Books* 54(19), December 6: 22–7.

Judt, T. (2008) Supercapitalism: An exchange. *New York Review of Books* 55(1), January 17: 61.

Kiondo, A. (1994) The new politics of local development in Tanzania. In P. Gibbon (ed.), *The New Local Level Politics in East Africa. Studies on Uganda, Tanzania and Kenya. Research Report no. 95,* 38–65. Uppsala: Nordiska Afrikainstitutet).

Kotthoff, H., and Spencer-Oatey, H. (eds) (2007) Intercultural Communication (= Vol. 7 in the series Handbooks of Applied Linguistics, G. Antos and K. Knapp general editors). Berlin: Mouton de Gruyter.

Kramsch, C. (2002a) In search of the intercultural. *Journal of Sociolinguistics* 6(2): 275–85.

Kramsch, C. (ed.) (2002b) *Language Acquisition and Language Socialization. Ecological perspectives.* London: Continuum.

Kramsch, C., and Whiteside, A. (2008) Language ecology in multilingual settings. Towards a theory of symbolic competence. *Applied Linguistics* 29(4): 645–71.

Lemke, J. (2000) Across the scales of time: Artifacts, activities, and meanings in ecosocial systems. *Mind, Culture, and Activity* 7(4), 273–90.

Mohan, G., and Stokke, K. (2000) Participatory development and empowerment: The dangers of localism. *Third World Quarterly* 21: 247–68.

Nyerere, J. (1973) *Freedom and Development.* Oxford: Oxford University Press.

Ochs, E. (1996) Linguistic resources for socializing humanity. In J. J. Gumperz and S. C. Levinson (eds), *Rethinking Linguistic Relativity*, 407–37. Cambridge: Cambridge University Press.

Pennycook, A. (2007) *Global Englishes and Transcultural Flows*. London: Routledge.

Poster, M. (1990) *The Mode of Information. Poststructuralism and Social Context*. Chicago: University of Chicago Press.

Prahalad. C. K. (2005) *The Fortune at the Bottom of the Pyramid*. Upper Saddle River, NJ: Wharton School Publishing.

Rampton, B. (1999) Styling the Other: Introduction. In B. Rampton (ed.), *Styling the Other* (= *Journal of Sociolinguistics* 3(4), special issue): 421–7. Oxford: Blackwell.

Reich, R. (2007) *Supercapitalism. The Transformation of Business, Democracy and Everyday Life*. New York: Knopf.

Robinson, D. (2003) *Performative Linguistics. Speaking and Translating as Doing Things with Words*. London: Routledge.

Sachs, J. (2005) *The End of Poverty: Economic Possibilities for Our Time*. Harmondsworth: Penguin.

Scollon, R., and Scollon, S. 2001. *Intercultural Communication. A Discourse Approach*. 2nd edn. Oxford: Blackwell.

Shivji, I. G. (2006) *Let the People Speak : Tanzania down the Road to Neo-Liberalism*. Dakar, Sénégal: Codesria.

Shivji, I. G. (2007) *Silences in NGO Discourse: The Role and Future of NGOs in Africa*. Nairobi and Oxford: Fahamu.

Truman, H. (1949) *Public Papers of the Presidents of the United States: Harry S. Truman*. Washington, DC: US Government Printing Office.

World Bank (2001) *World Development Report 2000/2001. Attacking Poverty*. New York: World Bank.

Yurchak, A. (2006) *Everything was to Last Forever until It Was No More. The Last Soviet Generation*. Princeton, NJ: Princeton University Press.

23 Unraveling Post-Colonial Identity through Language

RAKESH M. BHATT

Introduction

One of the defining features of globalization is the increasingly complex and multifaceted interactions of localism and globalism. The post-colonial contexts present us with a vibrant site where local linguistic forms – inflected by the nexus of activities taking place elsewhere in time and space – are constantly transforming in response to asymmetric exchanges, pluralized histories, power plays, and battles over polysemous signs. The transformation makes available a semiotic space where a repertoire of identities evolves in the inter-animation of the colonial–global and of the indigenous-local. This chapter will explore how ideological legacies of English colonialism in post-colonial contexts are transformed in communicative practices that allow the emergence of new identities, which are neither colonial–global, nor necessarily indigenous–local. Indeed the linguistic politics of post-colonial identity is, demonstrably, a continuous process of identification constituted through resistance and reconstruction, in a bid to subvert the discursive effects of colonization. Given this situation, the present chapter will focus on English and on the ways in which its local transformation has introduced hybridizations of cultural identities. Specifically, this chapter raises questions – and sets up possible scenarios of sociolinguistic analyses – related to how, for instance, post-colonial identities are re-shaped, renegotiated, and re-analyzed under pressures of globalization; particularly, as English dominates the "linguascape" of post-colonial contexts – to extend Appadurai's (1996) metaphor.

Drawing on contemporary linguistic practices in post-colonial South and Southeast Asia and in parts of anglophone Africa, I will present available data on various linguistic processes of indigenization as evidence of disruptions in the historical structure of center–periphery, as well as of transformations taking place today in global alignments of language and power. The most noteworthy exponents of post-colonial identity are visible in at least three dimensions of creative language use: linguistic, sociolinguistic, and literary. Taken together,

The Handbook of Language and Globalization, First Edition. Edited by Nikolas Coupland.
© 2013 Blackwell Publishing Ltd except for editorial material and organization © 2013 Nikolas Coupland.
Published 2013 by Blackwell Publishing Ltd.

these dimensions reveal how local cultural grammars displace standard linguistic grammars of the colonial masters, producing new, hybrid, post-colonial linguistic identities.

Colonial Contact and the Sacred Imagined Community

The spread of English in South Asia can be traced to an ordinance issued in 1835, which laid the blueprint of a colonial linguistic ideology designed to downgrade the cultural capital and values of the colonized. This ordinance, based on the recommendations of T. B. Macaulay and entitled *Minute on Indian Education*, decreed that English be the medium of all schools and universities in India. The motivation behind *Minute* was to create "a class who may be interpreters between us and the millions we govern, a class of persons, Indian in blood and colour, but English in taste, in opinion, in morals and in intellect" (Sharp 1920: 116). The logic of this language-in-education policy – restricting access to English to only a small number of Indians – was governed essentially by a colonial ideology of race and skin color. The assumption clearly is that the acquisition of English by the colonized may not change their biology (blood and skin color), but could create a new culture (taste, opinions, morals, and intellect) with which the colonizers could interact.[1]

The colonial contact thus established what I have referred to elsewhere (Bhatt 2002) as a "sacred imagined community" – roughly in the sense of Anderson (1991): the formation of a nation (or a community) based on a particular belief system – within which the subordinate groups acquiesced to large-scale relations of unequal power, especially between English and the indigenous languages. Subordination of indigenous linguistic groups within the English sacred imagined community was accomplished by the complex interplay of three axioms (Bhatt 2002; also Anderson 1991), which, roughly, are:

1   There is a standard language, English, which provides access to knowledge (= ontological truth).

2   Closely connected to this, only those few who speak English can command authority (social, linguistic, cultural, and political) over others.

3   Finally, myth and history are indistinguishable,[2] enabling prescriptions to be glossed as descriptions, since they are thought to be essentially identical.

These three axioms, and the sociolinguistic forms that replicate them, defined the parameters of linguistic etiquette within the colony. As long as these three conceptions kept their axiomatic grip on the indigenous people, the English sacred imagined community flourished (Bhatt 2002).

The acquisition, use, and subsequent hegemony of English within the imagined community subverted the inherited, traditional discursive practices and introduced new ones, with novel representations of self, society, and culture. The outcome was the creation of a 'cultural Other.' Pankhania (1994: 1–2), an articulation from the Indian diaspora, summarizes this point well:

> I remember speaking in English in my African school, for in many ways my friends and I were discouraged from speaking in an African or an Indian language. I remember learning about 'Humpty Dumpty,' 'Old Mother Hubbard,' 'Ba Ba Black Sheep,' and later about *Alice in Wonderland*, *The Wizard of Oz*, *Robinson Crusoe* and *The Adventures of the Secret Seven*. This education taught me that Africa and India have no children's literature worth pursuing in schools. At home when my mother sang Indian songs to me, I felt embarrassed and wished my parents would speak to me in English. *I hid my mother tongue in a world that was increasingly portrayed as ugly.* (Emphasis added)

Colonial discourses were thus actively engaged in teaching the virtues of the English language and culture to the indigenous people while devaluing local symbolic systems as vernacular languages and cultures. Not surprisingly, as the quotation above indicates, the educational system in the colonies was the most important instrument in the reproduction of English symbolic capital, since schools[3] had a monopoly over the reproduction of the market on which the value of linguistic competence depends (Bourdieu 1977). In colonial South Asia and West Africa, where education was the only source for the acquisition of cultural capital[4] and for apprenticeship into "fellowships of discourse" (see Foucault 1972),[5] the principal medium of that initiation was English. Formal institutions such as school, court, administration, and governance made the power and dominance of English visible to – and also tacitly accepted by – the colonial subjects.

The symbolic domination of English is most faithfully captured in Vikram Seth's novel *A Suitable Boy* (1994). The short extract below (from p. 501), a conversation that takes place between a farmer and the protagonist Mann, reveals how entrenched the power and domination of English in India is.

> "Do you speak English?" he said after a while in the local dialect of Hindi.
> He had noticed Mann's luggage tag.
> "Yes," said Mann.
> "Without English you can't do anything," said the farmer sagely.
> Mann wondered what possible use English could be to the farmer.
> "What use is English?" said Mann.
> "People love English!" said the farmer with a strange sort of deep voiced giggle. "If you talk in English, you are a king. The more people you can mystify, the more people will respect you." He turned back to his tobacco.

The power of English, in terms of its symbolic and economic profits, and the politics of its acquisition and use, in terms of its restricted access, were not lost on prominent political leaders in colonial India and Nigeria: they contested the use of indigenous languages in schools because that was perceived as denying them the linguistic capital necessary for the accumulation of both economic and political powers (see Kachru 1983, Goke-Pariola 1993). The colonial project was thus successful in securing for English the profit of distinction, in restricting its distribution to the prevailing caste hierarchies, and in creating, in the process, new criteria for establishing class identities (Bhatt 2005).

In sum, the imposition of the English language and literature during the colonial period represented claims to a superior culture. Colonial discourses activated the virtues of the English language and culture to the indigenous people while devaluing local symbolic systems as 'vernacular' languages and cultures.[6] Whereas the indigenous languages and literatures were devalued and to some extent displaced, the colonial subject was linguistically and culturally dispossessed (see Phillipson 1992, Skutnabb-Kangas 2000). Given the material realities of linguistic exploitation in the colonies, the natural question to ask is whether the former colonies are now free from colonial influence, especially in the age of increasing globalization and transnationalism. In other words, we need to explore the extent to which the ex-colonized can express their identities in English without engendering recolonization. I turn to these questions in the next section.

Post-Colonial Identity, Agency, and Awareness

Language choice in post-colonial countries reflects a complex and often contradictory linguistic identity-negotiation: on the one hand, the post-colonial subjects' desire for an identity that transcends, and at times even inverts, the politics of the linguistic and cultural dominance of English; on the other hand, a desire for a dual kind of identity – both local–indigenous and colonial–English – based on cultural negotiation, interaction, and appropriation. In Africa, for instance, the choice of English to articulate a post-colonial identity is categorically rejected by East African writer Ngungi wa Thiong'o, but accepted by the West African writer Chinua Achebe.

The abrogation model of linguistic identity-choice, as the one achieved by Ngungi wa Thiong'o, attempts to erase imperial representations of language, literature, and literacy, which had successfully devalued and displaced indigenous language and literatures and dispossessed the colonial subject culturally and linguistically. According to this model of post-colonial identity-politics, the silencing of the native through the imposition of colonial discourse can be resisted, and even erased, by actively recruiting native cultural concepts of meanings essential for decolonization. Thus, for Ngungi wa Thiong'o, a liberation of the imagination is only possible through his complete abandonment of the colonial language and adoption of his native language instead, Gikuyu, as part of the social (anti-imperialist) struggles of the indigenous populations of Kenya. He writes (1995: 290):

> I would like to see Kenya people's mother tongues (our national languages!) carry a literature reflecting not only the rhythms of a child's spoken expressions, but also his struggle with his nature and his social nature.

The abrogation position of Ngungi wa Thiong'o, however, contrasts sharply with Achebe's appropriation position. In his essay entitled "English and the African writer" (1965: 62), he notes the dilemmas of the post-colonial writers, especially in their choice of a medium for literary creativity:

> Is it right that a man should abandon his mother tongue for someone else's? It looks like a dreadful betrayal and produces a guilty feeling. But for me there is no other choice. I have been given the language and I intend to use it.

Further down he notes (ibid.):

> I feel that the English language will be able to carry the weight of African experience. But it will have to be a new English, still in full communion with the ancestral home but altered to suit new African surroundings.

For those writers who embrace the appropriation model of post-colonial identity-politics, the claim to a decolonized identity can in fact be effected in a colonial idiom if the idiom is altered sufficiently to reflect the local cultural ethos. These alterations reflect 'agency' on the part of the post-colonial writers: that is, the socio-culturally mediated capacity to act (Ahearn 2001), or the cultural confidence to write on their own terms, creating new literary canons and expressing an identity which is neither colonial nor necessarily indigenous.[7] Through sustained linguistic transgressions (to be discussed in the next section), these altered linguistic forms enable a new, hybrid voice, which has the capacity to articulate local cultural meanings. Thus, in their attempt to stay faithful to the cultural–semantic representation of the native (local) context in which the text is embedded, creative writers change the idiom from colonial English to other, local Englishes. It is this agency of intention (Ortner 2001) that Gabriel Okara (1963: 15–16) expresses in the following extract:

> As a writer who believes in the utilization of African ideas, African philosophy and African folklore and imagery to the fullest extent possible, I am of the opinion [that] the only way to use them effectively is to translate them almost literally from the African language native to the writer into whatever European language he is using as medium of expression. [...] Some may regard this way of writing English as a desecration of the language. This is of course not true. Living languages grow like living things, and English is far from a dead language. There are American, West Indian, Australian, Canadian, and New Zealand versions of English. All of them add life and vigour to the language while reflecting their own respective cultures. Why shouldn't there be a Nigerian or West African English which we can use to express our own ideas, thinking and philosophy in our own way?

In the context of post-colonial South Asia, the tension between abrogation and appropriation has been resolved in favor of appropriation. The appropriation, an exercise of agency, of the English language (and literatures) by ex-colonized South Asians has a long history of resistance and negotiation, of struggles over transformation, and over meaning, identity, and authenticity (Bhatt 2002). The cross-fertilization between English and local indigenous languages presents to the post-colonial Indian writer/speaker the possibility of choice, plurality, and bilingual creativity.[8] It is in the act of expressing linguistic agency that post-colonial subjects recontextualize the colonial idiom, giving rise to a hybrid sociolinguistic reality where the colonial norm is imbued with local–indigenous inflections. On this view, I argue that linguistic hybridity involves what Ashcroft (1989: 72) called the "devices of otherness":

> the devices which appear specifically utilized to establish the difference and uniqueness of the post-colonial text. [...] such devices include syntactic fusion, [...] neologisms, [...] the direct inclusion of untranslated lexical items in the text; ethnorhythmic prose; and the transcription of dialect and language variants of many different kinds ...

The very act of recruiting "devices of otherness" effects an appropriation of English by its local speakers, giving rise to new Englishes that express, as Green observes,

> a whole language, complete with the colloquialisms of Calcutta and London, Shakespearian archaisms, bazaar whinings, references to the Hindu pantheon, the jargon of Indian litigation and shrill Babu irritability all together. It's not pure English, but [...] the language of Shakespeare, Joyce and Kipling – gloriously impure. (Green 1998: 111, quoting Anthony Burgess)

The use of post-colonial Englishes carries the possibility of altering the structures of power by shifting the focus from colonial authenticity to appropriacy and appropriation (Kramsch and Sullivan 1996) and to authentic and local ideas and values. In fact Salman Rushdie's celebrated phrase "the empire writes back" sums up rather succinctly the confidence of post-colonial English writers in inverting the process of literary, cultural, and linguistic nourishment from the colonial masters. He correctly notes (Rushdie 1982: 8) that the English language needs to be decolonized,

> if those of us who use it from positions outside Anglo-Saxon culture are to be more than artistic Uncle Toms. And it is this endeavor that gives the new literatures of Africa, the Caribbean and India much of their present vitality and excitement.

In contemporary post-colonial India, English is "unselfconsciously" used, as Vikram Seth notes, since it "doesn't have any colonial associations for them [writers/speakers]. They use it as freely as their own language" (interview, in Seth 1993: 20). Indeed post-colonial Englishes have shifted the focus on identity, from parochial domesticity and exclusive colonial norms to global inclusiveness and egalitarian license to speak, and their users write in ways that meet diverse local needs (Seidlhofer 2001: 135). These Englishes, with their associated literatures, have come of age with their own identities – an amalgam of East and West, as Naik (1992: 290) correctly observes:

> In fact, the course of Indian English literature is an absorbing record of the steady march of the Indian writer in English from sheer psittacism to authentic literary expression. Far from remaining merely 'bastard bantlings of the British,' Indian English writers, struggling valiantly against prejudice, neglect and ridicule, have, at their best, proved themselves to be proud heirs to the two equally rich worlds of the East and the West.

The stability of post-colonial Englishes, which express hybrid identities, is now secured by forces of globalization, as they successfully compete with other Englishes (British/American) for profit-sharing in domestic, regional, and international linguistic markets. As a global tool, post-colonial English is used to express native/indigenous histories, ideologies, cultures, and current practices, as is evidenced in the works of contemporary Indian English writers such as Salman Rushdie, Shashi Tharoor, Amitav Ghosh, Shashi Deshpande, Firdaus Kanga, Vikram Seth, Arundhati Roy, and Rohinton Mistry. Even at the turn of the twentieth century, Vivekananda, the founder of Ramakrishna Mission, realized the global potential of the colonial idiom and used it to "put the ancient truths of Vedanta in it, [and] broadcast them to the world ..." Gokak (1964: 178) puts more forcefully this pragmatic function of post-colonial Englishes in globalizing local practices:[9]

> The English language has linked India with the world. It has conducted sparks of inspiration from the world outside to India and from India to the world. We are blessed with the two-way traffic that English has afforded us. We have paid a heavy price in the past for this privilege. But in our indignation over the price that has been paid, let us not throw away the privilege that is already ours.

The pragmatics of post-colonial English, through the hybridity of the language, draws both on the global and on the local, allowing its users to glide effortlessly among local, national, and international identities. This hybridity manifests itself through a complex of language behaviors, which produce and reproduce identity 'positionings' (*à la* Davies and Harré 1990) that link the global – the transnational English culture – to the local – the urbanized vernacular post-colonial English cultures.

In sum, post-colonial identity, as I have argued above, can be understood as the emergence of agency and self-awareness: a new semiotic process and ideology of plurality and hybridity, through which people imagine their identities as being dialogically constituted through resistance and appropriation. The hybrid nature of post-colonial identities – engaged at once as they are with anti-cultural imperialism and pro-cultural globalization – emerges in localized linguistic practices as a new differentiation, which welds colonialism with autonomy, past with present, and global with local. Hybridity involves the fusion of two relatively distinct cultural forms, styles, and identities, creating a discursive space – a *third space* (Bhabha 1994) – where competing representations of colonized–colonizer, indigenous–foreign, and local–global are constantly negotiated. It is specifically in this negotiation that a new orchestration of linguistic identities – say, Hinglish or Singlish[10] – emerges through subversion, transgression, and other forms of linguistic acts of resistance. The data in the next section offer evidence of hybridity – that is, of English linguistic forms that have undergone a process of transformation – of indigenization – in order to reflect the local cultural etiquette.

Post-Colonial Identity and Linguistic Acts of Resistance

This section presents data that show symbolic inversion of specific linguistic forms indexing post-colonial identity. The cumulative effect of such transgressions of linguistic forms, I claim, produces difference: variations associated with the specific local functions of resistance and appropriation. The data will specifically show that speakers/writers of post-colonial Englishes have altered the syntactic, discourse-pragmatic, sociolinguistic, and literary forms of metropolitan varieties to recreate, maintain, or represent more faithfully local cultural practices and culturally embedded meanings.

Linguistic indices of post-colonial identity

One of the striking illustrations of the linguistic act of resistance – and transformation – in syntactic form appears in the use of undifferentiated tag questions in post-colonial Englishes, where local English-language users subvert the standard form of tag to honor the grammar of local culture (see Bright 1968, Hymes 1974, D'souza 1988, Bhatt 2001, 2005). In standard varieties of English, tag questions are formed by a rule that inserts a pronominal copy of the subject after an appropriate modal auxiliary. A typical example is given in (1) below.

(1)   John said he'll work today, didn't he?

Tags express certain attitudes of the speaker toward what is being said in the main clause and in terms of speech acts and/or performatives. Functionally, tags in English generally behave like epistemic adverbials such as 'probably,' 'presumably,' and the like – as shown in (2) below.[11]

(2a)   It's still dark outside, isn't it?
(2b)   It's still probably dark outside.

On the other hand, undifferentiated tag questions such as in (3a) and (3b) subvert the colonial codifications of use to express local identities (compare Bhatt 2001, 2005).[12]

(3a)   You are going home soon, isn't it?
(3b)   You have taken my book, isn't it?

The meaning of the tags in (3) is not the one appended to the meaning of the main proposition; it is usually constrained by cultural constraints of politeness, by the politeness principle of non-imposition. In other words, such tags serve positive politeness functions (Brown and Levinson 1987), signaling deference and acquiescence. The evidence for functional difference can be found in the contrast between Indian English tags in (4) and British English tags in (5).

(4)   Unassertive/Mitigated
      (4a)   You said you'll do the job, isn't it?
      (4b)   They said they will be here, isn't it?
(5)   Assertive/Intensified
      (5a)   You said you'll do the job, didn't you?
      (5b)   They said they will be here, didn't they?

The perceptual–interpretational contrast between (4) and (5) is revealing: Indian Englishes speakers find the undifferentiated tag expressions in (4) as non-impositional and mitigating, while tags in (5) appear to them as assertive, direct, and intensified (Bhatt 1995, 2001, 2005). This claim is more clearly established when an adverb of intensification/assertion is used in conjunction with the undifferentiated tag; the result is, predictably, unacceptable (shown in the starred sentences below) to the speakers of different varieties of Indian English.

(4a*)   Of course you said you'll do the job, isn't it?
(4b*)   Of course they said they'll be here, isn't it?

In a culture where verbal behavior is severely constrained, to a large extent, by politeness regulations, where non-imposition is the essence of polite behavior, it is noteworthy that post-colonial Indian English speakers replace English canonical tags with undifferentiated tags. Variants of this undifferentiated tag are common in other post-colonial Englishes. In Hong Kong English, they are often used when seeking confirmation and involvement (see Cheng and Warren 2001), in mainly local positive politeness functions. Similarly, speakers of colloquial Singapore English (Singlish) use either the tag 'isn't it' or the tag 'is it' (Pakir 1994, Alsagoff and Lick 1998) mainly to signal local solidarity. Bamiro (1995) and Bokamba (1992) have discussed the case of West African English speakers using undifferentiated tags ('isn't it,' 'not,' 'no') to express deference in local interactional contexts.

Undifferentiated tags are not exclusive instances of innovations in the linguistic grammar of post-colonial Englishes that reflect a local linguistic identity of the users. The linguistic expression of agency and identity can be seen elsewhere in syntax, as in the use of the modal auxiliary 'may.' The data in (6), from speakers of Indian English, reflect an appropriation of the use of the modal auxiliary 'may,' to make it express obligation politely in local cultural contexts (see Bhatt 2001, 2005).

(6)   Indian English
    (6a)   This furniture may be removed tomorrow.
    (6b)   These mistakes may please be corrected.

Similar uses of the modal auxiliary are attested elsewhere in post-colonial Englishes: a polite softener 'may' replaces 'could' among Black South African English speakers (Mesthrie and Bhatt 2008); Singapore English speakers use 'would' as a polite form, as a tentativeness marker, and as a marker of irrealis aspect (Alsagoff and Lick 1998).

The linguistic expression of post-colonial identity is also available beyond syntax, for example in the use of pragmatic particles. Pragmatic particles have been analyzed as lexical adjuncts, peripheral to the clausal syntax in which they appear; their meaning is generally inferred from the context of use. Although they are non-truth conditional, these pragmatic particles do seem to contribute to the illocutionary force of the utterance, indexing speaker attitude or stance. One of the most visible indices of Indian English, for instance, is the use of the pragmatic particle 'only,' which appears immediately to the right of the presentationally (non-contrastively) focused constituent. The use of clause/phrase-final 'only' carries a specific semantic reading of 'least likely' and performs the pragmatic function of indexical assertion, drawing the attention of the hearer to a particular part of the speaker's utterance. In (7), the particle 'only' appears after the object phrase, marking presentational focus: 'only' (a) expresses the unexpectedness, the 'least likely' component of the meaning, and (b) makes salient a part of A's utterance.

(7)
    A: Why are these women dressed like that?
    B: These women wear everyday *expensive clothes only*.

The use of this pragmatic particle 'only' in Indian English is an important innovation, it asserts the presuppositional structure of an utterance (Bhatt 2000). Other post-colonial speakers have also introduced similar innovations as part of their appropriation of English. The particle 'la' is the most common discourse-pragmatic particle used mainly by speakers of local Singapore English (cf. Richards and Tay 1977, Gupta 1992, Wong 2004). 'La,' as shown in the data in example (8) below (taken from Wong 2004), occurs with a range of interactional functions such as requests, invitations, promises, suggestions, and so on, as long as the interlocutors share an element of solidarity. It is thus the very act of local identification that yields a new identity for speakers of Singapore English (Singlish).

(8)
>Daughter: Mum, it's private. How can I let you read it?
>Mother: Can la. I'm your own mother.

The data above show structural–linguistic subversions (for instance the undifferentiated tag questions, the use of modal auxiliary, discourse-pragmatic particles) that enable local linguistic appropriation, presenting new possibilities of articulating post-colonial linguistic identity and of establishing local solidarities.

Sociolinguistic indices of post-colonial identity

One key aspect of post-colonialism in late modernity is the unsettling of boundaries between different domains of social use of language, which results in a discoursal hybridity (see Chouliaraki and Fairclough 1999). Distinctive hybridizations emerging from the intermixing of colonial English with indigenous languages permit a cultural articulation of the mutual embeddedness of the local–indigenous and the global–colonial (see Dissanayake 1997). This hybridization, accomplished via code-switching and mixing, is able successfully to decolonize and democratize English language use, disrupting colonial claims to its cultural–linguistic authenticity. A new, hybrid code thus develops, offering multilingual experiences of cultural difference as well as a sense of the entanglement of different cultural traditions. In Bhatt (2008), the following evidence of this linguistic hybridity is presented (taken from *Times of India* at www.timesofindia.com, October 12, 2001):

(9)   There have been several analyses of this phenomenon. First, there is the 'religious angle' which is to do with Indian society. In India a man feels guilty when fantasising about another man's wife, unlike in the west. The *saat pheras* around the *agni* serves as a *lakshman rekha*.[13]

In this bilingual English–Hindi mode of news-feature presentation the Hindi idiom is left untranslated. Such untranslated words, according to Ashcroft and colleagues (1989: 53), "do have an important function in inscribing difference. They signify a certain cultural experience, which they cannot hope to reproduce but whose difference is validated by the new situation. In this sense they are directly metonymic of that cultural difference which is imputed by the linguistic variation." The code-mixed Hindi items in (9), rooted in the most important historical narratives, the Vedas, and in the great Hindu epic of India, the *Ramayana*, realizes an important sociolinguistic function: these words serve as vehicles of cultural memory, animating, simultaneously with the global–colonial, a local–indigenous identity. Code-switching between English and Hindi thus yields a hybridity that makes the semantic possibilities more flexible, movement between global–colonial and local–indigenous identities more manageable, and the goal of decolonization and democratization of English more realizable.

We find recognition and acceptance of this sociolinguistic hybridity, the new Englishes, in other genres as well, and particularly in popular – hip-hop – culture.

The linguistic choices in hip hop relate to the issues of identity politics and power struggles within the local contexts of the use of this global cultural product (see Berger and Carroll 2003, Lee and Y. Kachru 2006, Bhatt, in press). Pennycook's discussion of Japanese rappers Rip Slyme's rap 'Bring Your Style,' for instance, investigates questions of agency, identity, and the politics of representation (2003; see also Pennycook this volume). Blending African American speech styles with Japanese language, these rap artists not only manage to organize a genre that is simultaneously global and local, but also employ the language-blend locally as a form of "resistance vernacular" (see Potter 1995). Similar trends appear in creative articulations of post-colonial Englishes genre of hip hop: in East African hip-hop (Perullo and Fenn 2003), in West African (and diaspora) hip hop (Omoniyi 2006, see also this volume), and in East Asian hip hop (Condry 2000, Lee 2006). In these local genres of hip hop one notices a semiotic process of the social production of difference: local hip hop departs from the 'core' in its rejection of features that characterize the mainstream gangsta rap norms such as heavy sexualization, misogyny, politics, and monolingualism (Omoniyi 2006; see also Perullo and Fenn 2003). The linguistic production of difference in this genre relies heavily on the specific sociolinguistic choices that the artists make. The most dominant paradigm of difference is serviced by code-switching: the use of local languages in the global medium, English, extends the meaning potential of this genre to produce local indexicalities (Omoniyi 2006; Bhatt, in press).

Speakers in post-colonial contexts also switch between different English identities available to them to perform different sociolinguistic functions. Mesthrie (1992: 219), for example, discusses the case of downshifting in the use of the mesolectal variety of South African Indian English by a young Indian attendant at airport security in South Africa to a passenger of the same ethnic background, as shown in example (10) below.

(10)   You haven' got anything to declare?

The unmarked choice in this context would normally be the formal acrolectal equivalent, "Do you have anything to declare?," which closely approximates the colonial idiom. As Mesthrie notes, although the security guard and the passenger were strangers, the speaker was tacitly defusing the syntax of power (acrolect) in favor of mesolectal, ethnic solidarity, while still doing his duty. These subtle switches in everyday interactions exemplify the capacity of post-colonial subjects not only to subvert, and to resist, the symbolic domination of colonial English, but also to index local indigenous identity creatively.

Literary indices of post-colonial identity

Post-colonial creative writers, in experimenting with the English language, draw on their native sensibilities and inherited forms of culturally sanctioned discourse patterns. As such, post-colonial English literatures take different structural–textual forms, because literary texts as discourse reflect the underlying thought patterns, social norms, cultural practices, attitudes, and values of the people writing the texts and/or their intended audience. The connection between text and context not only results in cultural authenticity, but also enables a new way of meaning-making, of representation, which is different from traditional canons; consequently, English is ritually decolonized. In *Arrow of God*, creative writer Chinua Achebe (1969: 29) uses the following passage as an illustration of this decolonization process. In this passage the chief priest is telling one of his sons why it is necessary to send him to church:

(11)   I want one of my sons to join these people and be my eyes there. If there is nothing in it you will come back. But if there is something then you will bring back my share. The world is like a Mask, dancing. If you want to see it well, you do not stand in one place. My spirit tells me that those who do not befriend the white man today will be saying 'had we known' tomorrow.

Achebe then speculates: "supposing I had put it another way. Like this for instance":

(12)   I am sending you as my representative among those people – just to be on the safe side in case the new religion develops. One has to move with the times or one is left behind. I have a hunch that those who fail to come to terms with the white man may well regret the lack of foresight.

The first passage, according to Achebe, expresses the local rural sensibilities by the use of local proverbs and other culture-bound speech patterns, which express a local Nigerian discoursal identity. Achebe concludes that, although the material is the same, "the form of the one [(11)] is in character, and the other [(12)] is not."

As Kachru (1986) notes, the production of difference in post-colonial English discourse has more to do with the use of native similes and metaphors, the transfer of rhetorical devices, the translation ('transcreation') of proverbs and idioms, the use of culturally dependent speech styles, and the use of syntactic devices. So, while in Achebe's example above we notice the transfer of discourse and rhetorical norms of Igbo into literary Nigerian English, in example (13) below, from Raja Rao's *Kanthapura* (Rao 1938: 10), we observe a slightly different acculturation of text: a narrative loaded with historical and cultural presuppositions, which are different from the traditional historical and cultural milieu of English literature (Kachru 1987). References to local cultural–historical practices, juxtaposed with local contemporary political events of the time, result in a text that expresses an indigenous identity, with a highly culture-specific meaning system.

(13)   "Today," he says, "it will be the story of Siva and Parvati." And Parvati in penance becomes the country and Siva becomes heaven knows what! "Siva is the three-eyed," he says, "and Swaraj too is three-eyed: Self-purification, Hindu-Moslem unity, Khaddar."

More contemporary post-colonial Indian writers like Salman Rushdie, Arundhati Roy, Shashi Tharoor, or Kiran Desai (among many others) also use an English linguistic medium in narratives that are usually situated in local geographies requiring a linguistic fusion of the colonial and the indigenous. This fusion is made possible by these writers' actively introducing subtle inversions of English syntax, code-switching using liberal sprinkling of native terms and expressions, and linguistic and cultural transcreations – all of which reflect the complex multilinguistic realities of post-colonial India.

Rushdie, for instance, like his predecessors Raja Rao, Mulk Raj Anand, and R. K. Narayan, actively recruits Indian varieties of English – Bombay English in *Midnight's Children*, Babu English in *The Satanic Verses*, and Cochin English in *The Moor's Last Sigh* (see Goonetilleke 1998) – to present an indigenous identity. He also makes use of code-switching (generally unitalicized), using quaint Hindi expressions of the colonial era "as textual reminders of the colonial past and to portray aspects of contemporary Indian life which have continued after the colonial era subsided" (Langeland 1996: 17). The resulting hybridity derides colonial English by flouting its lexico-semantic constraints and by overwhelming it with linguistic plurality via code-switching.

For the most part, these transgressions of linguistic forms in Rushdie's work appear in shifts in voices, primarily in the movement from the narrator to a character voice – as shown in the data below, which are taken from his books *The Satanic Verses* (*SV*) and *Midnight's Children* (*MC*). In example (14), the semantic formulae characteristic of the speech act of showing appreciation in the native tongue are transferred in the performance of analogous speech acts in English. The nativized morpho-syntax and the native lexical form of address of Indian English are all packaged together in the character voice to express the authentic cultural realization of appreciation. In example (15) Rushdie uses a typical pattern of reduplication, pervasive in Indian languages, to animate the local character voice. The function of reduplication is to intensify and/or explicate the meaning, which is cleverly sociolinguistically engineered by using a Hindi code-switch accompanied by translative elucidation in English. The data in example (16) are particularly illustrative of linguistic experimentation, agency, and appropriation. Those incorporated in the character voice show evidence of local Indian English syntax (absence of inversion in matrix questions), and, in addition, a clever hybridization of Grace Kelly with the Hindu goddess Kali (Langeland 1996: 20), which creates lexico-cultural ambiguity.

(14)   "My God, Vallabbhai," he managed, and embraced the old man. The servant smiled a difficult smile. "I *grow* so old, *baba*, I *was thinking* you would not recognize." (*SV*, p. 65, emphasis added)

(15)   O God, Saleem, all this tamasha, all this performance, for one of your stupid cracks? (*MC*, p. 194)

(16)   What you waiting? Some Goddess from heaven? Greta Garbo, Gracekali, who? (*SV*, p. 25)

To sum up the discussion so far, hybridity in literary forms validates indigenous–local cultural voices in a colonial–global norm. Post-colonial contact of English with local indigenous languages presents a unique opportunity for creative writers to express agency, to articulate plurality, and to extend the meaning potential of the idiom of their choice. The tension between an abrogation of the English language and an appropriation of it in post-colonial context is resolved in favor of the latter – Indian Englishes – and its ownership is secured by intermittently code-switching to Hindi, as Rushdie does, effecting transient abrogations.

Conclusions

The discussion and analysis of data in this chapter demonstrate how post-colonial subjects become "hegemony's most successful discontents" (Erickson 2004) by acting against the inclinations of their linguistic habitus and, in the process, by breaking away with the order of things and carving out a niche, a new identity, which is neither global–colonial nor necessarily local–indigenous.

Cultural contact between the colonial and the indigenous has resulted in a cross-fertilization of languages, yielding a new alchemy of English in post-colonial contexts which represents a linguistic hybridity of form and function. Innovations in syntax, discourse, and pragmatics in post-colonial English contexts make possible an insightful study of linguistic acts of resistance and transformation: the socio-cultural practices of the indigenous community invest individual linguistic actions of English with local values, replacing the colonial representation with a hybrid representation, which includes multiple norms of literary styles, sociolinguistic strategies, and linguistic identities. The linguistic resources used to produce hybridity include: use of native similes and metaphors; transfer of rhetorical devices from local contexts; translation ('transcreation') of proverbs and idioms; use of culturally dependent speech styles; and extensive switching and mixing of English with local languages. All of these local linguistic resources collectively serve several pragmatic functions of post-colonial Englishes, such as new articulations of identity, values, power, and solidarity.

ACKNOWLEDGMENTS

Many thanks to Nik Coupland for his critical comments and suggestions on an earlier version of this chapter. His comments forced me to re-evaluate some of my assumptions, reasses my analysis on some parts of the data, and rethink some of the conclusions I had previously drawn. Thanks also to students in my graduate seminar on World Englishes for actively critiquing parts of the chapter that were introduced there. Finally, my thanks to Jennifer Cramer, for proofreading this chapter and for her other editorial comments. I alone take full responsibility for any errors of omission and commission.

NOTES

1 Such colonial projects are not specific to India but are also noticed elsewhere. Portuguese colonialism, for example, "tried to eradicate the African languages in institutional life by inculcating Africans through the educational systems in Portuguese only with myths and beliefs concerning the savage nature of their culture" (Macedo 2000: 16). Similarly, French colonization, motivated by a *mission civilatrice*, called on the services of the French language to civilize the colonized, whose languages were not considered adequate.

2 This relates to the general belief, at least in some quarters of the English-speaking world, that standard languages have sprung full-blown from a Garden of Eden and that non-standard varieties are flawed spin-offs from them (see Finegan 1992; also Williams 1992; Pyles and Algeo 1982).

3 It is in schools, argues Giroux (1981: 24), that the production of hegemonic ideologies 'hides' behind a number of legitimating forms. Some of the most obvious include: "(1) the claim by dominant classes that their interests represent the entire interests of the community; (2) the claim that conflict only occurs outside of the sphere of the political, i.e., economic conflict is viewed as non-political; (3) the presentation of specific forms of consciousness, beliefs, attitudes, values and practices as natural, universal, or even eternal."

4 'Cultural capital' here refers to the "system of meanings, abilities, language forms, and tastes that are directly or indirectly defined by dominant groups as socially legitimate" (Apple 1978: 496).

5 The function of "the fellowships of discourse" is, according to Foucault (1972: 225–6), "to preserve or to reproduce discourse, but in order that it should circulate within a closed community, according to strict regulations, without those in possession being dispossessed by this very distribution. An archaic model of this would be those groups of Rhapsodists, possessing knowledge of poems to recite or, even, upon which to work variations and transformations. But though the ultimate object of this knowledge was ritual recitation, it was protected and preserved within a determinate group, by the, often extremely complex, exercises of memory implied by such a process. Apprenticeship gained access both to a group and to a secret which recitation made manifest, but did not divulge. The roles of speaking and listening were not interchangeable."

6 The term 'vernacular' here is used in a restricted sense, as a colonial reference (see Macaulay 1957) to indigenous languages (and cultures).

7 Although several notions of agency appear in the literature, the specific model of agency, especially in post-colonial contexts, which I follow equates agency with linguistic actions that resist domination (see Abu-Lughod 1990, Scott 1990, and Dissanayake 1997), disrupting standard assumptions of English linguistic forms and functions and creating norms of English-language use that are appropriate to local cultural contexts (see Bhatt 2001).

8 These three possibilities, recruited individually or collectively, form the core of my understanding of agency.

9 It is important to note here that Gokak is making an argument to retain English as a language of wider communication in local Indian contexts, as a linguistic option available to members of an Indian speech community for interaction in global networks.

10 These coinages have gained local currency, although their use is still contested, especially in official discourses (see Kachru 1986, Wee 2005).

11   It is important to note that variation in the intonation of the tag (falling or rising pitch) can effect different semantic–pragmatic meanings in terms of assertiveness (Algeo 1988). Both (2a), the facilitative tag (with falling pitch), and (2b) seem to me to be mitigating the assertion – that it is still dark outside.

12   Nik Coupland points out that some varieties of British English, such as Welsh English, also have invariant tags. English-knowing bilinguals in India have both the canonical and the undifferentiated tags. However, their use is generally tied to the power–solidarity axis: in formal contexts the canonical tags are used, expressing a power function, while in informal contexts undifferentiated tags are used, expressing a solidarity function (Bhatt 1995).

13   The contextually appropriate translations of the code-switched items are:

saat pheraas: the term refers to the ritual in which the bride and the groom walk around the fire together, pledging commitment to each other for seven births;

agni: the sacred fire in the wedding ritual. Fire is believed to be the messenger (or priest) who operates on behalf of the people who perform the sacrificial ritual. Agni takes the prayers of the people to gods in the heaven, and brings back their blessings to the people;

lakshmana rekha: refers to the line of protection drawn by Lakshmana (in the epic, Ramayana) around Sita's hut to protect her from dangers of the external world. Maricha, the demon (in the form of the deer), disguised his voice as Rama's, and called for Lakshmana's help. This was a trick to lure Lakshmana away from Sita and to give Ravana an opportunity to approach Sita, who would be left unprotected. Lakshmana, however, draws a line around the hut and tells Sita not to cross it lest she will encounter a danger. Thus the phrase *lakshmana rekha* (literally, a line) has become a symbol of protection, and transgressing it has acquired the meaning of allowing undesirable results to occur.

REFERENCES

Abu-Lughod, L. (1990) The romance of resistance: Tracing transformations of power through Bedouin women. *American Ethnologist* 17: 41–55.

Achebe, C. (1965) English and the African writer. *Transition* 18: 27–30.

Achebe, C. (1969) *Arrow of God*. New York: Doubleday.

Ahearn, L. (2001) Language and agency. *Annual Review of Anthropology* 30: 109–37.

Algeo, J. 1988. The tag question in British English: It's different, i'n 'it? *English World-Wide* 9(2): 171–91.

Alsagoff, L., and Lick, H. C. (1998) The grammar of Singapore English. In J. A. Foley, T. Kandiah, B. Zhiming, A. F. Gupta, L. Alsagoff, H. C. Lick, L. Wee, I. S. Talib, and W. Bokhorst-Heng (eds), *English in New Cultural Contexts: Reflections from Singapore*, 127–51. Oxford: Oxford University Press.

Anderson, B. (1991) *Imagined Communities: Reflections on the Origin and Spread of Mationalism*. London: Verso.

Appadurai, A. (1996) *Modernity at Large: Cultural Dimensions of Globalization*. Minneapolis: University of Minnesota Press.

Apple, M. (1978) The new sociology of education: Analyzing cultural and economic reproduction. *Harvard Educational Review* 48: 495–503.

Ashcroft, B. (1989) Constitutive graphonomy: A post-colonial theory of literary writing. *Kunapipi* 11: 58–73.

Ashcroft, B., Griffiths, G., and Tiffin, H. (1989) *The Empire Writes Back: Theory and Practice in Post-Colonial Literatures.* London: Routledge.

Bamiro, E. (1995) Syntactic variation in West African English. *World Englishes* 17(2): 189–204.

Berger, H., and Carroll, M. (eds) (2003) *Global Pop, Local Languages.* Jackson, MS: University of Mississippi Press.

Bhabha, H. (1994) *The Location of Culture.* London: Routledge.

Bhatt, R. M. (1995) Prescriptivism, creativity, and world Englishes. *World Englishes* 14: 247–60.

Bhatt, R. M. (2000) Optimal expressions in Indian English. *English Language and Linguistics* 4: 69–95.

Bhatt, R. M. (2001) World Englishes. *Annual Review of Anthropology* 30: 227–50.

Bhatt, R. M. (2002) Experts, dialects, and discourse. *International Journal of Applied Linguistics* 12(1): 74–109.

Bhatt, R. M. (2005) Expert discourses, local practices, and hybridity: The case of Indian Englishes. In S. Canagarajah (ed.), *Reclaiming the Local in Language Policy and Practice*, 25–54. Mahwah, NJ: Lawrence Erlbaum Associates.

Bhatt, R. M. (2008) In other words: Language mixing, identity representations, and third space. *Journal of Sociolinguistics* 12(2): 177–200.

Bhatt, R. M. (in press) World Englishes, globalization and the politics of conformity. In M. Saxena and T. Ominiyi (eds), *Contending with World Englishes in Globalization*, 137–64. London: Multilingual Matters.

Bokamba, E. G. (1992) The Africanization of English. In B. B. Kachru (ed.), *The Other Tongue: English across Cultures*, 125–47. Urbana: University of Illinois Press.

Bourdieu, P. (1977) *Outline of a Theory of Practice*, translated by R. Nice. Cambridge: Cambridge University Press.

Bright, W. (1968) Toward a cultural grammar. *Indian Linguistics* 29: 20–9.

Brown, P., and Levinson, S. (1987) *Politeness: Some Universals in Language.* Cambridge: Cambridge University Press.

Cheng, W., and Warren, M. (2001) "She knows more about Hong Kong than you do isn't it": Tags in Hong Kong conversational English. *Journal of Pragmatics* 33: 1419–39.

Chouliaraki, L., and Fairclough, N. (1999) *Discourse in Late Modernity: Rethinking Critical Discourse Analysis.* Edinburgh: Edinburgh University Press.

Condry, I. (2000) The social production of difference: Imitation and authenticity in Japanese Rap music. In H. Fehrenbach and U. Polger (eds), *Transactions, Transgressions, and Transformations*, 166–84). New York: Berghan Books.

Davies, B., and Harré, R. (1990) Positioning: The discursive production of selves. *Journal for the Theory of Social Behavior* 20: 40–63.

Dissanayake, W. (1997) Cultural studies and World Englishes: Some topics for further exploration. In L. Smith and M. Forman (eds), *World Englishes 2000*, 145–59. Honolulu: University of Hawai'i Press.

D'souza, J. (1988) Interactional strategies in South Asian languages: Their implications for teaching English internationally. *World Englishes* 7: 159–71.

Erickson, F. (2004) *Talk and Social Theory.* London: Blackwell.

Finegan, E. (1992) Style and standardization in England: 1700–1900. In T. Machan and C. Scott (eds), *English in Its Social Contexts: Essays in Historical Sociolinguistics*, 102–30. New York: Oxford University Press.

Foucault M. (1972) *The Archaeology of Knowledge and the Discourse on Language*, translated by A. M. Sheridan Smith. New York: Pantheon Books.

Giroux, H. A. (1981) *Ideology, Culture, and the Process of Schooling*. Philadelphia: Temple University Press.

Gokak, V. (1964) *English in India: Its Present and Future*. Bombay: Asia Publishing House.

Goke-Pariola, A. (1993) Language and symbolic power: Bourdieu and the legacy of Euro-American colonialism in an African society. *Language and Communication* 13(3): 219–34.

Goonetilleke , D. C. R. A. (1998) *Modern Novelists: Salman Rushdie*. New York: St Martin's Press.

Green, J. (1998) English in India – The grandmother tongue. *Critical Quarterly* 40(1) 107–11.

Gupta, A. F. (1992) The pragmatic particles of Singapore Colloquial English. *Journal of Pragmatics* 18: 31–57.

Hymes, D. (1974) *Foundations of Sociolinguistics: An Ethnographic Approach*. Philadelphia: University of Pennsylvania Press.

Kachru, B. B. (1983) *The Indianization of English: The English Language in India*. Delhi: Oxford University Press.

Kachru, B. B. (1986) *The Alchemy of English: The Spread, Functions and Models of Non-native Englishes*. London: Pergamon.

Kachru, B. B. (1987) The bilingual's creativity: Discoursal and stylistic strategies in contact literature. In Larry Smith (ed.), *Discourse across Cultures: Strategies in World Englishes*, 125–40). New York: Prentice Hall.

Kramsch, C., and Sullivan, P. (1996) Appropriate pedagogy. *ELT Journal* 50: 199–212.

Langeland, A. (1996) Rushdie's language. *English Today* 45: 16–22.

Lee, J. S. (2006) Crossing and crossers in East Asian pop music: Korea and Japan. *World Englishes* 25(2): 235–50.

Lee, J. S., and Kachru, Y. (eds) (2006) *Symposium on World Englishes in Pop Culture* (= *World Englishes* 25(2), special issue). Oxford: Blackwell.

Macaulay, T. B. (1957) *Minute of 2 February 1835 on Indian Education* [1835]. In G. M. Young (ed.), *Macaulay, Prose and Poetry*, 721–4, 729. Cambridge, MA: Harvard University Press.

Macedo, D. (2000) The colonialism of the English only movement. *Educational Researcher* 29(3): 15–24.

Mesthrie, R. (1992) *English in Language Shift*. Cambridge: Cambridge University Press.

Mesthrie, R., and Bhatt, R. M. (2008) *World Englishes: The Study of New Linguistic Varieties*. Cambridge: Cambridge University Press.

Naik, M. K. (1992) *A History of Indian English Literature*. New Delhi: Sahitya Aakademi.

Ngungi wa Thiong'o (1995) The language of African literature. In B. Ashcroft, G. Griffiths, and H. Tiffin (eds), *The Post-Colonial Studies Reader*, pp. 285–90. London: Routledge.

Okara, G. (1963) African speech … English words. *Transition* 10: 13–18.

Omoniyi, T. (2006) Hip hop through the world Englishes lens: A response to globalization. *World Englishes* 25(2): 195–208.

Ortner, S. B. (2001) Specifying agency: The Comaroffs and their critics. *Interventions*. 3(1): 76–84.

Pakir, A. (1994) English in Singapore: The codification of competing norms. In Gopinathan, A. Pakir, H. W. Kam, and V. Sarvanan (eds), *Language, Society and Education in Singapore: Issues and Trends*, 92–118). Singapore: Times. Academic Press.

Pankhania, J. (1994) Making sense of inequalities in society. In J. Pankhania (ed.), *Liberating the National History Curriculum*, 6–25. London, UK and Washington, DC: Falmer Press/Taylor and Francis.

Pennycook, A. (2003) Global Englishes, Rip Slyme, and performativity. *Journal of Sociolinguistics* 7(4): 513–33.

Perullo, A., and Fenn, J. (2003) Language ideologies, choices, and practices in eastern African hip hop. In H. Bernger and M. Carroll (eds), *Global Pop, Local Language*, 19–33. Jackson, MS: University Press of Mississippi.

Phillipson, R. (1992) *Linguistic Imperialism*. Oxford: Oxford University Press.

Potter, R. (1995) *Spectacular Vernaculars*. New York: SUNY Press.

Pyles, T., and Algeo, J. (1982) *The Origins and the Development of the English Language*. New York: Harcourt Brace Jovanovich.

Rao, R. (1938) *Kanthapura*. London: Allen and Unwin.

Richards, J. C., and Tay, M. (1977) The *la* particle in Singapore English. In W. Crewe (ed.), *The English Language in Singapore*, 141–56. Singapore: Eastern Universities Press.

Rushdie, S. (1981) *Midnight's Children*. London: Vintage.

Rushdie, S. (1982) The empire writes back with a vengeance. *The Times*, July 3, p. 8.

Rushdie, S. (1989) *The Satanic Verses*. New York: Viking

Scott, J. C. (1990) *Domination and the Arts of Resistance*. New Haven, CT: Yale University Press.

Seidlhofer, B. (2001) Closing a conceptual gap: The case for a description of English as a lingua franca. *International Journal of Applied Linguistics* 11(2): 133–58.

Seth, V. (1993). Interview with Vikram Seth. *India Currents* 7(3): 20.

Seth, V. (1994) *A Suitable Boy*. New York: HarperCollins.

Sharp, H. (ed.) (1920) *Selections from Educational Records*. Calcutta: Bureau of Education, Government of India.

Skutnabb-Kangas, T. (2000) *Linguistic Genocide in Education – Or Worldwide Diversity and Human Rights?* New Jersey: Lawrence Erlbaum.

Wee, L. (2005) Intra-lingual discrimination and linguistic human rights: The case of Singlish. *Applied Linguistics* 26: 48–69.

Williams, J. M. (1992) "O! When degree is shak'd": Sixteenth-century anticipations of some modern attitudes toward usage. In T. Machan and C. Scott (eds), *English in its Social Contexts*, 69–101. Oxford: Oxford University Press.

Wong, J. (2004) The particles of Singapore English: A semantic and cultural interpretation. *Journal of Pragmatics* 36: 739–93.

24 At the Intersection of Gender, Language, and Transnationalism

INGRID PILLER AND KIMIE TAKAHASHI

Introduction

In this chapter we explore the ways in which language and transnationalism play out on the terrain of gender and sexuality. We are particularly concerned with the gendered nature of transnational migration and the unequal distribution of access to economic and social capital, to which language holds the key. Contemporary gender theory is informed by the idea that gender *intersects* with other aspects of a person's identity, such as class, race, or nationality (Burman 2003; Staunæs 2003; Valentine 2007; Yuval-Davis 2007). It has long been recognized that gender discrimination may be compounded by race, class, or age discrimination. However, rather than considering these identity categories as add-ons where one compounds the other, *intersectionality* describes a fusion of subjectivities:

> [...] gender is not always constituted coherently or consistently in different historical contexts, and [...] gender intersects with racial, class, ethnic, sexual and regional modalities of discursively constituted identities. As a result, it becomes impossible to separate out 'gender' from the political and cultural intersections in which it is invariably produced and maintained. (Butler 1990: 3)

Thus our concern is with the ways in which gendered identities are produced and maintained in transnational contexts and the ways in which they are intersected by linguistic ideologies and practices. It is the aim of our enquiry to establish how social exclusion or inclusion is achieved at the intersections of gender, language, and migration. We believe that the merit of a focus on intersectionality lies in its ability to illuminate power effects, as Brah (1996: 248) points out:

> What is of interest is how these fields of power collide, enmesh and configure; and with *what effects*. What kinds of inclusions or exclusions does a *specific articulation of power* produce? That is, what patterns of equity or inequality are inscribed; what modes of domination or subordination are facilitated; what forms of pleasure are

The Handbook of Language and Globalization, First Edition. Edited by Nikolas Coupland.
© 2013 Blackwell Publishing Ltd except for editorial material and organization © 2013 Nikolas Coupland. Published 2013 by Blackwell Publishing Ltd.

produced; what fantasies, desires, ambivalence and contradictions are sanctioned; or what types of political subject positions are generated by the operations of given configurations of power? (emphasis in the original).

Such an approach is particularly suitable to an inquiry into intersectionality in transnational contexts, which themselves can be characterized as consisting of "multidirectional flows of desires, people, ideas, and objects across, between and beyond national boundaries" (Constable 2003: 215f., following Appadurai 1990). Our view of language is similar in that we also see it as a circulating resource, or, as Heller (2007: 2) explains, as "a set of resources which circulate in unequal ways in social networks and discursive spaces, and whose meaning and value are socially constructed within the constraints of social organizational processes, under specific historical conditions."

Our paper is structured around two spaces that we identify as key transnational spaces: they are highly gendered and language and migrant status serve in them to inscribe social exclusion. These spaces are reproductive work and the commodification of sexuality. Our reasons for choosing these particular spaces and for structuring our paper around them are three-fold. To begin with, we recognize that there are significant linguistic challenges involved in each of these spaces; but, while there is some existing work to draw upon, these spaces are nowhere near to having received from applied linguistics and sociolinguistics research the attention that their importance warrants. Secondly, although language is a key space where gender, globalization, and language intersect, we have chosen not to concentrate on language and language education per se, because a fair number of overviews have been produced in recent years (see for instance Pavlenko and Piller 2001, 2007; Piller and Pavlenko 2004). Thirdly, these two spaces have been identified by a number of sociologists as the key intersections at which global gendered identities are produced. In a recent overview paper, Lan explains the intersection between paid and unpaid reproductive labor as follows:

> Migrant reproductive labor conducted in private households can be unpaid (migrant women as wives, mothers, and daughters-in-law) or paid (migrant women working as in-home nannies, maids, or caretakers). The paid labor is also done in institutional settings, including less skilled categories like caretakers in nursing homes and more skilled categories like nurses in hospitals. [...] [E]arlier literature has tended to treat these categories as separate subjects of research. Along with other scholars, I advocate an approach of relational thinking to highlight the structural and discursive continuities of migrant reproductive labor. I argue that these various links and circuits have manifested a new global politics of reproductive labor. (Lan 2008: 2)

From 'Women's Work' to 'Migrant Women's Work'

Recent years have seen a significant expansion of the care and service sectors. Reproductive work – that is, traditional women's work – has undergone significant transformations both in qualitative and in quantitative terms. Qualitatively, reproductive work such as child-care, aged-care, cooking, or cleaning used to be predominantly domestic work. However, in many developed countries there has been a significant shift to outsource such work outside the home, to childcare centers, aged-care facilities, catering businesses, or cleaning chains. Quantitatively, the need for reproductive workers has increased substantially as women have taken on paid work outside the home and thus have less time to spend on unpaid reproductive work in the home. Furthermore, the expansion of the leisure and tourism industries has resulted in the creation of new types of reproductive work, or at least in a substantial expansion of work such as hotel cleaning. As a consequence of its transformation and expansion, reproductive work, is no longer only women's work but has become migrant women's work – "a structural relationship of inequality based on class, race, gender and (nation-based) citizenship" (Parreñas 2001: 73). In developed countries, migrant women have taken on a substantial share of reproductive work, often to the extent of dominating certain sectors. Migrant women may undertake reproductive work in domestic environments as maids or nannies (Anderson 2000; Chang 2000; Hondagneu-Sotelo 2001; Parreñas 2001, 2005) or in institutional environments as childcare workers, aged-care workers, or nurses (Francis et al. 2008; Isaksen 2007; Malawian nurses struggle 2008; Pulvers 2008) or as hotel cleaners (Adib and Guerrier 2003; Adkins 1995).

The experiences of migrant reproductive workers are profoundly embedded in linguistic and communicative inequalities. Anderson (1997) points out that migrant women who join the global care chain as domestics are neither likely nor expected to speak the language of the people they are serving. As Piller and Pavlenko (2007, 2009) suggest, limited or non-existent proficiency in the majority language may even work to the advantage of employers by creating "the pretence of distance," rationalizing reproductive workers' inferiority, and maintaining their unequal status – as in the case of a Filipina domestic worker in Toronto, who described her Canadian employers as follows: "They think you're as stupid as your English is!" (England and Stiell 1997). Inability to communicate with the person whom the workers care for may also add psychological stress to an already strenuous domestic situation (Raijman et al. 2003).

At the same time, migrant women's linguistic backgrounds, or even a lack of proficiency in the local language, can be an asset in some contexts. For instance Filipina reproductive workers are more in demand than their counterparts from other countries of origin because of their ability to speak English, a highly privileged form of linguistic capital internationally (Piller and Pavlenko 2007; 2009). Lan's (2003) ethnographic study of foreign domestic workers in Taiwan demonstrates fascinating negotiations of power and identity between Filipina domestic workers and their newly rich Taiwanese employers on the terrain of English language proficiency. Lan (2003; 2006) shows that it became trendy to hire Filipina domestic workers in Taiwan as the English learning boom there intensified (see also Chang 2004). Thus the ability to hire a Filipina domestic worker who can speak English and teach it to the employer's family boosts the social and class status of newly rich Taiwanese. Many of the Filipinas interviewed by Lan (2003;

2006), who had not been maids back home but often were college-educated and even had professional work experience, felt humiliated and conflicted about their position. However, they also capitalized on their English proficiency as a means of resistance against the positions in which they found themselves. One maid said of her employers: "They have more money, but I can speak better English than most of them" (Lan 2003: 150). Lack of English proficiency on the part of the employers on the other hand clearly undermined their authority – they found it difficult to make requests of their employees in English, so much so that one employer ended up doing the work herself, while another had to invest time in improving her English in order to express dissatisfaction with her maid. The domestic workers also gained a sense of superiority over their Taiwanese employers either by correcting their English or by joking about their employers' poor English with their friends, as in this example:

> My employer called from the office and said, "Luisa, twelve hours, don't forget to EAT my children!" She actually meant, "twelve o'clock, don't forget to FEED my children!" [laugh]. [oh my God. Did you correct her?] No. Some employers don't like that. So I just answered, "Don't worry! I already EAT your children!" (Lan 2003: 154)

While jokes may provide some temporary release (Constable 2003), they act as a "hidden transcript" (Parreñas 2001: 194), to be performed by migrant domestic workers only among fellow maids. In interactions with their employers, migrant domestic workers mostly follow the expected script of deferential performance and engage in linguistic resistance "with disguise and caution" (Lan 2003: 154), for fear of losing their job. In fact, as Lan points out, Filipina domestic workers in Taiwan are rapidly being replaced by supposedly more "docile" Indonesian workers, who are less capable of making demands due to their limited ability to speak English (or Chinese; ibid., p. 156). The author goes on to state that this phenomenon provides an aspect of the harsh reality where "language becomes a means of symbolic domination to consolidate the employer's authority and silence the migrant workers."

Because of the unregulated nature of domestic reproductive work, which often leaves migrant women at the mercy of their employers, many transnational migrants in the global 'care chains' aspire rather to institutional work. Lack of linguistic proficiency often becomes a key obstacle to such aspirations – despite the fact that not all institutional reproductive work calls for substantial linguistic skills. This is particularly true of cleaning work. In hotels, for instance, migrant women of color are often assigned the 'invisible' – and hence also unheard – positions of chambermaids (Adib and Guerrier 2003; Adkins 1995). Adib and Guerrier describe how women's work in hotels is stratified along their ethnic and national background: while receptionists' work – which also has an element of caring and is heavily feminized – is 'white women's work' in British hotels,

> [...] ethnic minority and migrant workers are clustered in the lowest graded work in the hospitality industry [...] and it is common to find that all the chambermaids

in a hotel are drawn from the same ethnic minority or migrant group. While reception work is 'respectable' women's work, therefore, chambermaiding is not constructed merely as women's work, but as work to be undertaken only by certain groups of women. (Adib and Guerrier 2003: 420)

Access to 'respectable women's work' in such contexts is ostensibly a matter of skills, qualifications and experience. However, as Adib and Guerrier point out, "front-line" reproductive work – in their study, receptionist work – is often also framed as 'white women's work,' and women of color face substantial barriers. In a context where racism has largely become invisible and a majority of white people consider themselves and their societies to be non-racist or post-racist (Hill 2008), linguistic proficiency can sometimes substitute for racial or national discrimination. Racial and/or national discrimination are often illegal, and individual employers may genuinely feel themselves to be non-racists. Linguistic discrimination, however, is often a commonsense proposition, and it 'just so happens' that non-standard speakers – people "whose English isn't good enough" – usually are minority members, and, even more importantly for our discussion, transnational migrants (see Lippi-Green 1997 for an excellent overview of linguistic discrimination in the USA).

As a result of their lack of linguistic proficiency, skilled migrants frequently experience downward occupational mobility (for a recent overview in the Australian context, see Berman 2008 and Piller in press). In sectors such as nursing, the very nature of the transnational workplace – full of migrant workers – may even militate against language learning. The story of Nadia, a Latvian immigrant nurse in Norway, exemplifies this well:

> Last Friday I suddenly realised why my Norwegian still is so limited. Taking a look around the table I saw women from Poland, Ukraine, Bosnia and Africa. Only two ethnic Norwegians work in my unit. Even if I am a trained nurse I have to work as a nurse's aide until I can speak Norwegian more fluently. (Isaksen 2007: 54).

Language testing is the sub-discipline of applied linguistics that, to date, has responded most consistently to the linguistic challenges posed by labor migration. The development and implementation of tests such as the Occupational English Test (see http://www.occupationalenglishtest.org/), a language test for overseas qualified health professionals, which is necessary in order to practice in Australia, New Zealand, and Singapore, or more generic language tests such as IELTS and TOEFL, are motivated by a duty of care vis-à-vis citizens and employers of receiving countries, and particularly clients in (health) care contexts. These are obviously the constituency of the nation–states and registrations boards who assign a gate-keeping function to language tests such as these by making them mandatory requirements. At the same time, one of the main features of contemporary transnational migration is that care workers themselves, and their rights and needs, often fall through the cracks, as they are backed neither by the developing (or even failed) states from which they originate nor by the receiving countries

– for which they often are little more than a human resource in their marketplace and disposable non-citizens.

Despite a long tradition of language training for employment in many immigrant-receiving countries (for an Australian program, see Lo Bianco 2008, Martin 1998, or Piller 2009; for a Canadian program, Goldstein 1996; for a New Zealand program, Holmes et al. 2008, or Newton 2007), most of this work focuses on the production sector or on business contexts. There is a distinct lack of programs and materials that offer language learning support to migrants doing reproductive work. An excellent material is a multimedia language teaching resource produced for aged-care workers in Australia (Springall 2007), which is based on intercultural pragmatics (see particularly Wigglesworth and Yates 2007; Yates 2008) and on ethnographic work conducted by the author, Jackie Springall, in the aged-care industry. During the fieldwork, four language and communication issues emerged where targeted training was needed. First, there was an apparent lack of small talk: while many of the Australian residents appreciated their African and Asian carers because they were very respectful towards the elderly, they complained that they never 'chatted' with them. Secondly, there were significant occupational health and safety concerns. The resource therefore has units that focus on how to be proactive about following safe workplace practices such as manual handling and back care; units that suggest strategies on how do deal with practices in the aged-care industry which aged-care workers may encounter and which may not always be 'best practice'; and units that include scenarios where students need to question instructions if they have concerns (rather than go by the usual workplace language-training rule of 'following instructions'). A third communication challenge can be posed by the fact that, in the aged-care industry, high levels of duty of care may be placed on workers in entry-level jobs, or on workers who are new to the country and society and thus may not necessarily be able to distinguish between normal practice in a new culture and malpractice. Finally, the resource also provides pronunciation and intelligibility training.

The Sexualization of the World and the Commercialization of Sex

A form of reproductive work we haven't covered in the previous section is sex work. Like other forms of reproductive work, it is typical 'women's work.' We are devoting a separate section to it not only because its lack of regulation, frequent criminalization, and stigmatization raise a range of linguistic issues different from the ones discussed above, but also because we want to change tack slightly and focus not so much on transnational workers' language proficiency as on the way their identities are constructed discursively. We start by briefly providing evidence for the dramatic expansion of the sex industry in the context of globalization. We will then discuss some of the language issues raised by the high incidence of migrant women in the sex industry, before we move on to explore how the expansion of the sex industry goes hand in hand with a persistent sexualization of public life: we will focus specifically on the sexualization of language teaching and learning.

The phenomenal expansion of the sex industry has become a central – even if often ignored – aspect of globalization. Some of the population flows of globalization occur from the express aim to procure sexual services, as in the case of the so-called sex tourism (O'Connell Davidson 1995, 1996, 2001, 2004; O'Connell Davidson and Sánchez Taylor 2005). However, more often than not, the flourishing sex industry is incidental to other forms of movement. For instance the expansion of prostitution in Southeast Asia, particularly the Philippines and Thailand, in the 1950s and 1960s was a direct result of the Korean and Vietnam Wars (Enloe 1989; Seabrook 2007). Another example comes from the 'upper end' of prostitution: Swiss cities with 'high-class' escort services are considered more competitive in attracting business travelers, trade shows, and conventions than cities that lack such services (Piller 2010).

Language issues faced by sex workers in transnational contexts bear both similarities to and differences from those faced by other reproductive workers. In terms of differences, it is obvious that the transnational migrants here are not necessarily the sex workers: it is just as likely that their clients are the ones who travel. As Blake Willies and Murphy-Shigematsu (2008) rightly point out, globalization is happening to individuals even if they are not themselves on the move. While the language of the punter is likely to prevail no matter where the encounter takes place, it makes a substantial difference whether the language the sex worker is proficient in is the one of wider communication, particularly as sex workers are more likely than the general population to face encounters with the police, the legal system, health care providers, and providers of social services generally. In addition, migrant sex workers often have a precarious legal status, and their lack of proficiency in the dominant language may make them even more vulnerable to exploitation, as is described in a study of migrant sex workers in Switzerland (Le Breton and Fiechter 2005).

In terms of similarities, linguistic proficiency is crucially tied in with the type of sex work that may be available. Sex workers with low levels of proficiency in the language of the punter may find it more difficult to negotiate rates of pay, to insist on safe sex, or to negotiate the type of services to be performed. Consequently, non-governmental organizations working with sex workers offer language training focused on these scenarios, as is the case in an English and Japanese language teaching program aimed at sex workers in Bangkok (Seabrook 2001).

At the same time, access to more highly remunerated and less exploitative types of sex work, such as escort services or the provision of telephone sex, is dependent upon advanced linguistic and communicative proficiency. This is fairly obvious in the case of telephone sex, where an exclusively linguistic service is provided (Hall 1995). Less obviously, it is also true of physical sex work. First, the most desirable forms of sex work – in terms of working conditions, remuneration, safety, societal stigma, and personal satisfaction – involve a fairly high level of communication services, as punters are increasingly seeking a 'girl-friend experi-ence' when procuring sexual services (Bernstein 2005). Having sex almost seems to become incidental in the 'girl-friend experience,' where the focus is on being pampered, spending time, a meal or a drink together, and, most importantly, talking (Holt and Blevins 2007). As Lucas (2005) shows, US sex workers who can provide a 'girl-friend experience' – or companionship more generally – are likely to be self-employed and express high levels of satisfaction with their working conditions, remuneration, and their work generally. As it so happened, all the interviewees in Lucas' (2005) study were also white, native-born, and middle class, and many of them had college degrees.

Secondly, personal safety is a major concern for all sex workers, and many of them report that, in addition to practical precautions such as not accepting anony-mous clients or always having a mobile phone within easy reach, their main way of "handling clients" – in other words, ensuring their personal safety – is through talking their way out of difficult situations (Davies and Evans 2007). Talking your way out of a violent situation surely requires a complex set of linguistic skills and cultural knowledge – skills and knowledge which migrant workers are less likely to have available to them and the lack of which is likely to make work more dan-gerous for them. In sum, the linguistic identities of transnational sex workers intersect with their gender and nationality in such a way as to cluster them in more dangerous, more poorly remunerated, and more heavily stigmatized types of sex work. A good example of this process is provided by Filipina women in Japan. Filipinas come to Japan for various types of reproductive work, including sex work, and also for marriage (see Piller 2007 or Lan 2008 for an overview of the relationship between sex work and mail-order marriages in transnational contexts). Suzuki (2008) describes how, since the mid-1980s, Filipinas have come to be seen as problem migrants of shady morals and prone to exploit their Japanese partners. Another discourse that circulates about them denies them any agency and sees them exclusively as victims; as victims of their circumstances who are sexually (as well as socioeconomically) subjugated and exploited. In Japan, the term 'Filipina' has thus come to refer to an identity where a stigmatized gender and sexual, national, and class identity intersect. In an attempt to rewrite their stigmatized identity, Filipinas in Japan are increasingly re-training as English instructors (Suzuki 2008). By becoming community and home-based English instructors, Filipinas are partially reinventing themselves in the Japanese context, where English is typically associated with the powerful West. At the same time, the fact that the teaching course qualifies them as 'community and home-based instructors' rather than fully fledged language teachers points to the confined space in which they operate.

The expansion of the sex industry in the context of globalization can be seen as one aspect of a pervasive sexualization of public life in global consumer culture, a phenomenon that has been described as "raunch culture" (Levy 2005). One aspect of the sexualization of public life is the high visibility of the sex industry itself, as for instance described by Piller (2010) for Swiss cities. However, sexuali-zation has become a much more pervasive phenomenon at the intersection of globalization, language, and gender, as we will demonstrate with the following two examples of English language teaching programs and materials in Japan.

In Japan's multimillion dollar English-language teaching industry, whiteness and native speaker status are heavily romanticized and sexualized. However, the process works differently for males and females. Male white English teachers are eroticized as sensitive Prince Charmings in marketing aimed at Japanese women (Bailey 2006, 2007; Kelsky 2001, 2008; Piller and Takahashi 2006; Takahashi forthcoming). Female white English teachers, on the other hand, tend to be sexualized as exotic sex objects. A good example comes from the recent introduction of an online English learning service named "*Gaigo TV*" (Jeffs 2008). Targeting Japanese males, *Gaigo TV* is a form of edutainment that provides multimedia English learning materials led by "beautiful, sexy" white women. The job title of these characters, who are allegedly Hollywood models and actors, is 'hostess' rather than the more traditional 'teacher.' In the free sample lesson provided on their website (http://www.gaigo.tv; last accessed on 23/10/2008), the viewer sees a 'hostess' in a stylized classroom stripping her clothes off while enunciating the sentences "As an English teacher I do not speak too quickly," "As an English teacher I do not speak too quietly," "As an English teacher I do not take my clothes off too fast" in audiolingual exercise fashion. In our judgment as applied linguists, the language learning value of these materials is very limited. Consequently, the main reasons (other than curiosity) for perusing such materials must lie in the cheap sexual thrill they can provide. Their overall effect, however, is to contribute to a pervasive sexualization of white women and English language learning.

The eroticization of English and language learning is also achieved by teaching materials that serve a more clearly defined purpose: the establishment and conduct of an intimate relationship in English. English for Relationship Purposes (ERP) materials are probably the latest addition to the ever-increasing spectrum of English of Specific Purposes (Kubota 2008; Piller and Takahashi 2006; Takahashi forthcoming; Webb 2007). ERP materials are mostly targeting Japanese women and offer vocabulary, phrases, and communicative routines deemed useful for the purpose of conducting romantic and sexual relationships with foreign men. ERP materials are widely available today in various media forms, be it in women's magazines, on websites, as phrase books or as multimedia resources. The discourse-enabling ERP materials suggests that romantic and sexual relationships with foreign men are a key to success in English language learning and vice versa. The script of intercultural relationships, as espoused in these materials, is 'Meet – Fall-in-love – Have sex – Fight – Marriage or Break-up' and places the heaviest emphasis on the third step, 'have sex.' For instance, 45 out of 117 pages of the English language learning manga *Roppongi English* (Johnson 2006) are dedicated to sexual interactions. We will now describe *Roppongi English* as it pertains to our discussion of intersectionality (for a detailed analysis, see Takahashi forthcoming).

Roppongi English derives its name from Roppongi, a popular section of Tokyo which is famous for its nightlife entertainment and high number of international visitors. *Roppongi English* is a comi-style ERP phrase book with four main characters, who form two heterosexual couples: Tomoko and Kevin, and Naomi and Tony. Tomoko is a 'typically Japanese' middle-class university student whose English improves through her relationship with Kevin, a well-educated white American who teaches English in Japan. By contrast, Naomi is a cool bilingual woman of Japanese parentage who grew up in California, and partners with Tony, a divorced African American DJ and former marine. While Kevin emerges as a handsome, considerate, and caring gentleman,Tony, by contrast, is presented as an unsophisticated and insensitive "asshole" (Johnson 2006: 124). Both men take the lead in their sexual relationships, but where Kevin is romantic and accommodating to Tomoko's sexual needs, Tony is aggressive, egoistical, and portrayed as a sexual pervert. The two Japanese women's characters are also dichotomized, Tomoko being appropriately feminine and demure where Naomi is sexually demanding.

Despite its setting in the transnational and hypermodern space of Roppongi, *Roppongi English* presents an essentially national and traditional version of intercultural relationships: Tomoko and Kevin, the archetypal representatives of Japanese femininity and white American masculinity, enjoy a sexually satisfying and romantic relationship. Tony and Naomi, on the other hand, who as African and Asian Americans in Japan embody minority and hybrid identities, are portrayed as sexual perverts, unable to form a meaningful relationship. As with *Gaigo TV*, the actual language learning value of *Roppongi English* is doubtful. Many of our colleagues with whom we have discussed these materials are appalled by their racism, sexism, and/or pornographic nature. Again, like *Gaigo TV*, such materials may provide a cheap thrill to readers, but their overall effect is to sexualize language learning and intercultural relationships in ways that also racialize them and attribute high levels of morality to mainstream characters and low levels of morality to minority characters.

Conclusion

Our focus in this chapter has been on the circulation of both gendered people and gendered discourses. These do not circulate in isolation from each other, nor in isolation from language ideologies and other aspects of identity. The people we focused on are migrant women and the employment they have access to. The employment they have access to is circumscribed by globalized beliefs as to what constitutes women's work. Such beliefs limit both the aspirations of actual people and the employment situations in which the aspirations are being channeled. The employment options of these people are further constrained by their linguistic identities, national background, and citizenship status. Migration continues to be deeply embedded in gender inequalities both in the countries of origin and in the destination countries. Millions of women, who depart from their impoverished homes in Southeast Asia, Latin America, and Africa to work in the homes, factories, and sex and entertainment industries of more affluent countries, engage in low-waged women's work (Ehrenreich and Hochschild 2003) – women's work that is no longer just women's work, but has become migrant women's work. The international community has only recently begun to address the needs, challenges, opportunities, and rights of migrants at the intersections of gender, race, class, and nationality (Farah 2006; Piper 2006). The linguistic factor has increasingly been acknowledged as one of the most crippling obstacles to the social inclusion of migrants, leading to various forms of exploitation and discrimination in the host countries (UNFPA and IOM 2006a, 2006b); or, to phrase it differently, "[t]he language barrier seems to be the single most important reason: the 'original obstacle' that hampers all aspects of social inclusion." (Colic-Peisker 2005: 632).

REFERENCES

Adib, A., and Guerrier, Y. (2003) The interlocking of gender with nationality, race, ethnicity and class: The narratives of women in hotel work. *Gender, Work and Organization* 10(4): 413–32.

Adkins, L. (1995) *Gendered Work: Sexuality, Family and the Labour Market.* Buckingham: Open University Press.

Anderson, B. (1997) Servants and slaves: Europe's domestic workers. *Race and Class* 39(1): 37–49.

Anderson, B. J. (2000) *Doing the Dirty Work? The Global Politics of Domestic Labour.* London: Zed Books.

Appadurai, A. (1990) Disjuncture and difference in the global cultural economy. *Theory, Culture and Society* 7: 295–310.

Bailey, K. D. (2006) Marketing the eikaiwa wonderland: Ideology, akogare, and gender alterity in English conversation school advertising in Japan. *Environment and Planning D: Society and Space* 24(1): 105–30.

Bailey, K. D. (2007) Akogare, ideology, and 'charisma man' mythology: Reflections on ethnographic research in English language schools in Japan. *Gender, Place and Culture* 14(5): 585–608.

Berman, G. (2008) *Harnessing Diversity: Addressing Racial and Religious Discrimination in Employment.* Melbourne: Victorian Multicultural

Commission and Victorian Equal Opportunity and Human Rights Commission. Available at: http://www.humanrightscommission.vic.gov.au/pdf/Harnessing%20Diversity%20report.pdf (last accessed on October 22, 2008).

Bernstein, E. (2005) Desire, demand, and the commerce of sex. In E. Bernstein and L. Schaffner (eds), *Regulating Sex: The Politics of Intimacy and Identity*, 101–25. London: Routledge.

Blake Willies, D., and Murphy-Shigematsu, S. (2008) *Transcultural Japan: Metamorphosis in the cultural borderlands and beyond.* In Blake Willies and Murphy-Shigematsu (eds), 3–44.

Blake Willies, D., and Murphy-Shigematsu, S. (eds) (2008) *Transcultural Japan: At the Borderlands of Race, Gender, and Identity.* London, New York: Routledge.

Brah, A. (1996) *Cartographies of Diaspora: Contesting Identities.* London: Routledge.

Burman, E. (2003) From difference to intersectionality: Challenges and resources. *European Journal of Psychotherapy and Counselling* 6(4): 293–308.

Butler, J. (1990) *Gender Trouble: Feminism and the Subversion of Identity.* New York and London: Routledge.

Chang, G. (2000) *Disposable Domestics: Immigrant Women Workers in the Global*

Economy. Cambridge, MA: South End Press.

Chang, J. (2004) *Ideologies of English Language Teaching in Taiwan*. Unpublished PhD, University of Sydney, Sydney.

Colic-Peisker, V. (2005) "At least you're the right colour": Identity and social inclusion of Bosnian refugees in Australia. *Journal of Ethnic and Migration Studies* 31(4): 615–38.

Constable, N. (2003). *Romance on a Global Stage: Pen Pals, Virtual Ethnography, and 'Mail Order' Marriages*. Berkeley, Los Angeles, and London: University of California Press.

Davies, K., and Evans, L. (2007) A virtual view of managing violence among British escorts. *Deviant Behavior* 28(6): 525–51.

Ehrenreich, B., and Hochschild, A. (2003). *Global Woman: Nannies, Maids, and Sex Workers in the New Economy*. New York: Metropolitan Press.

England, K., and Stiell, B. (1997) "They think you are as stupid as your English is": Constructing foreign domestic workers in Toronto. *Environment and Planning* A29(2): 195–215.

Enloe, C. (1989) *Bananas, Bases and Beaches: Making Feminist Sense of International Politics*. London: Pandora.

Farah, F. (2006) An expert group meeting on female migrants: What's so special about it? [electronic version]. *Female Migrants: Bridging the Gaps throughout the Life Cycle* 23–8. Available at: http://www.unfpa.org/upload/lib_pub_file/658_filename_migration.pdf (accessed on June 9, 2008).

Francis, K., Chapman, Y., Doolan, G., Sellick, K., and Barnett, T. (2008) Using overseas registered nurses to fill employment gaps in rural health services: Quick fix or sustainable strategy? *Australian Journal of Rural Health* 16(3): 164–9.

Goldstein, T. (1996) *Two Languages at Work: Bilingual Life on the Production Floor*.

Berlin and New York: Mouton de Gruyter.

Hall, K. (1995) Lip service on the fantasy lines. In K. Hall and M. Bucholtz (eds), *Gender Articulated: Language and the Socially Constructed Self*, 183–216. New York and London: Routledge.

Heller, M. (2007) Bilingualism as ideology and practice. In M. Heller (ed.), *Bilingualism: A Social Approach*, 1–22. Basingstoke: Palgrave Macmillan.

Hill, J. H. (2008) *The Everyday Language of White Racism*. Malden, MA: Wiley-Blackwell.

Holt, T. J., and Blevins, K. R. (2007) Examining sex work from the client's perspective: Assessing johns using on-line data. *Deviant Behavior* 28(4): 333–54.

Hondagneu-Sotelo, P. (2001) *Doméstica: Immigrant Workers Cleaning and Caring in the Shadows of Affluence*. Berkeley: University of California Press.

Isaksen, L. W. (2007) Gender, care work and globalization. In M. G. Cohen and J. Brodie (eds), *Remapping Gender in the New Global Order*, 45–58. London and New York: Routledge.

Jeffs, A. (2008) Racy approach to English picks up speed [electronic version]. *The Japan Times*. Available at: http://search.japantimes.co.jp/cgi-bin/fl20080126a1.html (accessed on June 15, 2008).

Johnson, B. G. (2006) *Roppongi English*. Tokyo: Aoba.

Kelsky, K. (2001) *Women on the Verge: Japanese Women, Western Dreams*. Durham, NC: Duke University Press.

Kelsky, K. (2008) *Gender, modernity, and eroticized internationalism in Japan*. In Blake Willies and Murphy-Shigematsu (eds), 86–119.

Kofman, E., and Raghuram, P. (2006) Gender and global labour migrations: Incorporating skilled workers. *Antipode* 38(2): 282–303.

Lan, P.-C. (2003) "They have more money but I speak better English!" Transnational Encounters between

Filipina Domestics and Taiwanese Employers. *Identities: Global Studies in Culture and Power* 10(2): 133–61.

Lan, P.-C. (2006) *Global Cinderellas: Migrant Domestics and Newly Rich Employers in Taiwan*. Durham, NC: Duke University Press.

Lan, P.-C. (2008) New global politics of reproductive labor: Gendered labor and marriage migration. *Sociology Compass* 2(6): 1801–15.

Le Breton, M., and Fiechter, U. (2005) *Verordnete Grenzen – verschobene Ordnungen: Eine Analyse zum Frauenhandel in der Schweiz [Ordered Borders – Shifted Orders: An Analysis of the Trafficking of Women in Switzerland]*. Berne: eFeF.

Levy, A. (2005) *Female Chauvinist Pigs: Women and the Rise of Raunch Culture*. New York: Free Press.

Lippi-Green, R. (1997) *English with an Accent: Language, Ideology, and Discrimination in the United States*. London: Routledge.

Lo Bianco, J. (2008) Language policy and education in Australia. In S. May and N. H. Hornberger (eds), *Encyclopedia of Language and Education, Vol. 1: Language Policy and Political Issues in Education*, 343–53. New York: Springer.

Lucas, A. M. (2005) The work of sex work: Elite prostitutes' vocational orientations and experiences. *Deviant Behavior* 26(6): 513–46.

Malawian nurses struggle to cope with colleagues' overseas exodus (2008). *Nursing Standard* 22(33): 5. [no author].

Martin, S. (1998) *New Life, New Language: The History of the Adult Migrant English Program*. Sydney: NCELTR Publications.

Newton, J. (2007) Adapting authentic workplace talk for workplace intercultural communication training. In H. Kotthoff and H. Spencer-Oatey (eds), *Handbook of Intercultural Communication*, 519–35. Berlin and New York: Mouton de Gruyter.

O'Connell Davidson, J. (1995) British sex tourists in Thailand. In M. Maynard and J. Purvis (eds), *(Hetero)sexual Politics*, 42–64. London: Taylor and Francis.

O'Connell Davidson, J. (1996) Sex tourism in Cuba. *Race and Class*, 37(3): 39–48.

O'Connell Davidson, J. (2001) The sex tourist, the expatriate, his ex-wife and her 'other': The politics of loss, difference and desire. *Sexualities* 4(1): 5–24.

O'Connell Davidson, J. (2004) Child sex tourism: An anomalous form of movement? *Journal of Contemporary European Studies* 12(1): 31–46.

O'Connell Davidson, J., and Sánchez Taylor, J. (2005) Travel and taboo: Heterosexual sex tourism to the Caribbean. In E. Bernstein and L. Schaffner (eds), *Regulating Sex: The Politics of Intimacy and Identity*, 83–99. London: Routledge.

Parreñas, R. S. (2001) *Servants of Globalization : Women, Migration and Domestic Work*. Stanford: Stanford University Press.

Parreñas, R. S. (2005) *Children of Global Migration: Transnational Families and Gendered Woes*. Stanford, CA: Stanford University Press.

Patel, R. (2007) *Stuffed and Starved: Markets, Power and The Hidden Battle for the World Food System*. London: Portobello Books.

Pavlenko, A., and Piller, I. (2001) New directions in the study of multilingualism, second language learning, and gender. In A. Pavlenko, Blackledge, A., Piller, I., and Teutsch-Dwyer, M. (eds), *Multilingualism, Second Language Learning and Gender*, 17–52. Berlin and New York: Mouton de Gruyter.

Pavlenko, A., and Piller, I. (2007) Language education and gender. In S. May (ed.), *The Encyclopedia of Language and Education, Vol. 1: Political Issues*, 57–69. New York: Springer.

Piller, I. (2007) Cross-cultural communication in intimate relationships.

In H. Kotthoff and H. Spencer-Oatey (eds), *Intercultural Communication*, 341–59. Berlin and New York: Mouton de Gruyter.

Piller, I. (2009) Eigo wo tooshita shakaitekihousetsu: Gengoseisaku to iminkeikaku [The adult migrant English program: Language learning, settlement and social inclusion in Australia]. In C. Kawamura, A. Kondoh, and H. Nakamoto (eds), *Minseisaku eno approach: Raifusaikuru to tabunkakyousei [Living Together in a Multicultural Society: Approaches to Immigration Policy]*, 259–61. Tokyo: Akashi Shoten.

Piller, I. (2010) Sex in the city: On making space and identity in travel spaces. In A. Jaworski and C. Thurlow (eds), *Semiotic Landscapes of Globalization*, 123–36. London: Continuum.

Piller, I. (in press) Multilingualism and social exclusion. In M. Martin-Jones, A. Blackledge, and A. Creese (eds), *Handbook of Multilingualism*. London: Routledge.

Piller, I., and Pavlenko, A. (2004) Bilingualism and gender. In T. K. Bhatia and W. C. Ritchie (eds), *The Handbook of Bilingualism*, 489–511. Oxford: Blackwell.

Piller, I., and Pavlenko, A. (2007) Globalization, gender, and multilingualism. In H. Decke-Cornill and L. Volkmann (eds), *Gender Studies and Foreign Language Teaching*, 15–30. Tübingen: Narr.

Piller, I., and Pavlenko, A. (2009) Globalization, multilingualism, and gender: Looking into the future. In L. Wei and V. Cook (eds), *Contemporary Applied Linguistics, Vol. 2: Linguistics for the Real World*, 10–27. London: Continuum.

Piller, I., and Takahashi, K. (2006) A passion for English: Desire and the language market. In A. Pavlenko (ed.), *Languages and Emotions of Multilingual Speakers*, 59–83. Clevedon, England: Multilingual Matters.

Piper, N. (2006) Gendering the politics of migration. *International Migration Review* 40(1): 133–2.

Pulvers, R. (2008) Is aging Japan really ready for all the non-Japanese carers it needs? [electronic version]. *The Japan Times*. Available at: http://search. japantimes.co.jp/print/fl20080601rp. html (accessed on June 15, 2008).

Raijman, R., Schammah-Gesser, S., and Kemp, A. (2003) International migration, domestic work, and care work: Undocumented Latina migrants in Israel. *Gender and Society* 17(5): 727–49.

Seabrook, J. (2001) *Travels in the Skin Trade: Tourism and the Sex Industry*, 2nd edn. London, UK and Ann Arbor, MI: Pluto Press.

Seabrook, J. (2007) *Cities*. London: Pluto Press.

Springall, J. (2007) *Taking Care*. Melbourne: AMES Victoria.

Staunæs, D. (2003) Where have all the subjects gone? Bringing together the concepts of intersectionality and subjectification. *NORA – Nordic Journal of Feminist and Gender Research* 11(2): 101–10.

Suzuki, N. (2008) *Between two shores: Transnational projects and Filipina wives in/from Japan*. In Blake Willies and Murphy-Shigematsu (eds), 65–85.

Takahashi, K. (forthcoming) *Language Desire: Gender, Sexuality and Second Language Learning*: Multilingual Matters.

UNFPA, and IOM (2006a) *Female Migrants: Bridging the Gaps throughout the Life Cycle*. Available at: http://www.unfpa. org/upload/lib_pub_file/658_filename_migration.pdf (accessed on June 9, 2008).

UNFPA, and IOM (2006b) *State of World Population 2006: A Passage to Hope: Women and International Migration*. Available at: http://www.unfpa.org/upload/lib_pub_file/658_filename_migration.pdf (accessed on June 9, 2008).

Valentine, G. (2007) Theorizing and researching intersectionality: A challenge for feminist geography. *The Professional Geographer* 59(1): 10–21.

Webb, E. (2007) A foreign language for a foreign affair.' *Essential Teacher* 4: 14–16.

Wigglesworth, G., and Yates, L. (2007) Mitigating difficult requests in the workplace: What learners and teachers need to know. *TESOL Quarterly* 41(4), 791–803.

Yates, L. (2008) *The Not-So Generic Skills: Teaching Employability Communication Skills to Adult Migrants.* Sydney: NCELTR Publications.

Yuval-Davis, N. (2007) Intersectionality, citizenship and contemporary politics of belonging. *Critical Review of International Social and Political Philosophy* 10(4), 561–74.

25 Globalization and Gay Language

WILLIAM L. LEAP

This chapter considers how the linguistic practices through which people give voice to same-sex desires and identities are supported, enhanced, and/or silenced by the movement of economic and cultural capital within the global circuit. I examine specific nodes within the global circuit, travelling through Tonga, the Philippines, Hong Kong, Taiwan, Bolivia, Miami, Indonesia, France, Nigeria, and the United States of America.

Some settings in these national examples have explicit ties to forms of recreation and leisure associated with North Atlantic sexual cultures since the Stonewall period. Others are closely aligned with quality-of-life themes, although they also retain certain associations with North Atlantic blueprints. Whatever their function, each setting displays distinctive forms of linguistic practice, containing references to sexual sameness derived from 'local' and 'global' sources.

Read more broadly, these displays can be seen as distinctive accumulations of technologies, social practices, and ideological stances which can be described as local formations or, using Collier and Ong's terms, as territorializations of the *global assemblages* that regularly "articulate [...] the structural transformations" associated with globalization in various arenas world-wide (2005: 4).[1] In this chapter I examine instances where linguistic practices and discourses of sexual sameness move in assemblage with global capital in the global circuit. And I look at the *territorializations* that emerge when these assemblages engage linguistic practices and discourses related to sexual sameness that are embedded, or are becoming embedded, within particular locations inside that circuit.

A prominent element in the linguistic component of these assemblages, and in the linguistic components of the territorializations that they inspire, is the phenomenon I have elsewhere termed 'gay language.' Broadly defined, gay language designates a set of discursive practices associated with a subject position ('gay men'), and which has emerged in the context of gay liberation struggles in the 1970s. This subject position has changed dramatically in recent years, thanks to the politics of the AIDS pandemic and to the emergence of queer activism during the 1980s, and now under the growing neo-liberal pressures for "place at the

The Handbook of Language and Globalization, First Edition. Edited by Nikolas Coupland.
© 2013 Blackwell Publishing Ltd except for editorial material and organization © 2013 Nikolas Coupland.
Published 2013 by Blackwell Publishing Ltd.

table" gay conformity (Leap 2008). In effect, what began as ways of talking about sexual liberation and transgression has changed into ways of talking that equate sexual sameness with assimilation, mobility, achievement, and conspicuous consumption. In that sense, far from being limited to erotic desire, object choice, and sexual identity, gay language now gives voice to a broader ideological stance: *homonormativity*. This is "a politics that does not contest dominant heteronormative assumptions and institutions but upholds and sustains them, while promising the possibility of a demobilized gay constituency and of a privatized, depoliticized gay culture anchored in domesticity and gay consumption" (Duggan 2003: 50).

Within the current social moment, references to homonormativity are often constructed discursively through references to cosmopolitanism, mobility, self-reliance, and white gay privilege. These themes are prominently attested in the assemblages that accompany the movement of global capital – and gay language – within the global circuit (Altman 1997, Oswin 2007). Understandably, their presence helps explain why speaking subjects may reject the usefulness of adding fluency in 'gay language' to local linguistic repertoires. In some cases speakers may respond more favorably to the idea of a 'language' that articulates sexual sameness, but they may prefer to achieve that articulation through locally familiar linguistic practices. Of course, subjects may enthusiastically support an incorporation of linguistic practices drawn from the global circuit. This occurs for example when the discursive yearnings of local subjects are not entirely contained within the boundaries of the local sexual languages and cultures – at least in the sense in which those boundaries have been traditionally drawn.

These complex and contingent relationships, which connect linguistic practices and sexual sameness within contexts of globalization, are the topics of interest in this chapter. I begin by offering some examples of complexity and contingency, specifically reflecting on instances where cosmopolitan discursive practices and locally mandated 'reserved talk' about sexual sameness have become embedded within the contemporary dilemmas of sexual citizenship and within debates over subjectivity. From that basis, I use the lens of global assemblage to make broad points about 'gay language(s)' that widely appear in complex, contingent relationships with discourses of sexual sameness throughout the global circuit.

Cosmopolitan References and Tacit Subjects

Gay language has always been closely connected to the North Atlantic urban setting, and it is likely that cosmopolitan references have been part of gay-related linguistic practices for quite some time. These linguistic practices did not loose their cosmopolitan associations when they moved into the global circuit, and such associations make gay language an especially noticeable feature of territorialization.

Besnier (2002, 2007a) describes a situation of this kind in the Miss Galaxy context on the island of the nation-state of Tonga, South Pacific. Beauty pageants are not traditional cultural events in Tonga. The arrival of these spectacles in the mid-1990s was part of a world-wide circulation of public practices in which participants were asked to obtain audience endorsement while they performed demanding emotional and physical tasks. Unsuccessful participants endured severe audience criticism. Although the Miss Galaxy contest began as a small-scale event, it soon became so popular that it was held in Tonga's largest public building. In the contest described by Besnier, the winner received a round trip ticket to Los Angeles, California, sundry additional prizes, and enthusiastic validation from audience members. For the losers, criticisms were swift and brutal.

The participants in the contest are *fakaleiti* (hereafter *leiti*), male-bodied persons who identify themselves as transgendered individuals and frame their presentation of a 'feminine' self in terms of multiple practices, off-island and often US mainland-based. *Fakaleiti* is an indigenous gender construction in Tonga, but years of Christian missionization and related pressures toward heteronormative lifestyles have assigned a negative valuation to the Tonga-centered subjectivity. As one of its consequences, the Miss Galaxy contest opens a space where that negative sentiment can be confronted and challenged. The pageant setting gives *leiti* opportunities to claim positive valuation *as leiti* from a Tongan audience, and it enlists elements from the global circuit to assist in their efforts.

Especially important is the *leiti*'s use of English rather than Tongan during the question–answer segment of the beauty pageant. The association of English fluency with outside world discourses helps the *leiti* give voice to the status of sophistication, eloquence, worldliness, and cosmopolitan charm important within the context of the pageant. Claiming this cosmopolitan voice strengthens the authority of the *leiti*'s presentation of her gendered self in the beauty pageant in a manner that every audience member will recognize. By contrast, answering questions only in Tongan undermines and dispels any such claims to cosmopolitan authority, because it suggests that the candidate has been unable to achieve the cosmopolitan status which the globalized context of the beauty pageant purports to represent.

The English used in this case is not the language of the standard English-speaking mainland citizen. The pageant's English conveys the image of a sexual subject who actively transgresses Tongan male/female heteronormativity, while seeking public validation for her claims to an alternative set of gendered norms (*leiti* transgender status). In other words, a *leiti*'s success in the Miss Galaxy pageant, as contestant and as *leiti*, does not depend solely on the individual's linguistic performance, but on the audience's assessment of the effectiveness of that performance. That assessment cannot be obtained without the convincing embodiment of the discourses of gender transgression.

In Excerpt 1 we see that things started well for Masha, one of the pageant contestants.

Excerpt 1   *I enjoy working there with um … blowers …*

From Besnier 2002: 551 (following the original transcription)

EMCEE: What would you say about being a hairstylist or-being-a- working a-
what what does it mean, like, to be working at Joy's Hair Styles? ((*sotto
voce*, summarizes the question in Tongan)) […]

MASHA: ((takes cordless mike)) Well thank you very much. ((audience laughs
then shouts with admiration and encouragement)) If you want your
hair to be curled ((beckons with her hand)) come over (audiences
explodes in laughter and whooping. Masha laughs and then becomes
serious and requests silence with the hand.)) Uh, I like it very much,
and uh I enjoy working there with um ((pauses, word-searches, waves
her hand, audience explodes in laughter, drowning the remainder of
the answer)) blowers ((unable to finish, mouths)) thank you ((hands
back mike and returns to her position.))

Masha's poised use of English to deliver her well rehearsed opening lines won
accolades from the audience and the sexualized *double entendre* suggested by her
word choices ("to curl your hair," "come over") added to the entertainment value
of the statements for some audience members. But then Masha began to forget
her 'script.' At that point the refined image originally conveyed through her
English-language performance, and its allusions to gendered meanings beyond
Tonga, began to dissolve. This gave the audience "the expected proof of the
fraudulence of her claim to cosmopolitanism" (Besnier 2007a: 436). In response,
they began boisterously hooting and cat-calling, thus prompting Masha to end
her statement abruptly and to exit the stage silently in mid-sentence.

The cosmopolitan referencing invoked through Masha's use of English during
the Tongan beauty pageant is part of a broader contrastive valuation. It positions
Tongan and English fluencies as markers of 'local' and 'broader' subject affiliations, requiring the *leiti* to voice their status as sexual persons through both
options. Of course, Masha's *leiti*-related Tongan fluency is not in question in
Excerpt 1. But her presence in the cosmopolitan social practice of this pageant
obligates her to demonstrate proficiency in the corresponding cosmopolitan linguistic practice. Her failure to meet the task set for her leads to ridicule and
self-defeat.

English references with the sexualized associations discussed above provide
an indication of 'local' and 'broader' valuation in Excerpt 2. In this case, the languages used are English and Swardspeak. Swardspeak is spoken by same-sex
Filipino men who identify themselves as *bakla*. These men see *bakla* as a stance
of public visibility similar to the one associated with the notion of 'gay man.'
However, given its strong connections to Tagalog linguistic and Filipino
cultural traditions and national origin, *bakla* is not at all equivalent to 'gay.'
The terms are not used interchangeably, making flexible accumulation
(Leap, 2003) central to the linguistic work and social messaging reflected in
Excerpt 2.

Excerpt 2   *Growing muscles and going in drag*

From Manalansan 1998: 141

1   Noong nasa Manila ako,
     When I was still in Manila
2   kunyari pa akong pa-min ang drama ko
     I was putting on the macho drama
3   although alam ng lahat na bading talaga ang truth
     Although I knew that all the badings[2] knew the truth
4   Pag-step ng aking satin shoes ditto sa New York
     When my satin shoes hit New York
5   o biglang nagiba ang pagrarampa ko
     I suddenly changed the way I walked the ramp
6   May I try ko ang pagmumu and also nag-gym ako
     I tried going in drag and going to the gym
7   Ang sabi ng ibang Pinay na bading na parang lukresiya ako
     Many Filipinos (e.g. *bakla*) told me I was crazy
8   Bakit daw ako nagpap-muscles and then nagmumujer ako
     Why, they asked, was I growing muscles and going in drag?
9   Alam mo, pag wala ka sa pakikialam ng pamilya at kaibagan mo sa Pilipines
     You know, when you live far away from your parents and friends in
     the Philippines
10 kahit ano puwede.
     Anything is possible.

Tony is the *bakla* speaker in Excerpt 2. He was born in the Philippines and resides in Brooklyn, New York. Tony is one of the many Filipinos and Filipinas who have left the Philippines in recent years to find employment on the US mainland. While there are no data on the numbers of *bakla* in the Filipino diaspora, Tony's comments help explain why *bakla* subjects find voluntary displacement so attractive: "Living far away from your parents and friends in the Philippines, anything is possible." "Anything" refers to the new personal relationships and presentations of self that become possible in the metropolis and in its cosmopolitan setting.

He underscores the contrasts between these opportunities and the more limited social terrain in the Philippines through his placement of English-language references within the example. His description of the homeland setting is phrased entirely in words of Tagalog origin, except for the English function word 'although' and nouns 'drama' and 'truth.' The latter are regularly used in Swardspeak to identify key themes in *bakla* experience.[3]

But, when his "satin shoes hit New York," the range of English references used increases markedly. Here, however, these English words are added to, not embedded within, the Tagalog sentence structure. In the line "I tried going in drag and going to the gym," the base for the word meaning 'drag,' *pag-mumu*, is the Spanish loan word *mujer* ('woman'): *mujer* is turned to a plural formed according to the Tagalog rule, by duplicating the initial consonant vowel sequence *mu-mu*, and *jer* is dropped. Drag is part of Tony's life in the Philippines and in New York City. "Going to the gym" is something he began doing once he left the homeland. "Gym" appears with a Swardspeak prefix, *nag-gym*, but with no other Tagalog inflection. A construction with similar meaning appears in line 8: "nagpap-muscles." There the English word is turned to the plural with the English suffix for plural, not with the Tagalog reduplication, while 'drag' is again rendered with the Tagalog/Spanish loan *mujer* in a reduplicated plural: *nagmumujer*. "Ramp" occurs with reduplication, *pagrarampa*; but, by embedding the phrasing, Tony shows that "walking the ramp" is not unique to the cosmopolitan terrain and would not be expressed in cosmopolitan phrasing. "Satin shoes" is tied specifically to the new terrain and is appropriated from English without Tagalog framings.

Far from being a story about moving from 'here' to 'there,' Tony's narrative uses Swardspeak's unique linguistic accumulation to map out the direction of his diasporic movement, contrasting experiences in the homeland and in the displaced/cosmopolitan locale. With English terms limited solely to function words, certain *bakla*-specific discursive themes, and comments about a metropolis at distance from the homeland, Manila becomes textually positioned as a site seemingly free from the intrusions of the English-speaking global presence. This image of Manila's linguistic purity ignores a long history of US colonial and now neocolonial presence; but it contrasts with Tony's world of displacement, a world where English regularly penetrates his Tagalog and his Swardspeak as well as his linguistic embodiment of *bakla* identity.

Indeed, as Excerpt 2 suggests, the Swardspeak associated with Filipino displacement is very different from that associated with the homeland. In fact Manalansan (2003) reports that *bakla* who remained in the US for extended periods of time found that their language skills change. The most notable changes were too much reliance on English and too little reliance on the linguistic skills that kept Swardspeak more closely aligned with Tagalog grammar in earlier times. To address this problem, *bakla* try to return home once a year or make regular telephone calls to friends in the Philippines whose knowledge of Swardspeak has not been so heavily shaped by English expression.

Speakers do not always accept the messages about cosmopolitan experience associated with English-based linguistic practices. In some instances, speakers refuse to endorse those practices outright, or find ways of reshaping their discursive associations so as to ensure that cosmopolitan messages are more consistent with local assumptions and practices. One such instance has recently emerged in Hong Kong and on Taiwan: the growing popularity of a set of discursive practices occupied under the linguistic marker *tongzhi*. This concept integrates male and female sexual sameness, expectations of personal responsibility, and obligations to family and broader kinship networks, and it subordinates the former two to the latter. Apart from being the term for 'comrade' that became popular during the Chinese revolution, *tongzhi* expresses meanings of egalitarianism, cooperation, and selflessness, which have a conventional basis in Confucianism. *Tongzhi* positions discussions of sexual sameness within a sense of Chinese historicity, while affirming the indicated subject's rights to place as a sexual person within the all-important family and kinship ties (Wong 2005: 768–71).

In the 1990s, *tongzhi* was chosen by Chinese same-sex identified activists in Hong Kong and Taiwan who sought ways to create a sense of 'community' without duplicating the politics of confrontation and liberation aligned with gay/lesbian status in the global circuit (Wong and Zhang 2001). The choice was deliberate: Confrontation with, and liberation from, tradition, family, and kin are precisely what Chinese same-sex identified women and men do *not* want their sexuality to require of them. By appropriating *tongzhi* discourse, Chinese sexual subjects give voice to a culturally appropriate sense of sexual sameness, while emphasizing the distance separating them from their western gay/lesbian counterparts.

This distance surfaces repeatedly in the daily politics of sexual sameness in Hong Kong and Taiwan, as gay/lesbian-centered identity categories circulate widely in both settings, thanks to the internationalization of 'gay liberation politics.' This politics is instantiated through various media sources; through Chinese students' residence in North Atlantic university settings; and through persons coming from North Atlantic settings (often US citizens) to reside in Taiwan and Hong Kong – people who make it their 'cause' to bring 'gay liberation' to another segment of the world. From the perspective of this kind of gay/lesbian discourse, *tongzhi* appears as a reactionary and anti-progressive stance, since this discursive position does not *require* its subject to speak out about their sexuality. The essence of a gay/lesbian stance is its outspoken self-proclamation.

In contrast, the responsible *tongzhi* subject deftly avoids talking directly about sexual sameness, particularly with parents or other persons in positions of authority and respect. "Tongzhi would introduce their partners as good friends and let the parents understand their tongzhi relationship through actual practices in their everyday lives" (Chou 2001: 38). And, as Tat Ming's comments to Chou Wah-Shan indicate in Excerpt 3, parents may come to such understandings while maintaining appropriate Confucian restraint, and they may defer making any statement on the point until this becomes unavoidable.

Tat Ming is a 35-year-old doctor living with his parents in Taiwan. He carries the responsibilities of a dutiful Chinese son, including never discussing his sexual orientation with his parents. His father is concerned about the expectations imposed by Chinese tradition and its 'social obligation.' But his mother views things a bit differently, as Tat Ming's poignant description of last year's "most fascinating experience" reveals.

Excerpt 3   *Don't think I am dumb and blind because I didn't say anything*

From Chou 2001: 38–9

My parents should know it but I never tell them directly. I haven't ever dated women and only men phone me. It is so obvious! Once, when my mother and I were watching a TV programme on AIDS, she was so attentive, listening to every word. After the programme, she said to me: "Tat Ming, you must be careful. AIDS is a fatal disease. You are a doctor and know better than anyone. I never control your private life but I am too old, don't let me worry." And last month when the TV broadcast Xu You-sheng's marriage, my father said, "I really don't know what is in your mind, but we are Chinese. I think you should marry. It is a social obligation that obligates everyone." But the most fascinating experience was last year when I split up with Travis who had been with me for four years; my mother knows Travis as my best friend. One night my mother suddenly asked me whether I was very unhappy. I was really depressed at that time, so I didn't say a word. She then asked me, "is it because of Travis?" I was shocked and didn't know how to respond. She knew and she caught me and said, " Don't think that I am dumb and blind, just because I didn't say anything. You two are a good couple, a good relationship needs lots of effort." I was speechless.

Anecdotes like the one recounted by Tat Ming are widely reported in Spanish-speaking contexts (see Alonso and Koreck 1989, Carrier 1995, Cantú 1999, Decena 2008, Lancaster 1988, Murray 1996, Wright 2000). Same-sex identified speakers of Spanish repeatedly insist that it would be inappropriate and offensive for them to confront parents and family members with 'the truth' about their sexuality. It is preferable to let the unspoken reality remain until the facts emerge as they will.

This argument is greatly assisted by certain features of the syntax and pragmatics of Spanish, which make it possible for speakers to construct lengthy segments of text on different topics without having to specify the subject (the actor or agent) of the indicated events (Decena 2008). Instead, Spanish syntax allows the speaker to indicate the subject *tacit*-ly (in Decena's phrasing) by using verb endings to indicate person and number, by using inflectional ends on adjectives to indicate gender, and so on. Thus a conversation unfolds, messages are exchanged, and everyone may understand as much (or as little) of the subject-reference as they wish to. Conversely, such a tacit subject discourse allows speakers to ignore conveniently the information presented in the discussion, because the key elements in the text were never proclaimed. Audience silence is appropriate and understandable in such settings, as it was with Tat Ming's mother's observation of his break-up with Travis.

Wright (2000) offers a detailed illustration of Decena's argument in his discussion of "the tradition of reserved talk" that surrounds male homosexuality in the town of Santa Cruz, Bolivia. Unlike *tongzhi*, which is of quite recent origin, the tradition of reserved talk has been a part of Spanish discursive pragmatics for a long time. Wright explains:

> In Bolivia, male homosexuality and silence have been inseparable partners. This does not mean that homosexuality is never mentioned. On the contrary, within the confines of prescribed discourses it is part of the standard inventory. Tones of indignation, repulsion, anger or pity make it a safe topic in a wide range of public and private

forums, including nervous and degrading jokes and tabloid articles about immorality and crime. However, the more personal homosexuality gets, the closer to oneself, the less is heard about it. This quietness extends to one's relatives and close friends. The fact that male homosexuality has been shrouded in silence […] is not unique to Bolivia. However, it gains unique meanings as we consider the abrupt changes introduced into Bolivia by gay men's outreach. (Wright 2000: 91–2)

Similar to the situation in Hong Kong and Taiwan, the tradition of 'reserved talk' in Santa Cruz began to be challenged when a government-sponsored, internationally funded HIV/AIDS outreach program opened a 'gay community center.' These centers began sponsoring outreach events designed to unite the local 'gay community' and to encourage their participation in center functions. These events assumed that sexual subjects who identified themselves as 'gay' were already present in Santa Cruz and were ready to receive those messages. As messages began to circulate within the local community and community members began to accept the ideas about sexual sameness contained in them, 'gay'-identified subjects began to be attested there.

More than calling such subjects into being, these outreach projects also assumed that the subjects in question had willingly embraced cosmopolitan notions of a 'gay' community, public visibility, 'outness,' and confrontational politics. Such assumptions conflicted with the principles of tacit subject discourse. This inherent conflict discouraged many same-sex identified men in Santa Cruz from participating in the sponsored outreach events. Particularly reluctant were those men who pursued same-sex desires in the context of heterosexually married family life and/or the so-called *hombres* (men who enacted a hyper-masculine men role in erotic activity but would not participate in 'gay community' events).

Some same-sex men did visit the outreach program's community center, although they found it difficult to identify with the 'gay' subject position assumed by occupants of the center. Under local sexual discourse, those who are not *hombres* do not frame their sexuality in terms of hyper-masculinized themes, like public confrontation and political activism. In local parlance, those men are referred to as *maricones*. At one center a visitor made the point squarely: "*yo no soy gay, yo soy mujer*" ("I'm not gay, I'm a woman"; see Wright 2000: 102).

The center's outreach workers, and the few Santa Cruz residents who adopted the center's gay and cosmopolitan referencing, reacted to such remarks with scorn. They regarded them (and the subjects who made them) as reactionary, old-fashioned, and unenlightened. Thus, while "men-who-have-sex-with-men who were too rich or too poor or too masculine or too feminine were unlikely to be attracted to the gay center," these men were unlikely to be "welcomed as members of the emerging gay community" if they went to the center and tried to learn more about its activities (ibid.). Wright's example shows how easily gay-centered linguistic practices can create hierarchy and exclusion as they move through the global circuit, but also how practices like tacit subject referencing provide local subjects with ways of speaking out against disruptions of the kind exemplified by the statement "I'm not gay."

As Peña's (2004) work in Miami, Florida, on Cuban diasporic settings shows, the 'tacit subject' discursive stance is not inflexible. There are moments when such discretion is required, but there are also moments when a non-traditional, explicit, Spanish-language-based referencing of the sexual self needs to be proclaimed. Rather than embracing the English-based cosmopolitan discursive practices, the same-sex Cuban men from Miami whom Peña interviewed invoke *perra* – a diasporic variety of Spanish in which tacit subject formation is suspended and the explicit referencing of sexual desires, identities, and practices is now encouraged. What is not clear is whether *pera* builds on alternatives to tacit subject conventions that were in place at home, in the speakers' communities prior to their movement, or whether *perra* is entirely a diasporic product. But we know that the formation of *perra* allows Spanish-speaking diasporic subjects to step outside of the tacit subject boundaries while still remaining within the linguistic terrain of Hispanic tradition and not embracing the cosmopolitan mobility associated with a (gay) English fluency.

Remember that the incorporation of English was not problematic for the Tonga *leiti* subject (the failure to incorporate English *effectively* was the problem) or for the *bakla* sexual subject (until the *bakla* went back to the homeland, where the loss of *bakla* language may become apparent). Issues of racial/ethnic difference and class help to shape acceptance or rejection of cosmopolitan fluency even if these social features are not directly encoded within the details of linguistic performance.

Globalization, Sexual Sameness, and the Question of National Language

The movement of cosmopolitan linguistic practices and discursive meanings through the global circuit prompts new ways of talking about sexual sameness while it reconfigures ways of referencing sexual themes in local contexts. Out of this process of territorialization emerge new categories of sexual personhood, whose status within the local setting now needs clarification. Left unattended, these uncertainties quickly extend beyond the locality, into regional and national terrain, and beyond. With meanings of citizenship often under dispute in of these contexts, tensions between the '(homo)sexual subject' and the 'responsible citizen' become understandable and unavoidable (Alexander 1994, Cohen 2005, Jackson 2001, Leap 2004, Puar and Rai 2002).

In April 1996, the Indonesian government announced that motion pictures shown there could not be in any language except *bahasa Indonesia* (the national language). All subtitles in any other language would be eliminated, foreign-language soundtracks were forbidden, and all dialogue was to be dubbed in *bahasa Indonesia*. The legislative proposal, affirmatively nationalistic in its goals, was passed by the Indonesian parliament but was reconsidered after the Indonesian president refused to endorse it. The final version, approved by parliament in

December 1997, reversed the initial requirements. Now all non-English foreign films had to be dubbed in English, and all foreign films had to be shown with Indonesian subtitles (Boellstorff 2003).

The shift in position seemed curious, but it is understandable when examined in terms of questions of citizenship and national belonging. *Bahasa Indonesia* represents a point of unity for a nation composed of multiple languages and cultural traditions. The primary task in nation-building in such instances is to create a consistent 'image' of the nation, not to underscore its internal diversity. Instead of absorbing the foreign films into the national fabric via *bahasa Indonesia* dubbing, the mandatory use of English and Indonesian subtitles underscores the film's outsider character, reserving the national language for media projects that affirm the internal unity of the nation and its people.

Out of a similar discursive context has emerged *bahasa gay*, the variety of the national language spoken by Indonesian men who define their sexuality in terms of a "desire for the same" (Boellstorff 2005: 175). These men are usually urban residents (or wish to be so), they are middle class (or have middle class aspirations), and many are married to women and have children.

There is no term or phrase in *bahasa Indonesia* that identifies "men who profess a 'desire for the same.'" There are terms like *waria* and *banci*, but these refer to sexualized subject positions with a very different construction. *Waria* means "men with women's souls, who therefore dress like women and are attracted to men" (Boellstorff 2005: 57). They mark their *waria* status in public through a selective combination of cultural and linguistic practices identified as male and female; these include women's clothing, the use of make-up, and other feminine bodily presentations. They also use "typically masculine forms of bodily comportment and speech when the occasion demands" (Boellstorff 2007: 92). In contrast, men who express "desire for the same" do not cross-dress or present an explicitly effeminate persona in public settings. Instead, their use of *bahasa gay* is their primary public marker of sexual subjectivity. In most instances, the usage takes the form of a playful reshaping of the national language. This transforms a *bahasa Indonesia* statement like "*Aku tidak mau*" ("I don't want") into a *bahasa gay* statement of equivalent meaning "*Akika tinta mawar*," or a *bahasa Indonesia* sentence like "*Lelaki cakep [kamu] mau ngesong*" ("The boy is cute, do you want to fellate him?") into "*Lekes cekes meses ngeses*."

Indonesian men who share a 'desire for the same' and are presumably speakers of *bahasa gay* themselves have no problem decoding the meanings of such statements. Yet, while some the words may sound familiar to speakers of *bahasa Indonesia* who are not same-sex oriented, the meanings of the statements will be puzzling to those unfamiliar with the word-building processes through which these sentences are constructed (ibid., pp. 190–1). Features of syntax and vocabulary from Javanese, English, and other linguistic traditions also appear in *bahasa gay* sentences, further marking the distinctiveness of this code and the messages about sexual sameness that it conveys. Speakers of *bahasa gay* underscore this point when they refer to themselves by the term 'gay' rather than by using one of the extant Indonesian categories for male-centered sexual sameness, and when they define their personal relationships with North Atlantic-based and gay-centered vocabulary.[4]

That Indonesian sexual subjects modify national linguistic resources to incorporate cosmopolitan discourse of sexual sameness would appear to conflict with Indonesia's ongoing efforts at using the national-language project in order to build the nation. However, the emergence of *bahasa gay* as a distinct but embedded variant of the national language is consistent with the principles that shaped the anti-dubbing policy governing language use in the entertainment industry. Using a non-Indonesian term to mark the 'desire for the same' and the language through which this desire is articulated allows a gay language to be part of the national linguistic fabric, while ensuring that neither the subject position nor its linguistic practices will pose a threat to national unity. Listeners may not always know what speakers are saying in the discursive moment, but they can be certain that speakers are saying it in the national language.

Blackwood's work with Indonesian women who express a 'desire for the same' reminds us that visibility is also a key theme in *bahasa gay* usage (Blackwood 1999, 2005). The *bahasa Indonesia* term *lesbi* identifies primarily urban women who fashion their sexual sameness around a western rather than indigenous model of sexual sameness. Yet there is no *bahasa lesbi* as a named linguistic practice equivalent to that of these women's male urban counterparts. While the emergence of *bahasa gay* can be related to global circulations of linguistic and economic assemblages, the ensuing linguistic/economic territorializations have been quite uneven. Here as elsewhere (and see Chao 2000, Hall 2005, Hall in press, Jackson 2001), male privilege helps to direct emerging associations between 'local' and cosmopolitan meanings of sexual sameness, and so do distinctions created by urban or rural residence, class position, and other contrastive features of social location.

The tensions between language, sexual sameness, and citizenship unfolding in the French national context have led to outcomes rather different from those displayed in Indonesia or Taiwan. The idea of a national language in France is grounded in principles of egalitarianism whose points of emphasis are sameness and inclusion rather than difference and diversity (Provencher 2004, 2007). These notions of national belonging have been in place since the Third Republic; they obligate all French citizens to be French first, and only then to express whatever partisan or sectarian positions they may wish to hold.

No impediments within this ideological system prevent the formation of a French-based equivalent of *bahasa gay*. Unlike *bahasa gay*'s coding of sexual reference with altered syntax and accumulated lexicon, a French language of sexual sameness need only be unquestionably French in its linguistic and political affirmation, before any assertions of sexuality may unfold.

Implementing that mandate becomes complicated because, as is the case elsewhere in the North Atlantic region, English vocabulary is frequently employed in France too in discussions of sexual sameness. Admittedly French speakers do not need to make use of English words and phrases when talking about sexual themes;

French alternatives of the English gay vocabulary do exist, or could be formed. But translation and new word formation do not yield satisfactory results when the 'original' terms have established meanings in the global gay circuit. The English terms in question here, starting with the word 'gay' itself, are members of this category.

The alternative to translation/new word formation in French discussions of sexual sameness is to draw freely on words and phrases from English or other outside sources, while ensuring that discussions of the French gay experience "operate through the regulatory discourse of the nation's cultural and political system" (Provencher 2004: 26–7). What results is textual products like the printed advertisement in Excerpt 4, which invites readers to subscribe to the French gay magazine *Têtu*.

Excerpt 4 English words, French allegiance in a French gay magazine advertisement. From Provencher 2007: 40[5]

VOICI 12 CHOSES QUE VOUS NE POURREZ PLUS ACHETER
UNE FOIS DEPENSE L'ARGENT DE VOTRE ABONNEMENT A TÊTU ...
200F – UN AN 11 NUMEROS. 200F =

1/2 Levi's, 1 Caterpillar (pied gauche ou droit),
2 entrées dans un sauna, 4 places de cinéma,
4 gin-tonics dans un club, 2 entrées dans un club +
2 vestiaires + 1 Chupa, 13 paquets de cigarettes,
1/4 d'aller-retour Paris–Londres en charter,
1/10 d'aller-retour Paris–New York en charter,
28 quotidiens, 2 heures de 36. 15, 1 fois le tour du périph' en tarif de nuit.

EN REVANCHE, SI VOUS PREFEREZ ACHETER 200 CAPOTES À
1 FRANC, ON VOUS COMPRENDRA.

[PHOTO OF TÊTU MAGAZINE'S INAUGURAL ISSUE]

MENSUEL HOMOSEXUEL VRAIMENT NOUVEAU ET PLUTOT
INTÉRESSANT ...
200F – UN AN 11 NUMEROS.

'English' words that are recognizable in the text include: *Levi's, Caterpillar, sauna, gin* (and) *tonic,* and *club.* These words refer to commodities which are recognizable in the global circuit and which deeply resonate within the global gay terrain. Replacing them with French terminology would disguise both the fact of global circulation and the gay implications of that transnational flow. While English words are included, their 'outsider' presence is offset by the inclusion of references that give an unavoidably French framing to the gay-centered transaction. These include: pairing entry to a gay bath-house with entry to a cinema; noting that a lollipop (expressed here with the term *Chupa* – a word of Spanish origin and of questionable politeness) is part of the admission package at a gay club; the use of the vernacular *quotidian* for 'newspaper'; and the very Parisian allusion to the *tour du périph'*.

Similar combinations of references to sexual sameness and national placement can be found in French advertisements for gay pride events, alcoholic beverages, or designer clothing marketed toward French gay audiences, including the cover designs for *Têtu* and other gay-related French commercial publications. While the 'gay' message is never the dominant theme in these displays, the messages are sufficiently visible to affirm both dimensions of the reader's status as French (homo)sexual citizen. Excerpt 4 expresses this point with particular force, as such advertisements position these assertions of sexual citizenship within an explicit neo-liberal framework: the nationalist themes in the advertisement make a sub-scription to *Têtu* a more productive use of one's hard-earned francs than are such frivolous pursuits of anonymous sex, alcohol, vacations, and taxi-rides.

In the French example, language, sexual sameness, and citizenship combine to produce a speaking subject who is (or is expected to be) a responsible citizen. The same outcome is connected with the formation of the *yan daudu* in Hausa country, northern Nigeria. Here, and in a fashion more similar to what happens in Indonesia than in France, the linguistic articulations of sexual sameness involve coded refer-ences and indirect statements. Unlike in Indonesia and France, however, *yan daudu* linguistic practices are designed for private and concealed locations rather than for public usage.

This private focus is understandable, given the Nigerian government's active endorsement of the 'un-African status' of homosexuality. These arguments have been greeted enthusiastically in Nigeria's northern states, where Hausa is the dominant linguistic and social tradition and Islam the primary religion (see Gaudio 2009). The function of these anti-gay sentiments helps focus an otherwise fragile national unity by positioning post-apartheid South Africa's strong endorsement of lesbian/gay rights as evidence of its status as a client-state of Western financial and cultural interests. The contrast also works to strengthen Nigeria's leadership role among African nations intent on resisting neo-colonial influences.

These conversations assume the existence of 'homosexual' and 'gay men' as subject positions whose presence is not widely attested in the northern states. Instead, common subject positions are *yan daudu* (feminine-appearing men, who are sexually attracted to other men) and *masu harka* (masculine-appearing men, often married and with children, who 'do the deed' with *yan daudu*). *Yan daudu* and *masu harka* usually meet discretely: in a friend's home, in a bar or café that supports their presence, or in some other secluded location. These are not cosmo-politan notions of gay identity, nor are they expressed in publication locations. Consistently, neither *yan daudu* nor *masu harka* identify themselves as gay, or see themselves as part of some transnational visible community of men who have sex with other men. Gaudio tells the story of being introduced to a *mai harka*[6] in a discrete setting, by a mutual friend. The *mai harka* was made nervous by Gaudio's presence, until the mutual friend at the site explained that Gaudio also "did the deed." "White men do it, too?" the *mai harka* exclaimed, apparently surprised that the white experience of sexual sameness and those of the *mai harka* and his *yan daudu* partner would have something in common (Gaudio 2001: 40–1).

Interestingly, even though *gay* experiences are positioned at a distance from *yan daudu* and *masu harka* subjectivities, English language references are very much in evidence in *yaren harka*, the 'harka dialect.' This is the variety of Hausa that *yan daudu* and *masu harka* use creatively and playfully when talking among themselves about their experiences as sexual persons. Many words in *yaren harka* have English origins: *anti/* "aunty," *mandiya/*"my dear" (an imitation of British usage), *Indiya/*"India" (which brings into *yaren harka* discourse other references to Bollywood musical repertoire), *ji-sebin/*"G-seven" (which uses the nickname for this group of industrial super-powers to describe a *yan daudu* with exceptional style, e.g. *ji-sebin ce sosai/*"She's a real G-7"; (Gaudio 2009: 17). Other references in *yaren harka* make strong connections between *yan daudu* sexuality and commercial practices, for instance *Yaya hajoji?/"How are the merchandises?"* – which is the question that one *masu harka* might ask another when inquiring about the second party's *yan daudu/*"boy friend."

Besides *yaren harka*, *yan daudu* also make use of *maganar mata* and *habaici*. *Maganar mata* is Hausa 'women's talk' (Gaudio 1997). *Habaici* are the strategies of argumentation, widely used in Hausa society, allowing speakers to say much without stating the point of the message explicitly. *Yan daudu* have distinctive styles of *habaici*, just as they are not speaking *like* women or *as* women when they draw on *maganar mata* in their private conversations (Gaudio 1997). In other words, the 'language' of the *yan daudu* is a complex accumulation of linguistic practices, with cosmopolitan referencing as only one component in that accumulation.

In a context where opposition to homosexuality carries the force of law and the threat of religious sanction, it may seem inappropriate to refer to *yan daudu* linguistic practices as a language of sexual citizenship and to draw parallels between it and *bahasa gay*, *gai* French, or even Swardspeak. Its function seems more in line with *tongzhi* discourse or the tacit subject-marking of Spanish, yet *yan daudu* linguistic practices maintain an explicitness of sexual referencing that *tongzhi* and tacit subject-marking deliberately avoid. By speaking as *yan daudu*, subjects assert their rights to a place in Hausa society, but they also assert a willingness to act responsibly within that placement, by framing *yan daudu* discourse privately. This private framing of sexual citizenship raises the question: how can a language of sexual citizenship be effective if the only parties who witness and validate the linguistic expressions of citizenship are the would-be citizens (the *yan daudu*) and their partners (*masu harka*)?

Conclusions: Gay Language, Global Finance, Cosmopolitan Reference, and Masculine Privilege

Globalization never involves a simple "imposition of new forms of experience onto local contexts." Instead,

> globalization informs and transforms people's lives, creating new forms of agency
> as easily as it perpetuates structures that are continuous with the past. (Besnier
> 2007a: 425)

Globalization's authority to inform and transform people's lives has not been acquired arbitrarily. Globalization's "most striking feature" is its close ties to "the runaway quality of global finance, which appears remarkably independent of traditional constraints of information transfer, national regulation, industrial productivity, or 'real' wealth in any particular society, country, or region" (Appadurai 2001: 4).

With "private sector companies outgrowing their national territories and, as new 'multinational' or 'transnational' or 'global' forces, reshaping community life" (Coupland 2003: 467), "the runaway quality of global finance" has also encouraged new forms of sexual citizenship, These include a cosmopolitan-based citizenship tied to "privatized, depoliticized gay culture anchored in domesticity and gay consumption" (Duggan 2003: 50), as well as forms of citizenship that have more localized references, either preceding the cosmopolitan formation or emerging at the site in response to it.

Under Collier and Ong's framework, these "broad structural transformations or new configurations of society and culture" are examined in terms of transnational movements of global assemblages. These assemblages are not fixed and stable constructions, they argue, but are fluid, flexible, and subject to reshaping as they become territorialized by engaging conditions at particular sites in the global circuit. Importantly, Collier and Ong do not include linguistic practices within the characteristics that lend territorial visibility and vitality to global assemblages. Judging by the examples reviewed in this chapter, there is every reason to include these practices in such discussion. Linguistic practices help enable the visibility of new forms of technology, exchange, administration, and values that circulate broadly within the global moment. And, as far as globalization and sexual sameness are concerned, linguistic practices are deeply implicated in the work of territorialization: fusing the gay subject, the visible subject, and the cosmopolitan subject into new forms of local assemblage, which are then articulated, however diversely, with the subject positions, forms of discursive references, and attendant linguistic practices at the site. What results, adapting Collier and Ong's phrasing, are territorialized linguistic practices which may explicitly name sexual desires, conceal or encode references to these desires, or map certain linguistic practices and discourses within locally recognizable usages and social histories. Though English is often the framing 'source language,' linguistic traditions other than English are also employed to these ends.

Rather than imposing *a* single language of sexual sameness on local speech settings worldwide, the globalization of gay language is *broadening* the linguistic resources through which references to same sex desires, practices, and subjectivities are becoming territorialized.

Yet the broadening unfolds unevenly, as we have seen. To cite only one example: whether global or localized, gay language is likely to frame its discussions of sexual sameness in terms of masculine authority and privilege, often at the expense of non-masculinized subjects. Misogynist references were central to definitions of success and failure in the Tongan beauty pageant and to meanings of *bakla* subjectivity in homeland and in the diaspora. Tacit subject-marking keeps the subject's public masculinity uncompromised in Santa Cruz, whatever engagements may unfold privately. The *Têtu* advertisement specifically outlines activities of interest to male readers with disposable income, leisure time, and public mobility, activities from which women readers would in most cases be excluded. Moreover, connections between authority, privilege, and whiteness are underscored in these gay language-based formations of a masculinized sexual sameness. *Tongzhi* discourse prompts speaking subjects to reject a broader western identification as well as specific forms of western sexuality. And, while he was very secure in his identity as the partner of a *yan daudu*, the *mai harka* in the northern Nigerian bar was still surprised to learn that "white men do it, too."

Masculine privilege is another dimension of the consumption-centered, cosmopolitan-based subject references that gay language brings into the global circuit in specific territorial assemblages. But with the foregrounding of a gay-centered masculine privilege comes the marginalization of other subjects, only some of whom find alternative ways to (re)claim voice in the territorialized context. Those remaining on the sidelines regularly include women (regardless of sexual orientation),[7] transgendered persons, and men who are unwilling to claim 'gay' identity and have no recourse to tacit-like subject-marking. Serious studies of language, sexuality, and globalization need to consider how these subjects retain their vitality in the face of global and local exclusion, thereby disclosing the limits of masculine privilege in the relevant assemblage as well as demonstrating the depth of masculine authority.

ACKNOWLEDGMENTS

I developed this chapter in June, 2008, while I was a scholar-in-residence at the Institute for British and American Studies, University of Osnabruek, Germany. My thanks to my Institute colleagues Katherine Stark and Lena Heine and to the students in my seminar on 'gay language,' all of whom made helpful comments on earlier drafts of this chapter. I also thank Elijah Edelman (American University, Washington DC) for help with bibliographic research and Michelle Marzullo (American University) for invaluable assistance with manuscript editing.

NOTES

1   Assemblages are "distinguished by a particular quality we refer to as global," as they move worldwide, and become "articulated in specific situations – or territorialized in

assemblages," they promote constellations of "new material, collective and discursive relationships" that become "domains in which forms and values of individual and collective existence are subject[ed] to technological, political and ethical reflection and intervention" (Collier and Ong 2005: 4).

2   *Bading* identifies flamboyant, witty, sarcastic, effeminate Filipino men. The term is primarily used in the Philippines, but is also found elsewhere in the Filipino diaspora.

3   Truth means 'truth.' Drama refers to the particular pathway of life experiences, past, present and yet to come, over which a person usually has had and will have no control, for instance destiny or fate. Drama is always uttered with a more theatrical flourish. Leap (2003: 411–14) examines Excerpt 2 in more detail.

4   Because most Indonesian *gay* men have not travelled outside of the archipelago, their knowledge of North Atlantic gay culture has been acquired indirectly, primarily through internet resources, magazines, motion pictures and other media. The 'dubbing' issue mentioned above takes on particular significance within this context.

5   The advertisement appeared in the inaugural issue of *Têtu*, July/August, 1996, p. 11.

6   *Mai harka* is the singular form of *masu harka*.

7   Oswin (2006: 779) identifies particular problems related to studies of the "global lesbian."

REFERENCES

Alexander, M. J. (1994) Not just (any)body can be a citizen: The politics of law, sexuality and postcoloniality in Trinidad and Tobago and the Bahamas. *Feminist Review* 48: 5–23.

Alonso, A. M., and Koreck, M. T. (1989) Silence, Hispanics, AIDS and sexual practices. *Differences* 1(1): 101–24.

Altman, D. (1997) Global gays/global gaze. *GLQ: A Journal of Lesbian and Gay Studies* 3 (4): 417–37.

Appadurai, A. (2001) Grassroots globalization and the research imagination. In A. Appadurai (ed.), *Globalization*, 1–21. Durham: Duke University Press.

Besnier, N. (2002) Transgenderism, locality and the Miss Galaxy beauty pageant in Tonga. *American Ethnologist* 29: 534–66.

Besnier, N. (2004) Consumption and cosmopolitanism: Practicing modernity at the second-hand marketplace in Nuku'alofa, Tonga. *Anthropological Quarterly* 77(1): 7–45.

Besnier, N. (2007a) Gender and interaction in a globalizing world: Negotiating the gendered self in Tonga. In B. S. McElhinny (ed.), *Words, Worlds and Material Girls: Language, Gender, Globalization*, 423–45. Mouton de Gruyter.

Besnier, N. (2007b) Language and gender research at the intersection of the global and local. *Gender and Language* 1(1): 67–78.

Blackwood, E. (1999) Tombois in West Sumatra: Constructing masculinity and erotic desire. In E. Blackwood and S. E. Wieringa (eds), *Same-Sex Relations and Female Desires: Transgender Practices Across Cultures*, 181–205. New York City: Columbia University Press.

Blackwood, E. (2005) Transnational sexualities in one place: Indonesia readings. *Gender and Society* 19: 221–42.

Boellstorff, T. (2003) Dubbing culture: Indonesia gay and lesbi subjectivities and ethnographies in an already globalized world. *American Ethnologist* 30(2): 225–42.

Boellstorff, T. (2004) "*Authentic, of course!*": *Gay language in Indonesia and culture of belonging*. In Leap and Boellstorff (eds), 181–201.

Boellstorff, T. (2005) *The Gay Archipelago: Sexuality and Nation in Indonesia.* Princeton: Princeton University Press.

Boellstorff, T. (2007) Warias, national transvestites. In T. Boellstorff, *A Coincidence of Desires: Anthropology, Queer Studies, Indonesia*, 78–113. Durham: Duke University Press.

Cantú, L. (1999) *Border Crossings: Mexican Men and the Sexuality of Migration.* Unpublished doctoral dissertation, Department of Sociology, University of California, Irvine.

Carrier, J. (1995) *De Los Otros: Intimacy and Homosexuality among Mexican Men.* New York: Columbia University Press.

Chao, A. (2000) Global metaphors and local strategies in the construction of Taiwan's lesbian identities. *Culture, Health and Sexuality* 2: 377–90.

Chou, W.-S. (2001) Homosexuality and the Chinese politics of tongzhi in Chinese societies. *Journal of Homosexuality* 40(3/4): 27–46.

Cohen, L. (2005) The *kothi* wars: AIDS cosmopolitanism and the morality of classification. In A. Vincanne and S. L. Pigg (eds), *Sex in Development: Science, Sexuality and Morality in Global Perspective*, 269–304. Durham: Duke University Press.

Collier, S. J., and Ong, A. (2005) Global assemblages, anthropological problems. In A. Ong and S. J. Collier (eds), *Global Assemblages: Technology, Politics and Ethics as Anthropological Problems*, 3–21. London: Blackwells.

Coupland, N. (2003) Introduction: Sociolinguistics and globalization. *Journal of Sociolinguistics* 7(4): 465–72.

Decena, C. U. (2008) Tacit subjects. *GLQ: A Journal of Lesbian and Gay Studies* 14(2/3): 339–59.

Duggan, L. (2003) *The Twilight of Equality: Neoliberalism, Cultural Politics and the Attack on Democracy.* Boston: Beacon Press.

Gaudio, R. (1997) Not talking straight in Hausa. In A. Livia and K. Hall (eds), *Queerly Phrased: Language, Gender and Sexuality*, 416–29. New York City: Oxford University Press.

Gaudio, R. (2001) White men do it too: Racialized (homo)sexualities in postcolonial Hausaland. *Journal of Linguistic Anthropology* 11(1): 36–51.

Gaudio, R. (2007) Out on video: Gender, language and new public spheres in Islamic Northern Nigeria. In B. S. McElhinney (ed.), *Words, Worlds and Material Girls: Language, Gender, Globalization*, 237–83. Berlin: Mouton-de Gruyter.

Gaudio, R. (2009) Man marries man. In E. Lewin and W. L. Leap (eds), *Out in Public: Lesbian and Gay Anthropology in a Globalizing World*, 273–91. Malden, MA: Wiley-Blackwell.

Hall, K. (2005) Intertextual sexuality: Parodies of class, identity and desire in liminal Delhi. *Journal of Linguistic Anthropology*, 15(1): 125–44.

Hall, K. (in press) Boys' talk: Hindi, moustaches and masculinity in New Delhi. In P. Pichler and E. Eppler (eds), *Gender and Spoken Language in Interaction.* Houndmills, Basingstoke: Palgrave MacMillan.

Jackson, P. (2001) Pre gay, post-queer: Thai perspectives on proliferating gender/sex diversity in Asia. *Journal of Homosexuality* 40 (3/4): 1–25.

Lancaster, R. (1988) Subject honor and object shame: The construction of male homosexuality and stigma in Nicaragua. *Ethnology* 27(2): 111–25.

Leap, W. L. (2003) Language and gendered modernity. In J. Holmes and M. Meyerhoff (eds), *Handbook of Language and Gender*, 401–22. London: Blackwells.

Leap, W. L. (2004) Language, belonging, and (homo)sexual citizenship in Cape Town, South Africa. In Leap and Boellstorff (eds), 134–62.

Leap, W. L. (2008) "True things that bind us": Globalization, US language pluralism and gay men's English. In M. Bertho (ed.), *The Impact of Globalization on the United States*, 183–210. Westport: Praeger Publishers.

Leap, W., and Boellstorff, T. (eds) (2004) *Speaking in Queer Tongues: Globalization and Gay Language*. Urbana: University of Illinois Press.

Manalansan, M. (1998) *Remapping Frontiers: The Lives of Filipino Gay Men in New York*. Rochester, NY: Unpublished doctoral dissertation, University of Rochester.

Manalansan, M. (2003) *Global Divas: Filipino Gay Men in the Diaspora*. Durham: Duke University Press.

Murray, S. O. (1996) Male homosexuality in Guatemala: Possible insights and certain confusions from sleeping with the natives. In E. Lewin and W. L. Leap (eds), *Out in the Field: Reflections of Lesbian and Gay Anthropologists*, 236–60. Urbana: University of Illinois Press.

Oswin, N. (2006) Decentering queer globalization: Diffusion and the 'global gay.' *Environment and Planning D: Society and Space* 24: 777–90.

Oswin, N. (2007) Producing homonormativity in neoliberal South Africa: Recognition, redistribution and the Equality project. *Signs: Journal of Women in Culture and Society* 32: 649–69.

Peña, S. (2004) Pájaration and transculturation: Language and meaning in Miami's Cuban American gay worlds. In Leap and Boellstorff (eds), 231–50.

Provencher, D. (2004) Vague French creole: Cooperative discourse in the French (gay) press. In Leap and Boellstorff (eds), 23–45.

Provencher, D. (2007) *Queer French*. London: Ashgate.

Puar, J., and Rai, A. S. (2002) Monster, terrorist, fag: The war on terrorism and the production of docile patriots. *Social Text* 72, Vol. 20(3): 117–48.

Rofel, L. (2007) Qualities of desire: Imagining gay identities. In L. Rofel, *Desiring China: Experiments in Neoliberalism, Sexuality and Public Culture*, 85–110. Durham: Duke University Press.

Wong, A. (2005) The reappropriation of tongzhi. *Language in Society* 34: 763–93.

Wong, A., and Zhang, Q. (2001) The linguistic construction of the *tongzhi* community. *Journal of Linguistic Anthropology* 19(2): 248–78.

Wright, T. (2000) Gay organizations, NGOs and the globalization of gay identity: The case of Bolivia. *Journal of Latin American Studies* 5(2): 89–111.

26 Metroethnicities and Metrolanguages

JOHN C. MAHER

Negritude? A tiger does not proclaim its tigritude.

Wole Soyinka (1976: 74)

Transcultural performances show the links between idiosyncratic individual performances and the construction of transcultural linguistic, cultural phenomena within globalization.

Emi Otsuji (2008: xi)

Introduction

In the wake of the impersonal state and bureaucratic structures of late modernism, ethnic ties in the postmodern era show resilience and even revitalization. Essentialist ethnicity is still mobilising for many. Though the term 'ethnicity' is of recent coinage, Hutchinson and Smith (1996: 6) describe the typical features that *ethnies* exhibit: a common proper name to identify a community essence, a myth of common ancestry which gives a kind of fictive kinship or super family, shared historical memories, elements of a common culture such as religion or language, a link with a homeland or common territory, a sense of solidarity. Ethnicity is coming to be viewed as a residual category that people fall back on when everything else is found wanting (Hobsbawm 1990), while advanced communication (consumer culture, the internet, and the like) pays no attention to ethnic discreteness, rather driving it to the folkloristic margins (Featherstone 1990).

Despite the longevity of ethnic classification, there has been much discussion of 'transcending' ethnicity, or of an 'after identity' (Warnke 2008). Dynamic population movements of sojourners, ex-colonials and immigrants, a cultural shift toward polyethnic and multicultural states affecting language, civic membership, education, and so on has led to a gradual deconstruction of the notion of ethnicity. The repositioning suggests that "not only are all ethnic communities deeply divided, but also [...] ethnicity itself is an optional identity and is often

The Handbook of Language and Globalization, First Edition. Edited by Nikolas Coupland.
© 2013 Blackwell Publishing Ltd except for editorial material and organization © 2013 Nikolas Coupland. Published 2013 by Blackwell Publishing Ltd.

overshadowed by other (gender, class, regional) identities" (Melucci 1996: 12). The landfill loyalty that ethnic memberships traditionally demand is not viewed as obligatory by many people of the current generation. In Japan, wherefrom I will draw examples, such loyalty is viewed as uncool.

In the most recent census, one million young British identified themselves as 'mixed race.' Mixed race will become the largest ethnic minority population in Britain by 2015. Actors and actresses of ethnic ambiguity (EA) are in demand, and the ethnically ambiguous is a valency measure in what I term here 'metroethnicity' and 'metrolanguage.' The visual impact of EA is a form of micro-power: the *puissance* or vitality (Maffesoli: 1996b) that comprises urban/underground ('metro') sociality. Metroethnicity is experienced through the language of 'trivial vectors,' like Victoria Beckham's Chinese *hanzi* grrrrrrrrrrrl tattoo which decorates the social body. Metroethnicity is different from industrial strength ethnicity. Its manufacturing purpose is much more elusive/allusive. Metroethnicity is less ethnicity and more 'ethnicity.' It is a blurring of boundaries energized by sensuality of experience rather than by political experience. Butler, in a similar vein, rejigs the traditional essentialism of gender toward a performative semiotic of corporeality: "such acts, gestures, enactments, generally construed, are performative in the sense that the essence or identity that they possess is through corporeal signs and other discursive means" (Butler 1990: 136). Ludic ethnicity invites metrolinguistic play, and this constitutes the theme of this introduction to the notion of metroethnicity and metrolanguages.

Language, Society, Performance

Important to an understanding of the paradigm shift being undertaken by many post-colonial and 'third-eye' studies of nation and identity is what might be termed a shift from being to doing. Stuart Hall and Paul du Gay (1996, Introduction) have noted:

> the critique of the self-sustaining subject at the centre of post-Cartesian western metaphysics has been comprehensively advanced in philosophy. The question of subjectivity and its unconscious processes of formation has been developed within the discourse of a psychoanalytically influenced feminism and cultural criticism. The endless performative self has been advanced in celebratory variants of postmodernism [...] What, then, is the need for a further debate about 'identity'? Who needs it?

From a sociolinguistic angle, Pennycook (2003, 2007) and Cameron (1990) have highlighted the need to shift our perspective from the fatal attraction between language and a particular nation, territory, and ethnicity – from the "language reflects society" mantra; and Otsuji (2008) has effectively demonstrated how discrete ethnic and linguistic labels such as 'Japanese' and 'English,' as well as notions of 'code-switching' and 'bilingualism,' become problematic in the attempt to grasp the complexity of contemporary transcultural workplaces. How, then, can we describe things which receive value not from history, but from an ongoing cultural aesthetics; a superordinate category of music, dress, food, names, and language? How can we conceptualize the global shifting of sensitivities to cultural phenomena that are themselves not new?

Consonant with Pennycook's (2004) attention to linguistic and cultural performance ("performativity"), I suggest that the explanatory concept of metroethnic and metrolinguistic style might be a starting point. 'Metro' is a multiple signifier, which points to phenomena that travel below the radar of bordered perceptions of ethnicity and language; more underground (*métro*) than overground. Metroethnic/metrolinguistic style typically occurs in fast and fluid urban (that is, metropolitan) space – a conceptual and not necessarily a physical space. I also adapt the term 'metro' from the neologism 'metrosexual,' which (ignoring the criticism that it refers merely to rich and narcissistic men with an urban lifestyle, *à la* David Beckham) incorporates a new version of border-crossing for urban men whose lifestyle is no longer driven by a nagging concern to show and tell gender loyalty, but rather by a heightened aesthetic sense. The metroethnic and the metrolinguistic are a category of 'borrowing' born out of cultural movements, twists, and flows. Metroethnicities and metrolanguages are oppositional by virtue of their aesthetic placement. They are opposed to reified essentialist ethnic, religious, and cultural identities and in favor of a constructivist here-and-now. Naming and showing are important vehicles for metrolanguages: a Caucasian college student chooses to wear a T-shirt bearing *hanzi/kanji/hanja* (Chinese characater) design; a new baby is given a Chinese name Chinese by fourth-generation Chinese-heritage parents who neither read nor speak Chinese and who themselves have become ethnically ambiguous. The urge is straightforward. It's a nice thing. It's cool. They are doing metrolanguage.

Brazil! *Que bonito é!* Language as Play

Are there new values for variation and for style in the late-modern world?
Coupland 2007, Introduction, vi

An important starting point for the study of metrolanguages is the study of stylistics. Coupland has noted the "acceleration of sociolinguistic interest in [...] the socially meaningful" and has elaborated persuasively on how language users "inherit indexical resources and sometimes rework them creatively in interaction – structure and agency" (2007: Introduction, vi). In such creative rework we see that language is an ever-differentiating delight, an origami-world of action: folding and unfolding and refolding – like Chinese calligraphy, which unfolds its mercantile magic for the expression of emotion on baseball caps and restaurant signboards, and even on the human body. This is a social calligraphy where the linguistic meets the aesthetic. Speakers play with language, but also with the idea of language. This widens their circle of language life. As consumers, language users select dialects and styles and languages. Like the branding of rapidly reviving Manx Gaelic as a unique and 'neat' thing for newcomers to do, 'adding the Manx touch' to pronunciation, personal naming, house and business names, stationary signatures (Isle of Man Government 2006, Coonceil ny Gaelgey 2008, Cain 2008), all this deftly hooking up to the full-throttle boom in things Celtic.

Speakers manipulate 'language as historical property' as an accessory and for effect, according to an aesthetic principle. In such personal and reflexive action resides our explanation of language in society (sociolinguistics): "As human beings we are able to change our behavior; that we act as free agents is fundamental to our self-conception. Every word we say reinforces this conviction, for whenever we speak we make choices" (Coulmas 2006: 1). Language choice comprises philosophical choices based on the hermeneutics of gender, race, and sex identification. The challenge becomes immediately obvious when we begin to talk about identity: "History, institutional authority and social power have made me what I am yet why should I endorse a [particular] identity if I cannot justify it as a good one?" (Warnke 2008: 68).

On the one hand we have the languages of exalted patriotism and tribal loyalties and on the other the "uncritical celebration of diversity" (Hooks 1999). Metroethnicity eschews both dumb polarities. It is a more critical and plastic concept, although (as with the baby naming example above) its social critique does not come with an accompanying explanation. Metroethnic phenomena are critical because they put 'ethnic' in inverted commas: Baybayin (obsolete Filipino script) paraphernalia worn by nostalgia-tripping Californian Pinoy, like ethnic ambiguity and EA naming practices, the music of EA (ethnic ambiguiguity) pop Diva, like football songs and doing Brazil for the night … in Tokyo. Consider the following example:

> Excerpt 1   Discussion between two sports journalists. From World Cup, Tokyo Morning Show, FM Japan, July 6, 2002
>
> BRITISH FOOTBALL JOURNALIST: It struck a lot of foreign journalists as amazing. One night they were Japan supporters. Next night, the same people jammed the stands wearing Brazilian team shirts and face-paint, belting out songs and chants in perfect Portuguese. Like they were doing carnival. Lovers of Brazilian football.
>
> JAPANESE FOOTBALL JOURNALIST: Yeah. But this is much more than the old Japanese custom of imitation. Something bigger is going on with Japanese kids today. In my day, being Japanese – identity – was very clear. Nowdays, kids play with the idea of being Japanese. They think they can do what they want with identity. When they decide to be something else they devote themselves to it. Like singing Brazilian, like being Brazilian for the night.

Metrolinguistic play is employed as a form of on-the-spot knowledge. In the post-traditional order, self-identity is not a stationary object. It is open-ended and effervescent. Self-identity is an ongoing project toward a configuration of meaning: "an endeavour that we continuously work and reflect upon" (Giddens 1991: 81).

Ludic ethnicity seizes the same creative vitality and regeneration that language constantly provides. Compare a Braziliana football carnival in Tokyo to Bakhtin's description:

> While carnival lasts there is no other life outside it. During carnival time life is subject only to its laws, that is, the laws of its own freedom. It has a universal spirit; it is a special condition of the entire world, of the world's revival and renewal, in which all take part. Such is the essence of carnival, vividly felt by all its participants. (Bakhtin 1968: 7)

Metroethnicities are here and now, portable and temporal, built from identity ambiguity, from different contexts of meaning, and from the heterogeneity of emotion.

> I'm Irish when I can't explain myself and I'm Japanese when I can. Or maybe it's the other way round. My garage band speaks American and my computer speaks London. (Michael Endo, College Student, aged 19, Tokyo, to author)

Metroethnicity is relativistic. It discards the truth claims of traditional ethnicity. It is a restructuring. Metroethnicity involves a critique of ethnicity. This critique is a mode of what terms like 'self-reflection' or self-criticism imply regarding those ideological determinants of the self-formative process (*Bildung*) that instruct how we should behave in the world; and indeed metroethnicity is a critique of our very conception of the world.

To some, the embrace of metroethnicities may seem idle provocation or bourgeoise play, displaying ignorance of the realities of institutionalized injustice and everyday violence that accompany ethnicity and ethnic conflict throughout the world. However, it cannot be overlooked that multiple identity is not what was supposed to be in the age of exalted patriotism and tribal loyalties. This identity is not one but many. And the many are not discrete either. They constitute what Balibar terms "fictive," "ambiguous," "transnational" identities and citizenships (Balibar and Wallerstein 1994, Balibar 2004). In contrast to the categorical primacy of nation-state or racial membership, the world of overlapping identities presents individuals with alternative means of conceptualizing community and belonging. This is surely part of a bigger design, which might reside in what Lin and Luk describe as the benefit of "adapting Bakhtin's carnival laughter, i.e., the idea of undoing ideological certainties through human innovation to achieve freedom of consciousness" (2005: 78).

Ethnicity Lite: Beckham Bends It

> *Black like Beckham. Britain's most famous black man.*
>
> Channel 4 TV, 2005

It was inevitable, because libertarian 'crossing' (ethnic, gender-style, linguistic) shares the same territory in the age of globalization. David Beckham was shunted from being metrosexual to being metroethnic. The frontage was called 'comical' 'cuckoo,' 'tongue-in-cheek'and 'insulting' – namely the idea that shedloads of cash and bling make 'Becks' a black icon. People who played with such an idea were unfunny and merely demonstrated the very narrowest perception of black culture.

Beckham indeed bends it. His metrosexual (hybrid) style of David Beckham – androgynous and family-man look – feminized soccer in the same way in which the lovable lager-bloated fan epitomized soccer's hyper-masculinity. Favoring the occasional gender-bending sarong – as well as cornrows and crucifixes – as streetwear, Beckham helped football to be taken out of one category and slotted it into a larger circle, which epitomized multicultural Britain.

Beckham has been extensively discussed as a complex global icon (see for example Machin and van Leeuwen 2005). So what did post-ethnicities learn from the fuss over black Becks? It was surely the idea of 'ethnicity lite.' Namely, the idea that metroethnicity is ethnicity borrowed and made local through sensual experience (that is, through aesthetics) – something powered by style rather than by racial/mythic/historical orthodoxy. Wary of the constitutive assumptions of ethnicity and of the hubris of its boundedness, adopted metroethncities are thus (inverted commas) 'ethnicities.' In 1988, the late Peter Strevens told me the story below, about an ESP training course for Flight attendants in Norwich, England (Excerpt 2):

Excerpt 2   Put it on, take it off

FLIGHT ATTENDANT TRAINING MANAGER (THAI AIRLINES):	Teach them to speak properly but don't mess with the accent. Customers like the Thai accent.
EFL TEACHER	What about the two English-educated Thai women in the group?
TRAINING MANAGER:	I told them to work on it. Tone down the accent a bit. Sound less Milton Keynes and more Chiang Mai.
EFL TEACHER:	The girls are boarding-school British. Can't be done.
TRAINING MANAGER:	Yes it can. The ethnic thing's all about style. It's just like make-up. Put it on, wash it off.

Put it on. Take it off. Playful code-switching, for effect or ethnic irony, T-shirts logos, an interest in Tibetan script tattoos. Again, metroethnicities are here and now. They are style ethnicities, radically subjected to modification by their users. These metroethnicities provide the post-traditional contexts for ethnic crossing and language crossing (Rampton 2005) – a crossing based not upon careful deliberation but rather upon 'empathetic sociality' (Maffesoli 1996a: 11). Metrolanguages, like the metroethnicities they express, are motivated by sentiment and ludic vitality: "I just love talkin' Kansai-ben [Osaka-area accent]. It's cool. It changes the atmosphere. I'm not from Osaka. My dad is. It feels good" (Jun, aged 16, Tokyo High School boy, to author).

Osakan Japanese is racy, street, cool. The sideways step is brazenly "instrumental," in a felicitous explanation by Hewitt (2003); it is the adoption of a marked cultural form by a non-member of the group who is not at all aligned to the history and world-view of the group. Yes. On the one hand, the adoption of hip-hop in Japan – by Japanese as well as by many minority musicians in Japan (Nikkei Brazilian, Korean Japanese, Chinese Japanese) – is a signal of resistance to the patriarchal and obstructive myth of Japanese cultural homogeneity. At the same time, as Condry (2006) points out, the African or ethnic minority identity component itself has been left out. This is undoubtedly 'borderland' action, representative of what Willis and Murphy-Shigematsu (2008: Introduction, 6) felicitously describe as "multiple processes associated with globalization leading to larger hybridizations, to a global mélange of socio-cultural, political, and economic forces and to the emergence of what could be called trans-local Creolized cultures."

It Ain't Mix. It's REMIX

Who sings the nation-state?
            Judith Butler and Gayatri Spivak 2007: 34

Metroethnicities are not a 'mix' of simple ingredients, A plus B. They are a remix, because the identities they engage and the habits of speech, milieux, dress, eating, and personal associations are mobile; a continuous remixing. Metroethncities, like metrolanguages, do not make impossible demands but rather fulfill utilitarian needs. It requires social observation to know what is utilitarian and cool. You want to link up with, but avoid conformity to, an ethnic or group orthodoxy. Tricky. The residual primordial ethnic code is becoming a new code. The neo-tribes of metroethnicities are invited for social play and experiment with the very language affiliations that were hitherto fixed and immutable ciphers of identity. The importance of 'cool' must be underlined. Cool is crossing. Cool is mixed talk, as we are informed by Okinawan rockers and rappers. Cool is a discourse of the Creole, a discourse of the people, and the people is personal. Oiwa explains thus: "What is cool in Japan is the ability to play with traditional 'Japaneseness' and foreign elements at the same time. Not only is it their counterblow to social evils but an attempt to embrace identity [...] involving a reconstruction of identity" (2008: 2). This reconstruction is assisted by popular culture, and its new forms and styles are made possible by "the new form of globalization" (Hall 1991), which incorporates glocal affiliations and differences. Popular music is, therefore, "a site where identity is continuously deformed, desconstructed and reconstructed by the means to self-expression" (ibid., p. 4).

Style constitutes a re-scripting of experience, and thus it veers into creating new ways of translating our thought and action. As scholar Sharon Kinsella and novelist Oe Kenzaburo add, this immediately creates difficulty in accepting "the possibility that a different generation of people can be the bearers of new progressive theoretical approaches: styles of thought which are neither dependent on nor any longer closely derived from the remaindered logic of [the past]" (Kinsella 2000: 235).

Portable Ethnicity and Language Revival

Dress, ornamentation, dance and song – these may disappear as ordinary markers of group life while persisting (or re-emerging) as symbolic markers.

John Edwards 1985: 112

Metroethnicities turn away from the fortification of minority identities in order to regard ethnicity as an aesthetic project with internal validation. The *disponibilité* of the metroethnicity comportment may occur on a macroscale, as cultural choice – for instance when immigrants adopt new self-identities, which are hitherto empty of content but which look attractive.

Excerpt 3   The Manx language. Personal communication from A. Cain, Manx language officer, 2008

JOHN MAHER: Have new settlers helped Manx language revival? The story is that 80s [*sic*] young rootless expatriates brought up in the Middle East latched on to Manx identity and said "Hey, that's neat. I'll have that!"

ADRIAN CAIN: Right. Only 40% of the population is Manx so it would be point-less to articulate our identity any other way! Regarding new arrivals to the Island, historically it has been people from the UK but increasingly there are large numbers from South Africa and Eastern Europe. A number of new arrivals have been really important in the revival of Manx ... Some aren't interested in what we have to offer here but others are prepared to take on board the language and culture. Perhaps the children of these new arrivals will determine the future of the language.

This is not the same as the phenomenon of ethnicization (Tabouret-Keller 1999: 336), as for example in nationalist-driven discourse in the Autonomous Basque region of Spain and in the Flemish autonomous region of Belgium. The formation of metroethnicities, I have explained elsewhere, is an activity of the mainstream and of the minorities alike, who are

eager to embrace multiculturality, cultural/ethnic tolerance and multicultural life-styles, especially when it comes to friendships, music and the arts, eating and dress. It is a kind of post-ethnicity state whereby both Japanese and ethnic minorities 'play' with ethnicity (not necessarily their own) for aesthetic effect. It involves a cultural crossing, self-definition made up of borrowing and bricolage, a *sfumato* of blurred identities. (Maher 2005: 34)

This is sometimes found in metroethnic naming.

We gave the baby an Ainu name. 'Pirika.' We're not indigenous Ainu. We're just moved by Ainu culture and history. We've visited museums and things. I'm from

Hokkaido myself so I might have some Ainu background. Everybody's mixed. The naming also means that I care about indigenous peoples and maybe my daughter will too. Pirika means 'beauty.' (Postal worker, 24, Tokyo, to author)

Ethnolinguistic naming across ethnic boundaries asserts that symbols are rather portable. I can trans-port ethnolinguistic parts of myself across time and place. Portable ethnicity is everywhere. For example, it comes with being a migrant or a refugee. You take some, leave some. The symbols of identity, just because they are symbols, are detachable. Portable ethnicities are *de rigeur* in popular culture – for example in the (visual–textual) semiotics of rock music. In the globalized world of the openly ethnically mixed populations, a bilingual pop diva with electro thump and semi-operatic pitch pumps up the volume: The marketing of ethnicities is tried-'n-tested. Belasco (2001) has elaborated on this in her "shopping for identity." Postfeminist chic divas are from third or fourth-generation immigrant families, leaping over local musical boundaries and musical genre. The ethnic thing is careless, as scattershot as the mixed rhythms.

Lebanese–Colombian belly-dancing babe, Shakira, sings in Portuguese, English, French, Arabic, and other languages. She stepped out of the women's lounge to take the world stage during the time of the first Gulf War. Since then, her rock *en español* earned her a world-wide following. Or take the breezy and chirpy British Sri-Lankan Maya Arulpragasam (MIA), who is, likewise, multilingual and multicultural and floats her hip hop and improvised slang over a range of musical styles. Her definitive and plodding agit-prop bears the scars of refugee chic. Beyonce, Christina, Alicia Keys, Mariah, Faith, Shania, blah, blah.

A Lite Touch

The saliency of Okinawan ethnicity and its aesthetics is exceptional [...] reggae artists not only turn to archaic expressions of their own language but also employ foreign elements to distance themselves from mainstream Japan: interjection and calls in Jamaican Creole and English seem to provoke excitement from the audience [...] the effect is a sense of unity [of] both performer and audience.

Oiwa 2008: 52

Metroethnicity is a floating world, a light/lite touch. It knows the link between language and ethnicity and the truism that ethnolinguistic identity "is not a unit trait [...] [and that] implementation of our ethnic identity is not invariant but changes from occasion to occasion" (Fishman 1999: 154). Rather, it plays along the borders of the visual and artistic world of "contrastively recognizable identities" (ibid.).

Hard-core ethnicity is essentialist: we are fundamentally different – the difference could be racial, maybe biological, but it certainly is cultural. This is how WE are. Essentialist explanations claim the right to special sympathy and privilege from the mainstream. Get used to it. Essentialist explanations are mischievous and the world is familiar with them: the Northern Ireland bomber, like the Islamic terrorist of today, was an endemic–religious rather than a political phenomenon. For several decades, ethnic essentialist explanations for the downfall of Yugoslavia were *de rigueur*, and critical sociologists have tried to deconstruct them. The essentialist view posited a fundamental incompatibility based on the authoritarianism of nationality, on the emotional instability of any nationality, on ethnic stratification, on ethnic distance among the basic groups.

By contrast, ethnicity can be a toy. Something you play with. Hewitt (2003) has argued powerfully that Creole forms used by white working-class children mediate cultural difference and that such street-cred social adjustment is instrumental in shaping friendship. The adoption of Creole is a cultural synchronization (in this case, between white and black schoolboys). Thus ethnicity can be viewed as a holistic semiotic engagement: looks, talk, things valued.

The playful use of ethnic symbolism is a badge of friendship: singing, joking, formalized abuse, talk about the opposite sex signifies acceptance by black friends as well as desire to be accepted. Hewitt (ibid.) goes further by suggesting that, in jocular use, language is often treated as something external to the natural discourse of both parties, almost as a toy might be used, except that in this case the toy consists of a social relation.

Metroethnicity rejects the logocentric metanarrative of traditional ethnicity. It sidesteps the bruised-n-battered ethnic bollard around which an ethnic group assembles in order to construct an internally validated description of itself. It is no longer the rhetoric of contrast – here is majority society and there is minority society.

Metroethnics are Filipino-Californians who wear 'ethnic' T-shirts bearing the extinct Filipino Baybayin. Allusive play rather than primordial Filipino pride. Such persons are engaging less in an ethnicity than in what Maffesoli refers to as a unicity or shared cultural space. This sociality, or "underground centrality," "bestows, like the Freudian unconscious, strength, vitality, and 'effervescence' to social life" (Evans 1997: 227).

Ethnic *jouissance*: The Case of Japan

> *Metroethnicity is aesthetic resistance not political resistance. It is extremely difficult for elites to control because it is based on interpersonal interaction that plays with the social order and will not take it seriously.*
>
> J. Wasilewski 2008 (personal communication)

Metroethnicities signal a recovery of ethnic *jouissance*. Ethnicity becomes an open and polysemic text. Read it. Do it.

Metroethnicities critique ethnicity through a mode of what Habermas (1983) terms 'self-reflection' or self-criticism of those ideological determinants of the self-formative process (*Bildung*) that instruct how we should behave in the world and indeed inform our very conception of the world. In contrast to sociolinguistic theories that posit a binary relation between social role and fixed language use – as in Ferguson's diglossia involving H and L- language varieties – Tollefson and Tsui comment that "a constructionist perspective toward identity reveals the dynamic creativity inherent in changing contested discourses [and] multiple systems of meaning and representation present individuals with a wide array of changing identities" (2007: 260).

If, under the pressure of globalization, hard-core ethnicity and collectivism are now being exiled, in their place new forms of togetherness have emerged. This is nowhere more marked than in Japan. Power has been modernism's traditional weapon of choice (in politics, in religion, and in the rhetoric of "it's the economy stupid" economics), but in Japan there is stress on the *puissance* of style and on togetherness rather than on collectivity. An aesthetics of style derivative of inner strength. Networks based upon the cultural phenomenon of superflat, as well as on what Maffesoli terms "proxemic reality."

The Japanese younger generation, in particular, views cultural aesthetics as a serious challenge to contemporary political cliché, including standard ethnicity. In its place, metroethnicities permit (inverted commas) 'ethnicity' to be woven into a particular kind of linguistic *jouissance*. They are a form of micropower. They delve into a sensuality of experience rather than political experience, and they embrace an acceptance of the multiplicity of our sources of knowledge. They are the *petit mort* of traditional ethnicities in the sense that metrolanguages are their outcome. Out goes industrial-strength ethnicity. In comes a rethinking. Here forms of speech become a plastic entity, which shapes the personal world and places the self in changing interaction with the world. These forms constitute the metrolinguistic play of popular music. Reggae tells a tale in

> the layers of multiple identities constructed by the particular language use in the Japanese [and Okinawan] reggae scene: global citizen, Japanese, member of a local community, participant in the transnational reggae music scene [...] this cool hybridity of identifying with multiple groups at the same time on many different levels is characteristic of Japan. (Oiwa 2008)

Metroethnicities have a flattening effect. The remixing of speech styles (now you hear it now you don't!) provokes a shift in the perception of speech by which speech boundaries get flattened – figuratively. Cultural theorist Azuma (2001: 24) stresses that "superflat postmodernity" is rigorously hybrid and that "any nostalgic return towards its traditional, original, or 'pure' ethnicity [...] like Japaneseness seems a fake." Rather, "it is *otaku* culture that reflects most clearly this mixed, hybrid, bastardized condition; that is, the paradox that we cannot find any Japaneseness without post-war American pop culture." (quoted in Lamarre 2004). The new ethnicities try to dodge beneath the radar of "the society of control" (Deleuze 2006) and they are capable of relocating itself in various places. Metroethnicities finds perfect expression in Cultural Cool. No bourgeois flim-flam is this. On the contrary, cool is more accessible to ethnic minorities than to the middle class. It has been demonstrably employed in a big way in the wave of engagement/rediscovery (now twenty years on) of Korean pop/media culture. The opposite of bourgeois cultural capital: cool is street, readily accessible, and has been co-opted by hitherto marginalized Japanese minorities: Ainu, Korean, Brazilian immigrants, Okinawan. Brazilian immigrants (the working class who power Toyota factories) hitherto have found themselves cool, interesting, culturally powerful.

Beerkes (2007: 4) merges metroethnicity with Maffesoli's espousal of beauty, fantasy and profusion, pointing to the emergence of new social networks in which shared lifestyle, taste, or situation are the bonding principle.

> I believe that the being-together is a basic given. Before any other determination or qualification, there is this vital spontaneity that guarantees a culture its own puissance and solidity. Later on, this spontaneity can become artificial, that is, civilizing, producing remarkable (political, economic, artistic) works [...] [I]t remains necessary, if only to appreciate better the new orientations [...] to come back to the pure form of the 'undirected being-together.' (Maffesoli 1996a: 81)

Locality, temporality, and transitoriness are characteristics of these neo-tribalisms. Beerkes (ibid.) has invoked the notion of metroethnicity as an interpretive element is analyzing the most recent young Japanese men's street fashion,

> inspired by the almost structural presence in all the outfits: either urban young men 'dressed down' or they used all sorts of ethnic details, varying from Indian shawls to African prints; or they played with their masculinity by wearing female clothing; skirts, shoes, colors; either or not combined with 'tough' masculine elements. Considering these fashion choices of 'hip' urban Japanese men, I [am] curious about the role these style elements (ethnicity, class and gender) play in the formation and experience of their masculine selves.

Conclusion: Teach Yourself Irish

Markers of identity like race and place and speech continue to provide people with a muscular sense of belonging. Without them the world may seem merely like Coetzee's (1980), "waiting for the barbarians," or like the world emerging from Seamus Heaney's introduction to *Beowulf* – a world of people who inhabit an emotional geography with "no very clear map-sense of the world, more an apprehension of menaced borders, of danger gathering beyond the mere and the marshes ..." (Heaney 1999: iii). By contrast, metroethnicities bring a powerfully ironic presence to hitherto fixed loyalties and group affiliations. It is this fixedness that globalization undermines.

The shift from benign neglect to what is culturally cool became possible with the Celtic boom of the late twentieth century. The Breton-language Radio Kerne in Quevan, on the western coast of Britanny, is Celtic and world music, Breton talk. As half a million people gathered for a Celtic music festival in Lorient, Brittany, from Ireland and Portugal, Wales, Scotland, and Cornwall, it reported that, at the same time, the Council of Europe (1999) was legislating to encourage the use of Europe's local languages in school, media, and public life. In France the socialist government responded: "We are okay with that." However, the French Academy concluded that the new enthusiasm for regional languages was a trivial enterprise.

> Teaching regional languages is an enterprise that can destroy the unity of the nation. This will pulverize French. Why sacrifice a glorious language to local dialects? It's not a human rights thing. It's a fashion. (Académie Française, Maurice Druon, 1999; quoted in *International Herald Tribune*, October 30, p. 5).

The Académie Francaise was correct. It's about fashion and style. And yet, despite the monolingualist statements of the Académie and the "French Only" Toubon Law (1994), among Britany's four million people about 10 percent know Breton, but 10,000 are in language classes. The revivalist *Diwan* ('Seed') Movement has developed 34 Breton schools. Language diversity is, at least partly, about lifestyle. It is what Druon calls, dismissively, "fashion." It's not just about rights. Metroethnicities are driven by many kinds of motivations. Identity is about training, something you can sometimes teach yourself. My grandparents spoke Irish. My second-generation mother did not, but she was, culturally, both Irish and Leeds, West Riding. Whilst living in the Far East, I applied for an Irish passport to present it to my mother in her old age. I became interested in the Irish language and Irish culture. I bought *Teach Yourself Irish* and I got quite good. I had not yet visited Ireland when I gained citizenship. An English monolingual, passport-carrying Irish colleague was pained at all my cultural shenanigans: it looked like Irish amateurs night. For me it was curiosity, style, a neat thing to do – a something-more-of-me thing. Cultural consumption. Going metroethnic.

Metroethnicities are driven by cultural consumption and media activity. The increase in the demand for the study of Korean in Asian higher education was driven by Korean wave movies (Hallyu) and Korean-pop music in Asia. The good manners and sincerity of the surgically enhanced Korean (male) actors in *Winter Sonata* and *Jewel in the Palace* (no profanity, and *no* shagging please) catapulted Korean into college curricula across Asia. Likewise, BoA, a Korean female vocalist, blurred the boundaries of Asian pop, becoming Japan's top female pop vocalist to speak and sing variously in Japanese, Korean, and English.

Metroethnicities are 'ethnic' inscription on pendants and T-shirts, multimedia art, jewelry and compact discs printed up in Baybayin – the lost pre-Hispanic script of the Philippines, worn by enthusiastic but ethnically ambiguous (EA) Pinoy-Americans in California who have never been to the Philippines.[1] Metroethnicities are body tattoos and downjackets decorated in Chinese characters and worn by Hungarian martial artists who live and train in Budapest Chinatown. Metroethnicities invoke ethnicity not as a historical property but as a cultural reference.

The overlapping of identities reflects the new cosmopolitanism – a concept eloquently explained by Appiah. Cosmopolitanism has usually been limited to political issues, but is now a key concept in the articulation of civil society, migration, transnational space, and multiculturalism.

Metroethnicities are a form of cultural orthography that addresses the structure and organization of how ethnicity is written. Metroethnicities shove ethnicity between rabbit's ears. What was viewed with unblinking scriptural certainty is now an air-quote 'Scottish' or 'African' or 'Oriental.' From ethnic to 'ethnic.' 'Ethnic' is thus placed in an *Ersatz* world of the ironic; an inversion of traditional ethnicity; a comma of incongruity. And it may be humorous. In the postmodern, sardonic world ethnicity got stuck in a traffic jam and the new metroethnic forms are strutting along the sidewalk in the argot of "Hey, I'm 'ethnic' too but sorry guys I ain't got time to help yer out."

NOTES

1   'Baybayin' was the lost pre-Hispanic Filipino writing system, a member of the Brahmic family, which continued to thrive through the first century of Spanish occupation. It was eulogized by revolutionary Rizal thus: "this language of ours is like any other, it once had an alphabet and its own letters that vanished as though a tempest had set upon a boat on a lake in a time now long gone" (Rizal 2006: 54). It was the quintessential form of indigenous literacy, inscribed on bamboo, bone, and copper and used in correspondence, requests, and chants. It was replaced by the alphabet in the 1500s. Now it is found in California on the T-shirts of Filipinos. Ethnic cool. Baybayin exists on web sites, multimedia art, jewellery, compact discs, T-shirts, and logos.

REFERENCES

Appiah, K. A. (2006) *Cosmopolitanism: Ethics in a World of Strangers*. New York: Norton.

Arlidge, J. (2004) The melting pot. *Observer*, January 4.

Azuma, H. (2001) Superflat Japanese postmodernity. Lecture at the MOCA Gallery at the Pacific Design Center, West Hollywood.

Bakhtin, M. (1968) *Rabelais and his World*, translated by H. Iswolsky. Cambridge, MA: MIT Press.

Balibar, E., and Wallerstein, I. (1994) *Race, Nation, Class: Ambiguous Identities*, translated by C. Turner. London: Verso.

Balibar, E. (2004) *We, the People of Europe? Reflections on Transnational Citizenship*, translated by J. Swenson. Princeton and Oxford: Princeton University Press.

Beerkes, A. (2007) *Men in the Mirror: Japanese Men, Fashion and Lifestyle*. Amsterdam: Instituut voor Maatschappij en Gedragwetenschappen Universiteit van Amsterdam.

Belasco, W. J. (2001) Shopping for identity: The marketing of ethnicity. *American Jewish History* 89(1): 151–3.

Butler, J. (1990) *Gender Trouble: Feminism and the Subversion of Identity*. London: Routledge.

Butler, J., and Spivak, G. (2007) *Who Sings the Nation–State? Language, Politics, Belonging*. Oxford: Seagull Press.

de Pina-Cabral, J., and Lourenco, N. (1994) Personal identity and ambiguity: Naming practices among the Eurasians of Macao. *Social Anthropology* 2(2): 115–32.

Cain, A. (2008) The Manx language. Personal communication.

Cameron, D. (1990) Demythologizing sociolinguistics: Why language does not reflect society. In J. E. Joseph and T. J. Taylor (eds), *Ideologies of Language*, 147–60. London: Routledge.

Condry, I. (2006) *Hip-Hop Japan: Rap and the Paths of Cultural Globalization*. Durham: Duke University Press.

Coetzee, J. M. (1980) *Waiting for the Barbarians*. London: Penguin.

Coonceil ny Gaelgey (2008). *The Manx Have a Word for It*. Isle of Man: Manx Language Advisory Council.

Coulmas, F. (2006) *Sociolinguistics: The Study of Speakers' Choices*. Cambridge: Cambridge University Press.

Coupland, N. (2007) *Style*. Cambridge: Cambridge University Press.

Deleuze, G. (2006) *Two Regimes of Madness: Texts and Interviews 1975–1995*. London: Verso.

Featherstone, M. (1990) *Global Culture, Nationalism, Globalization and Modernity*. London: Sage.

Fishman, J. (1999) *Handbook of Language and Ethnic Identity*. Oxford: Oxford University Press.

Friedman, T. L. (2005) *The World Is Flat: A Brief History of the Twenty-First Century*. New York: Farrar, Straus and Giroux.

Edwards, J. (1985) *Language, Society and Identity*. Oxford: Basil Blackwell.

Evans, D. (1997) Michel Maffesoli's sociology of modernity and postmodernity: An introduction and critical assessment. *The Sociological Review* 42(2): 220–43.

Ferguson, C. (1997) A history of sociolinguistics. In C. B. Paulston and R.

Tucker (eds), *The Early Days of Sociolinguistics: Memories and Reflections*, 77–86. Dallas: Summer Institute of Linguistics.

Featherstone, M. (2007) *Consumer Culture and Postmodernism*. London: Sage.

Fishman, J. (ed.) (2001) Introduction. *Handbook of Language and Ethnicity*, 3–8. Oxford: Oxford University Press.

Giddens, A. (1991) *Modernity and Self-Identity. Self and Society in the Late Modern Age*. Cambridge: Polity.

Gumperz, J. (1962) Language problems in the rural development of Northern India. In F. Rice (ed.), *Study of the Role of Second Languages in Asia, Africa and Latin America*, 8–14. Washington, DC: Center for Applied Linguistics.

Habermas, J. (1983). *Theory of Communication and Society*. Cambridge: Polity.

Hall, R. (1966) *Pidgin and Creole Languages*. Philadelphia: Chilton.

Hall, S. (1991) Old and new identities, old and new ethnicities. In A. King (ed), *Culture, Globalization and the World System*, 41–68. London: Macmillan.

Hall, S. (1997) *Representation: Cultural Representations and Signifying Practices*. London: Sage.

Hall, S., and du Gay, P. (eds) (1996) *Questions of Cultural Identity*. London: Sage.

Halliday, M. A. K., and Hasan, R. (1987) *Language, Context and Text: Aspects of Language in a Social–Semiotic Perspective*. Oxford: Oxford University Press.

Heaney, S. (1999) *Beowulf: A New Verse Translation*, translated by S. Heaney. London: Faber and Faber. [See especially Introduction, pp. 1–7.]

Hewitt, R. (2003) Language, youth and the destabilisation of ethnicity [1992]. In R. Harris and B. Rampton (eds), *The Language, Ethnicity and Race Reader*, 188–98. London: Routledge.

Hobsbawm, E. (1990). *Nations and Nationalism since 1780*. Cambridge: Cambridge University Press.

Hooks, B. (1999) *Yearning: Race, Gender and Cultural Politics*. Ithaca: Cornell University Press.

Hutchinson, J., and Smith, A. D. (eds) (1996) *Ethnicity*. Oxford: Oxford University Press.

Isle of Man Government (2006) *Branding the Isle of Man: Culture and Heritage Survey amongst Residents*. Isle of Man: Isle of Man Government.

Jacobson, R. (1960) Linguistics and poetics, translated by T. A. Sebeok. In T. A. Sebeok (ed.), *Style in Language*, 46–67. Cambridge, MA: MIT Press.

Jesperson, O. (1922) *Language: Its Nature, Development, and Origin*. London: Allen and Unwin.

Kinsella, S. (2000) An interview with Oe Kenzaburo. *Japan Forum* 12(2): 233–41.

Lin, A. M. Y., and Luk, J. C. M. (2005) Local creativity in the face of global domination: Insights of Bakhtin for teaching English for dialogic communication. In J. K. Hall, G. Vitanova, and L. Marchenkova (eds), *Dialogue with Bakhtin on Second and Foreign Language Learning: New Perspectives*, 77–98. Mahwah, NJ: Lawrence Erlbaum.

Labov, W. (1964) Phonological correlates of social stratification. *American Anthropologist* 64: 164–76.

Lamarre, T. (2004) Introduction to Otaku movement. *Entertext* 4(1): 151–87.

Lamarre, T., and Nae-hui, K. (eds) (2004) *Impacts of Modernities*. Hong Kong: Hong Kong University Press.

Maffesoli, M. (1996a) *The Time of the Tribes. The Decline of Individualism in Mass Society [1988]*. London: Sage.

Maffesoli, M. (1996b) *The Contemplation of the World. Figures of Community Style [1993]*. Minnesota: University of Minnesota Press.

Maher, J. C. (2005) Metroethnicity, language, and the principle of cool. *International Journal of Sociology of Language* 175/176: 83–102.

Maher, J., and Macdonald, G. (1995) *Diversity in Japanese Culture and Language*. London: Kegan Paul International.

Melucci, A. (1996). *Challenging Codes: Collective Action in the Information Age*. Cambridge: Cambridge University Press.

Miller, L. (2006) *Beauty Up. Exploring Contemporary Japanese Body Aesthetics*. Berkely, LA, and London: University of California Press.

Oishi, N. (2005) *Women in Motion: Globalization, State Policies, and Labor Migration in Asia*, Stanford: Stanford University Press.

Machin, D., and van Leeuwen, T. (2005) Language style and lifestyle: The case of a global magazine. *Media, Culture and Society* 27(4): 577–600.

Oiwa, M. (2008) *Ethnicity Liberated: language Use and Restructuring of Group Identity in the Japanese Reggae Scene*. BA Thesis, International Christian University, Tokyo.

Otsuji, E. (2008) *Performing Transculturation: Between/within 'Japanese' and 'Australian' Language, Identities and Culture*. PhD thesis, University of Technology, Sydney.

Pennycook, A. (2003) Global Englishes, Rip Slyme, and performativity. *Journal of Sociolinguistics* 7(4): 513–33.

Pennycook, A. (2004) Performativity and language studies. *Critical Inquiry in Language Studies* 1(1): 1–26.

Pennycook, A. (2007) *Global Englishes and Transcultural Flows*. London: Routledge.

Pride, J. (1976) Sociolinguistics. In J. Lyons (ed.), *New Horizons in Linguistics*, 62–7. Harmondsworth: Penguin.

Rampton, B. (2005) *Crossing: Language and Ethnicity Among Adolescents*, 2nd edn. Manchester: St Jerome Press.

Rizal, J. (2006) *Noli Me Tangere (Touch me Not)* Harmondsworth: Penguin.

Soyinka, W. (1976) *Myth, Literature and the African World*. Cambridge: Cambridge University Press.

Tabouret-Keller, A. (1999) Bilingualism in Europe. In T. Bhatia and W. C. Ritchie (eds), *The handbook of bilingualism*, 24–52. Oxford: Blackwell.

Todorov, T. (2008) Civilized talk contends with politics, culture. *Japan Times*, Sunday June 1, p. 7.

Tollefson, J., and Tsui, A. (eds) (2007) *Language Policy, Culture, and Identity in Asian Contexts*. Mahwah, NJ: Lawrence Erlbaum.

Warnke, G. (2008) *After Identity: Rethinking Race, Sex and Gender*. Cambridge: Cambridge University Press.

Willis, D. B., and Murphy-Shigematsu, S. (2008) *Transcultural Japan: At the Borderlands of Race, Gender, and Identity*. London: Routledge.

Wolff, H. (1959) Intelligibility and inter-ethnic attitudes. *Anthropological Linguistics* 1: 34–41.

Yamanashi, M. (2008) *Personal Correspondence*. Tokyo: Asian Cultural Studies in Japan, Rikkyo University.

27 Popular Cultures, Popular Languages, and Global Identities

ALASTAIR PENNYCOOK

Popular culture is both facilitated by and facilitative of the shifting relationships between languages under conditions of globalization. The ease of cultural movement made possible by the transnational role of major languages such as English, French, Chinese, or Arabic, in conjunction with new digital media, allows popular culture to traverse the globe with speed and gregarity. At the same time, the attractions of popular culture draw people to those languages in order to gain better access to such films, music, or online environments. While studies of language and globalization often take economic or various utilitarian goals as primary driving forces behind the spread and take-up of different languages, it is also important to understand the roles of pleasure and desire, and the possibilities that popular culture may hold out for new cultural and linguistic relations and for new possible modes of identity.

We should of course be wary of mapping a simple relation between language and identity here – a relation whereby a particular language use implies a particular identification (using a particular language, say, German, implies a particular cultural attachment). The focus of this chapter, by contrast, is on the new possibilities opened up by new language uses in popular culture. That is to say, a study of popular cultures (cultural forms that have wide public appeal), popular languages (languages and styles that emerge in popular usage), and global identities (transcultural identifications made possible by global popular cultures and languages) allows for the study of how the take-up of different languages made possible by popular culture has significant implications for new forms of identification: not just new possible alignments along old linguistic lines, but rather new possibilities of local/global affiliation, which have not been imagined before. In contrast with the position which postulates fixity in some identifications between language and culture – on the assumption that language and culture are not only intertwined, but bound together in a knot-like grip – the position I shall argue in this chapter is one where new identifications made possible through popular cultures are never stable or permanent, but are always in flux.

The Handbook of Language and Globalization, First Edition. Edited by Nikolas Coupland.
© 2013 Blackwell Publishing Ltd except for editorial material and organization © 2013 Nikolas Coupland.
Published 2013 by Blackwell Publishing Ltd.

In this chapter I shall chart some of these processes, with a particular focus on hip hop, as one major contemporary form of popular culture. Several particular themes are important here: Although certain hubs of cultural production remain highly influential – the metropolitan centers of France and the USA, for example – the flows of popular culture are not simply from center to periphery, but rather operate in more dynamic circuits of influence. While the flow back into the centers may be limited, the directions and take-up of cultural production are many and diverse. Furthermore, once cultural formations such as hip hop become localized, the movement into local languages, and particularly the mixing of local and metropolitan languages, brings about new relations among languages and cultures. In addition, engagement with popular culture in diverse contexts is by no means a process of passive consumption; rather it is about the active construction of different possible worlds and identities.

Globalization and Cultural Flows

Given the widespread discussion of globalization elsewhere in this volume, there is no need to go over similar ground again. In brief, the position I shall be taking is this: We need to understand how languages operate in an uneven world (see Radhakrishnan 2003), how languages relate to the deep global inequalities of poverty, health, and education. Rather than viewing globalization as synonymous with economic disparity, however, it is more useful to explore the complexities of global flows of culture and knowledge. Unlike the argument of those who insist that globalization implies *"the homogenization of world culture* [...] spearheaded by films, pop culture, CNN and fast-food chains" (Phillipson and Skutnabb-Kangas 1996: 439; emphasis in the original), the argument in this chapter is that we need to deal with globalization beyond this dystopic, neo-Marxist critique, which is based only on political economy (Jacquemet 2005), and to deal with 'pop culture' in terms that go beyond the gloomy Frankfurt School image of the duping of the global masses (Jameson 1998). To suggest that globalization is only a process of US or western domination of the world is to take a narrow and ultimately unproductive view of global relations. Likewise, to view culture and language in terms only of reflections of the economic is to miss the point that new technologies and communications are enabling immense and complex flows of people, signs, sounds, images across multiple borders in multiple directions. If we accept a view of popular culture as a crucial site of identity and desire, it is hard to see how we can proceed with any study of language and globalization without dealing comprehensively with popular culture. The "real question before us," Scott suggests, "is whether or not we take the vernacular voices of the popular and their modes of self-fashioning seriously, and if we do, how we think through their implications" (1999: 215).

It is indisputable that flows of popular culture are dominated at one level by a weight and directionality that are part of the unevenness of global relations. Thus Pennay (2001: 128) comments in his discussion of rap in Germany: "Regrettably, the flow of new ideas and stylistic innovations in popular music is nearly always from the English-speaking market, and not to it." Similarly, in her discussion of the Basque rap group Negu Gorriak (which features the Mugurza brothers), Jacqueline Urla points out that "unequal relations between the United States record industry and Basque radical music mean that Public Enemy's message reaches the Mugurza brothers in Irun, and not vice versa" (2001: 189). Perry meanwhile critiques what she calls the "romantic Afro-Atlanticism" (2004: 17) of Gilroy's (1993) notion of the "Black Atlantic," with its view of multiple influences across communities of African origin around the Atlantic. "Black Americans as a community," she insists, "do not consume imported music from other cultures in large numbers," and thus ultimately the "postcolonial Afro-Atlantic hip hop community is […] a fantastic aspiration rather than a reality" (Perry 2004: 19).

While it may be the case that there is little take-up of imported music in US communities, there is also a strong case to be made that the circles of flow are far more complex than a one-way spread to the world – and for several reasons. Mitchell argues that, as hip hop has spread, it has become a vehicle through which local identity is reworked, and that indeed, "for a sense of innovation, surprise, and musical substance in hip-hop culture and rap music, it is becoming increasingly necessary to look outside the USA to countries such as France, England, Germany, Italy, and Japan, where strong local currents of hip-hop indigenization have taken place" (Mitchell 2001a: 3). According to Androutsopoulos, since "hip-hop is a globally dispersed network of everyday cultural practices which are productively appropriated in very different local contexts, it can be seen as paradigmatic of the dialectic of cultural globalization and localization" (Androutsopoulos 2003: 11; my translation). It is also important to note the history and current conditions of different regions of hip hop influence: While The US may be less influenced by external changes in global hip hop, countries such as France, with a very different post-colonial history, are far more influenced by the diverse francophone world which inhabits their urban environments.

Elsewhere in the world there are diverse linguistic/cultural circuits of flow. In the relations between Samoan, Hawaiian, Maori, and other Pacific Islander communities we can see, for example, a "pan-Pacific hip-hop network that has bypassed the borders and restrictions of the popular music distribution industry" (Mitchell 2001a: 31). These circles of hip hop flow are at times overlapping: Hawaii, for example, where Sudden Rush has developed "ne mele paleoleo, Hawaiian hip hop, a cut n' mix of African and Jamaican reggae rhythms, Hawaiian chanting, and subversive rapping in the English and Hawaiian languages" (Akindes 2001: 91), links the Pacific to the US, while French-influenced parts of the Pacific such as French Polynesia (Tahiti) and New Caledonia link the Pacific to the French circuit. Indeed there is now "scarcely a country in the world that does not feature some form of mutation of rap music, from the venerable and sophisticated hip-hop and rap scenes of France, to the 'swa-rap' of Tanzania and Surinamese rap of Holland" (Krims 2000: 5).

The French-language hip hop scene has been one of the most significant for twenty years – a complex interlocked circle of flow that links the vibrant music scenes in Paris and Marseille in France, Dakar, Abidjan, and Libreville in West Africa, and Montreal in Quebec. Hip hop in France developed in the *banlieues* – the suburban housing projects where many poor live, together with first and second-generation immigrant populations. Here, in multi-ethnic mixes of people of Maghreb (Algeria, Tunisia, Morocco), French African (Mali, Senegal, Gabon), French Antilles (La Martinique, Guadeloupe) and other European (Portugal, Romania, Italy) backgrounds, hip hop emerged as a potent force of new French expression. Rap, in France, "uses a streetspeak version of French that includes African, Arab, gypsy and American roots and is viewed with disapproval by traditionalists for its disregard for traditional rules of grammar and liberal use of neologisms" (Huq 2001: 74). While Paris became a center for many movements and crossings of French-language musicians, dancers and artists, the southern city–port of Marseille looked more resolutely southwards. Typical of the movement was the popular Marseille group IAM, which developed an ideology that Prévos (2001) calls "pharaoism" (p. 48); in this way it links to the Arabic background of many French immigrants and, as Swedenburg (2001) argues, it gives "Egyptianist Afrocentricity a Mediterranean inflection, asserting a kind of 'black Mediterranean'" (p. 69).

The rap scene in France, as Huq describes it, "stands out as the ideal soundtrack to accompany the post-industrial, post-colonial times ushered in by the new millennium, in which the new tricolore (the French national flag) is black, blanc, beur" (Huq 2001: 81).[1] While the many flows of immigrant influence into France have thus greatly affected French hip hop, the "diasporic flows" (Prévos 2001: 53) of hip hop back into the wider francophone circle of flow have in turn changed the music and linguascapes of other regions of the world. In Libreville, Gabon, rappers mix English, French, and local languages such as Fang and Téké. As Auzanneau explains further, English is never used on its own, but always in conjunction with French, while vernacular languages may be used on their own, with each other, or with French, but never with English. The use of vernacular languages signals a clear identitification with the Gabonese community, while at the same time it keeps a distance from France, which "is perceived as economically exploitative, culturally assimilating, and a former colonizer" (Auzanneau 2002: 114). By putting "Gabonese culture on a public and perhaps even international stage," Gabonese rap is also bringing about a revalorization of vernacular languages: "Formerly associated with out-of-date and archaic values (and thus with 'backwardness'), these languages are now becoming languages of 'authenticity' and 'roots' and thus claim for themselves an identiary role both in rap and in the city" (ibid.).

The French that is used in Gabon is subject to both endonormative and exonormative pulls, the former "departures from standard French" serving as "factors of social differentiation and thus identification" (ibid., p. 108). Libreville's "relexified French" uses "borrowings from Gabonese languages, languages of migration, and English (standard and non-standard, but especially slang)" as well as non-standard French lexicon, including various created forms, neologisms, and *verlan*. Not only is *verlan* a form of French slang that reverses standard French (hence the term *beur*, used to refer to people of Arabic descent, is derived from *Arabe*; and the term *verlan* itself derives from the French *l'envers*, which means 'the other way round'); but also, as Doran explains, it is "a kind of linguistic *bricolage*" formed from the multilingual and mutlicultural mixes of immigrants from North Africa, West Africa, Asia, and the Caribbean (Doran 2004: 94). When such codes are imported (or to some extent reimported) to the Libreville rap scene, there is a vast array of language and cultural influences at work. The choices they make between languages is crucial: "the place given to English or to French *verlan* can diminish in favor of terms taken from Libreville French or local languages when the song-writer wishes to negotiate his or her Gabonese identity through the interactions being represented in the song" (Auzanneau 2002: 117). By using re-lexified French, "speakers mark their attachment to Gabonese culture at the same time as they make their break with the values of both their own traditional society and the dominant Western society. This variety is the emblem of the rappers' culture and of their mixed [*métissée*] identity as young urbanites" (p. 118).

Another key point on this global circuit is Montreal, where the languages of popular culture reflect the city's location in North America (which renders African American English both easily available and rejectable), the locality within Quebec (which makes Quebec French a badge of difference from other parts of the French circuit), and the immigrant populations with their various connections to French. While immigrants from Mali, Senegal, and Gabon may find a space for their French, Africans from non-francophone nations – as Ibrahim (1999, 2008) points out in the Franco-Ontarian context – may often identify with black English, as their African identities are stripped away in favor of an identification as *black*. The large Haitian population, meanwhile, forge a new relationship between Haitian Creole and the other languages of Montreal. Sarkar and Allen (2007: 122) cite a Montreal rapper's view (interview with Impossible, April 6, 2004) that "[l]e style montréalais, moi, j'l'aurais défini comme, c'est la seule place où t'as un mélange culturel comme ça, que t'as un mélange des langues comme ça, que ça soit l'anglais, créole, pis le français, mais un français quand même québécois" ["I'd define the Montreal style as, it's the only place where you have a cultural mix like that, where you have a mixture of languages like that, whether it's English, [Haitian] Creole, then French, but all the same a Quebec French"]. While this mix of Quebec French, English, and Creole is unique in certain ways, it does not seem to be the case, however, that Montreal is so distinctive in supporting such levels of diversity.

While at one level this comment on the mixing of language may be taken as a reflection of the code-mixing on Montreal streets – according to J. Kyll of Muzion, *"en général, on chante, on rap comme on parle"* ["in general, we sing, we rap the way we speak"] (Sarkar and Allen 2007: 122) – at another level we also need to see such language use as productive as well as reflective of language realities. As Rampton (1995, 1999, 2006) has observed of urban contexts in the UK, such language use often involves 'crossing,' or the use of languages in which the rappers are not fluent. As another of Sarkar and Allen's participants explained, although he was not himself Haitian, he was often identified as such and felt free to speak and use Creole. As Sarkar and Allen also observe, rappers claim that, rather than such language mixes alienating listeners, they enable them to relate to diversity in new ways. Thus a line like "*Où est-ce que les patnais vont chiller ce soir?*" ["Where is the gang going to chill [hang out] tonight?"], which contains the Haitian Creole term *patnai* for 'good friend,' might now be heard from young Montrealers of many backgrounds. According to Sarkar (2009: 147), this new generation of urban Quebecers has integrated words from both Haitian (*popo* 'police,' *kob* 'cash,' *ti-moun* 'kid,' *kget* 'swearword') and Jamaican Creole (*ganja* 'marijuana,' *spliff* 'joint,' *skettel* 'girl, loose woman,' *rude bwoy* 'aggressive youth') into its everyday language and rap, whatever the ethnic background of its members.

Given these mixes, labels such as 'francophone' need to be applied with caution to such circles of flow. While at one level these music scenes are connected through their post-colonial use of French, this French is also widely divergent, and, as with English, cannot be easily assumed to be one entity. Edouard Glissant argues that

> there are several French languages today, and languages allow us to conceive of their unicity according to a new mode, in which French can no longer be monolingual. If language is given in advance, if it claims to have a mission, it misses out on the adventure and does not catch on in the world. (Glissant 1997: 119)

The languages and cultures that circulate within these flows are constantly mixed with other languages and cultures, so that new mixtures arrive in new places and remix once again as they become relocalized. Rappers in Libreville, Gabon, are thus "inserted into large networks of communication that confer on them a plurality of identities," using a wide "diversity of languages with their variants, along with their functioning as markers of identity (of being Gabonese, African, or an urbanite)" (Auzanneau 2002: 120).

360 Degrees: Other Circles, Other Flows

There are many such circles of flow, including the Spanish one, which connects the hip hop scenes in Cuba, Spain, Mexico, and South America (and which, due to the large Hispanic communities in the US, does have some effect on that market) (Cepeda 2003; Fernandes 2003; Pacini and Garofalo 2004), the Lusophone, the Chinese (Ho 2003; Lin 2009) and so on. These different circles also intersect in many places – above all, in Africa, where, as N'Dongo D from Senegalese group Daara J explains, "In Africa you will find Portuguese, Spanish, French, English all mixed together in the culture in the same continent" (Interview March 5, 2005; my translation).[2] For Daara J, furthermore, hip hop is an African art form that has returned home: "Born in Africa, brought up in America, hip hop has come full circle" (*Boomerang*). According to Faada Freddy, "this music is ours! It is a part of our culture!" Somali-Candian artist K'Naan similarly argues that, while West Africa has its *griots* and Somalia has a long tradition of oral language use, in "any given country in Africa, you will find an ancient form of hip hop. It's just natural for someone from Africa to recite something over a drum and to recite it in a talking blues fashion, and then it becomes this thing called hip hop" (K'Naan, Interview April 25, 2006).

Elsewhere in Africa we find similar patterns of localization. Higgins' (2009: 96) analysis of Tanzanian hip hop culture, for example, suggests that there is far more going on than a unidirectional influence from center to periphery: Rather there is a "two-way cultural flow," as "Tanzanian youths perform a range of identities" drawing on different local and global resources. As she points out, for example, the development of new "street Swahili" terms such as *"bomba"* ('awesome'; originally from Portuguese *bomba,* 'pump'), are likely affected by the African American term, common in hip hop circles, *da bomb* (the best). Similarly, in the Nigerian context, Omoniyi (2009) discusses the various discursive strategies that Nigerian hip hop artists use to construct local identities within the global hip hop movement. Code-switching, which, Omoniyi argues, needs to include not just language but modes of dressing, walking, and other patterns of social behavior, in particular marks forms of local Nigerian identity, with artists using Yoruba, English, and Pidgin with Igbo borrowings (Weird MC), English, Pidgin, and Yoruba (D'Banj), or Pidgin and Igbo (2-Shotz). In Weird MC's "Ijoya" [Yoruba: time to dance], for example, we find: "We own the dance/ Awa la ni ijo [Yoruba: we own the dance]/ *Ah trust us, we OWN dis dance*/ Awa la ni ijo/ Na we getam [Pidgin: We own it]/ Awa la ni *gini* [Yoruba/Igbo: We own *what*?]/ Awa la ni ijo" (Omoniyi 2009: 130).

Linguistic and cultural flows can also intersect with domains such as religion. Looking at rap produced by British and French musicians of Islamic background, for example, Swedenburg (2001) argues for "the importance of paying close attention to popular cultural manifestations of 'Islam' in Europe" (p. 76). British band Fun-Da-Mental's engagement with Islam is "central to its multipronged intervention: Islam instils religioethnic pride among Asian youth, serves as an image of antiracist mobilization, creates links between Asians and Afro-Caribbeans, and shocks and educates white leftists and alternative youth" (p. 62). Similarly, Swedenburg argues that French group IAM's Islamic engagement is part of their "effort to widen the space of tolerance for Arabo-Islamic culture in France, through its lyrical subject matter, its deployment of Arabic words and expressions, and its musical mixes, splattered with Middle Eastern rhythms and samples of Arabic songs" (p. 71).

In a rather different context, Malay rappers Too Phat saw both a spiritual and commercial opportunity in developing rap with lyrics from the Koran in Arabic. 'Alhamdulillah' (*360°*), as Pietro Felix explains, was originally conceived as "an R&B 'thankyou, praise Allah' kind of thing," which, they felt, "sounded very Arabic, it sounded very Malay, more prayer, religious kind of sound," so they got Yasin, an Arabic singer, to do the lyrics. The song is largely a critique of materialist values, with thanks to Allah for the gifts they have received – "I thank Allah for blessing me to be creative/ So here's a diss for me for bein' unappreciative/ Wanted a perfect life, yeah smile then die old/ Fame, money, women, phat cribos and white gold" – and a warning against not saying "alhamdulillah." As Felix Pietro goes on, "suddenly we thought 'this is great marketing.' A lot of Malay kids will love this, plus we can check this out to [...] all the way East kind of thing" (Interview December 12, 2003). This plan to gain sales in Middle Eastern countries such as Saudi Arabia, however, was not so successful: "they didn't want to play it because it seems their censorship board does not allow songs that have anything to do with praise Allah." Meanwhile, with less strict rules about what can and cannot be done in popular music, the song "gets great airplay" in Malaysia. "People were blown away with the song. They never thought a rap song would have Koran lyrics, Arabic lyrics" (ibid.). From rappers of Turkish background in Germany, such as Islamic Force (see Kaya 2001) to Malaysian Too Phat, from French bands such as IAM to the verbal intifada of Palestinian rappers (Sling shot hip hop 2006), it is possible to talk in terms of what Alim (2006) has called a "transglobal hiphop ummah."

Lin (2009) suggests that the language of hip hop also makes possible connections along class lines. MC Yan from Hong Kong uses predominantly colloquial Cantonese (rather than common mixed Cantonese/English code), especially the vulgar and largely taboo *chou-hau*. By defying the linguistic taboos of mainstream middle-class society, Lin suggests, MC Yan communicates his political message of linking Hong Kong slang and working class defiance with a broader, trans-locally defiant underclass – through hip hop. Meanwhile MC Yan becomes part of other circuits of flow: Hong Kong DJ Tommy's compilation "Respect for Da Chopstick Hip Hop" – the title itself is a play on global (Respect/Da) and local (Chopstick Hip Hop) elements – features MC Yan, K-One, MC Ill and Jaguar from Japan, and Meta and Joosuc from Korea, with tracks sung in English, Cantonese, Japanese, and Korean. Such collaborations are common. Too Phat's *360°*, for example, contains a track "6 MC's," featuring Promoe of Loop Troop (Sweden), Vandal of SMC (Canada), Freestyle (Brooklyn, New York), and Weapon X from Melbourne, Australia: "From sea to sea, country to country/ 6 MC's bring the delicacies/ It's a meeting of the minds to ease the turmoil/ 360 degrees around the earth's soil." Weapon X turns up again on Korean MC Joosuc's track Universal Language (Joosuc also featured on Respect for Da Chopstick), in which Weapon X uses English and Joosuc Korean (with some English). As DJ Jun explains, this track "is about different languages but we are in the same culture which is hip hop. So language difference doesn't really matter. So hip hop is one language. That is why it is called universal language" (Interview November 2, 2003). From this perspective, then, hip hop as a culture rises above different languages: The universal language is not English; it is hip hop.

Languages Remixed

One thing that also clearly emerges from these accounts of circles of flow is the constant mixing, borrowing, shifting, and sampling of music, languages, lyrics, and ideas. This process can include borrowings and imitations of African American English, as in Japanese group Rip Slyme's use of "Yo Bringing that, Yo Bring your style" (see Pennycook 2003, 2007), or Malaysian Too Phat's "Hip hop be connectin'

Kuala Lumpur with LB/ Hip hop be rockin' up towns laced wit' LV/ Ain't necessary to roll in ice rimmed M3's and be blingin'/ Hip hop be bringin' together
emcees." It is already worth observing, however, that, while Too Phat here use
African American-styled lyrics ("be connectin'" and so forth) and lace their lyrics
with references to consumerist cultural products (LV/M3s), they are at the same
time distancing themselves from this world through their insistence that hip hop
is about connecting MCs across time and space rather than about the accoutre-
ments of bling culture. Meanwhile more complex mixes of English with local
languages can be found in Rip Slyme's lyrics, when they describe themselves as
"錦糸町出 Freaky ダブルの Japanese": Freaky mixed Japanese from Kinshichoo, or
Korean singer Tasha's codemixed lyrics: "Yo if I fall two times I come back on my
third 절대로포기않지 [I never give up] and that's my word." What Tasha achieves
here is not just to move between languages, creating a set of new meanings by
doing so, but also to move in and out of different flows. By artfully integrating
the flows of English and Korean rap styles in a bilingual performance, she presents
English and Korean in new relationships.

"Now lisnen up por pabor makinig 2004 rap sa Pinas yumayanig lalong lumalakas never madadaig," rap GHOST 13 (Guys Have Own Style to Talk – 1 group,
3 rappers) from Zamboanga in western Mindanao in the Philippines. GHOST
13 use what they call "halo-halong lenguaje" ('mixed language'), which may
include Tagalog, Cebuano, Chavacano, and Tausug – as well as English. In these
lines, for example, they mix English (Now lisnen up/never), Chavacano (por
pabor) and Tagalog (rap sa Pinas yumayanig lalong lumalakas […] madadaig):
Please listen to 2004 Philippines rap getting stronger and never beaten. And they
are insistent that, in global hip hop style, they 'represent' Zamboanga, but at the
same time are not imitative: "Listen everyone we are the only one rap group in
the land who represent zamboanga man!/ Guyz have own style, style to talk a
while di kami mga wanna [we are not imitators] because we have own
identity."

Zamboanga, known as the City of Flowers, is home to Zamboangueño, one of
several Spanish-based Creole languages in the Philippines, usually grouped
together under the general term Chavacano (from the Spanish *chabacano*, 'vulgar'):
"Chavacano de Zamboanga siento porsiento […] kami magdidilig sa city of
flower" – in Chavacano, Tagalog and English: "One hundred per cent Chavacano
from Zamboanga […] we water the city of flowers." As can be seen from these
examples, Zamboangueño, the most widely spoken Creole in the region, has
predominantly Spanish vocabulary, with Cebuano as the substrate language.
And, like all Creoles, it never exists on its own, it is always in relation with
other languages. GHOST 13 also clearly take great pride in their version of
Chavacano, which, like many Creole languages, is often derided (with terms
such as 'Filo-Spanish'). For them it is a central means in the expression of a
Zamboangan hip hop identity, to be held up to display, paraded as a language to
be respected. To announce this identity, to place it centrally in their rap lyrics, is
a significant act of language politics. Not only are GHOST 13 on stage, but so is
Chavacano.

The use of Creoles in rap can be a sign of street credibility, of local authenticity. Since Creole languages are often viewed as non-standard, local languages, their very use also provides an avenue for an oppositional stance in term of language politics. While much is made of rap lyrics as the central means by which we can interpret the cultural and political stance of hip hop artists, it is equally important to look sociolinguistically at the linguistic varieties and mixes artists use. Most Creole languages are tied to slavery, colonialism, migration, and the African diaspora. From Jamaican *patwa* in the UK to Haitian Creole in Montreal, or to Cabo Verde (Cape Verde) rappers such as The Real Vibe and Black Side in Holland, and, arguably, from African American English to Aboriginal Australian English, to use Creole is to invoke a certain cultural politics, to take up a space within this historical and contemporary circle of flow. As with the hip hop crews in Libreville, whose mixing and use of languages was clearly overt, so the use of Creole and other languages by groups such as GHOST 13 is part of an explicit challenge to forms of identity. It is a reclamation of the non-institutionalized language world that has often been hidden beneath the patina of nationalist language policy, a world where language mixing and immanent variety are the historical and geographical norm.

Such a view ties in with the position on *créolité* argued by Glissant (1997) and Chamoiseau and Confiant (1999), who suggest that Creoles are not only a crucial form of expression for local, Caribbean and other populations, but also a model for understanding language diversity in the world, since they take *métissage*, mixing, and multiple origins of language as the norm, rather than focusing on diversity in terms of the countability of formalized language systems. Using the term 'Creole' more loosely, Kaya argues that Turkish rappers in Berlin

> have a peculiar language of their own. They speak a creole language. It is a mix of Turkish, German and American English. This new form of city speech in the migrants' suburbs is a verbal celebration of ghetto multiculturalism, twisting German, Turkish and American slang in resistance to the official language. (Kaya 2001: 147)

Creole linguists may object here and point out that this is not a 'true Creole,' but if we follow Mufwene's lead "to identify primarily those varieties that have been identified as 'creole' or 'patois' by nonlinguists" (2001: 10), we may be able to take seriously the notion that the transgressive language use of rap – mixing and borrowing, using language from wherever, deliberately changing the possibilities of language use and language combinations – may be seen as Creolizing practices.

In other words, the hip hop practices of *créolité* may be a force in the production of linguistic diversity, both in terms of diversity within languages and in terms of creation of new languages. While Chavacano in the Philippines or the Creoles of the Caribbean may be older and different in a number of ways, to reject the Turkish–German–English Creole of Berlin hip hop would be to overlook the ways in which languages are created. If, as many people rightly are, we are concerned about the decline of languages in the world (Skutnabb-Kangas 2000), we might then see hip hop not, as conservative critics would suggest, as an engine of linguistic degeneration, but rather as a potential driver toward diversity, both in terms of what Halliday has termed *semiodiversity* – the diversity of meaning within languages (Halliday 2002; and see Pennycook 2007) – and in terms of *glossodiversity* – the diversity of languages themselves. And if, as Mufwene (2001) argues, there is no reason to discount Creoles from the purview of world Englishes, then a nascent Turkish-based Creole, with German and English re-lexification, might just have to be considered as one of those 'Other' Englishes, as one of the many global Englishes.

Challenging Language Realities

The mixed codes of the street, and the hypermixes of hip hop, pose a threat to the linguistic, cultural, and political stability urged by national language policies and wished into place by frameworks of linguistic analysis that posit separate and enumerable languages (Makoni and Pennycook 2007). We need not only to understand contact linguistics, but to "examine communicative practices based on disorderly recombinations and language mixings occurring simultaneously in local and distant environments. In other words, it is time to conceptualize a linguistics of xenoglossic becoming, transidiomatic mixing, and communicative recombinations" (Jacquemet 2005: 274). Hip hop language use can therefore be read as resistant or oppositional not merely in terms of the lyrics, but also in terms of the language choice. Keeping it linguistically real (adopting the code of local authenticity) is often a threat to those who would prefer to keep it linguistically pure. For many communities, using a variety of languages and mixing languages together is the norm. The notion that people use separate and discrete languages is a very strange language ideology, which has arisen at a particular cultural and historical moment. Furthermore, to the extent that many hip hoppers come from marginalized communities, where the straightjackets of linguistic normativity have had less effect, their mixed-code language will probably reflect local language use. It would be strange for someone from Zamboanga not to use at least Chavacano, Tagalog, Cebuano, Tausug, and English in different daily interactions. This is not only a question, however, of reflecting local language use.

Choices in language use are deeply embedded in local conditions, from the economy and the local music industry infrastructure (limited recording facilities militate against local practices and languages) to language policies, language ideologies, aesthetics, and other social and cultural concerns, both local and regional. According to Berger (2003),

> while language choice in music may reflect prevailing language ideologies, that influence is often a two-way street; that is, rather than merely reproducing existing ideologies, singers, culture workers, and listeners may use music to actively think about, debate, or resist the ideologies at play in the social world around them. (xiv–xv)

Language choice and use, particularly in domains of public performance, need to be seen as far more than reflective of local circumstances, since "an appropriation of own or other cultures is an active and intellectually intensive and demanding exercise which mobilizes rational and sensual faculties, always" (Gurnah 1997: 126). With respect to language performances in general, Bauman (2004) argues that, when language is publicly put on display, made available for scrutiny, rendered an object of conscious consideration, it takes on different transformative possibilities.

Following Bauman, it is also important to take questions of genre and style into account here. A focus on genres – "the integrated, multi-level analyses that participants themselves implicitly formulate for their own practical activity" – Rampton (2006: 128) suggests, can provide the key for understanding the relationship between popular culture and linguistic practice. Drawing on the work of Bakhtin (1986), Rampton argues that these temporary stabilizations of form provide insights into the ways in which styles may transfer from the realm of popular culture to domains of everyday language use. Likewise, focusing on the active use of style, Coupland (2007) points to the importance of understanding "how people *use* or *enact* or *perform* social styles for a range of symbolic purposes" (p. 3). This enables us to see that "style (like language) is not a *thing* but a *practice*" (Eckert 2004: 43). A focus on style can thus shed light on several aspects of the role of hip hop in relation to everyday language practices: People engage in particular language practices because they are seen as having a certain style. Once a group of rappers puts a Creole language such as Chavacano on stage both as part of a profoundly local linguistic performance and as part of a global cultural performance, they give it a style that changes its status. And particular language styles, particular language varieties, are taken up in order to perform certain effects. Alim's (2006) research on copula use in what he calls Hip Hop Nation Language (HHNL) shows how "street conscious copula variation" is used to maintain a sense of staying "street" (connected to the linguistic and cultural world of hip hop). Language styles are practices that are performed as part of larger social and cultural styles. Language styles within hip hop are therefore precisely part of the process of change, making new language, new language mixes available to others, as well as taking up those styles that are deemed to have a particular street resonance.

Auzanneau (2002) argues that the language choices which the rappers in Libreville made were clearly intentional. Although at one level these language choices may therefore be viewed as reflecting local diversity, at another level they are also intentionally producing local diversity. Rather than merely reproducing local language practices, language use in hip hop may consequently have as much to do with change, resistance, and opposition as do lyrics that overtly challenge the status quo. This is particularly true of musicians such as rap artists, whose focus on verbal skills performed in the public domain renders their language use a site of constant potential challenge. The importance of this observation in terms of understanding popular cultures, languages, and identities is that it gives us an insight into the ways in which languages are used to perform, invent and (re) fashion identities across borders. Thus it is no longer useful to ask whether, in performing their acts of semiotic reconstruction, Rip Slyme are using Japanese English to express Japanese culture and identity, as if these neatly preexisted the performance; or whether Too Phat are native speakers of a nativized variety of English, as if such nationally constructed codes predefine their use; or whether Tasha's bilinguality is unrepresentative of language use in Korea, as if national language policy precludes alternative possibilities; or whether GHOST 13's lyrics reflect local language mixing in Zamboanga, as if language use was so easily captured and represented. When we talk of popular languages, we are talking of the performance of new identities. To be *authentic* in such contexts is a discursive accomplishment rather than an adherence to a pre-given set of characteristics (Coupland 2003; Pennycook 2007). And, like popular culture, these new identities are performances that are always changing, always in flux.

Once we understand languages from a local perspective, once we see language ideologies as contextual sets of belief about languages, as cultural and political systems of ideas about social and linguistic relationships, it becomes clear that the ways in which languages are used and thought about are never just about language but also about community and society, about what it means to be a person in a particular context (Woolard 2004). The performative nature of hip hop lyrics, therefore, may not only reflect local language conditions, but may actively resist current ways of thinking and produce new ways of thinking about languages and their meaning. Rap, Auzanneau suggests, "is a space for the expression of cultures and identities under construction." Indeed,

> it is itself a space creating these identities and cultures, as well as codes and linguistic units that will ultimately be put into circulation beyond the songs. Rap thus reveals and participates in the unifying gregarity of the city's activities, and works with the city on the form, functions, and values of its languages. (Auzanneau 2002: 120)

By working on the languages of the city while simultaneously being part of a larger global circuit of language and music, rap takes up and 'spits out' new cultural and linguistic possibilities, which are then made available again for recycling.

Mixing and sampling is a significant element of hip hop culture, extending not only to the use of sound samples, different backing tracks, and different instruments, but also to the mixing and sampling of languages. Just as lyrics may oppose social orthodoxies, the use of multiple languages may be purposive acts in opposition to ortholinguistic practices, performatively enacting new possibilities for language use and identity. The use of popular languages and styles within popular cultures questions commonly held notions of language origins (Pennycook and Mitchell 2009), of language purities, of possible code-mixes, and puts on stage new possibilities for identifications across borders. The unortholinguistic practices of popular culture display new and fluid linguistic, cultural, and identificatory possibilities that may then be taken up, reworked, and reprocessed back through the global circuits of cultural and linguistic flow. Once we take seriously the vernacular voices of the popular and their modes of self-fashioning (Scott 1999), we are obliged to rethink the ways in which languages and cultures work within globalization.

DISCOGRAPHY

Daara J (2004) *Boomerang*. Wrasse Records.
DJ Tommy (2001) *Respect for da chopstick hip hop*. Warner Music Hong Kong.
GHOST 13 (2004) *GHOST 13*. GMA Records Philippines.
Rip Slyme (2002) *Tokyo Classic*. Warner Music Japan.
Tasha (n.d.) *Hiphop Album*. Gemini Bobos Entertainment Korea.
Too Phat (2002) *360°*. EMI (Malaysia).

NOTES

1   This phrase, meaning 'black, white, Arab' ('Beur' derives from the common *verlan* inversion of the word 'Arabe') is a reference to the opposition that emerged to the French hyper-nationalism of the red, white and blue of the tricolore. Black, Blanc, Beur presents an alternative, multiracial, multilingual, multicultural vision to the monolingual, monocultural, monoracial view ascribed to French nationalists who cling to the traditons of the red, white, and blue.
2   Interviews were part of a research project on global hip hop between 2003 and 2006. See Pennycook 2007.

REFERENCES

Akindes, F. Y. (2001) Sudden rush: *Na Mele Paleoleo* (Hawaiian Rap) as liberatory discourse. *Discourse* 23(1): 82–98.

Alim, H. S. (2006) *Roc the Mic Right: The Language of Hip Hop Culture*. London and New York: Routledge.

Alim, H. S., Ibrahim, A., and Pennycook, A. (eds) (2009) *Global Linguistic Flows: Hip Hop Cultures, Youth Identities, and the Politics of Language*. New York: Routledge.

Androutsopoulos, J. (2003) Einleitung. In J. Androutsopoulos (ed.), *HipHop: Globale Kultur – Lokale Praktiken*, 9–23. Bielefeld: Transcript Verlag.

Auzanneau, M. (2002) Rap in Libreville, Gabon: An urban sociolinguistic space. In A.-P. Durand (ed.), *Black, Blanc, Beur: Rap Music and Hip-Hop Culture in the Francophone World*, 106–23. Lanham, MD: The Scarecrow Press.

Bakhtin, M. (1986) *Speech Genres and Other Late Essays*. Austin, TX: University of Texas Press.

Bauman, R. (2004) *A World of Others' Words: Cross-Cultural Perspectives on Intertextuality*. Oxford: Blackwell.

Berger, H. (2003) Introduction: The politics and aesthetics of language choice and dialect in popular music. In H. Berger and M. Carroll (eds), *Global Pop, Local Language*, ix–xxvi. Jackson: University Press of Mississippi.

Chamoiseau, P., and Confiant, R. (1999) *Lettres créoles*. Paris: Gallimard.

Cepeda, M. E. (2003) *Mucho Loco* for Ricky Martin: Or the politics of chronology, crossover, and language within the Latin(o) music 'boom.' In H. Berger, and M. Carroll (eds), *Global Pop, Local Language*, 113–29. Jackson: University Press of Mississippi.

Coupland, N. (2003) Sociolinguistic authenticities. *Journal of Sociolinguistics* 7: 417–31.

Coupland, N. (2007) *Style: Language Variation and Identity*. Cambridge: Cambridge University Press.

Doran, M. (2004) Negotiating between *Bourge* and *Racaille*: Verlan as youth identity practice in suburban Paris. In A. Pavlenko and A. Blackledge (eds), *Negotiation of Identities in Multilingual Contexts*, 93–124. Clevedon: Multilingual Matters.

Eckert, P. (2004) The meaning of style. *Texas Linguistic Forum* 47: 41–53.

Fernandes, S. (2003) Fear of a black nation: Local rappers, transnational crossings, and state power in contemporary Cuba. *Anthropological Quarterly* 76(4): 575–608.

Gilroy, P. (1993) *The Black Atlantic: Modernity and Double Consciousness*. London: Verso.

Glissant, E. (1997) *Poetics of Relation*, translated by B. Wing. AnnArbor: University of Michigan Press.

Gurnah, A. (1997) Elvis in Zanzibar. In A. Scott (ed.), *The Limits of Globalization*. 116–42. London: Routledge.

Halliday, M. A. K. (2002) *Applied linguistics as an evolving theme*. Plenary address to the Association Internationale de Linguistique Appliquée (AILA), Singapore. December.

Higgins, C. (2009) From Da Bomb to *Bomba*: Global hip hop nation language in Tanzania. In Alim, Ibrahim, and Pennycook (eds), 95–112.

Ho, W. C. (2003) Between globalisation and localisation: A study of Hong Kong popular music. *Popular Music* 22(2): 143–57.

Huq, R. (2001) The French connection: Francophone hip hop as an institution in contemporary postcolonial France. *Taboo: Journal of Education and Culture* 5(2): 69–84.

Jameson, F. (1998) Notes on globalization as a philosophical issue. In F. Jameson and M. Miyoshi (eds), *The Cultures of Globalization*, 54–77. Durham: Duke University Press.

Ibrahim, A. (1999) Becoming black: Rap and hip-hop, race, gender, identity and the politics of ESL learning. *TESOL Quarterly* 33(3): 349–70.

Ibrahim, A. (2008) The new flaneur: Subaltern cultural studies, African youth in Canada and the semiology of in-betweenness. *Cultural Studies* 22(2): 234–53.

Jacquemet, M. (2005) Transidiomatic practices, language and power in the age of globalization. *Language and Communication* 25: 257–77.

Kaya, A. (2001) *'Sicher in Kreuzberg' Constructing Diasporas: Turkish Hip-Hop Youth in Berlin*. Bielefeld: Transcript Verlag.

Krims, A. (2000) *Rap Music and the Poetics of Identity*. Cambridge: Cambridge University Press.

Lin, A. (2009) "Respect for Da Chopstick Hip Hop": The politics, poetics, and pedagogy of Cantonese verbal art in Hong Kong. In Alim, Ibrahim, and Pennycook (eds), 159–77.

Makoni, S., and Pennycook, A. (2007) Disinventing and reconstituting languages. In S. Makoni and A. Pennycook (eds), *Disinventing and Reconstituting Languages*, 1–41. Clevedon: Multilingual Matters.

Mitchell, T. (2001a) Introduction: Another root – Hip-Hop outside the USA. In Mitchell (ed.), 1–38.

Mitchell, T. (ed.) (2001b) *Global Noise: Rap and Hip-Hop Outside the USA*. Middletown, CT: Wesleyan University Press.

Mufwene, S. (2001) *The Ecology of Language Evolution*. Cambridge: Cambridge University Press.

Omoniyi, T. (2009) "So I choose to do Am Naija style": Hip Hop, language, and postcolonial identities. In Alim, Ibrahim, and Pennycook (eds), 113–35.

Pacini Hernandez, D., and Garofalo, R. (2004) The emergence of 'rap Cubano': An historical perspective. In S. Whiteley, A. Bennett, and S. Hawkins (eds), *Music, Space and Place: Popular Music and Cultural Identity*, 89–107. Hants: Ashgate Publishing.

Pennay, M. (2001) Rap in Germany: The birth of a genre. In Mitchell (ed.), 111–33.

Pennycook, A. (2003) Global Englishes, Rip Slyme and performativity. *Journal of Sociolinguistics* 7(4): 513–33.

Pennycook, A. (2007) *Global Englishes and Transcultural Flows*. London: Routledge.

Pennycook A., and Mitchell, T. (2009) Hip hop as dusty foot philosophy: Engaging Locality. In Alim, Ibrahim, and Pennycook (eds), 25–42.

Perry, I. (2004) *Prophets of the Hood: Politics and Poetics in Hip Hop*. Durham, NC: Duke University Press.

Phillipson, R., and Skutnabb-Kangas, T. (1996) English only worldwide or language ecology? *TESOL Quarterly* 30(3): 429–52.

Prévos, A. (2001) Postcolonial popular music in France: Rap music and hip-hop culture in the 1980s and 1990s. In Mitchell (ed.), 39–56.

Radhakrishnan, R. (2003) *Theory in an Uneven World*. Oxford: Blackwell.

Rampton, B. (1995) *Crossing: Language and Ethnicity among Adolescents*. London: Longman.

Rampton, B. (1999) Styling the Other: Introduction. *Journal of Sociolinguistics* 3(4): 421–7.

Rampton, B. (2006) *Language in Late Modernity: Interaction in an Urban School*. Cambridge: Cambridge University Press.

Sarkar, M. (2009) "Still reppin' por mi gente": The transformative power of language mixing in Quebec hip hop. In Alim, Ibrahim, and Pennycook (eds), 139–57.

Sarkar, M., and Allen, D. (2007) Hybrid identities in Quebec hip-hop: Language, territory, and ethnicity in the mix. *Journal of Language, Identity, and Education* 6(2): 117–30.

Scott, D. (1999) *Refashioning Futures: Criticism after Postcoloniality*. Princeton, NJ: Princeton University Press.

Skutnabb-Kangas, T. (2000) *Linguistic Genocide in Education – Or Worldwide Diversity and Human Rights?* Mahwah, NJ: Lawrence Erlbaum.

Swedenburg, T. (2001) Islamic hip-hop vs Islamophobia. In Mitchell (ed.), 57–85.

Urla, J. (2001) "We are all Malcolm X!" Negu Gorriak, hip-hop, and the Basque political imaginary. In Mitchell (ed.), 171–93.

Woolard, K. (2004) Is the past a foreign country? Time, language origins, and the nation in early modern Spain. *Journal of Linguistic Anthropology* 14(1): 57–8.

28 Global Representations of Distant Suffering

LILIE CHOULIARAKI

Globalization, Representation, Ethics

From tsunami-stricken beaches to bloody riots in Burma or Iran to war footage from Iraq or Gaza, our everyday experience of global events is largely the experience of human misfortune. It is the media that bring this experience in our living-rooms through their images and stories of distant suffering, throwing into relief the dramatic divisions of power that traverse the globe, between zones of prosperity and poverty, safety and danger, peace and war.

Whereas the role of the media, particularly news media, is often described in terms of instrumental obligations, for example as the duty to inform or to entertain western publics, spectacles of human misfortune bring into focus another important obligation. This is the ethical obligation of the news media to go beyond simply informing us of the facts of suffering, or simply entertaining us with exotic stories about distant disasters, and actually to turn these news dramas into occasions for reflection and potentially for action on the part of their publics (Silverstone 2007).

It is precisely this gap between showing scenes of suffering on-screen but not enabling audiences to engage in direct action on these scenes that renders the news media a crucial space for the symbolic performance of action at a distance (Alexander and Jacobs 1998: 28–32; Boltanski 1999: 7; Barnett 2003: 81–107). The symbolic power of mediation, understood in this ethical sense, can be productively conceptualized as the power of language and image to render suffering a cause of engagement for western media publics and thereby to constitute these publics as imagined communities of action toward the vulnerabilities of the non-western world (Anderson 1983: 9; Chouliaraki 2006: 44–6).

The ways in which news media represent the suffering of distant others have always made an object of research and controversy. In the past, this topic has raised moral questions about the power relations between the West and the 'rest,' about stereotypes of the 'poor South,' and about compassion fatigue among western audiences (Moeller 1999: 1–17). In the age of media globalization, the

The Handbook of Language and Globalization, First Edition. Edited by Nikolas Coupland.

symbolic power of global news to represent suffering reformulates these moral questions in new ways: to what extent do the representational resources of the media enable the expansion of the moral imagination of the West? What kinds of public action does the global narration of suffering propose to its audiences: action that tends to reproduce a sense of belonging to 'our' own local world – that is, communitarian action – or action that tends to expand our sense of responsibility beyond people like 'us' – cosmopolitan action?[1] It is these questions that the present chapter addresses.

I begin by reviewing three approaches to the relationship between mediated representation and public action, in the following section on the textuality of mediation. Then in the next section, on the analytics of mediation, I outline an analytical approach, which conceptualizes media representations as enactments of ethical discourse that selectively articulate specific proposals for action at a distance, thereby also configuring specific communities of viewing as imagined communities of emotion and action. The rest of the chapter is organized around the exposition of two paradigmatic types of imagined community available to us through global representations of suffering. In the sections devoted to the construction of communitarian publics and to the construction of cosmopolitan publics, I explore a number of examples that illustrate the role of representational practices in the construction of each type of community, by expanding on an earlier typology of such practices in terms of "adventure," "ecstatic," and "emergency" news (Chouliaraki 2006). In the conclusion, I return to the question of whether global news may act as a resource for the expansion of the moral imagination of the West, and I draw attention to those rare symbolic practices of the news that may indeed make room for some, albeit reluctant, optimism on the possibility of 'cosmopolitan publics.'

The Textuality of Mediation

Three approaches broadly engage with the textual nature of mediation and its relationship to public action: audience interpretation studies (a broad field, for overviews, see Alasuutari 1999, Livingstone and Lunt 1994, Livingstone 1998 among others); text analysis in the critical discourse analysis tradition (for example van Dijk 1987; Hodge and Kress 1988; Fairclough 1995, 2003; Scollon 1998; Jewitt and van Leeuwen 2001) and media sociology studies (for example Hall 1983; Hartley 1993; Jensen 1995; Bell and Garrett 1998; Wodak 1996, 1999; Couldry 2005).[2] As always with social scientific methods, there are advantages and limitations to all three approaches.

Audience studies regard the media text as the immediate context for people's understanding of social events and they emphasize the process by which people's own accounts of such events are both enabled and constrained by the discourse of the media. Analytical focus here falls on audiences 're-telling' various media genres, including the news; and it is these texts of interpretation that are taken as evidence of how the media influence social action.[3]

Textual research within critical discourse analysis takes both text production (the discourse of the news, for example) and text interpretation (audiences' accounts of the news) as its objects of study. Depending on the study, analytical focus may fall either on the media text as a locus of social struggle over meaning or on texts of interpretation as the locus of people's active construction of meaning. In the analysis of media texts, a conception of action lies within the text and is primarily understood in terms of the social relations of power involved in the construction of hegemony and in the legitimization of action as 'commonsense' through media discourse (Fairclough 1995; Wodak 1999). In the analysis of media interpretations, a conception of public action lies with the audience's capacity for appropriating the meanings of the news – in reproductive but also in resistant or subversive ways (Morley 1992; Fiske 1994; Katz and Liebes 1986).

Audience interpretation studies are often criticized for 'methodological individualism' – that is, for using a narrow conception of public action, which is defined exclusively in terms of how people understand news stories. What is lacking from this conception of action is a broader, societal explanation as to how the media may influence action. As Couldry puts is, "for all their virtues, there has been a tension in earlier accounts of how circulated media texts influence social action between (1) emphasising the moment of individual interpretation and (2) the desire to explain more broadly how interpretation is socially shaped" (Couldry 2005).

The tradition of textual analysis, on the other hand, does manage to capture the broad, societal dimensions of public action by using a Gramscian view of media powers as hegemonic articulations of meaning. What this tradition lacks, however, is detailed accounts of how such struggles of meaning are embedded in the specific contexts of practice which social actors live and act within – and therefore it often fails to account for the diverse and contradictory meanings that people attach to their actions, including their moral positions toward distant suffering.

Media sociology, the third approach outlined here, attempts to link media and public action by reference to concepts such as habitus, naturalization, and everyday life. Habitus, a concept originating in Bourdieu, refers to routine social practices that have become inculcated and embodied in people through socialization and habit – including the socialization of the media. Entailing a historicized conception of action as a 'structuring structure' that provides people with the categories by which they live their daily life, the notion of habitus seeks to explain how such categories become naturalized into taken-for-granted patterns of behavior and belief, and how they tend to reproduce certain preferred distinctions among spheres of activity in social life. Distinctions such as the one between the mediated and the ordinary, whereby the mediated carries more power, value, and prestige than the ordinary, come to organize hierarchical spheres of activity; the 'rituals' of reality shows or the 'liveness' of broadcasting are just two instances of a conception of the media as the 'social center' and the privileged locus of experience vis-à-vis everyday life. What such distinctions ultimately do is serve relationships of power; they come to "naturalise further the concentration of symbolic resources in media institutions that characterise contemporary societies" (Couldry 2005).

The advantage of this approach lies in its theorizing and historicizing of action in the social contexts where mediation and public life intersect. Paradoxically, however, the approach does not deal adequately with the question of power. Although implicit in the terminology of naturalization – the taken-for-grantedness of ways of acting upon the world – power is not thematized as an analytical category. This means that the conception of power in media sociology cannot explain *how exactly* the media may naturalize certain categories rather than others as spaces of ordinary life and *how*, in so doing, the media reproduce divisions that exclude far-away others from our sphere of responsibility and action (Silverstone 2004: 440–9).

It is particularly in relation to the ethical question of how the language of news media may forge relationships of care and responsibility to distant others that this type of media sociology remains limited. In focusing on the mediated/ordinary distinction, it addresses the agendas and concerns of those situated in the zone of safety, prosperity, and peace – those who are close to us; what it leaves aside is the key ethical question of how mediation may (if at all) enable and legitimize spheres of action toward the zone of danger, poverty, and war and those who are far away.

My argument is that, in order to theorize the link between public action and media representation, we need to attend to the specificity of media texts; we need to provide more concrete accounts of how their language and image inculcate in their publics a disposition to act, and how power in implicated in these processes of inculcation. Drawing on Aristotle's idea that engaging with the spectacles of public life is an important part of our moral education as citizens of the world – and it is indifferent here whether such spectacles are our contemporary media stories or the theatrical performances of classical Athens and its festivals – I argue that the link between media representations and public action may be usefully explored by analysing the ways in which such texts expose their audiences to specific "dispositions to feel, think, and act" in their everyday lives (Chouliaraki 2008: 831–52).

From this perspective, it is not the hegemonic struggles of meaning within media texts, nor is it the use of media stories as resources for audience re-tellings that can, per se, resolve – and adequately – the question of public action in the context of the media. It is rather the ways in which such struggles of meanings, and the re-tellings of these meanings, come cumulatively to articulate and naturalize ways of being for the spectator as a public actor that address the question of how media texts cultivate moral dispositions in the West.

The term 'habitus' can be understood, in this context, as having a significant textual dimension: as referring to the systematic repertoire of dispositions to action that media texts systematically propose to their audiences through the forms of agency embedded in their representations.

To be sure, the forms of agency embedded in media texts of distant suffering are not, in themselves, enough to constitute the spectator as a public actor. For this to happen, a broader chain of links to action must take place. Media texts are rather performative: they enact forms of identification that may (or may not) subsequently link up with other forms of effective action in the public sphere. However, this performative role of texts points to the fact that representations do not simply address a pre-existing audience, who waits to engage in social action; in the process of narrating and visualizing distant events, representations have the power to constitute this audience as a body poised for action. Media texts are, in this sense, conditions of possibility for social action.

The Analytics of Mediation

News stories of distant suffering best exemplify how the media may use the performative capacity of representation in order to transform a group of audiences into a collectivity with a will to act – a public. Because of the practical impossibility to act at the scene of suffering, the forms of engagement and action that media narratives propose to the spectator have less to do with immediate, practical intervention and more to do with patterns of imaginary, in other words projected, action on the part of the spectator (Barnett 2003: 102). Such patterns, as we shall see below, are infused with social value and ethical content, and it is by way of analyzing the embeddedness of value in language and image that we are able to evaluate the moral force of media representations in the global context.

The term 'analytics,' which Foucault borrows from Aristotle to distinguish his approach from a 'grand' theory of power, aims at describing how media discourse manages to articulate universal values of human conduct at any given moment in time and how, in so doing, it places human beings into certain relationships of power to one another (Foucault 1991: 102; Flyvbjerg 2001: 131–8). Media representations of distant suffering, for instance, operate as a strategy of power in so far as they selectively offer the option of emotional engagement with, and practical action on behalf of, certain sufferers, but they leave others outside the scope of such engagement and action, thereby reproducing western communities of care and global hierarchies of place and human life (Moeller 1999: 309–23).

Two implications follow from this analytical perspective on mediation. First, the *aesthetic quality* of representation – that is, the ways in which verbal and visual resources combine to tell the story of suffering – is inextricably linked to the moral stance toward suffering that the media propose to us (Sontag 2003: 16–35). As a consequence – and this is the second implication of my analytical approach to mediation – the exercise of power through the media cannot be understood solely in terms of habitus or hegemony. It should be understood more specifically, in terms of the options for *moral agency* the media make available: the subtle proposals for engagement with distant suffering that news stories introduce in the contexts of our everyday life. These proposals to action capitalize on a set of civil dispositions, which are historically available in our collective imaginary and can be used as resources in the public representation of suffering: for instance indignant denunciation toward the perpetrators of suffering, charitable tender-heart-edness toward its victims, or fear and shock at the sight of human misfortune.[4]

Following the Aristotelian principle, whereby the study of singular examples of mediation provides us with insight into the enactment of ethical discourse, I focus on the study of selected news stories on distant suffering in global news. My aim is to track down the practices through which each piece of news represents distant suffering, and, in so doing, to show how each case simultaneously evokes a normative claim as to whom it is important to care for and which community of action one should belong to. The study of the symbolic power of mediation as an ethical force in the context of globalization emerges out of this dual analytical focus in the particular properties of each news story and at the same time in the universal claim, which every story contains, as to which sufferings are worthy of action.

In the light of these methodological considerations, I explore the symbolic construction of community in six examples of news on suffering. Whereas the first four cases cluster around a West-oriented (or Eurocentric) image of community, constituting what we may call 'communitarian publics,' the final two cases suggest that alternative ways of managing the representation of suffering may lead to a 'cosmopolitan' expansion of the western imagination – a possibility which is, nevertheless, inevitably grounded in the premises and practices of western publics.

The Construction of Communitarian Publics

The construction of communitarian publics involves two clusters of representational practice: the minimalist cluster of 'adventure' news and the maximalist cluster of 'ecstatic' news.[5]

The representation of suffering in 'adventure' news

The first piece of news concerns a boat accident in India (BBC World, August 31, 2002). This is a brief story with a descriptive narrative: a river-boat capsized in river Baytarani, in the Indian province of Orissa, as it was making its way toward Jaipur town – "forty people are feared drowned – most of them office workers and school children."

The use of language and image in this piece is minimal. It does not involve on-location reports, but rather the use of maps – namely one of the Indian province of Orissa, showing it to be situated amidst neighboring provinces, and another one of India, showing it to be situated in the northern hemisphere. The aesthetic register here is cartography – a decontextualized representation of geographical space that abstracts the event of suffering from its experiential circumstances. This narrative of suffering involves mentioning no people, no action, no emotion. Such absences correspond to semiotic choices over where, when, and with whom the suffering is shown to occur, which in turn give rise to a particular type of moral agency: do nothing, care not. The geographical distance between western Europe and the river Baytarani is translated into another kind of distance: an emotional and moral distance between us and the Indian sufferers.

The second example is a piece of news on floods in Bangladesh (National Greek Television, July 23, 2002). It combines the visualization of the scene of suffering, as it reached national television via satellite, with a brief voiceover added for the Greek public. Two symbolic features stand out in this piece of news: the panoramic point of view and the lack of action. The panoramic point of view provides us with an overview of the flooded landscape from afar and above: this could have happened anywhere else, at any other time, and could have involved any other population. In creating this effect, the panoramic landscape also creates a distance from the lived reality, as the scene is all about water, trees and human figures in a static composition. This is not the footage of a catastrophe which, incidentally, affected 60 percent of the nation, but a *tableau vivant*, inviting distantiated contemplation of the flooded land rather than engagement with the urgency of suffering. At the same time there is no purposeful action, no voice: these people lack appellative power, the power to communicate the condition of their misfortune. Their dehumanization, echoed also in the voiceover's dramatic but brief linguistic text about the "biblical catastrophe," further participates in the aestheticization of this news story, effectively producing a spectacle of difference between cultures that lie beyond the possibility of contact.

These two examples of 'adventure' news share three key features: the minimal narration of suffering, the refusal to humanize the sufferers, and the interruption of emotion, denunciation or empathy vis-à-vis the events of suffering. Such symbolic features characterize most of our regular diet of daily news reports, on the grounds of the pragmatic argument of selectivity: the media do not always have access to sites of distant suffering, nor can they report on every event in the same order of importance (for the role of technological and economic restrictions on foreign reporting, see Livingston and van Belle 2003: 363–80). Yet these pieces of news throw into relief the fact that the interruption of emotion involved in this professional logistics is not only a necessity, but also one that makes a moral claim in its own right. They remind us of the fact that emotion is a scarce resource and that part of the capacity of news to represent the globe is its capacity to reserve the potential for emotion for some sufferers; to locate others outside our own community of belonging; and to place their suffering beyond the remit of our action.

The representation of suffering in 'ecstatic' news

There are, however, news stories with a different narrative of suffering. These exceptional stories include complex linguistic and visual representations that invite our exclusive engagement with suffering. The key feature of extraordinary news is the shift from the news bulletin to the rolling footage, which involves the suspension of an ordinary sense of temporality and the introduction of what

Badiou (quoted in Barker 2002: 75) calls "truly historic time: moments when a minute lasts a lifetime, or when a week seems to fly by in next to no time" – with reference to the shock and disbelief at the moment of the second plane crash on the World Trade Center. Let me briefly discuss the September 11 footage in Danish television, before I move on to the global media spectacle of the Iraq War in BBC World.

I concentrate on three distinct sequences from the September 11 Footage (Danish National Television channel, DR): the eye-witness account, the update of events and the panorama of the Manhattan cityscape. The *eye-witness account* is a 'right here right now' exposition of events. We are together with the expert panel at the Copenhagen studio and at the same time we are connected via telephone link with the Danish consul in New York. The visuals show ambulances and people walking away from the scene of the catastrophe, whereas the consul gives a dramatic, first-person account of chaos and mayhem in Manhattan. The genre of this sequence is that of raw documentary: camera and human voice combine in a complex act of witnessing, which invites national spectators to experience the events as if they were on location and to share the intensity of emotion as if they were themselves present at the scene of disaster. As a consequence of this intense proximity, the topic of moral agency is cast in the form of empathy, inviting us to engage in real time with the tragic fate of the American people and to feel for their unexpected vulnerability.

The update of the events of the morning of September 11 was inserted into the flow of the footage at regular intervals. The visuals took us everywhere where action took place: to New York, with the World Trade Center attacks; to Washington, DC, with the Pentagon burning; to Georgia, with Bush' first appeal to the American people. The cohesion of these sequences, particularly the use Bush's speech to conclude the update, already situates the attacks, the terrorism, and the promise of retaliation in one meaningful narrative. In terms of aesthetic quality, the last sequence differs from the previous ones in that it is not about events as breaking news, but rather about already authoring September 11 as history. The moral agency emerging from this narrative invites denunciation: it focuses on the tragic loss of human lives, separates between perpetrators and victims, and evokes the collective demand for justice as the only possible response to this instance of suffering (as in the concluding statement of Bush' first speech from a primary school in Florida: "we're going to hunt down those folks who committed that act").

The 'Manhattan panorama' is an extended sequence which provides us with a long shot of the cityscape in grey smoke, turning the scene of suffering into a phantasmagoric spectacle. The confrontation with the awe-provoking dimension of the imagery of suffering removes the urgency of the here-and-now and opens up a space of analytical temporality, where the events are being debated and reflected on (Boltanski 1999: 121). Indeed, the moral agency of this sublime aesthetics is devoid of empathy or indignation and turns to a tentative deliberation on the attacks: the voiceover consists of the expert panel explaining the causes and discussing the political implications of the event.

In sum, the September 11 satellite footage, characterized by a hectic alternation of aesthetic registers, complicates the moral agency of the Danish national public, inviting people to engage with this spectacle of suffering in multiple ways: to empathize, to denounce and to reflect on it as a human tragedy and as a political act. Importantly, the sufferers of September 11 are presented as thoroughly humanized and historical beings; as people who feel, reflect, and act on their fate. They are, in short, people like 'us,' who happen to live far away. We are united with them in denouncing the evil doers (recall *Le Monde*'s headlines "We are all Americans" on 12 September 2001) or in supporting them to alleviate their misfortune.

The shock and awe bombardments of Bagdad (BBC World, March–April 2003), one of the most visually arresting spectacles of warfare, were broadcast live on BBC World and were subsequently inserted as regular 'updates' in the channel's 24/7 live footage flow. The examples described here will focus on the common patterns of the updates throughout their three-week broadcasting span.[6]

The point of view is from afar and above: a steady camera captures Baghdad in its visual plenitude. Filmed at night, the sequences turn the screen into a dark surface, animated by yellow explosions and green flashes at the sound of bombing fire. The visual effect is that of a digital game, endowing the spectacle of war with a fictional rather than a realist quality – a similar quality to the Gulf War visuals that made Baudrillard (1994) famously conclude that the war never happened. The voiceover functions indexically toward the visual, following action closely, and uses the first person perspective of the eye-witness to draw attention to its detail. The extracts contain no visualization of human beings on the ground: no sufferers in their homes, in the streets, or in hospitals. At the same time, the linguistic choices that construe the sufferer and the bomber deprive both figures of any sense of humanness: the sufferer is mostly a collective entity ("city") or a non-living being ("compound"), and the bomber is either diffused in the activity of airwar ("planes," "missiles") or erased from the narrative. By cancelling the presence of the bomber and the sufferer, the footage presents the bombardment of Baghdad as a site of intense military action without agency.

This representation of suffering evokes a sublime aesthetics, which, as we saw, construes distant suffering less through emotions toward the sufferer than through a distantiated appreciation, derived from the awesome quality of the spectacle of warfare itself. The moral agency emerging from this first-person genre is one of engaging with the war in the mode of impartial contemplation, as a spectacle to watch rather than as a political act to take sides on. This attitude potentially blocks empathy toward the victims or the urge to denounce the bombing of civilians – or indeed the whole project of the war in Iraq. (For similar interpretations, see Lewis 2004.)

Communitarian publics

The two categories of news I discussed above differ substantially from each other. 'Adventure' news is about stories we hardly ever remember; 'ecstatic' news is about stories that are hard to forget. Despite radical differences in their representations of suffering, however, these stories share a key feature: they address their audiences as an already constituted community. This is a community united in blocking out emotions toward 'irrelevant' sufferings, or united in fully empathizing with sufferers who are like 'us.' Whereas the 'ecstatic' quality of representation in news such as the September 11 footage renders the far-away too close to us to ignore, the 'adventure' quality of representation in news such as the Indian accident or the Bangladesh floods removes suffering from the order of 'our' own humanity and weakens the capacity of such suffering to move us to a response. As a consequence, neither of these categories of news offers us connectivity of a quality that may bring with it a sense of responsibility toward forms of suffering registered outside the western communities of belonging.

The Construction of Cosmopolitan Publics

The possibility for constructing a cosmopolitan public emerges out of a particular cluster of representational practices: the 'emergency' news. This category differs from the other too in that it explicitly proposes action beyond the West as a possibility, or indeed as a necessity for western audiences.

The representation of suffering in 'emergency ' news

The Burma monk demonstrations (September 23–October 6, 2007, BBC World, plus various multi-platform media), which involved the violent crackdown of peaceful marches of people, mostly monks, against the tyrannical regime of Myanmar, became an emergency story across the globe. Two symbolic elements contributed to the construction of this story as an emergency:

1   the citizen-generated imagery of the peaceful demonstrators vis-à-vis the brutal violence of the state army, which elicited both feelings of empathy for the suffering of the monks and the urge to denounce the perpetrators of this suffering; and
2   the intertextual chains of this imagery across types of media, from mobile phones to broadcasting and to internet blogs and websites, which not only expanded the public visibility of the events but further contextualized them in powerful discourses of resistance against the Burmese junta.

Drawing on the aesthetics of the raw documentary, the footage gained significant news value by recording the long lines of the monks, dressed in saffron robes and marching quietly through army-populated city streets, and by capturing on camera the killing of a Japanese journalist by the rioting police. Illegal in its country of origin, this amateur and erratic footage acted as a transnational counter-narrative of power against the official accounts of events. As Cooper put it, "the pictures were often grainy and the video shaky, but in media terms, they were gold dust. [...] [T]hanks to them, we saw pictures of monks marching through the streets of Rangoon, and heard crackly phone calls with a chilling soundtrack of gun shots" (2007: 6).

The documentary's aesthetic of clandestine testimony simultaneously enacts and invites a particular type of moral agency, which we have not encountered so far: the dual agency of "seeing *and* saying" (Peters 2001: 717–23). This form of agency recognizes, in the passive act of witnessing, the active obligation to speak out in the name of those whose capacity to respond to injustice is limited and ineffective – to speak, in other words, in the mode of denunciation. This act of seeing is able to shift to the act of saying only because of the intense media activism of civil society organizations, which appropriated and recontextualized the images of monk demonstrations in a discourse of human rights and international solidarity – in Boltanski's words, they managed "to address the spectator's ability to consider himself as a speaker" (1999: 40).

The tsunami catastrophe, 2004, evokes a different quality of urgency, one that resembles the 'truly historical' temporality of the September 11 news. Given the magnitude and multi-dimensionality of the disaster, the rolling footage of this event involved a continuous alternation of locations, types of information, and genres of reporting, making the tsunami one of the most complex journalistic ventures ever. The result was an unprecedented amount of aid donations for the tsunami survivors – what Koffi Annan, then Secretary General of the United Nations, celebrated as a "unique manifestation of global unity" (BBC World, January 9, 2005).

A significant dimension of the footage, however, was the number of tourist video recordings that reached the websites of major news networks, making the tsunami a crucial turning point in the use of citizen-generated content by news networks (Gillmor 2004). The first-person perspective on such visual material lent the event an intense 'right here right now' quality and offered a powerful resource of identification for western spectators. Whereas the Burma demonstrations footage capitalized on a 'clandestine' witnessing unfamiliar to the western world, the tsunami material capitalized on the 'all too familiar' quality of witness accounts by people like 'us.'

In a characteristically amateur recording, shown across a number of networks around the world, the tsunami wave is approaching while the British tourist filming it from his hotel balcony shows no awareness of its imminent catastrophic consequences. What we see and hear on video is stuff reminiscent of what families do on holidays: the rough quality of the image; the casual conversation; the care-free attitude; the fascination with the exotic (Jaworski and Turow, this volume). This close-to-home aura suddenly snaps, as the recording culminates in fear and awe at the powerful wave blow, throwing into relief the immense potential for audience identification that citizen footage on distant suffering can bring about. In a different way from September 11, this aesthetic combination of the banal with the sublime created another sense of collective identification for western spectators (Hellman and Riegert 2006).

The construction of cosmopolitan publics

Emergency news inevitably construes the West as the imagined community to which its audiences belong. At the same time, however, this category of news further presents us with a demand for engagement that does not follow exclusively the implicit obligations of the communitarian bond. We are neither apathetic spectators to adventure news of distant suffering nor overengaged spectators to ecstatic news regarding the suffering of the West. We are simply confronted with the question of suffering as a problem to be solved. We are invited to consider our commitment to it as a matter of our own judgment. Are the Burma demonstrations a cause worthy of our action? What can we do to help the orphans of Banda Aceh? In posing these questions for our own reflection, emergency news also opens up a space that pushes us, even momentarily, beyond the concerns of our communities of belonging and beyond the obligations of the communitarian bond (Boltanski 1999: 35–8; Chouliaraki 2006: 188–9). But there is a difference between the two.

The emergency of the tsunami involves an intense management of visibility in global, multi-media environments, which became possible largely because of western tourists' use of technology and because of their subsequent involvement in the dissemination of images and narratives. Importantly, however, the extraordinary quality of this suffering is also due to the fact that, among the hundred thousands who lost their lives, nine thousand were citizens of western Europe on Christmas holidays: the tsunami emergency is proximal suffering at a distant location (Riegert and Olsson 2005). There is a Eurocentric bias in the construction of moral agency in this news, which ultimately throws into relief the very conditions of possibility for 'global unity': the care for the suffering of distant others expands beyond the West only insofar as the West is part of this suffering, both by experiencing and by witnessing it. Eldridge's observation that "the tsunami attracted more media attention in the first six weeks after it struck than the world's top ten 'forgotten' emergencies did over a whole year" (*Humanitarian Exchange Magazine*, March 11, 2005), and his mentioning of the number of western victims as one of the key reason for the West's philanthropic urge, come to confirm the following point: in the tsunami disaster, the West saw itself as partaking a global "risk community", sharing the loss of life with those zones of suffering directly involved in the disaster (Beck 2000: 79–105) rather than responding to the disaster in terms of cosmopolitan sensibilities, such as empathy and solidarity with distant suffering.

The emergency of the Burma demonstrations comes closer than any other example to what we might call 'cosmopolitan agency' – a proposal for public action on distant suffering, without reciprocity or guarantees. This is partly the consequence of a particular genre for the representation of suffering: clandestine testimony, which used new media technologies to shed public light on a military regime suppressing popular protest. Crucially, however, cosmopolitan agency is also the consequence of the voices of transnational governance and civil rights groups who strategically employed these new media to campaign and coordinate protests across the world (for a discussion of the use of new media and the development of civil society activism, see Tsagarousianou, Tambini, and Bryan 1998: 1–17; Tambini 1999: 305–29; Dahlgren 2001: 64–88).

Civil rights organizations, in this sense, enact the moral imperative of cosmopolitan citizenship in a dual sense: as a moral sentiment and as a political project (Kaldor 2000). It is precisely the capacity of this news, embedded as it was in a complex ecology of mediated communication, to appeal to a civil ethics of witnessing, in the scenes of violence and death, and to make the claim to justice, in the calls for action to 'free Burma,' that brought forth the moral agency of international solidarity. The management of representational practices across media in this particular piece seems to suggest that the cosmopolitan alternative may be a rare exception (Hafez 2006: 111–17), but it is certainly a possibility in the context of global mediation.

The Global Representation of Suffering

There is ample evidence in the study of the symbolic power of global mediation to confirm the skeptical argument, which challenges the capacity of global media to expand the moral imagination of western publics.

On the one hand, we saw that the reporting of suffering as 'adventure' suppresses emotional engagement and minimizes moral agency toward distant suffering. At the same time, 'ecstatic' news provides resources for identification and action that selectively reproduce publics with exclusively western affiliations. They do so either by fully humanizing the distant sufferers of the West, as if they were 'us,' or by dehumanizing non-westerners, as if their pain or death were not relevant to our moral consciousness.

On the other hand, the category of emergency news is the one that seems to bear the potential for expanding the existing images of community in western media. Whereas both examples of emergency news articulate the necessity for action, the Burma demonstration news in particular puts forward the normative claim of cosmopolitanism, whereby action toward vulnerable others involves no expectations of gratification in our part.

Two symbolic features of this piece of emergency news point to the construction of a cosmopolitan disposition: the renewal of the claim to mediated authenticity, grounded on an ethics of citizen witnessing; and the embeddedness of this claim in discourses of international solidarity.

Even though the aesthetics of first-hand documentary is as present here as it was in the previous examples, for instance in the Iraq War footage, its symbolic environment and hence its normative discourse are different. The immediacy and sensationalism of violence are now framed by a claim to clandestine testimony, by an awareness of the conditions of terror under which the recordings reached a global audience. At the same time, the call for action is not simply enacted through news texts, but comes through the mediated voices of civil society, in their blogs and websites, which provide concrete options for local action: signing a petition, participating in a protest. Without resorting to an uncritical celebration of the role of such media in enabling action, it is nevertheless important to acknowledge the multiply mediated dimension of practices of solidarity, online and offline, which ultimately manage the shift from watching to acting, from spectatorship to protest.

The civic disposition engendered by emergency news should be seen, then, as the product of a broader multimedia environment of satellite and interactive technologies. This complex technological environment suggests that the global representation of suffering as a cause for action may be an exception, but it is certainly a possibility in the global landscape of mediation. Insofar as it articulates an urgent claim to justice through forms of technological but effective action at a distance, it can indeed produce a kind of moral agency which abandons the West as an exclusive terrain of responsibility and action and extends beyond it, enabling what Gilroy calls a "wordly, cosmopolitan activism" (2006: 90).

Conclusion

The textuality of mediation, I argued in this chapter, is the central locus of the symbolic power of news media, insofar as such textuality does not simply address a pre-existing media audience but transforms this audience into a collectivity with the will to act – that is, into a public – in the course of narrating the news. Using news stories of distant suffering as exemplary illustrations of the symbolic power of the media, I addressed the sociological question of how global news stories produce forms of moral agency and participate in the imagination of community.

My analysis of the aesthetic properties of news stories, national and transnational, demonstrated that the symbolic power of western media consists in representing distant suffering in ways that reproduce a western imagination of community and devalue other places and human lives. Under certain conditions of possibility, however, the representation of distant suffering in the news may indeed produce a sense of moral agency that transcends the West.

NOTES

1   I draw on a social theory definition of cosmopolitanism broadly understood as "an orientation, a willingness to relate with the Other" (Hannerz 1996: 103), which demands nothing of the Other in return; which requires no reciprocation or guarantees (Linklater 2006: 19–36; 2007: 31–7; Beck 2000: 79–105).
2   For the distinction, see Couldry (2005), who juxtaposes his own approach to the study of media and social action to the Glasgow Media Group's interpretation studies and to

CDA-related work. The boundaries between these approaches, however, are rather malleable: for instance, Wodak's work can be seen as belonging both to sociological and to critical discourse analytical traditions.

3   For different approaches to the complex field of audience studies, from the early media effects to uses and gratifications tradition and to active audiences and resistance traditions, see Brooker and Jermyn 2003.

4   Boltanski (1999: 57–131), in a historical overview of the forms of the public representation of suffering – what he calls "topics of suffering" – produced a tripartite typology consisting of the topic of sentiment, the topic of denunciation and the aesthetic topic. Boltanski's threee topics have informed the description of the aesthetic quality of news in this piece of analysis. These topics can be traced back to classical Hellenism and, later on, to the emergence of the modern public sphere in Europe and to the Enlightenment ideal of universal moralism (Peters 1999: 33–62). Today, appropriated and reconfigured by modern technologies of mediation such as television, they still perform the crucial political function of presenting human misfortune in public, with a view to arousing the emotion of the spectators as well as to inviting their impartial deliberation on how to act upon the misfortune.

5   These two categories of news are part of a broader typology, which maps out the hierarchical distribution of representational resources in global news on distant suffering. Whereas adventure news, echoing Bakhtin's characterization of the early Greek novel, refers to news that represents suffering as a fictional curiosity irrelevant to the spectators' lives, ecstatic news, drawing on Badiou's description of extraordinary experience as "stopping time for a minute," refers to news that demands our exclusive and sustained engagement with suffering (Chouliaraki 2006: 158).

6   Examples drawing, specifically, on the March 27 and April 8 reports (Chouliaraki 2007a and b).

REFERENCES

Alasuutari, P. (1999) *Rethinking the Media Audience: The New Agenda*. London: Sage.

Alexander, J., and Jacobs, R. (1998) Mass communication, ritual and civil society. In T. Liebes and J. Curran (eds), *Media, Rituals, Identity*, 23–41. London: Routledge.

Anderson, B. (1983) *Imagined Communities. Reflections on the Origin and Spread of Nationalism*. London: Verso.

Aristotle (1976) *The Nicomachean Ethics*, translated by A. K. Thompson. Harmondsworth: Penguin. [Esp. 1140^{a}24–1140^{b}12 and 1144^{b}33–1145^{a}11.]

Barker, J. (2002) *Alain Badiou. A Critical Introduction*. London: Pluto Press.

Barnett, C. (2003) *Culture and Democracy. Media, Space and Representation*. Edinburgh: Edinburgh University Press.

Baudrillard, J. (1994) *The Gulf War Did Not Take Place*. Sydney: Powerful Publications.

Beck, U. (2000) The cosmopolitan perspective: Sociology of the second age of modernity. *British Journal of Sociology* 51(1): 79–105.

Bell, A., and Garrett, P. (eds) (1998) *Approaches to Media Discourse*. London: Blackwell.

Boltanski, L. (1999) *Distant Suffering. Politics, Morality and the Media*. Cambridge: Cambridge University Press.

Brooker, W., and Jermyn, D. (eds) (2003) *The Audience Studies Reader*. London: Routledge.

Chouliaraki, L. (2006) *The Spectatorship of Suffering*. London: Sage.

Chouliaraki, L. (2007a) The aestheticization of suffering on television. *Visual Communication* 5(3): 261–85.

Chouliaraki, L. (2007b) Spectacular ethics. In L. Chouliaraki (ed.) *The Soft Power of War*, 143–59. Philadelphia and Amsterdam: Benjamins Publications.

Chouliaraki, L. (2008) Media as moral education, mediation and action. *Media, Culture and Society* 30(6): 831–52.

Cooper, G. (2007) Anyone here who survived a wave, speaks English and got a mobile? Aid agencies, the media and reporting disasters since the tsunami 14th. Guardian Lecture, Nuffield College, Oxford.

Couldry, N. (2005) Media discourse and the naturalisation of categories. In R. Wodak and V. Koller (eds), *The Handbook of Applied Linguistics: Language and Communication in the Public Sphere*. Available at: http://www.lse.ac.uk/collections/media@lse/Word%20docs/MEDIA_DISCOURSE_AND_THE_NATURALISATION_OF_CATEGORIES.doc (accessed on February 3, 2010).

Dahlgren, P. (2001) The transformation of democracy? In B. Axford and R. Huggins (eds), *New Media and Politics*, 64–88. London: Sage.

Eldridge, C. (2005) The tsunami, the internet and funding for forgotten emergencies. *Humanitarian Exchange Magazine* 30. Available at: http://www.odihpn.org/report.asp?id=2724 (accessed on January 30, 2010).

Fairclough, N. (1995) *Media Discourse*. London: E. Arnold.

Fairclough, N. (2003) *Analyzing Discourse: Textual Analysis for Social Research*. London: Routledge.

Fiske, J. (1994) *Reading the Popular* [1989]. London: Routledge.

Flyvbjerg, B. (2001) *Making Social Science Matter*. Cambridge: Cambridge University Press.

Foucault, M. (1991) Governmentality. In G. Burchell, C. Gordon, and P. Miller (eds), *The Foucault Effect. Studies in Governmentality*, translated by Rosi Braidotti, 87–104. London: Harvester Wheatsheaf.

Gilroy, P. (2004) *After Empire*. Cambridge: Polity.

Gillmor, D. (2004) *We the Media. Grassroots Journalism by the People, for the People*. Sebastopol, CA: O'Reilley.

Hafez, K. (2006) *The Myth of Media Globalisation*. Cambridge: Polity.

Hannerz, U. (1996) *Transnational Connections: Culture, People, Places*. London: Routledge.

Hellman, M., and Riegert, K. (2006) Transnational and national media global crises. Paper presented at the Conference on Social Change sponsored by the Centre for Research on Socio-Cultural Change, 6–8 September, Oxford.

Hall, S. (1983) The rediscovery of ideology: The return of the 'repressed.' In M. Gurevitch (ed.), *Culture, Society and the Media*, 56–90. London: Blackwell.

Harrenz, U. (1996) *Transnational Connections. Culture, People, Places*. London: Routledge.

Hartley, J. (1993) *The Politics of Pictures*. London: Blackwell.

Hodge, R., and Kress, G. (1988) *Social Semiotics*. Cambridge: Polity.

Jensen, B. K. (1995) *The Social Semiotics of Mass Communication*. London: Sage.

Jewitt, C., and van Leeuwen, T. (2001) *The Handbook of Visual Analysis*. London: Sage.

Kaldor, M. (2000) Cosmopolitanism and organized violence. Paper presented at the Conference on Conceiving Cosmopolitanism, April 27–9, Warwick University.

Katz, E., and Liebes, T. (1986) Patterns of involvement in television fiction: A comparative analysis. *European Journal of Communication* 1(2): 151–71.

Kress, G., and van Leeuwen, T. (1996) *Reading Images. The Grammar of Visual Design*. London: Routledge.

Kress, G., and van Leeuwen, T. (2001) *Multimodal Discourse: The Modes and Media of Contemporary Communication*. London: Arnold.

Morley, D. (1992) *Television, Audiences and Cultural Studies*. London: Routledge.

Lewis, J. (2004) Television, public opinion and the war in Iraq: The case of Britain. *International Journal of Public Opinion Research* 16(3): 295–319.

Linklater, A. (2006) Distant suffering and cosmopolitan obligations. *International Politics* 44(18): 19–36.

Linklater, A. (2007) Public spheres and civilizing processes. *Theory, Culture, Society* 24: 31–37.

Livingston, S., and Bennett, L. (2003) Gate-keeping, indexing and live event news: Is technology altering the construction of news? *Political Communication* 20: 363–80.

Livingston, S., and van Belle, D. (2003) The effects of satellite technology on newsgathering from remote locations. *Political Communication* 20: 363–80.

Livingstone S. (1998) Relationships between media and audiences: Prospects for audience reception studies. In T. Liebes and J. Curran (eds), *Media, Rituals, Identity*, 237–55. London: Routledge.

Livingstone, S. (2004) On the relation between audience and public: Why audience and public? In S. Livingstone (ed.), *Audiences and Publics: When cultural Engagement Matters for the Public Sphere*, 17–41. Bristol: Intellect Books (Changing Media – Changing Europe series 2).

Livingstone, S., and Lunt P. (1994) *Talk on Television*. London: Routledge.

Moeller, S. (1999) *Compassion Fatigue: How the Media Sell Disease, Famine, War and Death*. London: Routledge.

Peters, D. J. (1999) Speaking into the Air. A History of the Idea of Communication. Chicago: Chicago University Press.

Peters, D. J. (2001) Witnessing. *Media, Culture and Society* 26(3): 707–23.

Riegert, K. M., and Olsson, E. (2005) The importance of ritual in crisis journalism. Paper presented at the annual meeting of the International Communication Association, Dresden International Congress Centre, Dresden, Germany. Available at: http://www.allacademic.com/meta/p91697_index.html (accessed on January 30, 2010).

Scollon, S. (1998) *Mediated Discourse as Social Interaction*. London: Longman.

Silverstone, R. (2004) Media literacy and media civics. *Media, Culture and Society* 23(3): 440–9.

Silverstone, R. (2007) *Media and Morality. On the Rise of the Mediapolis*. Cambridge: Polity.

Sontag, S. (2003) *Regarding the Pain of the Others*. New York: FSG Books.

Tambini, D. (1999) New media and democracy. The civic networking movement. *New Media and Society* 1(3): 305–29.

Tsagarousianou, R., Tambini, D., and Bryan, C. (eds) (1998) *Cyberdemocracy: Technology, Cities and Civic Networks*. London: Routledge.

van Dijk, T. (1987) *Communicating Racism*. London: Sage.

Wodak, R. (1996) *Disorders of Discourse*. London: Longman.

Wodak, R. (1999) Critical discourse analysis at the end of the 20th century. *Researh on Language and Social Interaction* 32: 185–94.

29 Global Media and the Regime of Lifestyle

DAVID MACHIN AND THEO VAN LEEUWEN

Introduction

In the literature on language and identity it has become common to challenge the notion of an essentialist self: "In a lifelong process, identity is endlessly created anew, according to various social constraints, social interactions, encounters, and wishes that may happen to be very subjective and unique" (Le Page and Tabouret-Keller 1985: 16). This model of identity has roots in the work of classic sociologists such as Durkheim (2002), Simmel (1971), and Tönnies (2001), who studied what happens to people's identity when they move from traditional rural communities to urban environments, which are characterized by change and anonymity and require people to play different roles throughout the day. But, unlike some of these predecessors, the new model celebrates complexity in all aspects of identity – gender, class, ethnicity, language group membership, and so on (Weeks 1990) – and it sees identity as a multi-faceted, flexible process of ongoing identity performance and as a liberation from monolithic, one-dimensional identity categories.

However, in embracing this new model of identity, we should not lose sight of the social and economic conditions that gave rise to it. In this paper we argue that the new model should not be seen as a sudden insight into what identity is and has always been, a sudden realization that everyone else has always had it wrong. As society changes, so do theories of society, necessarily. And at times theorists may even intuit changes well before they have made their full impact, and so they may contribute to change, doing their own little bit in helping it along. Like all ideas, the idea of a fluid, reflexive identity is rooted in a particular time and place. And, just as the older, monolithic model of identity served the interest of the institutions of the nation–state, so the new, flexible, and reflexive model of identity serves the new social order of global capitalism and is in fact systematically distributed around the planet by global media corporations.

In the following two interview extracts, women from two different countries talk about their identity. The data were collected as part of a research project investigating women's global media.

The Handbook of Language and Globalization, First Edition. Edited by Nikolas Coupland.
© 2013 Blackwell Publishing Ltd except for editorial material and organization © 2013 Nikolas Coupland.
Published 2013 by Blackwell Publishing Ltd.

Excerpt 1   Conversation I – Britain

WOMAN A   I am a confident person. I think that this is difficult for men.
INTERVIEWER   What do you mean by confident?
WOMAN A   Well, me and my friends, we are just confident and independ-
               ent. I guess we just really know ourselves. We are independent.
               Men don't know what to do with this.
INTERVIEWER   What do you mean?
WOMAN A   Well my friends just do anything they want, when they want.
INTERVIEWER   Like what?
WOMAN A   Well anything. They go to parties, they like dancing. I really like
               cars.
WOMAN B   They have whatever boyfriends they want. The men have been
               doing it for years and now we can do exactly the same. I have
               a friend who just picks guys up. She knows just what she wants.
INTERVIEWER   Are they independent in terms of political thinking?
WOMAN A   I just don't bother with politics, you have to get on with life, not
               be so heavy. Live a bit. You have to get out some.
WOMAN B   Well I think it's about really knowing yourself. You have to
               know who you are. I think my boyfriend has difficulty with
               that. I just say to him I am independent and I am proud of that.
               I just know who I am and what I want.

Excerpt 2   Conversation II – Spain

WOMAN C   I think that the role of the woman has changed so much. Women
               now have so many possibilities. The modern woman has so
               much independence and control. It was always very different
               for women when I was that age. The women in *Cosmo* look great
               and do whatever they want. They have just thrown out all the
               taboos. Take *Sex and the City*. These women are completely in
               control of their lives. They do whatever they want. They have
               a great group of friends and would never tolerate a sexist man.
               I think that all these things are really good as they show women
               what they can do if they wish.
INTERVIEWER   Do you think that women now have more say in how society is
               run?
WOMAN D   I think women now want to be free and do what makes them
               feel good. My friends in their late 20s like to take holidays
               together, spend money on clothes and on their flats. They don't
               want to be doing what their husband says.

In these interviews, identity is first of all female identity, positively contrasted to
male identity. Being a woman is fundamental to these women's view of who they
are. Other valued indicators of identity are 'psychological' rather than social,
'personality traits' such as 'confident' and 'independent,' or based on preferred

leisure time activities such as 'going to parties' and 'picking up guys,' or on con-sumer goods such as 'cars' and 'clothes' or taking holidays. In both cases, being able to 'do whatever you want,' in other words 'choice,' is a key aspect of identity. Many other potential aspects of identity, however, are *not* mentioned, for instance nationality, race, class background, family relationships (being someone's daugh-ter, wife, lover, mother, aunt), job, income level, education, religion, political convictions, and so on. As it happens, both of the women in the first example work in a child nursery. Their income is low, they do not have a fixed contract, and they live in rented accommodation. But they do not choose to see that as part of 'who they are.' The two women in the second example are unemployed and worried about their future, as the old local industries, which provide the major employers in their area, continue to close down. Striking in both cases is the absence of any sense of solidarity with a group. In a world where freedom of individual choice is a key value and where identity can be reflexively assembled, there seems to be little place for belonging.

The two interviews were part of a research project on the magazine *Cosmopolitan*, and this allowed us to observe that these women's views of their identity are highly compatible with the model of female identity propagated by *Cosmopolitan* (see Machin and Van Leeuwen 2003, 2004, 2005). This magazine, steered from New York by the Hearst Corporation and appearing in fifty different versions across the world, transmits a particular version of female identity, in which women are part of a global sisterhood of 'fun, fearless women' and are essentially on their own. The women in *Cosmopolitan* may have friends and colleagues, but they have no parents or children, and the few husbands who appear are usually a source of problems. Nor do they have political or religious beliefs or participate in any form of community. Their chief preoccupations are the pursuit of romantic adventure and sexual pleasure, of health and beauty, of consumer goods and pleasurable activities, and of career success, although the latter varies across dif-ferent versions. The 'career' sections in the Indian version of *Cosmopolitan*, for instance, address their readers as though they are company directors, managers, or self-employed designers, actors, and the like, while the career sections in European versions address their readers as though they are employees, usually in offices (Machin and Van Leeuwen 2004).

There is a link to be explored here: the link between the identities disseminated by large global companies and the way people describe their identities when asked to do so. In both cases the idea of a 'lifestyle identity' seems to play an increasingly important role. People are defined, and define themselves, not in terms of what they 'are' but in terms of what they 'do,' especially with regard to leisure activities, 'attitudes,' and the commodities they purchase or desire. At the core of this attitude is the reflexive ability to manipulate such factors, to 'choose.' Lifestyle identity is defined through reference to things you can change, things you can choose. And, as we have seen, more and more dimensions of identity are drawn into this, including our bodies, the color of our eyes, or the color of our skin. Global magazines such as *Cosmopolitan* and global television programmes are replete with advice and examples on choices of this kind. We will say more about this process and its origins shortly, but first we return to the older model of identity.

Monolithic Identity and the Power of the Nation-State

Below is an Appointees Payroll Details form that has to be filled in as part of applying for a job at Cardiff University.

| **Black or Black British** |
| Black African |
| Black Caribbean |
| Any other Black Background |
| **Chinese or other ethnic group** |
| Chinese |
| Any other ethnic group |
| **White** |
| British |
| Irish |
| Other White |
| **Asian or Asian British** |
| Indian |
| Bangladeshi |
| Pakistani |
| Any other Asian background |
| **Mixed race** |
| White & Black Caribbean |
| White & Black African |
| White & Asian |
| Any other Mixed Race |

Every time we have to fill in a 'diversity' form of this kind, we must declare a single identity. In the example above, you have to state whether you are (1) "Black," (2) "Chinese or other ethnic group," (3) "White," (4) "Asian or Asian British" or (5) "Mixed Race." If "White," you then have to declare whether you are (1) "British," (2) "Irish," or (3) "Other White"; if "Black," whether you are (1)

"Black African," (2) "Black Caribbean," or (3) "Any other Black Background." And so on. It is a curious list, mixing 'race,' 'ethnicity,' 'citizenship,' and 'history' (history in the sense of whether you or your ancestors hail from one of Britain's former colonies or not), and defining people as what they *are* on the basis of categories that are constantly reinforced by the way national media write and talk about identity. A closer look at the categories will bring this out more clearly.

Van Leeuwen (1996) has surveyed linguistic resources for constructing identity, investigating the words and expressions available to speakers of English for answering the question 'Who are you?' (or 'Who are we?,' 'Who is he/she?,' Who are they?'). He has distinguished two major categories of "categorization." One is "functionalization," which defines people's identity "in terms of an activity, in terms of something [people] do, for instance an occupation or a role" (Van Leeuwen 1996: 54). To express this, English allows us to turn verbs that denote activities into nouns, into fixed categories, by adding suffixes such as *-er*, *-ant*, *-ent*, *-ian*, and the like (for example 'asylum seeker,' 'immigrant,' 'insurgent,' 'guardian'), or to derive nouns from other nouns, which denote a place or a tool closely associated with an activity, through suffixes such as *–ist*, *-eer*, and the like (as in 'pianist,' 'mountaineer'). The other category is "identification," which defines people's identity "not in terms of what they do, but in terms of what they, more or less permanently, or unavoidably, are" (ibid.). Van Leeuwen then distinguishes three types of "identification": "classification," "relational identification" and "physical identification."

In the case of "classification," people's identity is defined "in terms of the major categories by means of which a given society or institution differentiates between classes of people" (ibid.). Such categories are historically and culturally variable. What in one period or culture is constructed as 'doing,' as a more or less impermanent and changeable role, may in another be constructed as 'being,' as a more or less fixed and unchangeable identity. As an example he cites Foucault's description of the way homosexuality changed from "the practice of sodomy" into "a kind of interior androgyny, a hermaphrodism of the soul." As Foucault said, "[t]he sodomite had been a temporary aberration; the homosexual was now a species" (Foucault 1981: 42). Such changes may occur slowly, appearing at first as new ideas, before they are incorporated into practices; but they always respond to the needs and interests of the institutions which introduce and promote them. Importantly, we always have to ask whose interests they serve and how they can do this.

"Relational identification" defines identity in terms of people's relations to each other (for instance kinship, work, friendship, 'connections'). Limited and culturally specific sets of nouns denote such relations: 'friend,' 'aunt,' 'colleague,' and so on. In English they typically come with possessive pronouns ('my friend,' 'his mother'), with the genitive construction ('the child's mother'), or with other means of denoting both the parties of the relationship. Van Leeuwen notes that relational identification plays an increasingly marginal role in western society; but anthropologists have shown that in many societies it is the single most important form of 'classification.' Von Sturmer (1981), for instance, has described how Australian

Aborigines, when they first meet, "search for relations whom they share and then establish relationships on that basis" (p. 13). This clearly differs from first meetings in western societies, where the opening questions tend to be 'Where are you from?,' followed by 'What do you do?.' In the past, however, relational identification was more prominent in British society. In Jane Austen's novels characters are constantly asked about their connections. In *Pride and Prejudice*, for instance, Lizzie is asked by Catherine De Bourgh: "Your father may be a gentleman, but who are your connections? Who are your aunts and uncles?"

Finally, in the case of "physical identification" identity is constructed in terms of physical characteristics. This is realized through a limited and specific repertoire of nouns denoting physical characteristics (such as skin color, color of hair) of specific groups of people – for instance women and blacks ('blonde,' 'redhead,' 'black').

The University Appointees Payroll Details form we reproduced above uses three of these types of categorization: the 'physical identifications' of certain 'races' ('black,' 'white'); classifications on the basis of provenance, which constitute 'ethnic' groups ('African,' 'Caribbean'); and classifications on the basis of citizenship ('British,' and perhaps also 'Irish'). Looking at the specific categorizations and at the way in which they combine, we can make a number of observations:

- Much as it may have been discredited by writers about racist practices in the colonial era, the form maintains the distinction between 'pure' and 'mixed' race.
- Going by the criterion of 'physical identification,' the form recognizes only two races, 'white' and 'black.' Other 'races' are no longer defined in this way. With respect to 'Asians,' for instance, there is no more 'yellow.' There has been a redefinition, a shift of emphasis from 'physical' to 'cultural' difference, which coincided with the rapid economic development of a number of important 'Asian' states (although the term 'Asian' still appears under the heading of 'mixed race').
- The form explicitly recognizes only one or two specific nationalities, "British" and perhaps "Irish," even though these nationalities are listed as subgroups of (the white) 'race.' 'Non-whites' from ex-colonies can be 'British,' albeit in a diluted, qualified form, but others cannot, even though many immigrants and descendants from immigrants from other places have been given British citizenship.
- Anyone who is not 'British,' or hailing from an ex-colony, or Chinese, is an "Other": apart from its complex and sometimes confused co-articulations of race, provenance, and nationality, the form also sets up a fine-grained pecking order among the groups it lists.

Classifications of this kind are designed for the service of specific needs and interests, in this case the needs of nation–states (and key national institutions such as health and education) and their current preoccupation with formulating and propagating a coherent sense of 'nationality' despite the 'diversity' that has resulted from the new patterns of immigration characteristic of the age of globalization. In these times, what on earth can constitute 'national identity'? In the case of this form, two factors play a role. The first is 'race,' which here plays an undiminished role, no matter how much racism has been debated and critiqued in the national media. The second is a shared history, more specifically the history of the British Empire, which allows 'Black British' and 'Asian British' people the status of citizens – albeit in a qualified way, which sets them apart from 'true' citizens.

On the form we find an absence of 'functionalization.' If 'functionalization' had been the dominant mode of categorizing people, it might have been easier to see that people from all these racial, 'ethnic,' and national categories *do* the same kind of things, even if they 'are' not the same. They go to school, set up households, purchase goods and services, work, pay taxes, and so on. But this is not the case. The nation-state and its institutions classify people in terms of what they 'are.' And these classifications are kept as permanent records. However long members of any of these intricately classified groups live in the UK, they will always have to reaffirm their identity in these terms, they will always have to reaffirm their difference. They will see this mirrored in the classifications used by the media, which continue to quote, for instance, 'Asian community leaders' and 'Muslim spokespeople,' as though all members of these groups think and feel the same. Critics of British Government Multicultural Policy (Singh 2001) argue that such monolithic categories gloss over the huge diversity of life experienced by members of this category – for instance single parents, long-term unemployed. Many of these people have more in common with those of other monolithic groups. Some argue that the use of such groups while promoting rights and equality in fact serves to conceal structural inequalities such as poor health, education, and opportunities for work, which cut across the lower socio- economic sections of such groups (Machin and Mayr 2007).

Members of these monolithic groups will always have to reaffirm these identities also in the private sphere. At the very least, they will continue to be asked "Where are you from?" even if they have lived in the UK all their lives. One of the authors of the present chapter grew up in the Netherlands, but has not lived there for over thirty years. When he meets new people, they notice his Dutch accent and immediately ask: "Where are you from?" If he answers "London," the question is repeated impatiently, "No, where are you really from?" The other author comes from the North of England, where his family always associated 'Britain' with the South and with London and fought on the streets with what they called the 'British police' during the miners' strike. As a result, he does not identify with Britain as a political entity. Yet he has no choice but to continue to tick the category 'White British.' The form of identity we have discussed here is one we can neither choose nor change, and the further it is removed from the privileged category of 'White British,' the more we will feel the consequences of the latter's power, both in the public and in the private sphere. While we may be able to be 'heard' as a member of an ethnic 'group,' this will background other socio-economic life experiences. Someone may have a voice as a 'Muslim community leader,' for instance, but not also (and at the same time) represent those who live in crime- ravaged areas now that local industries have transferred to South Asia.

This form of identity continues to play a key role in the destinies that are mapped out for us by nation–states and their key institutions. And, as the role of the nation-state changes as a result of migration and global forces, it is not surprising to find its institutions seeking even further to enforce things like 'British Identity' interviews for immigrants – who have to show knowledge on a range of matters such as the royal family, of which very few, even among those born in Britain, would have any knowledge.

Flexible Reflexive Identity and Corporate Power

While 'functionalization' does not play a role in monolithic identity models, in the 'lifestyle identity' model it does.

Our next example comes from an article in a Supplement of the British newspaper the *Guardian* (March 12, 2004), which explains how a particular marketing expert describes the identity of people as consumers. We include three of his eleven categories: "Symbols of success" (representing 9.6 percent of the population); "Ties of community" (representing 16 percent); and "Urban intelligence" (representing 7.2 percent).

Excerpt 3   Consumer identity. From *Guardian*, March 12, 2004

SYMBOLS OF SUCCESS

Their incomes have risen into upper income tax ranges, they have substantial equity and are most likely to be white British. They typically live in posh areas such as Kensington or Edinburgh's New Town, work as senior managers for large corporations, or have respected roles in professional practices. You only call them Smug Ponces because you're jealous. Likely to shop at: Waitrose, M&S, Sainsbury's, Tesco.

TIES OF COMMUNITY

This group lives in very established, rather old-fashioned communities. Traditionally they marry young, work in manual jobs and have strong social support networks with friends and relations living nearby. There is a sub-type of this group called Coronation Street, but not all Lee and Noreens live in back-to-back terraces or keep pigeons. Likely to shop at: Morrisons, Asda, Kwik Save.

URBAN INTELLIGENCE

Young, well-educated, liberal, childless and well off. They are mindful of career uncertainties but are often involved in high risk investments such as the buy-to-let market. Not all of them read the *Guardian*; many are in lifestyle thrall to Sarah Beeney. Likely to shop at Sainsbury's.

How do these classifications differ from those of our previous example?

- They are unsystematic. Despite the way they mix race, provenance, and nationality, the classifications in our previous example (the Cardiff University form) involves clear binary opposites: specific and unspecific identities ('others'), 'mixed' and 'pure' races, 'white' and 'black.' It would be possible to represent them in the form of a taxonomy. The form recognizes two kinds of white people, for instance – those with a named nationality and those without (the 'other whites'); it recognizes two kinds of named nationality ("British" and "Irish"); and so on. The classifications of consumer identities we cited above cannot be represented in this way, because they define identity in terms of clusters of features rather than in terms of single designations.
- Although it does use a number of traditional demographic categories, including race and nationality (and age), our second model does not do so systematically (for instance, race and nationality are only used as one of the co-categorizations in the case of "Symbols of success"), and it prefers categorizations which can change as people climb the social ladder: income, property, place of residence. It also includes a new, and even more easily changeable set of identity features, co-defining identity on the basis of what people think; on the basis of their 'outlook' ("liberal," "old-fashioned," and the like); on the basis of their 'independence' from people who might 'tie them down' (husbands or wives, children, relatives living close by); on the basis of the newspapers or magazines they read and hobbies they pursue; and, above all, on the basis of their consumer behavior.
- The identity features used by this second model include functionalizations as well as categorizations. People are defined not only on the basis of 'who they are,' but also, and above all, on the basis of 'what they do': their job, their leisure time activities, and of course their patterns of consumption. 'Ethnic' provenance matters less here. So long as you are a good consumer it is no longer important whether you are Asian, Chinese, Irish, or any kind of 'other.'

All of these features can be seen in the interview extracts (Excerpts 1 and 2) we presented at the start of this paper. Functionalization is predominant, and identity is about people's 'outlook' (are they 'independent,' 'confident'?), about where they live and what they own (do they have their own flat or their own car?). Possession of such commodities is then associated with 'freedom' and 'independence,' and these terms, in turn, are stripped of their political content and of their association with independent thought.

'Lifestyle' identities of this kind emerged as corporations looked for new ways of creating market demand. They were first formulated in the work of Arnold Mitchell (1978), who referred to them not as 'demographics,' but as "psychographics," clusters of "behaviours," "attitudes," and consumption patterns. Here is an extract from a report produced by marketing company Funsworth and Owler for the psychographic profile of a newspaper readership of the *Liverpool Post*. The aim of this research, which was carried out through interviews and focus groups, was to allow marketers to link opinions, values, and pastimes with consumer behavior. In this case the newspaper planned to re-brand in order to target a different lifestyle category.

> Excerpt 4   Consumer psychographic profile. From Funsworth and Owler market research

- They like to eat out regularly, hold dinner parties for friends and during the week often eat quality supermarket convenience meals.
- She is keen on personal fitness, socializes with like-minded friends and watches her weight.
- They are interested as a couple in active outdoor pursuits, which can involve their children, like, sailing, hiking or cycling.
- They are sophisticated or certainly aspire to be and like to go to the theatre or cinema, exhibitions and shows.
- Personal finance is a major issue in their lives, whether it is funding a house purchase, or major home improvements, putting a child through private school, college or university, or saving for retirement.

From their market research, Funsworth and Owler were able to formulate a template, a "DNA" for the re-brand (see table 29.1). This would allow the newspaper to be carefully redesigned so as to guarantee advertisers specifically targeted market segments.

The older *Liverpool Post* had in fact claimed to be a community newspaper. The re-brand recontextualized this feature as "social awareness" and "forward thinking" – in other words, as symbolic concepts. "Forward thinking" no longer related to concrete political strategies, but became a concept tied to the mood of neo-capitalism, to the buzz of the city as a commercial hub, to 'dynamic business solutions,' 'partnerships,' and 'stakeholders.' 'Open-minded' no longer referred to the world of ideas, but to a willingness to eat sushi and book exotic holidays. 'Social awareness' no longer meant attending to the increasing levels of poverty in the region, but referred to an awareness of market-defined trends and lifestyle issues. This is a world where the identity of the target reader is certainly reflexive, but also closely tied to the worlds of consumerism. The column on the right of the DNA profile contains only functionalizations in terms of what values people hold and what consumer practices they have.

Readers of newspapers will now find in news a reality designed to address them in the first place as consumers, as what they read, both in content and in form of address, connotes values such as 'creativity,' 'forward thinking,' and so on – values with which market profiling research will have shown that they wish to align. In other words, they are no longer addressed as citizens, as in the older, 'fourth estate' model of the press – where the press was to keep them informed, and where a sense of nation was maintained – but as consumers whose primary shared characteristics are lifestyle indicators. These marketing practices in news targeting are now found increasingly around the planet, especially as a growing

Table 29.1 DNA for *Daily Post* re-brand. Source: Funsworth and Owler marketing research

	Daily Post (English) brand DNA	
	Old	Desired
Characteristics	Tabloid; daily; some Welsh content	Tabloid; daily, recognised platforms; substantial regional news; sport; business and lifestyle
Benefits – rational (how the characteristics provide the rational advantage to the consumer)	Job seeking; earlier news than the *Echo*	Regional news round-up; more informed sport and broader sports coverage; in the know about regional business; professional regional jobs marketplace; regional arts and prestige property
Benefits – emotional (how the characteristics provide the emotional advantage to the consumer)	Mainly belongs to the Liverpool region	More intelligent perspective; belonging to the Liverpool region; thought provoking; entertaining and challenging; highly relevant and useful; a symbol of success
Personality	Retired male; dull; set in his ways	35+ professional ideal dinner party guest, i.e. interesting and interested; stylishly exciting; informed; self-assured; confident; intelligent; up-to-date; forward thinking; classically stylish with a sense of humour
Values	Reliability, tradition	Regional affinity (i.e. Merseyside) opinions; culture and heritage; intellect/analysis; indulgence; social awareness; success
Brand essence	Old informer	Intelligent, charismatic regional informer

number of nation–states become involved in the World Trade Organization, opening themselves up to the activities of global corporations and to the needs of their clients the advertisers.

Genre and Choice

The idea of choice and lifestyle changes not only the language of identity, but also the discourse genres in which it is expressed. For example, the advice column has long played an important role in women's magazines, and indeed in many other kinds of magazine. Traditionally it provided a single – expert, authoritative – solution to a problem of love, sexuality, beauty, and so on. It has been studied as an important example of the 'problem-solution' genre by several discourse analysts. This was part of the culture of professional authoritative advice, which informed us about many aspects of our lives such as childcare, managing our homes, and health. This authority is now on the decline, as such professions lose their power (Power 1999). Increasingly, it is replaced by what we have called the 'hot-tips genre,' where the reader can choose between a *range* of *alternative* solutions that are represented as what *you* can do, rather than as what the expert *tells* you to do. Handbooks of childbirth and health care provide lists of choices among options that all relate to lifestyle. This can be seen below in the Finish and Taiwanese versions of *Cosmopolitan* magazine (Excerpts 5 and 6).

Excerpt 5   Finnish *Cosmopolitan*: "Getting your voice heard"

Do your ideas go unnoticed because no one listens to you? Cosmo tells you how to get your ideas taken seriously.

- Think beforehand what you want to say. Practice a few opening lines, take a deep and calm breath in and breath out slowly. This way you can get a natural rhythm in your breathing and you can relax before the bog moment.
- If you are going to have to talk for fairly long, hum your favorite song for a while. Your voice warms up and stays clear and strong for longer.
- Do you need to sound assured and confident? People with a low voice are usually considered reliable. If you lower your pitch artificially, you end up with a dull nasal sound. You can hum your voice range up and down a few times a day. Eventually, you will have a more varied pitch.
- You can diminish mumbling with a simple tongue technique: Put the tip of your tongue out on top of your upper lip and then pull it back as quickly as possible. Practice this a few times a day and soon you'll notice that you'll never be tongue tied again.

Excerpt 6   Taiwanese *Cosmopolitan*: "Post-it for every month"

- **Tidy up the desk**   It always takes a long time to cope with piles of papers; thus, you should systematically sort them into three categories: use later, in use now, and useless.

- **Stand up**   Chatty colleagues will hinder your work. When they move in your direction stand up to show that you're terribly busy and they will shut up automatically.
- **Reduce time talking on the phone**   To reduce long and irrelevant phone conversations (to avoid engaging the line and wasting time), you should be friendly and reply directly, "how can I help you?" This will force the person on the other end of the line to get to their point and finish the conversation sooner.
- **Set goals**   Before leaving your work every day, write down one task which you want to perform the next day. Just in case when you arrive in the office in the morning you don't know where to start and thus waste time.

These hot-tips lists of solution never explain work-related problems in terms of organizational structures, management practices, and so on, but always as the result of individual choices. They suggest that we can assemble our desired lives in terms of career and relationships through making the right choices and taking control of our lives. The 'hot-tips' genre plays an important role in this context, as it has the power to naturalize individual solutions without any reference to workloads, performance reports, and all the other structural constraints that dominate the contemporary workplace.

The Regime of Lifestyle Identity

Sociologists (for instance Zablocki and Kanter 1976; Chaney 1996) have described lifestyle identities as less fixed and more freely chosen than traditional identities: "People use lifestyles in everyday life to identify and explain wider complexes of identity and affiliation" (Chaney 1996: 12). They have stressed the link with consumer goods. Lifestyle identity, says Chaney, is fundamentally based on appearances. It allows attitudes, values, and preferences to be signified by styles of dress and adornment, interior decoration, and so on, and it is situated, not in the realm of production, but in the realm of consumption. As Zablocki and Kanter note, lifestyle identities are chosen "by people for whom occupational and economic roles no longer provide a coherent set of values and for whom identity has come to be generated in the consumption rather than in the production realm" (1976: 270).

It may be true that "[p]eople use lifestyles," but such formulations make it easy to forget that lifestyles also use people. They are created and propagated to serve the interests and needs of powerful social institutions, in this case large corporations; and these institutions, like the nation–state, keep records of people's identities, in this case through marketing surveys and through the information consumers provide, wittingly or unwittingly, every time they use credit cards, 'loyalty cards,' internet shopping, and so on for their purchases. This information, like the classifications required by the nation-state, has material consequences, as it is instrumental in deciding what goods and services will be provided for whom.

Returning for a moment to the examples with which we started this paper (Excerpts 1 and 2), we can now see the role of the 'lifestyle' model of identity in the way the four interviewed women talked about 'independence.' They focused, not on traditional identity categories, or on their dependence on the patriarchal practices that still prevent women from receiving equal pay and equal access to many professions, but on 'independence' as an 'attitude' embodied in consumer goods such as cars, and lived out in leisure time activities such as clubbing and having casual affairs – exactly as in the *Cosmopolitan* discourse of the 'fun, fearless woman.' At times, however, the identification with this kind of independence, and with the devaluation of relational identification it entails (for example the devaluation of the 'relational' identity of 'wife' and 'mother'), seems only skin-deep:

Excerpt 7   Conversation III – Britain

INTERVIEWER   So you are happy to have casual relationships.
WOMAN B   I would like to fall in love and have family. I haven't met the right guy.
WOMAN A   It's hard in the clubs and pubs. Most guys are just after a shag really.
WOMAN B   Or they are just boring. You want someone who can have a laugh but is also pretty sensitive. Lots of guys are scared of us I think.
WOMAN A   We just end up having a laugh together. We have a drink, take the piss out of some guys.

Again, in a further conversation involving the same group of women in Spain – an extract from the Spanish interview – the interviewee comments positively on the television series *Sex and the City*, yet also hedges her alignment to the lifestyle model of identity ("it's not what I would like to do but ..."):

Excerpt 8   Conversation IV – Spain

WOMAN D   *Sex in the City* is just the best programme on the television. It is truly feminist. In many programmes women have very marginal role or are shown as simply housewives. Here the women do anything that they want. This is a really good message for young girls. I have a friend who just shags anyone she wants at any time. It's not what I like to do but it is great that she can just do whatever she wants. It's not what I would want to do right now but it is good that women feel that they can choose to do what they want. It's great to see that women are being shown with strong characters who are truly independent.

In Spain, the older identity regime is still more firmly established than in the UK. More generally, our interviews with women from different parts of the world have shown different levels of intrusion of the new identity model into the older 'nation-state model.' In the following extract, from an interview carried out in Taiwan, the interviewee positively acknowledges 'fun,' choice, and freedom, but also still values older, more stable identities for women and relational identities that entail responsibility and connections to others.

Excerpt 9   Conversation V – Taiwan

WOMAN E   It is good that women should be able to have fun and choose the lives they want to live. But it is also important not to forget our responsibilities to our family. A woman does have an important role in society. But then there is also a place for some freedom. I like to have a good time, listen to music. It's a good thing that women should be able to try different boyfriends before they get married. They can then find out what they want. *Cosmo* is good in this way. I don't think it is real. Women can't all be perfect like that, but the women get what they want, and that's a good message for young women.

A few other aspects of 'consumer identity' need to be pointed out. To do so, we will use a final example: an article in *Cosmopolitan* (November 2003) which introduced "Joseph Cohen, author of The Penis Book," who can tell "what kind of a man he is by the size and shape of his penis." He describes five types of man: the "Peanut," the "Banana," the "Baggy Jacket," the "Well Hung," and "Mr Average." Here are some extracts from his characterization of the "Baggy Jacket" (that is, a man whose penis has a loose foreskin):

Excerpt 10   Joseph Cohen on the "Baggy Jacket." From *Cosmopolitan*, November 2003

He is very laid back. He likes to be in a job where he can be as relaxed as his foreskin is […] He isn't a fussy lover and has plenty of ideas if the lady is willing […] But if you're looking for a laugh-a-minute kind of man, Cohen suggests you look elsewhere. "He is going to leave you feeling pretty empty in your heart and mind. He'll never suggest a restaurant or a weekend getaway destination," he says. "But on the plus-side, he's always up for some hot sex."

This extract illustrates a number of further points:

• Lifestyle classifications, especially in magazines but also elsewhere, are often presented in the tongue-in-cheek, humorous way that also characterizes many advertisements and, indeed, increasingly many of the texts that corporations distribute to their consumers or clients – for instance the brochures through which banks offer insurance policies. On the one hand the message is received. Men are reduced to their penis and to the skill with which they use it to provide women with pleasure. All else follows from this. On the other hand, the message can also be dismissed, laughed away: "it's only a joke, a bit of fun."

- The article is also an example of 'physical identification.' Reflection on the vocabulary of physical identification ('blonde,' 'black,' 'cripple,' 'hulk,' and so on) quickly reveals that it focuses on people who are deemed inferior, stigmatized, or otherwise held in low regard. The science that linked physical features to identities has been discredited precisely because it led to the racist theories that have legitimated colonialism, and eventually the Nazi genocides. Here it returns. As a joke. But, as we have already mentioned in relation to visual categorization, it is, today, precisely in entertainment contexts that the degrading stereotypes of 'physical identity' continue to flourish.

- Finally, 'pop psychological' classifications of this kind describe identity in entirely individualist terms. Neither 'Baggy Jackets,' nor 'strivers' can be said to form a social group. These classifications encourage people to think of themselves not in terms of the groups with which they may have some form of solidarity and community, but as isolated individuals, whose actions are determined either by fate (astrology, the color of your skin, the shape of your penis), or by active individual agency; and whose identity is to a large extent defined by the kind of 'personality traits' ('confident,' 'independent,' fun loving,' 'shy,' 'laid back'), which were developed for the purpose of personality tests by psychologists such as Eysenck and have now become ubiquitous in the lifestyle media: the latter constantly interpret people's taste in matters such as color, interior decoration, and so on as expressions of their unique personalities rather than (also) of the habitus of one or more social groups.

The Power of Classification

We began this chapter by pointing to the way in which contemporary social theorists critique essentialist static constructions of identity and celebrate the alternative: unique, individual, flexible, complex identities. In the course of the chapter we have argued that such theorists do so without taking into account the origins of this model in the work of 1970s marketing experts, and the way in which the model serves the interests of large corporations and informs their policies and practices. In our view, this link needs, at the very least, to be explicitly discussed and problematized. If people, in interviews such as those from which we have quoted here, use the 'lifestyle' model as a resource for describing themselves, then this is not so different from the way in which others may use the essentialist categories imposed by the nation-state and its institutions to describe themselves. Both can be 'owned' in the same way – and both can lead to fragmented identities and to contradictions, for instance the contradiction between identifying with the idea of 'independence' and yet also longing for 'Mr Right' and for 'having a family.'

This tendency is particularly noticeable in work that links identity to media reception. The same period that spawned the theories we have just discussed (it was the era of Reagan and Thatcher, let us not forget) also spawned a new direction in media and cultural studies, a new emphasis on reception rather than on production or product (see for instance Morley 1980, Radway 1987). The initial aim was to relate differences in reception to demographic factors. But this was soon abandoned for an approach in which reception was related to people's individual identities and histories (Radway 1988). It was an approach with clear predecessors in 1950s and 1960s American mass communication theory (compare for instance Berlo 1960, who coined the slogan "meanings are in people:) – and again, origins and affinities of this kind, and their implications, are not acknowledged or discussed.

Historically, there is a pattern here. As marketing experts and large corporations began to emphasize production over consumption, so did theorists of identity and meaning. As they abandoned singular, stable demographic identities in favor of complex, flexible, and individual identities, so did theorists of identity. As they championed the consumer's power of choice, so did theorists of identity. We do not want to argue here that these theorists are wrong. As we said, they have contributed a necessary and wholly convincing critique of the essentialist identity model. The greater emphasis on functionalization, on choice, and on identity as a cluster of features does have a positive potential. But this does not diminish the fact that the 'lifestyle' model is just as much produced and imposed by a powerful social institution as the older model, even if it propagates a different kind of identity and communicates it very differently.

So in conclusion we would like to argue for a different kind of complexity, a complexity in which at least two powerful 'regimes' of identity, driven by different needs and interests, operate side by side: that of nation–states and that of large, global corporations. The question, therefore, is not what identity *is*, in some absolute, indeed essentialist sense. The question is how nation–states and global corporations (re)*construct* identity in different ways, and what people do with this when they talk about their own identity. What agency people have in doing so has to be seen as constrained, to different degrees, by these socially constructed and imposed models of identity. And, while 'lifestyle identity' may have some genuine advantages over essentialist forms of identity, there is also a drawback here: just *how* agentive people can be within this model, how much they will or will not be constrained by it, depends to a great extent on the financial resources at their disposal.

ACKNOWLEDGMENTS

The research for this paper was part of the 'Language and Global Communication' research programme of the Centre for Language and Communication Research, Cardiff University. The programme was funded by a grant from the Leverhulme Trust.

REFERENCES

Advertising Statistics Yearbook (2003). London: The Advertising Association.

Berlo, D. K. (1960) *The Process of Communication*. New York: Holt, Rinehart and Winston.

Bhabha, H. (1990) The third space in identity. In J. Rutherford (ed.), 207–21.

Chaney, D. (1996) *Lifestyles*. London: Routledge.

Derrida, J. (2002) Faith and knowledge: Two sources of 'religion' at the limits of reason alone. In G. Anidjar (ed.), *Acts of Religion*, translated by S. Weber, 42–101. New York: Routledge. [Originally published in J. Derrida and G. Vattimo (eds) (1990), *La Religion: Séminaire de Capri*, 42–101. Paris: Editions du Seuil.]

Durkheim, E. (2002) *Suicide*, translated by J. A. Spalding and G. Simpson. London: Routledge.

Foucault, M. (1981) *A History of Sexuality*, translated by R. Hurley, Vol. 1. Harmondsworth: Penguin.

Hall, S. (1989) Cultural identity and diaspora. In J. Rutherford (ed.), 222–37.

Le Page, R., and Tabouret-Keller, A. (1985) *Acts of Identity: Creole-Based Approaches to Language and Ethnicity*. Cambridge: Cambridge University Press.

Machin, D., and Mayr, A. (2007) Antiracism in the British Government's model regional newspaper: The 'talking cure.' *Discourse and Society* 8(4): 453–78.

Machin, D., and van Leeuwen, T. (2003) Global schemas and local discourses in *Cosmopolitan*. *Journal of Sociolinguistics* 7(4): 493–513.

Machin, D., and van Leeuwen, T. (2004) 'Global media: Generic homogeneity and discursive diversity. *Continuum* 18(1): 99–120.

Machin, D., and van Leeuwen, T. (2005) Language style and lifestyle: The case of a global magazine. *Media, Culture and Society* 27(4): 577–600.

Mitchell, A. (1978) *Consumer Values: A Typology*. Menlo Park, CA: Stanford Research Institute.

Morley, D. (1980) *The Nationwide Audience: Structure and Decoding*. British Film Institute Television Monograph No. 11. London: British Film Institute.

Nederveen Pieterse, J. (1992) *White on Black. Images of Africa and Blacks in Western Popular Culture*. New Haven: Yale University Press.

Parmar, P. (1989) Black feminism: The politics of articulation. In J. Rutherford (ed.), 101–26.

Power, M. (1999) *The Audit Society*. Oxford: Oxford University Press.

Radway, J. (1987) *Reading the Romance*. London: Verso.

Radway, J. (1988) Reception study: Ethnography and the problem of dispersed audiences and nomadic subjects. *Cultural Studies* 2(3): 359–76.

Rutherford, J. (ed.) (1990) *Community, Culture, Difference*. London: Lawrence and Wishart.

Simmel, G. (1971) *On Individual and Social Forms*. Chicago: University of Chicago Press.

Singh, E. G. (2001) Multiculturalism in contemporary Britain: Reflections on the 'Leicester Model.' *International Journal on Multicultural Societies* 5(1): 40–54.

Tönnies, F. (2001) *Community and Civil Society*. Cambridge: Cambridge University Press.

Van Leeuwen, T. (1996) The representation of social actors. In C. R. Caldas-Coulthard and M. Coulthard (eds), *Texts and Practices. Readings in Critical Discourse Analysis*, 32–70. London: Routledge.

Van Leeuwen, T. (2000) Visual racism. In M. Reisigl and R. Wodak (eds), *The Semiotics of Racism: Approaches in Critical*

Discourse Analysis, 333–50. Vienna: Passagen Verlag.

Von Sturmer, J. (1981) Talking with Aborigines. *Australian Institute of Aboriginal Studies Newsletter* 15: 13–30.

Weeks, J. (1990) The value difference in identity. In J. Rutherford (ed.), 88–100.

Zablocki, B. D., and Kanter, R. M. (1976) The differentiation of lifestyles. *Annual Review of Sociology* 2: 269–98.

Index

The Handbook of Language and Globalization, First Edition. Edited by Nikolas Coupland.
© 2013 Blackwell Publishing Ltd except for editorial material and organization © 2013 Nikolas Coupland.
Published 2013 by Blackwell Publishing Ltd.